The Lonely Hunter

The Lonely Hunter

A BIOGRAPHY
OF *Carson McCullers*

By VIRGINIA SPENCER CARR

1975

DOUBLEDAY & COMPANY, INC.
GARDEN CITY, NEW YORK

Library of Congress Cataloging in Publication Data
Carr, Virginia Spencer.
The lonely hunter.
Bibliography: p. 580
Includes index.
1. McCullers, Carson Smith, 1917–1967—Biography.
I. Title.
PS3525.A1772Z58   813'.5'2[B]
ISBN 0-385-04028-8
Library of Congress Catalog Card Number 74-9478

Grateful acknowledgment is made to the following for permission to use copyrighted material:

Excerpts from *The Journals of Anais Nin Vol. 3*. Reprinted by permission of Harcourt Brace Jovanovich, Inc. and Peter Owen Ltd., London.

Excerpts from *The Heart Is a Lonely Hunter* by Carson McCullers, copyright 1940 by Carson McCullers, copyright © renewed 1967 by Carson McCullers; excerpts from *Reflections in a Golden Eye*, copyright 1941 by Carson McCullers, copyright © renewed 1968 by Floria V. Lasky, as Executrix of the Estate of Carson Smith McCullers; excerpts from *The Ballad of the Sad Café and Collected Short Stories* copyright 1955 by Carson McCullers; excerpts from *The Member of the Wedding*, copyright 1940 by Carson McCullers; excerpts from *The Square Root of Wonderful*, copyright © 1958 by Carson McCullers; excerpts from *Clock Without Hands*, copyright © 1961 by Carson McCullers; excerpts from *The Mortgaged Heart*, copyright 1940, 1941, 1945, 1948, 1949, 1953, © 1956, 1959, 1963, 1967, 1971 by Floria V. Lasky, Executrix of the Estate of Carson McCullers. Copyright 1936, 1952, © 1955, 1957, 1963 by Carson McCullers. Reprinted by permission of Houghton Mifflin Company.

"The Watchers" from *Waterlily Fire* by Muriel Rukeyser, copyright © 1962 by Muriel Rukeyser; "A Note on the Author" by Tennessee Williams, September 23, 1961, issue of *Saturday Review*. Reprinted by permission of the International Famous Agency.

Seven lines from Part II, Voyages, which appears in *Selected Letters and Prose of Hart Crane* by Hart Crane, copyright © 1933, 1958, 1966 by Liveright Publishing Corp. Reprinted by permission of Liveright Publishing, New York.

"Which Is My Little Boy?" from *In the Winter of Cities by* Tennessee Williams, copyright © 1956 by Tennessee Williams. Reprinted by permission of New Directions Publishing Corporation and International Famous Agency.

Excerpts from various issues of the New York *Times*, copyright © 1942–1967 by The New York Times Company. Reprinted by permission of the New York *Times*.

For LUCY QUILLIAN PAGE

Contents

A Note from the Author

For the past seven years I have been deeply immersed in the life and writings of Carson McCullers. I did not know this enigmatic woman personally, but I believe that I know her better now than most people who did. My keen interest in Mrs. McCullers evolved quite naturally as I worked on a critical study of her writings for a Ph.D. dissertation. Two years later, after I moved to her hometown, Columbus, Georgia, I began to meet and interview countless people with whom she had grown up. I knew then that a depth biography was inevitable. My research took me to a number of cities, towns, and hamlets in the Southeast where Mrs. McCullers' life—and her husband's—touched in some indelible fashion, then on to New York City, Brooklyn, Nyack, Saratoga Springs, and other communities in the North where she spent most of her adult years. Later, it seemed vital that I make the pilgrimage to more distant places where she had lived or visited, to the British Isles, France, and even the tiny village of Kirchstetten, Austria, to meet her old friend Wystan Hugh Auden.

For those who knew Carson McCullers personally and gave generously of their time and energies during the gestation of this biography, I am very grateful. For many people, she was, ambivalently, both a joy and a burden. For some with whom she had a meaningful relationship, sharing her with a biographer meant reliving painful memories; yet almost everyone who knew Mrs. McCullers well was willing to provide facts, impressions, reminiscences, and anecdotes to help reveal the facets of her that they knew best. Some gave bits and pieces; others shared in depth from their diaries, letters, notes, and other memorabilia. One of her friends gave me an original, unpublished manuscript; another, several letters she had written him and an autographed first edition of *The Heart Is a Lonely Hunter*. A few key people devoted hundreds of interview hours and spent additional time researching their personal archives so that this intimate portrait of Carson McCullers could be as accurate, sensitive, and honest as possible. Most shared cordially, enthusiastically, and candidly; some, hesitantly. Several asked for various reasons that they not be credited directly or acknowledged in this preface. To all who helped—and especially to those I should have publicly acknowledged, but somehow missed—I extend my deepest thanks.

Of the many who knew Carson McCullers intimately, six contributed more bountifully to this book than anyone else. To David Diamond, Jordan Massee, Edwin Peacock, Carson's brother, Lamar Smith, his wife, Virginia, and Tennessee Williams, I am especially indebted. Their support and co-operation were invaluable. I hold their friendship dear and thank them for their confidence in me.

My greatest appreciation goes to Lucy Quillian Page of Columbus, Georgia, who believed in me and in the reality of this book. Her contribution through each phase of the biography is inestimable. Mrs. Page worked almost daily during the book's early stages, reading, writing letters, collating materials, and performing myriad other tasks; promoting my research in countless ways, she also participated in interviews in this country and abroad and assisted in a study of other locales in which Mrs. McCullers had lived and worked; and, finally, she read and edited the manuscript chapter by chapter, not just once, but dozens of times as the book evolved. THE LONELY HUNTER is dedicated to her.

I am indebted to Aimee Alexander of Eastern Kentucky University for her helpful and generous research assistance through both correspondence and interviews, and for her encouragement and counsel from the time the book was first contemplated.

Special thanks, also, go to Lois Thompson and Jan Twichell. Miss Thompson assisted me with much of the early research, transcribed interview tapes, and helped with numerous secretarial chores—all in the name of friendship. Mrs. Twichell typed the manuscript through its several drafts, edited, read galley proofs, and performed other herculean tasks during the last three years of the book's preparation.

Indeed, I was most fortunate to have as my editor Ken McCormick, who knew Carson and Reeves McCullers. He was mentor and friend, as well, and I treasure our relationship. I appreciate, too, the valuable assistance of Doubleday editor Betty Prashker, copy editor Leota Diesel, and administrative assistant Joan Ward.

I am grateful to President Thomas Y. Whitley, Dean John E. Anderson, Jack Brown, Isaiah Moyel, the Columbus College Foundation for a research stipend, and to an anonymous donor for a grant that enabled me to take a three-month leave of absence so that I could be free to travel and write full time. During another critical period I was granted a lightened teaching load. To my colleagues at Columbus College who encouraged me and sometimes covered my classes, I also extend thanks.

In addition, I thank the linguists who translated foreign materials: Ursula Boyd, Jack Callendar, James Chappell, Mrs. Dexter Followill,

Albert Halley, Hans Jany, Philip Mankin, William Franklin Page, Patricia
Spano, and Mr. and Mrs. Donald E. Spencer.

The staffs of many libraries were generous in their assistance. I am
especially indebted to Virginia Lee, reference librarian of the Columbus
College Library, Columbus, Georgia, for her diligent research assistance
over a five-year period, and to her colleague Sally Brooker. Librarians from
other institutions also helped by sharing materials through interlibrary
loans. Very co-operative, too, were John R. Banister, Jeanne Hollis, Mrs.
Edward H. Storey, Joanne Sweeney, David Voss, and Michael Land, staff
members of the W. C. Bradley Memorial Library of Columbus.

I am grateful to Daniel Aaron, executor of the Newton Arvin Papers,
and to Dorothy King, curator of Rare Books, South College Library,
Smith College; Roy P. Basler, chief, Reference Department and Manu-
script Division, the Library of Congress; J. Terry Bender, director of
Special Collections, University Library, Hofstra University; Philip C.
Brooke, director, Harry S Truman Library, Independence, Missouri;
Richard M. Buck, assistant to the chief, Research Library of the Perform-
ing Arts, the New York Public Library at Lincoln Center; Penelope
Bulloch, King's College Library, Cambridge, England; Antoinette Ciolli,
chief, Special Collections Division, Brooklyn College Library of the City
University of New York; Alexander P. Clark, curator of Manuscripts,
Princeton University Library; Elizabeth L. Cox, research librarian, Satur-
day Review, Inc., Library; Rosalie J. Coyle, librarian in charge, Theatre
Collection, the Free Library of Philadelphia; David E. Estes, assistant uni-
versity librarian, the Robert W. Woodruff Library for Advanced Studies,
Emory University; Donald Gallup, curator, Collection of American Lit-
erature, Beinecke Rare Book and Manuscript Library, Yale University;
Holly Hall, head, Manuscript Division, Washington University Libraries,
St. Louis, Missouri; Juliann D. Hickerson, Botetourt-Rockbridge Regional
Library, Lexington, Virginia; Margaret Johnston, former librarian, National Library of Scotland, Edinburgh; Laurie Jones, Fort Benning Infantry School librarian, Fort Benning, Georgia; Sharon E. Knapp, Manuscript Department, William R. Perkins Library, Duke University; Elfrieda
Lang, curator of Manuscripts, the Lilly Library, Indiana University; Kenneth A. Lohf, librarian for Rare Books and Manuscripts, Butler Library,
Columbia University, New York City; June Moll and Sally Leach, Humanities Research Center, the University of Texas at Austin; Judith W.
Moore, assistant to the director of libraries, Boston College; Paul Myers,
curator, Theatre Collection, Library and Museum of the Lincoln Center
of the Performing Arts; Charles Niles, research assistant, Boston University
Mugar Memorial Library; Frank Paluka, head, Special Collections, the
University libraries, University of Iowa; Mary H. Proper, the Nyack Li-

brary, New York; Rutherford D. Rogers, university librarian, and Judith A. Schiff, chief research archivist, Manuscripts and Archives, Yale University Library; J. W. Reginald Scurr, chief, Humanities Department, the Chicago Public Library; the staff of the Manuscript Division of the New York Public Library; Mrs. William Tate, assistant, Special Collections librarian, the University libraries, University of Georgia; Mrs. Kelly Thurman, Eastern Kentucky University Library; John E. Via, assistant curator of Rare Books, Alderman Library, University of Virginia; Elizabeth L. White, local history librarian, Brooklyn Public Library.

I also am indebted to many others as well who contributed meaningfully in a variety of ways. Without their help, this biography could not have been completed:

Mr. and Mrs. John Vincent Adams, Cyrilly Abels, Herbert Agar, Edward Albee, Jonathan Aldrich, Al Alexander, Elizabeth Ames, Kingsley Amis, Jane Anderson, John H. Anderson, Alan Arkin, Mary Alice Arnold, Walter Aschaffenburg, Mary Louise Aswell, Louis S. Auchincloss, Wystan Hugh Auden, Leon Auerbach, Richard Avedon, Eli Avstrich, Jerome Bahr, Nona Balakian, Hazel Baldwin, Craig Ballantyne, Marielle Bancou, Nancy Banta, Mrs. E. S. Barbaree, Bill Barnes, Djuna Barnes, Danan Barnett, Margaret F. Baseman, Anne Baxter, Jean Baxter, André Bay, Sir Cecil Beaton, Simone de Beauvoir, A. Becker-Berke, Dan Beeland, Edith Behrens, Eugene Berman, Leonard Bernstein, Mrs. Charles K. Berry, Sr., Paul Bigelow, Mrs. James J. W. Biggers, Jr., Martha W. Billings, Dr. and Mrs. Francis B. Blackmar, Myrtle Blackmon, Betsy Talbot Blackwell, Albert U. Blair, Mrs. John Bloodworth, Kermit Bloomgarden, Winnifred Bodkin, George S. Bolster, Vance Bourjaily, Elizabeth Bowen, Paul F. Bowles, Mrs. John Thomas Boyd, R. Brahan, Mr. and Mrs. Henry A. Brannon, J. C. Bratton, Benjamin Britten, Joan Brooke-Smith, Kent Brooks, Andreas Brown, Mrs. James F. Brown, Dr. and Mrs. John Lackey Brown, Laura Ferris Brown, Helen Bryant, Mrs. Luther J. Bunge, Whit Burnett, Frederick Burrell, Mrs. Phillip Burrus, Mrs. Marion H. Burt, Brady Bynum, Scott Byrd, Mrs. Walter Byrd, Sr., Mary Margaret Byrne, Hortense Calisher, Polly Cameron, Truman Capote, Charles B. Carr, Mrs. Francis Carson, Mrs. Francis M. Carson II, Mr. and Mrs. Ricks Carson, Henri Cartier-Bresson, Mrs. J. Lucious Chadwick, Loretto Lamar Chappell, Andrée Chèdid, Brainard Cheney, Hazel Chrisman, John Ciardi, Eleanor Clark, David Clarke, Helena Clay, Hervey M. Cleckley, Mr. and Mrs. Aubrey Clements, Harold Clurman, Columbia Broadcasting System, Charles Cordova, Frances M. Cole, Marc Connelly, C. V. Cooksey, Aaron Copland, Katharine Cornell, Gaspero del Corso, Malcolm Cowley, Margaret Cox, Jack Crane, Tessa Craig, Cheryl Crawford, Mrs. Henry B. Crawford, Mrs. Leon W. Cunningham, Mrs. Harold Dale, Eileen Darby, Louise Dahl-Wolfe, Mrs. Alvin Davis, Mrs. Charles H.

Davis, Dorothy Salisbury Davis, J. B. Stringer Davis, Mabel Davis, Shirley Daw, Babette Deutsch, Mrs. P. B. Dexter, Mrs. William Diebold, Mrs. Charles E. Dimon, Sr., Harriet Doar, John E. Dobbin, Minnie Dobbin, Carl Doerr, Herman Dollar, Irving Drutman, Hugo Dryfus, Verna Dudley, Michael Dunn, Mrs. M. M. Dykes, Leon Edel, Mrs. Lewis A. Edge, Raymond A. Edward, Leonard Ehrlich, David Eisendrath, Ralph Ellison, Paul Engle, Margaret English, Albert Erskine, Helen Eustis, Mills Ten Eyck, Jr., Robert Faulke, Peter S. Feibleman, Nancy Ferguson, Harvey Fite, Janet Flanner, Gordon Flournoy, Jr., Mrs. Gordon Flournoy, Sr., Mrs. Robert Flournoy, Ruth Ford, the Ford Foundation, Mildred Miller Fort, June Fortess, Kenneth French, Lenemaja Friedman, Rowland F. Fullilove, Joan Gaskin, Marjorie Gamble, Mrs. Harvey Gardner, David Garnett, Jean Garrigue, Romain Gary, Felicia Geffen, Ruth Gikow, Rumer Godden, A. Godley, Max Goodley, Mrs. D. B. Gordon, Thomas Gossett, William Goyen, Shirley Ann Grau, Lillian Griffith, Graham Greene, R. B. von Guerard, Mary Rodgers Guettel, Albert and Frances Hackett, Mary Martin Halliday, Ernst Hammerschlag, Polly Hanson, Curtis Harnack, Mrs. James Harris, Julie Harris, Mrs. William Hart, Sr., June Havoc, G. Haver, Helen Hayes, Heaton Heffelfinger, Joseph Heller, Lillian Hellman, Eileen Hesse, Mr. and Mrs. Granville Hicks, Gladys Hill, Mrs. Vernon Hogan, Franklin Holcomb, Mrs. Gerald Holten, Elizabeth Jane Howard, Lelia Caetani Howard, Vera Howard, Helen Rose Hull, Kathryn Hulme, John Huston, Stella Hyatt, Mrs. A. Illges, Christopher Isherwood, Helen H. Jackson, Vannie Copeland Jackson, Mrs. D. G. James, Mrs. W. F. Jenkins, Mrs. Carlton M. Johnson, David J. Johnson, Uwe Johnson, Virginia Johnston, Charles Jones, Laurie Jones, Mrs. Hugh Jordan, Mrs. Robert Jorge, Peter Kaldor, Alfred Kantorowicz, Alfred Kazin, Daniel Keel, Marjorie Kellogg, the Reverend J. N. Kelly, Mrs. Kendrick C. Kierce, Mrs. Grafton Kimbrough, Mrs. Euell Kirkland, Lincoln Kirstein, Ella Kirven, Mrs. J. Dupont Kirven, Stanley E. Kramer, Richard Krebs, Werner J. Kuhn, Clason Kyle, J. Omaha Landrum, George Lang, Richard C. Larkin, Betty Lee, Harper Lee, L. Stanton Lee, Sr., John Leggett, John Lehmann, Rosamond Lehmann, Leo Lerman, Roy Lester, Elizabeth Lewis, James Lewis, Stanley Lewis, Alfred Linn, Mrs. Robert Linscott, Mr. and Mrs. R. T. Littlefield, Joshua Logan, Margaret Long, Nikolai Lopatnikoff, William Love, James Blair Lovell, Lucille Dudley Luetje, Andrew J. Lyndon III, Robert M. MacGregor, Mr. and Mrs. Edwin R. MacKethan, Juliette MacPhail, Gertrude Macy, Felicia Magruder, Ella Maillart, Jerre Mangione, Golo Mann, Marty Mann, Theodore Mann, Mrs. Frederick Markloff, Joseph Marks, Dr. and Mrs. Robert Marks, Albert Marre, Edward A. Martin, Robert Martin, Stanley Martineau, Monica McCall, Richard E. McClendon, the Reverend Anthony McCombe,

Charles R. McCullers, Sadie McCullers, David McDowell, Mrs. William McDuffy, J. Michael McGraw, John A. McKenna, Jr., Crawford McKethan, Mrs. Charles F. McLaughlin, Gay Noe McLendon, Beatrice McMillan, Mrs. Henry B. McMurria, Mr. and Mrs. Vernon McRae, Adele Menken, Victor Merkel, Mary Ann Meysenburg, Arthur Miller, Phoebe Moffitt, Michel Mohrt, Emily Montfort, Mario Monti, the Reverend Howard Moody, Alberto Moravia, Irene Spagg Morgan, Florence J. Moriarty, Alice Morris, Mr. and Mrs. Ira Morris, Susan Wilferd Morris, Theodore Morrison, Clarence L. Mullin, Mr. and Mrs. S. Robin Mullin, Carolyn Munro, Reg Murphy, Robert W. Murphy, Natalia Danesi Murray, Terry A. Murray, Susan Myrick, Anita Naef, Dink NeSmith, Edward Newhouse, William Nims, Anaïs Nin, Ken Norwick, Ann Novotny, John A. Oates, Edward P. O'Dell, Suzanne Schwarzenbach Ohman, Margaret A. O'Neill, Elizabeth Page, John Page, W. Marion Page, Virginia Parkhurst, Peter Pears, Lola Pergament, Kappo Phelan, Robert Phelps, the Philadelphia Fine Arts Association, Bentz Plagemann, Rebecca Pitts, Lester Polakov, Henry Varnum Poor, Frederick S. Porter, Katherine Anne Porter, William Z. Potter, Eric Preminger, Mrs. W. T. Presley, Francis Price, Sain Clair Pugh, Sally and Eva Quillian, Jose Quintero, Dotson Rader, Philip Rahv, Elizabeth Ralston, W. Jack Ray, Lee Reece, Rex Reed, Ida Reeder, Edge Reid, Ginger Storey Reiney, Howard B. Reiney, Mrs. Roy B. Revell, Mrs. Guy Rich, H. A. Robinson, A. Pancho Rodriguez, Emanuel Romano, Denis de Rougemont, Muriel Rukeyser, Thomas C. Ryan, Dame Margaret Rutherford, Arnold Saint Subber, Chris Sampson, Mrs. Roy Sasser, Fred Schomburg, Sr., Mark Schorer, Hans R. Schwarzenbach, Robert Seidel, Henry Senber, Vitorio Serini, Barbara A. Shattuck, Edward Shorter, Celestine Sibley, Tanya Siegelson, Mrs. Jean Paul Simmons, Francis Sitwell, Sir Sacheverell Sitwell, Robert M. Slabey, Lawrence Smith, Dr. and Mrs. Simeon M. Smith, Paula Snelling, Jamie Solinas, Mrs. Dudley Spain, Mrs. C. S. Sparkman, John R. Spencer, Wilma Bell Spencer, Jean Stafford, Sue Standard, Dr. and Mrs. Fred L. Standley, Maureen Stapleton, Gene Starlin, Max Steele, Wallace E. Stegner, Frances Stelloff, James and Tania Stern, Tommie Stevens, Jo Stewart, Paul Stewart, Ellen Stoianoff, Mrs. Earl Sturkie, Homer G. Suggs, Sarah Sutherland, Clara Svendsen, Emily Ransom Sweet, Mr. and Mrs. George Swift, Sr., Mrs. W. Edward Swinson, Gerald Sykes, Mrs. Frank S. Taylor, Mrs. Henry S. Taylor, Ida Thompson, Virgil Thomson, Mrs. Jack Thornton, Kelly Thurman, Arthur Tourtellot, Mrs. Dudley Trawick, Mrs. George R. Thomas, Geraldine Trotta, Ray E. Trussell, Ben L. Tucker, Linda Jordan Tucker, Mrs. Cliff Tucker, Sally Turner, Mrs. Richard W. Ulrich, Ricky Ulrich, Mark Underwood, Louis and Bryna Untermeyer, Alfred Valente, Jean Stein vanden Heuvel, Terence de Vere White, Gore Vidal, George Vincent, Mrs. Eliot Waddell, Mr. and Mrs. Tom Wade, Robert Walden,

Curtis Walker, Sir William Walton, Thomas R. Waring, Robert Penn Warren, Armitage Watkins, Ethel Waters, Constance Webb, Hattie Weeks, Lotte Lenya Weill-Detwiler, Ruth Wells, Eudora Welty, Glenway Wescott, Nancy White, Robert Whitehead, Sandra Whitley, Mrs. Arthur R. Wickmann, Alex D. Williams, Donald Windham, Mr. and Mrs. John T. Winn, Thomas Winship, Judson B. Wood, Marie Wood, W. C. Woodall, Emily Woodruff, James W. Woodruff, Jr., Mrs. George C. Woodruff, Sr., Harrell Woolfolk, Herman Wouk, Marguerite Young, John Zeigler, Jürg Zimmerli, Fred Zinnemann, and Robert Zuleg.

And, finally, without the co-operation of Roger Alton Carr and our three daughters—Karen, Catherine, and Kimberly—this book would not be a reality today. They cooked, mended, and meal-planned, shopped, nursed, and performed sundry other labors for each other while I was secluded in my study or away interviewing. Perhaps my children, more than anyone else, rejoice in the completion of THE LONELY HUNTER. My thanks, and my apologies, dear ones.

Virginia Spencer Carr
March 1974

Some Words Before

The author of this book, Mrs. Virginia Carr, entered the New Orleans scene of my life very quietly and tactfully a few years ago while she was still in the preparatory stage of her work on the book: the research, the interviews with old and close friends of the late Carson McCullers.

Despite the gentle quality of her voice on the telephone, I must confess that I consented to meet her with some hesitation, since I had recently read a professed critique of Carson McCullers' work which had placed its main emphasis on the physical illnesses which had beset her, and this critic had somehow contrived to make of their circumstance a base for attack on her stature as an artist. I recall that this piece of critical hogwash came from a female professor from a rather eminent seat of learning in the Northeast; that the writer of it was the recipient of a grant to permit her to take a "sabbatical leave" from the seat of learning in order to devote herself more fully to her duties of denigration. The most unfortunate aspect of this alleged *critique* was that it was the first upon Mrs. McCullers to appear in a consequential journal, at least in this country and after her death.

Certainly it was now time for a true appreciation of Carson McCullers to be written, and preferably by a writer less foreign to her background and nature, someone who did not confuse the implements of writing with a hatchet concealed in a kerchief moist with crocodile tears. And I was somewhat reassured by the pleasant southern tone of Mrs. Carr's telephone voice and by her apologies for intruding upon my time, which she judged to be more valuable than it was.

Still, it was with a somewhat guarded feeling that I kept a luncheon appointment with her the next day. She had not told me what color hat or dress she'd be wearing or where she'd be seated, but despite my rather poor eyesight, I spotted her at once. Her face had a certain smile which gave it a certain charm and within a minute or two I had dismissed my reluctance to share with her my many reminiscences of Carson, for I knew at once that this lady from Georgia, Carson's native state, was someone who valued the spirit and the writing of Mrs. McCullers as deeply as

I did, and it seemed to me that the preparation of this biographical and critical work had been undertaken by Mrs. Carr much in the way that the devout once made pilgrimages to sanctified places.

I pause here, for a moment, knowing that I will certainly be accused of romantic excess.

Mrs. McCullers was sometimes accused of that, too, but she was not deterred by the accusation, coming, as it did, from such alien sources.

Have you ever compared a *clinical* account of the experience of love to another which is invested with a tender and lyrical comprehension of that all-important matter?

Once Carson wrote a story called "A Tree. A Rock. A Cloud."—a mysteriously lovely title till you read it, and then no longer mysterious but lovelier still. The articles mentioned in the title were those things toward which, as first steps, a man or woman must learn to feel an emotional response before he is ready to undertake the dreadfully difficult problem of giving his love, his heart, to a being of the human kind. In this story Carson sounded her major theme: the huge importance and nearly insoluble problems of human love.

Now it is I who am intruding upon Mrs. Carr's work and not quietly nor gracefully, either.

I have used the word "heart," but it is not an adequate word to define the core of Carson McCullers' genius. It was a favorite word of hers and one of which she had exceptional understanding. Still I believe, in fact I know, that there are many, many with heart who lack the need or the gift to express it. And therefore Carson McCullers is what I would call a *necessary* writer: She owned the heart and the deep understanding of it, but in addition she had that "tongue of angels" that gave her power to sing of it, to make of it an anthem.

When physical catastrophes reduce, too early, an artist's power, his/her admirers must not and need not enter a plea nor offer apology. It is not quantity, after all, that the artist is to be judged by. It is quality of spirit and those occasions on which he/she was visited by assenting angels, and the number of those occasions is not the scale on which their importance is reckoned.

Finally, what have I to say that I haven't said to Mrs. Virginia Carr?

I am sure we discussed Carson's purity of spirit and her gentleness and grace, those characteristics of a lady of our southern states where the word "lady" is not a title but a kind of character, opposite to "red neck." Carson and I both had the fortunate circumstance of knowing ladies and gentlemen to exist among both blacks and whites, among migrants and sharecroppers, and among those physically twisted into deformity too often regarded with indifference and even contempt. And the mentally strange, too.

I hope that with increasing study of Carson McCullers it will be recognized, generally, that despite the early onset of her many illnesses, she was, in her spirit, a person of rare and luminous health.

I am not much given to quotation from Scripture but when Carson's *The Member of the Wedding* opened as a play, a bit of the Book of Common Prayer leapt into my mind as I composed a card to go with opening night roses:

"Let thy light so shine among men that they see thy good works and glorify thy father which is in heaven."

Carson's heart was often lonely and it was a tireless hunter for those to whom she could offer it, but it was a heart that was graced with light that eclipsed its shadows.

Tennessee Williams
February 1974

The Lonely Hunter

Chapter One

GEORGIA GIRLHOOD

*T*ell you what, Helen," said the lanky Georgia girl, "let's skip the cotton candy and hot dogs and save our dimes for the Rubber Man and all the freak shows this year. The Pin Head, the Cigarette Man, the Lady with the Lizard Skin . . . I don't want to miss a single one." Lula Carson Smith's best friend nodded in agreement and the two girls hurried on to be among the first at the midway, pausing only to gape momentarily at the garish billboard across the street proclaiming this year's Chattahoochee Valley Fair "The Greatest Show on Earth."

As a ten-year-old in the deep South in 1927, Lula Carson Smith viewed once more with terror and fascination the midway freaks who made their fall trek to her hometown, Columbus, Georgia. The child craved eye contact with these strange withdrawn creatures who sometimes stared at her sullenly or smiled and crooked a finger beckoningly. Yet she dared only to steal oblique glances, fearful of a mesmeric union. Lula Carson knew intuitively their abject loneliness and felt a kinship through some mysterious connection.

Deeply compassionate, the youngster was becoming increasingly aware that one's physical aberration was but an exaggerated symbol of what she considered everyman's "caught" condition of spiritual isolation and sense of aloneness in spite of his intense desire and effort to relate to others. By the time Carson Smith was seventeen (she had dropped at thirteen the embarrassing tag of Lula and a double name, part of her southern heritage), she was feverishly writing about lonely people. In 1940, at age twenty-two—now married to fellow Southerner Reeves McCullers—Carson McCullers, an unknown writer who previously had had only one short story published, burst upon the New York literary scene with *The Heart Is a Lonely Hunter*. The publisher's find of the decade, she was a star who had hoisted herself by her own petard from a South she ambivalently loved and hated. Within the next ten years the young author won accolades with three additional major novels—*Reflections in a Golden Eye, The Ballad of the Sad Café, The Member of the Wedding*—and converted her fourth book into a prize-winning Broadway play, both a box-office and literary success.

Along with the novels were dozens of short stories and articles published in some of the best slick magazines of the country, an additional Broadway play, and a final book which reflected a broadening of her vision: *Clock Without Hands,* published six years before her death. Yet through it all the motif of loneliness, isolation, and estrangement coursed unbroken, just as it underscored myriad facets of her personal life. To Carson, as to her fictional friends—and they were her friends—reciprocity in a love relationship seemed impossible. One could never be both lover and beloved at the same time. Some of her people never dared to assume either role, or to attempt an exchange.

Frequently in her writings a misshapen body was but a sign of man's incapacity to expand, to give of himself completely or to receive love—an impasse fraught with deep anguish. Countless misguided and fragmented people from her imagined world attempted to find meaning and purpose through personal attachments that ran a broad psychological gamut, but the author never thought such behavior abnormal. She saw their world as an inverted one, in which the norms were normlessness, meaninglessness, purposelessness, powerlessness, and alienation. In response to criticism regarding the apparent freakishness and grotesqueness of certain characters, Carson once wrote:

> One cannot explain accusations of morbidity. A writer can only say he writes from the seed which flowers later in the subconscious. Nature is not abnormal, only lifelessness is abnormal. Anything that pulses and moves and walks around the room, no matter what thing it is doing, is natural and human to the writer.[1]

To pulse and move and walk around a room, however, were not always possible for the author herself. When Carson McCullers died in 1967 at age fifty, she had been an invalid for over twenty-five years. Discomfort and pain had been a way of life since early childhood. Pernicious anemia, accompanied by a series of bouts with pleurisy and other respiratory ailments, had been an early affliction; at fifteen she was stricken with rheumatic fever, incorrectly diagnosed and thus improperly treated. Three strokes followed, and before she was thirty, the left half of her body was partially paralyzed and her mobility seriously impaired. During the next decade Carson's condition steadily deteriorated, and by the time she was forty, had she been any ordinary mortal she doubtless would have been dead. Nor would Carson have survived the many crises of her last ten years had it not been for the devotion, dedication, and professional help of her friend Dr. Mary Mercer. Other highly skilled doctors ministered to Carson's physical needs during this period, but Dr. Mercer also salved her soul. A score of surgeons and other specialists were called in during this time for the many intricate operations to relieve spasms of an atrophying left hand, wrist, elbow, and leg; to repair a shattered hip and elbow, and, later, to perform serious exploratory and corrective hip surgery; to cope with repeated sieges of pneumonia, a severe heart attack . . . and the cataloguing went on and on, reading like a hospital's monthly report.

Surely, if any Job had cause to curse his lot and cry out over the years, "Stop the world, I want to get off," it was Carson McCullers. Yet she seldom complained and clung tenaciously to life, just as she clutched with great dependency at people. Only a few minutes before her fatal stroke she was talking with her young friend Kenneth French, an actor-librarian who rented the basement apartment of her three-story home in Nyack, New York. He had stopped at her bedside to talk about his new role. "We're doing *Stop the World—I Want to Get Off*," French told her.

"Oh, darling, isn't that a marvelous title," Carson sighed, savoring the words in a whisper barely audible. Then she sank again into her pillows and gazed off with her great dark eyes into an imagined land called up at will. To the young man, it was as though she were thinking, "Ahh, to get off. Wouldn't that be something. Wouldn't that be marvelous."[2]

But no matter how tired she was, or how intriguing the idea may have been for the moment, Carson McCullers would not have "gotten off" for the world. Ironically, however, twenty minutes later the world did, indeed, stop for her. Only her faithful companion and servant Ida Reeder heard the startled cry. This time the attack was a massive brain hemorrhage. Forty-five days of coma followed, but the pain-ridden artist never regained consciousness.

Twentieth-century America had lost its lonely hunter.

Even before her birth Lula Carson seemed destined to be different. Her mother, Marguerite Waters Smith, had been alerted by the oracles that her firstborn would be unique. It was a prophecy which failed Marguerite only in that the name she had first selected, Enrico Caruso, would hardly do for a daughter. She confided to friends that there had also been secret prenatal signs that her child would be precocious and eventually achieve greatness as an artist. To Marguerite, even the infant's slightly misshapen head at birth (attributed by the doctor to an arduous delivery) presaged genius.

The local newspaper, however, put little stock in omens and handled the birth in routine fashion four days later:

> Mr. and Mrs. Smith are receiving congratulations of numerous
> friends upon the birth of a baby girl on Monday last. Mrs. Smith
> was formerly Miss Marguerite Waters.[3]

The announcement left the baby unnamed, included only the parents' surname—the most common name in America—and gave no address. Nevertheless, most people who had grown up in Columbus, Georgia, a town of some thirty thousand, knew who the former Miss Waters was, whom she had married, and where she lived. To be sure, Lula Carson Smith, born February 19, 1917, was fated not to be a common child—a destiny linked inextricably with her mother. When friends bearing gifts called upon Marguerite they were invited to gaze upon her infant as though she were a unique mortal whose veins pulsed with ichor, the élan vital of the gods. As Lula Carson herself grew old enough to appreciate and cultivate her destiny, she, too, delighted in perpetuating the image.

Marguerite took little notice that her daughter showed none of the so-called conventional signs of precocity. Moreover, for the child to have been predictable—even in genius—would have been unworthy. Daily activity, however, were it a bath, carriage ride, feeding, or simply a diapering—became, at Marguerite's hands, a studied ritual. Nieces of Lamar Smith, the infant's father, traveled by carriage the forty miles from Society Hill, Alabama, to Columbus, to spend the day with their baby cousin when she was a few weeks old, and as a special treat were allowed to witness the bath. An army could not have been brought more majestically to the field. The little girls beheld with wonderment the blond, straight-haired, squalling infant before them being gently stripped, immersed, patted, oiled, and anointed with violet toilet water. Accompanying the baby's fearsome cries was their aunt Marguerite's praise of her infant's alertness and phenomenal ability to focus on distant objects, to grasp eagerly at a rattle and scrutinize its mysterious parts, and even to cry "on key."[4]

Although it had not yet been revealed to Marguerite Smith just what artistic genre would be her daughter's forte, she was almost certain it would be related to music. Through the years Marguerite did all she could to encourage Lula Carson's development as a musician. The child had been named for her grandmother Lula Carson Waters, Marguerite's widowed mother with whom the Smith family lived. It now seemed fitting to Marguerite that her daughter's musical talent flower at the handsome, rosewood flat-top piano of Lula Waters. The piano had been handed down through several maternal ancestors. Even though Mrs. Waters herself was not a pianist, she loved music and urged guests to play at every opportunity. She had been unable to afford piano lessons for her own children and felt sorely the lack of music in her home. It pleased her to see her daughter ambitious for young Lula Carson as a pianist. When the child could barely walk and was too young to sit alone at the piano stool, Marguerite sat with her daughter on her lap, pressed the chubby fingers to the keyboard, and sang out, "Play, precious, play. Don't you know you'll be famous someday?"

No one in the Smith or Waters family had been famous, but

Marguerite Waters Smith was fiercely proud of her lineage and took satisfaction in knowing that her husband, also, came from good stock. Marguerite's mother had been a Carson, whose ancestors emigrated from Newry, Ireland, and settled in South Carolina before the Revolutionary War. The young men in the family had fought the British with great zeal and were rewarded for their valor with bounty land in Georgia. Later, their four grandsons defended the Confederacy, but only one Carson survived the Civil War.

In the South's ante-bellum days, the Carson clan had been a strong and highly respectable one. Ownership of land and slaves was the chief measure of a southern gentleman then, and by such a yardstick, as well as by their own charm, the Carson men stood tall. One of the biggest landowners of the family was Major John Thomas Carson, Marguerite's grandfather, who was killed in battle in Virginia. John Carson's two-thousand-acre plantation on the Flint River near Reynolds, Georgia, was worked by seventy-five slaves. During the Civil War, however, Wilson's Raiders ravaged his home, fields, and livestock, burned his valuable four-year-old cotton stores, and freed the slaves. The greatest emancipation was of the six Carson women who survived the onslaught. With all but one of their men dead, a matriarchal reign began with Susan Sophronia Carson, the major's widow, and continued through the generations until the scepter was relinquished over a hundred years later by Carson Smith McCullers, who died widowed and childless.

The youngest child—and only daughter—of John Thomas and Susan Sophronia Carson was Lula Caroline, who matured into a beautiful, charming, strong-willed woman, and married into a neighboring family of wealth. Charles Thomas Waters—known as Tom—Lula Caroline's husband, was the son of Elam Waters, a prosperous, benevolent "gentleman" cotton farmer, railroad magnate, and textile mill executive who traveled about Georgia in his private railroad car. Life had been easy for Elam Waters' three sons, who showed little inclination to hard work or interest in managing a mill or railroad someday. Tom Waters was a personable and rather dashing entrepreneur who saw to it that the physical needs and comforts of his growing family were met, but who was seldom at home to share in them himself. Alcoholic, he died before he was thirty; his brothers suffered a similar fate.

Although Elam Waters came to the immediate aid of his widowed daughter-in-law, who had four children and a fifth one on the way, Lula Caroline turned to her own kin for continued support. When her brother Robert Carson was declared guardian of the children, he urged his sister to move near him in Columbus so that he might better look after them. Columbus was a burgeoning border town situated on the east bank of the Chattahoochee River between Georgia and Alabama. One of the first planned communities in the South, it had been chartered in 1828 by the governor, who insisted that there be a systematic street pattern, land set aside for churches and public buildings, and a plan for orderly growth so that Columbus might eventually become an economic trading and transportation hub of the South. When Lula Caroline Waters arrived in 1891, the population had increased from its original three hundred inhabitants, at the time of chartering, to eight thousand. By then, Columbus was a prosperous mill town with a typically stratified southern society: many wealthy millowners, a large segment of whites and blacks who were agonizingly poor (the whites were millworkers and tenant farmers; the blacks, who made up almost a third of the total population, worked as domestics and laborers), and a relatively small middle class.

Lula Waters' brother Robert was considered upper middle class. He and his brother Alphonso ("Forney") had moved to Columbus in their teens. Forney struck out on his own first, and Robert walked the fifty miles from Butler, Georgia, to join him later. Now a successful wholesale and retail druggist, Robert was also a leader in civic and church affairs. Alphonso was a lawyer. Together they welcomed their widowed sister to Columbus and helped establish her, with Robert paying three thousand dollars for a large comfortable house for her a few blocks from his own in the downtown section. Although the town was aware that it was chiefly Robert who supported his sister's family, no one looked upon the newcomers as "charity." The elite of the social and intellectual community approved the young widow's manners, respected her well-bred background of southern gentility, and admired the fine pieces of furniture, elegant antiques, linens, china, and silver which she had brought with her. They also recognized Lula Caroline's ability as a clever, resourceful manager. She sewed carefully for herself and her children and gave the appearance of having a great deal more than people knew she actually had. The young Waters family walked proudly and securely in their new community, and everyone spoke well and affectionately of them.

It was in the old family homestead purchased by Robert Carson for his sister that Lula Carson Smith was born a generation later. By then, all of Lula Waters' children had left home except Marguerite, the youngest, who was born two months after her father's death. Elam married a Valdosta, Georgia, girl and left the South to work for Procter and Gamble in Cincinnati. Helen died in childhood of typhoid fever. Martha—whom the family called Mattie—finished high school, taught, then married C. Graham Johnson, a local druggist. Gorham Carson, the fourth child, died of blood poisoning when he was twenty.

After the other children were gone, Marguerite and her mother lived alone for almost six years in the sprawling, one-story, wood-frame home on the corner of Fifth Avenue and Thirteenth Street. By the time Marguerite reached her mid-twenties and still did not have a serious suitor, her friends stopped chiding her about being an old maid. It was one thing to be teased about it, and quite another to actually be one, they thought. Although Marguerite had lived through her share of infatuations, such pinings usually went unnoticed except at home. Marguerite was a pretty girl —as was her sister Mattie—and most of her friends could not understand why she had not married. Some decided that the men who might have responded seriously were deterred by what the girls called Marguerite's "harum-scarum personality" and a haughtiness she did not intend. Nevertheless, she was good company and well liked once a person got to know her.

Lula Waters was concerned about her daughter's spinsterhood, but Marguerite herself seemed not to mind. By the time she was twenty-five, however, and there was still no prospective husband in sight, her mother urged her to go to work. Mrs. Waters felt certain that her daughter would be happier in a respectable job than "idling" at home. Marguerite had shown no interest in going to college, teaching, or any other gainful employment, but she loved flowers and enjoyed gardening, reading, eating— she was just a little plump, she admitted—and storytelling. Sewing, needlepoint, and other conventional constructive hobbies bored her. She would rather be free to move around, to be with people and talk, visit in their homes, walk with them, or amble along neighborhood streets alone and look into the faces of strangers. Imaginative reverie was her favorite pastime, and she frequently sat on the front porch with half a dozen neighborhood children gathered about her, who listened avidly to her tangents of fantasy. Marguerite made up wonderful stories, with her daring protagonists always bearing unmistakable characteristics of the narrator herself. Years later, after her daughter Carson began to write and her books and stories were being read in Columbus, the older families who remembered Marguerite's own bent for storytelling felt certain that Marguerite was the real author of her daughter's fiction. It was only after Marguerite's death and Carson's works continued to appear that many people in Columbus ruefully admitted: "It must have been little Lula Carson after all."

In 1915, however, Marguerite decided that she would no longer stay at home indefinitely, but would go to work. Her mother heard that Schomburg Jewelers was looking for a shopgirl, and soon Marguerite was behind the counter. It was a happy experience for the most part, for Marguerite enjoyed the activity of the shop and the opportunity of seeing new faces. Schomburg's was one of Columbus' leading jewelry stores, and Fred Schomburg considered his new employee's friendly manner in dealing with customers a decided asset.

A fellow employee also took notice of the scintillating shopgirl in a manner that amazed everyone. Lamar Smith, twenty-six, was a shy, reserved watch repairman from Tuskegee, Alabama, who had never before shown any real interest in women. In the past, the inner workings of a fine gold watch or the chimes of an antique French clock which needed adjustment had intrigued him far more than the pulsing heart of a female. When Lamar began to see Marguerite away from the store, people were even more surprised.

In courting Marguerite Waters, Lamar was frequently invited to dinner by her mother, for not only Marguerite but Lula Waters, too, found his affable manner and quiet sincerity appealing. Mrs. Waters also recognized the young man as a potential husband who would be a sturdy, dependable provider for her daughter. Nothing would have pleased Lula Waters more than to have her daughter marry Lamar Smith so that the three of them might all live together in the old Thirteenth Street home. The more the two women saw of the kind and gentle watch repairman, the more they wondered if it might eventually become a permanent arrangement.

Lamar shared with them many anecdotes of his childhood in Alabama, but his taletelling usually lacked the imaginative quality of Marguerite's. Some of the facts were grim, for in Lamar's family, living had been a serious and practical affair. He had grown up with little supervision as the youngest son of ten children. His father, William Hooker Smith, had come South from Connecticut as a young man, prompted by chronic illnesses and the need for a more temperate climate. He had settled in Union Springs, a small Alabama farming community, and married well. His wife, Molly Gachet, was a member of the wealthy Stubbs family of Savannah, Georgia. For several years William Smith farmed hard and successfully; then his right arm was wrenched off in a cotton gin accident. With a handicap both psychic and physical, William felt severely maimed and believed that he could no longer provide adequately for his large family. In an effort to cope, he abandoned the farm and moved to Tuskegee, the county seat, where he was hired as a tax collector. William Smith's salary, combined with Molly's resourcefulness, might well have enabled him to meet his family's needs, but too frequently he squandered his money on liquor. Just as with Marguerite's mother upon the death of her husband, so it was with Molly Smith. Of necessity, a strong matriarchal figure emerged.

Too proud to acknowledge to her Savannah family her financial plight, Molly Smith pulled her large brood together as best she could, accepted her husband under their roof when he chose to be there, and with the aid of her children managed a bearable and dignified life style. All the boys except William, Jr., who had been born crippled and walked with heavy steel braces, worked at odd jobs. Lamar, inventive and curious, had tinkered as a child with everything mechanical within reach. Soon he began repairing bicycles, lawn mowers, and small motors for the townspeople, who understood and sympathized with the family's situation. At fifteen Lamar became an apprentice watch repairman to a jeweler. Then his father died in 1906, shortly after Lamar's graduation from high school, and one by one his mother and brothers migrated north to Buffalo and Detroit. Once his sisters were married or in college, however, Lamar—newly turned twenty-one in 1910—decided there was nothing more to hold him in Tuskegee and that he would cross the Chattahoochee and seek employment in Columbus, forty miles to the east.

Lamar had relatives in Columbus on his mother's side; thus it was to his cousin Rochelle Martiniere and her son Nick to whom he applied for room and board in exchange for a token payment and odd jobs around the house. Before long he put out a sign in front of the Martiniere home advertising himself as a repairman of bicycles, sewing machines, lawn mowers, clocks, and watches. There were few requests for his services, however, and the money only trickled in. Then he approached Fred Schomburg in his jewelry store and asked for a job. Lamar, wearing a visored repairman's cap, showed Schomburg his tools and said that he was ready to start that moment. The jeweler liked the looks of this large, slouchy country boy and appreciated his air of confidence. Lamar told him that he could repair almost anything that had movable parts. That the young man was kin to Rochelle Martiniere was a recommendation in itself, thought Schomburg. When he took Lamar to the clock department and showed him a number of old-style French clocks with chimes, which were difficult to clean and regulate, he said: "These clocks take a half day to repair. Can you work on them, son?"

"Yes, sir," Lamar replied assuredly, enamored of the beauty of their cabinets and intricate interiors and impatient to begin.

"Then you're hired," said Schomburg. Even Lamar's twenty-dollar-a-week salary—more than he had ever dreamed of earning—was less exciting to him than the opportunity to work full time as a craftsman of fine clocks and watches.

As the months passed the young repairman was happy in his new life in Columbus. Lamar was devoted to his work, but on weekends he looked forward to tramping in the woods alone or with his cousin Nick Martiniere. They picked berries, fished the river, skimmed stones across its surface, and often swam in the cool water. A restless man, Lamar needed to be doing something most of the time. Even in the store there was a vague uneasiness about him. He felt cramped and nervous after sitting and concentrating for long hours with his jeweler's glass in his eye. Three or four times a day Lamar bolted from his bench and walked up and down Broad Street, on which the shop was located, then down to Front Street and sometimes across the river, savoring the sun and fresh air. Fond of beer, he often stopped at Strauss's Delicatessen, where for a nickel the proprietor included a free sandwich with the beer.

He seldom stopped to talk to people, but they noticed him on his walks for he moved awkwardly, his gait resembling a shuffle, as though something were wrong with his legs. Lamar told Marguerite that his trouble was flat feet, which had bothered him all his life. Frequently a source of embarrassment, his feet had also kept him from participating successfully in sports in high school. He liked to walk, but did not do it well. Once Lamar attempted to accompany Schomburg and other hikers on a weekend walking tour deep into Alabama, but his feet became so lame that he had to abandon the group and return home by train. Weeks later he was still too crippled to walk easily and had to use a cane. Throughout most of his life, in fact, Lamar Smith looked, walked, and acted as though he were exhausted. Also, his clothes, though clean, never looked quite pressed. His posture was slumped, whether he was seated or walking, and his over-all appearance was that of a man who had been carelessly put together.

When Marguerite Waters came into his life, however, in 1915, Lamar Smith's whole psychic vision sharpened. Whereas before he had accepted his solitude and restlessness without question, he now wanted to be around people. No longer diffident, he would stretch his limbs in the shop and talk with Marguerite instead of taking long walks down Broad Street. A year of courtship followed; then Lamar asked Marguerite to marry him. He had been single long enough, he declared. He loved her and they would be good for each other. Marguerite's answer was an immediate departure for Jacksonville to visit an old friend, Mildred Salisbury, "because I need time to make up my mind," she explained coyly. Impatient, however, Lamar arrived unannounced on Miss Salisbury's doorstep two days later to push his suit, and Marguerite, delighted by an impetuousness she had not seen in him before, decided that they should marry at once. That it was Valentine's Day doubtless appealed to Marguerite's romantic and imaginative nature. They were married without family or fanfare in a simple ceremony in Jacksonville on February 14, 1916.

When Lamar and Marguerite returned to Columbus, there was never any question about where they would live. Lula Waters gave her "children" the large back bedroom and urged them never to leave. She wanted and needed their companionship, she said; moreover, she was in a position now to assist them financially if necessary, for she had inherited money from her brother Robert, who had died two years earlier. With two of her own children dead, Elam in Cincinnati, and Martha rearing a family in a home of her own, Lula Caroline Waters needed Marguerite and Lamar as much as they needed her.

Encouraged by his wife, Lamar now decided to open his own jewelry store. His reputation as an honest and highly skilled craftsman was unexcelled in his trade, and he had gained many friends during his six years at Schomburg's who admired his spirit in striking off on his own and gave him their business. At first Lamar rented a small shop at 19 Twelfth Street in the heart of downtown, but just off the main thoroughfare. Then he invested his small savings in jewelry stock so that he might expand his business. Marguerite assisted her husband by selling a small inheritance of Bibb Manufacturing stock and helping him choose silver, watches, and jewelry for his customers. Business was good, and when their first child arrived a few weeks after he opened his new shop, Marguerite was certain that little Lula Carson was their harbinger of new happiness, prosperity, and, eventually, fame.

Prompted by Marguerite's effervescence, the young couple communicated freely and dreamed and planned together for great success in the future. At home with her baby but much interested, also, in the shop, Marguerite queried her husband each evening about the various facets of the business. She wanted to know how many customers he had had that day, who had come to him *first*—instead of going to Schomburg or one of his other, larger competitors—which specific brooch, watch, or silver bowl had been sold, and to whom. The watch repair business was lively, but they both lamented that the location of his shop did not invite enough window-shopping traffic and potential customers for the jewelry stock. Suddenly Marguerite was taken by the idea of having a shop in the lobby of a movie theatre. Where else was there more flow both day and night, she reasoned. Lamar was persuaded to look into the possibilities, and almost before he knew it negotiations had been completed with the manager of the Grand Theatre on Broad Street for the construction of a tiny shop just off the theatre's lobby.

Once again business thrived, and in their new location Lamar employed a young assistant, Martha Hogan, to wait on customers and keep books so that he could work full time at his bench. The paper work end of a business had never appealed to him, but he loved his craft and it pleased him to see people delight in an old watch that formerly had defied running, or a clock that now chimed on the hour and half hour and kept perfect time. "It was a wonderful experience to work for Mr. Smith," said Mrs. Hogan. "The shop was postage-stamp size, not much larger than four by six feet, but we loved it. If we had two customers at once, one of us had to move out through a glass partition and stand in the alcove of the theatre lobby."[5]

On May 13, 1919, a second major change occurred in the Smith household. Lula Carson, now twenty-seven months old, found herself with a baby brother. Marguerite wisely had included her daughter in all the preliminary arrangements for the new baby, and her firstborn was intrigued by the chubby, red-faced infant who finally arrived. There was no reason for jealousy of her new sibling, for Lula Carson was always made to feel that she was foremost in her mother's affection and was encouraged to participate in the various affairs of the nursery. Lula Carson now became known as "Sister" to her mother and father, and young Lamar, Jr., was called "Brother-Man."

Whereas Sister had been very much her mother's child, Brother-Man was his father's. Now that there were four, Lamar, Sr., became more active with the family. At work he had always been sure of his position—and had an important one—but at home when there had been just the three, he often felt excluded. He did not know how to cope with his wife and young daughter together, for his serious nature and practical-mindedness kept him from fantasizing with them and entering freely into their childlike games. He felt safer at his jeweler's bench. With a new baby in the household, however, Lamar adjusted his hours and did not work so late at the store. He loved being with his children, especially when Brother-Man was big enough to be bounced on the bed and thrown in the air over the sofa. Sometimes he made up nursery rhymes and tall tales and chanted them to his children. A favorite of his young son's was a rhyme he adapted from the folk song "Old Dan Tucker":

> *Brother-Man Smith is a good old soul,*
> *Picks his teeth with a telegraph pole,*
> *Washes his face in a frying pan,*
> *Eats his supper like a man.*[6]

Lamar liked to take his family on Sunday excursions. Frequently they packed a picnic lunch and rented a horse and buggy to journey a few miles north of town to Blue Springs, where they picked berries, waded in the creek, and gathered wild flowers. Such outings delighted Lula Carson, who loved to roam outdoors and scrutinize every facet of nature. Occasionally, too, they rode over to Union Springs, Alabama, to visit Lamar's two sisters who had remained in the South. Every activity included Marguerite's mother. It was Lula Waters who insisted that the family participate in the various First Baptist Church activities: Sunday school and church, evening prayer meetings, church suppers, and congregational outings. Mrs. Waters had faithfully reared her own children in that church, and Lamar, too, had been baptized there upon his marriage to Marguerite. Although the Smith family dutifully followed Lula Waters' lead—for there was no questioning her matriarchal hand—Lula Carson and her father much preferred activities that involved only the immediate family.

When Lamar, Jr., was a baby, Marguerite expressed little concern that her firstborn's genius was not being directed into some explicit channel. She did not have time to worry that her child at age three had not astounded the community by reciting Greek or holding forth in Socratic manner to afternoon callers, but she did want Lula Carson at least to be exposed to a teacher who might encourage her talents to flower more readily. Consequently, the child was enrolled in kindergarten in September 1921 at age four and a half.

Lula Carson had always shown a lively interest in words, especially big ones that were a challenge to pronounce. She also happily made up stories for Brother-Man while turning the pages of her picture book. Although too young to understand the words, Lamar, Jr., was hypnotized by his sister's large, expressive, gray-green eyes that opened wide as she fantasized and "read" in her thick, soft southern accent. Even before kindergarten Lula Carson could recognize many words. When alone, she searched her books or the daily paper for familiar words; then at night she sat on the arm of her father's chair and "read" to him, making up the story as she went along, but astounding him with many of the actual words that she knew. Books had always been a springboard for Lula Carson's imagination. There was never a moment's hesitation when she was asked as a preschooler what she would like for her birthday or Christmas: "I want books—lots of books, Mama." Marguerite spent many hours reading aloud to her daughter, cradling her in her lap and pointing out especially "delicious" words, savoring and pronouncing each one carefully, explaining its meaning, and almost telling a new story in the process.

Except for the times she was out tramping in the woods with her father or playing with her cousins or her friend Helen Jackson, young Lula Carson showed a marked preference for solitude. She always played quietly when she was alone, and Marguerite frequently looked in on her to see what game or toy she might be engrossed with at that moment. It was not unusual for Marguerite to find her daughter sitting apart from books, dolls, and teacups, and facing a blank wall or looking out the window. "What are you doing, precious?" Marguerite would ask.

"Thinking, Mama, thinking. That's fun, too." Lula Carson's vibrant response revealed that her mental play was far more stimulating than any actual activity. What others thought of as shyness, aloofness, or even boredom in the child was, in reality, a preference and delight in fantasy. In truth, real people frequently did bore her. It annoyed Lula Carson when her mother urged her to "run along and play with the other children now" and said that she must not stay alone so much.

Even as a very small child Lula Carson experienced an ambivalence that possessed her the rest of her life. She yearned to belong to a group—or at least to be *able* to join one if she chose—yet she retained always a sense of her own separateness and the need to feel and remain unique. Many years later she wrote:

> To the spectator, the amateur philosopher, no motive among the complex ricochets of our desires and rejections seems stronger or more enduring than the will of the individual to claim his identity and belong. From infancy to death, the human being is obsessed by these dual motives. . . . After the first establishment of identity there comes the imperative need to lose this new-found sense of separateness and to belong to something larger and more powerful than the weak, lonely self. The sense of moral isolation is intolerable to us.[7]

Lula Carson felt a similar ambivalence toward her mother. She worshiped Marguerite and was seldom away from her side as a child. She basked in the contentment of her mother's praise and beatification, yet at times recoiled from the smothering influence that threatened the development of her own inclinations and personality. It was gratifying to be touted as a genius, but troubling, also, when the genius was not recognizable or had not emerged. "What is it you say I have, Mama? Tell me about it," she probed. The challenges and demands of a pedestal life were burdensome for a little girl whose formative years might well have been more sunny.

Lula Carson was not a happy child. In an essay written a number of years later, she recalled an incident when as a four-year-old she had been walking one day with her nurse past a Catholic convent. Surprised to find that, contrary to habit, the doors had been left open, Lula Carson looked inside the enclosure and saw children eating ice-cream cones and playing on iron swings:

> . . . I watched, fascinated. I wanted to go in, but my nurse said no, I was not Catholic. The next day, the gate was shut. But, year by year, I thought of what was going on, of this wonderful party, where I was shut out. I wanted to climb the wall, but I was too little. I beat on the wall once, and I knew all the time that there was a marvelous party going on, but I couldn't get in.[8]

That experience and the convent's inaccessibility became a symbol of the gulf that Lula Carson Smith felt for the rest of her life. Marguerite, by her adamant insistence that her daughter was different from everyone else, inadvertently encouraged her child's sense of self-estrangement and isolation. Even before Lula Carson began first grade, she had already experienced some of the group rejection she suffered in more bitter measure later from her peers. Had it not been for her friend Helen Jackson, Lula Carson would have been a far more unhappy and lonely child.

She and Helen had been thrown together almost daily since early childhood. Her friend, a year older, lived across Thirteenth Street and three doors down the block on Fifth Avenue in a large, white-columned ante-bellum home. Helen's father owned a lumberyard. When Lula Carson was five and old enough to recognize the signs of affluence, she envied Helen, with whom she sometimes argued about being rich or famous. Helen, squeamish about being thought rich, defended herself from her friend's accusing voice: "But Lula Carson, I'm not rich, honest."

"Oh, yes you are, you live in a big house—a lot bigger than mine," Lula Carson countered.

"Well, you all have a car—we don't have a car—we aren't rich," replied Helen.

Then Lula Carson announced with a note of defiance: "I'm going to be both rich *and* famous someday." To Helen, her friend's attitude was incomprehensible. She did not understand fame or riches. She did not understand Lula Carson either. It seemed that Lula Carson wanted fame more than anything else in the world, for her reasoning was that "famous people really *are* somebody!"

By this time a new conflict had developed, brought on by what she considered an intrusion in her own household: "the new baby sister."⁹ On August 2, 1922, Margarita Gachet Smith was born. Named for her mother and her father's maternal French ancestor, Dr. Charles Gachet, the infant sister posed an immediate threat to Lula Carson's security. Jealous of a new love object in the family and irritated by a crying baby who seemed always to be in her mother's lap, Lula Carson responded with both hostility and love. She had loved her baby brother, whom she could kiss and snuggle and sometimes even sleep with. She liked him, also, because they could play together, even if he were sometimes a tagalong. But "Baby Sister"—whom she called Bonny—was not good for anything that Lula Carson at age five and a half could figure out.

Had it not been for her friendship with Helen Jackson and, later, a catharsis brought about by Christmas fireworks, Lula Carson's psychic conflict might not have been resolved so successfully. In a *Mademoiselle* article years later, "The Discovery of Christmas," she wrote of the incident. She said that she and her brother were recovering from scarlet fever and were experiencing the misery of the long quarantine which followed. Her baby sister was "that hated rival" for whom her mother had deserted her, and along with that realization were two other simultaneous discoveries: that according to her mother, Santa Claus was "only parents," and that "Jesus is church . . . Jesus is as the holy infant—like Bonny." Believing that her two idols, Santa Claus and Jesus, had been reduced to "just family," Lula Carson repudiated them both, then wailed that she hated her baby sister.

It was Christmas morning, she said, and her parents had left the chil-

dren alone for a few minutes. Stimulated by a tale their nurse had told
her—that her baby son had burned to death on the fireplace hearth one
Christmas morning—Lula Carson lifted her sister from her crib and carried her to her grandmother's hearth, placed her beside the fire, and left
her, hoping that the infant might mysteriously be consumed. Then she
took her brother to the room in the back of the house where they had suffered their quarantine together and told him that she would show him
"how to have fun." Handing three-year-old Lamar, Jr., a Roman candle,
she helped him light it, then lit one herself:

> I thought I remembered the fireworks, but I had never seen any-
> thing like this. After a hiss and sputter the Roman candles, violent
> and alive, shot in streams of yellow and red. We stood on opposite
> sides of the room and the blazing fireworks ricocheted from wall to
> wall in an arch of splendor and terror. It lasted a long time and we
> stood transfixed in the radiant, fearful room. When finally it was fin-
> ished, my hostile feelings had disappeared. I was quiet in the very
> silent room.[10]

Then Lula Carson thought she heard her baby sister crying and rushed
into the living room to save her. But the child was all right. She had
turned over, away from the fire, and was crawling toward the Christmas
tree. It was the first time Lula Carson had seen her sister crawl, and now
she watched her with the "first feelings of love and pride, the old hostility
gone forever." Moreover, in her new tranquillity, she reasoned that it was
all right for Santa Claus to be "only family" and thought happily that perhaps her "family and Jesus were somehow kin."

During Lula Carson's early life there was no trauma of such complexity as the jealousy aroused by her sister, Margarita, feelings which she
tried to keep buried until years later when as an adult she chose to articulate and transform them into fiction and other writings. Doubtless more
justified was the resentment that Baby Sister and Brother-Man felt at
times in reaction to their mother's partiality to Lula Carson. According
to Lamar, Jr., however, if jealousy were felt toward their sister, it was
never actively expressed: "Not only were we proud that Lula Carson had
proved herself a genius in her writings, but we also believed that our
mother was almost one herself for recognizing it in our sister and helping
bring it to fruition. Our mother lived for Lula Carson, and Lula Carson
could not have been what she was without her."[11]

It never occurred to those in the downtown neighborhood, however,
that Marguerite Smith's eldest child was extraordinarily different. It was
Marguerite whom people in Columbus were more impressed by. She was
fun to be with, whimsical and unpredictable, but always genial and a lady.
There were times when she expressed her reluctance to leave an informal

gathering on a neighbor's porch: "I do hate to leave—I just know you're going to talk about me when I'm gone." And the town did talk, but their words were kind, for they admired and loved her. A stimulating conversationalist, Marguerite loved to have people in to talk. She was well read, appreciated good music, and had an excellent classical record collection which she shared in the evenings with friends. She also was conversant with community and world affairs, even though later, in the 1930s, she could not understand fully the significance of the Depression. (Sometimes impractical, Marguerite did not always understand why she could not keep spending money in the usual manner, even though her husband was bringing home rabbits, birds, fresh vegetables, and eggs in payment for watch repairs and jewelry.) Although Marguerite did not move in the social orbit of the most affluent in Columbus, she had many good friends who were wives of wealthy millowners and other business executives, and they visited freely in each other's homes.

Helen Jackson, Carson's cousins, and other children in the neighborhood loved especially to play in the Smith home, where they could always count on being welcomed with a sincerity that frequently did not ring true elsewhere. Marguerite encouraged the neighborhood children to call her "Bebe," an affectionate nickname which had started in her immediate family. According to Helen, "I'd much rather play at Bebe's than in my own home, where we were treated like sissy little girls and made to take naps and dress up in frilly clothes to go out visiting with grown folks." Instead, Marguerite gave the children her own good clothes and shoes to play dress-up in and frequently joined them in their fantasies. She sat with them at their tea parties and joined them in calling upon neighbors, the three of them clad in "dress-up attire," pretending to be emissaries from the Baptist Church calling upon fallen parishioners or suffragettes—missions in which Marguerite would never have participated.

The children in the neighborhood and Marguerite's adult friends loved the easy way of life of the Smith home, an atmosphere not regulated by clocks and schedules. Even though Lamar Smith's daily concern as a jeweler and watch repairman was with time, he was the lord of only one castle. The shop was his domain, but at home, the women reigned. Meals were cooked and chores performed because they were the acts of the moment, without rule or habit.

Such permissiveness, however, was not prevalent until after the death of Lula Carson's grandmother on November 21, 1923, a few months before the child's seventh birthday. Until then, Lula Waters had been the disciplinarian of the household and exercised the few controls that were in evidence. It was *her* home, and although she allowed her son-in-law to be the titular head for the sake of the census and city directory, one never forgot that Grandmother Waters was the family's ruling elder. What friends referred to as Marguerite's "flighty nature" had been only slightly subdued by her motherhood and responsibilities over the past seven years of marriage; her mother's practical conservatism, however, had imposed order upon the Smith family's affairs. Lula Carson was devoted to her grandmother—who had seemed more partial to her namesake than to her other grandchildren—and Mrs. Waters' death from pernicious anemia was a severe shock to the child. Allowed to attend her grandmother's funeral, Lula Carson was puzzled about death and tried to figure out how her grandmother's spirit could get out of the body and the blackness of that "awful, closed-up casket." Such enigmas were pondered over many times by young Lula Carson, just as they were later by her fictional creation Frankie Addams, who puzzled over her cousin John Henry's death in *The Member of the Wedding.*

Soon after Mrs. Waters died, several noticeable changes were apparent in the Smith household. No longer did family life pivot around the First Baptist Church and its activities. In fact, Lamar and Marguerite's churchgoing stopped almost entirely. Although the older children had attended Sunday school or the church nursery regularly since they were toddlers, Lamar, Sr., now walked his offspring to Sunday school, then went on to his shop to wind the timepieces and work for several hours. After church the children scampered up Broad Street to join their father. Accompanied frequently by Helen Jackson, who felt that she was not just Lula Carson's friend but a member of the Smith family herself, they asked permission to put on Mr. Smith's eyeglass and eyeshade and sit at his bench to examine the mysterious workings which lay before them. Then, ready to leave, they begged Mr. Smith to walk them the short distance over the Chattahoochee River bridge to gape—always with disappointment—at the sights in Phenix City, Alabama. The neighboring town was known as "Sin City" and often had been preached against by religious and civic leaders of Columbus as a modern Sodom and Gomorrah destined to fall. Weekly, Lula Carson expected to find that the town across the river had slid into the Chattahoochee. On Sunday mornings, however, it was calm and innocuous-looking, and on their walks Lula Carson admitted relief to her friend in learning once again that "all those innocent people had been spared another week."

Later, after Carson McCullers' fiction appeared, defensive Columbus residents were quick to point out that their naive little hometown girl had doubtless gotten her ideas for what they called "all those wicked, dirty old stories" in "Sin City." Columbus, however, had ample attractions of its own at the time, and Lula Carson did not, of necessity, have to go across the river to stoke her imagination with naturalistic details that were more than envisioned. Occasionally as a teen-ager she did go to Phenix City to drink beer, sit in the honky-tonks, and observe a more garish way

of life than she was accustomed to in Columbus, but the change in locale was purely a choice. Moreover, as a writer, she never sought out actuality of experience to reinforce her fiction. In fact, she usually avoided it.
When her husband suggested a few months after they were married that
he take her to a deaf-and-dumb convention in Macon, Georgia, so that
she might authenticate her concept of John Singer, the deaf-mute protagonist of *The Heart Is a Lonely Hunter*, she declined. She had already written that part of the novel, she said, and wanted to keep true her own
imagined image. Later, in 1949 when she was visiting in Macon while
Clock Without Hands was germinating, journalist Margaret Long offered
to take her to see "some lintheads on strike, some labor leaders, some Ne-
groes reorganizing the NAACP, some restless young people and the Council on Human Relations of black and white do-gooders," but the author
again said *no.* To Carson McCullers, imagination was far truer than reality.[12]

In spite of her parents' increasing disinterest in church and organized
religion after Mrs. Waters' death, Lula Carson went through a period of
being very much enchanted by them. On November 21, 1925, she joined
the First Baptist Church with her friend Helen Jackson, and the following spring they presented themselves for baptism. Lula Carson had
decided that if her grandmother had been alive then, she would have
wanted her to do that. Moreover, according to Helen, "Lula Carson took
her church-joining as serious business." Walking home after the service
that day, still dripping from their immersion, Lula Carson asked Helen
with great earnestness: "Do you feel different?"

"What are you talking about, Lula Carson?"

"I mean—we've just been baptized—we're supposed to feel different."

"No, I don't feel anything. But we get to take communion like everybody else now. We get to drink that ole grape juice and eat those little
bits of bread. That'll be fun."

"But we *are* different, Helen, no matter how we feel," Lula Carson
insisted. "When we die, we'll go to heaven now."

"Oh," said Helen, not at all concerned about that and surprised that
Lula Carson was.

For seven years Lula Carson was regular in her Sunday-school attend-
ance and took her church worship seriously. It also was comforting to be a
member of a group. She memorized Bible passages well and thoroughly
enjoyed reeling them off in her Sunday-school class, aware that she was
impressing both classmates and teacher with the fact that she had memorized many more verses than the week's assignment. If she were not in
the act of performing, however, she seemed to her teachers to be painfully shy. It was Lula Carson's habit to come into class a few minutes late,
for she did not like the socializing that preceded the class and the routine

preliminaries of getting settled. She slid quietly into her seat—usually one next to the door—and kept her eyes averted to her lap or in a vague gaze into the distance. Sometimes her teacher caught her eye and Lula Carson smiled back timidly and looked attentive. But she seldom fooled her teacher, who felt sure that her thoughts were elsewhere. When Lula Carson was about fourteen her teachers noticed that she simply had stopped coming. She had announced to her mother that she did not care to go to Sunday school or church again, and that was all there was to it. Her brother and sister continued, but Lula Carson stayed at home with Marguerite, read, and played the piano. She liked having just the two of them share the house on Sunday mornings.

Another important change in the life style of the Smith family after Lula Carson's grandmother died came about in 1925 when Lamar, Sr., bought his first car, a four-cylinder Whippet coupé, and a few months later moved his family to the suburbs. It was Marguerite's decision to sell the old homestead on Thirteenth Street and Fifth Avenue, which her mother had willed jointly to Marguerite, Mattie, and Elam, the three surviving Waters children. But Mattie and Elam had sold their shares to Marguerite soon after their mother's death and later, when the house was sold by Marguerite as the sole owner, she was pleased that the sale price was ten thousand dollars more than Robert Carson had paid for the house in 1891. (The property, however, included by this time a small adjacent tenant house and lot that Lula Waters had purchased in 1915 with a legacy from her brother.)

The exodus from downtown had already begun before Lula Waters' death, and now many prominent families were living in attractive, outlying areas. The old residential section in which Marguerite had been reared had declined as encroaching industrial businesses moved into the area with the city's increased prosperity of the mid-1920s. Moreover, residential growth in the Smith family's immediate neighborhood had been curtailed because of the north-south railroad lines which ran just a block away, and the business district and Chattahoochee River which bounded them to the west. The older sections, both to the north and south, were already overflowing, and there were a number of black homes in the immediate vicinity.

The thought of moving from the old familiar neighborhood troubled young Lula Carson at first. Although she had always been closely supervised by her mother, there were occasions when she was given permission to walk up and down the block with her friend Helen Jackson, or as a special treat, to go to the little store, run by a black proprietor, located a few doors up the street. Here the children bought penny candy and sometimes a watermelon or something their mothers had forgotten to get at the "big store" two blocks away. Lula Carson was curiously interested in the black people she met along the streets of her neighborhood. She had accompanied her mother and their cousin Marie Berry into almost every black home in the community in Marguerite's obsessive search for antiques, and Lula Carson felt a boldness in her jaunts that other children in Columbus might have been more timorous about. Sometimes she took short walks alone, and when she spotted a black woman in her yard poking laundry down into a pot over an open fire or making odoriferous lye soap, she squatted beside her to watch the mysterious process and questioned her closely about the various aspects of her labors. Even as a child she knew intuitively that the blacks were treated as second-class citizens, and sometimes she probed her father with such questions as why "colored people" had their own drinking fountains and why most fountains said "White Only." She wondered why white people were not supposed to drink after them, especially since "colored people cook for us and we *eat* after them." She also wondered why colored people lived in little brown houses and tar paper shacks and seemed so poor, and why white people never worked for colored people. She could never quite get the answers she wanted.

Even as a four-year-old, Lula Carson felt sympathy for the black man and tried to spare him degradation. Once when her mother sent her to the neighborhood black grocery to buy nuts for her Christmas fruitcakes, Marguerite said: "Get some niggertoes, Sister." But Lula Carson, troubled by the request and embarrassed to repeat the degrading word to her black friend—for she felt, indeed, that he was her friend—walked timidly to the counter and whispered: "A pound of colored-toes, please." She had no idea what a "niggertoe" was; she knew only that she did not want to ask for it. When she could not even point to the object she wished to buy, the puzzled proprietor sent her home. After a candid talk with her mother, Lula Carson returned to the store, this time beaming happily, and said, "A pound of Brazil nuts, please."

The child's compassion for the plight of her black friends incurred still another troubling ambivalence in her psychological make-up. Although she sympathized with them and regretted their status of servitude, Lula Carson was not so much the liberationist that she wanted to do her own work. She resented the fact that most of the other families in her neighborhood had servants full time, but that hers did not. In their new Wynnton neighborhood, Vannie Copeland Jackson, the black domestic who worked regularly for the family next door, came to the Smiths only part time, or when the Robin Mullin family was away. Marguerite, however, did not want a full-time servant or need one, she said. The "heavy" wash was sent out to a woman who laundered and ironed at home, and the personal wash and other household chores were done by another woman who came in two or three mornings a week. Most of the time Marguerite preferred to do her own cooking, and she was an excellent cook. Relatives of the Smith family were somewhat chagrined over the years that in Carson's fiction, as well as in conversation with friends in the North, she sometimes "poor-mouthed" her growing-up years in Columbus, as though her adolescence had been fraught with hardship and deprivation. According to her brother, Lamar, "We were not rich, but we lived in a respectable, upper middle-class neighborhood and had everything we needed. Lula Carson never lacked for a thing she wanted. She did not even have to wash out her underwear."[13]

When Marguerite Smith sold her mother's old family home on Thirteenth Street so that they could move to the suburbs, they first rented a small house at 2417 Wynnton Road. Here the family lived for a year while Marguerite searched for a suitable home to buy. Then, in January 1927, Marguerite purchased—again in her name alone—a one-story stucco house at 1519 Starke Avenue, two blocks from the Wynnton Road location. To class-conscious Columbus society, this address was much better than either of the former addresses of the Smith family, for many prominent professional men and businessmen lived on the street. The move, however, was in no way a calculated one on Marguerite's part to be socially advantageous. Marguerite Smith liked simple, unpretentious things and people.

Living on Starke Avenue and going to a new school was an exciting move for Lula Carson, but one that was accepted with mixed emotions. (In third grade she had transferred from the Sixteenth Street School to Wynnton Elementary, located a block from her house.) On one hand, Lula Carson liked her new neighborhood because it was quiet, the streets tree lined, and there were woods to tramp in nearby. There was also a small lake a few blocks away which was her special haven. Here she walked, sat, and meditated. But the move posed new problems for the sensitive, introverted child. It meant having to adjust to new playmates at school or not having any; giving birthday parties and going to them; having proms, into which birthday parties were transmogrified when the honoree became thirteen; and being asked out on dates, or being ignored and not asked to go anywhere. It meant social affairs given by her more affluent neighbors and parties and outings from which she might have preferred to be excluded. Yet if she were left out, a well-meaning friend or family member invariably sympathized that Lula Carson had not been invited and thus new feelings of rebuff and hurt were provoked. At age nine Lula Carson hated more than anything else being made to do "sissy things with sissy little girls," said Helen Jackson, and many times the child was thus mortified. Fortunately for Lula Carson, Helen, too, moved to the Wynnton neighborhood with her family the following year, and they again became almost constant companions.

Eventually Lula Carson found Wynnton a neighborhood that suited her preadolescent needs. She joined the "Wynnton girls" in skating on the sidewalks, playing hide-and-seek and kick-the-can in the street and yards until nightfall, and sometimes football and other tomboyish sports. There were fewer restrictions in the new neighborhood. Even more so in her new environment, however, Lula Carson was troubled by what seemed to be significant differences between her status and those around her. The fact that Helen Jackson and several others in the neighborhood had a horse or pony and she did not, that many others on her block had a full-time maid and her family did not, that some of the children seemed to have much more spending money than she, that her family seemed less secure financially than those who lived around her—all became exaggerated painful reminders that she was different, somehow an entity set apart from any group. Her identification with the alien, poor, and oppressed evolved as a natural accompaniment to such feelings. Although magnified in Lula Carson's mind far more than in actuality—just as the imagined continued to be more real for her than the actual—such self-identity was damaging to her psyche, while at the same time it helped mold her into the writer she became.

To cope, Lula Carson attempted to gain recognition, to be noticed, to excel in anything that interested her and could be made competitive. Just as she had outmemorized her classmates in Sunday school in their Bible verses, so, too, did she strain to win in physical endeavors. If it were a bicycle race, she pushed to ride faster and endure longer; if it were a swim across a pool, she struggled to get there first with strokes that defied identification. When swimming, she could always count on defeating Helen Jackson, her favorite competitor. In fact, Lula Carson seldom competed in any activity in which she was not reasonably sure she could win. She also excelled at tree climbing, and the tall elms on Starke Avenue were perfect for such feats. One day while climbing with Helen, however, Lula Carson became terrified. Although she was far more agile than her friend, who was much shorter than she and could not stretch to maneuver from limb to limb nearly so well, Lula Carson cried out for help in descending. Helen, on the ground at the time, tried to tell her just which hand and foot to place on each branch, but Lula Carson clung to her limb, afraid to move. To get her down, Helen climbed to her friend's perch, crouched precariously beside her, then demonstrated every move of the descent. Lula Carson quickly followed, this time with ease. Once on the ground she laughed nervously and urged Helen not to tell the other children how she had behaved. The sudden fear of the unknown, the fear that she might not be able to carry out a specific goal, the fear that she might be physically abandoned and not be able to survive on her own—such fears swept over Lula Carson intermittently throughout her life, always accompanied by gross embarrassment.

Fear of being laughed at, chided, or made fun of was an important aspect of her troubled childhood. Lula Carson knew that she often did things which incurred censure, but she usually responded with a devil-may-care attitude. Actually, she did care immensely. Painfully sensitive on the inside, easily hurt, she yearned to be accepted unquestioningly by the group. Also, she reasoned that if she were "a member," she could have whatever degree of anonymity she wished. It was similarly that her youthful protagonist Frankie Addams reasoned in *The Member of the Wedding,* in the book's opening lines:

> It happened that green and crazy summer when Frankie was twelve years old. This was the summer when for a long time she had not been a member. She belonged to no club and was a member of nothing in the world. Frankie had become an unjoined person who hung around in doorways, and she was afraid.[14]

Unlike Frankie, Lula Carson once had been a member of a group. In fifth grade some of the Wynnton girls formed The Loud-mouthed Dancers and invited Lula Carson to join them. Naive at first, the Smith child seemed pleased to belong. Then she realized that she was a member only because the group needed a piano player. "We asked Lula Carson to join the LMDs because piano players our age were hard to come by," admitted a fellow member. "But she wasn't much fun for us, and even when she did play, she was temperamental. She just played when she felt like it, and often things we didn't even want to hear. We didn't really like her." In high school the group was resurrected to include boys, this time the LMD stood for "Let Me Dance." Again, Lula Carson was a member.

The fact that Lula Carson could play, however, provided the balm that humans, in their inhumanity, could not have given her. Her talent had burgeoned at age six in an inexplicable manner. One Saturday, Lula Carson returned home with Helen Jackson after seeing a movie, a weekly habit for the girls. Impulsively Lula Carson sat at the piano and announced to her friend: "I can play that ole 'Prisoner's Love Song' just like it sounded in the movie today, Helen. Listen." And she did, almost perfectly. Helen was astounded, and Marguerite, thrilled that her daughter's genius had mysteriously blossomed—having sprung, it seemed, full blown—hastened to alert the neighborhood that the prophecy of the oracles had been fulfilled. Quickly Marguerite flew from porch to porch, calling out, "Come quickly, come hear my precious darling play the piano." Neighbors dropped their needlepoint and embroidering and went. Amazed, they found that Marguerite was right. "Look at little Lula Carson play— she really is a genius," they agreed.[15]

Lula Carson had been picking out tunes on the piano ever since her mother had put her on her lap and introduced her to a keyboard. Marguerite had urged her daughter to sit at the piano and simply caress the keys, to experiment freely, to create whatever sounds of harmony and discord she wished. Although Marguerite herself could not play, she had a good ear and knew that Lula Carson did, too. Frequently she hummed tunes, and the child, in turn, picked out the melody. Lula Carson's unrehearsed "recital" that Saturday afternoon at age six, however, was indeed phenomenal.

When the family moved to Wynnton and there was a little extra money, one of Marguerite's first resolutions was that her daughter be given piano lessons by an accomplished teacher. Selected was Mrs. Kendrick Kierce, a graduate of the local Chase Conservatory of Music and a personal friend of Marguerite's, who had become one of the leading piano teachers in Columbus. Lula Carson loved the richly toned Knabe grand piano on which she took one half-hour lesson a week. She was thrilled, too, when Mrs. Kierce allowed her occasionally to stay after a lesson and practice for several hours, for her teacher's grand piano was a remarkable contrast to her grandmother's old flat top on which she played at home. The child's passion for music became insatiable. Soon it was apparent to the neighbors that it was not Lula Carson's mother who *made* her practice long sessions—a rumor that abounded because of Marguerite's frequent conversations about her daughter's genius—but Lula Carson herself who chose to play with such frequency and determination. Some of the neighboring families were quick to resent the musical interruption of their settled, quiet way of life. They did not appreciate being awakened as early as 4:00 A.M. by the music of Liszt, Chopin, and Beethoven being played by a ten-year-old. Lula Carson, an inveterate worker, practiced four or five hours a day. It seemed to Mrs. Kierce, however, that her pupil's enthusiasm often ran away with her. Lula Carson did not spend enough time working on details. She practiced again and again the same mistakes and sometimes played too loudly, said Mrs. Kierce. Nevertheless, the child had marvelous hands, slender and flexible, with long fingers, and she knew how to use them. When it was time to prepare for a recital, she insisted that she be allowed to play Liszt's Second Hungarian Rhapsody. Mrs. Kierce had never given it to another child, for it was a difficult piece, colorful and showy, and having great range. "Lula Carson begged me for it," said her teacher, "and I gave in. She played it exceedingly well, not only for a ten-year-old, but for anyone." Mrs. Kierce never saw the Smith child as the musical genius that her mother did, but she conceded that the child had more talent and was a more serious musician than any of her other pupils "save one." To Mrs. Kierce, Lula Carson was a "loner," for whom music was both an art and a companion. It gave her confidence and was the means of acclaim.

Lula Carson continued as Mrs. Kierce's pupil until the fall of 1930, when she was thirteen. It was then that Marguerite heard of a woman reported to be a wonderful musician who had recently moved to Columbus. Mary Tucker was the wife of Lieutenant Colonel A. S. J. Tucker, the newly assigned commanding officer of the Infantry School at Fort Benning. Mrs. Tucker had had a career as a concert pianist, and as her reputation spread in Columbus—a city which prided itself on its fine arts— she was heartily welcomed. By now, Mrs. Kierce believed that she had taken Lula Carson as far as they could go together and recommended to her mother that the child audition with Mrs. Tucker. Again, Lula Carson insisted on playing her recital piece, the Second Hungarian Rhapsody, which she thought would impress her prospective teacher. "She played it loud and fast for Mrs. Tucker, but what she lacked in polish and control was compensated for by her girlish enthusiasm and determination," said Mrs. Kierce. Lula Carson Smith at thirteen knew without a doubt that she would be a concert pianist, a career that would fulfill a destiny created for her many years earlier by a confident and enterprising mother. Although Mary Tucker did not see the child as a *wunderkind* when Lula Carson first played for her, she did see great promise and accepted her as her only pupil. Lula Carson needed nurture and discipline if her talent were to flourish, and it was decided that the two of them would begin work immediately. The discipline which she experienced through her work with Mrs. Tucker was of inestimable value to her when she began to write. She later attributed her excellent sense of form and structure to her study of music.

It was at this time, too—the summer of 1930—that Lula Carson Smith decided she would no longer use her first name. She had traveled alone that July to visit Elam Waters, her mother's brother in Cincinnati, where the Waters children and their northern friends had teased her about her double name. It was all right to have one, but not to go by it. She should abandon the *Lula* immediately, they urged. When she returned to Columbus, Carson Smith insisted to her cousins, who were puzzled and amused, and to Mary Tucker and others with whom she was close that she should never be called *Lula* Carson again. When school started in the fall, she asked that the *Lula* be stricken from her records. From then on, almost every written record bore only the name *Carson*, even though over the years Columbus people persisted in saying *Lula Carson* and her family continued to call her "Sister."

Carson Smith's union with Mary Tucker was a bond entered into with her whole spirit, and for the next four years her piano teacher was the fulcrum of her physical and psychic existence. Never shy or self-conscious with the Tucker family, Carson embraced them as her *we of me* in the manner that Frankie Addams conceived of her union with her brother Jarvis and his bride in *The Member of the Wedding*. From Mary Tucker, Carson craved not only enormous technical training to help launch her as a musician, but also a demonstrable love. She could never articulate such feelings to her teacher, however, whose firm demeanor and demanding standards and discipline in music unwittingly created a barrier between them.

To compensate, Carson found solace in the companionship of Mary Tucker's daughter, Gin, who was a few months younger than she. On Saturdays after the first hour's lesson, Carson stayed on and spent the day, alternating serious keyboard work with child's play. The two of them also had long record-listening sessions. The Tuckers' quarters on Austin Loop at the post were near the riding stables and Officers' Club, and after the major piano work of the day, the two girls would ride bicycles or walk to the pool, swim for a while, and then move on to the stables for an afternoon of riding. Carson loved to ride, and in her teens was a good horsewoman. Her riding habit, however, often provoked mirth among her neighbors. On Saturday mornings she would be seen striding out to her father's Whippet in a black ascot and long flowing gown. "That's the way we ride at the fort," she responded flippantly to Mildred Miller and Leslie Mullin, her peers who lived on each side of her. To the neighbor girls, Carson's outfit was outlandish, and they giggled and questioned each other about where "Lula Carson might have found such a strange 'getup' in Columbus."

Besides a mutual love for horseback riding and swimming, Carson and her friend Gin delighted in books, music, art, and fantasy. Childlike in their daydreams, they argued about which famous artist they should marry, and whether Rachmaninoff's Second Piano Concerto was greater than Brahms's First. There also were discussions about what kind of gown Carson should wear for her debut at Carnegie Hall. An avid reader of biography, especially of women, Carson pored over the lives of famous people with her friend and searched for some means of identifying with them. After reading Isadora Duncan's life story, she spoke of the possibility of a career in dance. Of course she had not discovered the slightest aptitude for it, but the idea was appealing; thus she and Gin Tucker went through a fanciful period of dancing in white sheets to their own choreography.

Until Carson was fifteen she had not even remotely fantasized for herself a career in writing. Instead, she dreamed of going to Europe and studying piano under Dohnanyi.[16] Mary Tucker had urged her to consider studying at Juilliard in New York City or the Curtis Institute of Music in Philadelphia—which Mrs. Tucker saw as more realistic goals—but Carson's imagination knew no limit. It is difficult to ascertain just when Carson Smith, the writer, did evolve. The seeds doubtless germinated in childhood, when she frequently sat on her front porch with a book in her lap. Watching her brother and sister at play, reading, and reflecting, she found that books provided countless vicarious experiences and evoked phantasmagoric imaginings. As an eight-year-old living in her grandmother's home on Thirteenth Street, Carson had written and engineered pantomimes and skits for the neighbor children, creating plots that had evolved solely from her imagination. Later, after she had read more, much of her plotting came from the Marjorie Maynard series, the Rover boys, and the Tom Swift books, but she created new and even more harrowing situations for her protagonists.

In an article written for *Mademoiselle* in 1948, "How I Began to Write," Carson recalled her involvement in all phases of play production as a child. She was writer, director, and technician.[17] First she described how her Starke Avenue home lent itself to the production of plays. Using the front sitting room for an auditorium and the back sitting room for the stage—with the sliding wooden doors between for the stage curtain—she presented plays that starred the juvenile members of her family. Marguerite, immensely proud of all three children, helped by canvassing the neighborhood for an audience. Carson described their childhood repertory as "eclectic, running from hashed-over movies to Shakespeare and shows I made up and sometimes wrote down in my nickel Big Chief notebooks." Her cast was her most serious problem, she concluded. "Baby Sister was in those days a stomachy ten-year-old who was terrible in death scenes, fainting spells and such-like necessary parts. When Baby Sister swooned to a sudden death she would prudently look around beforehand and fall very carefully on sofa or chair." To the frustration of the playwright, the show frequently broke up before curtain time, with the cast compounding the insult by absconding with the hot raisin cakes and lemonade prepared for refreshments.

The fledgling writer's real awakening evolved at age fifteen following a serious illness. Doctors diagnosed the malady as "pneumonia with complications," but Carson, identifying with Eugene O'Neill, believed it was tuberculosis. Much later, the medical reports called it rheumatic fever. Whatever the disorder was, however, Carson required extensive bed rest at home and several weeks of convalescence in a sanitarium in another town. In an autobiographical sketch prepared for *Story* magazine in 1936, to accompany her first published story "Wunderkind," Carson alluded briefly to this period. She said that she began to think about writing during her convalescence, but gave it up and studied Bach fugues instead while still in bed. Soon, however, she was writing plays in imitation of O'Neill and dividing her time between writing and music. Accompanying Carson's convalescence was the nudging, and often annoying, question of whether she had the physical stamina necessary to be a concert pianist. She also wondered if she simply was a talented musician, not a genius. If she had been a *wunderkind*, was her genius now fading, she pondered. For weeks Carson considered what direction her life should take. Her miracle mother could not poof away her worries, nor did Carson care even to expose them to her. In December 1932, when Carson was still fifteen, Helen Jackson returned from Rome, Georgia, during her first semester in college and found her friend still on her sickbed. Carson called Helen into her room and said: "I've got something important to tell you, Helen. I've given up my dream of being a concert pianist. But it's O.K. I'm going to be a writer instead." She did not tell Mary Tucker then of her decision. That announcement was made a year and a half later after new anguish prompted her to break forever from a musical career. Instead, she continued her work with Mrs. Tucker with renewed energies, and again there was no meaningful life apart from her piano and the Tucker family. With Helen Jackson away, Carson's only friends among her peers were her cousins—the C. Graham Johnson children— Gin Tucker, and Gin's brother, Bud.

Seldom at ease with people her own age, Carson seemed aloof and diffident to her classmates at Columbus High. Many saw her manner as a pose prompted by a sense of inferiority. She did not date, nor had she even kissed a boy until Reeves McCullers began to court her. (By then, she was nineteen and had spent almost a year in New York City, returning home far less naive than when she had departed.) Before meeting Reeves, Carson's social life was limited to family outings, visits with relatives, and small neighborhood parties and proms. She usually shied away from proms, where refreshments and a little handholding and kissing were the primary attractions. Once or twice Carson herself was coerced into giving a prom, the arrangements having been made and invitations extended chiefly by her mother. More than one Columbus boy promised his concerned parents that he would be "nice" to Carson and "promenade" with her before the evening ended. Such affairs were agonizing ordeals for the self-conscious, gangly girl who was painfully aware of her lack of popularity. Carson never enjoyed proms unless something unusual happened, such as their breaking up into wild abandonment in the manner in which Mick Kelly's prom party disintegrated in *The Heart Is a Lonely Hunter*.

Most of Carson's high school classmates thought her eccentric. She usually stood out in a crowd because she dared to be different. Her skirts and dresses were always a little longer than those worn by the popular girls whose clubs and cliques gave them prestige among their peers. She also wore dirty tennis shoes or brown Girl Scout oxfords when the other girls were wearing hose and shoes with dainty heels. When Carson was younger, some of the girls gathered in little clumps of femininity and threw rocks at her when she walked nearby, snickering loud asides and tossing within hearing distance such descriptive labels as "weird," "freakish-looking," and "queer." "We didn't like the ugly white knee socks Lula Carson wore when the rest of us wore stockings or short crew socks. We also made fun of the knickers she wore. Even most of the boys in our neighborhood had stopped wearing them," said one former schoolmate. They ridiculed her, too, for her straight hair and bangs, which she cut herself. "Almost everyone else goes to the beauty parlor," they chided. "Why doesn't Lula Carson?" Later, Carson wore slacks, sagging pullover sweaters, and shorts in public when no one else would have considered leaving her yard in clothes comparable to what they called "Lula Carson's outlandish getups." To her schoolmates, it seemed that Carson did things differently only to shock them and to flaunt convention. What they failed to understand was that she had no interest in what people thought of her if they shared no personal relationship. If there were a meaningful rapport, she would do anything possible to enhance the union. The fact that she was stubborn and often highly argumentative tended to alienate potential friends. If she felt she was right she was inflexible, but she also had an open, curious mind, and if convinced she was wrong she admitted it and moved quickly to a new point of view. Then she would be as adamant as before.

Perhaps the characteristic that Carson was most self-conscious about—and a differentness she did not like—was her height. It had leveled off at 5 feet 8½ inches when she was thirteen; but each time she viewed the freaks at the Chattahoochee Valley Fair she feared that she might never stop growing. To herself she was the tallest girl in the world. Always the tallest in her class, she towered over the boys as well as the girls sometimes by a whole foot. One day she announced to her mother that she had started smoking in an effort to stunt her growth. Marguerite herself smoked and raised no objections to her fourteen-year-old daughter's joining her. Inadvertently, it was cigarette smoking that aborted a formal visitation of several women from the First Baptist Church, who called upon the Smith home one morning in an attempt to get Marguerite and Carson to return to active membership. By then, both mother and daughter had withdrawn all support of organized religion. The visiting emissaries abandoned their mission, however, when they saw Marguerite take out her cigarettes in front of them and offer one to Carson. As they abruptly retreated, they were shocked even further by Marguerite's dry admission: "Oh, yes, my daughter Lula Carson and I have such a good time smoking together. We do almost everything together, you know."

Neither Marguerite nor Carson attended church again in Columbus, but the two younger children continued regularly. Lamar, Jr., joined the church in 1928 and Margarita, two years later. The effects of Carson's rearing in the church, however, turned up occasionally later in her fiction, sometimes with embarrassing overtones. Before her final novel, *Clock Without Hands*, appeared, readers in her hometown worried, as they had in the past, fearful that she would poke fun at still another institution sacred to their way of life. Carson did not disappoint them. There, in full array, was the First Baptist Church of Columbus. Her ironic thrust was unmistakable in the dying druggist's thoughts as he turned to his church in an attempt to shore up the fragments of his bereft life:

> When tormented by the unreality of both death and life, it helped
> him to know that the First Baptist Church was real enough. The
> largest church in town, taking up half a city block near the main
> street, the property on offhand reckoning was worth about two mil-
> lion dollars. A church like that was bound to be real. The pillars of
> the church were men of substance and leading citizens. Butch Hen-
> derson, the realtor and one of the shrewdest traders in the town, was a
> deacon and never missed a service from one year to the next—and was
> Butch Henderson a likely man to waste his time or trouble on any-
> thing that was not as real as dirt?[18]

Many Columbus residents took the criticism as a personal attack. It was "just one more evidence of Lula Carson Smith's not being able to adjust or fit into a meaningful life pattern of her own," they concluded.

Carson's personality during her teen-age years no more endeared her to her teachers than it did to her contemporaries. Some teachers readily admitted that her personality irritated them. They disliked her aloofness and apparent disdain for the classroom and other formal school activities. The few who were aware that she practiced the piano for three hours every morning before school, and another three to five hours in the after-noon, made allowances for her, conceding that there was little time or energy left for academic studies. They also admitted that to Carson, school was simply unimportant.

To a few teachers, it seemed that she had a difficult time "trying to pass." Others thought of her only as an average or below-average student who had no aptitude for hard work and showed no unusual promise. Miss Lillian Griffith, her French teacher, thought her "a shy, sweet child who needed bringing out" and said that she showed a "good degree of competency in foreign languages. Had she not been so involved with her music, she could have done 'A' work for me," said Miss Griffith. Carson took a total of five years of Latin, French, and Spanish, studies that re-quired a discipline second only to her music. Most of her other subjects were also strongly academic. Carson's transcript reveals that her grades largely were "C's" and "B's," with a sprinkling of "A's." Regardless of the impressions of her teachers, she made no "D's" or "F's" on any course in high school. When Carson graduated in June 1933, she was sixteen years old, had completed the then required eleven years of public schooling, and had five credits more than necessary for graduation.

This hurdle over at last, Carson voiced no desire to go to college. Regardless of her deeply submerged thoughts about being a writer someday, there was no question in the minds of her mother and Mary Tucker that she would eventually go to New York and study at Juilliard for a career in music. In 1933, however, the country was in the throes of an economic depression, and even Marguerite was aware that there was not enough money in the Smith household to launch her daughter as she would have liked. There was talk about Carson's applying for a music scholarship, but she declined. She would rather stay home and continue her piano work with Mary Tucker, she insisted.

Some of her classmates went off to college or into the Army. Others sought work in the mills, shops, and offices in Columbus, or stayed at home, married, and had babies. Many could find no work of any kind and idled in the parks and streets. Carson, however, continued the rigorous practice schedule she had established when she first began to study with Mrs. Tucker. She also was filled—more than ever before—with an insatiable desire to read. This time she urged her cousin, Virginia Johnson Storey, who had graduated from college and was now a librarian in the local public library, to make up a list of all the books in the English language reported to be the "greatest literature in the world." She would read them all, she vowed, and within the next year and a half, it seemed to Virginia Storey that Carson, indeed, had read every book in the library. She read voraciously, poring over Greek philosophy and drama, French and German literature in translation, the works of the nineteenth-century Russian realists, and most of the British and American novels of esteem. In an article written for *Harper's Bazaar* in April 1941, "Books I Remember," Carson described the impact that Dostoevski had upon her:

> The books of Dostoevski—*The Brothers Karamazov, Crime and Punishment,* and *The Idiot*—opened the door to an immense and marvelous new world. For years I had seen these books on the shelves of the public library, but on examining them I had been so put off by the indigestible names and the small print. So when at last I read Dostoevski it was a shock that I shall never forget—and the same amazement takes hold of me whenever I read these books today, a sense of wonder that cannot be jaded by familiarity.

She expressed a similar enthusiasm for Chekhov, and to a lesser extent, Tolstoy, Gogol, and Turgenev, in whose books she found the "hot lazy Russian summers, the lonely villages on the steppes, the old grand-

fathers who sleep with the children on the stove, the white winters of
Saint Petersburg . . . as close to me as scenes from my own home town."
In another article written several months later, Carson acknowledged a
special indebtedness to those she identified as "the Russian realists," not
only for herself but for most of the other modern southern writers. To
her, the Russians were the original masters of the vivid and "outwardly
callous juxtaposition of the tragic with the humorous, the immense with
the trivial, the sacred with the bawdy, the whole soul of a man with a
materialistic detail."[19]

Carson was drawn during this period, again and again, to the writings of D. H. Lawrence, Gustave Flaubert, James Joyce, the Brontë sisters, and Katherine Mansfield, as well as to the writings of the early
American romanticists, Hawthorne and Melville, and the later Americans, Ernest Hemingway, William Faulkner, Thomas Wolfe, Sherwood
Anderson, and Gertrude Stein. She did not discover Isak Dinesen until
1937. Once having read Out of Africa, Carson returned to it every year,
finding in the Danish writer a new creative idol.

Not only was Carson reading deeply in all genres of literature and
playing the piano with what seemed the same old intensity and fervor but
she also had begun to write. In her essay "How I Began to Write," published by Mademoiselle in 1948 after she had four books and a handful of
short stories to her credit, she wrote:

> The sitting-room shows ended when first I discovered Eugene O'Neill.
> It was the summer when I found his books down in the library and
> put his picture on the mantelpiece in the back sitting-room. By au-
> tumn I was writing a three-acter about revenge and incest—the cur-
> tain rose on a graveyard and, after scenes of assorted misery, fell on
> a catafalque.[20]

Her first serious creative endeavor, she said, was a play called The
Faucet. It was set in New Zealand, where she believed anything could
happen. In a burst of youthful exuberance, she sent a copy of the play to
Eugene O'Neill, she admitted later in a radio interview with Tennessee
Williams,[21] adding that she was madly in love not only with O'Neill, but
also with his wife. (At the time, O'Neill was married to his third wife,
Carlotta, with whom he had recently eloped.) O'Neill reportedly did not
respond to Carson's manuscript, and no copy of this play is known to
exist.

Carson said in her Mademoiselle article that she read Nietzsche next,
and under his influence wrote a second play, The Fire of Life. Composed
in rhymed verse—a feat she took pride in—it had two characters, Jesus
Christ and Nietzsche. For The Faucet and The Fire of Life, Carson gave
"readings," explaining to her audience—her mother, father, and a visiting

aunt—that these plays did not lend themselves to stage presentation in the manner of her juvenile acting troupe's earlier performances in the Smith family's sitting rooms. Her family was somewhat shocked by the violence expressed by their budding playwright, but thought that the work showed promise of greatness. One of Carson's aunts, who was unable to attend the second reading, asked her niece later to tell her about it. Carson said that when her aunt was told that the cast included Jesus—and being unacquainted with Nietzsche—she gave what she considered a guarded but safe response: "Jesus? Well, religion is a nice subject anyway."[22]

Carson's next creative venture was a novel entitled *A Reed of Pan.* Set in New York City, the story disturbed the literary agent who agreed to attempt to market it for her. "I am puzzled by several oddities," he wrote, curious to know if the author was a senile man: "When were you last in New York?" Then he told her that most New Yorkers did not have front lawns and commuters did not hand tickets to subway conductors. To Carson, however, who had never been to New York but was accustomed to handing tickets to the conductor of the "beltline trolley" which circled Columbus, the procedure seemed perfectly logical.

She referred to this early creative effort a year later with some embarrassment, her fantasies about traveling now based somewhat on fact. She wrote a friend that at last she was writing prolifically. She intended to write and rewrite, perhaps, an entire novel that summer, as well as some short stories. She said that although she had a chance to get her first novel "printed" (naive to the trade, Carson apparently was not aware of the difference between having a work printed and published), it was so poor she probably would not allow it. Rather, she said she would spend a few years, possibly even five, working like a fiend and then perhaps she would have a work she could be proud of.[23]

Carson's first short story, or at least the one she took enough pride in to show to her parents, was entitled "Sucker." She had written it in longhand, as she had her earlier manuscripts, but this time she asked her father if he could have it typed for her. Lamar Smith responded by buying her a typewriter of her own. "Tartie, now you can type it yourself," he said, pleased to be able to give something to his child that was uniquely his gift. ("Tartie" was still another affectionate name used only by the family for Carson.) In her story, "Sucker" was the nickname of a small boy whose adolescent cousin Pete—with whom Sucker lived—believed that the child was too gullible for his own good; thus Pete shattered Sucker's illusions in a painful initiatory experience. Sucker's attempts to identify with Pete, whose emotions became consumed by his idol, Maybelle, and Sucker's efforts to get the older boy to acknowledge him "as a real brother" provide tension and pathos to the story. Pete, who narrated the tale in retrospect, acknowledged what evolved into a basic tenet in Carson's fiction: "If a person admires you a lot you despise him and don't care—and it is the person who doesn't notice you that you are apt to admire. . . . I suppose I was mean to him lots of times. I guess I wanted to ignore somebody like Maybelle did me."[24]

When things began to go right with Maybelle, Pete also became kinder and more loving to Sucker. Maybelle, however, was more impressed by a yellow roadster and its owner than by Pete and finally told him that she "was sick and tired" of him and "had never cared a rap" about him anyway. Inevitably, Pete turned on Sucker:

> Nobody cares anything about you! And just because I felt sorry
> for you sometimes and tried to act decent don't think I give a damn
> about a dumb-bunny like you! . . .
> Why do you always hang around me? Don't you know when
> you're not wanted? . . . You're too dumb. Just like your name—a
> dumb Sucker.[25]

Crushed, Sucker assumed a façade of hardness, and now it was Pete who suffered. Unable to apologize—for Sucker looked at him in a "new hard way"—Pete yearned to undo the damage. But it was too late:

> I don't care a flip for Maybelle or any particular girl any
> more and it's only this thing between Sucker and me that is the
> trouble now. We never speak except when we have to before the
> family. I don't even want to call him Sucker any more and unless I
> forget I call him by his real name, Richard.[26]

At about the same time Carson wrote "Sucker," she experienced one of the greatest traumas of her life. In the spring of 1934, Mary Tucker's husband received unexpected orders transferring him from Fort Benning to Fort Howard, Maryland. Not since Carson's acute jealousy had been aroused by her infant sister had she felt so undermined. The entire Tucker family would be leaving and she would lose her precious rapport with those who meant more to her then than anyone except her mother. Although devastated by what she considered her "abandonment," Carson maintained a surface calm in the wake of Mary Tucker's announcement and continued to play the piano and to take lessons with the inevitable separation hanging over her. She voiced her plaintive feelings to no one.

Suddenly, however, one day after the lessons had been temporarily halted while her teacher recuperated from a serious illness, Carson went to Mrs. Tucker's bedside and made a dark pronouncement: She was giving up music and her dream to be a concert pianist. Instead, she would be a writer. Unaware until now of her pupil's literary aspirations, Mrs. Tucker found the shock of Carson's admission as jarring as the news of her husband's transfer had been to Carson. Mary Tucker responded to her pupil's announcement with similar composure. She was deeply sorry, she said, for she could have helped Carson immensely with a musical career. But beyond that, she could be of no help. Restrained almost to the point of coldness, neither sought solace nor offered balm to the other's psychic wounds. Neither woman allowed the other to know how deeply she had been hurt.

When Carson returned home that evening there was no music in the house for the first time since she had begun to play. Relatives who came to visit found the mood in the Smith household mournful and gloomy. Carson merely sat and gazed into space, solemn and uncommunicative. The family tiptoed about the house and whispered to inquirers that Sister had given up her music. For weeks afterward Carson would not allow anyone even to mention her piano teacher's name in her presence. The Tuckers had been her *we of me*—a phrase that found voice when she was finally able to articulate her feelings some seven years later as she struggled to put *The Member of the Wedding* down on paper—and now she was a disjoined person. It was not until she transformed the agonizing experience of personal loss into the artistic catharsis of a book, and later, a play, that she was able to achieve a psychic release, to put her nemesis to rest, and to enter again into full communion with Mary Tucker.

It was to Mrs. Tucker Carson was indebted, also, for another important relationship: a friendship formed with a young man from Thomasville, Georgia, who became her lifelong friend, Edwin Peacock. Carson and Peacock met in the spring of 1934 before the Tucker family's departure for their new post. Peacock, twenty-four, was stationed at Fort Benning in the Civilian Conservation Corps, where he had become acquainted with the Tuckers through their mutual love of music. When he heard that the Russian composer and pianist Rachmaninoff would be playing a concert in Atlanta—a hundred miles away—he asked Mrs. Tucker if she could help find him a ride. The next day Peacock found himself en route to Atlanta with a fellow passenger, Carson Smith. The driver, a neighbor of Mrs. Tucker's, allowed extra time for the trip so that they might stop along the way to pick wild flowers on Pine Mountain. Carson and Peacock established an immediate rapport, and as they joked and laughed at each other's foolish antics she sensed that her new companion would become a friend. On the way home that evening they sang Christmas carols. Peacock was amazed at the strength and range of Carson's voice and that she could sing both soprano and alto parts equally well.

The summer after the Tuckers' departure, Peacock moved into town and rented a small apartment over the garage of the Columbus Woman's Club on Wynnton Road, a mile from Carson's Starke Avenue home. He had left the CCC to accept a civil service appointment in the finance office at the fort, where he not only made more money than before, but also had more leisure time. The young man began to come often to the Smith home, bringing with him records to play on their gramophone, eating dinner with them, and feeling, in a real sense, like a member of the family. He was immensely fond of Carson's mother, who found the young man warmly attentive and intellectually stimulating.

Once settled in his new location, Peacock yearned to own a piano. He wanted Carson to play for him, and to be able to practice on it himself. Although Peacock played the piano and the violin, he considered himself no musician. He declined when Marguerite asked him to play for her in the Smith home, but soon he was able to purchase an old spinet for one hundred dollars, and in his own apartment he sometimes played for Carson. She told Peacock about the Tucker family she loved and the musical career she had abandoned; but by summer she was playing again with much of her former enthusiasm. He marveled that his friend could make "such perfectly wonderful music" come out of the old piano. Never shy about playing for him, Carson seemed to Peacock to be the "finest nonprofessional pianist" he had ever heard. "I was thrilled that my very own friend had a musical talent of such magnitude," he said.[27]

They also listened for hours to records and held what they called "intellectual discussions" of books they both had read. When Peacock could afford them, he bought new records and invited others to join their informal "listening sessions." Sometimes they pooled their records, and eventually outsiders began to refer to the little group as The Record Club. Carson relished getting away from home, where her mother's strong personality usually dominated family gatherings. She loved Marguerite dearly, but sometimes her mother's hovering solicitude had a smothering effect. With Edwin Peacock, the evenings stretched warm and comfortable. With him she was herself—witty and whimsical one moment, deeply brooding and profound the next. They reveled in every facet of each other.

Carson never considered her various activities with Peacock as "dating." They simply were good friends. One of her contemporaries who had ignored her in high school but was fond of her now in their new coterie, sometimes chided her about "going out with that old man, Edwin Peacock," but Carson knew the remark was said in jest. She also valued increasingly her rapport with people. Music continued to be important to her—as it was for the rest of her life—but it was no longer her whole existence. Music and writing both were outlets for her troubled emotions, but more and more she was able to relate to people. A sense of her own worth as a musician, as a writer, and as a person grew as she became more articulate with friends and others outside of her home. Carson realized that many people were keenly interested in her, and accepted and appreciated her for exactly what she was.

Sometimes she and Peacock, along with others in their crowd, prowled at night about Columbus and Phenix City. Usually Carson was the only girl, but she dressed in dungarees or a pair of Peacock's fatigues and seldom stood out from the group. Occasionally they went to clubs "off limits" to Fort Benning personnel. Here the more adventuresome foot soldiers and paratroopers roamed freely. Carson preferred to sit quietly at a back table where she could smoke, sip beer, and watch intently the activities about her without being observed herself.

Neither Marguerite nor Lamar questioned their daughter's comings and goings at night. There was gossip in town that "Lula Carson Smith had absolutely no restrictions and did not behave as the 'nice' girls did," but if well-meaning friends voiced criticism or showed concern to Marguerite about her daughter's activities, Marguerite dismissed them lightly: "After all, Little Precious has to gather material so she can be a famous author someday." Carson had confided to her mother after the Tuckers left that in addition to keeping up her music, she also wanted to write. She might never be a concert pianist, she conceded, for the circumstances at present were conducive to a career in music, but she could always write, no matter where she was, she reasoned.

To Carson in 1934, Edwin Peacock was the best-read person she had ever known, and soon she began to show him the novel and stories she had been writing and to invite his comment. "Even from the beginning I thought Carson's work was good," recalled Peacock, who typed some of her stories for her. Perhaps Peacock's greatest contribution to her literary growth, however, was giving her a copy of *Story* magazine. *Story* had only recently moved to New York City after its founding in Vienna in 1931 by Whit Burnett and his wife, Martha Foley. The magazine had caught on well in New York and very quickly became the country's leading "little" magazine, a publication which welcomed new contributors, eschewed no subject matter, and experimented rather than conformed. Each issue was rich in exciting, original fiction, which Carson read voraciously as soon as it reached the Columbus newsstands.

Peacock also introduced her to many writers she had not had time to discover for herself. Attuned to the anticapitalistic fervor of the early 1930s, he urged her to read such social protesters as John Dos Passos, Erskine Caldwell, John Steinbeck, and James T. Farrell. He also put her in touch with Karl Marx. Later, when Carson was asked for a biographical sketch to accompany the publication of "Wunderkind," which Whit Burnett selected for *Story* as her first published work, she said she had done her share in proclaiming communism. She took pleasure in telling friends a few years later that as a sympathetic agitator she had marched in peace

parades in New York City and walked a picket line in support of striking waitresses at Woolworth's. It was Reeves McCullers, to whom Peacock
introduced her, rather than Peacock, who was more responsible for her
sharpened sensitivity for social reform. Carson's participation was most often vicarious, however, and executed largely in her fiction.

Another contribution to Carson's evolvement as a writer was a copy
of D. H. Lawrence's *The Rainbow*, which Peacock gave her one day. Fascinated by it, she then read *The Prussian Officer and Other Stories*. Two
of the characters she created a few years later, the homosexually inclined,
yet impotent Captain Penderton and the primitive, animalistic Private
Williams in *Reflections in a Golden Eye*, doubtless owed their genesis to
Lawrence's title story, as well as to Freud, in whose works she also was
steeped.

Vague stirrings that formerly had lain dormant now welled up in Carson as she fantasized herself in New York City among other writers. In the
essay "How I Began to Write," Carson told of how her literary unrest pervaded almost every waking moment during the winter of 1934–35:

> By that winter the family rooms, the whole town, seemed to
> pinch and cramp my adolescent heart. I longed for wanderings. I
> longed especially for New York. The firelight on the walnut folding
> doors would sadden me, and the tedious sound of the old swan clock.
> I dreamed of the distant city of skyscrapers and snow, and New York
> was the happy mise en scène of that first novel I wrote when I was fif-
> teen years old. The details of the book were queer: ticket collectors on
> the subway, New York front yards—but by that time it did not matter,
> for already I had begun another journey. That was the year of Dos-
> toevski, Chekhov, and Tolstoy—and there were the intimations of an
> unsuspected region equidistant from New York, Old Russia and our
> Georgia rooms, the marvelous solitary region of simple stories and the
> inward mind.[28]

By the following September Carson could restrain herself no longer.
Stimulated by her literary and musical intercourse with Edwin Peacock,
still bereft over her loss of Mary Tucker, yet complaining to no one, Carson persuaded her mother that only in New York could she achieve success
and recognition as a writer. Ambivalently, Marguerite wanted to nestle
her favorite child and keep her safely tucked away at home; yet she also
yearned to launch her in some grand manner upon her chosen career. Convinced that only New York City would meet her daughter's needs, un-
mindful of criticism by her sister and friends that a strange, hostile city
was no place for a naive seventeen-year-old child to flounder in alone, Marguerite settled down to the practicality of how to finance such a venture.
It was decided that Carson's father should sell a valuable family heirloom,

the diamond and emerald ring that had been given his elder daughter by her maternal grandmother, Lula Carson Waters. Carson's plan was not only to study at Juilliard, but also to take creative writing from Dorothy Scarborough at Columbia University. No, she would not abandon her musical studies even though she was no longer bent on a concert pianist's career, she assured her mother. Arrangements were made for her to stay with the daughter of another Columbus family—a girl she had never met— until she could choose another location.

With some five hundred dollars pinned to her underwear, Carson went by train to Savannah, Georgia, 275 miles northeast of Columbus, where she boarded an ocean-going steamer for the three-day voyage to New York. Other than her visit to Cincinnati, Carson had not ventured more than a hundred miles from home. Her trip to Savannah marked the first time she had ever seen the ocean, let alone set sail upon it. A courageous but timorous young woman loped up the gangplank, already a little bit homesick and having no one to wave good-by to. Grasping firmly the two old suitcases, which were her family's legacy, and her friend Helen Jackson's fur coat—for which she had traded a Dresden china dresser set— Carson took heart, for she recalled her mother's parting words at the station in Columbus where her family had seen her off. After a quick hug, Marguerite had pushed her daughter from her and dabbed at a tear. "Lula Carson, don't ever forget who you are. And know that soon you're going to be famous," she had said, beaming.

Chapter Two

APPRENTICESHIP
IN NEW YORK CITY

*A*s the gangling apprentice-author settled uneasily into a deck chair beside dozens of fellow passengers, she wondered how they viewed her— or if they noticed her at all. Would they recognize that it was her first trip to New York, guess that she had never even smelled the ocean before, or seen snow? Surreptitiously she glanced about her, observing and cataloguing every detail offered by her deckmates. Just as she had sat on her front porch throughout childhood and adolescence with book in hand, reading yet not reading, watching her brother and sister at play yet not seeing, dreaming about life, fantasizing situations in which she starred as protagonist and antihero, spinning her thread, weaving, and severing the cord at will, making reality of myth and oblivious of the transubstantiation—so, too, sat Carson aboard her vessel conveying her to the magical land of snow, skyscrapers, and concert halls, of the Metropolitan, Carnegie Hall, Broadway, Fifth Avenue, Washington Square, Tiffany's, and the Brooklyn Bridge. In her mind's eye she worked assiduously, an impressionistic painter whose shapes, textures, colors blurred pointillistically against a canvas of sea and clouds and sky.

Only vaguely did the seventeen-year-old girl know why she was going to New York City. To study at Juilliard, she had told her parents. To take courses at Columbia. And to write. But most of all she wanted to study the city, take its pulse, and, like her idols Walt Whitman and Hart Crane, fuse herself to it.

Steadily Carson's excitement, anticipation, fear, and anxiety mounted, and by the time her steamship entered Manhattan harbor, the lump in her throat had grown to goiterlike dimensions. When her pen pal, Claire Sasser, with whom she was to stay, greeted her at the dock, Carson could only respond inaudibly. Strangers, their single bond was their hometown, for their parents had arranged the meeting. Everyone in Columbus who had heard of "that poor Smith child being sent to New York City, alone and helpless," thought that Marguerite had grievously erred in this last foolish venture. But Carson's mother retorted that her daughter would be secure under the managing eye of a fellow Southerner with whom she had been invited to room until she could settle and decide for herself where she wanted to live.

Claire Sasser, from solid Columbus stock, was several years older than Carson, beautiful and talented. She had been in the city over a year. Miss Sasser wrote to both Marguerite and Carson that she would be delighted to act as mentor to the young novitiate. The relationship, however, proved an unhappy arrangement. Perhaps taking her charge too seriously, Miss Sasser allegedly suggested that Carson had no business carrying all her money about on her person as she tramped around New York, that she should bank it or let a person more experienced with the wiles of the city keep it. Happily Carson combined her money with her roommate's. Almost immediately, however, the purse was lost, either stolen or carelessly left behind on the subway. Now both were penniless.

Feeling responsible for the loss, Claire Sasser phoned her father for money for each of them. Carson had not dared let her father know her predicament. She was sure he would have sent her only a return bus ticket. From her roommate, Carson accepted only enough to survive in the city until she could find work and become self-supporting. If she had had any doubts before about whether to attend Juilliard, Carson's path was at last clear. She would work, take night classes, and write.

But now the cramped bedroom-sitting room that the two girls occupied over a linen store on the Upper West Side seemed even dingier, and Carson's spirits sagged more heavily than the ancient bed they shared. Uneasy, somehow blaming her roommate for her newly fallen state—in spite of the innocence of the incident—Carson decided to strike out on her own.

Her next location is only legendary. Carson told many friends about her unwitting move into a brothel on Thirty-fourth Street. In her new roominghouse, Carson found her fellow tenants friendly, yet she wondered about the late traffic and assortment of callers on her floor that first night. Naively she asked one of her new acquaintances what she did for a living, to which the response was raucous laughter. Finally, when her *landlady* brought an admirer to meet her in the parlor where she sat reading, and began to arrange an assignation, Carson hastily checked out. Whether this tale was one of those truths that she "took between her teeth and ran with," or a fact, went unchallenged by her friends; but Carson told the story frequently, with varying embellishments, to illustrate her naivete that first month in New York City.

Fear, loneliness, and a sense of her own anonymity pervaded her consciousness those first few weeks. The cacophony of city noises, the dirt and poverty, the bold stares and curt retorts of waiters, drivers, clerks, and tradesmen, the labyrinth of subways in which she almost daily became lost

—juxtaposed with the glitter and elegance of Park Avenue wealth, bedi-
amonded ladies, and gleaming limousines—all fascinated, yet repelled her.
Again and again Carson was driven back to the security of her room.

Although the Parnassus Club, a West Side girls' residence that housed
many Columbia University students, provided a more stable home for Carson for the next few weeks than the two she had left, she still was unhappy; moreover, she was sick much of the time with colds and pleurisy.
Still terrified when going out alone, yet feeling desperately the need to be
out, to be independent, she discovered safe harbor within the narrow confines of telephone booths. Particularly in Macy's department store did she
revel in the womblike niche in which she could hide away, pull up her
knees and hug them to her chest, feel the vibrations of a pounding heart,
and then gradually enjoy relaxed breathing. She never left her room without a book; it gave her security. In telephone booths she sat and read,
sometimes for hours. At Macy's there were so many booths that she never
felt guilty about taking up space or depriving someone of a phone. Here
she felt comfortable, the sea of faces not so threatening; the multitudes
pressed past, but they were oblivious of her.

"Just call me, Sister, if you need anything. Remember, I'm as close as
a telephone," her mother had shouted as Carson's train pulled away from
the station. Daily Carson fought off the compulsion to call home—not just
home, but her mother—to be caressed by her mother's deep-throated voice,
petted by her words, reassured of love, buoyed and strengthened by the
old familiar prattle. She wanted to ask what latest prank Brother-Man had
been involved in, if Edwin Peacock was still coming regularly to the house
evenings, and did Baby Sister miss her? But she could not call—would not
dare. Risk being laughed at? Allow the catch in her voice to become a
sob? Asked if she were homesick? Tricked into admitting that the city terrified her? Instead, feeling closer to home in a phone booth than anywhere
else, Carson sat and read and imagined brave and scintillating conversations over which she had complete control.

Jobs were scarce in New York City in the mid-thirties, especially for
unskilled workers and laborers. It was the decade of the Great Depression,
and although Carson had seen abject poverty in her mill town, Columbus,
Georgia, it had usually been across the tracks or over by the river. Now she
lived with it all around her and inevitably began to depict it in her
writings. Her early piece, "Court in the West Eighties" (published posthu-
mously in The Mortgaged Heart[1]), utilized much autobiographical material from her first year in New York City. In this story the young student-
narrator commented on the boy who sat next to her in an economics class,
who wore newspapers under his sweater all winter because he had no over-
coat, and on the man who lost his job while his wife was pregnant. She
watched the husband regularly bring home a quart of milk and put it on

the window sill, and then a pint, and then a half pint—until finally there was no milk at all. Carson's young protagonist observed:

> It is hard to tell how you feel when you watch someone go hungry. You see their room was not more than a few yards from mine and I couldn't quit thinking about them. At first I wouldn't believe what I saw. This is not a tenement house far down on the East side, I would tell myself. We are living in a fairly good, fairly average part of town— in the West Eighties. . . . From the street these buildings look almost rich and it is not possible that inside someone could starve, I would say: because their milk is cut down to a fourth of what they used to get and because I don't see him eating (giving her the sandwich he goes out to get each evening at dinner time) that is not a sign they are hungry. Because she just sits like that all day, not showing any interest in anything except the window sills where some of us keep our fruit that is because she is going to have the baby very soon now and is a little unnatural. Because he walks up and down the room and yells at her sometimes, his throat sounding choked up, that is just the ugliness in him.[2]

But the young girl in the story knew, in spite of her ratiocination, what the real problem was, and that neither she nor the strange man with the red hair who lived across the court from her could straighten out things for any of them, that life simply must be endured. The young girl and the redheaded man proved to be sensitively drawn prototypes of Mick Kelley and John Singer, who were germinating even then.

The young Georgia girl, too, was frequently among the unemployed. She got up at dawn, wrote all morning, worked in the afternoon—when she could find a job—and after the first of February, studied and went to school nights and late afternoons. Carson had paid her tuition money to Columbia University the very day before she lost most of her money; thus when the new term began, she was able to take courses in philosophy, psychology, and the art of the short story. Helen Rose Hull, author of mystery stories, novels, several books on the craft of fiction, and assorted miscellaneous writings, had established the School of Creative Writing at Columbia, and it was to her that Carson applied for her first formal literary training.

"Carson Smith was a nice little girl," reflected Miss Hull many years later, "but I don't remember what kind of a writer she was. I guess I didn't teach her much," she added. Apparently, neither Miss Hull nor Dorothy Scarborough, with whom Carson also studied, made a deep impression on the young writer; nor did they help her with her craft nearly so significantly as did the two instructors she encountered the following year, Sylvia Chatfield Bates, at New York University, and Whit Burnett, at Columbia.

Decrying the fact that she had had no training in anything worthwhile except music, Carson set about to prove how inept she could be on a job. She rarely lasted until the end of a regular pay period. Instead, she took pride in her record of never having resigned from a position; she was always fired. Sometimes she was hired to type, and for a brief period kept the general ledger and answered the phone at a real estate office. Her employer, Mrs. Louise B. Field—whom Carson described as "a mean old woman"—decided that her company's best interests were not at heart when she discovered Carson devouring *Swann's Way* beneath the giant ledger in which she was supposedly working. "You're fired! You'll never amount to a thing in this world," Mrs. Field reportedly shouted to her errant employee after pounding her head twice with the big book. Carson picked up her thermos and purse and moved sullenly to the door. She had just discovered Marcel Proust and she was not going to be intimidated or allow her enthusiasm to be dampened by what she considered a gross display of vulgarity.

Occasionally Carson worked as a waitress, but she always shunned any opportunity to serve as a short-order cook. She had never cooked at home, she told one prospective employer; furthermore, she did not intend to begin now, and certainly not for someone else. Even using her musical talents in New York City demanded of Carson a certain amount of prostitution. For a while she played as an accompanist for a dancing class in a settlement house, and later as an improviser for dancers, but these jobs were painful reminders of her rebellious stint in adolescence as pianist for her neighborhood clubmates, the Loud-mouthed Dancers.

More palatable to her talents, Carson decided, was an editorial position on a magazine. Such hopes were short lived, however. She found two comic magazines desirous of her services and worked for a short time on each, both of which she soon discovered were rapidly sliding down the fiscal drain into bankruptcy. Just before the creditors closed in on one, *More Fun*, she declined the opportunity the owner gave her of buying the magazine for a paltry sum. Whether it was her good sense not to, or the fact that she had no money, Carson was reluctant to speculate on later.

Perhaps Carson succeeded best that first year in New York as a dog walker. She liked dogs, had grown up with a big mongrel she had loved better than did anyone else in the Smith family, and she was always picking up Starke Avenue strays. Frequently she worked at her fiction until midafternoon, left for a class, and then returned home by way of Riverside Drive, where sundry dog lovers hired her to exercise an assortment of boxers, Airedales, chows, and Doberman pinschers. There were always more poodles, Pekingese, dachshunds, and Chihuahuas than she had time for, or wanted, for Carson hated small dogs. They were too poky and inquisitive; rather, she loved a brisk walk with large animals.

Carson's respiratory infections mounted during her first winter in the North. She had little resistance to the cold, although she often was out in it by choice. The piercing wind, sleet, and snow continually assaulted her health, but she was enamored of the snow and spent precious hours walking in it and daydreaming as she watched it settle upon the rooftops, awnings, and sidewalk shrubs.

Gradually she made friends, especially in her musical neighborhood near Juilliard. With music a common denominator, Carson never knew a stranger. Later, she described her aggressiveness in meeting people when music was an entree in her biographical sketch for Whit Burnett, editor of *Story*. She said that she began to hear some wonderful Mozart from a piano near her room and knocked on the door to discover its source. (Carson used the incident fictionally some twenty-five years later in *Clock Without Hands* when Jester Clane, the youthful protagonist, knocked on Sherman Pew's door after he heard his piano playing in the distance.) The musician was a young Jewish boy her age who had recently arrived from Vienna and was on a scholarship in New York City. Carson told Burnett that they immediately became friends. As she explored the city now with a companion, she found that she no longer even thought about telephone booths. Her whole perspective of life in New York City was dramatically altered.

Together they discovered the wharves, their pulse fascinating her, drawing her forward, a sense of urgency almost tangible as she moved among the cargo storage sheds and to the ship's side, activity at fever pitch. Carson watched each sling load of cargo go aboard as though it were the last, the dollies and forklifts in constant motion, carrying pallets from shed to ship, onto the apron, under the crane or boom; the longshoremen constantly chattering when not shouting or whistling signals, the whining of electric motors of the shore cranes barely perceptible over the squealing noises of the ship's winches, the ship impatient to be loaded, to slip her berth and point seaward. The wharf rats—some as large as house cats—startled her, darting from pallet to pallet, pilfering the cargo; and in a moment's lull she could hear the cooing of pigeons fluttering among the shed's rafters, restless until the next longshoremen's break when they could scurry about the floor and feed on grain or flour from a broken sack.

At night Carson frequently returned to the waterfront, watching the light fog drift in, thickening slightly, giving a halo to each light and the water's surface hidden below; listening to the forlorn sounds of fog signals from distant ships, their whistles and bells. At night the longshoremen almost stopped talking, their voices carrying half a ship's length with a whisper, their spirits dampened like the air itself, everyone working more slowly, seemingly lost in his own thoughts. She observed the crew wander back at all hours, looking as though they might collapse into a heap at any moment, smiled at their harsh expletives, listened to their ribald songs and drunken cries, envied their camaraderie, longed to be a part of them. Most of all, she yearned to travel, dreamed of the faraway, the unattainable . . . for now.

Filling the air were the pungent odors—brine from a leaking cask of ripe olives, salt water and oils wrung from the ship's hemp and jute mooring lines by their tautness—the droplets appearing on and between the strands like milky sap—salted green hides which smelled of unrefrigerated salt meat, a molasses odor rising from bags of raw sugar, aromatic teas and spices, coffee being roasted in a nearby packing house, an ever-present tallow odor like stale lard, woody smells from packing cases made of green lumber, filled with wood shavings, creosote from the wharf's pilings, and neatly strapped stacks of cured lumber awaiting shipment, gum turpentine and resin, stale urine as the longshoremen relieved themselves in the nearest corner—all discernible, heavy in the moist, balmy air of the waterfront.

Carson inhaled all of the smells, each distinct as she walked through the storage sheds, the odors clinging to her body and clothing. To leave the waterfront, to go home to her bland room at the Three Arts Club in the West Eighties, where she had settled after beginning her semester at Columbia, was too tame, almost intolerable. But sitting at her typewriter, she could escape again, return to the wharves, make that voyage.

Life at the Three Arts Club was shared with 150 girls who made their living acting, dancing, or working in the creative genres of painting, music, or writing—a requirement for residence. Although Mrs. Frederick Markloff, director-housemother, left the girls largely to themselves, she planned occasional mixers or teas at which she tried to help each newcomer find someone special for a friend.[3] Carson made one close friend, Jane Templeton, a fellow writer who lived on her floor; but usually Carson preferred to keep to herself. She read voraciously, wrote, and felt that she had no time to idle away in prattle. She did enjoy having an occasional companion to go places with, however, and she and Miss Templeton traveled freely about the city, frequently joined by artists Carolyn Haeberlin and Nancy Warren, who studied at the Art Students League on Fifty-seventh Street.

With new friends, enough work to allow her to eat and pay her rent—she had pawned Helen Jackson's old fur coat almost immediately, telling her friend later that it had kept her from starvation—a daily letter from her mother upon which she also fed, and a routine of dedication to her craft, Carson might have been tempted to stay on indefinitely in New York City.

She missed Edwin Peacock, but throughout the year he had written frequently, asking her about each new creative endeavor, encouraging her from southern sidelines. He also had a new friend, he told her, a young corporal from Fort Benning who was taking a sketching class from Peacock's friend Betty Fielder, who had introduced them. Soon he had written Carson all about James Reeves McCullers, Jr., a fellow Southerner who had completed one three-year army enlistment and was now on his second. But life was dull at the fort, and sometimes Reeves became gut sick of the regimentation, rules, and red tape. As often as possible he went into town to drink, take an art class, or sometimes just to spend a quiet day or evening in the town's public library. There he met Virginia Johnson, Carson's attractive cousin, with whom he began to have dates.

Edwin Peacock and Reeves McCullers shared a lively interest in books, music, and art. Reeves, too, was a great appreciator of music, although he himself played no instrument. His dream was to be a famous writer someday. Peacock took pleasure in telling Reeves about his friend Carson Smith in New York City, who was "greatly talented" and was at that moment taking writing courses at Columbia. The two men also fanned each other's political passions; both were disillusioned by what they considered the evils of capitalism and were ardently interested in the writings of Karl Marx and other social protesters popular in the 1930s.

Early in their relationship Peacock took Reeves with him to the Smith house. Marguerite Smith loved company, especially those with whom she could converse on music, art, flowers, world affairs, and her elder daughter, Sister. Sister had been dangled and flung at Reeves long before the two actually met. Throughout the winter and spring that Carson was away, the Smith home was open to Peacock and many of the other young people whom Marguerite encouraged to drop in for refreshments and an informal evening of talk and music. She was a gracious, chatty hostess who had a gift for making newcomers feel welcome and immediately at ease. Peacock often brought new records with him to share with the Smith family, and sometimes Marguerite read poetry aloud. She memorized easily and took pleasure in reciting poems. They also discussed gardening, cooking, books, politics, and sundry other topics of current interest. To Peacock, Marguerite seemed "pliable and affable, never dogmatic in her opinions." She often ventured judgments, but readily changed her mind if a more appropriate stand were suggested by someone whose opinion she respected. "Bebe was especially flexible where Carson was concerned," said Peacock. "I remember that shortly after *Gone With the Wind* came out Bebe thought it was one of the greatest books ever written. But Carson said, 'Well, I don't think it's so great.' Thereafter Bebe was the first to criticize it soundly when someone brought up 'that wonderful book, *Gone With the Wind.*'"[4]

Into this group in mid-June 1935 moved Carson, front and center. Overcome by a flood of relief and exhaustion when her term at Columbia University ended, Carson said good-by to her friend Jane Templeton, asked Edith Markloff, her housemother, to save a room for her at the Three Arts in the fall, and made the thousand-mile trek home on a Greyhound bus.

Once in Columbus, except for the small literary and musical coterie which gathered at the Smith home, Carson saw few people. Several of her contemporaries appeared and scrutinized her in an effort to determine if the big city had had "any beneficial effects upon Lula Carson," but they were not impressed and scurried off to report that it was highly doubtful that she would ever be any different. Most of all, Carson enjoyed being back home with Edwin Peacock, and now with Reeves McCullers, his young friend at Fort Benning. They resumed their relationship that summer as easily as if one had only stepped back from the Ping-pong table a pace and was waiting for the next serve. Joined now by Reeves, they hiked and swam, stretched out on the floor and read and discussed—as rapt new disciples—Joyce, Faulkner, and Marx, and listened for hours to Peacock's impressive classical record collection. They drank bock beer and got into eternal bouts of chess. Sometimes Reeves was invited to drive the Smith family's Whippet, and the three of them would motor into the country carrying a portable phonograph with them. Reeves once quipped, "I'll bet this is the first time Brahms's Fourth Symphony has been played in an automobile." But it was not the last, for they had many such musical drives. Invariably the three of them ended up in Peacock's apartment swapping yarns, with Carson determined to get a bare toe hold on truth and stretch it out of all proportion.

No one in Columbus with the possible exception of Edwin Peacock— for they had exchanged letters regularly—knew precisely what had transpired with Carson while she was in New York City alone for the first time. Probably not even Carson herself could ascertain the truth soon after it happened, for she immediately transposed reality into fantasy, distorted, polished, embellished, and presented her wildest imaginings as fact. Once the art had been created, she could not distinguish the tissue between actuality and imagination. She was unconscious, even, of a creative process having gone on, so natural was the flow.

To Peacock and Reeves she told anecdote after anecdote about the fascinating and evil life she had observed and encountered in the city. Her tales of seduction, prostitution, suicide, and other debaucheries of her friends smacked of the relish of naivete and hyperbole. Outsiders who heard her tales were usually too shocked to want to ascertain the truth, as was the case in 1944 when Carson returned to Columbus in mourning, the occasion, her father's funeral. World War II had been raging on both fronts, and transportation at home was at a premium when Carson made the sudden trip South by train. "You poor child, did you have to sit up all night in a day coach?" asked one solicitous relative at the cemetery.

"Oh, no," responded Carson demurely. "The nicest soldier shared his berth with me."

To Carson in June of 1935, the "nicest soldier" she had ever known was Reeves McCullers. Almost immediately the two of them became enamored of each other. Doubtless Reeves was half in love with her before they even met. Marguerite Smith, and her daughter Rita, too, had grown to love the handsome, fair-eyed soldier who had called regularly at their home for the past five months, sometimes bringing flowers—which especially endeared him to Marguerite—and fresh fruits and candy for the whole family. (To Carson, he usually brought beer and cigarettes.) It seemed only natural to them that Carson would love Reeves, too, for Marguerite felt as though they had become one big happy family. Surprising to outsiders, however, was that Reeves fell so completely in love with Carson. (That he would marry her two years later seemed incredible to most Columbus people who knew them both.) Carson had never dated before, except for a classmate, Omaha Landrum—who said that their "single date in high school was not really much of one"—nor had she even had a friendship with any young man until Edwin Peacock came on the scene. It was Reeves, however, who first made Carson feel like a woman. Moreover, he treated her like a lady, put her on a pedestal, and joined the Smith clan in single-minded worship.

At Wetumpka (Alabama) High School, where Reeves spent his senior year, he had been everything that Carson was not: popular, possessed of a sparkling personality, envied by his peers for his ability to get any girl he wanted (and his wants were many), charming and witty, a star halfback, one of five seniors singled out for football laurels, member of a half-dozen clubs, a Thespian, and a solid "B" student. He took girls to the Harigut Springs Pavilion out of town to dance to the jukebox, swim, and drink moonshine, and spent two weeks after graduation at a coed house party near Panama City, Florida, at which he gained both love and notoriety. In short, James Reeves McCullers, Jr., was Big Man on the Wetumpka campus—although in stature he was slender and of medium height, barely 5 feet, 9 inches tall.

After four years of seasoning in the infantry, Reeves was in top physical condition, hard-muscled and feisty; but with Carson that summer he was gentle, and she loved him, idealized him, and marveled that he had singled her out. Perhaps one of the things which drew her to him was his gift for storytelling. Whether he was relating an anecdote about "Big Mama" and "Little Papa," his paternal grandparents, both warm characters whom he loved, or an incident on post over which he had become heated and indignant, or a story of imagined heroics—all had the showman's sense of timing, suspense, and a near-professional narrative flow.

Reeves was a teller of tales in the best Homeric tradition, but he was not a writer; and therein, throughout life, proved the rub.

Frequently Carson and Reeves rode bicycles the ten miles up Whitesville Road to see Max Goodley. A bachelor some fifteen years older than Carson, Goodley had seventy-five acres of wild flowers surrounding his house in the country. Behind the house was a creek in which Carson and Reeves liked to wade and swim. According to Goodley, sometimes they "skinny-dipped." Those who recalled Carson in her youth as "wan and fragile" did not know her well during her late teens, particularly after she became acquainted with Reeves. According to Edwin Peacock, "While Carson was never robust, I never thought of her as frail. Her bravura technique at the piano certainly belied her physical condition as some people thought of it. Even so, she was no tower of strength. I will never forget when Carson and Reeves stopped by my apartment on their way home from a long bicycle ride out to the old Eelbeck mill on Macon Road—she was the picture of health: sun-burned, radiant, and happy with Reeves."[5]

By profession Goodley was a gardener; next to flowers, he loved books and aspired to be a published author of novels someday. Carson recommended that Goodley keep up with *Story*, saying, "That's the magazine to watch," offered him criticism on his stories—particularly when his plots and endings were not plausible enough—and frequently brought him stories to read that she had found especially good, such as two of her favorites, Katherine Mansfield's "The Wind" and "Violin Lesson." (Virginia Johnson Storey, Carson's cousin-librarian, said that she once had had to buy a new Mansfield book of short stories for the library because Carson had literally "read the pages to pieces.")

"How would it change your life if you had a book published?" Carson queried Goodley when she heard that Viking Press had once kept his novel manuscript for six months. Goodley thought for a moment without answering; then Carson asked, "You mean you wouldn't go to New York?"

"Never!" Goodley retorted. Carson thought such provincialism the silliest thing she had ever heard. She talked incessantly of New York to Reeves, Goodley, and Peacock that summer, and vowed that "when I become a famous writer, that's where I'll live all the time."

Max Goodley looked forward to Carson and Reeves's dropping in on him. Sometimes Peacock came, too. In fact, it was Peacock who had introduced them, for his special hobby was identifying wild flowers, and the two of them had methodically catalogued most of the flowers on Goodley's large acreage. To Goodley, Reeves was a source of humor and entertainment, as well as consternation. Clever at outlandish words,

Reeves frequently provoked Goodley to veiled laughter because of his tendency for malapropisms, of which Reeves himself was totally unaware. At other times, a frivolous incident ended fiercely, such as the day Carson, Reeves, and Peacock went out to Goodley's on a holiday and the men became intoxicated on his home-brewed blackberry wine. Reeves leaped high into the air to grasp a great crossbeam of the open ceiling of Goodley's living room, then began to swing from one to another. "Get down! You'll crack your head open," Goodley demanded, whereupon Reeves, resentful and angry at being called down, cursed abusively, flailed and hammered with his fists, and stomped off into the night.[6]

Querulous, sometimes vain, Reeves wanted desperately to be *somebody*. "Look at me! Notice me!" his whole being seemed to shout, and Carson knew precisely the feeling. But she had never had to shout it; instead, she had been looked at, noticed, adulated by her mother for eighteen years, recoiling from it sometimes, but also finding comfort in it. She reached out now to Reeves to soothe and to succor.

Reeves had known an insecure childhood, and he needed love. Born on August 11, 1913, in the home of his grandfather, Wiley McCullers, a dry goods clerk in Wetumpka, Alabama, Reeves had moved to Jesup, Georgia, as an infant, where his two sisters, Marguerite and Wiley Mae, and his brother Tommy were born as stairsteps behind him. His father, James, Sr. ("Bud"), had been a drugstore clerk, telephone lineman, penitentiary guard, unsuccessful farmer, and a railroad man; his mother was Jessie Winn McCullers, the daughter of John T. Winn, Sr., gentleman farmer who sold farming implements, mules, and horses through his prosperous firm, Winn & Co., of Jesup. Disapproving of the match but reluctant to criticize when it was too late, Jessie Winn's parents were convinced that their daughter had married beneath them and that the union was something only to be endured.

And endure it, Jessie did. When Bud McCullers left his job at the state prison in Alabama and moved back to Jesup, where he had met his wife while clerking in his brother-in-law's drugstore, he tried his hand first at farming a large acreage that his father-in-law had installed them on; but McCullers, reluctant to do any of his own work, imported blacks from Alabama and left them on their own resources to plant, till, and harvest his cotton and corn crops while he stayed in town most of the time to play baseball and to work on the side as a lineman with Postal Telegraph Company. For the next five years there was never enough money coming in from his own efforts to support his family, and McCullers was forced to accept help from his father, who clothed his family, and his father-in-law, who fed them.

Then Reeves's father was hired by Atlantic Coastline Railroad as a brakeman, and the money began to come in. When Reeves was nine the family moved to Lakeland, his father having been given a promotion and raise to relocate in Florida. In Lakeland, however, after a year there, McCullers fell from a coal car, suffered a crushed leg, and returned to Jesup in a cast, disabled and pensioned by the railroad. From then on, times were even more difficult for the McCullers family. With his railroad settlement money McCullers opened a bakery in Jesup, but the business soon failed and Jessie McCullers went to work at Nathan's Dry Goods Store for ten dollars a week. Both the senior Winns and McCullers helped support the family, with Mrs. McCullers' father trading a farm he owned for a house in town so that she and her family could live rent free. Enjoying poor health and essentially lazy, Bud McCullers began to drink more heavily, left his wife and children alone for increasingly longer periods, and eventually abandoned them altogether when Tommy, the youngest, was barely in grade school.

While Mrs. McCullers kept the two younger children at home with her, Reeves and his sister Marguerite were shifted about from relative to relative to help relieve the family's financial plight. When Reeves was ten, eleven, and twelve, he spent the summers with his aunt Ida Mae McCullers Lancaster, and her husband, John, who was president of the Wetumpka, Alabama, bank. Here he roamed the town and the cotton and corn fields of a two-thousand-acre plantation owned by his uncle's brother, rode horseback, and watched the slaughter of cattle and hogs for market.

Always small for his age, Reeves was frequently picked on or taken advantage of by his peers. But they seldom offended him twice, for Reeves fought fiercely for what he believed in—himself. During Reeves's first summer in Wetumpka, Horatio Robinson, the son of his grandfather's employer, let him join the sandlot football team. "Hey, boy, you play here. Boy, you play there. Boy, get out of the game," Reeves's teammates shouted, taking pleasure in the diminutive and nondescript nickname.

"My name's Reeves," the wiry youngster glowered, "not Boy. Don't you call me Boy again." And they did not. All of the McCullers men were small, the women, large and big-breasted. "Big Mama" McCullers, Reeves's grandmother, weighed over 250 pounds, her husband, "Little Papa," scarcely 120 pounds; but no one in the McCullers clan ever doubted for a moment who was boss. The little men fought for what they had and ruled the roost. But Bud McCullers, although small, seemed to be made from a different mold. Later, when his son James Reeves, Jr., met the eldest daughter of Lamar and Marguerite Smith, it was no contest, not in 1935 when they first met, or ever. Yet in her own way, knowing what a domineering woman can do to a man—had done in her own family—Carson at first did everything she could to preserve and protect Reeves's manhood.

When Reeves was twelve, he moved to Valdosta, Georgia, where he lived for three years with his aunt Emma Rosa McRae, his father's sister, and her husband, Vernon. Their son, Vernon, Jr., was a year younger than Reeves, and the two boys became constant companions. "Reeves was a hell-raiser even then," said his cousin. "Fun-loving, yes, but never really bad. And he was basically honest. Reeves borrowed my ties, shirts, and anything else he wanted. He beat me in everything he did, but fortunately we never competed for the same girl. Reeves could charm the skin off a snake. I loved him," McRae concluded. Reeves got drunk occasionally as a youngster, such as the time, at age fourteen when he borrowed the family car and wrecked it. "He cost us five hundred dollars, but he was sweet," said Mrs. McRae fondly.

In Valdosta, Reeves became a charter member of Boy Scout Troop No. 2. With his cousin and other troopmates he dug for arrowheads, pottery, and miscellaneous artifacts in the ancient Indian barrows that abounded in the area, camped at nearby Morgan Springs, and ate frogs that they trapped and cooked over an open fire at night. Determined to be the best Scout possible, Reeves earned scouting's highest award, the Eagle Scout badge, when he was barely thirteen. Jessie McCullers proudly made the one-hundred-mile trip from Jesup to Valdosta for the ceremony.

An ambivalence in Reeves's nature showed up as a child that was doubtless shaped by the times and his environment: his attitude toward money and his sense of responsibility toward making it. As a child in Jesup, Reeves worked hard; there was not a lazy streak in his body. He had his mother's energy, for Jessie McCullers was hard-working and resourceful. He had a job delivering groceries, sold sarsaparilla at the Saturday all-day-sings on the courthouse lawn, and redeemed the bottles later for the deposit, crawling about through the grass and shrubs looking carefully for each one. He also had a paper route. In short, Reeves did everything possible to help lessen his mother's financial straits. Yet, when he went off to live with relatives, either with the McRaes in Valdosta, or the Lancasters in Wetumpka, he felt no compunction about not working part time to help pay his room and board or to keep himself in spending money. In Valdosta, his cousin Vernon worked in his father's drugstore after school and on weekends, but Reeves did not. He never worked for money during his three years with the McRaes, but accepted gratefully whatever he was offered. In Wetumpka, during his senior year with the Lancasters, Reeves had plenty of spending money, financed a hobby of photography and developed film and printed his own pictures, dated freely and without restriction, dressed well, and never seemed to be in need. The Lancasters had no children, and Reeves was like a son to them. Although Horatio Robinson worked in his father's dry goods store—along with Reeves's grandfather—and most of his classmates also worked, at least for spending money, Reeves's every financial need was met by his well-meaning relatives.

Five months after Reeves was graduated from high school, in November 1931, he enlisted in the United States Army at Fort Benning, where he was stationed during his first five years of service. Discharged on November 2, 1934, he re-enlisted the next day for another three years and received a re-enlistment bonus of several hundred dollars. After meeting Carson during the summer of 1935 and feeling through her the contagious pull of life in New York City, however, Reeves resolved that he, too, would make his way North just as soon as possible. That summer he took a furlough and went home to Jesup for a few days to see his mother, then made his first trip to New York. He was determined to be a writer, a journalist perhaps. Reeves now began to keep a diary, making sporadic entries and writing sketches and a few prose essays about his observations, recollections, and army experiences.

In the meantime, during the summer of 1935, Carson was writing prolifically. Soon after her return home she resumed communication with her music teacher, Mary Tucker, who now lived in Virginia with her family. To Mrs. Tucker, Carson's remarks were always straightforward and honest; to Gin, Mrs. Tucker's daughter, however, Carson frequently embroidered, as she did in a long letter about Reeves soon after their marriage. Carson, writing now to Mrs. Tucker of the bus trip South, revealed herself as a scrutinizing observer and recorder. She said that the wretched discomfort of the trip was worth the opportunity of watching the fascinating people who got on and off during the hundreds of miles they wended through Baltimore, Philadelphia, Washington, Richmond, and on through the South. At one point during a change of buses she had become so entranced with her watchings, she said, that she almost missed her bus and left her luggage, typewriter, and manuscripts sitting in the station after she finally remembered to put herself on the bus. The items were retrieved, however, several days later, and immediately Carson began to record fictionally her trip home.

The story she wrote then became what she described to Edwin Peacock later as "Home Journey and the Green Arcade," an interior monologue by a young college girl on her way South by bus. "As I recall it, it was a good story," said Peacock.[7] The girl related what she thought about herself and some of the rural characters she had observed en route. She described herself as one who had been made over but not spoiled. Now she reproached herself for having given up too easily. She had run away and left her job on a comic magazine in New York City; and she wondered how she could find solace at home, which she identified as Columbus, Georgia. For Carson's fictional youths, to live in the South was to rot in boredom, to stagnate; yet there was ever an ambivalent pull, for home was also a balm that soothed, healed, enveloped, protected. As her sojourner approached home now, she recalled nostalgically the giant oak trees of the streets of Columbus—her "green arcade"—and her capitulation became less painful. There were worse places than home, she concluded.

A longer piece that also evolved from her journey home was "The Aliens."[8] Here the protagonist was a fifty-year-old Jew, a patient traveler who had boarded a bus in New York City and now sat alone in one of the rear seats, headed south to the town of Lafayetteville, where he meant to make his home. Carson described him as "an observant person," who already had scrutinized each fellow passenger. The author and her Jewish protagonist had several characteristics in common. First, she described his "one annoying habit":

> He smoked constantly and as he smoked he quietly worried the
> end of his cigarette with his thumb and forefinger, rubbing and pull-
> ing out shreds of tobacco so that often the cigarette was so ragged
> that he was obliged to nip off the end before putting it to his lips
> again. His hands were slightly calloused at the fingertips and devel-
> oped to a state of delicate muscular perfection; they were a pianist's
> hands.[9]

Carefully the Jew observed his fellow passengers, especially two blacks who got on at widely separate points. Gradually the story of the homeless exile unfolded as he became unwillingly engaged in conversation by a young southern man, a "redneck" with whom he superficially conversed. Yet the exile knew that the redneck could never know his pain, his sense of aloneness, or the real nature of his journey.

The maimed characters deftly drawn in this little sketch were two of Carson's earliest grotesques, for whom she showed deep empathy. The Jew was psychically maimed, and the black woman who climbed aboard later was a physical aberrant:

> Had she not been clothed in a filthy garment that served as a dress,
> even her sex would have been difficult at first glance to define. She
> was deformed—although not in any one specific limb; the body as a
> whole was stunted, warped and undeveloped. She wore a dilapidated
> felt hat, a torn black skirt and a blouse that had been roughly fash-
> ioned from a meal sack. At one corner of her mouth there was an
> ugly open sore and beneath her lower lip she carried a wad of snuff.
> The whites of her eyes were not white at all, but of a muddy yellow
> color veined with red. Her face as a whole had a roving, hungry, va-
> cant look.[10]

When the Jew asked "in a quiet, taut voice, 'What is the matter with her?'" the young Southerner took a long open look and responded blankly, "Who? You mean the nigger? . . . Why there's nothing the matter with her. . . . Not that I can see."[11] To be sure, the redneck was maimed, too, but in his crass insensitivity he would never know it.

Early that summer Carson wrote to Gin Tucker that she was thinking of starting a magazine with two friends, whom she identified as an amateur drama critic and a student. Although she conceded that it was a wild scheme—for they needed money as well as a definite political stand —they hoped to publish great fiction. She told her friend, however, that they must do something about political support besides talk. Edwin Peacock recalled that he always was "very bearish" about such plans when Carson suggested them to him—in spite of her enthusiasm—and that he offered only discouragement. "One of Carson's cousins had been editor of the literary magazine at Woman's College in Greensboro, North Carolina, and our friend John Zeigler was editor at the time of the literary magazine at The Citadel. Between the three of them, Carson became quite fired up," said Peacock.

Ultimately, however, the magazine did not go beyond the drawing-board stage; in the final analysis no one wanted to devote himself totally and selflessly to the task. According to Peacock, "When we were all together, our evenings were filled with talk, talk, talk—the Civil War in Spain, *The Nation* and *The New Republic*, Hemingway, Faulkner, Eliot, and the other 'in writers' of the period."[12] Although Carson had toured the mills and viewed with distress the squalid conditions and pervading hopelessness among the people of the mill district in her hometown, and had become increasingly aware of what she considered the weaknesses of her country's capitalistic system, she had not embraced Marxism so passionately that she was willing to give up precious writing time to become actively involved in politics. Nevertheless, she was much aware of the plight of the millworkers, and many of her views involving capitalism were graphically bared later in her first published novel, *The Heart Is a Lonely Hunter.*

Carson made other efforts, also, while at home that summer to see life in the raw in some of the offbeat areas of her hometown. She walked along the riverbank talking to idlers and ambled through the black sections and the old Fifth Avenue neighborhood where she had lived as a child. Sometimes her mother accompanied her on her ramblings and to the beer parlors on the edge of the downtown district. Although she rarely socialized during the daytime, Marguerite Smith loved to be where Carson was. When her firstborn was not at home, she usually sat indoors alone, smoking, drinking large quantities of coffee—which made her nervous, she conceded—and reading. Late in the afternoon she bathed and dressed again, hoping that she would have another houseful of "drop-ins." According to Edwin Peacock, who came more often than anyone else during the mid-1930s: "The evenings at 1519 Starke Avenue were not glamorous, but Bebe was very charming in a simple sort of way. She was certainly not ostentatious. I loved her like a mother. I remember once walking all the way from Fort Benning, gathering wild flowers along the way so that I could have a big bouquet to give her when I arrived. I ate often with the Smith family. Bebe's meals were always good. I remember especially her yellow squash cooked with celery."[13]

Carson hit upon still another idea that summer to help fulfill her writing ambitions. She decided to become a newspaper reporter, reasoning that she might acquire some valuable tools from working at close quarters in a newspaper office. She could observe news firsthand as it happened, follow fire engines, interview criminals, study the jurors' faces in court and the condemned murderer when he stood for sentencing. The imagined benefits of such experiences raced pell-mell through her mind and prompted her to approach Nelson Shipp, editor of the Columbus *Ledger*. She asked him if she might be a volunteer reporter without pay. Formerly a Mercer journalism instructor, Shipp was challenged by the opportunity to train another cub reporter and agreed to take her on.

For a little over a month Carson reported to the *Ledger* newsroom daily, wearing, like a uniform, a sailor middy blouse which always seemed to her associates to be "a little soiled." Carson worked on a variety of assignments, but the practicality of writing factual prose, the regimentation required by the rigid structure of journalese, the impossibility of embellishment—all intimidated her. In response, she daydreamed and moved about in a rarefied atmosphere that was almost impregnable to those around her. On August 15, 1935, for example, the newsroom became electric as crowds climbed the stairs and gathered in clumps, clamoring for news of the welfare of America's beloved humorist with the southwestern drawl, Will Rogers. The small plane piloted by Rogers' good friend Wiley Post had crashed in the wilds near Point Barrow, Alaska, while on a flight to the Orient, and now the news came in that both men had been found dead. The newsroom hummed with the labored excitement of getting out an extra. Presses rolled, waiting newsboys leaped eagerly upon their stacks of papers and dashed to the streets, yelling "Extra—Extra—Read all about it—Will Rogers killed," and finally, Carson—cub reporter—looked vacantly up from her desk where she had sat the entire afternoon, lost in copy and reverie, and asked, "What's going on? Has something happened?"

Carson told friends that what she liked most about working on a newspaper was police reporting and that she occasionally was asked to write a feature article. She remembered writing one on black widow spiders. She also recalled vividly having had her knuckles soundly rapped for failing to write such things as "the *alleged* murderer" or "the *accused* rapist." Latimer Watson, the woman's editor and an accomplished writer, little valued any assistance Carson might have given her, still smarting from the insult flung her way when Carson had draped herself against the door of her office and said, "I'd starve to death before I'd do what you do." Soon after the Rogers-Post tragedy, Carson abandoned her position as a journalist to those whom she considered hopelessly less imaginative than she, determined to leave not only her job, but the town as well as soon as she could.

Carson and her family had been living the last half of the summer of 1935 in the old downtown Woodruff home on Second Avenue while repairs were being made on their Starke Avenue home that had been partially destroyed by fire. She had gone to Jim Woodruff, prominent Columbus businessman, to seek advice about the mechanics of rebuilding their damaged house, and Woodruff had given Carson the key to his family's palatial old home as a possible haven for the Smith family for the next few weeks. Carson looked at the Woodruff mansion, announced that it was much too large for them, but suggested: "If you would construct a few partitions here and there, put in a kitchen, and do a little carpentry work, we could have our own small apartment on the second floor." Taken aback by Carson's audacity, yet amused by her direct manner and desire "to keep it all businesslike by paying rent—we don't want charity," Woodruff asked his young friend to name a rental fee. "I think fifteen dollars a month would be pretty fair, don't you?" Carson responded naively. "Sold!" he agreed, and as soon as the remodeling was accomplished, the Smith family moved in.

The fire itself attested to still another dimension of Carson's nature. Lying in bed in her room one afternoon, home alone and absorbed in a Dostoevski novel, Carson was unaware of anything amiss until loud snapping and crackling noises—which she first attributed to her brother—mounted to a roar and a portion of the ceiling collapsed at the rear of the house. Frightened, Carson fled from the house through the front door. Neighbors and passers-by had already converged on the sidewalk and now began rushing in to rescue the family's antiques and silver. When her parents returned home a few minutes later, unaware of the calamity, they responded with stunned apathy. The house had been ruined on the inside and much of the exterior structure damaged. While Lamar and Marguerite Smith sat on the curb looking like "forlorn waifs ejected by a cruel landlord," as one observer described them, accepting the sympathies of their friends, Carson leaped into the family car and drove the few blocks to the Woman's Club to tell Edwin Peacock, then returned home to take decisive action. No one who had known the eldest Smith child in Columbus could have guessed how capably Carson could cope with harsh reality in an emergency, but the proof was in the act. She arranged for their new homesite and also oversaw the restoration on Starke Avenue. With the insurance money, the house was not only rebuilt, but Marguerite was also able to save out enough to finance Carson's passage north again.

In September, after her family had moved back into their restored house, Carson reluctantly told Reeves and Peacock good-by and departed again by steamship for New York City. She and Reeves considered themselves engaged now, although he had given her no ring. Carson knew it was only a matter of time before they would be together writing and working in New York. Now she was a seasoned traveler. Upon arrival she moved again into the Three Arts Club and excitedly enrolled in school, this time at Washington Square College of New York University. Sylvia Chatfield Bates's evening fiction workshop had been highly recommended to her, and it was to her that Carson now applied. Miss Bates's writing course was in the Journalism Department of the School of Commerce, New York University having no bona fide creative writing department in the mid-thirties, and Carson happily became a commerce student. Not since Mary Tucker had she encountered anyone for whom she wanted to work other than herself; in Miss Bates's class, however, she was ecstatic. Here she found a sympathy, criticism, and discipline of constant work that proved invaluable, and under Miss Bates's encouragement and practical eye, Carson began to feel achievement and maturity as a writer for the first time.

For two semesters Carson studied with Sylvia Chatfield Bates, writing in earnest every morning, working each afternoon in the same haphazard fashion that she had the year before, and attending classes and observing the city at night. Her health was somewhat better this year. Although she missed Reeves, they wrote frequently and she seemed supremely happy.

Reeves, however, had become increasingly impatient to get out of the Army. Since his enlistment time would not be up until November 1937, he began to think now about an early discharge. A second termer could purchase a discharge by repaying the government his re-enlistment bonus and several additional hundred dollars, but Reeves had no way to finance such a move yet. Encouraging him, also, to come to New York was his old army friend John Vincent Adams, whom he had known since the spring of 1932 when they had been privates together at Fort Benning. Both men had been recommended for the West Point Prep School, but after the five-month course not one man of the forty-two-member class received an appointment to the Academy. Both Reeves and Adams had been bitterly disappointed. Adams, too, wanted to write the "great American novel," and he urged Reeves to get out of the Army and move to New York so that they could live and write together.

In the meantime, some of Carson's best work was germinating, but she made no attempt to publish it. These were apprentice pieces, she said, in which she was still feeling her way. Each manuscript that she submitted to Miss Bates was returned with sound, thoughtful comment, such as the one Miss Bates attached to "Poldi" and marked "Return for reading next time":

> This is an excellent example of the "picture" story—which means full dramatization of a short time scheme, the picturing of an almost static condition the actual narrative elements of which are in the past or in the future. The situation is rather trite, but not very. You can rescue it from triteness—as Willa Cather did in *Lucy Gayheart*—by the truth, accuracy and freshness of detail. Many a story sells on its detail; yours, so far as I have seen them, may be that sort. These details are good. Very vivid. Also a special knowledge story has a bid for success, and your special knowledge of music exhibited here sounds authentic. A musician can judge that better than I.
>
> The average reader will want more than your static picture vividly presented—movement forward, at the very least suggested for the future. But I like this as it is. For what it is it need not be much better done.
>
> S.C.B.[14]

"Poldi" and most of Carson's other early pieces remained unpublished until four years after her death. When her sister, Margarita G. Smith, edited and brought out many of the hitherto unpublished stories in *The Mortgaged Heart*, she included "Poldi" and nine other early manuscripts. Only "Sucker" and "Wunderkind" had been published during the author's lifetime. Juxtaposed with the stories published in *The Mortgaged Heart* were Miss Bates's critical comments of three of these early manuscripts: "Poldi," "Instant of the Hour After," and "Wunderkind." "Poldi" was the story of a female cellist and a young man, Hans, who futilely loved her. His was a pathetic and painful love, of which Poldi herself was not even aware. This story was perhaps the earliest in Carson's canon of writings about unreciprocated love.

"Instant of the Hour After" poignantly revealed the frustrations of a young marriage steeped in alcoholic bitters. Sylvia Chatfield Bates liked "Instant of the Hour After" least of anything Carson wrote for her. She thought that the story had no reason for being, that the reader was cheated, after all the disagreeable details, to learn only that the drunken husband loved his wife so much that it threatened to destroy him. Miss Bates encouraged Carson to rewrite the story, but cautioned her against the use of certain phrases "not printable in a magazine, Joyce or no Joyce." On the positive side, she commented on "the great vividness, the acute visibility" of Carson's story. "The dramatization of every little detail is excellent, and fresh. And the characters come through the objective scenes beautifully." What she called the "feature" of the story, a delightful "element of artistic piquancy," was the image of the two persons in the bottle, "skeetering angrily up and down the cold blank glass like minute monkeys."[15]

"Wunderkind" was Miss Bates's favorite. A mood story which also utilized Carson's special knowledge of music, "Wunderkind" depicted a fifteen-year-old protagonist, a piano prodigy, who teetered between adolescence and maturity in her unsuccessful struggle to play for her teacher with something of the passion, sensitivity, and technique she had once shown. Frances' painfully acquired self-knowledge led to her stumbling flight from the master's studio. Bewildered, she turned in the wrong direction in her simple route home. Yet the young woman had faced her impasse and recognized it, and now there was hope that she could collect herself and move forward in a new and more purposeful direction. Significant to this story was Carson's success in objectifying her attachment to her own music teacher, and the acknowledgment of what she feared to be the waning of her precious musical talent—that she had been a star struck too high, for whom the fall now was inconsolably painful.

Carson destroyed many of her early stories—everything which she was not satisfied with or felt was not salvable based on her writing teacher's critical comments. A number of these early pieces survived, which Carson's sister felt were appropriate for inclusion in *The Mortgaged Heart*. Three of them were published in *Redbook* (October 1971) just prior to the release of the posthumous collection: "Instant of the Hour After," "Breath from the Sky," and "Like That." "The Aliens," "Breath from the Sky," and a long narrative which Margarita Smith identified as "Untitled Piece" are direct predecessors to "The Mute," a long novel which began to take nebulous form the following winter and evolved eventually into *The Heart Is a Lonely Hunter*. Both "Breath from the Sky" and "Untitled Piece" contained elements of the girl Mick and many other characteristics of *The Heart Is a Lonely Hunter*.

"Breath from the Sky" was probably written while Carson was in Miss Bates's fiction workshop or the following winter while she was at home recuperating from what doctors thought was tuberculosis. Like Carson, her protagonist was a teen-age girl recuperating from pleurisy. It was Constance's first day outside and she sat in the sun, a Panama hat pulled over her eyes. She longed for "cool blueness that could be sucked in until she was drenched in its color," but her breath from the sky failed to refresh; instead, the sky was "a burning, fevered blue," symbolic of the troubled girl herself.[16] Juxtaposed between the sky and the painfully insecure, introvertive, and inarticulate girl were fragile sprays of white spirea, a fat, solicitous nurse who provoked only the girl's hatred, a seemingly insensitive mother—or perhaps an overly sensitive one who tried not to show it—and a brother, a sister, Mick, and a dog who seemed to Constance to be having all the fun and attention of the family. Although the story went nowhere, it was a sensitive mood story, a slice of life rich in sensory imagery and detail. The autobiographical elements were unmistakable. Carson, too, had been sent away to a rest home in Alto, Georgia, to recuperate after suffering a severe illness when she was a senior in high school; in the story, Constance dreaded the trip she must make—possibly alone—to Mountain Heights.

"Like That," which *Story* purchased but never published, the manuscript showing up many years later in the archives at Princeton University, was another early initiation story. In an interior monologue the young protagonist talked about her older sister who was eighteen and "grown-up now"; and if growing up meant acting *like that*, then she would not have a thing to do with it. "I know there's no way I can make myself stay thirteen all my life," she said, "but I know I'd never let anything really change me at all—no matter what it is." She told how she reacted when she found out that Sis had just "started with what every big girl has each month." Frightened and angry, she lied to her sister: "Anybody can tell. Right off the bat. Just to look at you anybody can tell. . . . It looks terrible. I wouldn't ever ever be like that." And now, five years later, the young narrator was upset about a new initiation of her sister's, a sexual one, although the younger girl herself did not actually know what had happened. She only knew that the relationship between her and her sister had changed, and she was hurt and resentful.[17]

Like this story's predecessor, "Sucker," the plot was the story of Sis's initiation, as it was Sucker's; but more importantly, it was the effect of Sis and Sucker's initiation upon each narrator—thus the narrator's initiation, as well. Just as Sylvia Chatfield Bates had thought that the language in "The Instant of the Hour After" was in poor taste for readers in the mid-thirties—in spite of what Joyce's *Ulysses* had done for literary freedom —so, too, in 1936 did Whit Burnett feel that a story whose central incident graphically referred to a young girl's menstruation should also be suppressed until more liberal times.[18]

In June 1936, after another laborious year in New York City, Carson returned to Columbus, again ill and exhausted. It was only a brief respite, however, for Miss Bates urged Carson to return to the city in July to attend Whit Burnett's short-story writing course at Columbia. Carson already knew Whit Burnett's reputation, for in *Story* he and his editor-wife, Martha Foley, had discovered and published more first writers than any other magazine on the market. Miss Bates had encouraged her also to submit "Wunderkind" to *Story* for publication, and Carson was anxious to present it to her teacher upon arrival in class. Carson longed to join the ranks, not just as a published author, but with such writers as William Faulkner, Erskine Caldwell, James T. Farrell, William Saroyan, Tennessee Williams, Jesse Stuart, Gertrude Stein, and other quality writers who were appearing in the pages of *Story*. Although leaving Columbus so soon also meant leaving Reeves, she knew that more than anything else in the world she must not compromise her writing. As she explained in her biographical sketch for Whit Burnett later that summer, there were two things she needed to do more than anything else: to write directly from her own being and to concentrate and avoid any waste of passion that could be used in writing. At the risk of sounding silly or childish, she said that she believed most of all in love and its many facets, and then, secondly, in a meaningful rendering of her creative drives. Thus it was not surprising that the first of July, as soon as she felt well enough, Carson was on the Greyhound bus again, returning once more to New York City and "home" at the Three Arts Club—settling in this time to work under the direction of Whit Burnett.

Reeves, too, was making plans to go to New York. His aunt, Mrs. John Lancaster, with whom he had lived in Wetumpka while he finished high school, had died in January 1936, leaving him three Alabama Harbor bonds. Taking his aunt's legacy just as soon as it could be released to him, Reeves sold his bonds for fifteen hundred dollars, then quickly purchased his discharge from the U. S. Army. On August 27, 1936, Reeves was a civilian once again. After a brief trip home, he gathered up his few personal belongings and moved to New York City. His friend Vincent Adams welcomed him into his tiny apartment at 439 West Forty-third Street, and Reeves made plans to go to college and to write. On September 15, he enrolled at Columbia University in courses in journalism and anthropology. By this time, however, Carson felt that her college days were over. She needed only to put into practice the lessons that Sylvia Chatfield Bates and Whit Burnett had so successfully driven home. She felt that *now* was the time for her to be her own critic and to perfect her craft.

Reeves's first college experience was aborted after five weeks when on November 12, 1936, he withdrew from Columbia University to take Carson, once again seriously ill, back to Columbus by train. She had refused Reeves's offer to finance her for the fall term at Columbia, insisting, instead, on her own rigorous, self-imposed work schedule. Encouraged by her sale of both "Wunderkind" and "Like That" to *Story*, with "Wunderkind" slated to appear in December, Carson had been getting up at dawn and writing for several hours, her body sustained largely by coffee and cigarettes. By now she was chain-smoking almost three packs a day. Barely eating, she had lost weight, become nervous and highly irritated by trifles, ran chronically a low-grade fever, and suffered a deep respiratory infection.

Once home, Carson was put to bed for the winter and told that she must stay there indefinitely if she were to recover fully. The local doctors vaguely diagnosed her ailment as tuberculosis; in reality, it was rheumatic fever. Her New York doctors believed later that had this disease been correctly diagnosd, her life style might have been altered to at least include more rest; subsequent damage to her heart and her crippling strokes might have been avoided.

Reeves stayed only a few days, promising to return for Christmas. Immediately upon getting home, Carson wrote to Whit Burnett and Martha Foley to thank them for her check. She took pride in the twenty-five dollars she received for the purchase of her two stories. Before leaving New York, she celebrated her success with the purchase of two bags of chocolate almond cakes, a bottle of wine, and a book, Sir Thomas More's *Story of Three Decades*. Some twenty-five years later when she wrote Whit Burnett to give him permission to reprint "Wunderkind" in an anthology he was preparing—having received by this time fifteen hundred dollars for the sale of her story "Sucker," an earlier, more juvenile effort than "Wunderkind"—she told him that she was reminded of the twenty-five dollars she had received from him for her first literary success and the chocolate cakes she had bought with the money.

The Burnetts took a personal interest in Carson and wrote her that winter in Columbus to ask how her book was coming that she had told them about earlier. She replied that she was not dissatisfied with her progress, but that she had written only a few pages. Then she explained that she was convalescing from a serious respiratory infection and had chewed her pencil more than she had written with it. But even if she should work for six months and discover that the writing was not good, at least it would not be time wasted, she assured them. Hopefully, however, enough of it would be good so that they could see merit in her efforts.

Carson's novel had been gestating for many months. She told the Burnetts that it was a long work which rambled. She was troubled by it constantly, but she could not leave it alone. It was about a man in a southern town to whom various people kept talking and relating their troubles. First, she conceived him as John Minovich; then, he became Harry Minowitz, a Jew. It was a strange creative process, admitted Carson. She had been writing at random, with the characters simply appearing and forcing themselves upon her pages. Although she wrote every day, the whole thing made no sense. Then one day, as she musingly paced the living-room hooked rug, stepping on some designs and skipping others—all in a state of great agitation over the mystery of her book—a great light seemed to flash in her mind.[19] Excitedly she called to her mother and announced that at last she knew that Minowitz was a deaf mute and that his name was John Singer. Her mother, bewildered by Carson's pronouncement, thought for a few moments then asked, "How many deaf mutes do you know, dear?"

"I've never known one, but I know Singer," she replied. At that moment Carson knew that the work had defined itself and she was safe. *The Mute*, which eventually became *The Heart Is a Lonely Hunter*, had at this moment been born.

Carson described these sudden illuminations as "the grace of labor." In an essay, "The Flowering Dream: Notes on Writing," written many years later, she further identified the process:

> It is like a flowering dream. Ideas grow, budding silently, and there are a thousand illuminations coming day by day as the work progresses. A seed grows in writing as in nature. The seed of the idea is developed by both labor and the unconscious, and the struggle that goes on between them.
>
> I understand only particles. I understand the characters, but the novel itself is not in focus. The focus comes at random moments which no one can understand, least of all the author. For me, they usually follow great effort. To me, these illuminations are the grace of labor. All of my work has happened this way. It is at once the hazard and the beauty that a writer has to depend on such illuminations. After months of confusion and labor, when the idea has flowered, the collusion is Divine. It always comes from the subconscious and cannot be controlled.[20]

Carson stayed in bed or in her room most of the winter of 1936–37. Lying there, she listened to the voices in her novel talk around her, impatient to get up and record what they were saying. Her mind raced even though her body languished. When Reeves came at Christmastime, he hoped to be able to take her back with him, but the recovery had been slower than expected. She would stay at home and rest and work, she told him, then join him in New York in the spring. At home Carson lacked no creature comforts. She could not have had a more attentive nurse than her mother, who brought her thick nourishing soups, kept a thermos of hot tea at her bedside, and served fried chicken and creamed potato dinners—her favorite—almost every night.

Although the appearance of *Story* in December had brought Carson some notice in Columbus, the magazine, not having the circulation of the popular slicks, was seldom read by the general reader. When Carson was given the opportunity of submitting to *Story* a list of persons to be notified that her story was being published, she responded with only four local names: her friends Edwin Peacock and Max Goodley, her former employer at the *Ledger*, Nelson Shipp, and Mrs. DuPont Kirven, the mother of one of her high school classmates. Others on her list included a few out-of-town relatives, Colonel and Mrs. Tucker, Sylvia Chatfield Bates, her housemother at the Three Arts, Reeves—who by then was living in Long Island City—and a handful of New York acquaintances. For Columbusites to take notice of the budding young author, it took not only her first novel, *The Heart Is a Lonely Hunter*, but also the second, *Reflections in a Golden Eye*—and even then her fame at home was not so much for her artistic achievement as it was notoriety for the uncomfortable exposure of what appeared to be her hometown and the nearby fort.

Meantime, Reeves and Vincent Adams had moved to an apartment in Sunnyside, New York, where they spent most of the winter. Reeves was taking classes at Columbia, both men were writing, and Adams had a salaried job on the side. In the spring they rented a cottage in Golden Bridge at Lake Katona, fifty miles north of New York City, where Reeves had a small studio and there was room for Carson when she was well enough to join them. Together the two men purchased a 1931 Model A Ford roadster with most of what was left of Reeves's legacy from his aunt, and in March Reeves drove into the city to meet Carson and take her home with him. He would take wonderful care of her, he had promised Carson's mother, and Carson could rest and write as she saw fit. Adams, too, was fond of Carson and the three of them got on well together. The men had tentatively planned a trip to Mexico for the summer, for Reeves had in mind a novel to be set there and he needed local color. In April, however, Adams decided to get married, and the trip was called off.

After only three and a half weeks in Golden Bridge with Reeves and his friend, Carson became ill again and Reeves accompanied her to Columbus, this time by ocean steamer. New York simply did not seem to be the place for them to live—not yet, at least, they reasoned—and Reeves, now out of money, decided to relinquish temporarily his plan to become a writer. He would marry Carson as soon as he could save some money, but first he must get down to the practicality of earning it, he resolved. He settled Carson with her family in Columbus, then went to Valdosta, Georgia, to look for work. He had a few connections there, he said, having lived in Valdosta with his aunt and uncle for three years as a teen-ager. The salaried insurance job he hoped to get failed to materialize, however; he was too young, he was told. He would be next in line for another position with the company in July, officials promised him, but he was skeptical. While in Valdosta his paternal grandfather died, and Reeves went to Wetumpka, Alabama, for the funeral. Then he traveled about Alabama and northern Florida looking up old friends from the Army and his high school days, telling them his troubles and how badly he needed a job. Most of them needed good jobs, too, they conceded.

The end of May Reeves arrived unannounced on his uncle's doorstep in Charlotte, North Carolina, suitcase in hand. He asked his mother's brother, John T. Winn, Jr., if he could move in with him and his family for a few weeks. The Winns—John, his wife, and two young sons—were suffering acutely from the Depression, as were most of their contemporaries, and they looked with alarm at their nephew's appearance. To keep from losing their home they had divided their small brick house on Chestnut Avenue into two dwellings, lived in one unit, and rented out the other. Reeves assured them that he would find work soon, would help around the house, and would contribute money toward the family's living expenses.

In the meantime, he asked Vincent Adams to ship his belongings south. Apprising his friend of his present situation, Reeves admitted that fate had not been kind to him in recent weeks; in fact he needed money desperately, he added. His grandfather had left him a piece of property, but he had found no buyer for it yet. If Adams should sell the car they jointly owned and could send him a little cash, he could get by until he had a steady income again, he ventured. Reeves had rushed from Valdosta to Charlotte on the wild hope that he might secure a position with the Charlotte *Observer*, one of the leading newspapers in North Carolina. Unfortunately, the owner of the paper had hired one of his in-laws the very day Reeves had arrived in town and applied for the job. He tried next to get on at the *Observer* as an assistant feature writer, but again he was turned down. The job required someone from the community who already was well acquainted with people in Charlotte's upper social stratum, from whom personality features could easily be generated. Through it all "Uncle Sam" still had his arm around his shoulder and beckoned, said Reeves ruefully, but he was adamant about not returning to the Army. If he could find any kind of work in Charlotte he would stay until he could save enough money to move elsewhere, perhaps to Atlanta or even Washington, D.C., he told Adams. He admitted parting company with his seventeen-jeweled wrist watch for enough cash to allow him to survive with dignity for a few more days, at any rate.

Vincent Adams responded to Reeves's request with $275, money which he himself had had to borrow. When the two men had lived together in New York, Reeves had contributed far more than his share of their living expenses, and he had been generous with his money. "Reeves had helped me when I needed it, and now I could help him. That was the way our friendship worked," said Adams.[21]

After a few days of intensive job hunting, Reeves was hired by Retail Credit Corporation as a credit investigator. For over a month he received no money; his pay was to come strictly from commissions, he lamented to Adams. He was not particularly proud of being a "snooper," as he referred to himself now. The pay was poor, the hours long, the work hard; yet it was interesting, he conceded, because he was reminded again and again of the quirks in human nature. In the course of a day he usually talked to some thirty to fifty people and walked twelve to fifteen miles. The job demanded that he keep his feet on the ground and his head out of the clouds, he said, and at night he usually was too tired to do otherwise.

Reeves's light breezy manner, which he assumed in his letters when

times were hard, was typical. His complaints were never bitter, his pleas
to Vincent Adams for help never pathetic. He knew that his friend was
having a difficult time financially, too, in his new role as husband and
wage earner, and Reeves urged Adams not to become discouraged. Although he admitted that he himself had little self-respect by the end of a
day, he said that his lot could be worse: He could be back in the Army.
Nevertheless, walking kept him in shape, he told Adams, and he expected
never to be bothered by constipation. He kept hoping that an editorial or
reporter's job would materialize with the *Observer*; to Reeves's optimistic
spirit, his credit work was only temporary. He also confessed to Adams
that since his temper still came into play occasionally he could never be
sure of the permanency of any situation.

In July, Reeves wrote Adams that he was living solely off commissions
and economizing in every way possible. He was still with his aunt and uncle, did his own washing and ironing, ate some of his meals at home,
bought his share of the groceries, and helped with the house and yard
work. He was particularly good with his young cousins, John Thomas II,
eight, and Ed, six. The youngsters were interested in scouting, and they
were thrilled to have an Eagle Scout as their mentor. One night the senior
Winns came home to discover Reeves and their sons having a cookout.
The trio had caught a large bullfrog in their lawn pool, skinned it, roasted
it over an open fire, and eaten it for supper. To the little boys, Reeves was
their hero and idol.

He lived most of the summer with the Winns, who found him affable
and a good conversationalist. Although he seemed reticent to talk about
himself and his personal experiences, they noticed that he never hesitated to voice his opinion. Dogmatic, Reeves sometimes said to his uncle,
"No, you don't understand that—you don't know how to look at that in
its proper perspective, Uncle John, because you haven't taken the right
courses in college and read up on things." It seemed to John Winn that
Reeves thought his having studied anthropology and journalism at Columbia University for a few weeks had guaranteed him a proper perspective on the world. In retrospect, Winn was certain that Reeves and Carson
—whom he met later—"were living thirty years ahead of their times, and
that they doubtless would have been highly principled demonstrators in
today's society."[22] Winn did not know that even in the 1930s and 1940s
Carson carried picket signs and marched in peace parades.

It was not until John Winn and his wife returned from a two-week vacation late in the summer of 1937, having left their children at home in
Reeves's charge, that they learned about Carson. Upset by finding several
long-distance calls on their telephone bill, they asked Reeves for an accounting. He told them that he had called his fiancée in Columbus,
Georgia. They were not pleased and told him so, and soon after the incident Reeves left the Winn home—without reimbursing them for the calls,

his uncle recalled—and there was a brief estrangement. Reeves told Adams that he had moved because he had had a falling out with his aunt after he had cuffed one of the boys. His next home was a private room at 343 Clement Avenue, which he told Adams was in a good, middle-class section of the city.

Reeves eventually became fond of Charlotte, North Carolina. He told Adams that he at least was getting enough to eat so that his pants stayed up around his middle. Just as he became somewhat complacent, however, he was jolted by news that he would lose his job within a week if he did not have a car. With an automobile he could cover more territory and earn up to $150 a month on commissions alone, he wrote his friend. Then he made a new plea for money. If Adams could send him only seventy dollars more, he would have enough for a down payment on a car. He would repay the loan in three or four installments out of each pay check, he promised. Again Adams sent money—this time enough for the car—and Reeves purchased an old Chevrolet. Later, Reeves admitted that he had made a bad bargain, but the car ran, at any rate, and his position was secure once more. Throughout the summer he wrote Vincent Adams almost weekly, but each letter was laced with apologies and accounts of why he was unable to begin making payments. Adams, however, never considered the money a loan; it was only what was rightfully Reeves's.

By the end of August Reeves's spirits had dropped considerably. Things had gone much worse than he had expected, and he wrote Adams that he had been without cash for ten days. Even more regrettable was the fear that he had put excessive strain on his friend's pocketbook. Reeves told Adams that he was barely able to keep a clean shirt on and had no idea how he could save money. Disillusioned, discouraged, melancholy, he now depicted Charlotte as a barren little island too much like thousands of other ragged communities across America which were livable only by dint of one's unique human resources. His own were very thin, he admitted. Only two weeks earlier Reeves had written in a lighter vein. He said that he liked Charlotte much better than Carson's hometown of Columbus. Charlotte's climate was superior, and even in the summer he could sleep under a blanket, he bragged. He wrote Carson that he was never bothered by asthma there, as he had been elsewhere, and his appetite was so good that he never seemed to get enough to eat. In his almost daily letters to Carson he minimized his adversities and told her the good things about life in North Carolina. He acknowledged that he knew she did not like her part of the South, and that she was greatly bothered by the heat. He told her that he wanted very much to get her located with him in Charlotte, where the climate would surely be more curative. If she could have a year of rest there while he worked and saved enough for them to move north again, he felt that her physical ailments would be over. Of course, she would still have him to cope with, Reeves teased, but if all went well he promised that they would marry by late summer.

To Adams, Reeves wrote that he spent most of his spare time reading or doing homework for his job; occasionally he took a night out to drink beer or to go dancing at one of the country clubs. He told Adams that he had encountered a good many futilitarians in Charlotte who scoffed at the vanity of human strivings, but that he had managed to remain on the fringe. He still clung to a few of his old ideals and hoped to keep them until he had children of his own, he vowed; then he would no longer try to recast the world, but would try to keep the world from changing him. He felt that his real salvation would come through Carson, he told Adams. He would marry as soon as he could, for marriage to Carson would complete him. Until then he felt he was only a fragment of a man and would not be able to accomplish anything first-rate. His hopes were still foolishly high that someday he might find his particular niche, his star, but it was difficult to see much light at present, he admitted.

Carson, in the meantime, recuperated rapidly in Columbus this time. By June 1937 she felt well enough to begin a lecture-study course in music appreciation for a dozen culture-loving Columbus ladies who were friends of her mother's or of Mary Tucker's. The women showed a lively interest in the Smith girl's career. Carson played the piano for them, gave them music history, and put records of chamber music and other pieces on the old gramophone to illustrate her lectures while the women sat around the dining-room table taking notes and reveling in the music and Carson's talent. She wrote Reeves that she expected to make enough money from her course to buy a wedding trousseau. It was one of the few occasions as a young woman that Carson expressed to anyone an interest in clothes.

One of her pupils with whom she became good friends that summer was Mrs. George Woodruff of Columbus. When Carson learned that Kathleen Woodruff had lived in Paris she was intrigued. In breathless, little-girl fashion, she urged Mrs. Woodruff to tell her all about life in France, and later she wrote Reeves about her new friend and told him that they, too, would have to live in Paris very soon. Kathleen Woodruff told Carson that she had lived on the Left Bank near St. Germain, where she had eaten most of her meals outdoors. The weather was delightful, she said, the people gracious, and the sidewalk scenes an unending source of entertainment. She assured Carson that in Paris a writer could always find "grist for his mill."[23]

Almost immediately after this conversation, Carson invited her friend to lunch. "There were just the two of us," recalled Mrs. Woodruff. "Carson led me into the back yard where the kitchen table had been placed. It was spread with a red-and-white-checked tablecloth and heaped with food. There were intriguing-looking dishes, wine in an ice bucket, and a 'waitress' standing demurely in the background under a tree, waiting to serve us. It was Marguerite, of course, Carson's mother, who had cooked the meal, pretended not even to be there, entered into no conversation, and now waited on us."

Over wine, Carson told Kathleen Woodruff that she was going to be a writer. "I'm going to be very famous," she said, squinting her eyes narrowly and looking intently into her friend's face. Then she tried to tell Mrs. Woodruff the story she had conceived which she called now "The Mute."

"Carson was not articulate and did not tell her tale at all well. There were long pauses as she thought, regrouped her words, and tried to explain the nature of her characters. I listened and wondered whatever made Carson think she could be a writer," said Kathleen Woodruff. "How wrong I was, I learned later." Carson also told her friend about Reeves McCullers and how he was struggling to work and save money so that they could marry. She explained that he, too, wanted to write, and that someday they both would be rich and famous. To Carson there were no qualifications to her aspirations. She never said that she *hoped* to be a success, or *hoped* to be rich and famous. She simply was going to be. It was a fact to be reckoned with and acknowledged.

On September 20, 1937, Reeves arrived in Columbus by train at 6:00 A.M. Carson had not known just when to expect him, and his arrival that morning at daybreak came as somewhat of a surprise. They quickly talked over their situation with each other and with Carson's mother and decided to marry immediately. There was no longer any question of when Reeves could afford to support the two of them. He had wrecked his car in a collision with another vehicle a few days earlier, and although the judge ruled that the accident was unavoidable and that neither driver was at fault, it had cost Reeves fifty dollars for repairs, and again he had no money. He wrote Adams a few weeks later that he could not foresee when conditions would have ever been precisely right for him and Carson to marry; it had almost reached the point where it was now or never, he conceded.

The events of the morning were hurried as Reeves and Carson made last-minute arrangements for the ceremony, which they decided to have at home at high noon with just the family present. While Reeves was at the courthouse getting the license, Carson knocked at a neighbor's door and asked if she could wash her hair in their lavatory. "The water's off at my house," she explained, "and I'm getting married today."

"Of course," said Mrs. John Miller, never surprised by anything that Carson or any of the Smith clan had ever said or done. Then she went to see what she could do to help the family get ready. "I found Marguerite sitting in a housecoat at her sewing machine, trying to make Carson a nightgown or two at the last moment," said Mrs. Miller. "I said to her, 'Marguerite, what are you going to feed your wedding guests?' "

"Oh, I don't know. I haven't had time to think about that—there'll just be the family, my sister and her children, and our friend Edwin Peacock," Marguerite replied. Immediately Mrs. Miller went home and prepared a lunch of salads, open-faced sandwiches, and a casserole, then returned with the food only moments before twelve. She also sent her daughter Mildred to town to buy gowns for Carson's trousseau and a white orchid for her wedding suit.

At noon the ceremony began. Peacock, Reeves's best man, was to start the gramophone with one of the couple's favorite pieces, Bach's Concerto for Two Violins in D Minor. But instead of the *largo* movement, in his excitement he dropped the needle on the *vivace* side. Quickly he flipped the record over as Carson and Reeves entered the living room arm in arm, Reeves dressed in a dark business suit and Carson in knee socks, brown Girl Scout oxfords, and a tailored suit. A few of the neighbors who had been alerted by Mrs. Miller of the impending event gathered outside at the windows to watch Dr. Frederick S. Porter, pastor of the First Baptist Church of Columbus, where the family still had their membership, unite them in marriage. After the ceremony and lunch, Peacock drove the couple to the train station, where they departed for Charlotte and an apartment Reeves had rented for them. Carson wore her wedding suit and a sailor hat she had brought back from New York. Her family and a few Starke Avenue neighbors waved good-by in front of the house as the three of them drove off, and Carson twirled her orchid at them in return. Although Marguerite Smith quipped merrily as her "children" departed that "a son is a son 'til he gets him a wife—a daughter's a daughter all her life," she feared that her role as a mother to her firstborn, a role that had sustained her own psyche for twenty years, would now be slight— and painfully inadequate.

To Marguerite, the people she loved seemed almost perfect, and through the years she had done everything she could to nurture and protect them. To her, Carson could do no wrong. Marguerite had devoted her life to keeping what she referred to as the "ungentle winds" from her firstborn, and had she been able to, she would have spared Carson every pain and suffered it happily herself. Yet, more and more, Marguerite realized that she was unable to fend off the hostile forces—both from within and without—which would continue to threaten her daughter, and that neither Carson's physical problems nor her psychic tensions could be resolved by anything within a mother's power. Her daughter was in Reeves's hands now. Marguerite had great love for the young man who had married her very heartbeat, and she had faith in his ability to cope well with her daughter's ambivalent needs. To Marguerite, Reeves was more than a son-in-law—he seemed to be her own blood.

Chapter Three

MARRIAGE AND THE HEART

*L*ife in Charlotte, North Carolina, for the young couple during the first eight months of their marriage proved to be the closest thing to idyllic living together that they would ever experience. Although Reeves's salary was only twenty-two dollars a week and he had returned to his apartment with his bride with a bare three dollars in his pocket, neither felt apprehension nor misgivings over the suddenness of their marriage. After all, they reasoned, why should they waste time preparing for marriage in the face of obstacles they could not control when they could already be sharing precious life with each other.

One of Carson's first letters was to her friend Gin Tucker, to apprise her of her marriage and the wonderful man with whom she had begun to share her life.[1] Although her panegyrics doubtless were sincere, whether she was aware of it or not, she was greatly fantasizing again. The impression she conveyed to her friend was colored by Reeves's own bent for exaggeration, and Carson herself may not have known the truth. She said that it would be almost impossible for her to think of words to describe him adequately, but she would do her best. His parents were divorced and he had been fending for himself since he was a little boy. He had traveled widely, rambling around the country on his own, doing unusual things, she said proudly. At fourteen he had been hired to drive a bootlegger's truck, and later he had been a printer's apprentice. He was a writer, too. For a few years his interests had centered on political science, philosophy, and literary criticism. After two semesters of college he had gone into newspaper work. Finally he had impulsively enlisted in the Army and ended up at Fort Benning, but that was a facet of Reeves's life that she thought would be better not to comment upon. Through it all he had studied hard and already had filled dozens of carefully kept notebooks and journals.

If, indeed, Carson knew the facts of Reeves's existence as he grew up —his being cared for by his mother, grandparents, aunts and uncles, never on his own until he joined the Army at seventeen (five months after graduation from high school, without most of the interim experiences she had enumerated to Gin Tucker), she chose, nevertheless, to make of her husband what she wished him to be.

In a description of Reeves's physical being, she was more accurate. He was less than an inch taller than she and very slender. His face was sensitive, his nose and chin pointed, and he was curly-haired and blond. It was quite a handsome face, Carson bragged; one friend had told her that he might well have been the subject of a fine eighteenth-century Italian portrait. It was also the most expressive face she had seen, a face which sometimes exploded and was easily provoked. Finally, Carson changed subjects in her eleven-page letter, but before doing so she added still another note of praise: He had read more wisely and widely than anyone his age she knew; moreover, his mental agility was marvelous to watch when it came to arguments and casual conversation.

Their first home was one into which Reeves had moved a few days before their marriage. The large, two-room, furnished apartment at 311 East Boulevard near downtown Charlotte was the strangest dwelling Carson had seen since she left New York. The refrigerator was in the bedroom, stuck away in one corner some distance from the tiny kitchen in which there was barely room to cook and work at the sink. The bedroom was oversized and accommodated well the massive pieces of old furniture installed in the apartment by the landlord. A huge iron bed was surrounded by three large dressers, one of which Carson had appropriated for her papers and paraphernalia, two bookcases the landlord found for them when Carson had made a special request, a large table at which they both worked and ate—the kitchen having no eating area—and a smaller table designed for a lamp but now bare, Reeves having tied the ancient table lamp to the head of the bedstead so that they might read in bed at night. Otherwise, there was no decent light in the room. Assorted overstuffed chairs completed the furnishings.

Although it seemed to Carson and Reeves that the rent for their apartment was too high to allow them to plan on staying indefinitely, they set about to make it their own for the time being. First, they hung their precious store of prints, a Brueghel, which her mother had given her, a Renoir, a Picasso, a Chirico. They also proudly displayed the small Donatello statue that Marguerite had given them as a wedding present, long a favorite bit of mantel decor at Starke Avenue, and a bronze plaque of St. Cecilia, Carson's patron saint of music. The bookcases were crammed with books, the mantel was lined with them, and extra books and manuscripts were stacked along the wall on the floor and on the tables.

Carson wrote her friend Gin Tucker that Reeves was violently opposed to allowing any volumes whatsoever to be banished to the attic, even for temporary storage. Vincent Adams had just shipped the store of books that Reeves had left at their cottage in Golden Bridge, and now

Carson mentally threw up her hands at the very thought of six more crates
of books arriving, knowing that her husband would be equally adamant
about their remaining in constant sight and touch. She wanted to share
with Gin all the details of their life, even little things such as how the sun
shone in their Chinese bowls on top of the refrigerator and cast golden
bars across the room. It was impossible to tell her how good everything
was, said Carson.

When Gin Tucker wrote to ask who did the housekeeping, Carson responded proudly that she did, but that it was a struggle. Sometimes she
made games of her housewifely chores. In emptying the trash and garbage,
for example, she said that she usually approached the cans while singing
something loud and aggressive, such as the Funeral March from *Götter-
dammerung*. The garbage was slung into the can and the lid slammed shut
with an imagined clash of kettledrums and cymbals. The various abortions
of her creative endeavors at the typewriter were disposed of with a lively
tune from Haydn or Schubert.

Carson told her friend that she was less successful in her career as
cook. Many of her pans, with remnants of charred food in them, were in
soak on the kitchen floor. She was sporting a bandage on her right hand,
she said, as a major badge of valorous action, and there were some half
dozen burns in other sundry places. One of her best friends was her
butcher, she admitted, who selected her meat for her and told her how to
cook it. They did not have meat every day, but the eggs, milk, and bread
they ate daily were playing havoc with their budget. They were trying to
get along on $3.50 a week and had made great sacrifices, she said, such as
eating vegetable fat instead of butter. In spite of a number of incongruous
schemes to stretch both the dollar and the food, they were still voracious
four times a day, Carson added. After a few days of niggardly meals, they
usually ended up stuffing themselves on Schraffts candy.

Although they could buy a gallon of wine for fifty cents, which tasted
like iodine and sugar water, she told Gin Tucker that they sometimes
splurged on their wine buying. They intended to nurse their present jug
of sherry all winter. It had an interesting history, Carson volunteered. They
liked a glass with dinner every evening, but Reeves was very particular
about the quality of his wine. On a recent Saturday night they had made a
thorough shopping tour of various delicatessens and wine shops on their
quest for some especially good wine. Finally, at one shop the Roumanian
proprietor insisted on their sampling many different brands, standing back
without a word and watching with interest while they tasted from each
bottle and earnestly discussed the quality of each. When they had at last
made up their minds and Reeves reached across the counter with a bill,
the merchant rang his cash register, put his hand in the till, then pushed
some coins back into Reeves's hand. The bill, however, had merely been

converted into change, except for a fraction of the stated price of their selection. Reeves protested that the Roumanian had made a mistake, but he
was not allowed to return the money. Instead, the shopkeeper smiled
subtly and moved away. His gesture was spontaneous and generous, said
Carson, in fact, one of their nicest experiences in a long time.

In spite of her talk about budgets, burns, and cooking, she spent relatively little time in the kitchen in meal planning or preparation during her
first year of marriage, or ever, for that matter. She and Reeves ate inexpensive delicatessen fare for the most part during their stay in Charlotte
and kept iced tea on hand by the gallon. Similarly, for the rest of her
life Carson largely "played" at housekeeping and cooking. Recipes she
preferred to talk about, to envision the results rather than to actually cook
from them.

A few weeks after their marriage, Reeves's aunt and uncle, the J. T.
Winns, invited them to dinner. They had never met Carson, but they
were prepared to receive her favorably and were curious about the girl
their nephew had chosen to marry. "We had not anticipated being stunned
by her, however," said Winn, who found Carson's "unusual outfit shocking." They had never seen anything like the white tailored blouse with
its elaborate embroiderings on the long sleeves and the front of the bodice,
which Carson wore with a man-tailored coat. Even stranger were the
sleeves of the coat, which hung open at the seams from the elbows down.
Reeves's aunt viewed askance, also, the long skirt, which seemed to be at
least four inches longer than the length then fashionable. "You mustn't
stare at Reeves's wife so," she admonished her young sons, but the adults
were having difficulty in repressing their own surprise. It amazed them
that Carson was not only far ahead of her time, but oblivious of it as
well. In personality the Winns found Carson shyly appealing. Although
she gave the appearance that she wanted the Winns to like her, she nevertheless dressed and acted to suit herself, they concluded. Yet she apparently suited Reeves in the process. "Reeves was never apologetic about his
wife's nonconformities when we knew them, nor did he appear disturbed
or embarrassed by her in any way," said Winn. "We began to like her, too,
in fact," he added.[2]

The one thing Carson missed most in her new life was her piano. The
fact that her landlady had a piano in the living room and invited Carson
to play it whenever she liked did little to alleviate her ache. She wrote to
Gin Tucker that fourteen keys of the ancient instrument did not work.
She could stumble through Scarlatti in a strange, shrill key in the upper
register, but Beethoven came off very badly in the bass, she said. To Carson, her landlady's invitation was a mixed blessing. Not only was the
music itself frustrating, but her benefactor annoyed her by asking absurd
questions just as she sat down to play. The entire situation was impossible,

said Carson. As soon as they could afford it, she vowed to rent a piano of her own; or if that were impossible, she would rent one in someone's house or store for an hour or two each day.

Unfortunately, however, Carson found that there was no money for luxuries that winter, and acquiring a piano in any fashion was out of the question. Instead, she became immersed in her novel. She wrote friends that she had frittered away the entire preceding year because of her chest ailment and many months of recuperation, but that at last she felt robust, and now was working feverishly to catch up. Reeves had been ill much of the winter himself, suffering from pleurisy, but they survived by nursing each other, trying to get more rest, sleeping regular hours and eating the proper foods. Before cold weather set in, they changed apartments and moved into the upstairs of an old, white clapboard, Pennsylvania-Dutch house at 806 Central Avenue. This home was much more to their taste. Here Carson was able to sit and work at a large kitchen table which overlooked the valley to the east and enjoy what she thought of as a Parisian view. This time there were two rooms in which she and Reeves could work separately. She also could close off the kitchen from the bedroom and their small sitting room, features which they had found sorely lacking in their other apartment.

To Carson's thin blood, however, the apartment on Central Avenue always seemed to be too cold. On the most severe days of the winter she chose instead to work in the Charlotte Public Library, where she frequently warmed up her insides by surreptitiously sipping sherry from her ever-present thermos. Daily Carson measured out her ration of sherry from their gallon jug that was supposed to last them throughout the winter, but which had to be replaced more than once. At night Reeves picked her up in their decrepit Chevrolet, stopped at the delicatessen for their supper, and later, after they had eaten, Carson read aloud to him what she had written that day. Then she typed the dozen or more sheets and revised as she went along in response to Reeves's praise or criticism. He was good with words, Carson thought, although like her, he frequently made words up when he could not think of an appropriate one which already existed. Reeves's syntax often was awkward, but he, too, was an accurate observer, a good listener, and a storyteller whose sensitivities caught the nuances of language and the rhythms of speech.

He wrote Vincent Adams that winter that Carson wrote constantly, learned from her own writing, and improved each day. Although he admitted that he was by no means a professional critic, he thought her novel read beautifully. There was little time for his own writing, he conceded. He worked hard as an investigator, and they got by on what he made, but each time he wrote to Adams he commented on their financial difficulties and apologized for his outstanding debt. When he was not at work or preparing his reports and handling other paper work essential to his job,

Reeves helped Carson with the housework and did much of the cooking. In the meantime, he took in cheerful stride the fact that his own literary aspirations had been shelved temporarily. As he explained it to Adams, he really did not mind the delay because he felt that his day would come. What if he did have to spend all his time now making a living and helping keep house—he was with the only person who truly mattered to him. Just to be with Carson and to help her in every way possible was the important thing, he said, even if his own name did not go down in history. He told Adams, furthermore, that he probably was too lazy to stick to what mattered most where work was concerned.

Reeves both admired and envied Carson's single-mindedness in her dedication to her muse. Sporadically, he, too, worked on several personal experience prose pieces that winter. He told Adams that by spring Carson would have sold her novel and that he hoped to be able to market his own book of essays. Then they would go to New York and visit Adams and his wife and make plans to move North permanently. Reeves admitted that he lacked the passion and the drive for fame and literary success that constantly pushed Carson in her writing. He needed self-esteem—he had always needed it and fought for it—but he cared little for a reputation that extended beyond his own personal existence and rapport with the people he loved. If he was loved and admired by a close few, it was all that mattered.

During the eight months that Carson and Reeves lived in Charlotte, they were quietly happy. The times were too difficult for them to be exuberant, but they were hard-working and in love with each other. Years later Carson wrote her friend composer David Diamond that she had done everything possible during her first year of marriage to make it work, and that it had been a good year for them both. In spite of their hard work, they also played. It was Carson's habit to stop writing in the midafternoon and take a long walk. At night after dinner she usually read in bed, listened with Reeves to her favorite music on their new Victor electric phonograph, and went to sleep early. Reeves appreciated music, but he was not as enchanted by it as she was. Carson loved all musical instruments except the harpsichord. Although she loved the music of operas, she did not like the lyrics; Reeves cared for neither. In awe of composers, she wanted to know their private lives, their personal habits, and to read about their art— not just listen to it. She was usually deeply moved by their works.

Mick Kelley, the adolescent girl Carson was creating that winter in her novel, was very much the girl Carson herself had been, and still was. Mick's whole life was tied up with music. She wrote music, spent her lunch money for private piano lessons, and yearned for a piano of her own. She dreamed of being a famous musician, wanted to travel to romantic distant lands, and planned to have her initials on all her personal possessions. Late at night Mick took long walks and listened from lawns to other people's radios. One night she sat under a window of a strange house and thrilled to a Beethoven symphony. To Mick, the opening of the Beethoven piece reminded her of "God strutting in the night":

> After a while the music came again, harder and loud. It didn't have anything to do with God. This was her, Mick Kelley, walking in the daytime and by herself at night. In the hot sun and in the dark with all the plans and feelings. This music was her—the real plain her.
> . . . The whole world was this music and she could not listen hard enough.[3]

Carson wrestled with music as Mick did, who held that it was "the worst hurt there could be." Yet it also salved Carson's soul when everything else failed.

During their first year of marriage, music, Reeves, and her devotion to writing seemed balm enough. Once a week Reeves set aside an evening for what he referred to as their siesta. That winter he described to Vincent Adams one such typical evening. He said that it was a merry night of fun and games. Arguments usually flew, he admitted, lubricated by winebibbing. That particular night they had listened to Toscanini; he had had a little too much to drink, and Carson had had to put him to bed. It was nothing to worry about, said Reeves, so long as it did not happen too often. Earlier, Carson had almost prophetically described such an evening in her short story "Instant of the Hour After," which she had written in Sylvia Chatfield Bates's fiction workshop. Although she had conceived the story and submitted it for criticism before her marriage, the characteristics of the young husband in her fiction too closely resembled Reeves to have been coincidental, just as the wife—from whose point of view the story was told—was a facsimile of Carson herself. The young couple, indeed, knew each other's personalities by the time Carson wrote this story—they had already spent a summer together—but the actual situation, of course, had been imagined. And now, a little over a year later, the two people depicted had begun to act out the vignette.

In March 1938, Reeves came home one evening with news of a raise and a promotion, but it would mean their leaving Charlotte. He had thought he would be sent to the western part of North Carolina, but orders came now for him to manage the territory in Fayetteville, in the eastern part of the state, and set up a new office there. Neither Carson nor Reeves had ever been to Fayetteville and they had no idea what the town was like; but it was Reeves's job that was at stake, his advancement on the line. There was no question in Carson's mind. Of course they would go. It was the last time in her life, however, that she accompanied Reeves anywhere at his initiative as Mrs. James Reeves McCullers, Jr. When she became Carson McCullers, novelist, it was a different story.

When it came time for the move, Carson had reached a good stopping point in her novel. She had finished the first six chapters and also had a detailed outline of the entire book. Her former writing teacher, Sylvia Chatfield Bates, had heard of a new contest for undiscovered authors, the Houghton Mifflin Fiction Fellowship Award, and now she urged Carson to submit her outline and completed chapters to the competition. She also recommended that the material be sent first to novelist William March, whom Carson had met earlier in New York through Miss Bates. Carson should ask for his opinion and invite his criticism, her teacher suggested. When March read the manuscript, he reportedly could hardly believe that the work was the effort of an unpublished novelist. He praised it generously and assured the writer that it would surely win a prize and be published. On this optimistic note, Carson posted the manuscript to Houghton Mifflin and departed with her husband for Fayetteville, North Carolina, and a new life.

Once there, however, the honeymoon was over. The unhappy *mise en scène* of Carson and Reeves as they settled in the spring of 1938 on Rowan Street was set by the wails of infants through paper-thin walls, ill-trained children, fighting neighbors, and yards of diapers, tricycles, and clutter. Carson could hardly believe the almost squalid conditions of their apartment building, the dirt street, the town itself, in fact—all of which dampened their spirits and jangled sensitive nerves. She and Reeves found that they were arguing and reconciling repeatedly, struggling to recapture their old happiness and delight in one another while seeking at the same time to retain their own identities—to work separately, yet together. It was impossible for either of them to put a finger on precisely what had gone sour in their marriage, but the ferment was unmistakably there.

From the beginning, life in Fayetteville was difficult. Disillusionment set in almost as soon as they drove into the flat, humid town in southeast North Carolina. They missed the hills of the Piedmont, the high, cool air which they had found so invigorating. During the summer of 1938 they were certain that Fayetteville was the hottest, most God-forsaken land they had ever known. Reeves reasoned that it was just like the Army to plop another military base into such an area as further punishment for its troops. Nearby Fort Bragg did little to boost the sagging economy of a town stagnant even before the Great Depression had set in. (It took World War II to do that.) The natives chose to think of their community as a traditional southern one—no narrower than the next—which had just the right number of churches, schools, lodges, and civic organizations. To them, Fayetteville was a cultural town; it was also a politically influential town that had just missed being the capital of the state. To Carson and Reeves, Fayetteville was an economically depressed town. When they arrived in 1938, it had fifteen thousand inhabitants, most of whom were poor. Reeves very quickly resented his transfer to the area. Although he had to admit that the new job was a challenge, it was one he could well do without. A livelihood which depended upon establishing the financial credit of sharecroppers and struggling tobacco, cotton, and truck farmers was destined to fail, he was sure. The small branch of Retail Credit Corporation that he worked hard to establish floundered, nor did his civic-minded position as secretary of the Merchants' Association help his standing in the community as he had hoped.

Carson was not an asset to his business, either. She missed her mother, complained bitterly about their plight there, and frequently articulated to local residents her criticism of Fayetteville and the life style of its people. Potential friends were put off by her aloofness and honest, but tactless remarks. "If you don't like our town and keep finding fault with it, why do you stay?" probed a nettled woman, tired of Carson's disparaging remarks directed at her at a small social gathering one night.

"For a special reason I couldn't expect anyone to understand—but believe me, I won't stay a minute longer than I have to," Carson retorted.

The young couple hated the town and prayed for early relief. Into Reeves's usually cheery letters to Vincent Adams, who with his wife had recently spent the night with them in Fayetteville while en route to Florida, crept now a note of futility. He said that everything in the office remained the same, never changing, and that business was bad, bad. The previous week's continuous rain would probably cause starvation among the farmers during the winter. To Reeves, the town of Fayetteville was the same today as it had been years ago and probably would be years from now. All a man could do there was work all day, go home, read, go to bed, get up, and work all day again. The only slight change was getting a little bit drunk on Saturday night. But just a little bit—just a little bit, he said. It was this same sense of monotony and boredom that was a part of the genesis of not only the book at which Carson was presently at work, but also of her next two novels, *Reflections in a Golden Eye* and *The Ballad of the Sad Café*. Reeves realized, as did Carson, that their only hope for liberation lay in the sale of her fiction.

Carson's spirits sagged, too, as the summer's heat intensified. She had become increasingly depressed and petulant. They had little money and few friends. She fretted, also, because she had had no word in over two months regarding her manuscript and the Houghton Mifflin contest. Even though Sylvia Chatfield Bates and William March had thought her embryonic novel first-rate, she worried that her chapters were being too hastily read or perhaps overlooked entirely. She was afraid she had not sent the publisher enough to evaluate and that her outline was insufficient. At last, in early July, the long-awaited letter came. She had not won the important first prize, but the publishers had decided to grant her a second award contingent upon her finishing the novel to their satisfaction. Carson, only momentarily disappointed, was elated by what she did get—a contract with Houghton Mifflin for publication of her novel and a promise of a five-hundred-dollar advance against royalties. She told her family and friends that half of the money would be sent immediately and the other $250 would be paid upon receipt of the completed manuscript.

Carson aimed for the summer of 1939 to have her book in the publisher's hands, and Reeves did everything he could to help make it possible. He kept house, shopped, and cooked most of the evening meals. When they could afford it, they sent the laundry out; if not, Reeves also washed and ironed. Carson had never cooked, laundered, or kept house before they were married, nor did she intend to spend any more time at it now than she could help. She was an artist, she reasoned. Reeves, knowing her reluctance to be bothered by mundane activities that sapped her energies or otherwise distracted her from her writing, understood. Walking, talking to people, observing life—all were a part of the creative experience. Housework was not.

It was only a matter of time before Reeves became acutely aware that everything—everyone—was subordinate to Carson's dedication to her art. He knew, too, without their even talking about it, that they had abandoned forever their plan to alternate roles as writer and breadwinner. According to the agreement, she was to have been the writer the first year of their marriage while he supported them. Once the novel was completed, it would be time for them to reverse roles, for by then almost two years would have elapsed. Yet Reeves knew there would be no exchange —right or wrong, it would never be any other way than it was right now. Without illusions to cling to, how could either of them exist, he pondered. Carson's illusions were in her fiction and could be preserved there; his were in actuality, and they were being shattered daily. To Reeves, the future was grim. Their plan to migrate to New York City seemed hopelessly far away. It would be late 1939 or even 1940 before they could leave—and it would be Carson who would get them out. Displeasure swelled as Reeves mentally ticked off grievances against his wife and their way of life.

In July, Reeves was able to take a week off with pay, and Marguerite urged them to come home. In spite of Carson's ambivalent feelings toward her hometown, they looked forward to their first trip to Georgia in almost a year. Although she and her mother had written to each other practically daily during each separation since Carson's first departure in 1935, it seemed that Carson missed her mother's physical presence now more than ever. The war news in Europe troubled the young couple, too, and they were anxious to talk with Edwin Peacock and Reeves's friends from his old army company who were still in Columbus.

Once at Fort Benning as an outsider, however, Reeves was disappointed to find that everything important to him had changed. He wrote to Vincent Adams that most of their old buddies were no longer there;

even their little shack and cache of corn whiskey seemed like a dream. Georgia had become wet during his two-year absence. Reeves lamented that the old dives had changed and that a liquor store stood on almost every corner. It was good to return once, but *that* was it; he had *had* it, he observed.

Most of all during their vacation, Carson and Reeves simply enjoyed the comforts of home. Marguerite Smith was still the *belle dame* of her informal Starke Avenue "salon of the arts and intellect," although most of her neighbors never knew the home as such and would have been astonished to know how others regarded it. This summer there were several new intimates in the household. One was Aubrey Clements, a young friend of Edwin Peacock's who worked for the National Biscuit Company and ate Sunday dinner with Peacock at Mrs. Grubbs's boardinghouse. Early each evening the two men went to the Smith home to talk with the family and to listen to the war news on the radio. With Carson and Reeves home for a few days, a number of their contemporaries gathered to exchange ideas. The entire Smith family were avid followers of world affairs and freely articulated their views. Lamar Smith was afraid that the United States would get into the war; Carson and Reeves were afraid that it would *not*. Marguerite's fear was for the lives of *her* young boys, although she empathized with the plight of the oppressed for all countries. To her, Reeves, Edwin Peacock, Aubrey Clements, Lamar Smith, Jr.—all were her "sons" and their lives were too precious, she said, to be lost in senseless aggressions or killings.

During the past year Carson had become passionate about the European situation, zealous in her attack on fascism and nazism, and indignant at racism and what she considered the gross mistreatment of blacks in Fayetteville and in her own hometown. She longed to do something to help her country's allies, and soon both she and Reeves were talking of adopting a refugee child. Carson believed her country to be criminally negligent and immoral for not getting involved directly in the war. Although England and France did not declare war on Germany for another year, Anthony Eden and Winston Churchill had already spoken loud words of warning to both Europe and the United States. The fearsome news of the moment was that Hitler had marched into Austria and annexed seven million Austrians to the Third Reich. Germany was scrambling to complete its mighty fortification, the Westwall, to protect its borders from France. Poland, Denmark, and Norway were soon to be invaded, and all Europe was on the brink of World War II. Much of the indignation and anger that Carson felt concerning the social injustices and military aggressions of Fascist and Nazi powers was now being embodied explicitly in her novel.

In spite of the precarious world situation, life in the Smith household on Starke Avenue in Columbus continued much as it always had.

The atmosphere was now more charged, however, with the electricity of ideas and social concerns of the war and man's role in the world than it had been in the past. Lamar, Jr., had returned home from a year at Georgia Tech, and he, along with his sister Rita, who was entering her senior year in high school, found it far more interesting and exhilarating to spend their evenings at home with the family and the endless stream of company there than it was to seek entertainment elsewhere. After the grimness of the war news and the serious conversations that ensued, Rita helped her mother serve cookies, coffee, and punch or lemonade, and frequently they popped corn or made sandwiches. The evenings were further lightened by music. Carson often played the piano for the group, or they listened to their favorite records and talked of books, antiques, and art. Both Lamar, Jr., and Rita Smith acquired more *savoir-faire* and *savoir-vivre* through their exposure and participation in such evenings of discussions of world affairs, music, art, and literature then they ever could have gained through books or a less gregarious household. When Rita went to Alabama Polytechnic Institute the next summer to begin her freshman year, she was far more sophisticated and knowledgeable about life and the arts than Carson had been when she went to New York City at a comparable age.

Carson would have liked to stay on alone in Columbus for a few days, but Reeves was due at a four-day convention of the North Carolina Merchants Association in the mountains at Blowing Rock as soon as his vacation was over, and he wanted her to go with him. Carson had never stayed in the mountains before, and to her the novelty would be almost as good as seeing snow again, which she loved. It was a good trip. The Blue Ridge mountain scenery was breathtaking, and the young couple felt a renewed sense of union as a result of having gotten away from the grimness of life in Fayetteville for a while.

En route home from Blowing Rock, they stopped in Charlotte, where they were joined by Reeves's mother and his sister Marguerite. Jessie McCullers had never met Carson, and she decided that it was time to have a look at her daughter-in-law. John Winn had reported to his sister that he and his wife liked Carson very much, but he allowed that she was "certainly different from every other young woman we know." When queried about Carson by Reeves's mother, the Winns had hesitated to call her eccentric, but they indicated that to meet her would be "an experience." Quickly Jessie McCullers arranged a trip to Charlotte and a visit with her brother to coincide with Reeves's vacation and convention plans.

Carson's first advance royalty check on her novel had arrived just before her departure for Georgia, and she carried it about with her on her trip to display proudly to their various friends and relatives. Whereas Reeves's sister looked with some reserve at the unusual girl her brother had married, who spent most of her time writing and dreaming of being famous, his mother took an immediate liking to Carson. The attraction was mutual. "It is all right for writers to be a little odd," reasoned Jessie McCullers as she became acquainted with her daughter-in-law that weekend, "especially if they are successful." She had a feeling that her son's wife would be just that.

Jessie McCullers was now divorced from Reeves's father and had been living alone for some time in Jesup with Wiley Mae and Tommy, her two younger children. Marguerite, her older daughter, had left home early, having married at age sixteen a Jesup man, Stanton Lee. Life had not been easy for Reeves's mother for many years, and she yearned to reunite her remaining family. Bud McCullers had remarried, and there was little rapport between father and children. Jessie had been especially fond of Reeves, her firstborn. She was proud of him, and she felt remorse for having seen so little of him during his growing-up years. Reeves had not lived at home regularly since he was twelve, and his mother hoped desperately that he would know love and a new kind of security at last in his marriage to this strange, artistic girl. To Jessie, it seemed that her son worshiped Carson.

Back in Fayetteville, the townspeople had no idea that Carson was writing a novel until they read reviews of *The Heart Is a Lonely Hunter* months later. In 1938–39 they knew only that a rather queer and curious girl had arrived in their town with a handsome, personable husband to whom she seemed ill-suited. They observed her prowling about their town, going out in the mornings on long tramps either before daybreak or a few minutes after her husband left for work. Sometimes she stopped people on the streets to probe them about their way of life, their political views, families, and grievances. They were sure that she was "stirring up trouble, acting in some common way unbecoming to a wife whose husband is trying to establish himself as a young businessman in the town." They watched her engage blacks in earnest conversation, sympathize with them, and attempt to allay their suspicions, for they, too, wondered why she sought them out. Once the townspeople observed a black enter Carson and Reeves's apartment, and they felt certain he was there at Carson's invitation. Surely some secret insurrection was at hand. After news of the incident spread about the town, no one willingly socialized with her. To Carson, on the surface, it did not matter. Her friends, her *real* friends, were those in her novel or those with whom she corresponded in actuality. In every letter she wrote now she urged her friends to come visit them. This craving for company, to be the genial hostess, was a characteristic of Carson's all her life. If she entered into a relationship, it was with her whole heart and spirit. She could not be bothered with a casual affair. She demanded much of a relationship, and if she met with rebuff or felt a lack of reciprocity, she withdrew instantly, hurt, resentful, and often bitter and unforgiving.

Like her father who impulsively left his jeweler's bench to walk about the town, so, too, did Carson bolt frequently from her typewriter and worktable and go out among the people. Sometimes it seemed as though she were proselytizing. The character in her novel with whom she was obsessed now was Jake Blount, who exhibited similar, though exaggerated characteristics of Carson herself. Blount was driven to the point of near madness by the inequalities of the working conditions of the masses and the indifference displayed by the victims of such injustice. Yet he was misunderstood and rejected by the very people he wished to help. In a similar manner, another fictional friend from her book, Dr. Copeland, a black physician was repudiated by the people of his own race, as well as by the whites. The vehemence and strength of their obsessions doomed them to isolation, and both became outcasts within their town, exiles, strangers wherever they found themselves. So, too, did their young creator find herself.

In the fall, Carson and Reeves moved to a different neighborhood, taking the upstairs of a large, white-columned home at 119 North Cool Spring Street. Here, they were temporarily happier. The house was rich in local color, having been built a century and a half earlier as the Cool Spring Tavern. It was the oldest standing structure in Fayetteville. Carson loved hearing tales of the rogues who had fought, drunk, and loved within its portals, and of the Indians who washed their feet in the cool spring behind the tavern, then came upon the porch to sell their beads and trinkets. In 1938, the old tavern was a private home in which the upstairs had been converted into a spacious single-unit dwelling. Although the apartment was in need of repairs, was torrid in the summer and in the winter almost impossible to heat, Carson and Reeves liked it as much as they could like anything in Fayetteville at this stage in their lives. They loved the open fires in their living room and bedroom, even though they suffered from the cold if they were seated out of range of the crackling sparks that shot from the hearth. They also marveled that Carson's health seemed better during the winter of 1938–39 than it had been in almost three years.

Apparently her reputation had preceded their move into the Cool Spring Street neighborhood, and Carson lost no time in living up to the image. From their homes and yards her neighbors listened to Beethoven's Third, Liszt's Hungarian Rhapsody, and her favorite Bach and Schubert pieces, amazed that the strange girl of whom they were so critical could play the beautiful music they heard daily coming from her landlady's piano in the downstairs parlor. Then, incongruously, they saw a tall, straggle-dressed figure emerge with a portable typewriter and sit at a small table near the railing of the wide, upstairs veranda, which ran across the front of the house. Carson usually worked outdoors for several hours when the weather was good, and sometimes ate her lunch out on the porch. Sporadically the sessions were interrupted by solitary jaunts about the neighborhood. The women recognized Carson from afar, for she wore what they had come to think of as her "winter outfit"—a pair of high-topped tennis shoes and knee socks, an ancient-looking, shin-length coat trimmed with a fur collar, and a khaki, knitted army hat which had seen better days on Reeves.

Not only did the local ladies not admit to being Carson's friends, but they also were reluctant to be seen in conversation with her on the street. Although they talked to her, more frequently they talked *about* her, speculated on her personal life, and ruefully shook their heads at one another as she walked by. Since they seldom saw Carson and her husband together, they agreed that the young couple had a miserable marital relationship, if, indeed, one at all. Their sympathies lay with Reeves, whom they continued to like. It disturbed them, however, that they had seen them only a few times in church—the Methodist, in which Reeves had been reared—and concluded, finally, that the McCullers were both God-forsaking and forsaken. The townspeople did not see much hope in being able to salvage the young couple, either. Reeves told Vincent Adams that he had even gone to church for a while in an effort to get better established in the community, but that it had not been fruitful and he had stopped going.

Near the end of December 1938, Edwin Peacock took the train from Columbus to Fayetteville to visit Carson and Reeves at their North Cool Spring Street apartment. Although they were delighted to be with their old friend again and assumed an air of joviality and satisfaction with one another, Peacock could tell that there was a strain and tenseness in their relationship that was foreign to the happy couple he had known and loved in Columbus. "Reeves never discussed their financial plight with me, but I knew that times were rough for them, as they were for everyone then, of course. I wonder now how I afforded the train ticket to North Carolina and back on my thirty-dollar-a-week salary," said Peacock.[4]

They did not complain, however. Carson seemed cheerful, was proud of her housekeeping, and did most of the cooking while Peacock was there. He remembered one meal of poached eggs nestled in corned beef hash which she called by the fanciful name "eggs in a nest." On New Year's Eve Reeves suggested that they go out to celebrate, and that night he and Carson appeared to Peacock to be their old selves, laughing, happy, healthy, content for the most part with themselves in a world which had problems, but which they, personally, could do little to remedy. It came as somewhat of a jolt to Peacock the next day when Carson and Reeves approached him with a small suitcase laden with their wedding silver. He was getting ready to leave for the train station when Carson spoke up: "Please take this back to Columbus with you, Edwin, and sell or pawn it for us—it's all we have of any value, and we do need the money." When Peacock returned to Columbus, however, he could not bring himself to dispose of it. He was certain that most of the silver had come from her father's store, and he regretted the idea of his dearest friends having to part with precious wedding gifts that would be irreplaceable. Instead, he waited a few days then sent the silver back by express. The incident was never mentioned among them again.[5]

The following spring Reeves wrote to Vincent Adams, whose wife had just had a baby, and likened her delivery to their own experience. Carson's novel would be ready to go to the publisher in another three weeks, said Reeves, and it would take a load off both of them. By the end of April 1939, the manuscript was ready. Exhausted, Carson sent it to her New York editor, then went home to Columbus alone to recuperate for a few days. But she could not seem to rest at home, either. The pace at which she had worked for the past year and a half could not be slowed. Already there was another story boiling inside that had to come out. She thought of it as *Army Post*. Its genesis had come from a chance remark Reeves made to her about a voyeur who had been arrested at Fort Bragg, a young soldier who had been caught peeping inside the married officers' quarters. Carson told her mother that she had to get back to Fayetteville quickly. Now that the manuscript was in, she was expecting the other half of her royalty advance any day. They needed it badly, she admitted.

It was almost a year later, however, when Carson received payment. In a version doubtless modified by the passage of time, her imagination, and a lack of knowledge of the facts of the situation, she wrote her German friend, Alfred Kantorowicz, a few years later that her publisher had treated her like a stepchild. She said that when she had finished her novel it was many months before she had a response from her editor, and that then it was only to suggest bizarre changes. She consented to minor changes, but most of the suggestions were completely out of the question, she said. After another long wait she heard again from her editor, this time to say that the book would, in fact, be published—as though there had been some question—but she told Kantorowicz that no reference was made to the $250 still due her as the other half of her royalty advance. Moreover, it was months later before the galleys were set, she complained. The publisher acted as though he was sure the book would be a failure and planned almost no advertising, said Carson, until advance copies were enthusiastically received by reviewers. At that point the company delayed publication until the book might be launched more appropriately. Then, finally, she received her remaining $250, she wrote Kantorowicz.[6]

Carson's rendering of the publication history of *The Heart Is a Lonely Hunter* reflects her ability to mix fact and fantasy. According to Lee Barker, a salesman and literary scout for Houghton Mifflin at the time, both he and Harwick Mosely read the manuscript and were enthusiastic about it. There was a kind of electricity running through the publishing house upon the knowledge that they had discovered a thrilling first novelist. Moreover, she had one of the best fiction editors of the country who was rarely fooled about talent. It is highly unlikely that payment to Carson would not have been made according to the contract. It is more likely that Carson's contract called for the second half of her advance upon publication of the novel, rather than upon receipt of the completed manuscript.

Carson, tense, upset by what appeared to be unnecessary delays by her publisher, and piqued that there was no money to finance the vacation trip to New York City which she and Reeves had dreamed of for so long, plunged impetuously into her next novel. She told her editor later that writing *Reflections in a Golden Eye*, as her *Army Post* was eventually entitled, was simply for fun, that it was as easy as eating candy. It not only served as relief from the long, arid months of labor of *The Mute*, but it also was a kind of therapeutic diversion from the emotional strains of what had become a disillusioned marriage and its increasing dissatisfactions brought on largely by poverty and the constrictions of their life style in a region in which they resented having to live.[7]

While Reeves fretted about his impending transfer with Retail Credit Corporation from Fayetteville to Savannah, Georgia—a move he did not want to make, for it would mean going still farther south and he felt certain that his wife would not consent to go with him—Carson used the Fayetteville and Fort Bragg setting, as well as her memories of Fort Benning, as the setting for her next fiction. It seemed to her that *Army Post* almost wrote itself. All of its characters seemed to burst full grown from their creator, like Athena, who sprang full blown from her father's brow. She did not know what they were going to do until they told her or showed her, nor did her characters themselves until they did it. Yet with her uncanny ability to transcend reality, she identified completely with each of them. Carson wrote in her essay "The Flowering Dream: Notes on Writing":

> I am so immersed in them that their motives are my own. When I write about a thief, I become one; when I write about Captain Penderton [the protagonist in *Reflections in a Golden Eye*], I become a homosexual man; when I write about a deaf mute, I become dumb during the time of the story. I become the characters I write about and I bless the Latin poet Terence who said, "Nothing human is alien to me."[8]

After only two months of arduous writing, she finished the book and put it away in her dresser. It did not occur to her then that anyone would want to publish it. Whereas Reeves had labored with her over *The Heart Is a Lonely Hunter, Army Post* was entirely her own creation. When she spoke of it to friends, she referred to it as her "fairy tale," a story in which everything was done "very lightly." A year and a half later, however, upon publication, the book was not lightly taken. Carson said that her father threw the magazine in which it first appeared across the room in disgust and wondered how a child of his could have spun such a tale. Those in Fayetteville who had known Carson nodded their heads in agreement: "It is just as we suspected—the McCullers girl is a queer duck." The novel caused some embarrassment in Columbus and at Fort Benning where people speculated about the source of her weird tale. General George Marshall, who had been a commanding officer at Fort Benning and had met Carson through the Tucker family, extended some good-natured teasing to the Tuckers after both families had left and wondered if "the whole post had gone to pot." More than one Fort Benning officer's wife recalled that Mrs. George Patton had canceled her subscription to *Harper's Bazaar* in protest over the story and had encouraged other wives at the fort to do the same thing. Most readers, however, according to Mrs. Tucker, saw the story as pure fiction and marveled that a person Carson's age could write it. Although Marguerite and Lamar Smith suffered a few personal slights in Columbus because of the novel, they were quick to defend their daughter. The response of the author, herself, to the furor was simple. She had written the novel as she felt she must. Although she had typed out the actual story when she was twenty-one, she said that the story had germinated when she was an adolescent and had first stepped upon the alien territory of Fort Benning. She could no more have *not* written the story than she could have stopped the earth on its axis.

But at the time Carson wrote the story as *Army Post*, she did not think about it as a tale to be published. The work simply was finished, over and done with. She tucked it out of sight and mind and resurrected, instead, several of her old manuscripts written under the tutelage of Sylvia Chatfield Bates and Whit Burnett. Several of these she revised slightly and decided to submit for publication. To Maxim Lieber, New York literary agent, Carson mailed "Sucker," her earliest story, and "Court in the West Eighties." Lieber accepted the manuscripts, which he admitted to Carson later had made the rounds rapidly from magazine to magazine. According to Lieber, "Sucker" was read and rejected by most of the major magazines of the decade. He told Carson that it had been rejected by *The Virginia Quarterly, The Ladies' Home Journal, Harper's, The Atlantic Monthly, The New Yorker, Redbook, Harper's Bazaar, Esquire, The American Mercury, North American Review, The Yale Review, The Southern Review,* and *Story.* The markets to which "Court in the West Eighties" was sent were only slightly different: *The Virginia Quarterly, The Atlantic Monthly, Harper's, The New Yorker, Harper's Bazaar, Coro-*

net, North American Review, The American Mercury, The Yale Review,
Story, The Southern Review, Zone, and *Nutmeg.* On November 10, 1939,
Lieber abandoned his quest with a succinct note: "We are returning
the two stories herewith."[9] The failure by Lieber to place them doubtless worked to Carson's advantage, however, at least monetarily. When
"Sucker" finally appeared in *The Saturday Evening Post* in 1963 (September 28), she received fifteen hundred dollars, a sizable leap from the
twenty-five dollars she was paid for her first published story, "Wunderkind," in *Story.* "Court in the West Eighties" was not published until its
inclusion in the posthumous collection, *The Mortgaged Heart.*

When Max Lieber's letter rejecting her stories arrived, Carson was
back in Columbus without Reeves. In times of great stress she felt that
she simply had to be near her mother. Her loneliness had increased, and
her inner turmoil was still turbulent. Nor could she rest in Columbus this
time, either. She knew that she had yet another story she must write, one
which had nudged and prodded and tormented her for several years.
Once again in her hometown, myriad thoughts pushed hauntingly to the
surface. She remembered anew her sense of rejection when Mary Tucker
told her that she was leaving Columbus, and her emotional wrenching
from the family and music which had become the fulcrum of her whole
existence during her highly impressionistic early teen-age years. She realized, too, that her old and precious love for Reeves seemed spent. Almost
everything which had been meaningful in the past now seemed gone.
Marguerite Smith comforted her daughter as best she could, but the deepest thoughts of each could not be articulated.

Carson had been able to express something of her sense of loss, which
she had nursed over the years, in a letter to her girlhood friend Gin
Tucker soon after she and Reeves had married.[10] Carson had asked in
detail about each member of the Tucker family and said, reservedly, that
she would like very much to hear from them directly, too. Then she told
Gin Tucker in a carefully controlled statement about a puzzling and saddening experience she had had several years earlier which had involved
her friend's parents. She said that she and her cousin had been walking
down the street in Columbus when a car passed by her and its occupants
waved, but did not stop. Carson believed that it was Colonel and Mrs.
Tucker and that they were doubtless on their way to her house to visit.
She had not seen them for several years, and their sudden appearance
now had been startling. She said that she had rushed home and waited
all afternoon and evening for them, but that they had not even called.
Although Mrs. Tucker later assured Carson that she and her husband had
not been in Columbus at that time and that they certainly would never
have done such a thing, the trauma had long been fixed in Carson's psyche. And now a nebulous plot began to evolve during the fall of 1939 in

Columbus, a fiction that Carson thought of as *The Bride and Her Brother*. She was anxious to get it on paper, but it was five years before the story—transmuted finally into *The Member of the Wedding*—was ready for the publishers.

As of now, however, in late 1939, Carson was still an unpublished author except for her one short story, "Wunderkind." Restless to get on with her "bride story," she returned to Fayetteville and Reeves and forced herself to sit at her typewriter. For hours and hours she worked daily, yet seemingly got nowhere. She strained at each new frustration of not being able to get to the center of her novel, to catch its focus. To Carson, the way in which a work gathered momentum and power was as mysterious as the manner in which sex was determined in an unborn child.[11] Although she always worked energetically as a writer, she also knew that hard work was not enough, for "in the process of hard work, there must come an illumination, a divine spark that puts the work into focus and balance."[12]

In the spring of 1940, Carson's mother rode the bus from Columbus to Fayetteville to visit. She had always loved Reeves as though he were her own son, and it grieved her to know that her children were unhappy. Carson, usually open and honest with her mother—as she was with everyone—spared Marguerite most of the details of their difficulties, but made it clear now that her marriage left much to be desired. Marguerite had taken Reeves into her heart even before Carson had, having been won over by him when he used to visit the Smith household with Edwin Peacock as far back as 1935 while Carson was first in New York, and she had encouraged the relationship when the two of them eventually met and began to see each other frequently. Marguerite felt now that the failure of their marriage was also *her* failure, and if there was anything she could do to save it, she would.

Once in Fayetteville, she noticed that on the surface the relationship seemed smooth enough. With the three of them together, it was almost like old times. They teased and laughed and told funny stories that she and Carson had entertained each other with for years. Carson had a passion for small-town stories, and Marguerite told her anecdotes about life in the old downtown family home on Thirteenth Street as her mother had related them to her, stories about her father's maiden aunts, and tales of the female heroics on the plantation in Reynolds, Georgia, when General Sherman's men had been fitly rebuffed by Carson maternal ancestors. Carson wanted to hear the same stories over and over again. If a new one was introduced, there was a slight impatience and she usually said, "Now I want to hear about those brothers again." Then later, after the new story had had time to sink in, she would remind her mother: "Remember the story you told me last time? Well, tell me that one once more." Soon both stories became part of the repertoire. Carson loved, especially, the legend of the seven brothers of a prominent Columbus family who became convinced that their brother-in-law had mistreated their sister. Plotting vengeance, the brothers promoted a horse race that was attended by the whole town except the brothers and their waylaid in-law. The seven boys fired their pistols in unison at their offending relative. Later, no one could determine whose shot had killed their sister's husband. In fact, no trial was even held. The sentiment of the town was that the boys had acted on "a point of honor," and they were not condemned. The tale was told with various embellishments over the years, and by the time Carson heard it, the story bore little resemblance to any factual prototype, which made her appreciate it even more.

Reeves sometimes entertained them, too, with yarns about army life, of the camaraderie of the barracks, of the strange characters he had met across the miles—doubtless exaggerated—and of his experiences with his cousins and other relatives with whom he had spent much of his life. Juxtaposed with tales of the past were Reeves's observations of experiences of the day. He talked about his various "credit snooping" assignments he had been engaged in, and though he never revealed names, he was proud of the ingenuity he showed in completing a mission. There was humor in the way Reeves narrated an incident. Many people over the years thought him to be a master storyteller, and they sympathized with him for never having time to write fiction as Carson did. There was pathos in his tales, too. He empathized with the people he met and observed in the town as he went about his work. He pitied the poor farmer who lost his tractor because he could not make payments when his crops failed and the pregnant black who sat outside the doctor's office with a half-dozen "yard" children, a "lap" baby, and one still being suckled. He hated the system that allowed a man to work and sweat and harvest a crop, yet provided no market for it, or a system that rewarded a man for his labors with only half enough money to cover his costs. Reeves sometimes paced the room, hammered a fist into the palm of his hand, and shook with rage at the injustice of it all.

Marguerite Smith watched her children in Fayetteville that spring and silently grieved. She knew how badly the South depressed them, yet she did not think the North would be a panacea either. The whole country was afflicted, and she hated to think of Carson's being exposed to such sickness. If her daughter would be happier in another environment, however, she would again send her North with her blessings. Near the end of her stay, Marguerite suggested that the three of them drive to Charleston to visit Edwin Peacock. She felt that Peacock, too, was her son, and she knew it would be good for all of them to be together again. Also, visiting Charleston would not stir up the old loves and antipathies for Carson that visits to her hometown did. It would not be charged with the painful memories of her youth. Edwin Peacock had written to them enthusiastically about the town to which he had moved a few months earlier, and now he urged them to visit. He was sure that Carson would be fascinated by the old fruit stands and the fish marketplace, the wide, beautiful harbor where numerous ships could be seen at anchor in the bay, the islands off the mainland, the countless historical sites of pre-Revolutionary days.

Upon her arrival in Charleston, however, Carson paid little attention to the town. Peacock, who was living on Sullivan's Island just off the coast, arranged for them to have two rooms in the huge, old boardinghouse where he was staying. It was a quiet, restful weekend for the four of them. Carson was more interested in staying on the island and reveling in the small-town stories about Thomasville, Georgia, where Peacock had been reared, than in sightseeing in Charleston. They also talked for hours of the books, music, and composers they loved. Carson played once again for her friend one of her favorite Chopin etudes, "The Winter Wind," and they listened to the music of Scarlatti, Bach, and Beethoven from Peacock's record collection. She and Reeves felt rich that weekend, their troubles less oppressive than they had seemed for months. Their friend's gentle manner and quiet optimism regarding the bright future he foresaw for them made each feel as though he were the luckiest and most loved person in the world.

When they returned to Fayetteville on Sunday night, accompanied by Marguerite, the couple felt a buoyancy they had not experienced since the first weeks of their marriage. To Reeves, Marguerite seemed more like a mother than his own. He loved Marguerite for the way she loved him, and for the way she loved Carson, too. Although Reeves sometimes thought that Marguerite was remiss in never having trained her daughter to be much of a homemaker or culinary artist, he recognized that Marguerite herself had never worked hard at the roles. She was a good cook, certainly, but she admittedly was not a housekeeper. To Reeves, both Carson and her mother were wives who had to be true to their artistic temperaments, and the devil could take the hindmost. Whereas Carson's father was never seriously bothered by his wife's neglect of the physical aspects of the home because there was always a servant to do the menial chores and he himself was never pressed into such services, Reeves had been chafed since the early days of his marriage by the constant friction in his own mind regarding the way he thought things ought to be done, and the way they actually were. When Reeves suspended thought and judgment about their situation, he was contented; but when he intellectualized, he knew that he was tired of being the dishwasher, cook, housekeeper, and provider. Reeves had already weathered many storms as Carson's nurse through her various illnesses, but he could not even wildly imagine what lay in store for him. He sometimes thought of Carson as a prima donna to whom her mother paid unnecessary homage; yet he, too, had done his share of curtsying, and he was painfully aware now that he suffered from a stiff knee.

Reeves had begun that spring to put out feelers in New York City in hopes of continuing there in the credit field. He told Edwin Peacock that being a credit snooper in the South was a very poor way to make a living; perhaps in New York it would be better, he said hopefully. Reeves considered going back into the Army, but the thought of possibly stagnating in uniform while his country apathetically viewed the mounting crisis in Europe with a "thank God it is not happening to us" attitude was more than he could stomach. Nor could he hope to keep Carson with him in the South much longer, or anywhere else where he was not free to accompany her when she chose to go.

It was fortunate both for their economic situation and personal relationship that Carson was notified in May by her publisher that *The Heart Is a Lonely Hunter* would be out in early June 1940. Regardless of Carson's version of how Houghton Mifflin was handling her book, it definitely was not slated for a routine release. The book was fittingly launched to match the company's enthusiasm and the plaudits of reviewers, who saw the novel as one of the most exciting books of the decade. Interviewed in Fayetteville and asked by her editor and the Houghton Mifflin promotion department if she would be going to New York soon, Carson responded, "Just as quickly as I can get there." The only thing holding her back was money. A few days later, with the remaining $250 royalty check now in hand and fifty dollars that Reeves managed to wangle for their old Chevrolet, the couple hastily prepared to move North once again. As far as Carson was concerned, she was ready to jump on a train that night, but Reeves gently restrained her. Quickly he notified his company that he was terminating, closed the office before his replacement could arrive, left his books in order and a note for his successor— wishing him luck and extending his sympathies.

In mid-June 1940 the two of them boxed up their store of books, paintings, dishes, cookware, linens, and silver, shipped them by railway express, and boarded the Atlantic Coast Line Champion for New York City, determined never to live in a small town in the South again.

Chapter Four

NEW YORK'S
NEW LITERARY DARLING,
SUMMER 1940

*In spite of her eagerness to get away from the South, Carson felt timor-*ous over her impending return North. Self-confidence yielded to doubt as she considered her re-entry into New York City. Today, she would be noticed in a new and exciting way. She had a name and a novel to her credit, yes, but would people like her? Would it be any different from the way it had been in Fayetteville? Regardless of her apparent unconcern over what other people thought, Carson quivered inside and yearned for acceptance. Would they wonder how such a naive young girl could write *The Heart Is a Lonely Hunter,* and would they think any less of the book once they had met its author? En route on the train with Reeves, Carson daydreamed constantly, imagining what life would be like in New York City this time. In most of her dreams she saw a single image: a girl sur-rounded by admirers, reading fan letters, attending parties hosted by her publisher, granting requests for interviews, receiving the New York lit-erary coterie—whom she saw welcoming her into their sanctum—lunch-ing at the Algonquin, being the honored guest at cocktail parties, inti-mate dinners . . . and the fancies danced on and on. Herself a onesome, not a twosome, she did not see Reeves in the crystal ball.

For once, actuality almost matched Carson's fantasy. She and Reeves arrived in New York City just two weeks after *The Heart Is a Lonely Hunter* burst upon the literary scene amid reviewers' accolades that the book's young author was the most exciting new talent of the decade. Hurriedly settling into their fifth-floor walk-up apartment at 321 West Eleventh Street in Greenwich Village, Carson and Reeves went out to survey their kingdom. Jubilant in her success, they walked arm in arm through midtown Manhattan, pausing at windows of bookshops to thrill at the sight of stacks of her novel and blowups of her picture on promi-nent display.

She had been photographed at a table as she sat autographing copies of *The Heart Is a Lonely Hunter,* looking like a drowsy-eyed child who had not been long out of bed. Carson did not like the picture, for she thought it made her face appear pouchy—"almost possum-jawed," she called it. (Later, the British actress Maria Britneva Saint Just referred to Carson as "Choppers.") Her public, however, found Carson freshly appealing and boyish-looking, dressed in Reeves's shirt and a dark man-tailored corduroy jacket. New York's new literary darling had a natural, fresh-scrubbed look. Her straight bangs and long brown hair—tousled and gleamingly clean—well-shaped eyebrows, slightly upturned nose, full lips which parted invitingly into a half smile, all contributed to the wondering look of a sixteen-year-old with captivating charm, a press agent's dream. Both the book and the person took New Yorkers by storm.

That she could publish a best-selling novel at twenty-three was feat enough, but to write with a knowledge and insight that so obviously transcended her years and experience was just short of miraculous. New reviews had been appearing almost daily since the book's release on June 4. Although they were not unanimous in their plaudits, all the critics recognized her sizable talent. Life with Reeves was sweet-tasting all over again in New York City, and she thanked God that the ugly chapter of their wretchedness in Fayetteville was over.

Every day seemed to bring news, invitations, and unexpected opportunities. Several weeks after their arrival in New York, Robert Linscott, Carson's editor at Houghton Mifflin, reported that the book was selling marvelously well. He asked if she would like a fellowship to Bread Loaf Writers' Conference, an annual summer program of Middlebury College which convened the last two weeks of August. Here, promising young poets and authors could work, either on their own or under the tutelage of older, more established artists. Linscott wanted Carson at Bread Loaf so that she could exchange ideas with other writers and be seen and talked about as well.

Carson had only recently heard about the prestigious writers' school nestled high in the forests of the Green Mountains near Middlebury, Vermont, and she was pleased to be invited, to be given an opportunity to be a member of a group—even though as a member she frequently rebelled and tried to see how unlike the rest of the group she could be. Bread Loaf was known for its distinguished faculty and talented students. The students came as contributors, auditors, or fellows. To be invited as a fellow meant that the artist had exceptional ability and had met with extraordinary success in publishing or in having had a book-length manuscript accepted. Carson had both, and she was proud of it. As a published novelist of less than a month, she was already being acclaimed for a second major manuscript that had been accepted by Houghton Mifflin.

The work was *Army Post,* now retitled *Reflections in a Golden*

Eye. It had been discovered early that summer upon her arrival in New York by George Davis, literary editor of *Harper's Bazaar*, when, impressed by *The Heart Is a Lonely Hunter*, he had gone to see her and had pushed for other manuscripts. Carson had given little thought to her army post tale lying dormant in a dresser drawer for almost a year, but Davis found it while rummaging among her early pieces and urged her to let *Harper's Bazaar* publish it. The story was novella length, just right for two installments, he insisted. According to the contract for her first novel, Houghton Mifflin also had rights to her second. Her editor, however, saw advantages to allowing a prepublication serialization in the fall and thus scheduled *Reflections in a Golden Eye* for an early February release.

Even though her second novel seemed a polished, completed work of art in Carson's judgment, Robert Linscott suggested slight revision. To him, Bread Loaf would be an ideal environment for Carson, both a place to work and a marvelous retreat from the summer's heat and hubbub of the city. Quickly Linscott saw to it that Carson received a fellowship which paid all of her Bread Loaf expenses. Moreover, Houghton Mifflin was anxious to have her second book in press as soon as possible so that readers would know that their young author had not only written a great first novel, but also had followed it with an even more tightly controlled and precision-chiseled second novel within the year.

As the summer progressed and Carson heard more about Bread Loaf, her excitement mounted. She was struck by the list of distinguished staff members she would be meeting soon, men such as Louis Untermeyer, Robert Frost, Wallace Stegner, John Marquand, and John Gassner. She had also heard that Bread Loaf was something of an escape, an exciting and stimulating get-together for those who found it important not only to work hard, but also to have spots of time in which to play. Carson had missed the enthusiasm and creative vitality that came from sharing with a group, whether it was a creative writing class such as she had feasted on with Sylvia Chatfield Bates and Whit Burnett, or her mother's informal salon on Starke Avenue in which Carson had enthusiastically participated, or even her Carson Smith days as instructor of the private music study course she had created for wealthy Columbus matrons. Carson accepted the Bread Loaf invitation and looked forward to basking in new glories under a Vermont sun.

By August, too, she had still another reason for wanting to get away. She had fallen in love, but Reeves was not the recipient. It had all started only a few days after they had settled in New York. Through Reeves and her own lively interest in international events, Carson had become increasingly aware of the vast numbers of refugees who were pouring into New York City in flight from fascism. Poland, Norway, Denmark, France—all had fallen by midsummer 1940. Germany was bombing British ports and cities, yet America still had not gotten into the war.

Angered by what she considered her country's weakness and lack of compassion for humankind in the rest of the world, Carson became even
more estranged from her homeland, the South. Obsessed by her sense of
exile and estrangement from Georgia, North Carolina, and all that the
South seemed to represent, she identified now with other exiles.

In her uniquely impulsive manner, Carson began to call upon some
of the more prominent ones in arts and letters. One of her earliest attempts to welcome and pay tribute to a fellow exile, however, met with
rebuff. She called on Greta Garbo, whom she idolized as a beautifully
masculine female who pulsed with sensitivity, talent, and élan vital. She
admired everything about Miss Garbo—the way she dressed—in handsomely tailored pants and long-sleeved men's shirts softened at the collar
by a scarf—and the way she walked, talked, and successfully made her
way in a male-oriented world. Carson took her a copy of her novel,
sought a personal meeting, and loved her mutely as a kindred spirit. Miss
Garbo received Carson, but made it clear that she was not interested in
a developing friendship.

It was not Miss Garbo who complicated Carson's life, however, but
a stunningly beautiful, talented Swiss girl, Annemarie Clarac-Schwarzenbach, long a friend of the exiled Thomas Mann family. The first of July,
Carson called upon two of the Mann offspring, Klaus and Erika, and
Wystan Hugh Auden, the young, self-exiled British poet to whom Erika
was married. Visiting the Manns was Annemarie, a thirty-two-year-old
novelist, journalist, and travel writer who had recently arrived in New
York. She had come to see Erika and to negotiate the sale of photographs
to *National Geographic* and *Life* magazines that she and Ella Maillart, a
colleague, had taken on an expedition through Afghanistan, Bulgaria,
India, Russia, and Turkey. Klaus Mann recorded his impressions of Carson after that first visit:

> July 5, 1940—Reading among other things *The Heart Is a Lonely
> Hunter*—the melancholy novel by that strange girl, Carson McCul-
> lers, who came to see us the other day. Very arresting, in parts. An
> abysmal sadness, but remarkably devoid of sentimentality. Rather
> grim and concise. What astounding insight into the ultimate incon-
> solability and incurability of the human soul! Her style and vision
> remind me some of Julian Green. Wonder if she may know him. . . .
> I hope she'll write that story about the Negro and the refugee, to
> which she referred as one of her next projects. Uncannily versed in
> the secrets of all freaks and pariahs, she should be able to compose a
> revealing tale of exile.[1]

Carson's response both to Erika Mann and Annemarie Clarac-Schwarzenbach was love at sight. The qualities of Annemarie which Mann had
captured in his journal some ten years earlier were still immediately ap-

parent. In 1930, he had referred to her as "our 'Swiss child,' Annemarie, the eccentric scion of a patrician house. She is delicate and ambitious and looks like a pensive page."[2] The better Carson got to know these two unusual women the more sacred grew her discipleship. She joined them frequently for dinner and spent long hours at their feet, enthralled by their tales of adventure and woe.

What had been fantasy for Carson in the 1920s as she playacted on her front porch in Columbus, Georgia, Erika had lived. Tall, handsome, mannish-looking, she was the oldest child of Thomas Mann. She had married Gustaf Grundgens in 1925, a prominent left-wing actor who had collaborated with her brother Klaus on a book and was now director of the Berlin State Theatre. Finding Grundgens incompatible with her own anti-Fascist sympathies, she divorced him. Erika had led several lives simultaneously during the past decade. Trained for the theatre, she acted, staged her own satiric revue which toured all over Europe, traveled widely as a journalist and lecturer, and was a leader in anti-Fascist movements. A spirited adventuress, she once participated in a race of Fords around Europe in which she won first prize for driving six thousand miles in ten days while sending in newspaper stories of her progress at the same time. Her prize? A Ford.

In 1935, Erika Mann had married Wystan Auden, whom she had never met. It was a marriage of convenience that Auden extended to her so that she might have British citizenship and be free to travel. Their marriage had never been a matter of living together as man and wife—Auden needed his freedom as much as she—but they were good friends and usually looked each other up when their paths crossed. Miss Mann had been in the United States off and on since 1936 when she brought to New York her *Pepper Mill* show, a bevy of females led by a German burlesque actress, Therese Giehse. The satiric musical played over one thousand performances in Europe before opening in New York's Chanin Theatre. The show had soon closed in America, however, when it became apparent that Miss Giehse's rotund curves and thick accent were not appreciated by New York audiences. After war in Europe broke out, Miss Mann traveled behind the lines disguised as a peasant and helped refugees escape to Switzerland and America. In the United States she met with other exiles and sympathizers who were concerned with rescue work and war relief. As Carson got to know Erika and Annemarie and the exciting and often dangerous nature of their lives, she begged them to let her help, too. There was little that Carson could do, but they did take her with them to some of the Emergency Rescue Committee meetings and introduced her to other exiles.

Especially with Annemarie did Carson feel an instant affinity. No one in her entire life had seemed so fascinating or more deserving of her total commitment. Seeking always to identify with those she loved, Carson soon discovered that with the exception of travel, she and Annemarie had much in common.

Like Carson, Annemarie had been a sickly child, pampered by an overly protective mother who nursed her through bouts of scarlet fever, whooping cough, and a heart ailment. As the two women revealed themselves to each other, they compared and contrasted backgrounds and environments. Even though their life styles and cultures were vastly different, they found that the inner tensions which sprang from them and their methods of coping were similar.

Annemarie as a child had written stories and fairy tales to relieve difficult emotional strains. In constant conflict with her mother, she avoided home as much as possible. Maria Renée Schwarzenbach was a proud, impulsive, strong-willed woman who lived zestfully by instinct. She was the daughter of the Supreme Commander of the Swiss Army during World War I, whose home had long been a cultural center of Europe. Visiting freely in Annemarie's grandparents' palatial estate, Mariafeld, had been such eminent guests as Johannes Brahms, Richard Wagner, and Alfred Nobel. In contrast to her mother, Annemarie's father, Alfred Schwarzenbach, had a superior intellect and lived solely by reason. He was one of the wealthy and cultured owners of the largest silk-weaving industry in Switzerland, Robert Schwarzenbach and Company. Carson listened avidly to Annemarie's stories of life in Switzerland, of her parents and their fascinating backgrounds. Never had she known anyone so worldly, aristocratic, sophisticated, and privileged as Annemarie.

The fact that Annemarie was from Switzerland had first stimulated Carson's unabashed hero worship and passion. Switzerland was the magical land of snow and adventurous exploits from which Carson's childhood fantasies had been shaped. Almost all of Carson's youthful fictional characters—those she had already created, such as Mick, and others yet to be born—yearned for snow and a mountainous Swiss terrain in which they might perform heroic feats for their beloveds.

Also like Carson, Annemarie had shown precocious talent as a pianist. She could play beautifully before she was six and had amazed large audiences as a child. Many nights Carson and Annemarie sat about the Mann apartment with Klaus and Erika, sharing their favorite music and talking about composers as though they were old friends. One weekend the four of them visited the family home of Thomas Mann in Princeton, where Annemarie played the piano for Carson, and Carson responded with her childhood recital piece, Liszt's Second Hungarian Rhapsody. Out of practice, Carson did not play nearly so well as she once had, but she poured body and soul into it, her libation for a goddess.

Annemarie, too, had published early. Her first book appeared when she was twenty-three, and she gained immediate literary fame. In rapid succession six other books of travel and autobiographical adventure followed, including a lyric novel and a long fairy tale, which Carson saw as comparable to her own work *Reflections in a Golden Eye*. By 1940, Annemarie was the literary sweetheart of Switzerland. To Carson, it seemed as though they were fated to be the stars of their respective hemispheres.

Even Annemarie's taste in clothes coincided with Carson's. According to Annemarie's sister, their mother had always dressed Annemarie as a boy and "encouraged the boyishness in her character and in her enthusiasm for other girls."[3] The third of five children, Annemarie had an older brother and two younger ones, but the oldest boy was a sickly child, and Annemarie was treated by her parents as the "little man" in the family. Fairly close to her father, although frequently misunderstood by him, Annemarie accompanied him often on business trips throughout Europe and to America. Alfred Schwarzenbach found it far more convenient to travel with a *son* than a daughter. Annemarie appreciated the male image imposed upon her by her parents and did all she could to perpetuate it; she was also very much aware, and pleased, that to her admirers she was a beautiful and sensuous woman.

As a child she was noticed by everyone. Painters asked to paint her; photographers, to take her picture. At eleven she was offered a seat next to the German director Arthur Nikisch, so that she could watch him closely as he conducted Beethoven's Ninth. Young and old competed to do as much as possible for her pleasure. At the institute in Fetan, a private school in Zurich, Annemarie took only the subjects that interested her: history, German, and music. As her sister put it, "Annemarie did not need to darn even her own stockings. Her friends did it for her."[4] (Three of the Schwarzenbach children earned Ph.D.s—Suzanne, Annemarie, and Hans. Annemarie's degree was from the University of Zurich, where she majored in history and minored in literature.) In short, everyone who came into contact with Annemarie fell at her feet. Nor was Carson an exception. When *Reflections in a Golden Eye* appeared in book form the following February, its dedication was to Annemarie.

That Carson's new beloved was married posed no problem. Her marriage to Claude-Achille Clarac in 1935 had been an unhappy one. He had arrived in Teheran a stranger as the new chargé d'affaires and they had known each other only a few weeks when they married. Moving immediately to an isolated area far from Teheran, they lived for many months without a car and a great distance from European neighbors. Annemarie was miserable. Unable to cope with her restricted life there, bitter and rebellious over her narrow confines, she became addicted to morphine. She had experimented with it while a student at the University of Berlin in 1930 and had been using it intermittently ever since to help assuage painful psychic and physical disorders.

By 1940, Annemarie and her husband had been estranged for three years. She had preceded him to Switzerland for a holiday and never went back. The plan had been for Clarac to join her in Switzerland, but she knew that she could never return with him to a life of physical and moral isolation. Traveling alone by car from Teheran, she journeyed home by way of an extensive trip to Russia and the Balkans. In Moscow Annemarie acquired the diary and films of Lorenz Saladin, famous Swiss mountain climber who had frozen to death while attempting to climb the Khan Tegri on the Russian-Chinese border. With these, she returned home to resume writing. What ensued was Annemarie's most successful book, *Lorenz Saladin: Ein Leben für die Berge.* Upon finishing it, she was off to the Far East on another expedition to the Balkans, Turkey, Afghanistan, and India with journalist Ella Maillart, and then on to America to join Erika Mann.

Annemarie had become disillusioned quickly by her visit to the United States this time, unlike the several other trips she had made in recent years. Just before meeting Carson she had written to her friend Ella that "in a little over four weeks I have seen enough of New York, its busy life, committees, social contacts, etc., etc., to feel deeply discouraged." Annemarie had arrived in mid-May, stayed with Erika and Klaus Mann for a while, visited the Mann family in Princeton, and then worked vigorously with the Emergency Rescue Committee. Torn between taking out "first papers," which would allow her to stay on in America, and returning home where she might be able to become more directly involved in refugee relief, Annemarie welcomed Carson into her complex life as a temporary respite and found strength and spirit in her exuberance and devotion.

She would stay on for the time being, she decided, but she was reluctant to become deeply involved with Carson in a relationship that she knew could not be sustained. Annemarie did not want to hurt her, and she knew that eventually Carson would be hurt. Annemarie had had many loves and had been the object of female pursuits all over Europe. Throughout her young life she had been saturated by people and found herself constantly having to withdraw to preserve her individuality and sense of well-being and security.

Caught up in the spirit of her new friends' lives, Carson found that she was staying away from Reeves and the apartment for longer and longer periods of time. She had also largely stopped writing. Reeves had become aware very quickly of his wife's infatuation with her new friends, but felt powerless to cope with it. He confided in his old friend, Vincent Adams, whom he saw frequently now that they both were living in the city, that Carson apparently was "having an affair of some sort" with them. Adams' solution was simple: "Go see those females and tell them to get the hell out of your wife's life—then pop 'em in the jaw if necessary." Reeves hoped, instead, that Carson would be able to handle it herself, that time would be the great curative. He would weather it, just as he had weathered other storms of their marriage.

Carson had even included her husband in the relationship that was developing with her new love. Annemarie and Reeves became very fond of each other, in fact—another instance of an echo from Carson's fiction now being actualized in reality, a situation reminiscent of *Reflections in a Golden Eye*, in which Captain Penderton "had a sad penchant for becoming enamoured of his wife's lovers." Carson was later to say that "everything significant that has happened in my fiction has also happened to me—or it will happen, eventually."

As the time approached for her to leave for Bread Loaf in August, she had become almost physically ill from the psychic tensions that had evolved again in her marriage, compounded now by the anxieties and uncertainties evoked by her involvement with Annemarie. Carson also had begun to drink heavily for the first time. Yet through it all, Reeves had remained uncannily patient. He knew well his wife's capacity for love, knew that it was her nature to love intemperately, voraciously. Carson rarely had simple likes and dislikes; rather, she loved with passion, adoration, single-minded devotion, or she disliked with vehemence, detestation, hatred. There was no continuum, no sliding emotional scale. Reeves could put up with his wife's frequent crushes on women with stoic resignation so long as they stopped short of the bed. Now he was no longer certain of anything. Before Carson left for Bread Loaf on August 14, they talked vaguely of divorce. Reeves did not want it—he was willing to accept almost any substitute if it meant hanging onto his marriage.

Carson was anxious to get away, to be free of the apartment and Reeves's questioning eye. In Vermont she hoped she would be able to work again, for with Reeves it had seemed, increasingly, an impossibility. Ambivalently, however, she was reluctant to leave, for she felt intuitively that Annemarie would not be there upon her return. She could not restrain her feelings of jealousy either because of Erika Mann's apparent hold over Annemarie, just as Annemarie's own family had been apprehensive for many years about "Erika's strong, perhaps not always good, influence on her."[5] At the last minute Carson urged Robert Linscott to arrange a Bread Loaf fellowship for Annemarie also. Linscott complied, but, caught up in a whirl of activities and commitments that did not include Carson, Annemarie failed to go. Carson went on to Bread Loaf without her, clinging to the illusion that Annemarie would somehow see fit to join her there later.

Annemarie, too, needed a rest, needed to remove herself from everyone with whom she was involved. Before Carson left, Annemarie had taken a cottage at Siasconset, Nantucket, for a few weeks and was writing again. Then Erika Mann suddenly decided to leave for London on August 19, and Annemarie rushed to New York City to tell her good-by. She stayed on in the city a few days to meet again with the Emergency Rescue Committee, spearheaded by concerned Europeans, to investigate the procedure for acquiring the proper papers in case she should choose to remain in the United States, and ultimately, to talk with Reeves about Carson and Carson's destiny.

When Annemarie had called Carson to tell her she would not join her at Bread Loaf, Carson begged her to meet her in Boston instead, saying that she would leave Vermont immediately. Both of them wanted to see Robert Linscott in Boston, for he was not only Carson's editor and friend, but he was also Annemarie's friend, and Annemarie wanted to talk with him about her own manuscript in progress. Carson had arrived exhausted at Bread Loaf, however, and in Reeves and Annemarie's judgment, it was foolish for Carson even to think of leaving the writers' conference early, both because of the fellowship and how it might appear if she should not stay, and because of her own poor health. The trip by bus from Bread Loaf down to Boston, with its changes and uncertain connections, would be long and wearying, Reeves pointed out. Instead, she should stay on in Vermont and get a rest there. In typical fashion, Carson had worked it out in her own mind that after she and Annemarie saw Linscott, they would go together to the seashore and have a few idyllic days at Cape Cod. Annemarie was hesitant to agree to that suggestion, either, and at last the impact of what possibly was now total rejection by her friend hit Carson.

When she talked with Annemarie several times by telephone from Bread Loaf, she was unable to understand why Annemarie could not come to her, or why Annemarie would not allow Carson to make the trip to her, either. Even more damaging to her psyche was the fact that Annemarie seemed to be "on Reeves's side," to be his advocate. Annemarie's loyalty to Reeves seemed to be the ultimate betrayal, a betrayal that was repeated more than once in a triangle involving other loved ones, a triangle she ultimately objectified in *The Ballad of the Sad Café*, her next novel, and still later, in *The Member of the Wedding*. Carson loved Annemarie passionately. Yet it had been an unfulfilling and destructive liaison, too, for there had been no real reciprocity. During the summer of 1940 Carson was experiencing what became for her eventually a basic tenet: that for love to survive, passion must mellow to friendship or to a love and devotion that do not depend upon reciprocity, in which there is nothing hoped for, no fear of rejection, no jealousy. But it was a year later before she could gain any measure of perspective that might allow such a philosophy, and even then, it was largely lip service.

What Carson could not understand or accept at the time, either, was Annemarie's involvement with Baronessa Margot von Opel, wife of the

German car manufacturer, whom she had known in Europe and who had a summer home on Nantucket Island. Frustrated by what she considered mistreatment by the Baronessa, upset by Erika Mann's abrupt departure, unable to make any concrete decision involving her own life at present, tired and depressed, Annemarie knew simply that she did not want to go anywhere or become any more fragmented than she already was. In a long letter to Robert Linscott on August 23, 1940, Annemarie apologized for her failure to go either to Bread Loaf or to Boston, for which Linscott had made careful plans: "This *was* a mass of planning & changing plans & telephone calls and a zero result! I feel very bad about it, & I wish you would be indulgent and forgive me." She briefly explained her involvement, then told Linscott something of her feelings for Carson and their hapless situation:

> As Carson had planned to have a few days at the sea with me, after
> August 18th,—and I cant get away from here,—I wonder if you
> couldn't propose to take her to some nice place at Cape Cod. I feel
> so bad being unable to do anything for Carson. I'm deeply fond of
> her, & I wish the world would be different, easier for her to face. I
> wish I would be able never to hurt her. But she is very innocent &
> cannot admit certain fatalities—it frightens me to think it quite
> through, but I know she will be hurt. I had a long talk with Reeves in
> New York. He is a fair person, and tries hard to "live up" to his be-
> ing with Carson. But somehow I feel he claims her life . . .[6]

At Bread Loaf, weary of the whole situation, Carson determined to plunge herself again into hard work—to her the one great healer, the only truth.

When Carson's name was proposed to the Bread Loaf staff in the early summer of 1940 as a fellow, Louis Untermeyer was the first and loudest to speak up for her. Several members of the staff had read her typescript of *Reflections in a Golden Eye*, after which it was presented to Theodore Morrison, Bread Loaf director, for assessment. Morrison recognized its extreme brilliance as a piece of writing, but he was put off by the macabre incidents in which a rejected wife cut off the nipples of her breast with garden shears and a kitten was stuffed live into a mailbox. Morrison was "less than enthusiastic" about the work, nor was he able to take her "defense at face value"—for Carson had maintained that those incidents were "hilariously funny."[7] Writer Wallace Stegner, who conducted some of the fiction sessions, recalled that Carson attended several meetings with his group, but that she did not contribute a question or comment: "I had talked with her about *Reflections in a Golden Eye*, but probably not to her satisfaction, for its distortions were things I could grant as legitimate grotesque without especially admiring."[8] Untermeyer, however, stoutly defended Carson's manuscript. They had already corresponded, in fact, for she had written him a warm and thankful letter in response to his praise of *The Heart Is a Lonely Hunter*. Untermeyer was the first great artist in America to hail Carson as an enormous new talent.

Once at Bread Loaf, the two of them quickly became friends. An immediate rapport, a feeling of kinship and love flowered instantly between the sophisticated fifty-five-year-old poet from Brooklyn and the shy twenty-three-year-old girl from the South. Carson could not have been more pleased that she had come. Although there were over a hundred students at the conference in 1940, the group of fellows was small. In addition to herself, there were five others: Eudora Welty, who had had a number of stories published in the little magazines and whose first collection, *Curtain of Green and Other Stories*, appeared the next year; John Ciardi, an obscure twenty-four-year-old poet who was just beginning to be published (Ciardi became director of Bread Loaf in 1955); and three novelists, Edna Frederickson, Brainard Cheney, and Marion Sims.[9]

Others on the Bread Loaf staff in 1940 included Edith Merriles, a popular fiction contributor to women's magazines; Fletcher Pratt, pulp writer and military expert; Hershel Brickell, book editor of the New York *Herald Tribune*; and visiting lecturers Katherine Anne Porter, James Still, John P. Marquand, Bernard De Voto, and Wystan Hugh Auden. Scouts for various publishing houses and editors were also in and out. When Carson met editor Ken McCormick at Bread Loaf, she asked him if Doubleday would like to have *Reflections in a Golden Eye* if Houghton Mifflin decided not to publish it. "She put all this very coyly," said McCormick, "and I told her that of course Houghton Mifflin would be mad not to want to do the second book but that if for some unbelievable reason they didn't want to do the book, I would. We both recognized that this was just a little exercise in flattery."[10]

The *genius loci* of Bread Loaf was Robert Frost, who had been a major force in creating and sustaining the conference since its beginnings in 1926 under the direction of John Farrar, then editor of the *Bookman*. Bread Loaf had come into being when the land and a dozen buildings, along with thirty thousand acres of forests, were willed to Middlebury College by Joseph Battell, philanthropist, who bred Morgan horses and believed in the preservation of trees. The college quickly began two summer programs at its new Bread Loaf campus, eleven miles from Middlebury: the Bread Loaf School of English, a six-week summer school for the study of literature and expository writing, and the two-week Bread Loaf Writers' Conference, the first school of its kind in America.

Frost's good friend, Theodore Morrison, professor of English at Harvard, had been Bread Loaf's titular head since 1935, assisted by his wife, Kay, "who had no title or official position" but "did everything possible to help keep the conference on an even keel," said Morrison. She also served as Frost's secretary. Frost and Untermeyer were advertised as the consultants in poetry, but according to the latter, Frost was not much of a mingler (except at night, when he "mingled like mad," added McCormick), and Untermeyer superintended the poetry sessions. "Frost rarely sat in at the manuscript sessions and I sometimes joined in the discussion and analyses of (fanciful term) Creative Writing," said Untermeyer. Students could attend any of the group lecture and discussion sessions, in which instructors held forth on the principles and techniques of their particular craft and shared some of their personal practices with them. Students also participated in workshops in which their manuscripts were criticized and met privately with the staff member who had evaluated their work as a condition of admission.

Carson sat in on several of Untermeyer's poetry sessions, usually held under a great tree. Although not inarticulate in them, she rarely raised her voice and preferred not to criticize adversely. She told Untermeyer that she was stimulated by his sessions, but he suspected that such comments may have been "nothing more than friendly flattery." After a few appearances in his classes, she informed him that she would have to forgo the group conferences for the rest of the session. She had to spend most of her time going over her own writing, working alone, she said.

Carson was especially in awe of Frost, as she was in her early literary career of all famous artists. Frost and Untermeyer were the most prominent literary figures she had ever known, and she hesitated to seek their advice or to share with them her own poetry, which she had been writing sporadically since she was sixteen. Had Frost been a novelist, she would have eagerly shared her work. At Bread Loaf Carson spoke of her poetry only once to Untermeyer, "with extreme reluctance, as though she did not want to inflict it" upon him, he recalled. She was at Bread Loaf as a fictionist, she reasoned; poetry could come later. Moreover, Carson was always sensitive to criticism. She knew that her own tightly twisted poems, heavy with metaphor, were more in the manner of Hart Crane or Emily Dickinson—the latter, her favorite poet of them all—than in the lucid diction and syntax of Frost, although she loved the depths of Frost's symbolism and greatly admired his poetry.

What she enjoyed most about Bread Loaf was her relationship with Untermeyer. It seemed as though she had always known him. He could see that she was anxious about *Reflections in a Golden Eye*, on which she had ostensibly come to work. Although she was aware of Theodore Morrison's response to the novel, she was not apprehensive so much about it as she was afraid that Untermeyer would not like it so well as *The*

Heart Is a Lonely Hunter; she worried, too, that her public might feel
let down by her second novel. Untermeyer reassured her. He was so enthusiastic over her new book that he compared her to James and Tolstoy.
Untermeyer never forgot Carson's look of pleasure when he told her that
he would write to her publisher about "her strange combination of simplicity and dark insight." What he wrote to Robert Linscott a few days
later became the blurb on the dust jacket of *Reflections in a Golden Eye:*

> The story proceeds from some inner compulsion which is as un-
> planned and as inevitable as life itself. It is a story which flows in
> every paragraph, flows with strange and sinister twists and sudden
> humorous flashes, but flows always to its certain and incalculable end.
>
> I find it utterly unlike anything produced in our time. It is one of
> the most compelling, one of the most uncanny stories ever written in
> America.
>
> Louis Untermeyer

With Untermeyer, Carson also shared a love of music. As a child, he
had expected to become either a concert pianist or a composer; it did not
occur to him until he was eighteen that he might be a writer. Most precious to them both were the few moments they set aside daily to sit at the
piano in the parlor of the Bread Loaf Inn, playing and talking about
music, keyboard technique, and their favorite composers. They both fa-
vored the German romantics and seemed to have discovered Mahler
simultaneously.

Untermeyer, between wives at the time, or rather, vaguely still married to Esther Antin, described his relationship with Carson that summer
as "a platonic affair intensified by not-so-platonic embraces." He was
aware that the strain in Carson's marriage was "due greatly to their confused sexual relations." To Untermeyer, "Carson's bisexual tendencies
were obvious."[11] It was difficult for her not to talk about her private life
with him, for when she liked a person immensely, she immediately took
him into her confidence as though he were an intimate member of the
family; thus it was his life, too, that they were sharing. To Carson, there
was no such thing as a vicarious experience: "If you wanted it for your
own, it was yours," she seemed to say. She told Untermeyer about her
uncertain relationship with Reeves, and "told it rather ambiguously," but
she made no direct reference to her Swiss friend, Annemarie Clarac-
Schwarzenbach. It was as though Carson was trying to put Annemarie
out of both her life and her mind.

Carson's method of coping with her sexual ambivalence while at
Bread Loaf struck Untermeyer as "amusing and pathetic." One such incident occurred at the end of a long session on the porch of Tremayne

Cottage, nicknamed *Delirium Tremayne,* where the staff and students assembled frequently for drinking parties after the evening lectures:

> We had been drinking a bit and going over passages of *Reflections.*
> The party inside was breaking up—it was well after midnight—and
> Carson gave me a goodnight kiss. Then she said, "Would you like to
> sleep with me?" I said (ungallantly but honestly), "I'm afraid I'm too
> tired." "Me, too," said Carson. "But I thought it would be nice to
> ask."[12]

Other "Bread Loafers" speculated on the nature of Carson and Untermeyer's relationship. Although Brainard Cheney acknowledged that he knew nothing of her intimacies with others, "there was, however, a breath of gossip about her irregularity. She spoke freely of her husband, from whom she was then—I believe—separated. He was, or had been a Boy Scout leader, and she spoke of him, it seemed to me then, a bit ambiguously. . . . The suspicion with us, among the fellows, then was that Untermeyer (who enjoyed the reputation of a tom cat) was seducing her (or at least, trying to). Several of the fellows occupied the same lodging house, including Carson. On at least one occasion (and it seems to me no more than once) when Marion, Eudora, Edna, my wife, and I were in some one of our rooms socializing, we could hear 'for hours,' Louis' murmuring but carrying voice coming to us from Carson's room. We couldn't hear Carson's responses, if any. But then, Louis talked incessantly—indeed, it seemed to me substantial evidence against his being engaged in seduction."[13]

In his own relationship with Carson, Cheney found her "friendly enough . . . her personality likable and, indeed, winsome . . . quite gregarious and talkative. She seemed to have opinions on most topics that came up and was quite ready to give them." The image of Carson he chose to remember best, however, involved a late afternoon stroll on the mountains before dinner. Cheney, his wife, Eudora Welty, Edna Frederickson, and Carson were together, and there was an early moon in the sky: "The crowd was scattered, and for some reason Carson and I were lagging behind. On impulse she grabbed me by the hand and we ran up on top of a large haystack in a roadside field. Playfully, she put my arms about her waist and we danced around together, and looked up at the moon. . . . Her gesture was fanciful, not lustful, and there was a sort of pixie appeal and grace about it."

According to Untermeyer, "Some of the Bread Loafers found Carson self-centered. I found her shy but not unduly egotistic . . . not reclusive, but not a joiner, either." Eudora Welty liked Carson that summer and regretted that she did not get to know her better.[14] Miss Welty saw her again at Yaddo in 1941, but that second summer was spent under the watchful eye of Katherine Anne Porter, whose protégée Miss Welty had then become; thus Carson and Miss Welty's friendship never developed. John Ciardi confessed that his memories of Carson were blurred:

> My first session at Bread Loaf seems to have been a binge, produced as much by excitement as by alcohol, though heaven knows I was a prime consumer. I think I went through that first conference on a fifth of whiskey per day and two hours of sleep per night. I was twenty-four at the time and it then struck me as a normal way to do things. In the course of that blur, and some generalized girl chasing, I didn't see much of Carson. My one clear memory of her is of descending a flight of stairs at the Bread Loaf Inn in the company of Richard Brown, the assistant director. There was a pug-nosed little girl with black bangs at the foot of the stairs reading the bulletin board. I said to Dick Brown, "My God, whose 'enfant terrible'?" And he said, "That's Carson McCullers." Then we drew back into the alcohol fumes that purified us.[15]

Brainard Cheney remembered, too, the alcoholic fumes: "The fellows and faculty members made up a pot to supply liquor for conviviality at Tremayne Cottage. Gin seemed to be the least expensive liquor, so our pot was turned into gin. Each afternoon at the cocktail hour a large pitcher of martinis appeared. . . . We all imbibed freely, but Carson no more conspicuously than myself and many others."

According to Wallace Stegner, Carson was something of a phenomenon that summer, with *Reflections in a Golden Eye* circulating around Bread Loaf in galley proofs and *The Heart Is a Lonely Hunter* recently out:

> She was young, gifted, "odd," and in the view of some of the staff who watched her with interest, fey. She was a gangling, skinny girl who wore boys' white shirts and changed them three times a day. . . . I knew her only during that hectic two-week Bread Loaf session, when all of us were working our heads off, and playing tennis or drinking in every off half hour. Louis Untermeyer called her the *fleur de mal* and predicted that she would die young. I think that was not undue prescience on his part, but an extrapolation from the amount of liquor she drank, and the hours she drank it at. Even then, young as she was, she was drinking straight gin out of water glasses.[16]

Stegner did not find Carson easy to talk to, conceding that he was "neither from the South nor a celebrity," but that he and Carson were "distantly friendly." The only evening that he could admit to Carson's being "animated and talkative" was when he observed her retired in a corner with Wystan Auden—having taken with them Stegner's only bottle of bourbon. "They talked and drank like mad, somewhat to my dismay, since the next day was Sunday and the only liquor store in Brandon would be closed," he said. Auden, never a regular member of the full-time staff, was at the conference only as a weekend guest artist to give a reading from his poems. Morrison remembered that Auden "joined amiably in a softball game (in which Robert Frost was captain of one side) and performed effectively, though his batting swing was that of a cricketer rather than a baseball player."[17]

Although Stegner did not see Carson engage in the group's usual physical activities such as their "high jinks" at Texas Falls, where they swam in marble basins and jumped off marble brinks beside waterfalls, he did once see her riding a horse through the Bread Loaf campus, "clad in her clean white shirt," he added. "I also remember her somewhat awkward, angular way of moving, those glasses of straight gin, and that air of secret, bemused, withdrawn self-communion that she wore much of the time. She was my first personal contact with a confirmed devotee of the grotesque, and I found her very interesting, but not easy to know. . . . She seemed to me a twilight figure, old beyond her years, bizarre, everything about her just a little crooked, and hence interesting, but not necessarily what I would have liked to be myself."

On August 28 when the conference closed, Carson was reluctant to leave the beautiful Vermont countryside and her new friend Untermeyer, but Robert Linscott had invited her to return to New York by way of Boston and Cape Cod. It would be her first trip to that area of New England, and she was anxious to visit it and to go over the changes with Linscott that she had made in the *Reflections in a Golden Eye* manuscript. She did not know that it was Annemarie Clarac-Schwarzenbach who suggested that her editor take her to Cape Cod for a holiday and said, "Please look after her health." When Linscott saw Carson, he, too, was troubled by her wan look and deep cough. Carson herself never worried openly about her physical well-being; if she ignored it, ill health usually went away, she reasoned. She was chain-smoking still and had no incentive to stop, even though she realized that it provoked the cough. She was thinner now, too, than she had been a few months earlier, and her face lacked the plump, round look of the child whose picture was on the publicity posters for *The Heart Is a Lonely Hunter*. She had learned that the lonely hunter is never well fed.

In Boston, everyone at the Houghton Mifflin office was eager to catch a glimpse of Carson when she first appeared with Linscott, for they considered the young author their brightest new discovery. She shocked the secretaries, however, when she came in wearing a stocking cap and knee socks and thus became—even more than before—the talk of the

publishing house. Already she was something of a legend—even before
the appearance of *The Heart Is a Lonely Hunter*—for someone from the
Houghton Mifflin office had seen her on a train en route to New York
City, drinking from a flask and marching up and down the parlor car aisle.

Invited to stay at Linscott's apartment on Pinckney Street in Boston,
where it was planned that she would do some writing, Carson discovered
that her editor had forgotten about inviting one of his daughters and her
two young children to stay there at the same time. Thus, instead of
working, Carson played the piano and sang southern ballads to the
children.[18] After escorting Carson about Boston for two days, Linscott
took her to Cape Cod for a holiday in the salt air and sun.

She had been happier at Bread Loaf—and then in Boston and Cape
Cod—than she had been in months, she wrote Louis Untermeyer later.
She said that because she loved German lieder and remembered with
pleasure Mahler's "Songs of a Wayfarer," which the two of them had
shared at Bread Loaf, she bought the entire song cycle as soon as she
reached Boston. She whistled the last song almost constantly while she
was with Linscott, she told Untermeyer, adding that it probably drove
her editor mad; and even upon her return to Manhattan the melodies
continued to haunt her.[19]

Once back in New York, Carson found it difficult to settle down to
work. She had returned to Reeves and their apartment on West Eleventh
Street, but she was restless and impatient. Although her husband did
everything he could to make life easy and uncomplicated for her, to divert
her mind with pleasantries, little gifts, informal entertaining, and dinner
parties for which he did all the work, they still were not happy as a couple.
Her new freedom at Bread Loaf had been precious, her friendship with
Untermeyer warm and stimulating. Now, having to account to someone
for her day, to stop for a meal, even—although she did not have to prepare
it—simply talking with Reeves, all seemed to demand too much of her.

The weather was hot and sticky, the city stifling and almost overwhelming in September. Carson identified with Mahler's wandering youth
in "Songs of a Wayfarer," missed the Vermont hills, and longed to get
away again quickly—anywhere. With the manuscript of *Reflections in a
Golden Eye* out of her hands at last, she tried to sit at her typewriter
and work again on the novel that had been gestating for almost seven
years. Still referring to her story as "The Bride and her Brother," she
lamented to Untermeyer that somehow she was not able to get down to
work because the real design and technique of the novel had not yet
evolved, and until it did, life was an unhappy experience.

When the writing did not go well, Carson liked to back away from
the manuscript and read and sip a glass of sherry and ruminate, wandering in forests of words with her various characters. She read insatiably,
often comparing and contrasting her own style, characterization, and fic-

tional situations with other writers. More often, she climbed into the narrative she was reading and became the character with whom she most identified—as she had done so often with Dostoevski, Tolstoy, Isak Dinesen, D. H. Lawrence, Katherine Mansfield, and others who had become her favorite authors.

In early September she took time out, also, to read a book Untermeyer had recently sent her. It was his own autobiographical *From Another World*. Untermeyer's personal reminiscences of other famous poets, writers, and friends from the artistic arena had transported her from the sooty, gray Manhattan surroundings which she viewed from her fifth-floor apartment into the artists' world—a world she yearned to know more intimately firsthand. On September 3, 1940, she wrote to Untermeyer that she had finished reading *From Another World* and thought it extremely good. It had fascinated her, she said, not merely because she was so fond of the author personally, but because he had experienced life fully and with such vitality. She thanked him, even, for her own experience in being able to read the book, which was a privilege. While she wrote to her friend, Carson watched a woman across the alley pull in her washing from the roof, noted that the factory nearby was quiet for the time being, and basked in the peaceful atmosphere that prevailed. Her glass of sour wine had made her relax a little, too, and she told Untermeyer that she yearned to have him nearby so that they could touch glasses once again.

Yet the poet's book had stimulated Carson in still another way. She longed to find her own *other world*, to move out of their Greenwich Village apartment and take her own place. She felt that she simply had to get away from Reeves. It was no longer a matter of choice—as she had once thought—between a life with her Swiss friend or a life with Reeves. Annemarie had left New York for Washington and was possibly already bound for Europe. They had seen each other only twice since Carson's return from Bread Loaf, and Carson was devastated by Annemarie's apparent indifference, but accepted what seemed the inevitable.

Desperately lonely without her, void of hope of any meaningful relationship again, Carson sought solace in simply being around other people. Fortunately for her at this time, George Davis, whom she had met when *The Heart Is a Lonely Hunter* first became an Algonquin Round Table conversation piece, came frequently to the apartment. Davis was a young, personable bachelor whom everyone seemed to love, and as literary editor at *Harper's Bazaar* and a novelist himself of some note, he had many friends to whom he introduced Carson at every opportunity. Davis knew well her discontent, for he had suffered several rejections himself and was well acquainted with thwarted love. He tried many ways to lift her spirits. One day Davis called to ask Carson if she would like to go up to Suffern with him to visit his good friend, Kurt Weill, the German composer, and Weill's wife, Lotte Lenya, actress and singer who had starred in the United States and abroad in her husband's *Threepenny Opera.* Davis had been seeking a change of quarters, and he hoped that he and Carson might find something together. While in Suffern they also looked at some rustic cottages that could be rented cheaply for the winter. Cheap they were, but totally unsuited for them, they concluded. They decided they would rather be closer to the city.

A few days later, Davis startled Carson with an account of a strange dream. In his sleep he had visualized an old, Victorian brownstone large enough for him and any of his friends with whom he might wish to share it. It was for rent, and exactly what he had been looking for. The dream had been so vivid that the next morning Davis impulsively took a subway to Brooklyn Heights to the neighborhood he already knew well and where he felt intuitively he would actually find such a house. For twenty minutes he walked up and down the blocks near the Brooklyn Naval Yard, and then, at 7 Middagh Street, he suddenly spied a "For Rent" sign. The house was precisely as he had visualized it.

When Davis discovered that the ancient three-story brownstone was both a reality and available, he immediately arranged to lease it. Then he invited two of his favorite people to move in with him—Carson and his old friend, Wystan (W. H.) Auden, whom Davis had known well in Europe and who had come in 1939 to the United States to live permanently. Auden, too, had been looking for a more suitable place to stay, and as soon as Davis completed a few renovation chores, the three of them made their exodus to Brooklyn Heights.

Carson's ambivalent feelings toward Reeves as she attempted to explain to him her rationale and emotions brought to a head by the impending move were heartrending for them both. She cared deeply for Reeves, and she knew that she would continue to love him tenderly, gently, as she would love a brother, as she loved Edwin Peacock and her own brother, Lamar, Jr. They would continue to be good friends, she assured him, better friends, actually, than when they attempted to live together. She did not want a divorce, she said, nor did he, but they both realized and accepted the need for the separation. Vulnerable, still not strong physically, Carson felt that at 7 Middagh Street she might find herself, and in the process, possibly rediscover her husband. Yet to Reeves, in spite of the truth behind their decision, to be abandoned was devastating. A troubled and quietly angry husband helped box up and move his wife's belongings from their apartment—packing away, too, his dreams of their joint climb to the pinnacle of literary fame—no longer knowing how to compete for her affection and attention, and pretending that he did not much care.

Chapter Five

7 MIDDAGH STREET,

A QUEER MENAGE

*M*oving *in September 1940 into two rooms on the second floor of* George Davis' house at 7 Middagh, in an area known as Brooklyn Heights, Carson loved what she called "living in a real neighborhood." Lined with giant maples, Middagh was a short little street, a hyphen in the shadow of the Brooklyn Bridge. Tree shrouded, the large comfortable houses with their gingerbread façades belonged to the late eighteenth and nineteenth centuries. Some of them were on foundations laid before the Revolutionary War, carved into a hook of land on which Aert Middagh had settled and erected a mill in 1710—a promontory from which his Dutch descendants could view the Manhattan and Brooklyn bridges, the dazzle of Lower Manhattan, and ship-infested waters. Shady back yards limp with willows, the sound of distant foghorns on the river, sailors who wandered into its quiet lanes from gaudy Sand Street, neighbors who smiled and paused to exchange the day's trivia—all seemed to beckon Carson as a kindred spirit.

She set out immediately to prowl the declining, Old World neighborhood. The ancient, weathered homes in her block of Middagh—a dead end—gave way to a fire station, convent, and small candy factory in the next, and then, just a little beyond, lay Sand and Fulton streets. Sand Street stretched from Brooklyn Bridge to the Navy Yard, a glittering haven for sailors in search of liquor, women, and dancing—although not necessarily in that order. Sand was one of the most exciting streets Carson had ever seen, and now she visited it daily.[1]

Less than a week after she had settled, Carson received another letter from Louis Untermeyer, forwarded by Reeves from their Village apartment. Overjoyed to learn that Untermeyer was coming down from his Adirondacks farm for a weekend in the city and wanted to see her, Carson replied with a hasty note. She told him of her move from Manhattan to George Davis' pleasant and quiet old house in Brooklyn. She looked forward to his coming, for there was much she wanted to talk over with him, she said.

Untermeyer was among the first of countless dozens who trekked out to the old brownstone at 7 Middagh to visit, spend the night, or move in for a few weeks or months. What began as a tranquil little household soon attracted others and assumed a new face. Davis and Auden quickly discovered that having a woman in the house did not automatically mean that they also had a cook. That Carson had no culinary skills or even a willingness to learn, however, bothered them not at all. The men sometimes cooked the evening meal, but more often they ate their meals in the various little cafés nearby. Frequently Gypsy Rose Lee, a statuesque striptease artist and burlesque entertainer who had long been Davis' friend, joined them. At night the four of them frequented the Sand Street bars—talking, drinking, watching, and participating, even, at times in the entertainment of the house and that which sprang up spontaneously among its patrons. Carson was fascinated by Gypsy Rose Lee, who had known public acclaim since her vaudeville days as a three-year-old. She had been a burlesque dancer and show girl since she was fifteen, when her mentor, "Tessie, the Tassel Twirler," taught her to "leave them hungry for more—you don't just dump the whole roast on the platter." Miss Lee had never failed to heed the advice. She was not really an ecdysiast —a word H. L. Mencken coined especially for her—but an artist who knew when to stop. Gypsy Rose Lee's charisma was as magnetic without lights and tassels as it was with them. She towered over Carson, her remarkable, slender body almost six feet tall, beautifully proportioned except for rather small breasts. Carson, too long discomfited as a child by remarks about her gawky height, found it amusing now to be the short half of a Mutt and Jeff relationship as they strolled down Sand Street and into the shops and bars. Her friend moved with leonine grace, spoke with a peculiar but appealing lisp, and smiled from a prominent mouth that glowed with warm intensity. To Carson, she was an exciting gypsy queen.

The Middagh Street trio found Miss Lee an engaging comrade, an interesting combination of intelligence and sophistication, wit and reserve. A stimulating conversationalist, she held her own well in the gay repartee of Auden and Davis. Auden's dry humor, his flair for histrionics, love for role playing, mimicking, and clowning endeared him to the others, although his acerbic tongue was known, also, to slash with rapiered swiftness. Davis looked out from a soft, round, smiling face, but his genial manner yielded when provoked to acrid observations of his fellow man which dropped with guillotine precision. Had some of Louis Untermeyer's expertise at verbal thrusts and parries not rubbed off on Carson at Bread Loaf a few weeks earlier, she would have been hard pressed to keep up with her new companions.

Gypsy Rose Lee was pleased when George Davis invited her to join the Middagh colony in residence. Her career was at a new height at the moment—she had just appeared in the 1939–40 New York World's Fair in *The Streets of Paris,* and was starring now in *Du Barry Was a Lady* at the Club Petite—yet she was also intrigued by the possibility of a dual role as entertainer-writer. Miss Lee was a competent artist and portrait painter, as well, having just finished an excellent portrait of Max Ernst. Under Davis' encouragement, she had begun to write a novel, a story fittingly dubbed *The G-String Murders.* Davis, a brilliant editor and teacher, offered to assist her with it, and he was presently editing and advising her on the techniques of conflict and tension, character development, and otherwise helping her sharpen the book for publication. (At one time Gypsy Rose Lee and George Davis had allowed a mystery story collaborator to work with her—an unfortunate alliance, for eventually Miss Lee had to go to court to terminate the agreement and extricate herself from a difficult situation. As a result, Davis worked closely with her to see the book through publication.) Although she continued to maintain an apartment in Manhattan, she thought of 7 Middagh as her "hideaway."

Apparently it was such a good hideaway that even her family did not know about it. Her sister, June Havoc, quoted Miss Lee later as having said flatly "that she had never lived in Brooklyn Heights and there was apparently some confusion in somebody's mind about this."[2] Untermeyer, however, among other visitors and residents at 7 Middagh Street, remembered very well her staying for a time with "that queer aggregate of artists" in Brooklyn Heights:

> I did indeed visit Carson at Middagh Street. I do remember an evening there . . . a gay (in both senses of the word) occasion at which Auden and Gypsy Rose Lee were present. (Gypsy did not strip, but Auden did plenty of teasing.) Carson was more voluble and euphoric than usual.[3]

With Gypsy Rose Lee's arrival, the whole tempo of the house changed. Just as she was not really a stripper on stage, but a titillating tease, she was not a coquette offstage, either. With Carson, she was a warm, responsive woman, kind and sympathetic. Miss Lee was just the antidote Carson needed to help combat the loneliness and thoughts of Annemarie that wafted into her consciousness that fall in unguarded moments. Just as Carson had sat entranced at the feet of Annemarie Clarac-Schwarzenbach and Erika Mann, listening to tales of high adventure in Europe, so, too, she now sat at the feet of Gypsy Rose Lee, devouring in wide-eyed wonder her stories of show business and the striptease world. Carson loved her, but she was determined not to lose her soul in anything like the consuming passion she had experienced with Annemarie. With Miss Lee life was light and bright. Neither of them would have had it otherwise.

As word got around that George Davis had a three-story house in Brooklyn Heights, in which Wystan Auden presided as poet laureate and housefather, other artists quickly petitioned for membership. Those who were accepted had Davis' invitation, Auden's approval, and Carson's awe. By Thanksgiving the group included three of Auden's friends and countrymen: Louis MacNeice, poet, with whom Auden had spent a summer in Iceland several years earlier; Benjamin Britten, composer; and Peter Pears, a talented tenor who frequently performed Britten's music. Auden had met Britten in the mid-1930s when they worked together on documentary films in England and then in the British Group Theatre productions, with Britten composing music for Auden's plays. They had combined talents often, with Auden writing librettos for Britten, and Britten setting many of Auden's ballads and art songs to music. Auden, too, had had a sound musical education and played the piano competently. In spite of the formidable talent that surrounded her, Carson was never too shy when prevailed upon to play snatches of her own favorite composers, particularly Bach, whom she felt she played especially well. The old Middagh neighborhood resounded with music, arias, oaths, and feverish conversation—the likes of which it had never known before—and after these tenants left, its climate would never be duplicated.

On Thanksgiving Day, 1940, Carson invited Reeves out to Brooklyn Heights to join the group for dinner and to help celebrate her purchase of a case of champagne. On occasion at 7 Middagh Street, Carson was known to splurge on good liquor. She had seen Reeves fairly often during the first weeks of their separation, and he had come frequently to the house in Brooklyn at night after work. Fond of each other in spite of their differences, they remained on friendly terms. Far better friends than lovers, especially when they were not living together, each showed the other more respect now. Reeves called Carson frequently, and sometimes they met at a favorite haunt, the sidewalk café of the Brevoort Hotel, at Eighth Street and Fifth Avenue, for drinks and lunch.

Reeves, knowing how much his wife enjoyed the excitement and stimulation of her new environment, was both jealous and envious. He would have given anything to have been a part of the fabulous menage himself. He felt that the artists who lived and worked and played there were his kind of people, too, that they were separated now only by circumstance. Usually before Reeves left 7 Middagh Street, he had drunk considerably and worked himself into a good sulk, bringing an extra tension into an already high-strung household. He probed Carson, too, about her writing, and whether she felt she could successfully work in her new location. Reeves took pleasure in hearing that the house in Brooklyn Heights was not the best place for her to write in, either, and he rationalized that she could not create well without him. Work on *The Bride and Her Brother* was not going well there, and she told Reeves honestly that she still was struggling to find the heart of the book. She had not yet had the incisive moment of illumination, which she knew would eventually come.

Thanksgiving afternoon 1940, however, proved crucial to her work. After dinner, over brandy and coffee before the fire in the great, ground-floor drawing room with Gypsy Rose Lee, Reeves, Auden, Davis, and newcomers MacNeice, Britten, and Pears, Carson heard the screaming siren of a distant fire engine drawing closer as though its destination was their street. Carson and Miss Lee, always alert to the extraordinary and exciting, rushed outside to view the spectacle. Running three or four blocks, Miss Lee's long strides leading the way, Carson suddenly caught her arm and shouted breathlessly for her to stop. Then she exclaimed: "Frankie is in love with her brother and the bride, and wants to become a member of the wedding!" Miss Lee stared at her friend as though she had suddenly lost her mind, but as the two walked silently back to the house, Carson was trembling. She was certain now of the style and theme of her book. Its focus had sharpened at last.

Until this sudden illumination, Carson had not worked well on her manuscript. One reason was that she had been caught up in a whirl of friendships and activities revolving around a new magazine erupting in their midst. Writer Klaus Mann was planning what he called "a review of free culture," a phrase which became its subtitle upon publication three months later. In Germany Mann had been editor of a literary review, *Die Samnling*, which flourished from 1933–35, a period Mann considered the most fruitful and productive of his life. During this time, he had not only edited his own magazine but also published three novels, made lecture tours throughout Europe and the United States, and contributed to scores of other periodicals. Klaus Mann was a liberal writer, as was his father, Thomas, but with a war spreading across Europe and threatening to disrupt the entire world, he knew that he had no chance—in Europe, at least—to resume a literary career for many years.

Anxious now to begin a new magazine in America, he talked with George Davis, whom he had known in Paris in the mid-1930s when Davis was "frail and young and writing his first novel," said Mann. Auden, of course, was not only his brother-in-law, but his friend, too, from their days in Europe together. Delighted now to find Davis a successful editor and champion of other artists and the center of a rare menage of intellectual and artistic fervor, Mann began planning sessions for his magazine with Davis and Auden, and Carson, too, who sat in enthusiastically with the group. Having failed in her own attempt to start a literary magazine in the South a few years earlier, she was thrilled to participate in the evolvement of a bonafide magazine with writers of stature behind it. Soon Mann pulled in others from the New York literary coterie: Janet Flanner, Horace Gregory, Ernest Boyd, Eleanor and Eunice Clark, Robert de Saint-Jean, and Glenway Wescott—all of whom agreed to help in some way. Still in the planning stage, the magazine's name evolved now from *Zero Hour* to *Cross-Road*. Wescott, a latecomer to the group, suggested that the name *Cross-Road* itself sounded undecided. Suddenly Mann hit upon what the group considered the perfect name, *Decision*.

The first issue of *Decision* appeared on December 18, 1940, with new fiction, poetry, and essays by such established writers and poets as William Carlos Williams, Somerset Maugham, Sherwood Anderson, Noël Coward, Robert Sherwood, and Archibald MacLeish. Others also rallied to help. Muriel Rukeyser said that she would contribute poetry regularly, Christopher Lazare, art, and Tom Curtiss, a theatrical column. Indeed, most of the artists, writers, poets, and musicians who gathered, visited, or lived at 7 Middagh Street began to make literary contributions and to plan for features unique to their own creative genre. By the first of the year subscriptions and plaudits were pouring in.

Another contributor to *Decision* was Chester Kallman, a nineteen-year-old, pimply-faced American poet who had begun to publish in the little magazines. Kallman, a student at Brooklyn College, was attracted by Auden to the Middagh commune, and soon he, too, was invited to move in. When Auden left in the fall of 1941 to teach at the University of Michigan and be the poet in residence, Kallman went with him. Eventually the two men lived together, both in Austria and America, and collaborated to become two of the most distinguished librettists in grand opera of the twentieth century. An earlier collaborator of Auden's— with whom he was not quite so successful as he later became with Kallman —was British playwright Christopher Isherwood, who spent several days in the household during the summer of 1941. Isherwood, Auden's schoolmate in England, boyhood companion, and close associate for over twenty-five years, had emigrated to the United States in 1939 a few months ahead of Auden, but chose to settle in California instead of New York.

The house on Middagh Street was an exciting place to visit, but its confusion and sheer numbers were enough to set awry any serious artist who attempted to work there. Yet the singular household in Brooklyn Heights became that fall and winter an important center for dozens of creative men and women. Soon there was a waiting list for permanent occupancy and countless visitors drifted in and out of 7 Middagh day and night. For a few weeks, even a trained chimpanzee and his keeper held court there.

When Davis first talked about his house to Janet Flanner, the talented and precocious "Genêt" whose crisp, tart "Letter from Paris" essays had appeared regularly in *The New Yorker* since 1925, she responded, "That's admirable," for Miss Flanner admired Brooklyn, which had preserved its old-fashioned shapeliness much more than most New Yorkers realized. Then she asked, "And what is it like, George?"

"Well, it's an old house, quite a handsome old house, a boardinghouse, really," Davis replied, but Miss Flanner thought he had said: "It's a 'bawdy' house."

"Why, George, how did you find one? That's just priceless for the pack of you."

"Well, I don't know why that's so appropriate," growled Davis.

"Boardinghouse—bawdy house, it's just the same, George—it's all so in character, you know."

When Miss Flanner saw the establishment for herself, there was no reason to alter her opinion. "It was a household that confused itself almost immediately without any difficulty," she said. Miss Flanner knew the principals of 7 Middagh Street very well, in addition to most of the other artists who congregated there. She could see, too, how Carson would be enough "to drive any small town right off its rocker. Carson stood out with New Yorkers, even, as an eccentric of the first water." According to Miss Flanner, her friendship with Carson developed "without any difficulty—she was always so eager, so full of the energy of affection. In that she was gifted, perhaps overgifted."[4]

When Erika Mann returned to the United States later that winter, she went frequently with her brother Klaus to Brooklyn Heights to see Carson, Auden, and her brother Golo, who had recently joined his fellow exiles in residence at Middagh Street. Golo—another of Thomas Mann's talented sons, this one a novelist and historian—was released from a French concentration camp in October 1940 and brought to the United States by his parents. Golo Mann was not popular, however, at 7 Middagh, recalled Janet Flanner. Perhaps it was the result of his recent deprivation, but to Miss Flanner, "Golo seemed greedy about everything. He would go into the kitchen every morning ahead of the others and drink all the cream off the milk." She admired Klaus Mann, but found him an egotist and hard to get along with. To Miss Flanner, "the prince of the Manns"—and she knew them all—was Erika. Several times that winter, Annemarie Clarac-Schwarzenbach also reappeared. Once Carson saw Annemarie again, all the love she had felt before was released with new surges of stored-up energy. That it could come to nothing, that Carson loved Annemarie far more than Annemarie could ever requite, was indubitable. This Carson knew and accepted as one more evidence of the veracity of her evolving thesis of love and the beloved-lover relationship that she treated at length in *The Ballad of the Sad Café* some two years later.

As the group at 7 Middagh grew, an austere Auden insisted on certain household regulations. Chaos had begun to reign among the assorted artists, and the craggy poet stepped up authoritatively to impose order. Although George Davis was the titular landlord, he was away daily at his office. Auden, however, was at home each day, functioning without benevolence as an inflexible proctor and house manager. He collected the rent, paid bills, devised menus, hired servants, and insisted that all meals be served on time and sat down to promptly. He who was not there at the stroke of the hour did not eat. If Auden announced to the guests that it was time for them to leave—be it morning, noon, or night—they left. On handwritten social invitations hosted by the entire group, he frequently added: "The carriage will depart sharply at 1:00 A.M." It did not matter what stage the festivities had reached by that hour, the party was abruptly halted, often to the disgruntlement of its other Middagh hosts, who spilled out into the night and adjourned to a neighborhood bar or invited their guests to come upstairs to their rooms for a smaller, more intimate affair.

Auden saw to it that each of the regular inhabitants shared equally in the expenses of food and service, whether he was there for meals or not. Rent varied slightly, depending upon the size of the quarters. Auden recalled that for his sitting room and bedroom on the top floor he was assessed twenty-five dollars a month. "I believe the others paid about the same. Two black servants were employed by the household: a general cook, Eva, who slept in the basement, and Susie, a daily. Their wages were fifteen and ten dollars, added Auden, who had no objection to sharing impersonal facts about life at 7 Middagh, but believed that personal details about an artist were his affair only. "Contrary to rumor, Carson had absolutely nothing to do with housekeeping—she simply lived there, as did the other paying guests," he said.[5]

Although Auden was obdurate in his house rules, the mechanics of meals and fiscal arrangements, the intellectual and artistic atmosphere of the menage crackled. Newly arrived exiles from Europe came to 7 Middagh to see what was going on in the United States. They found that the group breathed a European intellectual element full of Marx, Freud, Nietzsche, Jung, and Kierkegaard, and were doing the most exciting work in the arts to be found anywhere. When Denis de Rougemont, Swiss novelist and critic, visited the house early in 1941, he concluded that "all that was new in America in music, painting, or choreography emanated from that house, the only center of thought and art that I found in any large city of the country." There were other cells of culture in the United States at the time, but 7 Middagh Street was an extraordinary one. To De Rougemont, the exaggeration was unintentional. He described Carson as a "touchy sensitive adolescent" who lived in "an unlikely household—Kafka and the 'Enfants Terribles'—with an atmosphere that was definitely old New York":

> There was always a flurry of activity. Some of the residents were writing, some were composing, some were doing sculpturing, and the piano students were always practicing with their doors ajar. They all had their meals together around a very long table served by two or three enormous black women. Wystan Auden, the greatest English poet since Eliot, presided over the table with malicious dignity. At the other end George Davis, the editor of *Harper's Bazaar*, played a proprietary role. Benjamin Britten and Paul Bowles represented the new music, Gypsy Rose Lee, the dance and striptease, and all the others with one title or another were "creative people" who talked of Kierkegaard, Jung, the ballet, or pre-Columbian sculpture.[6]

Bowles, who then was composing music rather than writing, and his novelist-and-soon-to-be-playwright wife, Jane, were invited to bring their piano and join the group in the spring. According to Bowles,

> Our moving in was somewhat retarded by a disagreement Davis had with Gypsy Rose Lee, who was, and was not, going to stay there any more, back and forth, for some time. (She had used the place as a hideaway while she was writing *The G-String Murders*: now the book was completed, and eventually she moved out entirely, so that Jane and I were given her two rooms.)[7]

Bowles and his wife stayed at 7 Middagh Street for almost a year, where his presence attracted other musicians, composers, and patrons of the arts, such as Virgil Thomson, Aaron Copland, Leonard Bernstein, Marc Blitzstein, Lincoln Kirstein, Kurt Weill, and later, David Diamond. All dropped in frequently, and Blitzstein took up permanent residence for a few months.

Perhaps most exciting among the artists who came were surrealists Pavel Tschelitchev, Salvador Dali, and Dali's striking wife, the beautiful Gala, who became a celebrity in Europe as a model. Convinced by this time that they were the reincarnated Zeus and Hera, the *gods* entertained the menage with wild tales from their other life. Auden, like Carson, especially delighted in fairy tales, fantasy, and any level of reality that transcended common sense and natural law. They listened to the Dalis with rapt enthusiasm.

Indeed, the whole atmosphere of 7 Middagh became surrealistic.

Carson called it "campy." Auden played the role of a benign wizard who exorcised devils, but enjoyed them at the same time and loved their wizardry. Tschelitchev made his contribution one evening when he decided that the huge drawing room wall lacked character with its look of blankness and drab sterility. Gathering his paints and brushes around him, he decorated the wall with a great surrealistic mural, a splash of color and grotesque form that delighted the guests. Some of the tenants, however, were not sure that they wanted to live with it every day. Other painters were attracted, also, to the strange household. Eugene Berman and Oliver Smith, who were yet to gain the serious recognition that was soon their due as scenic designers and painters, came to see what was going on, and young Smith, whom Carson referred to as a "recluse," moved into the fourth-floor attic as soon as Davis could make that portion of the building habitable. The house was shabby, the floors were bare and rough, but no one seemed to notice—or if he did—to care. Davis renovated and furnished as time and money allowed, beginning with his own apartment, which he decorated in plush Victorian splendor.

Davis was a collector of all kinds of things, a man of "great talent for spotting valuable *objets d'art* amid a mess of junk," as Lotte Lenya, the woman he later married, described him. Always a gregarious host, he took pride in showing off his apartment to visitors, who knew well his reputation as a bluejay collector of curios and liked to see what new and weird acquisitions he had made. Davis especially loved American antiques, Edwardian pieces, Victorian porcelain hands holding roses, old-fashioned stationery scented and strewn with flowers, and lacy Valentines. In Canada on his honeymoon a few years later Davis was ecstatic over his discovery of a figurine camel whose humps moved.[8]

Like Carson, Davis was fascinated by freaks. He watched for them on the streets and in the bars and went miles out of his way to see a circus, which he attended primarily for the P. T. Barnum sideshows. Here his eyes searched out physical aberrations he had never seen before. He had another hobby, too. Over the years Davis accumulated an enormous photograph collection of freaks. Carson discovered his strong attraction for the sick and maimed when they first met over a glass of sherry at his visit to talk about *The Heart Is a Lonely Hunter*. Davis' interests were similar to Biff Brannon's, her character in *The Heart Is a Lonely Hunter*, who was attracted to John Singer because he was a deaf mute. Davis especially empathized with Brannon in this passage from the novel:

> He would offer to treat Singer to a slug of whiskey before he
> left. What he had said to Alice was true—he did like freaks. He had
> a special friendly feeling for sick people and cripples. Whenever
> somebody with a harelip or T.B. came into the place he would set
> him up to beer. Or if the customer were a hunchback or a bad cripple,

then it would be whiskey on the house. There was one fellow who had had his peter and his left leg blown off in a boiler explosion, and whenever he came to town there was a free pint waiting for him. And if Singer were a drinking kind of man he could get liquor at half price any time he wanted it.[9]

Carson and Davis sat together for hours poring over his picture album of strange creatures. She told him about the midway at the Chattahoochee Valley Fair back in Georgia, where she had spent more dimes on the freaks than all the other attractions combined, and Davis shared with her details of the great midways in Europe he had seen in the early 1930s, when he first began his study. Doubtless, Carson's fictional character evolving then—Frankie Addams in The Bride, who ambivalently was both attracted to and repelled by freaks—owed much of her genesis to Carson's long sessions with George Davis.

Carson and novelist Richard Wright also shared a special affinity. Wright had moved in with his wife, Ellen Poppell, a white German Jew, and their infant daughter Julie during the summer of 1941. Having a married couple with a child in residence was an exception to policy, but Davis had met Wright when, as fiction editor, he had selected one of Wright's earliest stories, "Almos' a Man," for publication in Harper's Bazaar a few months earlier. Then Wright's first novel, Native Son, had appeared, also in 1940, and propelled him into public notice and critical acclaim. The two men now were good friends.

Wright had reviewed The Heart Is a Lonely Hunter in New Republic before he ever met Carson. In it he applauded her "astonishing humanity that enables a white writer, for the first time in Southern fiction, to handle Negro characters with as much ease and justice as those of her own race."[10] Now it was not only her writing that attracted Wright to Carson, but also her "tortured soul, her zest for the ordinary moments of life," Wright said.[11] Frequently moody, Wright found his spirits invariably lifted when Carson greeted him, as she always did upon her return from long daily saunters down Sand Street and to the river, saying, "Isn't it wonderful to live in a real neighborhood and breathe fine salt air!"

The Wrights did not really consider themselves part of the Middagh menage. They took their meals separately in their own apartment, which spilled over from the parlor floor into the basement of the building. At first Wright was stimulated by his social and intellectual intercourse with Davis and others in the household. The only racial prejudice had come from a fellow black who brought in coal and stoked the furnace: "I'm not waitin' on no nigger," he said defiantly upon discovering Wright living in the house. But intolerance was not to be tolerated at 7 Middagh, and the black servant was given no second chance.

Wright's fellow artists always welcomed him into their rooms. He felt a sense of brotherhood with them, for they shared his social concerns, spoke out fearlessly on vital issues, and were not afraid to be involved. Wright also liked to talk with Oliver Smith, who stayed alone most of the time in his attic room. When Wright admired a large semicircular desk that Smith had inherited from his ancestral cousin Henry James, Smith reportedly told him, "Someday I'll give it to you."

As the tenants came and went, the atmosphere of 7 Middagh Street changed with them. Carson herself was forced to leave during the winter of 1940–41, having become seriously ill again. Marguerite Smith went up on the train from Columbus to nurse her daughter and then to take her home to recuperate. When Carson returned again to Brooklyn Heights, it was only for a weekend visit during the fall of 1942. At this time she came down from Yaddo, the artists' colony in Saratoga Springs, New York, where she had been in residence during much of 1941 and 1942. At Middagh Street in 1942, she was surprised to see so few people living there and the pace of the house markedly different. She wrote Newton Arvin upon her return to Yaddo that the atmosphere had completely changed. It was no longer campy, but sedate and respectable. She told Arvin that Richard Wright's family now had the first two floors, Oliver Smith, the tiny attic floor, and George Davis, the third floor. Except for Davis, all of the charter members of the establishment had left. Auden and Kallman had gone to the University of Michigan for a year; MacNeice had returned to England during the winter of 1940–41 to help his war-torn homeland in whatever manner he could, short of actual combat; Britten and Pears had also gone to England; and the other regular occupants had, in time, drifted elsewhere.

Davis' third-floor quarters consisted of two back rooms, a bath, a large hall which had been converted into a pantry-kitchen with an electric grill and refrigerator, and a beautifully decorated front room which Davis assured Carson he had been saving just for her. Many of his friends had asked if they could rent the room, but he had declined their generous offers because he wanted the room available for her on weekend visits or as a permanent home, whichever she wished. Deeply touched, Carson told Davis that if she decided to leave Yaddo that winter—as she was then considering—she would love to live at 7 Middagh Street again. The house was quiet now as it had never been before. She wrote Arvin that Davis never brought people home with him any more and that the Wrights hardly made a sound. She felt confident that if she should return now to Brooklyn Heights, she could write there in a way that had been impossible in the past. The room itself was conducive to creativity with its rich, velvet curtains at the windows, walls painted a deep blue green, a little separate alcove with a work table that, to Carson, would be just right for writing, and many pieces of heavy antique furniture that reminded her of home. To her, most thrilling of all was the handsome grand piano Davis had recently installed in the room.

On January 17, 1943, Carson left Yaddo, ill again. She went immediately to Brooklyn Heights and found solace in the warm, genial friendship of George Davis and the room he had reserved for her. According to Richard Wright, however, Carson was a disruptive personality in the house that winter. She seemed to be a compulsive talker, he complained. Moreover, he decided that she drank too much liquor and that he was tired of her monologues, which invariably centered on herself or her work. Wright told friends, also, that he feared for Carson's health—not so much for Carson's own sake, but that she might collapse at the feet of his young daughter and inflict some deep psychic wound on her. To Wright, who formerly had been fond of Carson, his friend from the South had changed considerably in less than a year. She appeared to be driving herself to destruction, he concluded, and he did not want his family around when it finally occurred. As soon as he was able, Wright moved out of 7 Middagh Street into a more private apartment elsewhere in Brooklyn.

It was at this time that Anaïs Nin, internationally noted diarist and novelist, visited 7 Middagh Street for the first time and described it in her diary:

> March, 1943—An amazing house, like some of the houses in Belgium, the north of France, or Austria. He [Davis] has filled it with old American furniture, oil lamps, brass beds, little coffee tables, old drapes, copper lamps, old cupboards, heavy dining tables of oak, lace doilies, grandfather clocks. It is like a museum of Americana which I had never seen anywhere before.[12]

George Davis had told Miss Nin that Carson wanted to meet her, but the spring afternoon that the 7 Middagh Street group sat in chairs under the trees in the back yard talking amiably to the diarist, Carson gave no indication that their guest was even present. "Our friendship did not develop at all," said Miss Nin, without regret.[13] Her diary entry that day continued:

> Carson came in . . . I saw a girl so tall and lanky I first thought it was a boy. Her hair was short, she wore a cyclist's cap, tennis shoes, pants. She came and pushed through the group like a bull with its head down, looking at no one, not saying a word. I was so put off by her muteness, and by her not even looking at me, that I did not even try to talk with her.[14]

Miss Nin, of course, was accustomed to being noticed, and when Carson failed to be impressed, the diarist would have no more to do with her. Carson, too, was accustomed to homage. According to Eleanor Clark, who saw Carson fairly often during the early 1940s but did not consider herself to be in Carson's "circle" of friends, "Favors and admiration alike were supposed to flow her way. . . . Carson had to be the whole show, and somehow there was not room for any other real artist around her." To be in Carson's "gang," Miss Clark found that one had to be "willing and able to sit around and admire, be in the position of an inferior or better yet, a worshipper."[15] When Carson walked out into the Middagh Street back yard that afternoon and found the handsome Miss Nin holding court with admirers surrounding her, there is little doubt what lay behind her aloofness. Many people over the years defended Carson's muteness and called it shyness or modest reserve, but those who knew her best have said that her jealousy and sense of rivalry with other writers—unless they worked almost exclusively in different genres, such as her friend Tennessee Williams—were well known to the literary world with whom she had intercourse. If her coterie did not revolve attentively enough around her, Carson's response often was chilling.

Miss Nin bestowed a new name upon the house in Brooklyn Heights during her visit. When she found out that Davis, Auden, and Carson all had been born under the sign of Pisces, she called their curious home "February House." Many persons have since referred to 7 Middagh Street by that name, but no one except the little group who lived there that spring was aware that it was Miss Nin's dubbing. Earlier residents were puzzled by the name when they heard it later. Golo Mann asked, "What was 'February House'? . . . The name of the place where I lived with Auden, Davis, Pears, and Britten was not February House."[16] Paul Bowles's response was similar:

> Where did you hear that the place was called February House? Who called it that, I wonder, and at what period? I ask because I am curious to know if anyone actually ever referred to it by that name during its existence, or if the name were invented after its demise.[17]

Although 7 Middagh Street lost much of its eccentric flavor during its last two years of existence, the demise of the fabulous old house came abruptly. Early in 1945, the entire street was condemned and all the houses razed to make room for a new and wider automobile approach to the Brooklyn Bridge. The charter members of the artists' establishment had already left it for good, and only Oliver Smith remained from among the first-year residents. Carson had settled permanently by this time into her own home in Nyack, New York; Gypsy Rose Lee was touring military establishments with USO shows; Wystan Auden, an emissary of the United States Air Force, had been sent to Europe to investigate the effect of strategic bombing on German morale; and George Davis had moved to Yorkville in Manhattan. Visitors who searched Brooklyn Heights later for the site of the famous "February House," or "House of Genius"—as writer Marguerite Young and others sometimes referred to it—found no trace, even, of the charming, old neighborhood.

When Carson had left 7 Middagh Street the first time—barely four months after becoming a part of the strange menage—she was on the verge of physical collapse and exhaustion. For much of the autumn of 1940 she was listless, pale, unable to sit her usual four or five hours at the typewriter without restless wanderings, compulsion for conversation, cravings for sweets, and her ever-present thermos of hot tea mixed with sherry. She told Janet Flanner that she had a habit of analyzing the ingredients of the various wines she drank. She had become such a connoisseur, she admitted, that she could roll a sip around on her tongue, narrow her eyes, concentrate, and then announce the "blend." A brand she called "Sonnie Boy," for example, she was sure was a combination of sorghum sugar, water, wood alcohol, and a dash of urine. Carson combined it with hot tea to cover the taste.[18]

During the winter of 1940–41 she became increasingly ill with a fierce cough, aching chest, and chronic fever. Carson resented her sickly childhood and having had precious time taken up by doctors and a variety of physical ministrations; yet she admitted, too, that she derived unmistakable pleasure from the attentions accompanying an illness. It was with similar feelings that she was persuaded to see a Manhattan doctor in early December. After X rays were taken, she learned that she had become what the doctor called "slightly tubercular." The malady was in her joints, he told her. He also said that she apparently had been suffering from dormant grippe for over ten years. She must go to bed and take better care of herself if she did not want to become an invalid permanently, he admonished her.

Upon the first inkling that Carson might again be seriously ill, Marguerite Smith hurried to New York and her daughter's bedside. She had worried about Carson's frail constitution since her daughter had first ventured North alone in 1934. She urged Carson now to return South with her for the two or three winter months that lay ahead so that she might recuperate in a milder climate. At least in Columbus she would not have to contend with blizzards, piercing winds, and hazards of sleet and ice. Seldom in South Georgia did temperatures stay long below freezing. Snowflakes usually turned to rain or melted on contact with pavement or grass, and winters were brief.

Marguerite knew how much her daughter hated even the *thought* of leaving New York again so soon. Carson had been back only six months this time, and she dreaded leaving George Davis, Gypsy Rose Lee, and other fellow Middaghers and friends with whom she had become close. Marguerite, too, was impressed by the illustrious residents and visitors at the house. She was thrilled that her daughter could live with other stimulating and talented people. Yet that was as it should be, she reasoned, for genius attracted genius. As Marguerite saw it, the Middagh menage was simply an extension of what Carson had already become accustomed to in her own home on Starke Avenue. To her, Carson's genius had been intensified by the artistic and cerebral fervor of the Smith household.

Whenever Marguerite could divert the other Middagh artists from their creative energies, she chatted with them briefly about their projects, then turned the conversation back to her own gifted child. Only a mother could sing such paeans of ardor about Carson amid a household brimming with brilliance. Typical, too, were Marguerite's conversations with strangers she met on buses and in restaurants and stores. On one occasion several years later, Marguerite was riding a bus from Nyack down to New York City. Seated next to her was an elegantly dressed, sophisticated-looking woman with whom Marguerite soon launched a vigorous conversation about her favorite subject—Carson. She talked on and on about her remarkable daughter until finally the woman volunteered: "I'm very much interested in this famous author. You see, my father, too, was a writer."

"Oh, I didn't get your name," Marguerite ventured.

"I am Countess Tolstoy" was the demure reply.

Carson's reaction to her mother's presence in New York City that winter was an ambivalent one. To her, Marguerite was an intruder, a threat to her new life style, for she had come to nurse her daughter and to take her home; yet Marguerite herself was also a refuge, a loving guardian who promised solace. Her mother had talked with Reeves upon her arrival, and he too felt that Carson would be much better off at home in Georgia than in the house in Brooklyn Heights. Although Marguerite sympathized with Reeves, she knew that if her children had separated, it must have been for good cause. To her, of course, it was Reeves's fault. Marguerite would never have questioned the rightness of Carson's act, but she would not allow the separation to keep her from looking upon Reeves as an errant son who was still worthy of a mother's love. Among Carson's housemates, Marguerite especially loved George Davis. She appreciated what seemed to be his brotherly concern for her daughter, as though he were looking after a defenseless sibling in an alien land. Davis also generously showered Marguerite with gentlemanly gestures which further endeared him to her.

Carson's mother nursed her at 7 Middagh Street as best she could, administering medicines and bringing nourishing soups, fruits, and Carson's hot tea concoction to her bedside throughout the day. "Here, precious, a little toddy for the body," Marguerite sang out as she brought in the sherry tea. Marguerite's cliché became Carson's, also, a phrase both women used for many years.

The doctor, too, advised Carson to recuperate in a more temperate climate. Even though she would have found staying indoors all winter almost impossible—her compulsion was strong to tramp long distances daily, no matter what the weather was—Carson might have done so. Yet had she remained in the North, her health would have suffered. The big rooms with their high ceilings at 7 Middagh Street were drafty and difficult to keep warm, and the gurgling, noisy radiators gave off either too much heat or none at all. Even Marguerite recognized that Carson needed sunshine and a less hectic pace than that afforded by the confusing household in Brooklyn Heights.

Another source of Carson's anguish that winter which contributed to her own poor physical condition was her anxiety over Annemarie Clarac-Schwarzenbach. Now desperately ill herself, Annemarie had been hospitalized since late November in the psychiatric wing of a Connecticut hospital. She had succumbed again that fall to a heavy dependence on drugs. Since leaving her husband in 1937, Annemarie had fought her addiction to drugs and voluntarily placed herself repeatedly in various clinics. Yet at the same time she was defeated by the very people from whom she sought help. According to her sister, "Nurses, doctors—everyone—fell in love with her and became her willing tools." Annemarie, whose personality and emotional pattern was schizophrenic and manic-depressive, tried that winter to kill herself by slashing her wrists. She had come close to succeeding, and now she was under maximum security and unable to have visitors. Friends attributed her death wish and suicide attempt to a variety of factors: drugs, deep despair over the unsatisfactory relationship with her baroness friend from Nantucket Island, and guilt feelings expressed over not going home to Switzerland earlier that month for her father's funeral.

Although Carson wrote often to Annemarie in the hospital, she never knew whether her friend was given the letters to read. She believed, however, that Annemarie was in good hands and was being well cared for medically. Surely she would get well, Carson prayed. Only now did she consent to go home with her mother. Carson reasoned, too, that if she went South temporarily, she could concentrate on shoring up the fragments of her own life, which she admitted was in bad shape.

At last strong enough to travel, she boarded the Seaboard Seminole with her mother a few days before Christmas, her first trip in a Pullman. Lamar Smith, Sr., was at the station in his little Whippet coupé to take his sojourners home. Awaiting them, too, were Carson's sister, whom Marguerite called "Little Pretty," who was home for the holidays as a

French major at the University of Miami (where she had transferred in the fall after a summer at Auburn), and Brother-Man, Lamar, Jr., who had dropped out of school at Georgia Tech and worked locally in a furniture store. Little Pretty and Brother-Man stood now in awe of their frail sibling, from whom their lives seemed far removed. It was hard for them to understand how Sister had achieved success and fame almost overnight in New York City and had lost a husband in the process. They envied what they saw as a glamorous life in the magical Bagdad of America. To their sister, however, life was anything but exciting at this point. It was a sad, dejected young author who stepped heavily off the train that cold, gray afternoon in her native Southland.

Still, in spite of her illness, Carson continued to write. V*ogue* had published a timely, nonfiction article, "Look Homeward, Americans," in its December 1940 issue, her first short piece to be published since "Wunderkind" had appeared exactly four years earlier. With *Reflections in a Golden Eye* now being talked about after its serialization in the October and November issues of *Harper's Bazaar*, Carson was presently being sought after by several magazine editors for other short fiction or essays. Publishers also began to send Carson books to review. The only request she responded to during the early 1940s, however, was a book she reviewed negatively for *Saturday Review* (March 15, 1941), Howard Coxe's *Commend the Devil*.

In "Look Homeward, Americans," Carson wrote in a warm, personal tone about her friend Lester, a young man she had known in North Carolina. Lester's passion for travel, his yearning to know the world, was but a lever for Carson's acknowledgment of her own polarities:

> We are torn between a nostalgia for the familiar and an urge for the foreign and strange. As often as not, we are homesick most for the places we have never known.
>
> All men are lonely. But sometimes it seems to me that we Americans are the loneliest of all. Our hunger for foreign places and new ways has been with us almost like a national disease. Our literature is stamped with a quality of longing and unrest, and our writers have been great wanderers.[19]

Lester realized, too, that war changed one's outlook. "Look at what happened to the places I meant to go," he said. "There is certainly one thing about this war. It leaves you no place to be homesick for." Carson's conclusion was a clarion call:

> So we must turn inward. This singular emotion, the nostalgia that has been so much a part of our national character, must be converted to good use. . . . We must make a new declaration of in-

dependence, a spiritual rather than a political one this time. . . . We must now be homesick for our own familiar land, this land that is worthy of our nostalgia.[20]

Carson's acute social consciousness, her deep feelings for the oppressed of any nation or ethnic group, her conviction that the United States should no longer put off aid to its European allies, her sensitivity to exiled friends with whom she shared such kinship—all made her poignantly aware of the responsibilities for which she held herself accountable as a writer.

The January 1941 issue of Vogue carried still another nostalgic piece, this one the brief "Night Watch Over Freedom." Written in a conversational tone as though she were the celebrant on the eve of the new year, Carson spoke to the free people of the world. She urged them to listen to the tolling of Big Ben bidding farewell to the old and welcoming the new, sounding "the heartbeat of warring Britain—somber, resonant, and deeply sure":

> Nor will the echoes stop there. The time will not actually be midnight everywhere. But the twelve slow strokes will for a moment seem to effect a synthesis of time throughout the world. In the defeated lands Big Ben will bring hope and, to the souls of many, a fevered quiver of rebellion. . . . Yes, Big Ben will ring again this New Year, and over all the earth there will be listeners.[21]

The March (1941) issue of Vogue carried yet a third nonfiction article by its distinguished young author. Written at 7 Middagh Street back in November 1940, Carson had submitted "Brooklyn Is My Neighborhood" to Vogue soon after her return South. In it she described some of the curious and likable people who lived about her in Brooklyn Heights, such as the Duchess and Submarine Mary, the dowagers of the doxies, who regally plied their knitting needles in the brawling bars while awaiting the attentions of their favorite sailors who roamed Sand Street. Submarine Mary's smile was always bright, perforce, because every tooth in her head was of gleaming gold. And then there was the hunchback, the pet of a nearby bar who was freely wined and beered.

Carson also told of the corner druggist, Mr. Parker, whose desperate voice could be heard nights from behind the counter as he grimly worked at his daughter's arithmetic: ". . . the square of the hypotenuse of a right triangle is equal to—." Likening the druggist to a cat, she continued:

> And when I weigh myself, he sidles up quietly beside me and peers over my shoulder as I adjust the scale. When the weights are balanced, he always gives me a quick little glance, but he has never made any comment, nor indicated in any way whether he thought I

weighed too little or too much. . . . On every other subject, Mr. Parker is very talkative.[22]

Carson said in her essay that she had furnished her rooms at 7 Middagh from another favorite haunt, Miss Kate's junk and antique shop on Fulton Street. Here she usually found the proprietress "hovering over a little coal stove in the back room." Miss Kate, the bearer of "one of the handsomest and dirtiest faces" Carson ever beheld, told her young customer that she slept every night wrapped in a Persian rug on a green velvet Victorian couch; nor had Carson any reason to doubt her. When she visited Miss Kate's competitor across the street, she was told that "Miss Kate is a good woman, but she dislikes washing herself. So she only bathes once a year, when it is summer. I expect she's just about the dirtiest woman in Brooklyn." To Carson, the comment was not a malicious one; rather, it had a "quality of wondering pride." Such acceptance of uniqueness was one of the things she loved best about Brooklyn. "Everyone is not expected to be exactly like everyone else," she concluded.[23]

But in Columbus, Georgia, Carson's singularity was not at all appreciated. She had learned to live with her own uniqueness, to embrace it, and to find purpose and meaning in a life of nonconformity. On the other hand, her literary critics and southern neighbors judged her now by her second book, which had been brought out in mid-February by Houghton Mifflin. The reviewers had not responded to *Reflections in a Golden Eye* when it was serialized in magazine form, but they pounced upon Carson now with both feet. Some chastised her for her "obsessive preoccupation with abnormality." Others felt that all the characters were "too preposterous" and suggested the author take a reading course in Twain and Chekhov. Another attacked her as an artist who had much to learn about reality, concluding that "if this is a fair sample of army life, and if the country is soon to pour itself into the army, then God save the Union!"[24] Yet even those who believed that the book fell short of the promise expected of the young author of *The Heart Is a Lonely Hunter* agreed that *Reflections in a Golden Eye* was a beautifully sculpted, chilling *tour de force*.

Home in Columbus, Carson was not disturbed by critics. She had written the book as she felt she must. To her, *Reflections in a Golden Eye* was a funny story, written in the manner of the Russian realists, whose works were rich in tightly controlled tragicomedy.[25] *Reflections in a Golden Eye* was her fairy tale, she maintained; people could take it or leave it. An anonymous telephone call at home a few weeks after the appearance of *Reflections in a Golden Eye* upset her family far more than it did Carson. An alleged Ku Klux Klansman called to say that he and his friends were going to get her that night. She had been a "nigger lover" in her first book, he said, and now she had proven herself "a queer," as well. Carson's indignant father waited all night on the front porch of their Starke Avenue home to greet the Klansmen with a loaded shotgun and was disappointed when no one attempted to carry out the threat.

Far more distressing to Carson than such unneighborliness, however, was news from New York City that Annemarie Clarac-Schwarzenbach had fled without permission from the psychiatric hospital and spent a harrowing night alone in the Connecticut woods. Cold and penniless, she convinced a taxi driver the next morning to drive her to Manhattan, where she would find friends who would pay him, she promised. The raw exposure to the New England winter made Annemarie physically ill, as well, and she was immediately put to bed by two of Carson's friends with whom she found temporary refuge. Carson, in Columbus, was notified immediately of Annemarie's dilemma, and although still ill herself she caught the next train to New York City to be with her friend and to help nurse her back to health. Word leaked out, however, regarding Annemarie's hiding place, and one day while Carson was away from the room, a doctor and policeman came for Annemarie with new commitment papers. Forced to accompany them to Bellevue, Annemarie was placed in a general ward with other patients afflicted with a variety of acute mental illnesses. What followed, Carson told friends, was too awful to think about. Annemarie was finally transferred to a hospital in White Plains, but once there she was unable to write or call anyone in New York. Certain that Annemarie received none of her mail, Carson brooded over her inability to communicate with her. Unable to help further, and ill herself, Carson returned home to Georgia. The only word she received later from her Manhattan friends was that Annemarie was "quiet."

Carson was optimistic, however, that Annemarie eventually would get well. "I know it," she declared defiantly over and over again to her mother, and in letters to Robert Linscott and others who knew how much Annemarie meant to her.[26] Carson's childlike faith in the face of adversity, her fighting spirit, her clinging to some thread of hope against predictable odds—all were exemplified again and again throughout her life. She was much like Mick, her youthful protagonist in *The Heart Is a Lonely Hunter*, in whom she had sown germinal seeds of hope at the novel's close[27]:

> But maybe it would be true about the piano and turn out O.K. Maybe she would get a chance soon. Else what the hell good had it all been—the way she felt about music and the plans she had made in the inside room? It had to be some good if anything made sense. And it was too and it was too and it was too and it was too. It was some good.
> All right!

O.K.!
Some good.

Mick felt somehow cheated because things had not gone as she had expected. She argued with herself about the truth of the human condition, but wanted to believe that everything that had happened to her had unique meaning and would somehow serve a useful purpose.

Carson was mercurial, just as young Mick Kelley was. In a letter to Robert Linscott she told of her acute melancholia because of Annemarie's illness and her inability to help. Then, in almost the same breath, she began an exultant paean about her own work. She told Linscott that she was insanely happy for she was working hard on a strange new tale that was better than anything else she had ever done. She was also deriving more pleasure from her writing than she had previously. She had even put aside *The Bride of My Brother*—as she referred to it now—and resolved not to go back to it for another half year, or until the new story was ready.

For Carson, once an illumination came and she had focused clearly on her subject, there were few variables. She needed only the time and good health to follow through. She felt secure in her writing now for she knew very well what the story was about. It was another tale of thwarted love—one which involved this time a trio of lovers and beloveds—and again, there was no real reciprocity. It was a story that she, in her own way, had lived. In her actual relationships with people, particularly with those she loved, she felt insecure. In the confusion characterized by life at 7 Middagh Street that fall and winter, unhappy and fragmented in her emotionally entangled relationship with Annemarie, Carson wrote very poorly. Passion was necessary, as was tension, but she needed it in more moderate amounts. Carson told David Diamond the following summer that she had nearly killed herself in her involvement with Annemarie during what she considered her slothful year of 1940–41. Carson's genius and psychological makeup required large feedings, for her appetite was insatiable, but she could survive healthily only if she felt psychically attuned to her love object and had a sense of well-being and security. With Reeves, there had been too much tension; passion had dissipated, replaced by ennui, disillusionment, and at times, even disgust.

Carson revealed still another facet of her personality and chameleon-like moods in the same letter to Robert Linscott in which she had spoken dejectedly of Annemarie and then, exuberantly, about her writing. She described a mild, wintry Sunday morning in Columbus and her appreciation of what she often called her "Sunday morning wine." She said that she had arisen at six o'clock, as was her custom, eaten fish roe for breakfast, and listened to the Beethoven C Sharp Minor Quartet. The day had dawned gray and cool, and the first camellias were in bloom, their pink,

silky blossoms cheerful and comforting as she viewed them from her bedroom windows. Then she sat about the house for a while and puttered
until she began to drink a little of her special wine. She said that it was
unique in that it seemed richer in color than the wine she usually drank,
and that it also warmed her insides in a special way, which she likened
to the radiant warmth that stained glass windows of a church give off to
worshipers within. Carson's paragraph in Linscott's letter was unmistakably the germination of a passage that appeared later in the novel she had
just begun. In *The Ballad of the Sad Café* Carson described Miss Amelia's home-brewed liquor as so "smooth" that it livened up one's "gizzard":

> For the liquor of Miss Amelia has a special quality of its own. It is
> clean and sharp on the tongue, but once down a man it glows inside
> him for a long time afterward. And that is not all. It is known that
> if a message is written with lemon juice on a clean sheet of paper
> there will be no sign of it. But if the paper is held for a moment to the
> fire then the letters turn brown and the meaning becomes clear.
> Imagine that the whiskey is the fire and that the message is that which
> is known only in the soul of a man—then the worth of Miss Amelia's
> liquor can be understood.[28]

With wine like Miss Amelia's liquor inside Carson that Sunday
morning, her writing flowed. She told Linscott that her new book was an
odd work, true, but also fantastic and passionate.

Carson continued to write well until the work was interrupted by a
new and frightening illness. In February 1941, her vision was suddenly impaired, and she was overcome by stabbing pains in the temples and blind-
ing headaches. Terrified that she might be going blind, she feared that
she might never again be able to write. She was afraid that her brain, too,
had been affected. For several days doctors were unable to assure her of a
complete recovery, nor could they even be sure of her malady. Years later,
specialists concluded that the attack that winter when she was barely
twenty-four had been her first cerebral stroke. For days Carson could not
see to read or even to make out the numbers on the face of a clock.
Gradually her sight returned, but her over-all convalescence was slow. Although there was not the paralysis that accompanied her later strokes,
she was too weak to move from her bed to the living-room sofa for over
a month.

Marguerite had notified Reeves of his wife's illness when she was first
stricken and he wanted to come immediately, but Marguerite insisted that
he wait until Carson was better. By late March she at last was ambulatory,
and again, Reeves pressed to be allowed to come to Columbus to see her.
He hoped that she had regained enough strength to be able to return to
New York with him in a few days. The weather had begun to turn mild
again in the North, and he counted on her wanting to go back. Anxious

to be reconciled with his wife, lonely and tired of their separate exist-
ences, he assured both Carson and her mother that he loved her dearly
and would always take kind and gentle care of her. Reeves told them,
too, that he had changed jobs and was selling insurance now, and rather
successfully, he added. He promised to work hard to support the two of
them so that she could continue to devote all her time to writing or any
other pursuit she might choose.

Memory does strange things to people, and the passage of time since
their initial separation over a half year earlier had been kind to them both.
Carson realized that she needed Reeves, perhaps as much, even, as he
needed her. She was ready to return North, and she knew that she would
always need someone close at hand to provide affection and the necessary
creature comforts. She would never cook or housekeep again in any conventional way; this Reeves realized, but it did not matter. He had already
demonstrated his skills in both areas and now accepted unquestioningly
his role in her life.

Another problem that had bothered Carson earlier, too, seemed
solved. Reeves had a habit of pocketing bits of money which he found
lying about the apartment, money that Carson considered solely hers. She
had not been disturbed, however, until she could not find a fairly large
sum that had disappeared mysteriously, nor did Reeves acknowledge any
part in its absence. Now, months later, Reeves told her that the money
had shown up among some of her old letters which she had left behind
in their Village apartment. Reeves sent the money to her that spring
while she was recuperating in Columbus. With it, Carson concluded
that still another disturbance had been resolved, and the less said about
it, the better.

Willing to make amends, to attempt again some kind of meaningful
life together, Carson and Reeves returned North in April 1941 to their
old West Eleventh Street apartment that Reeves had continued to occupy.
The young couple's return this time bore little resemblance to their last
entry into New York City. Feelings now were muted. They had both
matured considerably, and this time there were no pictures in bookstore
windows of the impressionable young author of *The Heart Is a Lonely
Hunter* to greet them. Although Carson's future was uncertain in view
of the relatively poor reception by critics of *Reflection in a Golden Eye*,
her self-esteem in her own intrinsic worth as an artist was still undaunted.
She knew she could write, and she would. They had each other, and they
had friends who believed in them. Life might be sweet in New York City
again after all.

Chapter Six

NEW YORK CITY AND YADDO, 1941

C*arson could not have endured another summer in Georgia.* From past experience she knew that from the middle of May until September, the days in Columbus—to her, at least—were like scorched nightmares, depressing and feverish. Also, in spite of her acquiescence in returning North with Reeves, she did not anticipate spending another summer in the heat of New York City, either. In New York, she felt as though she had been flayed alive. One avenue of escape about which she had recently heard was a working retreat for gifted writers, composers, and artists: Yaddo, an artists' colony founded in 1900 in the beautifully wooded hill country just outside Saratoga Springs, New York.

Before leaving the South, she had been recommended to Yaddo (pronounced to rhyme with *shadow*) by Marjorie Peabody Waite, the adopted daughter of George Foster Peabody, a distinguished philanthropist from Carson's hometown. Peabody had established Yaddo with his wife, Katrina Nichols Trask, a wealthy turn-of-the-century *grande dame,* on the five-hundred-acre estate of the old Trask family. Carson had met Mrs. Waite while recuperating at home from her stroke, and Mrs. Waite had become extremely fond of her and recommended her to Yaddo's executive director, Elizabeth Ames: "Please meet this shy, sweet girl from Columbus who wants so badly to work at Yaddo, but who wouldn't dream of asking anyone to let her come."

Mrs. Ames was Marjorie Waite's widowed sister, who had served as the colony's director since its inception. Soon after Carson had settled again with Reeves in their walk-up Village apartment, she began to correspond with Mrs. Ames, who proposed a meeting with Carson the next time she was in the city. In the meantime, fearful that the opportunity to work at Yaddo might not materialize, Carson said nothing to Reeves about the possibility of another imminent separation.

In early May when the appointed date arrived, it was all Carson could do to arrive bodily at Mrs. Ames's hotel. Seized by an almost hysterical paralysis of the vocal cords, she could barely whisper. Mrs. Ames waited in her room for her young visitor, but some thirty minutes later Carson had still failed to appear and Mrs. Ames ventured downstairs in search of her. Unable to accept the possibility that she might simply have forgotten the appointment, Mrs. Ames asked at the desk and then looked about the lobby. Even though the great hall was crowded and Mrs. Ames had not seen so much as a photograph of the young author, she immediately spotted her. There in a corner, with head bowed almost to her lap, alone and looking pitiably withdrawn, sat Carson. Mrs. Ames approached the forlorn-looking girl and addressed her gently, "You *are* Carson McCullers, aren't you?"

The answer was almost inaudible: "Oh, please forgive me, Mrs. Ames. I have been so frightened at meeting you that I have lost my voice." The interview, however, once embarked upon, was a success. Carson was able to relax within the confines of Mrs. Ames's room, warm to her motherly hospitality, and gradually regain her voice. Two hours later, the two women embraced and parted as old friends. Although Carson would have to be voted upon by the Yaddo Board of Directors for her official invitation, she was assured by Mrs. Ames that she would be able to come to Yaddo for whatever portion of the summer she wished.

Usually, two groups of twenty artists each were invited to Yaddo every summer, with one aggregation coming in mid-June and staying a month, the second in July after the first group vacated. Carson was told that she could come in June for the entire summer, a privilege afforded to only a few, depending upon the nature and scope of the creative project. Carson told Mrs. Ames about the two novels she had in progress: her new fairy tale, *The Ballad of the Sad Café*, which she hoped to complete by midsummer, and the much belabored *The Bride of My Brother*, which she knew was still several years from completion.

Carson had always thrived in anticipation of a grand event—even something as simple as a birthday or Christmas—and now Yaddo loomed large upon her horizon as an emotional Shangri-la and literary Mecca. Disappointed by her inability to remain the winter of 1940–41 as part of the original Davis-Auden menage in Brooklyn Heights, having to leave 7 Middagh Street dissipated and ill, Carson was certain that life at Yaddo would be productive. The young writer knew well how much she needed the discipline Mrs. Ames had insisted she would find at the artists' colony. There, the working guests were assured of absolute privacy from daylight until 4:00 P.M. They were not allowed to visit each other's studios except by invitation, and then only in the late afternoons and evenings when their private lives were accountable to no one. One either worked and lived by the rules at Yaddo or got out. The matriarchal Mrs. Ames made it clear to Carson that she reigned over her subjects with a gentle, but firm hand and would put up with no foolishness.

Financially, Yaddo would be a boon for Carson. To be a working guest meant that she would have her room and board free, no living expenses or household duties—simply the obligation to be on time for meals—and would have to provide only her transportation to and from Saratoga Springs. Carson had always been fascinated by the opportunity of going anywhere she had not been before, and now she enormously anticipated seeing upstate New York for the first time. Except for her two weeks at Bread Loaf and the ensuing weekend in Boston with Robert Linscott in 1940, Carson had not been north of the New York City area. When she returned that evening to the apartment to tell Reeves of her acceptance, she was in a state of near euphoria. She was sure that Reeves would understand her need to go away again. It was her way of life, her whole existence—with him or apart, she had to write.

Carson was jubilant the next few weeks in anticipation of Yaddo and a summer of dedicated work. At first Reeves took the news of her departure in stride. He was better adjusted to their present mode of life than he had been in a long time. He was selling insurance now, although not so successfully as he had a few months earlier, and he had made several new friends in the city apart from Carson. More important, he had gained anew some sense of self-identity. He was Reeves McCullers, whose wife was a writer. She, too, was working again with renewed energy, spending five or six hours at the typewriter each day. In the late afternoon she left her manuscript and relaxed with a drink, then ambled over to the Hudson River to watch the ships or down to Washington Square to observe people in her Village neighborhood. Frequently she arranged to meet someone for drinks or rode the subway to 7 Middagh Street for cocktail parties and dinners at the invitation of George Davis or Gypsy Rose Lee—who stayed with Davis off and on after Carson left—and then spent the night. Weak from her stroke of last winter and perpetual bouts with respiratory infections, Carson still suffered from a great hacking cough which she treated with large doses of cough syrup, laced heavily with codeine to "quiet it," she told a friend who was concerned by her near addiction to the cough syrup.

Carson nursed sherry through most of the day while she worked, for she needed a certain amount of alcohol in her system to function creatively. At twilight she shifted to bourbon on the rocks and listened on her phonograph to Mozart, Beethoven, Schubert, and Mahler. To Carson, such moments as these—drinking and reveling in her favorite composers—were precious, and achingly, she missed having a piano of her own. She knew that one of the things she loved best about life in Columbus was being able to play the piano whenever she felt like it. In New York she went weeks sometimes without getting near a piano. Yet every chance she got she visited someone's apartment in which there was a piano. If she were not invited immediately to play, after several drinks she sat down unbidden and began.

Her repertoire always included her favorite sacred piece, Bach's "Jesu, Joy of Man's Desiring," some of the Bach preludes and fugues—for Bach was her favorite composer—and also the Chopin nocturnes and snatches of Scarlatti.

As people met Carson and got to know her well that spring, they responded to her either with admiration and infatuation or extreme dislike. Those who allowed themselves an intimate relationship liked her in spite of her foibles. Many loved Carson immensely, yet to a number of acquaintances, she seemed a bitch. They found her vain, tiresome, shallow, and unreasonably argumentative. Some thought her sentimental, even though they usually agreed that she managed to keep sentimentality out of her fiction. There were a few who knew her casually—but never allowed or encouraged a relationship to develop—who did not like her. Lincoln Kirstein, writer, publisher, and promoter of the American ballet, knew Carson rather well when she lived in Brooklyn Heights and saw her occasionally afterward. His succinct comment about her was simply: "I did not like her—you see, I knew her." Another artist who became highly agitated in Carson's presence was Gore Vidal, who, like Carson, was full of his own sense of worth. Although Vidal admitted that he knew Carson "only slightly," he found her "vain, querulous, and a genius— alas, her presence in a room meant my absence: five minutes of one of her self-loving arias and I was gone."[1]

Like a child, Carson craved attention, totally lacked reserve, and was disarmingly honest—frequently to the chagrin of her host or companions. But those who knew her well understood that she was the natural product of a home situation in which she had been the constant and much loved recipient of a mother's extravagant praise. Narcissism had readily flowered under cultivation wrought by such bountiful showerings, aided substantially by Reeves's conviction of her great intrinsic worth as an artist—a fact which he voiced generously to others. Carson was also greatly affected by the adulation heaped upon her by an adoring reading public and literary coterie who had responded similarly to the two early novels that had propelled a twenty-three-year-old girl to renown amid cries of *wunderkind*.

Carson's evolvement had been cyclic: her sense of differentness having been curried by her mother since infancy, she was made to believe that she was *in fact* a genius. A favorite child, she was, in turn, rebuffed by peers and resented by neighbors and relatives who felt that Carson's brother and sister were receiving "short shrift." As an adolescent, she violated many of the norms imposed upon her by her contemporaries who rejected her; then, successively, she further rejected peers and traditional values and retreated into an even deeper awareness of her uniqueness. As her shyness, awkwardness, and sensitivity to her 5-foot-8½-inch, gangly frame intensified, she was driven still further from the crowd and into a haven of private worlds—of books, music, fantasy, and writing. Yet Carson yearned to share her "inner room," as she called it, to find someone with whom she could commune and bare her soul.

In New York City during the spring of 1941, Carson joined again the literary group that centered around Klaus Mann and his avant-garde magazine, *Decision*. Her closest friends now included Muriel Rukeyser, who had become Mann's chief assistant, and Henry Varnum Poor. Poor had painted an oil portrait of Carson in 1940, soon after the publication of *The Heart Is a Lonely Hunter*. He was one of her oldest friends in New York; he had known her since 1935 when she first arrived in New York City at the age of seventeen. Reeves, too, was fond of Muriel Rukeyser and Henry Varnum Poor. He felt that they were his friends, as well as his wife's. Through Klaus Mann and Miss Rukeyser, Carson also became acquainted with members of the magazine's editorial board. The list of *Decision*'s advisers was an impressive one to Carson, who found that most of New York City's vigorous intellects and current writers either were on the board or were contributors to the magazine. Several board members, like Mann, were European exiles. Assisting Mann that spring, in addition to Muriel Rukeyser, were associate editors Christopher Lazare and Alan Hartman, his father, Thomas Mann, his good friend Wystan Auden, Sherwood Anderson, Stephen Vincent Benét, Julian Green, Horace Gregory, Frank Kingdon, Freda Kirchway, Somerset Maugham, Robert Nathan, Pierre van Passen, Vincent Sheean, and Robert Sherwood. Soon Carson's intellectual and social life revolved around these people, along with Janet Flanner, short-story writer Rebecca Pitts, *Mademoiselle* feature writer and columnist Leo Lerman, and a handful of others. British writer James Stern and his talented wife, Tania, who frequently gave what became known among the literary set as "fabulous parties," were good friends of this group, too. Carson and Reeves were invited out often, but her preference —either with, or without her husband—was small, informal affairs in private homes of friends where she could relax over drinks, dinner, and good music.

Ever since her return North with Reeves this time, Carson had been alert for someone to fill the psychic void experienced after her separation from Annemarie Clarac-Schwarzenbach, who returned to Europe in February while Carson was still ill in Georgia. Annemarie had recuperated from her physical and mental disorders enough to convince her doctors that she could travel home to Switzerland if she were accompanied by a nurse. Just before departure for Lisbon by ship, Annemarie wrote Carson that to be chaperoned home and handed over to her family was the only way she could get out of "that hell of a hospital." Relieved to hear of Annemarie's new freedom yet distressed by an overpowering sense of loss,

Carson tried to compensate. She found that she was sipping sherry less and less and bourbon more and more. She craved companionship, sometimes prowled the bars alone, and began staying away from the apartment overnight and for longer and longer periods with no accounting to Reeves of her time or with whom she spent it. Her husband's response alternated between righteous indignation and studied indifference. Bitterly unhappy, Reeves sought release by drinking more hard liquor than ever before, making no secret of his assignations with other women, and accepting once again the fact that he was an abandoned and unloved spouse.

One night in May 1941, Carson and Reeves were at a party at Muriel Rukeyser's apartment, an affair that proved momentous to them both, for at Miss Rukeyser's she met her new love—this time, a man. David Diamond was a young composer and violinist from Rochester, New York, who at twenty-five had already won Guggenheim and Juilliard prize honors. He had studied in Paris for two years and had been at Yaddo, the artists' colony in Saratoga Springs, the preceding fall and winter, having just returned to New York City in the spring. When Diamond heard of Carson's interest in Yaddo, he told her how exciting and stimulating it would be for her to live and work there with artists of all genres. It would be quite different from her Bread Loaf stay the summer before, he pointed out, since Bread Loaf was a conference only for writers. That evening Diamond entertained Carson with a variety of tales of Yaddo life. He felt she would enjoy, especially, the Sunday night gatherings in the great library of Yaddo's "Mansion," where guests shared with others their various current creative endeavors and listened to records or live music. Even better, said Diamond, was the informal camaraderie over a bottle when they got together in intimate groups after the day's work.

Diamond had impressed his audience at the artists' colony when he conducted his own recently composed Concerto for Small Orchestra, which had been featured at the Yaddo Arts Festival in September 1940, and now Carson, too, was much taken by him. She had already heard about the young conductor-composer from Benjamin Britten and other musicians who had lived or visited at 7 Middagh Street, and she listened to Diamond now with rapt enthusiasm, immensely pleased, too, by his gentleness, senitivity, and unabashed delight in her.

He told Carson that evening about another great artist he admired who had come to Yaddo for the first time during the summer of 1940 and was now thought of as the "queen" of the colony—Katherine Anne Porter. Carson, too, had met Miss Porter the preceding summer when she was at Bread Loaf as a visiting artist one weekend. They had seen each other only briefly, but Carson had become completely enamored of her,

1 Portrait of
Carson McCullers
by Emanuel Romano,
New York City, 1949.

2 Portrait of drawing of
Carson McCullers by
Marcel Vertès
(1895–1961);
date of sitting unknown.

3 ABOVE: Lula Carson Smith,
with her mother,
Marguerite Waters Smith,
and her brother, Lamar, Jr.

4 LEFT: Lamar Smith
(Carson's father) at seventeen,
Tuskegee, Alabama, just before he
moved to Columbus, Georgia, to seek
his fortune.

5 The home of the
Smith family from
1926–44,
1519 Starke Avenue,
Columbus, Georgia.

6 Lula Carson at
age eight on a
neighbor's pony.

7 ABOVE: Lula Carson, eight, at the birthday party of a classmate and neighbor, Ella Kirven, October 9, 1925. Left to right: Eula Wade, Lula Carson, Margaret Schomburg, Ella Kirven, Mildred Edge, Caroline Callaway, Carrie Dudley.

8 ABOVE LEFT: Riding Daniel Deronda, owned by her friend Helen H. Jackson, was a favorite activity when Lula Carson was thirteen.

9 BELOW LEFT: Lula Carson Smith, age thirteen, Columbus, Georgia.

10 ABOVE: Reeves McCullers' father and aunts;
Emma Rose, Ida May, James Reeves, Sr.,
and Berta Rose McCullers,
proud of their dress and social status in
their small Alabama hometown, Wetumpka,
in the 1910s.

11 RIGHT:
At fifteen,
Carson dropped the Lula from her name;
at sixteen, she is pictured
in her senior yearbook
at Columbus High School, 1933.

12   Carson's mother, Marguerite Waters Smith, Columbus, Georgia, 1940.

13 Carson Smith with James Reeves McCullers, Jr., Columbus, Georgia, a few weeks after they began dating, 1935.

14 ABOVE:
The McCullers'
family home in which
Reeves's father
was reared, 105
North Bridge Street,
Wetumpka, Alabama.
Here Reeves spent his
senior year in high
school and several
summers as
an adolescent.

15 LEFT:
James Reeves McCullers, Jr.,
thirteen months, with his father
outside their home
in Jesup, Georgia.

she told Diamond. Miss Porter's beauty and charm were legendary, and Carson had responded with a great show of affection. Admittedly she admired Miss Porter, too, because she was the most famous American prose writer Carson had yet met. Still naive and impressionable, Carson had not fully developed her tendency to ignore other artists who worked in her own genre. David Diamond assured Carson that Miss Porter would be at Yaddo when Carson came, and that he hoped that they might become good friends. To be sure, Carson looked forward to being at Yaddo while Miss Porter was there, but she also felt a tinge of jealousy.

For Carson and David Diamond at Muriel Rukeyser's that night, the attraction to one another was mutual. When he returned to his apartment afterward he made a careful entry in his diary:

> May 22, 1941: I have met Carson McCullers, and I shake as I write. KAP [Katherine Anne Porter] was for me at our meeting last summer the fulfillment of a strange love which I carried about in my heart in Paris when I first read "Flowering Judas." Now I have met *this* love—this lovable child-woman—whose loneliness hit me the moment I entered Muriel Rukeyser's apartment. I cannot write here more of Carson. I gave her my ring, which she asked about. I met her husband, whom I know I love. As we share the days together, I'll know more about them. I wonder what my destiny is in relation to Carson.

Nineteen years passed before David Diamond knew the full answer to such ponderings, but the meeting that night was the beginning of another meaningful we of me triangle for Carson that eventually found poignant literary expression when *The Bride of My Brother* came to published fruition five years later as *The Member of the Wedding*.

The ring of which Diamond wrote that night had been given impulsively to his new friend when she admired it. Carson exuded a curious mystique that inexplicably prompted friends, admirers, and sometimes total strangers to give her extravagant gifts. If she admired a cigarette case, picture, ring, lighter, shirt, sweater, or even a pair of tennis shoes someone was wearing, the owner often responded by stripping it from his person, wall, or coffee table and giving it to her. David Diamond, Tennessee Williams, Truman Capote, and many other friends over the years gave to Carson with a similar immediacy. In his diary the next day, Diamond wrote of his quickened feelings for "my new friend, my new beloved one":

> May 23: I gave Carson my ring. With it went my adolescent suffering. This amazing child and woman is a part of me. I cannot erase her look of pleasure when I spoke of her, when I declared my feelings for her work.

Diamond had read *The Heart Is a Lonely Hunter* almost a year earlier when it first came out. Overwhelmed then by the book, he now was completely taken by its young author.

Carson and Reeves invited Diamond to a party in their apartment the next night. They were doing their favorite kind of entertaining—a small group of friends in for some lively conversation over drinks and with music. Carson loved this kind of a party—with people she cared about who were stimulating and free in their opinions and ideas. The evening ended on a volatile note, however, the party punctuated by an altercation between Reeves and one of the guests. Reeves tended to argue unreasonably when he had had a few drinks. His temper flared this night as he exchanged scathing remarks with a young Englishman, Geoffrey Avery, who—like Reeves—had apparently consumed more liquor than he could handle. The two men scuffled briefly, and in the encounter Reeves's hand was bitten rather deeply by his feisty guest. Coming to Reeves's aid, Diamond soothed him with reassuring words, then led him into the bathroom to cleanse the wound and bandage his hand. Afterward, Diamond took Reeves to a neighborhood bar to calm him further with a drink and gentle talk. Very quickly the composer's ambivalent feelings toward both Carson and Reeves crystallized that night. He realized that his "destiny lay now not only with Carson, but with Reeves, as well."[2]

The next day Diamond again entered in his diary his intimate thoughts concerning his new friends:

> May 24—Saturday: What has happened to me since meeting Carson and now Reeves, her husband. Carson, whose magnetism and strange sickly beauty stifles me, gnaws at me, and I know it is that I love these two human beings. It is a great love I feel. It will nourish me or destroy me.

Haunted by the new involvement and somewhat fearful of what might ensue, Diamond continued to record his daily thoughts and activities:

> May 25—Sunday: Since last night I think only of Carson and Reeves and the way Reeves looked at me. Took Reeves and Carson to dinner at Rochambeau. We were very, very drunk. Carson wanted Djuna Barnes to have a bottle of champagne.[3]

Almost immediately Carson realized, too, that her new relationship with David Diamond would have to be a threesome. At dinner that night she said to her husband, "Reeves, David is a part of our family. We love each other." It was typical of Carson to make such candid statements of her emotions. To Diamond, her tremendous capacity for love was gratifying. In his diary May 25, he continued: "And how I love them both, Carson above all. She has the loneliness of a woman's woman, that does not allow my feelings freedom." Diamond, through his own sensitivity, felt her needs and respected them.

Both Carson and Reeves urged Diamond to spend as much time with them in their apartment as possible, and Diamond, loving them both, readily acquiesced. For Carson, Diamond was also someone dear with whom she could talk of music and composers, someone who would listen with her, hear what she heard. He also talked with her and instructed her in some of the facets of musical composition about which she knew little. She was interested in counterpoint, Diamond recalled, which she used both as a symbol and for the design of a short story she wrote that summer, a work entitled "Madame Zilensky and the King of Finland."[4] To David Diamond, Carson rejoiced that she could bare and share her inner room with him, just as Mick Kelley did with John Singer, her deaf mute, in *The Heart Is a Lonely Hunter*. With Diamond, however, the reciprocity was real, not imagined.

On May 26, 1941, the composer came early to Carson's apartment, arriving before Reeves left for work. First, he drank coffee with Reeves and talked with him as he dressed. After Reeves's departure, he stayed on with Carson and spent the day. That evening he recorded a new dimension in their relationship:

> May 26—Monday: I think only of Reeves and Carson. After he left
> for work, I crawled into Carson's little bed and held this child, this so
> tender, this so great artist in my arms, felt her cracking lungs as she
> coughed miserably. We had a fine breakfast together. . . .

For Diamond, however, the encounter was not the beginning of a sexual tryst. Each wanted only a warm, human body to snuggle up against. Carson desired his tenderness, his love, but rejected any sexual involvement.

Loving Reeves desperately, too, David Diamond viewed Carson's husband as a kind of omniscient gift. On May 26, his diary entry continued: "Thank you, dear God, for bringing me to Reeves. My feelings and thoughts are so full of love for this sweet, gentle man. I think I shall never have the right to self-pity again. I have almost everything I need now—and Carson is so fine about it all." To be sure, Reeves had his gentle moments, but Diamond found that he could not always apply the *gentle* epithet as he got to know Reeves better.

A week after their first meeting with Diamond, Carson and Reeves visited his apartment on Bleecker Street. Diamond had a grand piano and he urged Carson to play for him. For the first time in years she felt nervous and apprehensive about her performance, but after several drinks, she played. Delighted by her sensitivity to music and what he later termed her "moderate technical ability" at the keyboard, Diamond wrote his impressions of the evening:

> May 29: . . . Carson played some Bach inventions beautifully. Her ear is fine and true. And her love of music so great that she fairly trembles speaking of a chord. . . . It is a strange love we three feel for each other.

Late that same evening, Carson and Reeves invited David Diamond to come home with them and spend the night. In their one-bedroom apartment they had a double bed and also a little single bed in which Carson usually slept. In his diary, Diamond recounted the evening and the following day:

> I woke early without a hangover. Reeves lay next to me. He went to work. Carson and I had breakfast. I left, went home, and met Carson at the Brevoort for lunch. Warm and sunny. I looked at this girl whom I love so dearly, and inside myself asked God to be good to her, to her body, to her career, to keep the venomous hearts away from her. Muriel Rukeyser and Eleanor Clark passed by, and we hailed them for brandies and coffee. Carson seemed so happy, but her hands shook so.

Diamond loved being in public with Carson. He was proud of her and basked in her obvious devotion to him. Yet he worried constantly about her health for she smoked continuously, and it seemed to him that she drank enough liquor to stagger most men, yet she seldom appeared to be even slightly drunk. Carson's marvelous physical control when she was drinking amazed him.

One night, early in their relationship, after dinner in the open air at Nino and Nella's, a favorite restaurant, Diamond accompanied Carson and Reeves back to their apartment for more drinks and to listen to a Beethoven symphony. As the evening progressed, however, Reeves and Carson suddenly began quarreling. "It was as though they were two beasts," said Diamond. Reeves, in his anger, put his fist through a pane in the door. Diamond was never sure just what had stimulated the outburst —and the innumerable others he witnessed in the future—but Carson and Reeves shocked him that night by their verbal brutality to one another.

Although Diamond said that he never saw Reeves "out and out hit Carson," he did witness him "slap" her once. "It was not a wounding slap in any way, but rather, a slap of frustration. I sympathized with Carson, but I could see how exasperating and unreasonably stubborn and demanding she could be on occasion," he recalled. To Diamond, it seemed that

Reeves and Carson seemed to take pleasure in taunting each other, and it was painful to be with them at such times. His role throughout their stormy sessions was that of peacemaker, both to control and calm Reeves —who responded well to Diamond's tenderness—and to gently caress Carson and assuage her tears and resentment. After an explosive bout with her husband, Carson frequently broke down in hysterics. Then, when the tension had abated and they were calm again, Reeves looked gratefully at his friend, touched him gently, and said, "You are tops, David, in everything."

Not only was David Diamond ambivalent in his own emotional responses to Carson and Reeves, but he also was troubled by his sense of loyalty to each. Although he was not fully aware of the marital problems that had beset them in the past, Diamond could see that Carson was taking Reeves more and more for granted as a husband. She had emotionally abandoned him and her own role as his wife. Many years later as Diamond attempted to assess their situation rationally, he concluded:

> Carson did not even seem aware that she had rejected Reeves to the extent that she now was losing him. She appeared far more interested in everything else going on about her, in the celebrities she was meeting, in the hangers-on, in her pseudofriends who swarmed about her. Although her work, of course, took her away from Reeves, at least 75 per cent of it was caused by *people*. Charmed by a smile, adulation, or kind remark, Carson at this time loved almost everyone she met.[5]

Eventually Carson told Diamond that she was no longer having a sexual relationship with Reeves because she "felt either too weak or too ill most of the time." To Diamond, it seemed that Carson still loved Reeves deeply, but simply was not interested in him sexually. "She did not seem to care that she was threatening his whole sense of manhood, or even to be aware that it was happening," he added.

Feeling more keenly now than ever before his role of abandoned husband, Reeves freely roamed the bars and night clubs of Manhattan in search of female companionship or a casual affair. In June, he became attracted to Judy Holliday, who was appearing as Judy Tuvim with "The Reviewers" at the Village Vanguard on Seventh Avenue. Enamored of both Miss Holliday and Betty Comden, the only girls in the revue—thinking them beautiful and talented—Reeves often watched the show and talked to them backstage. Later, Judy Holliday told Diamond that Reeves had frightened her, particularly the night he followed her home and attempted to kiss her at the door of her apartment. "But I rushed inside and slammed the door," she related. Another time she observed to Diamond: "Reeves has such crazy eyes—why does he stare at me that way?" To Diamond, Reeves's eyes were beautiful: "They changed color readily, from gray to blue or green, depending upon his mood and temper rather than upon what color he was wearing. They had a 'steely' look when he was dejected, however, and he appeared to be on the verge of tears. I never saw Reeves cry, but I often watched his whole face become darkened and take on an anguished, tortured look."

Many people who knew Reeves well and had read *The Heart Is a Lonely Hunter* could see multifacets of him in the novel in the character of Jake Blount, a fanatic Marxist who was totally frustrated in his obsession to communicate his needs to society or to help the poor millworkers who seemed content to wallow in their misfortunes. Reeves, like Blount, cast out many warnings, but his indignation usually fell upon deaf ears.

By the time Carson left her husband in New York City to go to Yaddo, Reeves, too, had found the situation intolerable. In his search for solace, he confided to David Diamond what seemed to lie at the heart of the matter:

> We simply are not husband and wife any more, David. It just doesn't make sense our staying together. When I come home, she either is there or is not there, without any explanation. Sometimes she comes home early in the morning, sometimes not. After all, she sleeps with whom she pleases, sees whom she wants. I'm not a husband any longer.[6]

Diamond sympathized with Reeves, for he knew the truth in what he was saying; yet Diamond also was fearful of becoming more involved with Reeves than he already was. Although he loved both Carson and Reeves deeply, he felt himself being sucked into their excessive drinking habits. He had never drunk so much, it seemed, as he had with them over the past few weeks. Too, Diamond hated to see Carson bent upon what appeared to be a self-destructive mode of life and Reeves holding on more and more to him for emotional support and drifting further and further away from his wife. "How I loved those two human beings," said Diamond, "and wanted so desperately to be able to help." He hoped that the separation of the summer—with Carson at Yaddo and Reeves working in the city—might have some beneficial, miraculous effect upon their marriage. Diamond, too, would be at Yaddo for several weeks. Although he yearned to resume the discipline that Yaddo would enforce upon him, he quivered in anticipation of Carson's being there, too. His work had suffered greatly since Reeves and Carson had come into his life, yet by this time it seemed impossible for Diamond to conceive of his own future apart from either of them. It was apparent, however, that they could never be the threesome in the old manner. Carson realized, too, that triangles could no more work in real life than they could in the short novel on which she was at work then, *The Ballad of the Sad Café*. "Darling, *The Ballad of the Sad Café* is for you," she told Diamond, to whom she knew the work would speak more directly than to anyone else. Diamond pondered deeply about his fate with Carson and Reeves that spring and arrived at what seemed to be the inevitable conclusion: A life with Carson would be difficult at best, but it would doubtless be a more successful liaison than a permanent relationship with Reeves could ever be.

On June 14, 1941, Carson stepped down from the Greyhound bus at the diner-terminal in Saratoga Springs and into the waiting station wagon sent by Elizabeth Ames to fetch her and several other Yaddo-bound artists who had made the four-hour trip from New York City. Carson knew no one else on the bus, and she felt a little apprehensive and frightened by it all. Also, her thermos of sherry had given out before the journey was over, and she was impatient to get settled, have a drink, and stroll among the blue spruce and tall white pines of the heavily wooded estate. Perhaps most precious of all, she thought, was the opportunity to be alone again, to completely control her environment, to see people only when she chose to.

The unusual name for this wonderful haven for resident artists had come about in an unusual way. It had been named by a little child, Christina, the four-year-old daughter of Katrina and Spencer Trask, its philanthropic donors, who used to sit and dream in front of the great stone fireplace of the original Yaddo mansion, a hideous Queen Anne villa which the Trask family had purchased in 1881 and begun to refurbish. Fascinated by the leaping, forked flames, Christina was sometimes frightened by the strange shapes of fire shadows on the wall which invaded her fancies, and she called out in fright, "Mama, Mama, the yaddo [shadow] will get me!" Later, when her parents were choosing a name for their newly acquired estate, Mrs. Trask consulted her daughter: "What shall we name the place, Cuckoo?"

After a moment the child reportedly responded: "Shadow, Yaddo— Yaddo, shadow. Call it 'Yaddo,' Mama. It sounds like shadow, but it's not going to *be* a shadow any more, is it?" The child had heard her parents sigh and say that their lives were "shadowed," for the family had undergone a series of bereavements. Two of the Trask children were already dead, and Mrs. Trask felt that Christina associated the word "shadow" with her own life, yet unconsciously shrank from it. Elizabeth Ames's sister, Marjorie Peabody Waite, said that the child unconsciously gave a prophecy for the years to come; "yet it grew less and less to mean *shadow* until at last, in the radiance of the life here, it came to mean *light*.[7]

The original mansion burned to the ground in 1891, but a new Yaddo, a huge, turreted, gray-stone Victorian mansion with fifty-five rooms, a music room to seat three hundred, and a great baronial hall was rebuilt in 1893 on the same site. Yaddo quickly became a center of festivities and house parties for visiting statesmen, authors, artists, and musicians. According to legend, countless poems, plays, and musical compositions were created by talented guests who sometimes extended their stay for months. Katrina Trask wrote poetry, and it was with great enthusiasm that she entertained artists of all genres. Tragedy again struck the Trasks, however. Within a week their two surviving children died from diphtheria. Soon Katrina Trask became a permanent invalid, and in 1909 her husband died in a railroad wreck. Long before Spencer Trask was killed, the couple had decided to have Yaddo converted after their deaths into a working community for artists and writers. At first they made elaborate plans for the colony, but Trask's fortune foundered in 1907 and he was unable to recover his former financial worth before his death. Forced to adjust their dream to a more modest scale, Mrs. Trask moved out of the great mansion into a smaller house on the estate, West House, so that funds could more easily accumulate for what eventually became The Corporation of Yaddo. Later, Mrs. Trask married George Foster Peabody, who had been a lifelong friend of the family and a business associate of Trask's. In 1926, four years after Katrina Trask Peabody's death, the artists' colony of Yaddo became a reality, administered by Elizabeth Ames, the sister of Peabody's adopted daughter, Marjorie Waite Peabody.

Yaddo lay two miles east of Saratoga Springs. In addition to the mansion, a large garage with kitchen and additional quarters in which guests lived during the winter, three smaller houses, and a number of separate studios, the five-hundred-acre estate contained four small lakes well stocked with fish, a beautiful marble-statued rose garden open to the public, a rock garden and fountain, and several hundred thousand trees, including 250,000 planted by Trask himself over the years—the most splendid specimens of deciduous and coniferous trees indigenous to the northern hemisphere.

Carson walked alone through the woods the afternoon of her arrival, watched George Vincent, the great estate's caretaker, land two large speckled trout from the lake beside the tower studio, then returned to the huge dining hall of the mansion for dinner. When the guests were introduced that night, Carson marveled that there were apparently so many talented artists she had never heard of before. Most of them were from the New York City area. A few were European exiles, a group with whom she immediately identified.[8]

To Carson, only the names Colin McPhee and Eudora Welty meant anything at all, other than David Diamond, who arrived a week later, and Katherine Anne Porter, who had been in residence since the summer of 1940. It was love at sight again as Carson beheld the chic Miss Porter, small, slim-hipped, beautiful. Although Carson had sat in the audience when Miss Porter appeared as a visiting lecturer at Bread Loaf the summer before, she had hung back and made no attempt to know her, awed by her fame, but also a little envious. Now, however, she lost no time in making her infatuation known to the prominent author. Carson began following Katherine Anne Porter about the colony in much the same manner as the characters she created that summer did. Cousin Lymon, the little dwarf in *The Ballad of the Sad Café*, mooned foolishly over the despicable Marvin Macy and traipsed after him through the countryside. Carson told friends that she had written the "music" for her folk tale years earlier through her own experiences with people she had loved; her lyrics were more recently inspired, however. "I love you, Katherine Anne," Carson declared to Miss Porter that summer with unabashed candor. Then she added, as though to justify the infatuation, "You're the *only* famous writer I have ever known." Carson would have stood on her head and wiggled her ears to get Miss Porter's attention had she only known how, just as Cousin Lymon did in his futile efforts to attract Marvin Macy.

Miss Porter's rebuttal was simple: "No, I'm not famous, Carson—I've just had the good luck to have critics who like what I write."[9]

Indeed, Miss Porter, like the critics, had thought *The Heart Is a Lonely Hunter* a remarkable novel for one as young as Carson to write. "It had the mark of genius," she added. Yet the novel had already alerted her to expect some aberration in the author herself. According to Miss Porter, her husband, Albert Erskine, declared to her upon finishing the book a year earlier, when it first came out: "Katherine Anne, that woman is a lesbian."[10]

Indignant over such an abrupt and seemingly unjustified judgment, Miss Porter retorted, "You can't assume that—what makes you think so?"

Erskine replied with a generalization that explained nothing, but implanted, nevertheless, the thought in his wife's mind: "I can tell from the author's mind in that novel and by what she makes her characters do and say."

Miss Porter had stoutly defended Carson and was prepared to like the Georgia-born writer at Yaddo and prove her husband wrong. The seed having been planted, however, Miss Porter soon decided that the young author's infatuation with her was offensive and fully supported what Erskine had surmised. "But perhaps I simply misunderstood Carson," Miss Porter ruefully recalled later. "I have many friends who are homosexual and the fact does not bother me at all, but with Carson then, the thought seemed intolerable." Those who knew Miss Porter well, however, and also knew Carson, believed emphatically that Carson's infatuation that summer was definitely misunderstood.[11]

Miss Porter had a way of permanently chilling a relationship she did not want developed or maintained. One story that circulated about New York City was that some years back when she was a struggling reviewer for the New York *Herald-Tribune*—possibly her only source of income at that time—Katherine Anne Porter was routed from her bed when the doorbell was rung at 4 A.M. by the wealthy and beautiful Elinor Wylie (Mrs. William Rose Benét), who seemingly had all of the material advantages that Miss Porter lacked then. "Katherine Anne," Miss Wylie began, "I have stood the crassness of this world as long as I can and I am going to kill myself. You are the only person in the world to whom I wish to say good-by."

Miss Porter reportedly looked Miss Wylie dispassionately in the eye and responded: "Elinor, it was good of you to think of me. Good-by." Then she promptly closed the door. Miss Wylie did not commit suicide, but she doubtless decided then that the world was even more crass than she had guessed.

The day that Carson pounded on Miss Porter's door of the mansion and pleaded forlornly, "Please, Katherine Anne, let me come in and talk with you—I do love you so very much," Miss Porter demanded that Carson leave. She shouted from within that she would not come out until Carson had vacated the hall. It was 6:30 P.M., however, and time for dinner. Both women knew not to risk Mrs. Ames's displeasure by being a minute late. Soon Miss Porter heard her devotee's feet shuffling off down the corridor. After a brief interval, the elder woman cautiously opened the door and stepped out. To her astonishment, there lay Carson sprawled across the threshold. "But I had had enough," said Miss Porter. "I merely stepped over her and continued on my way to dinner. And that was the last time she ever bothered me."[12]

Another newcomer to Yaddo in June 1941 was Eudora Welty. Carson had been fond of Miss Welty since they met at Bread Loaf the summer before, but Eudora Welty was Katherine Anne Porter's protégée, and the older woman now kept a vigilant eye to discourage any friendship from developing between the fellow Southerners. To Miss Porter, Eudora Welty was "a marvelous person, a most talented writer—moreover, she was 150 per cent female." Miss Welty, however, regretted that over the years she never became better acquainted with Carson. They were only to see each other during those two summers at Bread Loaf and Yaddo. Later, Miss Welty lamented: "I wish Carson's and my own paths had crossed more. . . . We were never to know each other very well, though I do know we always liked, right along, each other's work."[13]

Both Carson and Miss Porter had rooms the beginning of the summer in the mansion, but the latter soon persuaded Elizabeth Ames to let her move into what was known as the farmhouse, located a few hundred yards down the drive and away from the main flow of traffic. It had the advantage, too, of having its own kitchen, and its tenants did not even have to walk to the mansion for meals if they did not choose to. The farmhouse was actually two separate apartments. Mrs. Ames, who considered it a paramount duty to see that Yaddo's guests did not bother each other, quickly consented to move Miss Porter into the upstairs living quarters. When David Diamond arrived—who got on well with Miss Porter—Mrs. Ames moved him into the lower quarters. "I was crazy about David," said Miss Porter. "We were so happy together off by ourselves in the farmhouse. He was one of my favorite people—and still is."[14]

Carson, disappointed that she was unable to see Diamond as often as she had hoped, and now considering Miss Porter something of a rival, determined not to inflict herself upon the woman any longer. By this time, they were not even speaking to one another. Walking one day with her friend Newton Arvin, who was a writer, director in residence, and Smith College professor, Carson caught his arm and nodded toward Katherine Anne Porter on the path ahead of them: "She may be the greatest female writer in America now—but just wait until next year."[15]

Recalling the antagonism between Miss Porter and Carson, Mrs. Ames reflected that "over the years the female artists at Yaddo always got along better with the men than with each other":

Women artists are usually not very tolerant of each other. They're temperamental, and Katherine Anne was always very temperamental. She was, of course, very attractive, and she and Carson had personalities that would naturally be a little antagonistic to one another. Carson was much younger than Katherine Anne [about twenty-five years], who was already a much-established writer when she and Carson met.

Another characteristic of Carson's that put off Miss Porter considerably was her masculine attire. At Yaddo as at Bread Loaf, Carson almost always dressed in dungarees or men's pants. With them she wore a man's white dress shirt buttoned at the top. Her shoulders were narrow, and the long sleeves usually hung down to her knuckles. On top of this she frequently wore a boy's jacket with sleeves so short that they ended well up on her forearm. Other residents of Yaddo referred to this outfit as Carson's "dress-up city garb," which she usually wore into town at night.[16] Mrs. Ames recalled that "while Carson usually wore pants, sometimes she would wear a dress at night for dinner. But no matter what she wore, she was always very clean and always combed her hair. She was brought up that way," Mrs. Ames added.

David Diamond still saw Carson frequently, but he worked hard all day and often took his meals with Katherine Anne Porter in the farmhouse. Soon Carson set out to make herself a new friend in the person of Edward Newhouse, a handsome and sophisticated writer of short stories for The New Yorker. Newhouse had been a bridegroom only a few weeks, his wife having departed on a South American concert tour soon after their marriage. Newton Arvin, as a director in residence, had invited him to work at Yaddo during his wife's absence and enjoy a vacation, as well. Newhouse said of his first morning there, having joined Arvin, Colin McPhee, Carson, and several others at their breakfast table:

> I never dreamed that I was at the "Table of the Sensitives"—so it had been dubbed by some presumably heterosexual wag. Katherine Anne Porter usually sat with Eudora Welty at the other end of the room. Although I had read Proust with great absorption, I must have thought he was kidding. In any case, I was not very good at recognizing a homosexual when I met him. Or her. I had known Newton for years, and the notion that he might be one had not crossed my mind. I was surprised when Colin McPhee told me about the Balinese boy he had loved, surprised that he made no bones about it. You can see that this was a long time ago. I was not surprised when Carson told me about herself. She sometimes wore a man's trousers and often a man's jacket, and even I was able to make the connection. I had not read a line she had written, and I'm afraid I did not take her very seriously. Still, she must not have minded being treated like an obstreperous, engagingly goofy kid sister, because for those two or three weeks at Yaddo, she decided to appoint me her caretaker.[17]

With Newhouse selected as her new friend and champion, Carson asked him if he would like to see "a little story I have just written that has Saratoga Springs as its locale—and though I've never seen a horse race, this story is about a jockey, a lonely and bitter little man." Newhouse liked what he read and immediately took it into the city with him to show to Gus Lobrano, then fiction editor of *The New Yorker*. When he returned to Yaddo a few days later, he happily handed Carson a check for about four hundred dollars. On August 23, 1941, "The Jockey" appeared in *The New Yorker*, and Carson was ecstatic.

Proud of the results of what she considered an easy creative effort, Carson carried her *New Yorker* check about with her for several nights on her rounds with "the boys" to the various night spots on Congress Street in Saratoga Springs. Almost every afternoon Mrs. Ames sent the official Yaddo car, a station wagon, to town so that guests could shop, bank, see a doctor, go to a hairdresser, or perform other sundry errands, and then get back in time for dinner. At night the car made a second trip to take those into town who wanted to prowl the night clubs or otherwise socialize.

Almost every evening a group from the artists' colony visited Jimmy's Place, the Golden Grill, the Hi-De-Ho, or, occasionally, the respectable Worden Bar at the resort hotel, the Worden. The Worden was the only bar of the better sort in which they spent any time. Carson had found her setting there—and in the hotel proper—for her jockey story. One morning a bartender at the Worden called Mrs. Ames on the telephone: "One of your authors has left a check down here on the bar—and *he* must be a good one because it's for a lot of money." Carson was amused that her name frequently misled people into thinking she was a man. She also could be deadly serious about her masculine nature, which she felt was more real than her feminine one. Discussing her bisexuality with Newton Arvin that summer, Carson declared: "Newton, I was born a man."[18]

Habitually careless with her money even though she liked to have a strict accounting of it when it came to record keeping, Carson had not even missed her check on this occasion until the telephone call. But upon recovering it, she waited a few days, then sent the check to Reeves to deposit to her account in New York City. Unfortunately, the check never reached the bank, as Carson learned later. Instead, Reeves forged her signature and cashed it himself. "The Jockey" was almost in print and on the newsstands that summer before Carson had any inkling that she, personally, had derived not a penny from its payment.

Although Carson's nights were spent largely in long drinking sessions and friendly antics in the bars in town and in the various artists' studios, especially the atmospheric stone tower nestled in the tall trees beside Lake Spencer in which Colin McPhee lived, her days were full and productive. She worked most of the time on *The Ballad of the Sad Café*, which she had begun the preceding winter in Columbus. The work was progressing well and she was almost through with it, she wrote to friends in New York that summer. *The Ballad of the Sad Café* never gave her the problem that *The Bride* had, the novel she decided to lay aside temporarily while she devoted her full attention to the story of the hunchback and the Amazonian woman.

As was her habit back in Georgia, Carson usually began her day with a long tramp through the beautiful Yaddo woods before breakfast, which was served strictly between the hours of eight and nine. At breakfast, Carson sat alone most of the time and appeared to be shy and withdrawn, reluctant to enter into conversation with those around her. She looked melancholy and appeared frequently to be brooding. As soon as she finished her meal, she left, picked up a box lunch from the kitchen—available for all guests who wished to work through the day without returning to the mansion for lunch—and went immediately to her studio. According to Elizabeth Ames, Carson was one of the most disciplined artists while she was working that Mrs. Ames had ever known:

> Nothing could keep Carson from her desk at half-past nine in the morning, and she stayed there throughout the day. She was very, very disciplined. She could turn against or grow cold toward anyone who was ever thoughtless enough to try to break in on her.[19]

As director, Mrs. Ames always stressed the rule that guests were in no way to socialize or interfere with their fellow artists during the working day, and on a few occasions she had to be stern with her charges. Rarely did drinking parties in the evening become too raucous, said Mrs. Ames, who recalled that it had been years since anyone drank so much that he made "a disgusting, boring fool of himself." Fewer than a half-dozen guests during all of Yaddo's years of existence were ever told that they must terminate their scheduled stay early, she admitted.

Many guests thought it surprising that Carson got on so well with Elizabeth Ames, "who liked things tidy. People, too," said Edward Newhouse. According to Newhouse, "Nothing about Carson was tidy, but Mrs. Ames appeared to be devoted to her."[20]

It seemed to Carson's fellow artists that she consumed a great quantity of alcohol during her various stays at Yaddo, yet for her, the amount was never excessive. The same quantity might, indeed, have been too much for someone else. In the summer of 1941—she was to be in residence at Yaddo on five later occasions, as well—Carson usually started her day with a glass of beer which she carried with her to her typewriter. To Mrs. Ames, she seemed to need a mild stimulant to sharpen her creative process—almost "a quietening," to allow her to focus on her subject. From beer, she shifted to sherry, which she sipped off and on the rest of the day. At four-thirty or five, she put away her work, bathed, and looked forward to joining the men for cocktails before dinner. Usually Newton Arvin, Edward Newhouse, Colin McPhee, and sometimes writer Gerald Sykes got together.

Even though Carson was writing extremely well and enjoying a social rapport with her Yaddo friends, by mid-July she became increasingly concerned about Reeves. Although both realized that they could no longer live together compatibly, when apart their psychic life was a failure, also. Carson could get along well as long as she knew that Reeves loved her and was in relatively good mental health. But he had written to her only twice during her first month at Yaddo. Whereas Carson thought it perfectly all right for her to leave him so that she might write and be with other artists at the Saratoga colony, she expected his faithfulness when they were separated. Naively, she could not seem to comprehend Reeves's overwhelming loneliness and sense of estrangement while she was away. For him not to write—when he had been such a reliable correspondent in the past—she could not fathom.

Carson had interrupted her *Ballad of the Sad Café* a few days earlier to write a short piece entitled "Correspondence," a story doubtless prompted by her extreme anxiety over not hearing from Reeves. "Correspondence" was the story of a teen-aged girl, Henky Evans, whose Brazilian pen pal failed to answer a single letter. The entire tale was told by the letters which Henky wrote to Manoel Garcia. Finally, the girl wrote her fourth epistle, revealing a disappointment and bitterness she could not hide:

> I have sent you three letters in all good faith and expected you to fulfill your part in the idea of American and South American students corresponding like it was supposed to be. Nearly every other person in the class got letters and some even friendship gifts, even though they were not especially crazy about foreign countries like I was. I expected to hear every day and gave you the benefits of all the doubts. But now I realize what a grave mistake I made.
>
> All I want to know is this. Why would you have your name put on the list if you did not intend to fulfill your part in the agreement? All I want to say is that if I had known then what I know now I most assuredly would have picked out some other South American.
>
> Yrs. truly,
MISS HENRIETTA HILL EVANS
>
> P.S. I cannot waste any more of my valuable time writing to you.[21]

To a distraught Carson, Reeves was defaulting on his contract, too. She had thought many times that if he had not come into her life, she might have been far happier with someone else. But since that was not possible, she was determined now to get along as best she could.

Again, Carson turned to her new friend Ed Newhouse for solace. To Newhouse, Carson at Yaddo in 1941 was emotionally very much a child, a characteristic she never seemed to outgrow: "I would call her *childlike*, although people who didn't like her thought her *childish*. She could drop people suddenly or pick them up with a tremendous show of affection." Newhouse said, "I saw her as a very dependent child who developed a bit of a crush on me during my two or three weeks there." He found that she had a disarming way of throwing herself on a person, as though to say, "Take care of me. I am helpless." Yet to him, she was bright enough and sweet enough never to run out of people who could be, if only for a time, depended on. He also remembered her as one who would very much rather talk than listen:

> Midway through some relatively brief interposition, I would realize that she was merely waiting for me to stop so that she could go on talking, usually about herself. It was not often that she wished to hear what anyone else might be saying. Her attention span appeared to be that of a small child. And when she was off on say a rhapsody about that Swiss girl, Annemarie Clarac-Schwarzenbach, she was unstoppable. Annemarie was lovely. Annemarie was charming and witty. Annemarie was sheer enchantment, the essence of, well, the con-

tinental. What continent? I asked. Carson said, "Joke about God. Joke about anything you like. Not Annemarie."[22]

Carson's tremendous ego regarding her powers to attract another female blossomed that summer, too. When she met Newhouse's wife a few weeks later, she said to him: "Ah, but you never told me she was a great beauty. If I'd met her six months ago, I would have given you a run for your money." Newhouse laughed, but Carson said gravely, "I mean it, I could have, and I *would* have."

Carson could, however, make some men insecure in the affection of their wives. Alfred Kantorowicz, for example, a German exile who fled to the United States in 1941 and became Carson's good friend at Yaddo two summers later, had a wife, Friedel, whom "Carson liked very much—so much that I was jealous," said Kantorowicz.[23] Other husbands also felt threatened off and on throughout Carson's life. It was not so much that they feared an actual bed liaison, but rather, the entangling emotional involvement that consumed their wives' time, energies, and attention.

Not only was Carson given to great outpourings of love that summer to Katherine Anne Porter and to David Diamond, but also to people she did not know very well. Carson told Newhouse about a several-hundred page letter she said she had written to "the woman she was in love with at that particular time—Greta Garbo. She pronounced it 'Greeta.'" Carson's having said that she wrote such a letter might, in fact, have meant:

One, she actually wrote it. Two, she didn't. Three, the letter had been several thousand pages long. Four, it ran to nine pages. Five, today is Wednesday. As I told you, our girl was given to saying pretty much anything that came into her head. If I were given the choice of writing her biography or being shipwrecked on a desert island with Spiro Agnew . . . well, I don't know.[24]

Carson sometimes could be talked out of her infatuations, as was the case during the winter of 1940 when she was living in Brooklyn Heights with George Davis and Wystan Auden. She had developed a tremendous crush upon a young ballerina who was dancing with the New York City Ballet Troupe. Carson had never met her, but she used to stand out in the snow beside the stage door evenings on end, waiting to catch a glimpse of her new beloved, to speak to her, or at least to establish eye contact with the young woman. Finally, after Carson's influenza and respiratory ailments had intensified and threatened her total health, Davis sat her down one day and said: "Now look, Carson, you're simply no longer in love with that woman. She's not for you. You're not to go down and moon outside her door any longer—do you understand?" Carson did understand, and she ceased her vigils without protest.[25]

Everyone who ever knew Carson remarked upon her wonderful verbal storytelling abilities of anecdotes that she frequently presented as truth. At Yaddo that summer, Carson once told Edward Newhouse a harrowing tale of having walked into the living room of her home in Columbus and discovered her father sitting on the sofa, nonchalantly smoking while the entire piece of furniture was engulfed in flames. At this point, Carson's tale was interrupted when another guest came up. Later, curious about her father and the extent of his burns, Newhouse sought out Carson and asked, "What finally happened, Carson?"

Amused, she looked quizzically at him and replied, "Oh, you believed all that? You are so good yourself, that I must be a marvelous storyteller to have convinced you. I only wanted to illustrate how absentminded my father was when he was drinking." Carson's uncanny ability to mix fact with fantasy led almost everyone who knew her to accept with reservations her personal experience tales. Yet she also was painfully honest with her friends. Her cousin Jordan Massee, a native of Macon, Georgia, who was living in New York City in 1941 and became acquainted with her that year for the first time, shared perhaps the longest and most constant and loyal relationship with Carson of anyone in her entire life. Massee felt that Carson was always totally honest with him, as well as with most people. "She never lied to me, I am sure. If it were something inconsequential, she might attempt a fib just to see if she could get away with it, but she couldn't tell one with a straight face. Afterwards we always had a good laugh over what she had tried to put over on me."26

In fact, the way Carson met Jordan Massee was a tale in itself. It was while she was living in Brooklyn Heights with George Davis and Wystan Auden. She was sitting in a drugstore having a cup of coffee and dish of ice cream and chatting gaily with the young man at the soda fountain. Another customer came in, sat at the counter, and began to talk about her brother, whom she identified as "a famous author." "Well, there's another great writer," said the man behind the fountain, who knew Carson because of her frequent stops for sweets, ice cream, and sundry medicines. "That's Carson McCullers," he indicated, pointing to the figure perched on a stool nearby.

"*That's* Carson McCullers?" queried Mabel Wheaton incredulously. Then she slid off her stool and moved to Carson's side. "Why, I'm Tom Wolfe's sister," she said. "Honey, I want you to come back to the hotel and meet Mama." A few minutes later, Carson accompanied Mabel Wheaton to the nearby Franklin Arms Hotel, where she met Thomas Wolfe's mother, Julia Wolfe, and Paul Bigelow, a young man employed by the hotel. Bigelow had endeared himself to Mrs. Wolfe when he had summoned for her a friend of his, a psychoanalyst, to treat her for a cold.

Mrs. Wolfe, convinced that she was dying, urged Bigelow to send, also, for Mabel Wheaton, who was living in Washington, D.C. When Bigelow was introduced now to Carson, he responded:

"How perfectly wonderful—my roommate is a cousin of yours, but he has never met you. His name is Jordan Massee."

"Why get him on the phone, won't you—he's a legend in my family. I can't believe he actually exists!" Carson, however, was thinking of Massee's father, who, indeed, *was* a legend to the Smith family. A few nights later, Massee and Bigelow called upon Carson at 7 Middagh Street.

"She was very quiet then," recalled Massee. "She played the piano for us, and I remember that when her housemates came in she introduced me, saying: 'This is my precious cousin.'"

Massee said that Carson sat holding his hand most of the evening. "She did not know how to communicate with me, nor I with her. That was something we learned later, through letters and through Bebe, her mother," he added.

In the middle of July 1941 when Ed Newhouse left Yaddo to rejoin his bride, a great wellspring of loneliness came over Carson. While he was there, she could usually count on someone special to be with her. They had never been simply a twosome, for Newhouse preferred not to be that involved with her, but they usually traveled in a small group that included Colin McPhee and Newton Arvin. She also saw a good deal of Gerald Sykes, a Kentucky writer, and John Slade, who was president of The Corporation of Yaddo. Slade lived in Saratoga Springs and frequently joined the Yaddo group with his wife, Caroline, for parties and informal gatherings. Even the new group of artists who rotated in for the second half of the summer did little to remedy Carson's sense of separateness.[27] She knew none of the guests among the new arrivals. Only the Russian composer Nikolai Lopatnikoff became her good friend during the second half of the summer. Thirty years later, Lopatnikoff found Carson still indelibly etched in his memory: "I was fascinated by this somehow elflike girl of great charm, whose face looked older than her general appearance would suggest, betraying her inner problems and difficulties." Carson's great love of Russian literature and a renewed interest in Russian art and music again surged because of what she thought of as a "kinship" with Lopatnikoff. They talked of books, music, and the war. It was the time of the Hitler-Stalin pact, and Carson was deeply depressed by the turbulence in Europe. The United States still had not entered the war—it took the bombing of Pearl Harbor that December to do that—but almost everyone at Yaddo had strong feelings about the country's lack of involvement and took a lively interest in politics in general.

Yet despite those somber times, Carson never suppressed the lighter and often whimsical side of her personality, which sometimes found an

outlet in unexpected pranks. Lopatnikoff recalled that one Sunday afternoon as twilight approached, Carson's fey side was uppermost. There had
been an unusually large spate of gaping sightseers and visitors to the rose
garden, and more could be spied down the road headed for the grounds
of the Yaddo mansion. Impulsively, Carson persuaded a group of her cohorts gathered on the Yaddo terrace waiting for dinner to impersonate in-
mates of an insane asylum for the onlooking flock. To the amazement
and delight of the excited spectators, their suspicions regarding the sanity
of the Yaddo residents were confirmed.[28]

Another whimsical exploit of Carson's, which she related to Lopatnikoff that summer, involved her alleged encounter with a mounted policeman tending a Manhattan beat somewhere on East 57th Street. She
said that she had been with Gypsy Rose Lee and was returning home
alone well past midnight. As she stood on a corner and rested, having a
number of blocks yet to walk, she said that she watched the officer approach, then hailed him. He dismounted and leaned against his horse
while they talked amiably for a few moments. Then, by a ruse she did
not explain, she told Lopatnikoff that she managed to distract the man
and get him to move away from his horse, whereupon she leaped into the
saddle and galloped away. The tale doubtless was fantasy, thought Lopatnikoff, for he knew that Manhattan's mounted policemen prided themselves on being able to control their steeds by verbal commands. But it
made a good tale, and to Carson—after a few tellings—it actually had happened.

The main reason that Carson had been so lonely at Yaddo after Edward Newhouse's departure was that David Diamond also had left. Diamond, who had been at Yaddo from the winter of 1940–41 until the middle of March, had become somewhat estranged from Elizabeth Ames and
decided that he would prefer to work at the MacDowell Colony in Peter-
boro, New Hampshire. Carson and Diamond wrote each other frequently,
however, and each of her letters was filled with great outpourings of how
much she missed him and what she had been doing in his absence. One
Sunday she wrote him that she was going to dress in costume that night
for dinner and could hardly wait to see the surprised looks on everyone's
faces. She had borrowed a sarong and Chinese jacket from Colin McPhee
and planned to pin bunches of white flowers behind each ear and walk in
barefooted. It was not a costume party; however, her tendency to do the
unexpected and to thrive on the element of surprise which she sometimes
sprang on her fellow artists was one of the things that most of Yaddo's
guests remembered her best for that summer.

Carson was especially fond of the informal Sunday night buffets at
the mansion, which always contrasted with the more formally served meals
the rest of the week. There was a hilarity on Sunday evenings that even

Mrs. Ames encouraged "so long as the guests did not do anything too shocking," she explained.[29] "Sometimes our people dressed in outlandish costumes, just as Carson did, but her outfit that night was out of character even for her. After dinner the guests sometimes imitated a fellow artist—all in good fun, of course—or they might put on an impromptu skit. They were most resourceful. We had a wonderful cook and the food was plentiful in those years. The buffet spread always included some twenty different dishes. I remember that Carson's appetite was usually splendid at the buffets," Mrs. Ames continued.

Before the meal, guests frequently gathered in the large music room and sang, and afterward, they convened there for more music. Sometimes a composer played his work, or the group listened to Yaddo's excellent record collection or to a piece that one of the artists brought in. Sometimes Carson played, but usually if she were asked she demurred, saying that she was too much out of practice. To Elizabeth Ames, Carson seemed very shy about playing before others; Ed Newhouse recalled, however, that Carson needed little prompting to perform. In fact, he felt that she revealed a "lack of good judgment" and "a childlike attitude" in her occasional insistence that a concert pianist of such distinction as Colin McPhee should sit and listen to her, who seemed to Newhouse to be "a comparatively small talent. The 'Moonlight Sonata' was 'her piece' and she played it for us rather too often, Colin thought. I didn't mind."[30]

Elizabeth Ames considered Carson a modest woman when it came to her musical ability: "She did not think of herself any longer as a musician, but as a writer. Her playing was lovely, although it usually seemed to me that she liked music that was a little solemn or sad. At Yaddo she played Chopin more than Bach. It was usually the Chopin preludes."

Those who drank with Carson and watched her experiment with cigars and attempt unsuccessfully to keep a pipe lit ("She experimented with all the manly arts," recalled Newhouse), found her far from modest in her life style as an artist. Carson had tremendous self-assurance, knew her worth as a writer, and did not hesitate to remind a listener of the fact. Yet she often strove to demonstrate a prowess she did not have in an act which sometimes proved discomfiting or embarrassing. On one occasion, Carson described in a letter to David Diamond the aftereffects of a party when, amid the bourbon, scotch, and gin bottles, various members of Carson's group attempted strange feats. She cloaked the event in an apology for not having written to her friend in a few days. She explained that she fell on a stone floor and cut open her chin so badly that it needed several stitches to close it. She discreetly avoided telling Diamond the entire tale, however. Actually, Carson's mishap occurred in the tower studio when she tried to duplicate a resident sculptor's little trick of falling rigid to the floor on his face, as though in a swoon, but catching himself with his hands at the moment of impact without injury. "That's nothing spectacular, just watch me," she announced, impatient to show off her own skills. Urging the others at the party to clear a space for her "trick," Carson fell forward, her body a dead weight, hands at her side. She made no effort to catch herself until it was too late. The blow knocked her unconscious. Although Newhouse himself was not a heavyweight, he hoisted the 130-pound girl over his shoulder and carried her, bleeding profusely from a cut on the chin, back to the mansion and up the stairs to her room. The next morning Mrs. Ames examined her errant artist and ordered her driven to the doctor in Saratoga Springs. Carson told Diamond that she not only had a badly hurt chin, but that a bad gum infection had set in and she had been going daily to the dentist in Saratoga Springs for treatment.

For Carson at Yaddo during the middle of the summer 1941, there was little humorous relief in a world of reality. She felt disassociated from the real world; to cope, she fantasized over her typewriter in the daytime and she fantasized at night. Reeves had become very remiss in his correspondence with her, and she admitted that she felt forsaken and unhappy. Increasingly anguished as her doubts concerning his loyalty grew, she felt an abundance of love stirring again for those who had been significant to her in the past, for her Swiss friend, Annemarie Clarac-Schwarzenbach, for Gypsy Rose Lee, for her piano teacher, Mary Tucker, and for her mother. Yet she knew, too, that she still loved Reeves, that she was inextricably bound to him. She realized also, however, that her ambivalent nature demanded, craved, a reciprocal love relationship with a woman.

On July 19, 1941, Carson wrote to David Diamond a deeply touching letter in which she bared many facets of her inward and outward life. A long letter, it began in nostalgia. She had not heard from Diamond in several days, and she wanted him to know that she greatly missed him and the good times they had shared at Yaddo. She had just been out walking around the lakes and among the beautiful silver-green poplars, haunts they had enjoyed together. She also longed to be with him down at Jimmy's Place, she said, where they had perched on stools and drunk coffee and cognac.

The old terror had returned, too, she admitted, and she did not know to whom she might turn next. She was such a child, she confessed, and the people who loved her had to put up with much. Their patience and understanding had to be in large measure. Carson told Diamond that her need for love was awesome, that it was an insatiable craving; nor did she expect ever to feel differently. She also spoke of herself as an invert and wondered if she would ever know the love of a woman who might answer her multileveled needs. She told Diamond that her love for Annemarie

Clarac-Schwarzenbach was deep and abiding, but that she realized there could be no true reciprocity in their relationship.

She had just finished reading Havelock Ellis' book, *My Life,* a tragic story which chronicled Ellis' relationship with his wife, who also was an invert and whose situation was much like her own, she told Diamond. Even though Ellis had a profound understanding of his wife's needs and showed great compassion, she went mad and he was powerless to help. If only Reeves could understand her as Ellis had understood his wife, lamented Carson, they, too, might have had a better life. Carson may not have known it at the time, but Reeves was already well acquainted with the writings of Havelock Ellis and his dilemma with his wife. Reeves and their friend Edwin Peacock had talked at length about Ellis and his understanding of the psychology of sex. Reeves told Peacock that when he was stationed at Fort Benning he had persuaded a librarian at the Columbus public library to allow him to sit in a little back room where books were mended and read the Ellis book, which was kept, along with a few others, separate from the books circulated to the general public.[31]

Diamond responded to Carson's letter with an outpouring of his own love for her. He understood her ambivalent needs, yet proposed that the two of them consider getting married when she was eventually free from Reeves. He was sure that it was only a matter of time before Carson would divorce him. Diamond knew that he himself loved Reeves, but he realized, too, that he and Reeves could never have a satisfactory life together. A life with Carson, however, was a decided possibility. He deeply loved Carson, he told her now, and he wanted them to share all aspects of their lives in some meaningful union. He yearned to take care of her and to try to protect her from the harsh elements that had assailed her in the past. Diamond also told Carson that they would have to be bound by "more than just brotherly love."

Diamond's letter, which reached Carson on July 23—only four days after her own letter had been written—was somewhat overwhelming. She pondered over how to answer it, for she said that he had not made his own feelings completely clear. Finally she began her letter. She said that she would first have to explain to him how she viewed her own life at present in relationship to other people. At last she felt in command of herself in a way she had not experienced before. She could work now because she had accepted unquestioningly that her life would always be an awful loneliness; ambivalently, however, came a new sense of well-being and strong purpose. In her letter to Diamond she reviewed the facts of her marriage. She said that she had speculated long and hard on why her marriage had failed, but that many of the questions lay unanswered. Her first year with Reeves had been richly rewarding. Happy and compatible with her husband, she had worked indefatigably on her novel since the first week of her marriage, and he had encouraged her and helped in every way possible. Yet when the book was finished, something vital in her life seemed to leave her, too. In Fayetteville her nerves had become strained to the breaking point. It was as though she had suddenly discovered that it was impossible to work and be creative if she were in any physical proximity to Reeves. While with him, both her psychic and physical life were out of kilter. Carson told Diamond that she felt great compassion for Reeves, for she knew that he suffered, too. They had reached a point where she was no longer good for him. She could no longer help him, and if they attempted to continue in a marital relationship, the results could be devastating for them both. Although Reeves seemed to her now a much loved brother who was incapable of taking care of himself, instead of a husband, she felt that his very survival demanded that he be independent of her.

What would a relationship with David Diamond be like? she asked herself. If he expected a passionate involvement, he was mistaken, she told him. Passion was the last thing she wanted at present. With Annemarie she had known passion, she declared, but the involvement had been so intense, filled with emotional peaks of rapture and depression, that she had nearly destroyed herself. With God's help, that kind of life was over for good, she vowed. Carson asked Diamond if he had read Dostoevski's *The Idiot* recently, and if so, he would understand what she meant when she said that she had felt like a cross between Rogozhin and Myshkin. Strangely, however, it was not Annemarie as a human being she had loved so desperately, she admitted, for with her, inexplicably, passion caused the beloved to become anonymous. Moreover, passion obviated any possibility of fulfillment in spite of one's dreams and pinings.[32]

Carson had once told Diamond that she felt it wrong, impossible even, to attempt to make love fit into neat little slots or classifications. She likened love to jam, explaining that there were all kinds of jams. There was fresh quince and blueberry and cherry, jams that seemed just right, and there was jam that did not jell properly. Some jams caught a few stray insects—but it all was jam, just as love was love. And sometimes it tickled and tantalized the palate and fulfilled her gnawing hunger, and sometimes it scarred and maimed both the lover and the beloved. Carson conceived each role as separate. The Holy Grail of reciprocity was elusive to the hopeful pursuer, and impossible to the one who tired of the pursuit and abandoned hope.

In her letter to Diamond now she wanted him to know that she loved him very much even though she could not quite define such a love. They had felt a special connection from the very beginning which had brought them quickly to an emotional peak. Yet there was also Reeves in the middle of their relationship. Carson admitted frankly to Diamond that she did not know how deeply involved the two of them were, but she sensed that she should withdraw from both of their lives and wrap herself up in her own loneliness as best she could. Therein lay still another paradox, she admitted. She loved life, but at times felt compelled to withdraw from it. She loved people, yet felt that she sometimes repelled them. There were times when she felt she could draw no nourishment from any human relationship, that she was inexorably set apart—as though she were locked inside a very small room in which there was no light. She was sure that something marvelous was going on just outside her door, but after a few vain attempts to get out, she decided that it was safer and warmer within. Locked in her inner room, she would not have to risk being an object of ridicule, sympathy, or even worse, indifference.

Carson told Diamond that if she had never married Reeves, she might have made a life with Diamond that would have been pleasing to them both. The way things were, however, she could not hazard a guess. In the meantime, they should be together more, she suggested; they should learn to know each other better. She was not a complicated person, she told him. Her needs and longings were for simple, homely things. If Diamond should see Reeves, she pleaded, he must not mention her letter or any of the things she had told him. A broken marriage was a very painful thing, said Carson, and even though she had told Reeves much of this directly, there still was much to be talked over and worked out with him.

In spite of Carson's newly gained sense of independence, she was vaguely disquieted, she admitted to Diamond, because Reeves had not written to her in some time and she felt that she needed to hear from him. That Reeves had somehow changed in his affections for her now seemed obvious, yet she could not quite account for it, and it was painful to admit that it could even be possible. Diamond, however, knew explicitly what the problem was and why Reeves had not been writing. Reeves's ego had suffered grievously over the past few months, for he felt abandoned by Carson. He had remained in New York City only a few weeks after her departure for Yaddo. Very soon he had found himself not only out of money, but out of a job, as well.

When Diamond returned from Yaddo and a series of lectures at Smith College in early July, having stayed at Yaddo only three weeks, Reeves took a train to Rochester to join him. Reeves, too, had pondered where his destiny lay, just as Diamond had recorded his own feelings in his diary back in May, the day after the three of them had met. Perhaps for the first time Reeves became aware of his own bisexual nature and realized that his intense attraction for the young composer was more than platonic. Far more conventional than Carson in his attitudes and values, however, Reeves was troubled and deeply stirred by his ambivalence. He told Diamond that he knew he loved him; yet he also knew that their relationship transcended anything so limiting as sex. Carson, on the other hand, could not understand or even envision the possibility that her husband might love someone else. The triangle that haunted her fictional characters now haunted her in reality, as well. A we of me relationship was good only as long as it suited Carson—and included her—but it was devastating if it left her out.

In the past, in an attempt to overcome Reeves's puritanical nature, Carson had frequently preached to him that it was perfectly all right for a person to love a member of the same sex. To her, nothing human in nature was alien or abnormal. A love relationship between two men or two women could also be a very spiritual union that should be above petty jealousies. Yet it was a difficult philosophy for Carson herself to live with. When she finally realized that it was David Diamond whom Reeves now loved, she did not object because Diamond was a *man*, but because he was *their* best friend. Had Reeves gone off with a ballet dancer or a truck driver, had an affair with some vague male figure, Carson's attitude would have been simply: "Why, Reeves, that's just lovely—it rounds out your personality and has nothing to do with us, our marriage or our love for each other. You'll have a good time for a while, then you'll be back." But for her husband to have loved *their* best friend, to have gone off to Rochester with him and removed him from the we of me relationship that had been so meaningful to them both, was gross and unfair.

The situation that Carson was fantasizing daily at her typewriter, *The Ballad of the Sad Café*, which she told David Diamond was for him, was reminiscent of her own experience. In her novella, Miss Amelia was abandoned by Cousin Lymon, the little dwarf she loved inordinately, and Marvin Macy, her husband, whom she loathed, when the two men teamed up against her. The situations were by no means parallel, of course. The theme of abandonment also served as the fulcrum of her still unfinished novel, *The Bride*, in which Frankie Addams was abandoned by her brother and his bride, whom Frankie had conceived as her we of me. Carson strongly objected to Reeves's loving David Diamond. She feared its potential intensity, for she knew that it might develop into a permanent relationship for the two of them that completely excluded her, which, indeed, became the case years later when Diamond formed a meaningful and lasting liaison with someone else.

David Diamond soon realized that his chances for happiness with Reeves were nil. Like Carson, he found his own creativity as an artist suffering when he and Reeves were together for extended periods, a situation attributed largely to Reeves's excessive drinking and great waves of depression. Diamond did not think they could ever live together harmoniously. Reeves had stayed with him for several weeks in Rochester in the home of Diamond's sister and brother-in-law, but he returned usually on weekends to Manhattan to date a young nurse there. Reeves told Diamond that he slept with the young woman, but that the affair was simply the meeting of a sexual need. She satisfied his virile cravings, yet also met his need for a maternal figure. She had been a virgin, Reeves said, and he felt very tender toward her. Reeves also told Diamond that Carson knew about his affairs with other women, which had begun soon after their move to New York the year before. When Carson had begun to seek out other relationships and to keep company with the New York literary coterie and to exclude him, he had compensated by forming his own attachments elsewhere. She seemed to accept his purely sexual liaisons with others since she admitted that she herself was giving so little as a wife, but a deeply meaningful psychic union in which love was involved was completely out of the question, she said.

When Diamond came home from the MacDowell Colony, where he had worked during the latter part of July and early August, Reeves moved all of his personal belongings to Rochester. Carson was unaware of her husband's new location, but Reeves himself was completely serious in his intent to establish a permanent relationship with Diamond and hoped that they might live together in Diamond's family home on Edgerton Street. At first Reeves stayed with Diamond at his sister and brother-in-law's house. After a few days, Diamond's brother-in-law got him a job at Samson United, a chemical plant in Rochester. Once Reeves had an income again, he moved into a furnished room on East Avenue, and later to an apartment on Argyle Street, but he yearned to move in permanently with Diamond.

Reeves confided to his friend that summer his abandoned dream of being a writer someday and his disillusionment when he realized that the plan he and Carson had made for them to take turns writing while the other supported them as the official wage earner would never materialize. Reeves admitted that it was only logical that the plan had not worked, for their creativity simply could not be turned on and off like a spigot to coincide with the calendar. Yet while Carson's talent continued to flower, Reeves's psyche churned and subterranean resentment swelled. One night Diamond urged Reeves to begin to write while he was in Rochester and to attempt to fulfill his personal ambitions apart from Carson. The thought was not completely altruistic on Diamond's part, for he knew that his own creativity was suffering and he needed greater freedom to work. Seemingly pleased by the encouragement, Reeves sat hunched over a desk for several hours in what appeared to be labored creativity. When he finally got up, Diamond asked him with much interest: "Would you like to share with me what you have written, Reeves?"

"No, it's terrible—it's nothing at all," Reeves muttered, crumpling his manuscript and hurling it into a wastebasket. This aborted effort was the only attempt at creative writing which Diamond ever knew Reeves to make while with him. Reeves told others, however, that he had made many attempts to write, but that something always interfered.

Reeves was torn by his actions that summer. He knew that Carson would be deeply troubled because she had not heard from him in several weeks, yet he could not bring himself to acknowledge his betrayal in going to Rochester and seeking sanctuary and love with David Diamond. He told Diamond that he could not possibly write to Carson while he was admittedly still emotionally involved with them both. He loved Carson deeply, he said, and talked about her often, yet refused to communicate with her. His moods of melancholy and depression increased the longer he stayed in Rochester. One night after Diamond picked him up from work at the Samson plant, they drove to a neighborhood bar, the Tick-Tock on East Avenue, for drinks and dinner. Across the table, Diamond looked intently at Reeves and was struck by a sudden anguished expression that darkened his whole countenance. "I miss Carson terribly," Reeves said softly, ". . . so much so that I can hardly bear it."

The abject loneliness which Reeves felt at this moment lay in his inability to hold in balance his dual quest which had been activated by very human tensions in no way unique to him: his compelling need for a separate identity, yet his craving to belong entirely to someone else. A weaker person than Carson, according to those who knew them best, Reeves was far more dependent upon her than she ever had been on him.[38] Certainly in the future, after their reconciliation, the roles might have appeared to be reversed, for Carson was consumed by many illnesses later in life and was physically very dependent upon others for her well-being and daily comforts; but even then, she was the stronger figure. Tennessee Williams likened her strength to his handsome, marble-topped table in Key West, which he pounded for emphasis, and producer Arnold Saint Subber, who knew her well in the mid-fifties when they worked together on her play *The Square Root of Wonderful*, found her not at all the "wounded sparrow" that some persons had made her out to be, but called her, instead, an "iron butterfly." Reeves himself, in 1953, after Carson had been partially paralyzed for six years, replied to Tennessee Williams' question "And how is Carson?" with a long pause, followed by one explosive word which told all: "Indestructible!"

During the summer of 1941, however, Reeves's anguish was intensified because again and again he was reminded that Carson bore a name, *McCullers*, that had become more hers than his. It was *her* life and works that had made the name famous. He yearned to be an important entity himself. A few weeks later, Carson herself rebelled against the name. She found that she had become so psychically disturbed she could no longer write the last half of her signature. The check forgings that Reeves soon became engaged in, in which he wrote the name *Carson McCullers* and assumed her identity, in a sense, were also a part of his deeply troubled psyche. Such polarities caused Reeves to brood more and more until, eventually, he began to speak of suicide to David Diamond. One night in August while the two of them strolled leisurely across the Rochester Driving Park Bridge, Reeves paused, looked at his friend, and declared haltingly: "I think, David, that suicide is the only answer . . . it might be best for me." Then he put his arm about Diamond's shoulder and mumbled somewhat incoherently, "But don't you believe, also, that two people who love each other as we do, David . . . should die together?" Then, in a sudden movement, Reeves tightened his grasp on Diamond, hoisted him off his feet, and pulled him toward the railing of the bridge.

"No, Reeves, no!" shouted Diamond, ducking under his arms and out of Reeves's embrace.

The climactic moment over, Reeves quickly composed himself and reassured his friend, "I'm sorry, David. Please don't worry. I would never harm you." Years later, in Rome in 1951, Reeves told Diamond that he was certain he would kill himself someday. He also related just how he planned to do it. He said he would take an overdose of the drug, Antabuse, which sometimes is given to alcoholics to keep them from drinking. On top of that he would "down as much of a fifth of whiskey as possible." The combination would be sure to kill him, he said.

At the end of July 1941 Carson wrote to David Diamond that she was deeply disturbed since she had not heard from Reeves in over a month. She had no idea that Reeves had been with Diamond in Rochester during part of this time. Even worse than not hearing from him, however, was something else that alarmed her. She apologized to Diamond for sounding so mysterious, but she said that she could not tell him precisely what was troubling her yet for she needed to talk with Reeves himself first, or to hear some explanation from him in a letter. A few days later she sent Diamond a trenchant telegram. He must not mention her to Reeves or contact him in any way. It was desperately important. She would tell him all about it as soon as possible, she promised.[34]

Diamond, still at the MacDowell Colony at this time, called Carson at Yaddo to get to the bottom of her distress. She told him she had discovered that Reeves had been forging checks in her name. He not only had forged her signature and cashed the check she had received from *The New Yorker* in payment for "The Jockey," which she had sent him to deposit, but he also had forged and cashed other checks, including royalty payments sent to her at their apartment that had come from Houghton Mifflin for her first two books. Diamond assured Carson that he had been unaware of Reeves's latest disloyalty. After the telephone call, Carson mailed Diamond a hastily written note. She said that she would have to take immediate corrective steps, but did not want to file a criminal suit against her husband. To avoid the criminal charges she would have to pay several hundred dollars, she told Diamond, but she wanted secrecy no matter what the cost. There was no doubt about it—she would have to divorce him, she confided. Although she had known for weeks that a divorce was inevitable, she had not anticipated Reeves's unmanly betrayal—as she considered it—and his action was deeply offensive and humiliating. She told Diamond that everything worthwhile between her and her husband was over for good. She would leave Yaddo immediately and meet with a lawyer in New York City.

For Carson, the next few days were nightmarish and without number. She talked with Reeves briefly by telephone, saw her attorney, and initiated divorce proceedings. She resented that she would have to use the only grounds for divorce legal in New York in 1941—adultery. To her, the actual reasons were far more important. Of her cohorts in the city she sought out only Muriel Rukeyser, whose friendship she cherished. Miss Rukeyser was Reeves's friend, too. Devoted to them both, the poet was troubled by the unhappy turn of events. She was also aware of Reeves's liaison with David Diamond, a relationship which had been unsettling to all concerned. To Miss Rukeyser Reeves confided that he intended to enlist in the Coast Guard before the end of the week. He would get out of the city and out of his wife's life as soon as possible.

Carson, too, left New York City immediately after a second meeting with her lawyer. From Yaddo the next day she wrote Miss Rukeyser that she had cried practically the entire trip under the full view of everyone on the train. At first she had retreated to the water closet to weep privately, but the room was so tiny and stuffy that she had gotten sick instead. She had not been able to pull herself together until the train was less than an hour away from Yaddo, when a dining car was finally added. In it she found sanctuary and a large stiff drink and regained a small measure of self-control. No one else—no mother or close sister—could have been more dear and compassionate than her friend Muriel Rukeyser had been throughout the ordeal, Carson told her.

In spite of her bitterness and hurt over Reeves's latest deceit, she was still concerned for his physical and psychic well-being. Since her husband would not be able to think of practical concerns at present, Carson suggested to Miss Rukeyser that she hoped her friend would do certain things for Reeves to help make his transition to military life as smooth as possible. He would no doubt forget to take any civilian clothes with him, Carson said, and it would be months before he could save for a new wardrobe. Being able to dress well when off duty would help give him the identity and self-respect he craved, she reasoned. Would Miss Rukeyser please help him pack his things and give him money for a month's supply of tobacco to carry him through pay day? she asked. Enclosed in Carson's letter was ten dollars for Reeves, but she urged her friend not to let Reeves know its source. It would be better for him to think of it as Miss Rukeyser's loan as a friend, for which she expected reasonably prompt repayment, Carson suggested. It would help his self-respect, she added. Nor would it be wise to give him more, for he would only drink it up. She also sent money which she asked Miss Rukeyser to keep—a few dollars to help defray the cost of the many meals she knew Reeves to have eaten in the poet's apartment when he was without funds.

Back at Yaddo Carson rested, stayed quiet, did not work—was physically unable to work, she wrote Miss Rukeyser—and went to see her Saratoga Springs doctor about what now seemed to be a chronic malady. Her heart hurt and bumped and skipped dreadfully, she told him. When she mentioned that some of her Yaddo friends had asked her to go to Canada with them, he advised her that to get away for a little while, to have a complete change of locale, would help relieve her distress. Newton Arvin had invited her to accompany Yaddo director Granville Hicks, Hicks's wife, Dorothy, and their daughter Stephanie to Quebec. Although they had originally planned to leave while Carson was in New York City, Arvin assured her that they would await her return.

Duly encouraged, Carson dashed off another hurried note to David Diamond to apprise him of the trip and then typed a long letter to her editor at Houghton Mifflin, Robert Linscott, who had written that he would visit her at Yaddo the end of August. She told Linscott, too, about her problems with Reeves and the suit for divorce. She said that she had made restitution on all the checks he had forged in her name, which had overdrawn her checking account. Had it not been for the money she received from *The New Yorker*, she told Linscott, for two stories ("Madame Zilensky and the King of Finland," her tale of a pathological liar who was obsessed by music, and "Correspondence," the epistolary story of Henky Evans and her Brazilian pen pal who never wrote her a letter), she would not have had the money to cover Reeves's abuses. She said that she had received almost five hundred dollars for the two pieces.[35] Carson also thought that her editor would be pleased to know that she had finished a work about the same length of *Reflections in a Golden Eye*, her fairy tale *The Ballad of the Sad Café*, but she did not want to show it to anyone yet. After she wrote two more tales of about the same length, she thought Houghton Mifflin might like to make a book of them; but first, upon her return from Canada, she wanted to finish *The Bride*.

The trip to Quebec had developed in an interesting manner. Although she apparently had known about the journey and had planned for some time to make a trip, Granville and Dorothy Hicks had no inkling that anyone except Newton Arvin and their daughter Stephanie intended to accompany them. Practically on the eve of their departure Arvin had casually asked Hicks if it would be all right for Carson to come along, too, adding that "Carson asked if she might join us." Very likely Carson did decide on her own, without consulting anyone, that she, too, was going to Quebec, just as Carson's fictional Frankie Addams planned to accompany her brother Jarvis and his bride on their honeymoon. Hicks, in fact, had not even met Carson until a day or two before their scheduled departure—a departure which was delayed until Carson could return from her trip to New York. Like Newton Arvin, Granville Hicks was a director of Yaddo. He was never a resident artist as Arvin had been that summer, but he had heard a great deal about Carson and looked forward to knowing her in person.

On August 22 Carson departed with the Hickses, their daughter Stephanie, and Arvin in the Hickses' car. When they had driven only a few miles—to Glens Falls—Carson and Arvin tapped Hicks on the shoulder and announced that they wanted to stop at a liquor store. The two of them went in and emerged a few minutes later carrying several gallon jugs of sherry and three or four bottles of brandy and whiskey. "The car was already brimming and there was no room in the trunk, but Carson and Newton settled the bottles and jugs in around their feet and on the seat beside them and seemed not the slightest bit discomfited," said Hicks.

The trip to Quebec took two days each way. Hicks usually drove thoughout the morning and his wife in the afternoon. When Dorothy Hicks drove, her husband joined Carson and Arvin in the back seat for sherry and conversation. Hicks always felt relieved not to drive because he often became so fascinated by the strange conversations going on between Carson and Arvin that he could hardly keep his eyes and mind on the road. It seemed to Hicks that Arvin lectured Carson on all manner of things, "both intellectual and otherwise." Sometimes he and his wife overheard something they thought especially amusing, such as Arvin's comment: "But, Carson, that isn't Montaigne—it's La Rochefoucauld," or "But I really don't believe Yaddo could be called baroque, Carson."[36] According to Hicks, Arvin spent much of the travel time trying to persuade Carson to go through with her divorce, as though she had some misgivings. Hicks's daughter, who had known Arvin since she was a baby, adored him, but she confessed to her parents on the trip that Arvin and Carson's conversations seemed "a little crazy" to her. Frequently the five of them played word games, such as "Pig," a simple identification game that Carson and Stephanie delighted in especially.

On the trip up, Hicks decided that they could make better time if they skirted Montreal and took a less traveled route. It proved a poor choice. The roads were terrible and the countryside relatively uninhabited.

Their situation would not have bothered them except that as twilight approached they could find no suitable lodging. Finally they came upon the little village of Sorel, where they took rooms in a quaint old hotel. That particular stop was the most amusing of the entire trip, said Hicks. The rooms in the hotel had an assortment of signs posted for the benefit of the guests. Intended as behavioral guidelines, the signs provoked hilarity because of the manager's literal translation of French into English. Some of the signs read: "Please do not lie on the bed with your shoes on. You should not do this at home. Why would you do it here?" Another one said: "If you desire to make friends, please consult the management first." The next morning Carson was fascinated by the chatter and haggling of the town market being set up just outside their windows. The women jabbered and quibbled in French amid the carts of fresh vegetables, fruits, cheeses, and chickens. "It was all quite wonderful," said Hicks, "very picturesque in a European sort of way."[37]

Upon their arrival in Quebec the second evening, Arvin astonished the Hicks family by stepping up to the register and signing himself and Carson in as "Mr. and Mrs. Newton Arvin." "Nothing was said, but we were a bit shocked," admitted Hicks, "for by this time even Stephanie realized that Newton didn't like women—at least not in the bed. But what surprised us even more, perhaps, was Newton's returning to the registry the next morning and asking for a separate room."[38] Speculating later, Hicks said that he never could decide if Arvin's breach with Carson had occurred simply because "he was an insomniac and Carson had not had a good night's sleep, or if they had had some kind of sexual experience when one had perhaps pushed the other further than he wanted to go." One thing the night did accomplish was that Carson became convinced that she would sleep better if she adopted Arvin's habit of wearing a night shade to bed. Her practice of sleeping with a night shade began soon after the Quebec trip, for she, too, had often found it difficult to go to sleep.

On the journey up, Carson remarked to the Hickses that she intended to stay on in Quebec indefinitely—all winter, perhaps, or at least for a month. In a letter to Robert Linscott she had said the same thing, for she felt that a change of environment would help her put aside her unhappiness and adjust to a new way of life. By the end of their first day in Quebec, however, Hicks was certain she would stay no longer than they did, and by the second day, Arvin agreed with him. Carson had no interest in sightseeing. She accompanied the group only once, on a boat trip the first day. Earlier she had announced to them that she could hardly wait to get the feel of Quebec, but according to Hicks:

> We soon discovered that her idea of doing that was sitting in her
> room all day and drinking and fantasizing. Carson talked as though

she had a whole series of plans—all in typical childlike fashion. We knew almost immediately that those dreamlike plans would fall through. . . . The day we went to Ile d'Orleans, which I think Carson would have liked, she said she wanted to write letters and wander around the lower town. We got back, of course, to find she had done neither.[39]

Carson did write at least one letter that day, however. In a note to David Diamond she said that she had talked with Reeves in New York, who told her he was going on to Rochester. Perhaps he was there now, and if so, she urged Diamond to mention her in no way to Reeves. The whole situation was unspeakably painful, she admitted. Then Carson shifted her tone in a manner that never ceased to amaze her correspondents, who marveled that she could appear to be abjectly depressed one moment and then buoyant and enthusiastic the next. This time she wrote euphorically about Quebec and the charming towns they had seen en route. The city swarmed with smiling soldiers and priests wearing long black robes. It made her think about the war in Europe. She observed that people in the larger towns in Canada seemed to show excitement and awareness of the war, whereas the villagers took little note of it. She told Diamond that Arvin and the Hickses were far more energetic than she, who preferred ambling about the town by herself.

Although Carson had been physically transported to a new environment, which Newton Arvin hoped would distract her from her anxieties, the trip to Quebec did little to alleviate her psychic suffering or to take her mind off Reeves and Diamond, whom she resented being together. She spoke of Reeves to Arvin and the Hickses with great hostility. She admitted, too, that even though she wanted the divorce, she still loved Reeves. He must have been mentally ill to have done the dreadful things he did, she reasoned. Granville Hicks recalled quite vividly one of Carson's conversations about Reeves:

> Carson talked all one evening about Reeves—how he had forged her checks and spent the money on parties, had beat her, pushed her into the hall naked, tore up her clothes, etc. (All of this can be taken with due skepticism, I'm sure. I think I can see now as never before that one thing Carson and Reeves had in common was a taste for melodrama.) After all her horrid revelations, Carson still would say, "He is a very charming person, and I love him dearly. . . . I love him like my own brother." Although Newton urged her strongly to get the divorce, I thought she would never follow through with it, and I was surprised when she did.[40]

When the Hickses and Arvin announced that they were ready to leave Quebec, Carson, too, appeared eager to depart. There was never any question of her asking if she might ride back with them. She simply packed her suitcase and was ready to go when they were. En route, Arvin invited her to stop off with him in Northampton, Massachusetts, for a few days. He wanted Carson to meet his good friend and colleague at Smith College, Al Fisher, a fellow English professor, whose wife, Helen Eustis, had just begun to publish fiction. Carson welcomed the interlude, for she did not want to return to Yaddo until Katherine Anne Porter vacated the farmhouse, which Elizabeth Ames had promised her when it again became available.

On August 30, 1941, the Hickses dropped Carson and Arvin off in Northampton and continued to their home in Grafton, New York. The weather had been lovely and the scenery beautiful, said Hicks, but at no time could he recall Carson's having taken any notice of the physical world about her. Although she almost always revealed in letters a keen sensitivity to nature and an aesthetic appreciation of her external surroundings, she usually did not remark on nature to people with whom she was in casual conversation. When alone, she chose to think creatively, to write fiction, to write long letters to those she loved in which she might express her deepest thoughts. With stimulating companions such as Newton Arvin and the Hickses, Carson would much rather talk about ideas and tell anecdotes of real and imagined happenings. When Arvin summed up the trip to Granville Hicks a few days after their return, he confided: "The trip for me was one sustained conversation with moving scenery."[41]

Carson left Northampton after spending the weekend with Arvin and returned to Yaddo for only a few days. The farmhouse still was not available. It did not bother her, however, for she knew she had more important things to do at the moment than write. Buoyed by Arvin's urging that she proceed with the divorce as soon as possible, Carson discussed the matter thoroughly with Elizabeth Ames, who had acted over the years as a kind of "Mother Superior" to troubled Yaddo guests if they sought her help. Mrs. Ames, almost as distressed as Carson, agreed that her young friend should return to New York City at once to press for the necessary court action.

Quickly Carson packed the few personal belongings she had taken to Yaddo with her, not knowing when she would return, and caught the next train into the city. As soon as she checked into the Bedford Hotel on East Fortieth Street, she made an appointment to see the lawyer she had consulted before going to Quebec. Carson habitually was indecisive, but once she made her mind up to a thing she was capable of resolute action. The next night she wrote a joint letter to Mrs. Ames and Newton Arvin to apprise them of the latest developments. She said she had spent all morning with the lawyers and was now exhausted. She had trouble sleeping, she told them, but she had written to a doctor she knew on Long Island, William Mayer, to see if he could help her. Surely he could do her some good if anyone could, she reasoned. The divorce proceedings would take about three weeks. In the meantime, she would wait it out and try to work quietly in her hotel room. Once settled, Carson did try to work, but each time she sat at her typewriter she found herself in a state of perpetual agitation. She told Arvin that she simply could make no sustained effort now. Moreover, she could not think well. She had begun to stammer, she said, and felt as though she were becoming psychically unstrung. As her stay in New York City lengthened, she began to tremble uncontrollably, could seldom sleep, and experienced wild, hallucinatory dreams whether awake or asleep. Arvin responded with a soothing, reassuring letter and said that he would come to her if necessary. Carson assured him in her next letter, however, that she was better. She said that she had carried his letter about with her all day in her shirt pocket. Just having it on her person gave her a sense of security and made her feel less lost, she admitted. Moreover, she had gone to a doctor who was a friend of William Mayer's. Anyone who had undergone the pressures she had been subjected to over the past months would have behaved the same way, he assured her. Carson told Arvin that her mind was once again clear and in good shape in spite of her anxieties. She was amused when her new doctor told her that if she had gone to see Dr. Mayer, he simply would have invited her to come home with him to play Beethoven quartets. Soon after this letter to Arvin, Carson's condition suddenly worsened and she did go to see William Mayer. A psychiatrist in Amityville, Long Island, Mayer eventually became her good friend, but by the time she saw him, the emotional entanglement involving the divorce had become almost devastating to her.

In order to divorce Reeves on the grounds of adultery, she was told that she would have to produce evidence that he had had a sexual assignation with someone else; mere verbal assent on Reeves's part was not enough. Advised to hire a private detective to get evidence that would hold up in court, Carson reluctantly complied and acquired the necessary data. The whole sordid affair was sickening to her. She did not want to see Reeves if she could avoid it; she wanted only to conclude the legalities as soon as possible and then to retreat home to her mother and to some margin of safety where she might repair her mind and body and put Reeves behind her for good.

Reeves, in the meantime, had returned to New York City from Rochester to consult his own lawyer, but he had no intention of contesting the divorce. He had given up the old apartment on West Eleventh Street and had no permanent address in the city. He felt disassociated and almost destitute, even—which was a reason he gave Carson for having forged her checks in the first place. She had abandoned him, closed out the checking account, and left him with no money, he argued. Reeves stayed that fall in various cheap hotels and spent a few nights in a room next to Muriel Rukeyser's apartment, an arrangement Miss Rukeyser made to help ease his financial plight. The young poet's relationship with Reeves and Carson was a delicate one for she loved them both, felt loyalties to each, and empathized with them in their dilemmas. She had written a poem for Carson and Reeves a few months earlier, moved by what seemed to be the impossibility of a harmonious marriage and the tragedy of their lives. Entitled "The Watchers,"[42] the poem revealed much of the ambivalence and dichotomy of the young couple's troubled relationship and of Miss Rukeyser's tender attitude toward each:

THE WATCHERS

for Carson and Reeves

She said to me, He lay there sleeping
Upon my bed cast down
With all the bitterness dissolved at last,
An innocent peace within a sleeping head;
He could not find his infant war, nor turn
To that particular zoo, his family of the dead.
I saw her smile of power against his deep
Heart, his waking heart,
Her enmity, her sexual dread.

He said to me, She slept and dreaming
Brought round her face
Closer to me in silence than in fire,
But smiled, but smiled, entering her dark life
Whose hours I never knew, wherein she smiles.
Wherein she dim descending breathes upon
My daylight and the color of waking goes.
Deep in his face, the wanderer
Bringing the gifts of legend and the wars,
Conspiracy of opposing images.

In the long room of dream I saw them sleep,
Turned to each other, clear,
With an obliterated look—
Love, god of foreheads, touching then
Their bending foreheads while the voice of sleep
Wept and sang and sang again
In a chanting of fountains,
A chattering of watches,
Love, sang my sleep, the wavelight on the stone.

I weep to go beyond this throne and the waterlight,
To kiss their eyelids for the last time and pass
From the delicate confidence of their sly throats,
The conversation of their flesh of dreams.
And though I weep in my dream,
When I wake I will not weep.

Carson remained in New York City for three difficult weeks. She saw Muriel Rukeyser, Tania and James Stern—whose parties Carson had enjoyed immensely with Reeves that spring—and Greta Weiskopf, who had been her closest female friend at Yaddo that summer. She purposefully saw as few others as possible. She did not even want to go out to the house in Brooklyn Heights and be with George Davis and Wystan Auden —whom she dearly loved—for there would be too much to explain and to have to talk about.

Among her letters forwarded from Yaddo were two that were particularly cheering: a letter with an application for a Guggenheim Fellowship, which David Diamond and Newton Arvin had urged her to seek, and a letter at last from Annemarie Clarac-Schwarzenbach. Elated, she wrote to Arvin that her missive from Annemarie had taken three months to reach her. It was the first that any of their mutual friends had had since she had gone to Africa. Annemarie had known great deprivation, loneliness, and fear, but she no longer felt the abject desperation and terrible sense of finality to her life that she had felt before, she said. She had been traveling for many weeks into the middle of the Congo. For months she had had no news of the outside world. She urged Carson to write and to tell her what was going on, especially in New York City. She assured Carson, also, that they would someday see each other again. She said that she appreciated now the simple rules of life that she had violated in the past, and that she knew what it was like to feel pride once more.

Carson was deeply grateful for Annemarie's letter, for she had feared that the person she felt she loved then more than anyone else in the world had been lost to her forever. In the same letter to Arvin in which she had rhapsodized about Annemarie, she admitted to being only mildly dismayed that *The New Yorker* had turned down her latest batch of pieces with the comment that they were too grim. *The New Yorker* had accepted the first three stories Carson had written at Yaddo that summer, the first of her stories to be published anywhere since "Wunderkind" had appeared in *Story* magazine in 1936, but the magazine published no more of Carson's fiction. She did not like to be turned down, and she decided that she simply would not submit anything else to *The New Yorker* again. It was their loss, she reasoned, not hers.

Carson also saw Robert Linscott while she was in New York. She had missed him when he had gone to Yaddo in August while she was in Quebec, but now, among the forwarded letters, was one from her editor written from the very hotel in which she herself was staying: the Bedford. When she found that Linscott was still there, she called him and he came to see her immediately. They talked of her work and Linscott told her that Houghton Mifflin would publish her *Ballad of the Sad Café* separately if she would like, instead of in a collection with a few of her other stories, as she had once proposed. Again, however, she told him that she did not want any other full-length work to come out before her story of *The Bride*. She had given her body and soul over to that book, she said, and she had to write it out of her system if she were ever going to be sound again.

In order to finish the book, Carson felt that she would need financial help. If only she could get a Guggenheim Fellowship, she fretted, but the deadline for submitting the necessary papers was only two weeks away and she needed to secure sponsors. Carson wrote Newton Arvin for suggestions. Before her second book came out, she had applied for a Rosenwald Fellowship but had not received it. In the process, however, she had used up the sponsors she might have called upon now. She told Arvin that he was the only person with academic prestige she knew. Then she thought about Theodore Morrison from Harvard, whom she had met at Bread Loaf. She asked Arvin if Geenslet, another editor for Houghton Mifflin, might also be a good person to name, along with Louis Untermeyer, Granville Hicks, and Amy Loveman. Van Wyck Brooks was also a possibility, she suggested, but she did not know if he had read any of her works. Carson asked Arvin for advice about each person as to whether or not he would make a good sponsor.[43] The list must have been satisfactory both to Arvin and the Guggenheim people, for the following spring she was awarded a fellowship.

After a week at the Bedford Hotel, Carson moved into her favorite hotel in New York City, the Brevoort. When at last her role in the divorce proceedings was over, however, she discovered that she could not sign her name. She trembled uncontrollably, then grew very rigid when she tried to write her signature. She was alarmed, too, for she had a train to catch. She had already called her mother and told her that she was returning home immediately, but now she could not even sign her traveler's checks so that she could check out of the hotel. Frustrated and embarrassed, Carson finally telephoned Rebecca Pitts, a literary acquaintance she had met through Muriel Rukeyser: "I'm unable to write a check—please come over and help me get out of the Brevoort," she pleaded mournfully.

Miss Pitts, thinking Carson was out of funds, replied as gently as possible: "Carson, you know I haven't any money—I'm surely not the one to help."

"That isn't it," Carson wailed. "Please come over and I'll explain."
Rushing to Carson's room, Miss Pitts discovered her friend in the grip of
"some kind of hysteria which prevented her from signing her check in the
only acceptable signature—*Carson McCullers*. She could write *Carson*,
and anything else she wanted, but not her last name," said Miss Pitts.
Finally, after some fruitless conversation about the ridiculousness of the
whole situation, Rebecca Pitts had to swear to the desk clerk that the
woman who stood in front of him was, indeed, Carson McCullers—a fact
the manager knew very well. Then, by dint of Miss Pitts's holding Carson's writing hand firmly with her own, she managed to guide Carson
through a reasonable facsimile of her ordinary signature.[44]

Once home with her family in Georgia, Carson felt free at last, shed
of a marriage steeped in bitters. Carson was not so naive that she took no
blame for the deterioration of her marriage, yet she believed strongly that
she was very much the injured party. Marguerite and Lamar Smith were
greatly relieved to have their daughter back in Columbus. From such a
distance it had been impossible for Marguerite to keep the "ungentle
winds" away from Carson, and Marguerite had suffered heavily from her
inability to bear her daughter's burdens for her. Cradling Carson to her
now—the child-woman who always would remain her "little girl"—Marguerite wrapped her daughter in love, compassion, and tender care. But
even her mother could not ward off Carson's next afflction. Although
1519 Starke Avenue was *home*, it still was not the haven Carson sought.

Chapter Seven

COLUMBUS AND YADDO,
FALL 1941 – WINTER 1942

*C*arson *arrived in Columbus on October 14, 1941, the self-styled exile* returned, a sensitive artist grateful to be home at last. Exhausted from the twenty-hour train ride, she picked at her supper, bathed, and fell into bed. Her parents understood well their daughter's need for sleep now more than anything. Carson had brooded deeply during her trip South, reflecting intensely upon the recent months and asking questions which demanded answers: Why was she going home? What could she accomplish there that she could not have done in New York? How might she redeem herself? Her only certainty was that the last year and a half in New York had been a period of sloth and corruption. She could not reason away her terrible waste of time, emotions, and creative genius, nor could she understand her bent for self-destruction. She was merciless in her self-appraisal. She felt constantly, and in all ways, that she had failed in her work, in her relationships with those she loved, and in everything most precious to her. But she would prostitute herself no longer. She resolved that she must—and would—hold herself to account at last. Through work, loneliness, and adherence to the truth of her own inward life—these mortifications would meld into a singular path through which she might pay penance daily.

Above all, Carson felt that she needed God, that she must be able to pray again if she were to effect her own redemption. Carson wrote to David Diamond that she could no longer ask anything of people. She had asked twice before, and both times there had been no response. Her love and petitions had ended only in dreadful suffering and broken faith. She could call now to no one except God—yet she lamented that she could not even bring herself to do that.

Once home, Carson was relieved not to have to share the house on Starke Avenue with anyone except her parents. Her sister, Rita, had returned that fall to the University of Miami and would not be home until Christmas; Lamar, Jr., had recently married and was living with his wife's family several miles away. Carson's other relatives in the town now discreetly kept their distance, for Marguerite had made it clear that her daughter did not want to *have* to talk with anyone. For the first days she saw no one. Her father had never questioned her actions, and she did not have to make small talk with him now. With her mother, there was instant communion, even if a word was not spoken. Best of all was the sanctity of her own room.

Carson basked in the comforts of her room, surrounded by the safe, material things she could count on and held dear. In one corner of her bedroom was a fireplace. Although the mid-October weather was still mild, she went out early the morning after her arrival into the back yard to chop wood for her bedroom fireplace. There was nothing that could dispel gloom and make her feel more right with the world—and with herself, she said—than a fire flickering and turning the walls of her room a warm, shimmery orange. One thing was missing from her bedroom, however, which Carson had already resolved to rectify—she wanted a new piano of her own. She would take some of the cash she had salvaged from her marriage and her own profligate spending, she decided, and buy one, then give her mother most of the rest of the money to cover her living expenses for the next few months. Carson arrived home with a little over $1,300, which she hoped would see her through the completion of her novel.

On Saturday morning, the day after her arrival, Carson announced her intention to take a bus to town and select a piano. She asked her mother if she might trade in the old family Linder, which had been in the home for years. "Of course, precious," said Marguerite. "Anything you want to do is perfectly all right with us—you know that." Carson played on all of the spinets at Humes Music Store that day, choosing, finally, a forty-inch mahogany Gulbransen. She gave her name as Mrs. Lula Carson McCullers—the first time she had used her double name in over ten years—and peeled off $300 in cash to add to the $100 trade-in that Humes allowed on the family's piano. She bought a stack of new music, too, having lost almost all her old pieces in New York when Reeves had vacated the West Eleventh Street apartment and left her music and many of her other belongings behind. That night she wrote Newton Arvin to please try to locate some of her other music which she had forgotten in Northampton. Jubilant for the moment, Carson felt that music and hard work with her "Frankie" might salve her soul even if God would not.

She played on her new piano almost all morning the next day, interspersed with conversations with her mother. The upper register seemed a bit sharp to her, she told Marguerite, but she loved the tone and said that her little spinet would hold her until someday she might purchase a small Steinway. Carson had revealed to her parents the night of her arrival most of the sordid story behind the divorce—or, at any rate, *her* side of it—for she was unable to give a completely objective, rational account of all the psychic factors that had led up to it. Nor did she acknowledge her sexual ambivalence that had contributed to the estrangement. She had not gotten over Annemarie Clarac-Schwarzenbach in spite of her good intentions and reckless attempts to replace her with other relationships. She found, instead, that she had merely clutched hysterically at people, clung tenaciously to life—any life. Eventually her mother knew of Carson's ambivalences and accepted them unquestioningly, but her father did not know, nor is it likely that he would have understood.

Once home, Carson brooded over Reeves and how sad and wrong their marriage had been. Although the final decree was not to be granted for several months, she felt as though she had been lifted from a great pit in which she had been entrapped for years, a pit that she herself had helped dig. Loyal to Carson, Marguerite and Lamar, Sr., concluded that Reeves was "something bad that had happened to their daughter—and the sooner forgotten, the better."[1] Carson's parents were embittered over Reeves's latest behavior, and they wrote off their son-in-law as one who no longer existed. Carson, too, felt even more victimized than she had before after her mother told of one of Reeves's more recent shenanigans of which Carson herself had been unaware. Marguerite said that Reeves had borrowed money from her, which she had set aside for her daughter Rita's schooling. To Carson, Reeves's action was a dastardly deceit, and she vowed to make up the loss—a sizable amount—as soon as she could. She had already given her mother all the cash she had. In a letter to Newton Arvin, Carson lamented that her mother had never had any money to speak of, and that Reeves had taken what little she had. Such assertions by Carson over the years prompted some of her relatives to resent her attitude of "poor-mouthing the family's economic situation," exaggerating to make it appear as though she had been reared in a deprived home. "She was not. If anyone was deprived, it was her brother and sister," said one of Carson's cousins from Columbus.[2]

The family had scraped to send Rita back to the University of Miami, for Lamar, Sr., was still methodically repaying his creditors, having refused during the Depression to take his banker's advice and declare bankruptcy. Other small businessmen in Columbus who had declared bankruptcy were now operating thriving new businesses upon the wake of more prosperous times in a country preparing for war. Carson's brother, proud of his father's reputation for honesty and personal integrity, recalled that "before my father died in 1944, he had paid off every dime he ever owed—which was a lot, for during the Depression he owed ten times what he was worth."[3]

A few months before Carson returned home, her father moved his jewelry and watch repair shop back to its 1918 location, where Marguerite had first pushed him into business for himself. An economy move, this time he shared the ground-floor office of the Murrah Building at 19 Twelfth Street with a loan company, a location he kept until his death three years later. (Smith's shop was on the right side of a partial wall, the Walter Park Loan Company on the left.) Lamar Smith was still a plodder. He went to work early regularly and came home late, keeping his store open long after most of the other downtown businesses had closed. He brought home the profits of his business, which were substantial, and never questioned his wife as to how she spent them. Nor had his personality changed much since he was a young man, except that he was more taciturn now and inclined to melancholia. Although seldom an outwardly happy man, Carson's father expressed pleasure at having his elder daughter home again. With Rita away at school and Lamar, Jr., now married, 1519 Starke Avenue had become a quiet and lonely household in recent months. Lamar, Jr., had married Virginia Standard, a local girl who deeply loved her father-in-law and made over him in a way that his own daughters had not; but soon after the marriage the young couple had moved in with Virginia's parents, and Lamar, Sr., missed his affectionate, robust son who had always taken time to visit with him, who made it a point to share bits of his day with him, to listen with him to the war news in Europe, to seek his advice—in short, to make his father know that he was a recognized and much-loved entity in the Smith household.

The last three or four years of Lamar, Sr.'s life were lonely ones, for his son enlisted in the Seabees and spent the rest of the war years in the Pacific. (Brother-Man—as he still was known by the family—was not even able to return for his father's funeral.) The elder Smith had felt increasingly a sense of estrangement from a family which seemed to revolve in an alien orbit, an orbit which once again pivoted almost exclusively around Carson. To cope, he began to drink heavily for the first time in his life.

Rita had always been more gregarious and outgoing than Carson in the Smith household, and Carson had played more exclusively the role of her mother's companion and confidante, a liaison that the family thought perfectly normal since she was five years older than Rita. But Carson's communion with her mother was at her father's expense, and inadvertently her presence at home again contributed to her parents' further estrangement from each other. It was never a sharp cleavage, but a gradual drifting apart, their lives quite separate even though they lived under the same roof. Carson had not communicated with her father in any deeply personal way since propelling herself as a child into a world of books, fantasy, and music. Whereas Marguerite had always intruded upon Carson's private world—her inner room—and made herself a part of it, Lamar, Sr., would not have dreamed of it, nor would he have known how. Carson had already depicted in *The Heart Is a Lonely Hunter* a father who felt cut off from meaningful communion with his family, who sat aimlessly drinking beer each night and occasionally making inadequate gestures at communication. In the novel, Mick, her youthful protagonist, tried one evening to talk with him, having suddenly realized his abject loneliness; but her thoughts stuck in her throat and neither of them could say the things in their hearts. Frankie, whom Carson was creating then in her story *The Bride*, also felt set apart from her father. Frankie loved her father, but looked at him in "a slant-eyed way." Carson could articulate in her fiction sensitivities she could never express in actuality. In this way, the fiction became her reality.

She was sensitive to her father, however, in ways he never guessed. She mentioned him in letters to her friends, voicing often her concern for his welfare and speaking of his goodness. In a Thanksgiving Day letter to Newton Arvin, Carson told of her father having gone that day to the funeral of an old crony of his, for whom he had been asked to be an honorary pallbearer. But the gesture had saddened and provoked him, for he felt that to be an honorary pallbearer meant that he was getting old, although he was only fifty-one. Carson felt pity for her father as he brooded over the people who were invited to carry the coffin, maintaining that he was as strong and agile as they were.

In actuality, Carson, too, was detached from her family, although she could leave or join them at will. Part of her ability to do so was in knowing that they were always there. "I cut myself off from my family when I was six," Carson told Janet Flanner before leaving New York that fall. The comment had so impressed Miss Flanner that she had written it on the bottom of a poem Carson gave her, a comment which seemed applicable not only to Carson's life, but to the poem, as well.[4]

"The Twisted Trinity," Carson's first published poem, was a personal expression couched in richly metaphoric language. She said that there had been a time in her life when "stone was stone," "a face on the street was a finished face," and the trinity of "a leaf, my soul, and God alone/ Made instant symmetry." Suddenly, all things failed; the trinity was twisted. Faces were dreamlike, incomplete, and stone no longer stone, but splintered fragments. Yet in "the child's unfinished face," the poet could recognize "sudden eyes"; a stranger's climb up a stairway left a familiar shadow, and somehow, "the delicate autumn hill and the slant star" received "a new dimension" from the "exiled intellect": "something of you." It was a different trinity now, as well as a twisted one, but the exiled wanderer could take comfort in it. She now realized a love that transcended human ties—in which reciprocity was never an issue.

Although Carson had cut herself off from her family when she was six, as she told Janet Flanner, had accepted her sense of separateness, loneliness, and alienation, and known that she must find within herself what she most needed, she remained, paradoxically, the quester. Her Grail was reciprocity—of love, compassion, communion, and commitment —regardless of her protestations, on occasion, to the contrary.

Carson's body mended quickly at home. Her strange, hysterical paralysis had inexplicably been left behind in New York City—a symptomatic quirk of the whole hellish experience, she decided. She now craved sleep more than she thought possible, getting ten or eleven hours each night. Hers was a woodchuck's sleep, untroubled now by dreams or nightmares. Each morning, she was up two hours before daybreak, alert and eager to start the day.

To Carson, the predawn was a wonderfully mysterious time. She loved, especially, to get up to a black, starless sky. On first arising, she usually walked out on the porch in the crisp October air, still dressed in her pajamas and bathrobe, stretched, looked up at the dark heavens, and silently thrilled at the unfathomable mystery of things. Her father, also, was an early riser. Usually up first, Lamar Smith built a fire and had hot oatmeal waiting on the stove for his daughter. Soon Marguerite was in the kitchen, too, fixing sausage and eggs and strong black coffee, which Carson habitually drank from the ceramic mug her friend Henry Varnum Poor had made for her. Her father left the kitchen then and the two women in his life whom he little understood. Carson ate a large breakfast while she and her mother listened to the music of Mozart, Scarlatti, and the record she considered her favorite of them all, a Beethoven quartet. After breakfast, Carson walked in the woods while it was still dark, the first streaks of pink barely showing in the sky. Her walks were never hikes or a matter of physical fitness; rather, she climbed the hills and rambled through the woods so that she might breathe deeply and more freely— absorbing, listening, scrutinizing, and becoming at one with the sounds and textures and hues of nature.

Although Carson rarely dated letters—usually she simply wrote "Tuesday, 1519 Starke Avenue"—one could trace in them the evolvement of the seasons in Georgia as she saw them, for her letters abounded in rich, sensory impressions of the out-of-doors. On Thanksgiving 1941, she wrote to Newton Arvin of roller-skating up and down the streets of her Wynnton neighborhood, but of having to watch for the acorns which tripped her if she were not careful. The leaves in the gutters which she leaped over with great agility were gold and bright brown, she said, and she marveled that for days the skies had been cloudless and blue, the winds crispy cold. Inside, delicious smells of baked hen, dressing, and sherry permeated the house.

In February, Carson wrote that the days had become bleak, gray, cold, and dreary. Yet she found relief in the rice birds that came almost every morning. Hundreds of them swooped down into her father's dried-up garden then moved to the mistletoe in the giant oak trees around the house and pecked the holly berries outside her window in their incessant search for food. The winter days of late February were brilliant and clear, she said, and the trees had already begun to swell with lacy, red buds. She told Newton Arvin how lovely her yard looked with the first signs of spring, and that her father was looking forward again to planting another vegetable garden. As an added enticement to get Arvin to visit her in Columbus, she said that her mother would make homemade gumbo out of the vegetables and herbs from the garden. Everything except the veal would come from her back yard, she promised.

To David Diamond, Carson wrote about the shrill little sparrows who quarreled in the garden in the late afternoons. In the early spring the sky was lavender. It was a time when she was often aware of thunder echoing faintly and lazily in the distance. Carson told Janet Flanner that she knew spring had come even before the calendar had said so because the mockingbirds were singing at noon and the garden was abloom with honeysuckle, pansies, and the first azaleas. She even distinguished spring shadows from those cast during other seasons. The spring ones, she told Miss Flanner, were tinted a delicate pale blue; yet she could not help questioning if it were just her fancy that seemed to make the shadows adapt their color to the seasons. Those who received her letters were aware that it was Carson's attention to detail and thoughtfulness about it that made her the masterful descriptive artist she was in her fiction. Even the very early pieces she wrote at age seventeen and eighteen proved that.

Carson had begun to write letters to her friends the day after her arrival home in the late fall of 1941. First, she answered Newton Arvin's letter, for he had written that he was worried about her, having heard no word from her directly since her last hectic days in New York City. Carson had wired him and Elizabeth Ames a "joint telegram" immediately upon her arrival in Columbus, but now she took time to detail her homecoming. During her first week at home Carson wrote similar letters to Newton Arvin, Janet Flanner, and Muriel Rukeyser, letters which at times included almost identical phrasing, especially if she wrote to more than one person on the same day. This often happened with her, for she did not just *answer* letters; she wrote only when there was something special she wanted to share. And if that was the case, she usually wanted to share it with more than one person. When Carson wrote to Newton Arvin on October 16, 1941, two days after getting home, she urged him to visit her in Columbus before he returned to Northampton. Nothing would make her happier, she pleaded. In her letter to Janet Flanner, Carson used much identical phraseology that she had already written to Newton Arvin a week earlier.

The little-girl quality was unmistakable in these early letters, particularly in her pleadings with friends to please come to see her. She said that Georgia was not far away and that it would take less than a day and a night from New York. She promised her friends that they would have music together and share long talks and walks in the woods. Best of all, they would be happy together again, she vowed. A little later, she sent similar letters to David Diamond, but in the early winter when she first came home, she could not write him. Still uncertain over Reeves's whereabouts and situation, she suspected that he was with David Diamond in Rochester. If that was the case, she did not want to make herself vulnerable emotionally to either of them again.

Carson wrote Janet Flanner that she had found home very much the haven she had envisioned from afar. Writing to Miss Flanner had a soothing effect on Carson, for she loved and greatly admired her older friend who seemed infinitely wiser. Moreover, Miss Flanner had a brilliant intellect, sharp wit—which fascinated Carson—and impeccable taste. Carson's several letters to Miss Flanner during the winter of 1941–42 revealed a sensitive artist grateful to be home once more. Her letters were mood pieces, warm and mellow and filled with vivid descriptions of nature, her home life, problems encountered in her writing, and an assortment of philosophical reflections. One day she wrote a manifesto to Miss Flanner's friend Solita Solano, a letter of some twenty pages which she admitted later she had put into the fire instead of mailing.

In her first letter to Janet Flanner that winter she explained that she had not written immediately, but had waited purposely for a peaceful time when she did not feel hurried. She wanted first to describe her room and the good feeling she had in being back in it. She said that she had grouped her three favorite things together: Her new piano was on one side of the corner fireplace, which was the focal point of her room, and her worktable was on the other side. In the corner opposite the fireplace was a beautiful antique French walnut bed and bureau she loved. A chaise longue stretched out into the room a few feet from the fireplace, where Carson sat in the afternoons to read and ruminate and listen to music from the family phonograph. Soft brown chintz curtains hung at the windows, shaded by ivy and a large holly tree which she looked out on from her worktable and bed. Her room was exactly the way she wanted it, she told Miss Flanner, and she wanted to stay in it in Columbus for a long time. The women's editor of the Columbus Enquirer, who interviewed her in her bedroom the next spring, described her room as "Spartan in its decoration—nothing to turn her thoughts from her work."[5] Indeed, Carson needed no pictures, wall plaques, or tapestries to free her thoughts for imaginative wanderings or to distract her from reality. No matter how ascetic her existence, fantasy was the very essence of her art.

Having returned home on a Friday, Carson allowed only the weekend in which to rest and get settled. On Monday her daily regime began. She shut herself in her room before 8 A.M. and worked at her typewriter until well past noon. Although she kept a cigarette lit constantly, she smoked very little. Carson inhaled deeply as she thought, played with the cigarette in her ashtray, watched the smoke curl into the air, and sipped from her ever-present thermos of hot sherry tea. Yet in spite of her efforts, Carson realized from the beginning that she was struggling with every page. As the bright autumn leaves dropped and a cold, damp Columbus winter set in, so, too, dropped Carson's spirits. She reasoned that part of her trouble was that she could not pray. She admitted that she had always felt a need to be close to God, yet for too many months—years, in fact—she had ignored Him. As she struggled now with her new book, she experienced a heightened sense of loss of her creative powers, an uncontrollable sluggishness which seemed inextricably bound to her awareness of divine deprivation. Carson felt certain that her inability to proceed well with *The Bride* was symptomatic of her greater spiritual loss. She longed to pray, she told Newton Arvin. She had rewritten the first part of the novel five times, yet still did not have the timbre. If only God would help, she exclaimed, but instead, she felt a sense of abandonment, a loss of God and godliness which haunted her, intermittently, much of her life.

Although deeply religious in a natural sense, Carson had accepted since age fourteen the fact that her Christian beliefs must, of necessity, be divorced from church or dogma. She recognized God as an omniscient being, a supreme creator who imposed order on the universe, but she sometimes saw Him as a capricious deity whose specialty was freaks. Laboring now with *The Bride*, Carson created Honey Brown, the fair-skinned son of "Big Mama," who described her offspring as "a boy God had not finished. The Creator had withdrawn His hand from him too soon . . . and so he had to go around doing one thing and then another to finish himself up."[6] Just as in *The Heart Is a Lonely Hunter, Reflections in a Golden Eye,* and the then unpublished *The Ballad of the Sad Café,* the young author again depicted an inverted, nightmarish world—a World War II world—which a deterministic God had peopled with fragmented beings, unhappy grotesques who realized that their destiny was to achieve no lasting joys or satisfaction. They formed a community of pariahs. When Klaus Mann had looked into Carson's eyes the first time they met, he recognized her instantly as a wanderer, he said, just as other sensitive artists intuitively knew and identified with the exile. Each lonely character in Frankie Addams' world was locked inexorably in a realm which barred fruitful communion.

16   James Reeves McCullers, Jr., five and
a half, with his sisters,
Marguerite, three and a half,
and Wiley Mae, fifteen months;
Jesup, Georgia, March 1919.

17   Reeves, fifteen,
on his father's horse;
Jesup, Georgia, 1929.

18 Carson and Reeves's second home after their marriage: the upstairs apartment at 806 Central Avenue, Charlotte, North Carolina. Here Carson wrote the early chapters of *The Heart Is a Lonely Hunter*.

19 In the fall of 1938, Carson and Reeves moved to an upstairs apartment at 119 North Cool Spring Street (formerly a tavern), Fayetteville, North Carolina. Here they lived until June 1940, when they moved to New York City upon publication of *The Heart Is a Lonely Hunter*.

20   Carson and Reeves in their North Cool Spring Street apartment, Fayetteville. Here Carson finished *The Heart Is a Lonely Hunter*, then wrote *Reflections in a Golden Eye* in two months.

21   Carson with Louis Untermeyer, Bread Loaf, August 1940.

22 Publicity picture of Carson upon the appearance of *The Heart Is a Lonely Hunter*, 1940.

23 ABOVE: Carson with her good friend George Davis, Nyack, New York, 1946.

24 BELOW: Carson at Bread Loaf Writers' Conference, August 1940. Front, left to right: Edna Frederickson, director Theodore Morrison, Carson McCullers. Standing, left to right: Eudora Welty, John Ciardi, Brainard Cheney, Marion Sims, Louis Untermeyer.

25 Annemarie Clarac-Schwarzenbach (1908–42), Carson's Swiss friend to whom she dedicated *Reflections in a Golden Eye*.

26 The Mansion, Yaddo Artists Colony, where Carson spent many summers.

27 The Pine Tree Studio, Yaddo Artists Colony; Carson's favorite studio, where she finished *The Member of the Wedding*, 1945.

Frankie Addams and Honey Brown in *The Bride*—as well as Mick, Singer, Brannon, Penderton, Miss Amelia, and countless other characters Carson created later—were victims in an inchoate world, where an irresponsible cosmic maker had suddenly become infatuated with someone else—or some *thing*—and abandoned His creative task at hand. Instead of fashioning man in His mirror image, who would behold Him with love and adulation, Carson's fictional creator had become distracted by a love object already existing on a still higher plane, whom He, in turn, worshiped and adored. Such a spiritual hierarchy of gods had already been presented by Carson in *The Heart Is a Lonely Hunter* in the dream allegory experienced by her deaf mute, John Singer.

In actuality, Carson conceded that there *had* to be a God in operation in the physical world about her. Exceedingly sensitive to the beauties as well as to the harshness of nature, she had an acute sense of harmony and balance and the rightness or wrongness of moral acts. Yet for Carson, there was no salvation of the soul, no afterlife to be hoped for. Death simply was "one trillion, billion zeros which added up to naught."[7] She felt intensely her need for the presence of God in this world—for to her, there was no other.

Sometimes her sense of urgency, a craving for a benevolent, forgiving God gave way to a doleful wail for help. Rebecca Pitts, who had relieved Carson in New York of her distress when she was unable to sign her name and check out of the Brevoort Hotel, recalled an evening at Yaddo two years later when a group of artists were sitting around the old tower studio sipping sherry before dinner. "I've lost the presence of God!" Carson cried out suddenly in an outburst irrelevant to the conversation and addressed to no one in particular. Nor did anyone respond. Her anguished lament simply terminated the cocktail hour and the group moved quietly off to dinner.

Many people associated such cries with the novel she continued to wrestle with for over five years before it was finally shaped to her satisfaction as *The Member of the Wedding*. Just as she had with Rebecca Pitts and others that summer at Yaddo, so, too, did Carson wail audibly —and in letters—many times in the future for divine assistance. When God seemed indifferent or inaccessible, sometimes she cried out to her mother for guidance or release in much the same way that she groped for a deity. During the summer of 1945 at Yaddo, Carson sat talking with Eleanor Clark about how she had suffered so over *The Member of the Wedding* and of her great difficulty in getting it right. She told Miss Clark that she had lain on the grass and cried, "Mother! Mother!" Carson's "anguish of integrity in art was a side of her I liked and admired, even while aware at times of the element of self-dramatization," said Miss Clark.[8]

Besides Carson's feelings of estrangement from God that fall upon her return to Columbus, she also felt cut off from David Diamond. In November, she learned that although Reeves had been with Diamond in Rochester, Diamond had recently left him and returned to New York. The composer found that he was no longer able to live with Reeves with any degree of serenity and productively create as an artist. Reeves, knowing well the essentially destructive nature of his part in their relationship, sent Diamond a consolatory message. He told Diamond that he agreed with his conclusions relative to ending their close relationship, but pointed out that the outcome doubtless would have been otherwise had he, Reeves, been older. He wished his friend well, asked that he please not think too ill of him, and invoked God's blessing.

At last Carson felt that she could write to her friend whom she had missed so much. She told Diamond that she still felt exceedingly tender toward him and greatly valued his friendship, but she wanted him to realize that when Reeves had been with him, she could not write, could not communicate with Reeves, or be thrown with him in any way, her emotions still too exposed and raw. She also echoed what she had written to her friends Newton Arvin and Janet Flanner a month earlier. But now, however, she felt close to God at last and was thankful to Him that she could work hard and well again every day. She said that in going home she had done the only thing possible in honesty to herself as a writer and as a person of honor, and when her book was finished, she intended to live in some more normal way. Then she hoped she could return to New York and prove that she could live there, too, with dignity and honor. Carson also thanked God that she had been able to shelve Reeves neatly away from her thoughts. Her family, other relatives, and the very few friends she saw occasionally in Columbus were careful to avoid all reference to Reeves, nor did her correspondents allude to him, either.

Carson assumed that he had gone back into the Army when he finally left Rochester, but she knew nothing for a fact. Yet in spite of her being able to work well on her manuscript now, Carson was not happy. To find no radiance or buoyancy in her daughter was distressing to Marguerite. Carson's mother seemed ubiquitous; although she fluttered in the background, she was always available to minister to Carson's every whim and need. She also gently chastised her daughter and told her that she had not once seen her smile. She urged Carson to go out and be among people who might help bring some light and happiness into her life. She had found Carson weeping in the afternoons and ached that she could not alleviate her suffering. Marguerite reasoned, however, that if she could not cheer her daughter's psyche, she could at least help keep her body strong. Every meal was designed to please Carson's palate. Marguerite wrote to David Diamond that winter that she loved to cook vegetable soup, mashed potatoes, stewed tomatoes, and the other foods her daughter liked best. She told him that Carson was very lonely, but that she was looking well. Marguerite at times could view her daughter quite objectively, as though she had nothing to do with Carson's birth and rearing. She wrote Diamond that she considered it a great privilege even to be near her, and that she did not want ever to stand in her way or cause conflict with what Carson felt in her heart had to be done.

During the winter of 1941–42, Carson wrote often to David Diamond and Newton Arvin and, occasionally, to Muriel Rukeyser and Elizabeth Ames. But more frequently than writing, she held imaginary dialogues with those friends who were most precious to her. She told Arvin that she was terribly remiss in not writing Granville and Dorothy Hicks, with whom they had gone to Quebec, Al Fisher and his wife Helen Eustis, whom she had met in Northampton, and Gypsy Rose Lee. Carson said that she had talked half of one day about them to her mother, but that all her love seemed to go into talking about them, instead of writing letters.

To her mother now, Carson could also talk easily about Annemarie Clarac-Schwarzenbach, whom she had begun to hear from in the fall of 1941. When Annemarie had been released from the psychiatric hospital in White Plains in February, she had gone first to Lisbon. By mid-March she was back in Switzerland, where it was rumored among her friends that she was working with Erika Mann in a secret shuttle to help anti-Fascists escape into Switzerland through the little valley of Engadine near her parents' home. In April, Annemarie started the long trek to Africa, first to join her husband in Tetuán, Morocco, so that she might talk with him about a divorce, and then to go by river boat and foot deep within the Congo jungle. She had remained with Clarac in Tetuán for several weeks. It had been an amiable meeting. They decided that it would be better for Annemarie if they remained legally wed, for she could travel with greater freedom as the wife of a foreign service officer than she could as an independent woman adventurer and writer. It was actually a journalistic assignment that had summoned Annemarie to Africa. Her destination was Thysville, in the Leopoldville province of western Belgian Congo.

Through letters written in late 1941 and the spring of 1942, Carson's Swiss friend became once more the old Annemarie she knew and loved. Carson elatedly told many friends that she and Annemarie were writing to one another again, and to Newton Arvin, David Diamond, Janet Flanner, and others she provided countless details of Annemarie's new layer of life that had evolved in the tropics. Her friend wrote that she had begun to discover anew her true being and to develop a strong, viable sense of purpose. She said that in the past she had prostituted and worn herself out in myriad ways through what amounted to cheap compromises with civilized society. She had abused even her language through humdrum intercourse with people, and she had become thoroughly disgusted and ashamed of herself. She told Carson that in Africa, however, she had begun to regain some of her old verities of truth and honor and could write again with a heightened sense of integrity.

In her conversations and letters to friends, Carson likened her own retreat South to Annemarie's inward journey into the depths of the human heart, as well as into a more primitive condition of human existence. To Carson, Annemarie was like Joseph Conrad's Marlowe, whose psychic and physical journeys took him deep into Africa and "the heart of darkness." Carson found solace and inspiration in her friend's sensibilities and sensitivities in coming to terms with herself.

Each time Carson heard from Annemarie, her psyche thrived. In late November, however, there had been no letter for several weeks, and she was depressed and out of sorts both with herself and her work. She wrote to Newton Arvin on Thanksgiving 1941 that she had been very unhappy and could not seem to get into her work no matter how long and hard she tried. She likened her book to a pot watched too closely, which she hovered over anxiously, only to find that it still had not even simmered. As though to offset her mood of gloom, Carson again begged her friend to come South and visit, promising that her entire family would spoil him if he would come. She said that her mother would cook him good things and they would have hot rum toddies before the fire. They could stretch out before a huge Christmas tree, which Carson envisioned as black and mysterious, and they would listen to records. She was sure Arvin would be happy with them, or at least she thought so, she added.

Almost immediately after extending the invitation, however, Carson's spiritual and creative malaise was accompanied by a physical illness more threatening to her life and work than anything she had yet experienced. First she had simply looked wan, was nervous and indifferent to work. Then she came down with a high fever and a severe ear and streptococcal infection. Just as these maladies began to heal, double pneumonia, pleurisy, and the most severe chest pains she had ever felt set in. In December, Carson was hospitalized, delirious and feverish. As Christmas approached, she asked her mother to bring her radio to the hospital. David Diamond's First Symphony was to be premièred on December 21 by the New York Philharmonic, under the direction of Dimitri Mitropoulos, Diamond's good friend whom Carson had met and was much taken by. The afternoon of the performance, however, she knew nothing that was going on, was wildly delirious, and the doctor had removed the radio. Later, Carson regretted bitterly that she had been unable to hear her friend's symphony, but it was a month before she could even write to him and acknowledge her illness.

In late January, Carson also wrote to Janet Flanner, summing up her latest brush with death and explaining the complications. When her lungs finally cleared and it seemed as though she were getting well a second time, she said she suffered a fresh attack of pneumonia and went through the whole agonizing ordeal again. Carson took pleasure in telling Miss Flanner that for weeks everyone thought she would die; but she had survived, and was proud of the good fight.

Although a nurse came home with Carson from the hospital, she succeeded only in getting in her mother's way. Marguerite anticipated her patient's every need. She brought Carson's meals on a tray to her bedside, read to her, played her favorite music, kept the fire going in her bedroom fireplace night and day, spent many nights asleep on the chaise longue beside her bed, gently exercised her bedsore limbs, and, at last, accompanied her daughter with cautious steps about the room. Later, when cousins and an occasional friend came to call, Marguerite saw to it that visits were limited to ten minutes. Ambivalently, this wise woman to whom Carson owed so much yet who demanded so little yearned to press her eldest child to her bosom and prayed that she might be able to protect her always from adversity; yet Marguerite knew, too, that she must release her daughter, urge her to go, when stronger, to a milder climate. South Georgia weather had treated Carson no more kindly than that which she had encountered in New York. It had been her habit for many years to walk daily, no matter what the temperature. She wrote Janet Flanner that the last two winters she had stayed in Columbus she had been ill with the same maladies as this year's siege—except in milder degree—and that earlier, she had required a rest cure for almost a year. In despair, Carson confided to Miss Flanner that she simply did not know what to do or where to go.

Carson's illness left her in a state of inertia for weeks. She wrote David Diamond and Newton Arvin almost identical letters in late January, telling them that she was blank and weak, but that such a state would not last long. She had been told that she must gain twenty pounds, but even if that were not possible she vowed that with her great recuperative powers she would soon be robust again. Carson, of course, was never robust or husky. On January 28, Arvin sent her roses, a gesture which touched her more than she could express. She wrote him that because of her depressed spirits and weakened state she was crying when the flowers arrived; however, her spirits lifted immediately and she stayed up all day working and happy. Surely the roses were a portent for better times, she told Arvin, for her strength was returning in good measure.

Carson enjoyed being petted and fussed over, and Arvin, who had been devoted to her since their meeting at Yaddo, was always thoughtful and generous to her. On Valentine's Day he sent her a warm, loving greeting, and on the nineteenth, a birthday card. Carson was especially sentimental about Valentine's Day because it was her parents' wedding anniversary; but she loved, even better than Christmas, being the center of attention on her birthday. All of her life she anticipated birthdays with a childlike enthusiasm that one could neither forget nor ignore. She was disappointed by cards alone, but presents delighted her—many presents gaily wrapped, no matter how small. If a gift did not especially please her, she revealed it by facial expression or tempered comment, after which the perceptive giver usually left and returned later with a new present. As Carson got older, there was less subtlety. When her cousin Jordan Massee—knowing how well Carson loved German lieder—gave her a recording of Mahler's "Die Zwei Blauen Augen," by a female vocalist, she responded: "Thank you, darling, I've wanted this more than anything else in the world." But when Massee got ready to leave, Carson picked up the record and asked, "Don't you think it's better when a man sings it?" Another time, Massee gave her an album of the forty-eight preludes and fugues of Bach played on the harpsichord. Carson seemed ecstatic over her present, but when he prepared to tell her good-by, she said, "Darling, it would be even more beautiful on the piano." And, again, her cousin made the appropriate exchange.

Carson's sense of psychic well-being increased as her physical recuperation became more complete. Although she still rarely smiled or laughed, her joys were inward. It was more the reminiscence of good times rather than anything immediate that brought a look of pleasure to her face. In one letter, she reminded Newton Arvin of the foolish sunbath they had taken at the end of the season at Yaddo when everyone else was as bronze as a penny. They had both thought it a marvelous joke at the time, but in hindsight, Carson decided that if she had been sunbathing all summer like the others, instead of doubled over a desk all day and perched on a bar stool at the New Worden every night, she would not be in the state she was now.

By mid-February 1942, Carson had resumed her old work schedule and her writing was going well. She decided that Newton Arvin's roses had been the presage of good times. Soon she reported that she was through with the short, first part of her novel, which she called "The Listener," and was at work on the long middle section, "The Nigger with the Glass Blue Eye." What bothered her most at this point was technique. She wanted to use two levels: one, objective—combined with a free poetical form—and the other, subjective. But to entwine them and bring about an artistic synthesis was a problem. Carson felt that eventually she would have an illumination, just as she had had others, but in the meantime she simply would stick to her typewriter and keep struggling, she reasoned.[9]

At times, however, it seemed to Carson that she had reached an impasse. On February 19, she took a holiday from The Bride, not just because it was her birthday, but because she had another story erupting. To help celebrate Carson's twenty-fifth birthday, her friend Kathleen Woodruff arranged a dinner for her. At the last minute, however, Carson backed out of it, too distraught over what she considered her sick world and, at the same time, too caught up in the creativity of her new story "A Tree. A Rock. A Cloud." to stop for anything. Again, the setting was a southern mill town like Columbus, the time, the present. The story's protagonist was not a child like Mick or Frankie, however, but an old man, a beer-soused tramp. Had it not been for Annemarie Clarac-Schwarzenbach and Carson's own experiences regarding human rejection, she doubtless could not have written this particular piece of fiction. Although her red-nosed protagonist was over sixty, he still was much like Mick Kelley and Frankie Addams. Twelve years earlier, the old man had married a woman who made him feel needed and complete:

> Nothing lay around loose in me any more but was finished up by her. . . . There were those beautiful feelings and loose little pleasures inside me. And this woman was something like an assembly line for my soul. I run these little pieces of myself through her and I come out complete.

But after a year of marriage, she had left him and run away with another man, and now he was more lonely and fragmented than before. At first his mania was simply to get her back, and he pursued her in vain all over the country. Finally, to cope with his loss, he developed his "science" of love, the theory that love must begin with something inanimate—a tree, a rock, a cloud. He had started with a goldfish, and eventually his science had expanded to include all creation.

> Son, I can love anything. No longer do I have to think about it even. I see a street full of people and a beautiful light comes in me. I watch a bird in the sky. Or I meet a traveler on the road. Everything, Son. And anybody. All strangers and all loved!

Yet his boast was a meaningless one. He was not ready for a woman, he conceded, nor had he been able to relate to anyone on a one-to-one personal basis. Ironically, the old man was still isolated and lonely *because* of his science, not in spite of it. Loving in this fashion ran no risks—but it not only failed to warm his heart; it also alienated any possible human recipient of love because of his monomania to explain it. Carson's protagonist was like Coleridge's Ancient Mariner, whose listeners were unable to comprehend. Although the old man could communicate, he could not commune. The little newsboy whom he had stopped abruptly with a grip on his shoulder and a sudden declaration of love could respond only with uncertainty and insecurity as he listened to the incomprehensible monologue. After the sterile delivery, and after its orator had vanished into the night, the lad made the only remark that he hoped would not cause embarrassment to himself: "He sure has done a lot of traveling." "A Tree. A Rock. A Cloud." was accepted immediately by *Harper's Bazaar* for publication the following November.[10]

The old tramp in her fiction could boast that he had found the science of love and survival in such a world, but ironically, his existence since its discovery gave testimony to its utter impossibility as a meaningful way of life. Carson knew that she simply could not go out among people yet. Although she had recovered from her terrible physical sickness and, like Annemarie, had found a new layer of life within herself, she was still much like her beer-soused tramp: not yet ready to reckon with man. Letters were safe; distance was necessary. For Carson, to anticipate a pleasure was always better than the real thing. In letters, as in her fiction, she could fantasize and have her truth at the same time. She and her Swiss friend had known intuitively from the beginning of their relationship that they were attuned psychically, almost mirror images of one another, comparable in thought and habit. Yet Carson felt that she and Annemarie were destined to live apart, to write to each other and to commune in spirit, each from her separate jungle.

Although Carson worried about Annemarie and wrote frequently, she was never certain that her letters were getting through to her. She did not hear from Annemarie for a month during her crucial illness and depression in January, but in February, Annemarie wrote again. She said that whereas she had been very restless when she had first gone to Africa, she had gained strength through the many months of solitude deep within the jungle. She had left Leopoldville, moved up into the hills, and now was living completely alone. It has been an inward journey of psyche as well for Annemarie, and in the process she had gained a deeply meaningful and creative inner life, which she termed "soul." She felt that only through suffering and adversity was the soul actually freed. To Annemarie, the strong bond between two people who shared an abiding love and spiritual affinity could survive any kind of physical separation.

In a letter that spring to Carson, Annemarie said that in her seclusion she had begun to translate into German the novel which had been dedicated to her: Carson's *Reflections in a Golden Eye*. Also in progress was a book of her own, a work which she likened to Carson's poem "The Twisted Trinity." She said that her book opened with a man looking at a tree. His scrutiny was to discover what she called the "instant symmetry" of the man's soul, the tree, and "God's silence." To Carson, her story "A Tree. A Rock. A Cloud." seemed but a synthesis of Annemarie's ideas; yet each had expressed herself without knowing explicitly what the other was thinking.

Annemarie told Carson that when she finished her own book, she hoped that Carson would attempt to translate it for her. She also had asked Carson earlier if she would translate her Congo River poems. Actually, Carson did not know German. She could quote Rilke in German—and did, endlessly—and she knew every word of Mahler's "Die Zwei Blauen Augen," but before she could work on the Congo River poems, she would need someone who knew both languages thoroughly so that she would not miss the nuances. Then from a literal translation, she would be able to make her own poetic transliterations. Although Annemarie's prose book would be a more difficult task, Carson reasoned that nothing was impossible. She simply would learn German and do the best she could. She felt strengthened that Annemarie had such faith in her.

In the late spring, she heard again from her Swiss friend. Restless, Annemarie reported that she had left the Congo and was in Lisbon, but she was anxious to return to London and find out what was going on in the rest of the world. Although relieved to hear that Annemarie was out of what seemed a dangerous and sinister place, Carson felt that her friend would not be safe until she returned to neutral Switzerland.

During the winter and spring of 1941–42, Carson identified completely with Annemarie and Annemarie's discovery of her true essence. She told friends that in sharing with Annemarie a conviction that man must be true to his highest nature, regardless of the cost, she realized how like Annemarie's words was her own struggle. She had been wrestling not only with Frankie's problems in her book The Bride, but also with the seeds of another novel that had germinated, watered now by Annemarie's thoughts—a work which did not reach maturity until some twenty years later as Clock Without Hands. Carson told a reviewer in 1951 that for ten years she had been wrestling with the theme of how much responsibility a person may take on himself.[11] This theme became the story of Malone, a grief-stricken druggist who knew that he was dying of an incurable disease, yet could not bear to die in his fragmented state since he had only half lived, having been a "yes man" nearly all his life. Malone, like Annemarie, eventually was able to overcome difficulty and suffering and free his soul.

There were times, too, in Columbus that winter when Carson yearned to get away again. Hearing from Annemarie had a dual effect: She dreamed of unknown places which tempted her from her work; yet at the same time she resolved even harder to stay at home and keep writing. David Diamond, too, contributed to her sense of restlessness and nostalgia for the faraway. He had gone to Hollywood in January with clarinetist Artie Shaw. Carson liked to fancy herself out there with them, writing for the movies, being sought after, and meeting stars who were introduced to her. She urged Diamond to talk about her in Hollywood, to brag handsomely if he saw anyone who even looked like he hired authors. She calculated that she had only enough money left to hold her if she could finish *The Bride* in nine months to a year. Then she would have to do something else, perhaps some more *New Yorker* stories or a Holly-wood script. Again, with childlike simplicity, she romanticized the possibilities of David Diamond and Artie Shaw coming to Columbus to visit. She envisioned the three of them as a happy triangle, another we of me. She said that they would listen to music, walk in the woods, and drink in the clubs downtown, which were now filled with soldiers. Above all, she urged him to come because it had been such a long time since she had laughed or talked with anyone with whom she could communicate—except, of course, her mother, she added.

David Diamond did talk about Carson that winter in Hollywood, and soon she received a letter from an agent asking her about possible manuscripts. She decided not to get involved, however; until her *Bride* was ready, she would be no good to anyone. It was a strange book to write, she told Diamond. She had worked like a dog, but so little had come of it. If it had not been for her handful of friends who had corresponded with her over the long troubled months since her return South, Carson acknowledged that she could not have endured. Other than satisfaction when her work was going well, she had known no real joy except through her devotion to people and constant reassurance that she, too, was loved. Almost every letter that Carson wrote during this period in her life contained a peroration of how much she valued her correspondent's friendship and love. She reminded Newton Arvin frequently that she thought of him always with great tenderness and that her mother and her few precious and real friends were all she felt she had in the way of any outward happiness. She wrote David Diamond to please remember how much their friendship meant to her and to know that she loved him deeply. At the end of her letters she now began to scrawl large hearts, the beginning of a habit she continued the rest of her life. For those with whom she shared a special kinship, she drew a scrawny, lopsided heart about an inch high, placing within it either an X or a heart pierced by an arrow. In many letters she scrawled dozens of Xs across the bottom of a page. Sometimes she drew broken hearts, with jagged edges and arrows coming out the other side. Nor was she apparently consistent in her heart drawings, regardless of the recipient or mood.

Sometimes Carson admonished Diamond—and herself as well—that they must hang on to the good things in spite of their crazy world. She saw the world now essentially from the existential posture, in which meaninglessness, purposelessness, normlessness, loneliness, and alienation reigned. If there was a norm, it was abnormality. The United States was now deeply entangled in war. Whereas Carson had felt guilt for her country in its failure to enter into the world conflict earlier, she had taken little interest in the politics or ideologies involved. Now she felt anguish because of the pain and suffering of hundreds of thousands of tortured, deprived human beings whom she mourned as sinless and helpless. One day she wrote to both David Diamond and Newton Arvin that even thinking about the war made her almost insane. Her days had become a strange and terrible personal hell. In spite of Gabriel Heatter's "Ah, there's good news tonight," Carson wept that all Europe was starving and that Greece, Poland, and France were in the throes of defeat. She felt that even though the Allies would eventually win, could there be anything of value left to inherit?

Carson tried not to waste time and brood, but she vowed that when she finished *The Bride* she would do something worthwhile for her fellow man. One possibility she had had in mind for months was a career as a foreign correspondent.[12]

By March, another worry nudged its way to the surface of Carson's consciousness—money. Her agent had written that in some mysterious way every penny she had earned in 1941—all six thousand dollars of it— had disappeared. How, Carson did not know. Grateful that she had come home this time with a thousand dollars to give to her mother for her living expenses, Carson figured that at least there was some of that left; if necessary, she could borrow from Houghton Mifflin. Such outside help proved unnecessary, however, for on March 24, 1942, Carson was notified that she had won a Guggenheim Fellowship. Out of fifteen hundred applicants, eighty-two had been successful. When the New York *Times* made the announcement public on April 7, listing Carson along with John Dos Passos, Gustavus Myers, W. H. Auden, and Dorothy Baker (author of *Young Man With a Horn*) as the best-known recipients from the literary world, it commented also that "it seems that a writer of English can become quite famous and still need a scholarship in order to have leisure for creative work. More encouraging, it appears that some writers need help because they insist on writing to satisfy their own artistic rectitude and will not take formulas from editors or publishers."

Carson was ecstatic when she received news of her Guggenheim. Immediately her whole sense of direction and complacency in staying in Columbus changed. She told David Diamond that whereas she had been skeptical that she would receive any literary award in which money was involved, she now felt suddenly young again and had a wild and insatiable longing to leave home and see another part of the world. Carson wrote to Diamond as though he needed convincing. She explained that once her need for home had been alleviated, she could no longer write there —in fact, that she had never been able to work or write well in Columbus. Then she explained the paradox: Away, she always suffered great homesickness; it enabled her to write about her native scene; but once home, all she had to do was ride a bus downtown and she had had enough. Then she yearned to write about New York and other distant places. A separation and a sense of exile were necessary, and it was time to go away, she explained.

Her thoughts turned now to Mexico as she made tentative plans and rationalized about where to go. She wrote to both David Diamond and Newton Arvin that she had selected Mexico; then she asked Diamond if it would be possible for him to come immediately to Georgia from California so that they could talk over her plans. She also asked him and Arvin, as well, to seek counsel from others who had been south of the border. It might save her from wandering forlornly about the countryside without proper direction. She begged her friends not to think her a child, or at least not to be exasperated at her for being one. Her need to leave was immediate and urgent, she said. Columbus had trebled in size during the past year and was thick with soldiers. It was simply not her old hometown any more, she explained. Carson likened herself to a little dazed animal who had hidden in the protection of her mother's burrow for too long. She had never been completely free, having both money and independence, she told Diamond. When she left home the first time there had been barely enough money to send her to New York; later, there was Reeves. She lamented that she and Diamond did not both have fellowships so that they might hike off together somewhere, but she was hopeful that he might join her later. To Newton Arvin, the invitation was more explicit. She would go immediately to Mexico, she proposed, and settle in a little house somewhere. As soon as the school term closed at Smith, Arvin should meet her there. She would send him railroad fare out of her allowance, she promised. They would be able to live cheaply together in Mexico. With Arvin she envisioned mule trips in the mountains, good high air, beautiful scenery, and great creativity.

Carson's letters to David Diamond and Newton Arvin with their bubbling enthusiasm and little-girl wonderment sounded much like those which Henky Evans wrote to her Brazilian pen pal, Manoel Garcia, in Carson's short story "Correspondence." Soon, however, Carson's dreams mellowed. Henry Moe, a trustee of the Guggenheim Foundation, cautioned her that Mexico had not proven to be a good place for creative work, that artists frequently became restless and unproductive because of the seven-thousand-foot altitude in Mexico City and other areas to which she might be attracted. Carson, deciding to seek advice from her doctor, told him that she planned to stay a year in Mexico and wanted desperately for it to be all right. He advised her not even to consider it. Pneumonia affected the heart peculiarly, he said, and even now it was impossible to determine how much damage had already been done during her various illnesses. Once in Mexico, she might suffer even more severely. With two such negative attitudes, as well as Diamond and Arvin's lack of enthusiasm, Carson settled down again and became reconciled to the idea of staying in Columbus and working without pause for six months. She was certain that by then *The Bride* could be finished. She reasoned that if she wanted to, she still could go to Mexico for a short time to see how the climate and altitude agreed with her.

Carson now began to write letters to thank those who had nominated her for the fellowship. She told them that she would stay in Columbus, work like a fiend, and see her friends in New York before too long. To Louis Untermeyer she wrote that she knew what Jacob felt like when he wrestled with his angel. Carson thought about Untermeyer frequently, even though they seldom wrote. In April, she urged him, since she was not yet going North, to please make a pilgrimage South and come to see her. She promised him her room, her piano, and breakfast outside under the trees every morning. They would drink sherry, listen to Mozart, and take long walks in the woods. But Untermeyer did not come either. Only one of all the people Carson wrote to and pleaded with to visit her from among her friends in her artists' world of New York City, Brooklyn Heights, or Yaddo made a special trip to Columbus to see her: her friend and editor, Robert Linscott. Before long she did not even have a home in the South.

Carson began to think of where else she might go with her Guggenheim money, but with a war on, she reasoned, there was no place but Mexico that would satisfy her wanderlust. She might just as well stay in Columbus. Elizabeth Ames wrote to ask if she wanted to return to Yaddo, but Carson declined. She said that it seemed too selfish and greedy of her to have fellowship money and also live an expense-free summer at Yaddo among friends. As soon as Carson mailed the letter, she was stricken with remorse. That night she had fitful dreams and barely slept. She wanted desperately to go to Yaddo. She could no more conceive of remaining in Columbus for another nightmarish summer than her Frankie would have willingly stayed. In *The Bride*, Carson described Frankie's world in the South as "a silent crazy jungle under glass" that she longed to break out of. She told Arvin that her view of Columbus and Frankie's were identical. Carson knew that she, too, could not stay in the South much longer.

Unable to restrain herself, Carson wrote again to Elizabeth Ames and begged her to please let her change her mind and return to Saratoga Springs. Finally the answer came: Yes, there was still a vacancy, and she should come on July 2. If things went well, she could stay through the winter if she wished. Once Carson knew she could leave home, she settled down and worked harder than she had all spring. Still getting up at daybreak and at her worktable by eight o'clock, she sometimes did not stop until four in the afternoon. David Diamond wrote to invite her to join him in California, suggesting that they might take a cottage somewhere together and work, but Carson knew that she wanted to return to Yaddo to work more than anything else. California would be stranger than a Malayan island to her, she admitted. At Yaddo, there would be no need to adjust to anything new; she would simply keep on writing. She also found that two other books were pressing very close and demanding attention. In more than one letter she made reference to the book that eventually became *Clock Without Hands*. The other, less clearly defined in her mind at the time, finally became a part of *The Bride*.

No longer were Carson's letters heavy with reference to personal unhappiness or creative struggles. She wrote that spring of going out among people, making new friends, reading Yeats, Chekhov, Jane Austen, Djuna Barnes, and Céline, playing Bach fugues and Chopin nocturnes, and listening to music—to Mahler's Second Symphony, which she thought one of the greatest ever written, to Beethoven's Choral Symphony, to his Quartets, and to Schubert, Mozart, and Scarlatti. She also took great joy in counting David Diamond and Newton Arvin her two dearest and most talented friends. On April 26, she accompanied Marjorie Peabody Waite, Elizabeth Ames's sister, to Warm Springs, Georgia, for Mrs. Waite was philanthropically interested in the treatment center for polio there; and while in Warm Springs, they had listened to another première of Diamond's music, this time his "Elegy in Memory of Ravel" in the version for strings. Carson also learned that Diamond had won the 1942 Prix de Rome in Music for his Symphony No. 1 and his even more recent String Quartet No. 1. She had already told him that her novella *The Ballad of the Sad Café* was for him, and he, in turn, had set her poem "The Twisted Trinity" to music. Now nearing completion of his Second Symphony, Diamond wrote that he would be back East very shortly and would come to Yaddo and be with her. He had also sent Carson the score of his ballet *The Dream of Audubon*, which had won him in 1941 a renewal of his Guggenheim Fellowship. Carson played the piano score of the ballet over and over. She wrote to Diamond that her father's eyes had welled with tears from pride as he examined the music, even though he could not read a note. Lamar Smith had heard much about David Diamond and felt a special connection with him. Examining now the magical, intricate score gave him a feeling of being in on wondrous things.

Newton Arvin, too, would be at Yaddo, and Carson was beside herself with anticipation. In early June, he had sent her a copy of his new book just published, a biography of Hawthorne. Unlike most critical works, which she felt pinned a subject down—like a butterfly on a board

—Arvin's book was mothlike. To Carson, Hawthorne breathed, as though he were a moth drawn against a window screen at night—held by the light, fluttering and alive. Never had Carson so warmly and sincerely praised an author's work as she did her friend's *Hawthorne*.[13]

Carson was still getting fan mail occasionally herself. Usually there were two or three letters a month, and for almost a year she had been the recipient of long-distance telephone calls from a man in Texas who had read *The Heart Is a Lonely Hunter* and called her every time he was intoxicated. She told Janet Flanner that he had called her the previous summer in New York, Yaddo, Quebec, and now Columbus, talking sometimes for a half hour or forty-five minutes on every imaginable subject. Carson's attitude was bewilderment; she could not penetrate his endless ramblings, and the whole thing stumped her, she said. But it did not occur to her to hang up and not talk to him. She took her fan mail and fans seriously. Later, she received an anonymous letter accusing her of anti-Semitism in *The Ballad of the Sad Café*, an unfounded accusation which upset her almost as much as anything Reeves had ever done to offend her. Perhaps Carson's best-known fan at the time—with whom she had not yet established a personal acquaintance—was novelist Henry Miller. He wrote her several admiring letters that spring, impressed by the psychology in her books, and sent her all of his own books as well—an overture which astonished her.

In late spring Carson met another admiring young man, Robert Walden, an army private stationed at the Infantry School at Fort Benning. Edwin Peacock introduced them, and soon Walden was spending all his free time in the Smith home. He became another of "Bebe's young men," for Marguerite Smith welcomed him warmly. Once he was a guest for a week, with Carson spending most of her time working on her novel or simply lying in bed not feeling well. In the afternoons, however, she emerged, and then there were long sessions of talk about people, books, and music, often lasting late into the evening. At night they sometimes drank burgundy and read poetry aloud to one another. When Walden found out that Carson had met Djuna Barnes and admired her work, he gave her a copy of Miss Barnes's recently published volume of poetry, *Nightwood*. Walden was most impressed, however, when he learned that Carson and David Diamond were good friends, for he already knew well Diamond's music and esteem. Carson took pleasure in telling the composer later that she had talked about him all one evening with her new friend, and that now they both were enamored of him. Only once did they go out for drinks and dinner, said Walden, occasioned by a weekend visit by his friend Edward Newberry, who eventually became Carson's good friend, too.

In June, Carson's sister, Rita, came home from the University of

Miami, having completed her junior year.[14] Rita, a French major with minors in Spanish and education, also aspired to write professionally or to have an editorial career on a New York magazine. She, too, felt the magical lure of the publishing world in New York City and yearned to go there when she graduated. That summer the two sisters shared warmly the anticipation of being in New York together in the near future.

With Rita home, Carson found that she spent less time alone in her room and more leisure with her family. Occasionally she even helped in the kitchen. One afternoon she wrote David Diamond that she was planning to cook the entire meal that night. She mentioned also that Rita, who played the piano too, was at that moment playing Haydn. Carson used the same image in her letter to describe Rita's playing that she had written in "Wunderkind" six years earlier and would repeat in *The Bride*—the rattling of "notes . . . falling over each other like a handful of marbles dropped downstairs."[15] Rita's playing had doubtless triggered the old image, and Carson called it up now for use not only in her letter, but in her *Bride* manuscript as well.

The last two weeks in Columbus were difficult ones for Carson. She felt skittish, edgy in her anticipation of returning to Yaddo. It was a feeling somewhat akin to the timorous excitement experienced on her first trip by steamer to New York. There were no fears or wonderment about this journey, however; this time she would see old friends, favorite haunts, and retreat to the safe, comfortable, and scenic environs of the artists' colony. She was sure that the writing would again flow in the disciplined, yet free atmosphere of Yaddo.

In spite of her having turned down Elizabeth Ames's initial invitation to Yaddo that summer, there had been no real cause for Carson to doubt for a moment that a place could now be found for her. Mrs. Ames was fond of Carson, and she would have made room for her even if she had had to string someone else from a rafter. But psychically, it suited Carson's nature to worry. She was a good worrier, for her fantasies leaped pell-mell as she discarded alternates. To have stayed in Columbus would have killed her, she was sure. It pleased her, however, to imagine herself a forlorn waif with no sanctuary. She took comfort and an almost sadomasochistic pleasure in identifying with the outcast, with the quester whose Grail was always elusive. She believed it her destiny not to find reciprocity. She liked being the lover for the very reason she had expressed in *The Ballad of the Sad Café*: "The value and quality of any love is determined solely by the lover himself":

> It is for this reason that most of us would rather love than be loved.
> Almost everyone wants to be the lover. And the curt truth is that,
> in a deep secret way, the state of being beloved is intolerable to

many. The beloved fears and hates the lover, and with the best of
reasons. For the lover is forever trying to strip bare his beloved. The
lover craves any possible relation with the beloved, even if this experience can cause him only pain.[16]

The time in Columbus could not pass fast enough for Carson now.
She found it impossible to stay in her room and write—even for the three
or four hours in the morning to which she had become conditioned. Instead, she talked compulsively with her mother and sister, listened again
and again to David Diamond's music, played the score of his ballet, and
longed to be with him.

Arriving in New York by train the end of June, Carson took time
only to see Muriel Rukeyser, Janet Flanner, Henry Varnum Poor, and
two or three other special friends before going on to Saratoga Springs. She
wanted to catch the pulse of the city, but she was determined to view it
dispassionately; she would not stay long or in any way get involved, she
vowed. It was not time to return to New York City permanently, she
reasoned. Carson still wore her albatross of penance, although more lightly
than when she had donned it the preceding fall. But where else could she
better learn what was going on in the world, she mused. She had missed
what she thought of as the exciting artistic world of Manhattan and the
literary coterie from which she had felt vaguely excluded while she was
South. Carson also longed to spend an evening with George Davis in
the atmosphere of his den of unpredictable artistes at 7 Middagh Street,
but there was no time. She had a drink with Klaus Mann at the Bedford
Hotel—Mann's "second home"—and saw for only a few moments Gypsy
Rose Lee, who had married several days earlier. It was Gypsy's second
marriage, this time to Broadway actor Alexander Kirkland. Gypsy herself
was back on Broadway in a new show, Star and Garter, which theatregoers said, "gave full scope to her talents."

With Henry Varnum Poor and Muriel Rukeyser, Carson talked about
Reeves. She learned that he had re-enlisted in the Army in March at
Camp Upton, New York. Afterward he had gone to Fort Jackson, South
Carolina, but soon was to report to Fort Benning for Officers' Candidate
School. Reeves had volunteered for the Rangers, reputed to be the tough-
est and most fearless assault outfit in the U. S. Army. Hearing of her
former husband again, Carson was surprised to discover that she had not
dismissed him from her emotional life as thoroughly as she had imagined.
The old rancor was there, yet she felt a secret pleasure in knowing that
he was performing a useful and courageous service for his country. If
there was one thing Reeves was, she said, it was a good soldier. Her
thoughts of him were now more charitable than she had guessed possible
in view of their recent months of conflict, betrayal, and bitterness. In

spite of herself Carson wished him well and prayed that he would be safe in combat and return to live a good life with some nice girl with whom he could be happy.

Carson arrived at Yaddo on July 2 by train, going straight to David Diamond's studio. Elizabeth Ames had invited Diamond back this summer, also. Carson had written to him that spring in generalities about the future and their life together once her book was finished. Reeves and Diamond had not corresponded since Diamond's abrupt departure from Rochester the preceding November; but now, with the war on, the composer had worried about him and wondered where he was. "He is a sergeant in the United States Army," Carson told him, proud that Reeves was trying to make something of himself once more.

Newton Arvin, too, was back, but only for a few days. A director of the colony, he was there more than most of the other directors, but he seldom stayed in residence all summer. Again, as last year, Carson knew few of the artists, but this time it did not matter. Nathan and Carol Asch were back, and it was good to be with them. Asch had gained prominence as a writer in Europe and was one of the earliest and most successful Jewish-American novelists and short-story writers, who rivaled even his own father's considerable reputation. (Nathan Asch's father was Sholem Asch, a novelist-dramatist whom Carson admired as a beautiful, sensitive writer. Intrigued by father and son, she found that her identification with the Jewish exile was intensified by her friendship with the Asches.) Carol Asch, who worked part time as Elizabeth Ames's secretary, had typed *The Ballad of the Sad Café* manuscript for what Carson referred to as pocket money. Alfred Fisher, Arvin's good friend and Smith College colleague whom Carson had met in Northampton the preceding fall, was in residence in June, and in July his wife, writer Helen Eustis, came. The Fishers had staggered their Yaddo residence so that one of them could be at home with Adam, their young son. Franz and Greta Weiskopf, Carson's friends from Prague whom she had met at Yaddo the preceding summer, were back, too. Writer Leonard Ehrlich, almost a year-round resident, was joined later that summer by his brother, Gerald. In all, there were some thirty-five people at Yaddo while Carson was there in 1942, although usually no more than twenty were there at a time.[17]

Carson found not only that she had a place to stay at Yaddo—contrary to her unfounded anxieties—but also that her quarters were the most highly esteemed of the colony: the tower room, which had been Lady Katrina Trask's boudoir. An enormous room, it had seventeen mullioned bay windows which formed a semicircle at one end and afforded a panoramic view of miles of valley, trees, and hills. To skate down the sidewalks of Starke Avenue, dodging the acorns, to walk in her Wildwood Circle woods in Columbus, to view the changing seasons in the trees and flowers of Georgia and upstate New York as a scrutinizer and disciple of nature—all had no relationship to the emotion Carson felt now as she looked out the windowed expanse. Terrified, she made a new discovery: She had agoraphobia, a phobia that had never before been put to the test. She knew now why there had been such comfort in phone booths at Macy's when she was seventeen and why the ocean voyage to New York as a teen-ager had vaguely disquieted her. Overwhelmed by the fear of working, sleeping, and living in such a great open space, Carson begged Helen Eustis to change rooms with her. She said that just leaving her shoes on the far side of the room meant taking a long walk to retrieve them. Nor could she sleep with the windows undraped. Since the two women shared a bath, Carson told Miss Eustis that no one would even have to know that they had exchanged rooms. Again, she revealed her fear of being criticized or laughed at, just as she had when she asked her friend Helen Jackson in childhood not to tell the other children that Helen had had to climb the elm and demonstrate limb by limb her descent. Helen Eustis readily agreed, for she was pleased to have the better room. It did not bother her, for she loved the light and open space, as well as the huge Victorian bed and other accouterments accompanying the exchange.

Carson was delighted, too, to be back with Elizabeth Ames, who had witnessed and shared her heartaches the preceding summer. She told Mrs. Ames now that with luck and hard work she was sure she could finish her *Bride* by the first of the year. She needed Elizabeth Ames just as she had always needed someone with whom she might articulate her problems. Although Yaddo's executive director appeared fearsomely autocratic to most of the guests, she and Carson had felt a special affinity for one another and had enjoyed a warm personal relationship since their first meeting in New York City in the spring of 1941. Mrs. Ames never put herself upon people and usually stayed out of her artists' professional progress, but she exercised less restraint in watching over their personal affairs. To her, it was all in the guise of following the rules.

Good at nipping incipient romances, Mrs. Ames preferred to avoid face-to-face confrontations with the principals. Rather, she sent little "blue notes," typed messages on blue note paper in which she indicated that the offender had in some way stepped over the line, had deviated from the pattern, and that a change was in order. Usually the notes appeared in lunch boxes. If an artist had taken an evening stroll through the Yaddo pines after dark with a fellow resident, he was apt to find a blue note tucked in among his sandwiches and deviled eggs the next day, suggesting that it would be unwise to form youthful attachments. A writer who may have decided to skip the evening's chamber music and seek pleasure, instead, in shooting craps at Jimmy's Place in town might receive the cryptic message: "Everyone else enjoyed some very fine music last night." Another might imagine that his sojourn into the rose garden or a turn around the lakes with a young poetess had been unnoticed by everyone and too irrelevant to be remarked on by *anyone*, but a note on his door usually caught his eye the next morning when he arrived at his studio. The missive made the subtle observation that he had missed an interesting discussion in the parlor.

Certainly one's offenses did not have to be horrendous for him to fall from the director's grace. By grace, too, he was frequently reinstated. In spite of Carson's foolish pranks throughout the summer of 1941, she received few reprimands from Mrs. Ames, or so it seemed to the other guests who were continually amazed to see that the errant author continued to stay in the director's favor. When Elizabeth Ames retired at 10:00 P.M., as was her habit, she generally expected her charges to do so, too. It was not "good breeding" to slip into Saratoga Springs and perch on bar stools or gamble in the iniquitous dens on Congress Street, the "red light" district and black section of the town. Over the years, Mrs. Ames gradually became less vigilant—as well as less critical of what she did see and know to go on—but during the 1930s and 1940s, guests were expected to follow the rules or get out. More often than not, they simply were careful to avoid getting caught.

Carson was a far different girl at Yaddo in 1942 than she had been before; she worked hard, socialized little, and refrained from most of her antics of the preceding year. She was there to work, she resolved, not to play. The responsibility of the Guggenheim also imposed upon her a certain seriousness. When she left her parents this time, she told them she would not return South until she had finished her *Bride*. Her plan was to stay at Yaddo as long as it took. Although Yaddo was essentially a summer colony only, she hoped that Mrs. Ames would let her stay on through the winter if necessary. Elizabeth Ames was *Queen* Elizabeth, and her matriarchal reign carried far more weight than the titular board of directors over which she presided. She not only made the final decision in the selection of guests, but also vouched for and insisted upon their monastic conduct once there.

Each spring the board met to pass judgment on the applicants who wished to work that summer at Yaddo. Their talents and creative works in progress, as well as laurels already earned, however, were usually subordinate to Mrs. Ames's personal opinion regarding the prospective guest's character and his apparent compatibility with others. If she liked him and could vouch for his personal conduct, she might say: "Now, I happen to know that this person is going through a difficult period in his life emotionally, and I think he is just the kind of person we should take in and help." General assent of the group would follow. Then another name might come up for discussion about which she could make a similar comment: "Now I happen to know that this applicant is going through a very stormy personal experience." But instead of a recommendation for acceptance, she would sedately add: "So I think we should not invite him—he might be disruptive to our Yaddo life." That application would promptly go into the reject pile. Elizabeth Ames prided herself on her intuitiveness in deciding who would fit in and who would not—and she was seldom wrong.

Carson relied upon Mrs. Ames's critical judgment, also, on her *Bride* manuscript that summer. Upon arrival, she presented the director with all the drafts she had written to date. There were three, and she sought her friend's advice on small points as well as the overview. More often, Carson simply wanted an ear. She also liked to read aloud to Mrs. Ames, who was an alert critic to the sounds, rhythms, and nuances of language. Eventually the director of Yaddo read every draft Carson wrote, and told her, finally, when she felt that the perfect one had been achieved. But that was not until the summer of 1945. When it got to be the fifth or sixth version, in 1944, Elizabeth Ames said, "Carson, I think it would be much better if you would get other people to pass judgment on it. We are both too close to it now." Carson's face fell. She had been despondent again about the work, for she agonized over her *Bride* as a mother would whose time for delivery had long since come and gone, yet who had still delivered no child.

"Oh, Elizabeth, I could never do that. You are a part of this book, of Frankie and me."[18] To Mrs. Ames, it seemed as though Carson would give up the work rather than share it with anyone else; it would be like changing jockeys two days before the big race in Saratoga Springs.

There had been a time, however, when Carson had welcomed any listener's ear and eye for her manuscript. The summer of 1942 she shared it with several. David Diamond read many parts of *The Bride* when he joined her in Saratoga Springs, and Newton Arvin was consulted frequently that summer. But next to Elizabeth Ames, perhaps the one on whom the book was inflicted most often was Helen Eustis, the young writer with whom Carson had exchanged rooms. Miss Eustis read at least three different drafts that summer during the five weeks she was there. By then she was so weary of it that she hoped she would never even see the title again; nor did it take restraint *not* to read the book when it finally appeared.

When Carson was not at work on her manuscript, in the late afternoons and evenings, she craved companionship and sought out her fellow artists. She seemed to plead constantly for approval and to make enormous, open statements of her need for dependence upon others. Just as she had attached herself to Edward Newhouse the summer before, so, too, did she approach other fellow artists now. To one Yaddo guest she seemed like a large puppy who kept falling over her feet and her emotions. Carson readily took people into her confidence, and when they sympathized with her she responded with great loyalty and devotion.

Katherine Anne Porter was also very much in evidence at Yaddo that summer. Two "camps" had been loosely established the preceding summer with Miss Porter and Carson squared off in opposite corners as the matriarch of each. David Diamond, who had a beautiful rapport with each woman separately, found his relationship threatened with both because of the friction between them. One simply could not be Carson's friend and also Katherine Anne Porter's and comfortably remain in the close proximity in which they all lived. The cleavage finally became so deep that Elizabeth Ames interceded with more than a "blue note." She asked Diamond to leave Yaddo that summer, for she blamed him for much of the unrest. The friction had become highly personal and the offenses more imagined than real, said observers, or as one writer put it, "It was impossible to have two prima donnas at Yaddo at the same time." Mrs. Ames was exceedingly fond of both Carson and Miss Porter, and there was no question of either of them leaving; therefore David Diamond, whose estrangement from Elizabeth Ames had begun the summer before, was the one asked to go.

It was the threat of Carson's becoming a burden to a person that caused one to try to maintain a certain distance from her; and again and again people withdrew before being sucked into a position they could not support. Carson told more than one fellow artist that summer about a fantasy that had persisted as both daydreams and nightmares. She said that she had dreamed she was very sick and that it would be necessary for her to have constant care and attention by someone else for the rest of her life; yet in the dream she always feared that there would be no one who would care for her. "Of course it was only a dream, but it seemed so real," she said, with a kind of breathless urgency. To her listener it seemed that the necessity of having someone nurse her all her life was a craving, rather than simply a foreboding. Carson also told friends that summer about a short story she might write someday. Its protagonist was a beggar who faked that he was a cripple. Each day he rode the subway to his begging station where people generously doled out money and sympathy. The attention he received there was even more important to him than the monetary rewards which supported him. At night he returned home, and in the confines of his room stood erect and moved without a limp—psychically maimed, but physically whole. If Carson wrote such a tale, it was never published. Yet those to whom she told the story wondered if Carson recognized its psychological implications, or if the fictional beggar himself knew his true condition. Later, when her Yaddo acquaintances heard of Carson's crippling strokes, there were some who could not help wondering if her physical ills had been—at any point in her life—psychosomatic. She had told many people that eventually she would experience everything that her characters did—if just given enough time.

There were times when Carson was not working that she liked being alone. She usually took Sundays off, from both her typewriter and her room. She loved especially to walk in the autumn afternoons, for the woods in September were a warm wash of yellows, russets, crimsons, and golds. She spent hours tramping around the Yaddo estate. In the fall the apple orchard was a special attraction. Sometimes she would leap up, catch a low-hanging apple limb, and swing until she dropped from exhaustion. Afterward, she would stretch out among the fallen leaves, doze, and daydream. To climb a birch would have been more challenging, but Carson decided that to be a vicarious swinger of birches with her friend Robert Frost would suffice. Just before the dinner hour she would return with pockets bulging, having squirreled a half dozen apples for bedtime snacks. Carson loved to savor, too, the pungent odor of the ripening fruit in her room.

By late September barely a handful of resident artists were left at Yaddo. Only Carson, Kenneth Fearing—poet and writer of mystery novels—and novelist Nan Lurie remained through the winter. One of her favorites, Langston Hughes, stayed until November. Hughes and composer Nathaniel Dett were two of the first blacks ever to be in residence at Yaddo, and Carson thoroughly enjoyed her friendship with them over the summer. Another guest writer who stayed into the autumn was Alfred Kantorowicz, a forty-three-year-old German Jew who had been a law student, literary critic, foreign correspondent, and writer. Carson made him her new idol, enthralled by his tale of flight from Germany when the Nazis came to power, his sanctuary in France—then internment there by the Vichy regime in 1940—and finally, his harrowing escape from the Gestapo in 1941 and safety in the United States.

She fell half in love with Kantorowicz, and, later, even more so with his beautiful wife, Friedel, who had shared his plight. At Carson's urgings, he told many of his experiences during, what seemed to him, Europe's darkest times. To Kantorowicz, "The child from Georgia responded as though she had never before heard such tales." Wide-eyed, she asked again and again for details of his life of exile, underground, concentration camp, civil war in Spain (against Franco), prison, flight, and book burnings. To Kantorowicz, Carson lamented that Hitler's Germany was no more "the land of Goethe and Schiller, and that France was no more the land of Liberté, Egalité, and Fraternité," but what fascinated her most that summer were the details of what was really happening. It was as though she had heard little, and had read nothing, of Brecht, Heinrich Mann, or Malraux, he thought. Every day for weeks, Carson met Kantorowicz and "sucked all the true stories I could tell her, anecdotes, too, for instance, of how Ernest Hemingway's bathroom in Madrid was destroyed by a shell—all like a child listens to fairy tales," he concluded.[19]

With Kantorowicz Carson listened also to the war news of the moment. The small group sat about the radio in the mansion several times a day, eager for details. Then they stayed on and discussed the latest ravages of each front. What was happening in Stalingrad was a miracle, Carson thought, but she had begun to believe in miracles, she said. Stalingrad had been suffering some of the heaviest losses of the war from massive tank assaults upon the city for almost a month. Thousands were slain daily, outlying towns taken, and portions of the city itself occupied intermittently in seesaw action through fierce, close-quarter combat. Finally the Nazis decided not to attempt to save the city for their own occupation, but rather, to destroy it through massive artillery battery. Each letter Carson wrote to friends during the fall and winter of 1942–43 abounded with concern and compassion for those on the Stalingrad front, in Africa, and the Pacific theater. One can almost date her letters from her references to what was happening in the war. Frankie Addams, in Carson's *Bride* manuscript, exuded the same anxieties over the war and its hapless victims that Carson herself made explicit almost daily in her letters and conversations.

She was uneasy, too, about the fate of her friends. David Diamond expected to be drafted any day. Klaus Mann had enlisted in the Army and was a correspondent for *Stars and Stripes*. Edwin Peacock, her friend from Charleston, had enlisted in the Navy in California, and soon Henry Varnum Poor joined a special Artists' Unit of the Alaskan Theater in the U. S. Navy. Carson's brother, Lamar, was in the Seabees and on his way to the Pacific, and the rest of the men of the Smith-Waters clan in Georgia were away from home, too, in the service of their country. Carson worried about them all. More and more, she fantasized about being a foreign correspondent and in the thick of it, even if she could not fight.

In spite of the tragic world events her writing on the *Bride* manuscript was going better that fall and winter than it ever had gone before. She found that she was working not only every morning, but throughout the afternoon as well, rarely going into town any more except to buy a few provisions for her room: a stock of tea, raisins, and a gallon jug of sherry or white wine. (According to Ruth Gikow, everyone at Yaddo that summer took for granted that "Carson had to be a little high to work."[20])

In September, Newton Arvin returned to Smith College for the fall teaching term, and without him Carson found that she could seldom even force herself to go into the lounge and bar of the New Worden any more.

She wrote David Diamond—for whom it had also been a favorite haunt —that when she walked into the Worden she felt like a ghost stalking the pair of them. One day she reported that she had gone in alone but had become inebriated on only four martinis. During one of her jaunts into town, Carson was accompanied by Robert Linscott, her friend and editor at Houghton Mifflin, and his son Roger, on leave from the Navy. Linscott came to talk with several of his authors and to search for new manuscripts for his publishing house. After they finished shop talk, Carson took them to shoot craps at Jimmy's Place and to wander into some of the more atmospheric bars on Congress Street, well known for its sleazy night life. Linscott and his son were duly impressed by Carson's way with dice. She spit on them, canted over them with a few sonuvabitches, and rolled them hot in front of an admiring crowd. Her luck had been even better a week earlier, she boasted to Diamond in a letter. Her prowess as a crapshooter had won her over six dollars at Jimmy's, she said, and she had spent it all at the bar afterward, setting her fans up to drinks. But most of her play was behind her, Carson ventured. (According to Leonard Ehrlich, Carson "spent many pleasant hours at Jimmy's," many of which he had shared with her. Twenty years later when Ehrlich returned to Saratoga Springs and to the old hangout one evening, Jimmy came over to him and asked fondly: "How's that nice girl, what's her name, the tall girl, the writer? . . . Yes, that's it—Carson!"[21])

When she wrote to Klaus Mann in September to congratulate him on his newly published autobiographical journal, *The Turning Point*, she said that she had no special news, only that she was working hard, reading, walking, playing the piano, and going to bed early. Carson had immediately shared Mann's book with the few European exiles still in residence, with whom Mann—and Carson, as well—had an affinity. She never got over the idea that she was always the exile from somewhere. Carson wrote to Newton Arvin that she no longer went in for evening shenanigans, but plugged along steadily both night and day with her *Bride*, her ideas spilling over so constantly when she was not even at the typewriter that sometimes she felt she simply had to go to sleep just so Frankie could get some rest. To Arvin, she was ever grateful that he had introduced her to sleeping with a night shade.

As cold weather moved into upstate New York, the front part of the mansion was closed off. Carson felt the cold earlier than everyone else. Before the move to the back of the house, where she occupied a small attic room, she sat hunched over her typewriter wearing a sweater and leather jacket, drinking scalding sherry tea and an occasional double shot of whiskey. She told David Diamond that she was not only cold, but also hungry all the time. She thanked Jesus, she said, that she was getting on with her book. With luck, it would be ready in three months. She said that she sat over her desk and struggled, the book sounding like Frankie's piano, which she had tuned and tuned. Then Carson quoted some of her novel to her friend. She said that the more Frankie tuned her piano, the stranger it sounded. Finally her piano played weird, unknown music, and Frankie had become so disquieted that she closed the piano lid and put away her tools. But Carson was not going to tune herself out of a piano or her book, she resolved, and her novel coursed relentlessly on.

In November, her story "A Tree. A Rock. A Cloud." appeared in *Harper's Bazaar* and brought new fan mail and an invitation for its inclusion in the *O'Henry Prize Stories of 1942.* Carson was especially pleased by Kay Boyle's congratulatory letter. Miss Boyle wrote that she was expecting another baby any day and that she planned to name it for Carson.[22]

A few days later Carson decided to make a trip into New York City. She thought that everything at Yaddo would be closed after the first of the year, and that soon they might be snowed in. Ostensibly, Carson wanted to see about a place to stay in the city, and to shop, she said; but what she really wanted was to be with other people again, with David Diamond, who was also in the city, with Muriel Rukeyser, and with Janet Flanner. In New York, she also talked with Gus Lobrano and with George Davis about a possible job for Helen Eustis on *The New Yorker* or *Mademoiselle,* where Davis had recently been made fiction editor. Davis invited her out to 7 Middagh for dinner and to see the upstairs front room which he had furnished just for her, he said, then closed off so that it would be ready whenever she decided to come back to the city. This time the house in Brooklyn Heights appealed to her as a practical and sensible place in which to live. Its only inhabitants were Richard Wright and his family, who had leased the first two floors, Oliver Smith, who had the top attic floor, and Davis. Carson could stay as long as she wanted, David urged.

It was not an agreeable trip for the most part, however, for Carson came down with dysentery and fever in the city and returned to Yaddo earlier than planned. She wanted to recuperate in her own bed, she said. She did manage to shop a little, for she needed a sturdy pair of winter shoes and a new suit. She also bought velvet material and resolved to find a dressmaker in Saratoga Springs who would make just what she wanted. Carson loved the sensuous feel of velvet and had always wanted a suit with long pants made of it.

On November 5, Carson moved to the Pine Tree studio, a little cottage several hundred yards away from the mansion. It was at the edge of the woods, set amid huge pines which shaded the little house from the sun, creaked and moaned in the wind, and dropped their needles noisily upon the roof. In the morning Carson frequently found deer and pheasants just outside her door, and in the evening she sometimes caught the reflection of eyes peering at her from the brush. She loved her new quarters, which had a large worktable, a deep pile red rug on the floor, and a stove, which she kept going all night. For the first time since cold weather set in Carson now felt completely comfortable. It was a lonely existence away from everyone else, for she saw almost no one except at mealtime. She seldom even saw Elizabeth Ames, who was busy nursing her sister, Marjorie Peabody Waite, who had suffered a stroke and was badly paralyzed. Mrs. Waite struggled to talk, but it was agony for both her and her sister as she tried unsuccessfully to communicate. In a letter, Carson posed to Newton Arvin the thought that perhaps psychiatric treatment would help. Soon Elizabeth Ames and she both wrote to Carson's friend on Long Island, psychiatrist William Mayer, who had once treated her, to ask if he would come to Saratoga Springs and examine Marjorie Waite.

The first day of December Carson's warm, encapsulated little world in the Pine Tree studio crumbled. She had been walking in the woods that afternoon—almost all day, in fact—for it had started snowing that morning, and she was anxious to be out in it. There in the woods and in the snow, Carson felt especially close to her Swiss friend, for the rapidly falling flakes seemed to be Annemarie's snow, and the black firs, her forest. When finally Carson walked to the garage late that afternoon, she found a letter awaiting her from Klaus Mann. Annemarie was dead. She had died in Sils, Switzerland, on November 15, but Mann could offer no details. He had received only a cable from a Swiss friend, delayed ten days because of the war. Her response was disbelief and a terrible chilling numbness.

That night Carson wrote to Mann, but what was there to say? He knew what Annemarie had always meant to her. She had had no love, no emotion, no life, it seemed, apart from Annemarie. Nor could belief pierce the numbness. And over all, the snow kept falling, blanketing her mind, her body, the studio, the trees, her vision of life. All night the snow fell, and the next day and the next day, and the days and nights were without dimensions. She could not sleep, and the sleeping powders only dazed her even more. On December 3, Carson managed to write letters to David Diamond and Newton Arvin. It was as though a robot had typed them. They were almost identical in phrasing, syntax, and punctuation. She had not slept since Mann's letter. Her only hope, she said, was to try to walk, and exhaust herself. And to write. She would write no more letters for a while, but try to work instead. She could not go on like this, she knew. There was no running to Elizabeth Ames for pity or solace, only the abject loneliness of housing within herself the grief. Mrs. Ames knew of Annemarie's death and something of the depths of Carson's love for her, but sensed that verbal condolences would mean little.

A week later (as soon as the Christmas holidays began at Smith), Newton Arvin came. Arvin, work on her *Bride*, and letters to and from

Diamond and Mann helped maintain Carson's tenuous hold on reality and sanity the next few weeks.

By Christmas Day, it was clear to Mrs. Ames and to Arvin that Carson would survive, that her great powers of resilience had proved themselves again. Carson wrote to David Diamond Christmas afternoon about her day of quiet festivities. Arvin, Mrs. Ames, and the handful of other winter guests at the colony gathered for dinner over the garage, where Carson opened a stack of presents from home—then ate too much and drank too much, she confided. Afterward, she dressed up in her new Christmas shirt, knee socks, and sweater and looked splendid, she told Diamond.

Eventually Carson learned from Klaus Mann most of the details of Annemarie's death, but for weeks she knew nothing. At first, it was rumored that her friend had committed suicide, but Carson refused to accept such a possibility. Then in January she received a cable from an unidentified respondent to her inquiries: Annemarie had had a bicycle accident, followed by a severe brain illness. She died in the care of nurses, alone and shut away from friends in her home in Sils, Switzerland. According to Annemarie's sister, Suzanne Ohman, suicide was in no way involved unless Annemarie felt a subconscious desire for death and thus gradually let go of her will to live.[23] Miss Ohman's account of the bicycle accident was as follows:

> On 6 September [1942], Annemarie had hired a carriage and driver
> to visit friends in Silvaplana. She rode by Miss A. Godli's and
> chatted happily with her before driving on. Shortly thereafter a friend
> of Annemarie's [Miss Isabelle Trümpi] rode by on a bicycle and in-   .
> quired about her. Miss Godli told her she could surely catch up with
> Annemarie, which she did. As Annemarie and her friend were riding
> side by side, Anne wanted to show her that she, too, could ride a
> bike. So they exchanged vehicles. Anne pedaled, and to really show
> her ability let go of the handlebars and rode with no hands. The
> bicycle struck a sharp stone before or after a small bridge. Anne fell
> and hit her temple on this sharp stone. Immediately she was uncon-
> scious and bleeding severely from the wound. I do not want to go
> into any further details here. In any case, she died on 15 November
> of the same year without ever gaining consciousness.[24]

Pondering the tragic events, Carson told Arvin that she had not heard from Annemarie for two months before her death. It distressed her to realize that during that time she had no way of knowing that Annemarie lay ill and dying. The cable Annemarie sent her the end of August and a letter Carson received about the same time had been filled with confidence. Knowing that her questions could never be answered, Carson "wondered" to Klaus Mann if Annemarie had died quite suddenly, without fear, or if she had been sick and tormented and possibly locked away somewhere. In August of that year Carson had written a long letter to her friend which she described as "a small manuscript." It was a comment upon Kierkegaard's *Fear and Trembling*, almost a paraphrase, but Carson had arrived at a different hypothesis.[25] How strange it seemed to her that that particular letter should be the last one she had written, and it grieved her that she had no way of knowing if Annemarie had received it before her accident. Nor could she bear to think of a stranger reading her letters addressed to her friend. She told Mann that no one else could possibly have understood them, for in most of them she had written little stories, and her personal messages had been oblique. She longed, too, to know what had happened to the Congo River poems that she had been asked to translate, or if Annemarie's book *The Miracle of the Tree* had been completed in Africa and could now be published. Much later, the poems did turn up. They had been preserved, and eventually Mann sent her a copy of them to translate. For years, however, it was thought that all of Annemarie's manuscripts had been destroyed by her family. Annemarie's sister finally learned that Anita Forrer had been given the manuscripts according to Annemarie's will, but that most of the letters found in her effects had been destroyed. According to her sister, no direct reference to Carson appeared in any surviving piece of writing by Annemarie.

With the death of her beloved, Carson felt again that she was without shelter. It was time to move on and attempt once more to shore up the fragments. George Davis now urged Carson to come to 7 Middagh. They would look after each other, he promised. On January 17, 1943, Carson packed her belongings and returned again to the city. Only Kenneth Fearing from among Yaddo's winter artists remained after Carson left. In the meantime, Elizabeth Ames had all she could do caring for her paralyzed sister, and she did not have time or energy left to supervise meals and households for anyone else. William Mayer went to Yaddo for eight days in January to study and diagnose Mrs. Waite's illness, but the prognosis was that she would never get any better. (She died December 6, 1944.)

Upon Carson's relocation in New York City, another major phase of her life had passed: marriage, literary success, love, divorce, and death of a loved one. She wanted no further complications—only to be left alone so that she could continue her life's work as as artist.

Chapter Eight

RECONCILIATION AND REMARRIAGE:
COLUMBUS AND NYACK, 1943 – 45

*W*hen George Davis received Carson's wire on January 17, 1943, that she was leaving Yaddo and was on her way to 7 Middagh Street, he was in the midst of refurbishing the old house. She arrived to find her room empty of furniture and the overwhelming odor of paint everywhere. Davis had not expected her to arrive until early February, and her quarters had not been painted. Two of his friends, however, pitched in to help and they worked late into the night. Carson insisted on adding a few deft touches herself, a bourbon on the rocks in one hand, a brush in the other. In another day the room was dry, aired, and again tastefully decorated with Davis' antique furniture, Edwardian *objets d'art*, and grand piano.

The room set aside for Carson was the large front one on the third floor, separated from Davis' sitting room and bedroom by a small hall in which he had installed an electric grill and refrigerator. She could hardly believe that the household of which she was again a part had once been the fabulous and sometimes testy menage of Brooklyn Heights that she had helped George Davis and Wystan Auden colonize in 1940. Men and women endowed with some of the greatest genius and eccentricity of twentieth-century America had wined, dined, and bedded there—some only for hours, others overnight, and many for a fortnight or months at a time. But now the entire setup had changed. Richard Wright and his family, who had the two lower floors—including the regular kitchen facilities —were quite independent from the rest of the establishment. Oliver Smith kept largely to himself in his two rooms on the fourth floor, and Carson and Davis shared the third floor. She loved being back in Brooklyn Heights. The quiet neighborhood, which seemed not to have changed a bit, the hoarse and sometimes shrill sounds from the harbor, the harsh raw smell of salt air—all greatly pleased her fancy.

Carson's simple, idyllic life in what now seemed almost like home was abruptly interrupted a few days after her arrival when she became bedridden with influenza and what she called "a mean grippy cold."

She and Davis had been taking most of their meals out, for they rarely ate more than delicatessen food in the apartment, neither of them being much interested that winter in hot-plate cooking. There were no decent places in which to eat in the immediate neighborhood, and they frequently walked over a mile in the snow for their evening dinners after Davis got home from the city. They liked especially to walk up to Borough Hall to a Chinese restaurant for egg rolls and sweet and sour pork. But prolonged exposure to the cold and snow, particularly after the sun went down, made Carson more susceptible than usual to throat infections. Stricken again severely, she was put to bed for ten days and allowed up only to ride the subway into Manhattan daily to see her doctor for cold serums and sulfa drug treatment.

Worst of all, she could not write. For most of the rest of January and February, Carson was either ill in bed or convalescing. Just as she began to feel well enough to think seriously about sitting once more for long stretches at the typewriter, she suffered a new malady. During a seemingly innocuous molar extraction, her dentist cracked and broke her jawbone. Of course, it was not his fault, Carson assured Newton Arvin, who was much concerned by her whole predicament. Her dentist was splendid, she said; had her bones not already been unhealthy and brittle, it would never have happened.[1] Then a bone infection in the jaw ensued, and she was forced again to make daily trips into Manhattan to have the bone scraped and dressed.

The pain seemed almost unbearable to Carson, yet she never whiningly complained of it. To Arvin she wrote with restraint and objectivity about her discomfort, acknowledging simply that she was afraid to take sufficient sedatives to quiet the pain because they were dangerous and addictive. Perhaps what helped most, since she had little stamina for writing, was a new friendship that was evolving. She had recently met Cheryl Crawford, whom she liked and admired immediately and immensely. She and Miss Crawford shared the same dentist and saw each other frequently, Carson told Arvin. A former student of Arvin's at Smith College, Miss Crawford had been a cum laude graduate in 1925. Because of her friendship with Newton Arvin, Carson felt that she and Miss Crawford had a special connection. Fifteen years older than Carson, Miss Crawford had been active in various facets of the theatre since she first played Lady Macbeth in high school the year of Carson's birth. From Smith, she had gone directly to the Theatre Guild, where she served as secretary and appeared in several Guild productions. Miss Crawford had also worked as a stage manager and director, had been a founder of the Group Theatre in 1930, and by the time she and Carson met, was one of the most successful and shrewdest producers on Broadway.

It was through Cheryl Crawford that Carson got her first taste of the theatre and an appreciation for what went on behind the scenes. To Carson, it was a baffling and mysterious new world. In telling Arvin about her new friendship with Miss Crawford, she said that they had been going about the city together and that she had a feeling they would become special friends. A few months later, Carson wrote Arvin that their relationship had been taut and strangely disquieting, at least for her. She had no reason to believe that Miss Crawford had any sexual feelings for her, and it was not that she was in love with Miss Crawford, Carson said, but she did feel edgy and tense. There were vague stirrings within that she could not put down, feelings that she thought had been outgrown or had died with Annemarie, she admitted. It was discomfiting for Carson to realize that she was once again attracted to a female. Surely it was the devil at work in her, she told Arvin, and she hoped that she had not completely ruined her new friendship.

In February, Carson's mother joined her in Brooklyn Heights for a few weeks, no longer able to withstand the temptation to be at her daughter's side. In a rather muted, plaintive letter Carson had written home that one of her main problems was food, that when she was sick, it had been almost impossible for her to go out to eat. George Davis was good about bringing food in for the two of them, she said, but for weeks they had eaten ham sandwiches off the top of the piano, had allowed dirty dishes to pile up high in the bathtub, and had lived a rather sordid existence. Once Marguerite arrived, their lives became more ordered. Carson ate well again and her health began to mend. Her mother tried hard to prevail upon her to return South to recuperate. Marguerite promised to fix the nutritious homemade soups Carson loved and to bring hot sherry tea or coffee laced with rum to her bedside or worktable as often as she wanted it throughout the day. They again could listen together to music, her mother told her, which to Carson had always been a soothing balm. Adamant, however, that she was not ready to leave Brooklyn Heights, to capitulate and go home, she told Marguerite that she felt she had to stay North and work; she had made few friends and had begun to see David Diamond again. To retreat to her isolated way of life in her hometown when she was enjoying a new sense of independence was more than Carson could envision, and finally Marguerite returned to Columbus alone.

The most important thing that happened to Carson's psyche that winter after her arrival in Brooklyn Heights was a conciliatory letter from Reeves. To her it was a noble letter—and even though she did not consciously regard it as such, it was a long-awaited one. Judging from its tone, Reeves had found himself, she thought. His spiritual life appeared to be secure. He said that he had faced God and arrived at a satisfactory spiritual reckoning. He also assured Carson that he was over his strange sickness, which he identified as a mental illness, that had made him do the ignoble things which led to their divorce. The fact that he was a soldier again and had found a meaningful role in life had been his salvation, he said. He had been commissioned in November 1942 at Fort Benning, and as soon as the present maneuvers were over at Camp Forrest, Tennessee, he expected orders for overseas duty. He was looking forward to combat, he said, to leading his company of men, to proving himself worthy, and to dying, if need be, for his country, his woman, and the men he led and loved. It was a moving letter, and a difficult one for Reeves to write, thought Carson. She told Newton Arvin that she was thankful she could again write to Reeves after all these months of silence. Her former husband still seemed like a strange brother she had always loved, whose welfare she felt deeply responsible for. She admitted that during their two years of estrangement and divorce she had suffered great anxiety on his behalf and prayed for a safe recovery from his psychic problems and alcoholism. It was good to have an open line of communication again.

Had their reconciliation "of spirit" not occurred, Carson could not have written the article requested by *Mademoiselle* that winter. George Davis conceived of Carson's writing a kind of universal message to an embarking soldier, an anonymous letter with which all war wives and combat-bound husbands could identify, for hundreds of thousands of American troops were en route to combat areas throughout the world and many units were already in action in Europe and the Pacific. *Mademoiselle* would run Carson's article just as soon as possible, Davis said. In April 1943, Carson's "Love's Not Time's Fool" appeared, signed simply "By a War Wife." The tone was perfect, the message beautifully controlled, poignant and devoid of sentimentality. The letter began:

> Somehow I feel that this will be the last letter that will reach you while you are still here in America. During these last days, through the long journey of the troop train, my heart has been with you each hour. And now, tonight, I have such an insistent premonition that your embarkation will come off sooner than human reason can grasp. Yet I feel no panic. I hear within me no crying out. I realize that I cannot hope to know any details of your departure, and that it may be weeks before you may be able to write me where—on what island, what continent—you have been sent. But this suspense is part of the suffering we must face until the war is won.

Carson had wondered what she herself could do to serve her country. She anticipated the conscription of women to military service soon. She also wanted desperately to be a foreign correspondent and told friends that she had gone to the top in writing letters of application. Perhaps her "Open Letter" published in *Mademoiselle*, however, was one of the greatest things any woman could do for the war effort. It gave hope and strength to thousands of American women who identified with her, and a pledge of love, reassurance, and commitment to the men who left them behind.

Carson's "War Wife" affirmed that physical aloneness was not unbearable except when accompanied by moral isolation, and only through a "profound spiritual experience" could such suffering be alleviated:

> For you and me, and for all of us, there is an urgent necessity to believe in something larger than ourselves and our individual destinies. We know a deep necessity to affirm life, to believe in a future of creation rather than destruction, to have faith in ourselves and in the future of mankind. Because never have the forces of destruction and hate been so intricately organized. Never has there been more need in the world for love.

She then attempted to explain the nature of love, but acknowledged that it was like "trying to put down a definition for God." Her "War Wife" was able to define it, however, in honest and honorable terms. In no way was love an inexplicable honey-coated accident; rather, it was "a creative experience." She called the war a fight for their love as husband and wife, and as such, there were bound to be casualties, psychological casualties as well as physical ones. Carson's "War Wife" pledged that she would not be such a casualty, maimed by fear and strain:

> I can, and will, maintain a bulwark against the insidious threats that lie in wait for me, as they do for all the women of men at war. It will mean a conscious, determined, fiercely vigilant effort; and I believe that it is fine that it should be so. I shall feel nearer to you that way.

Yet she vowed never to lie that she did not feel fear:

> Fear is one of the prime realities of these times. When we were too lazy or too ignorant to know our enemy and fear him, we came near losing the world that is blessedly ours. It is right to fear, when it brings courage and fury to a job that must be done. . . . You see, darling, I feel fear, but somehow I am not afraid. It's a funny distinction maybe, but you will understand. To be afraid means to me a panicky yielding to anxiety; it means cowering in nightmarish shadows. . . . This will not happen to me, I promise you. I have found that against fear and loneliness work is an indispensable weapon.

Moreover, she kept in mind constantly that she was not alone, that all around her were other women faced with identical situations: "And as a soldier can find protection in the spirit of camaraderie that always accompanies the horrors of war, so those of us who are working together here at home can find strength in the knowledge that our emotions are shared by all of those around us." To be sure, her love was "not time's fool," for love has "the tenacity and power to overcome even the conditions with which we are now faced. . . . And in the final victory I know we will have won our own triumph—the preservation of our love, our life together."

Carson herself was beginning to feel like a war wife—she would always be married to Reeves, psychically though perhaps never again physically. He would be leaving Camp Forrest soon, going to his staging area for embarkation. He wrote that he would like to see her again before he went and asked if she possibly would be coming South soon. Marguerite, too, urged her daughter to come home. There were veiled references to the fact that Carson's father was ill, as well. Carson learned that her father was drinking more heavily than ever before; he also believed that he was dying of cancer, yet would not see a doctor. She worried, too, about Elizabeth Ames and her ability to continue indefinitely to bear the burden of caring for her sister, whose condition was steadily worsening. Carson urged Mrs. Ames to come to the city and stay with her at 7 Middagh Street for a few weeks to rest and regain her strength, but she knew that Mrs. Ames would be reluctant to leave her sister's bedside. Carson felt that she, too, had to go somewhere, for the mental pressures upon her were mounting. Again, she was getting no real writing accomplished, her creative energies sapped by the prolonged influenza and jawbone infection. Too, she felt edgy at remaining in the city when it had become obvious to her that she was becoming increasingly distracted by the people around her. She would leave before prostituting herself once more with false values and a life style incompatible with her dedication to art, she promised herself.

Then, on April 9, 1943, Carson received an unexpected boon—a letter from the president of the American Academy of Arts and Letters and the National Institute of Arts and Letters informing her that she was to be awarded a one-thousand-dollar "Arts and Letters" Grant to further her creative work in literature. The award would be presented at the Academy's Annual Ceremonial on May 12, and it was the Academy's hope that she would be there in person to receive it.[3] Thrilled, Carson intended to delay her trip home so that she might attend the Ceremonial. The announcement was made public on April 14 by the New York *Times*. Ten awards would be presented that year to creative workers in the fields of music, painting, sculpture, and literature. The four in literature were to be given to Carson; to Jose Garcia Villa, a young Philippine poet; to Virgil Geddes, poet and playwright; and to Joseph Wittlin, a Polish writer whom the Academy chose to honor for his "many years of literary accomplishment."

Carson's citation read:

> To Carson McCullers, born in Georgia, in recognition of her new
> voice of eloquence and power describing the American spiritual scene,
> in such books as *The Heart Is a Lonely Hunter*.

The new money came just as her Guggenheim Fellowship expired.
Carson told Newton Arvin in February that she would not try to renew
her Guggenheim, for she had sold *The Ballad of the Sad Café* to *Harper's
Bazaar* and would try, instead, to support herself without additional help
this year. The price for the new manuscript had not been settled, but the
editor loved it, she told Arvin, and she was sure it would bring a good
contract. But the manuscript would have to be cut some, she was told,
even though it was planned for two issues, as was *Reflections in a Golden
Eye*, which *Harper's Bazaar* had published in October and November of
1940. Carson hated to allow even a single word to be deleted. It was
already a tight story. She consented at last, however, to let the cuts stand.
It was David Diamond's story, she told friends. She had written it for
him, and he was to have the manuscript when *Harper's Bazaar* was
through with it.[4] She had originally wanted to finish *The Bride* and
have it out first, then take time to polish her little jewel, which she had
already chiseled to near precision the preceding summer at Yaddo. But
Frankie's story was still elusive, and she did not want to delay any longer
her ballad of the hunchback and the Amazonian woman who loved him.
The Ballad of the Sad Café was slated to be published in August, with
Mary Lou Aswell, literary editor, pushing to have it appear all in one
issue.

Carson decided that she should put off her trip South no longer. She
would not wait for the National Institute of Arts and Letters' Ceremonial
but would send a substitute in her place. On April 22, 1943, Carson again
boarded an afternoon train for Columbus, Georgia.

Carson had written Reeves to let him know she was coming, and on
May 5 he got a weekend pass and asked Carson to join him in Atlanta. It
was a good meeting, on neutral territory where they had not been together before. He had never looked so good—well, strong, and in command of himself again. Later, when she better understood the nature of
the rigorous and dangerous Ranger training and his position of leadership
with his men, Carson knew why.

A week later, Reeves secured a five-day leave and went to Columbus.
Marguerite and Lamar Smith greeted their former son-in-law warmly, as
though he had merely been away for a while, stationed elsewhere but now
home with his family on leave. If Carson loved him and welcomed him
back into her life, then Marguerite would receive him the same way. It
was good for Reeves to be back in the Smith household. He had always

felt at home there; the whole family was his family. They were good listeners, too, anxious to hear about his new work and life as a Ranger. Reeves had great pride in his men and his new outfit, and he loved to talk about them. He explained that he was the commanding officer of "I" Company in the newly created Second Battalion of Colonel William O. Darby's Rangers, an all-volunteer unit which specialized in commando-assault tactics, night fighting, and silent reconnaissance landings. He told them of the nature of the Ranger missions: to assault, confuse, terrorize, and demoralize the enemy. They were taught to kill quickly and swiftly, to use their bayonets as much as possible, to leave their mark, to destroy life with their bare hands if necessary, and above all, to work as a team.

Reeves, like the others, had been handpicked from volunteers already in the Army. The requirements were that each soldier possess physical prowess and a high moral character, and be mentally adaptable for making quick decisions under unexpected circumstances. To qualify, each man was adjudged to have a psychological proclivity for dangerous action, to be athletically inclined, to have good wind and stamina, and to be a strong swimmer. Reeves not only had these traits, but also the extra quality of being an able and inspiring leader of men. Marvelously caught up in the esprit de corps of the outfit, he believed that not since Marion's Swamp Foxes or Mosby's Confederate Rangers had an American fighting unit experienced such camaraderie. Highly competitive, each of Darby's Rangers believed that he was in the best section, platoon, company, and battalion of the entire American Army. Their training was with live ammunition under exacting and highly simulated battlefield conditions. They made their way over grueling obstacle courses, up steep-slanted rocks, across canyons, through forests, and down jagged cliffs. A grappling hook was as much a part of their equipment as bayonet or knife.

The men of the Second Battalion did not know their immediate destination, but thought that it might be Africa, where two other newly formed Ranger battalions were already in training. Reeves was looking forward to proving his mettle in combat, he told Carson and her family. He loved his men and felt great confidence in facing what lay before them with only a minimum of fear—honest fear that any intelligent man would logically have. Again and again, the Rangers had made a name for themselves in daring behind-the-lines missions and nighttime assaults on Dieppe, France; Arzew and El Guettar, French Algeria; and Italy, all with a minimum loss of men. No other outfit in the United States Army had so low a ratio of lives lost in proportion to the magnitude of the mission and the number of enemy killed.

Soon Reeves's outfit would go overseas to join the newly formed Fifth Battalion for training in England, Northern Ireland, and Scotland. While the Third and Fourth Ranger Battalions were being formed in Africa from volunteers already overseas, the Second was recruited wholly within the United States, but trained by seasoned veterans of the First Battalion and led by Lieutenant Colonel Max Schneider, also from the First. The Second and Fifth Battalions underwent even more rigorous conditioning and readiness than had been possible in the States. Groomed for the invasion of the Normandy beachhead on June 6, 1944, these two units found that a vital part of their training was in making amphibious landings and scaling the giant rocks of Dundee, Scotland, in preparation for the steep perpendicular cliffs which rim the French coast line. The Sixth Battalion soon formed and served in the Pacific Theatre.

Carson loved being with Reeves again and was filled with pride and awe at his accomplishments as a soldier. But it was sobering, too, for them to reflect upon their former days of love and happiness and to know that what they once had could never be recaptured. She felt now, more than ever, that it was her destiny to live the rest of her life alone. She was sure, however, that Reeves needed a woman he could love and marry, an uncomplicated wife who would give him children. In Columbus, Carson gave Reeves a copy of her "Letter from a War Wife." She hoped he would like it, would not think it a sham since she herself was not a "War Wife," but a "war divorcee." Yet who ever heard of "A Letter from a War Divorcee," she ventured. Her letter was within the province of the fictionist— she wrote what she felt, wife or no wife—it had to be. Reeves loved her letter, and loved her for writing it, for giving of herself to every other woman who could identify with her. She was his wife, he knew, marriage bond or not. In a few weeks, he, too, would be embarking as had her "War Wife's" husband, and the love, the union, would be just as strong.

Soon after Reeves left Columbus and returned to his unit, Carson again was restless. She felt that she, too, should go somewhere. She sent David Diamond Reeves's address and urged him to write, for Reeves needed the strength of friends and loved ones now more than ever. There was no longer rancor in Carson's mind as she reflected upon Reeves and Diamond, their former relationship, and her own exclusion. It was a thing of the past—just as all things pass, as had her we of me with Mary Tucker and Annemarie, with David Diamond and Reeves—all, her truths of the past. But to Carson, there was a more important present and a future. She hoped that she would never again expose herself so vulnerably. Her maturation had come painfully, as had Mick's in *The Heart Is a Lonely Hunter*, Miss Amelia's in *The Ballad of the Sad Café*, and now Frankie's, in her *Bride* manuscript. Carson, too, was evolving very much like F. Jasmine Addams, and then Frances—into whom Frankie was eventually transmogrified—living again her spring and summer in Columbus when she was twelve years old.

Finally, Carson decided to return North. Her father's condition had improved, and she felt that Yaddo was the only inspiring place where she could work. There was not the aesthetic distance necessary to her manuscript while she stayed in Columbus, and she had bogged down in spite of her good intentions to write at home again.

On June 8, 1943, Carson returned to Yaddo, where Elizabeth Ames had assured her of a standing invitation. En route from Columbus, she stopped in New York City only long enough to see Ann Watkins, her new agent, and to meet with editors from *Harper's Bazaar* about several changes in *The Ballad of the Sad Café* manuscript. She also wanted a little time apart from her writing to be with her friends. Muriel Rukeyser had already left for California, having received a Guggenheim Fellowship that spring, but she saw Cheryl Crawford and George Davis, and Davis had urged her to come out to Brooklyn and spend a few days with him at 7 Middagh Street. Tired and unstrung from the long trip and what she called "a hectic day in the city," Carson called David Diamond and asked him to meet her at 7 Middagh. Diamond refused, although he said he would meet her elsewhere. "I resented the grotesquerie of the life at 7 Middagh Street, Davis' charades, the drinking, and I felt that Carson must cease to expect me to go rushing to her side whenever she was in despair," he said. Now both were offended, and they did not see each other before Carson went on to Yaddo.

Carson stayed two nights in the old boardinghouse in Brooklyn Heights, where Davis had always made her feel that she had a second home; then she went into the city and checked into the Bedford Hotel. Before she could even unpack, however, a sudden sense of loss and isolation swept over her and she began to cry hysterically. Far more unstrung than she realized, but determined to keep moving and not succumb to the new despair, she called Alfred Kantorowicz and asked if he could go at once to Saratoga Springs with her.[5] Again, Yaddo was her refuge. She needed Elizabeth Ames as well, and she felt that Mrs. Ames needed her.

With a war on and a blackout over New York City and much of New England, Yaddo hosted only a small group the summer of 1943. For the first few days, besides Mrs. Ames and her sister, Marjorie Peabody Waite —still hanging on by some miracle—only Kantorowicz and Carson were there. She was given the octagonal room, south, of the mansion. It, too, had many windows and a magnificent view of the Vermont mountains, but she was not bothered here by the agoraphobia she had experienced in Katrina Trask's boudoir the year before. She and Kantorowicz simply rested, read, played, and talked. In the afternoons, they took long hikes and swam in the Yaddo lakes. It seemed that the days had never been more brilliant and beautiful. Soon other guests arrived. Carson was especially pleased to see Langston Hughes back. A newcomer was Agnes Smedley, a writer and lecturer who had lived for many years in China and now was passionately in support of Chinese communism. An old-line revolutionist, she was totally undisciplined and doubtless would not have made a fit member of the American Communist Party, about which she was completely negative. Carson was fascinated by Mrs. Smedley's tales of her life in China and listened thoughtfully to her ideologies. A friendship ensued, also, between Carson and Danish writer Karen Michaelis, who shared Carson's great admiration for Isak Dinesen. Other Yaddo guests included Isabella Howland, Kappo Phelan, Tomaras Kerr, Hans Sahl, Harold Shapiro, Margaret and Paul Zucker, Jean Stafford, and Rebecca Pitts, whom she had not seen since Miss Pitts had helped her check out of the Brevoort Hotel. Alfred Kazin had returned, too, as a director in residence for a few weeks. Newton Arvin did not come, but Carson wrote him frequently to apprise him of Yaddo life. Soon after her arrival she wrote Arvin that Katherine Anne Porter was there for the weekend and that they had even played poker together one night. Miss Porter was surprisingly pleasant to her, Carson volunteered.

Perhaps her closest friendship that summer developed with Alfred Kazin, who recalled later that it was often hard to be "judicious" about Carson:

> From the moment I met her at Yaddo during the war, I was moved by her *Southern* feeling against injustice. . . . She had such an intense need of love, and we were so sympathetic to each other in a funny kind of way, that there is almost nothing to say but that we "loved" each other. My relationship with Carson was personal without being intimate, sentimentally intense. She was unhappy to the point of catastrophe—and when we met I was so grateful for her sympathy, as for her art, that it was great being together. But we weren't together very often, actually, or very long; a deep part of her life—her sexuality—always a mystery to me and perhaps to her—was outside of my ken, as were a lot of her friends.[6]

Carson's good friend William Mayer—who had helped her with minor emotional disturbances, played the piano with her, and had earlier examined Elizabeth Ames's sister—was at Yaddo the last two weeks of June to work on his biography in progress of Emily Dickinson. Dr. Mayer agreed with the prognosis of Mrs. Waite's Saratoga Springs physician—that she would live on indefinitely, dying a little each day with painful slowness. Carson found herself questioning medical ethics in cases like Marjorie Waite's, which allowed a patient to exist so hopelessly. Euthanasia would have been such a sensible and humane solution, implied Carson in a letter to Arvin, since Marjorie Waite's mind, as well as her body, had become damaged and confused.

In the meantime, Carson's *Bride* manuscript was progressing well in the disciplined Yaddo environment. She and David Diamond had made amends without any difficulty, for their friendship was precious to them both. Soon after her arrival she had written him to explain how upset she was when there was friction between them. Why could not two people simply love each other without complications and be, she wondered. In answer, Diamond called her at Yaddo to reaffirm his love. Again, everything seemed good and right between them. Her personal affairs in order once more, Carson could share with Diamond and Arvin the unexpected changes and developments that were taking place in her book that summer. Frankie's plight as a member of the wedding had become only one of three main themes. A new character had emerged unbidden, she discovered, an adolescent boy whom Carson was much taken by. She described him as Frankie's inverted double. With the new proliferation, it seemed that the manuscript might require still another year of work. Perhaps she would stay on at Yaddo again all winter, and, hopefully, until the book was finished.

By midsummer, Carson had struck a good pace, writing mornings and reading Chekhov, Dostoevski, and Tolstoy during the lazy, hot afternoons. She wrote Diamond that she wished she could get away from such readings, but that the Russians were caught up in her blood. Sometimes she felt abominably lazy, like a Russian peasant lying about scratching and catching flies. The summer heat, however, had become so oppressive, damp, and sour that she felt tempted to grab a butcher knife and go berserk. It was the same feeling that Frankie experienced in the final version of *The Bride*. In *The Member of the Wedding*, Carson had Frankie picking at a splinter in her foot with a butcher knife. Then, irritated by Berenice's teasings that she had a crush on the wedding, Frankie had taken careful aim and thrown the knife into the door across the room. "Frances Addams, you are going to do that once too often," said Berenice.

"I never miss outside of a few inches," the girl replied.[7]

On August 12, a little over two months after her arrival, Carson abruptly left Yaddo. She had telephoned her mother the preceding weekend in response to Marguerite's indirection in letters about her husband's condition. Yes, he was worse, but just how, she could not say. Worried and anxious about her family, Carson had felt for some time that things were not well at home and that she should be there. In a sense, she felt as though she were the head of the family, responsible and needed when problems arose.[8] She had not seen Newton Arvin all summer, however, and hated to leave without saying good-by. She wrote him that once home, she would doubtless stay for nine months to a year. She was tired of all this running back and forth; instead, she would stay at home and work where she could also keep an eye on her family. Arvin came down from Northampton almost immediately to be with Carson for three days before she left. It was the extra effort that her friends took to be with her, to help her out of various dilemmas, to assure her that she was much loved and needed, that endeared to her the men she loved. Again and again Car-

son made great open statements of how she cherished her friendships with
Edwin Peacock, Newton Arvin, and David Diamond. Later, she wrote
similarly to her new friend Alfred Kantorowicz, to Alfred Kazin, and to a
score of others with whom she formed deep relationships.

Before leaving Yaddo, Carson wrote a hurried note to David Diamond to tell him that *The Ballad of the Sad Café* had just come out in
Harper's Bazaar. She also wanted to see him in the city, if only for a day or
two before going home to Georgia. In her letter, Carson again invoked
God to come to her aid in finishing her book since she had continued to
meet with adversity. All else seemed to have failed, she implied. Carson
and Diamond met in New York on August 14 and shopped for music for
Carson to take to Georgia. Then they went to see Diamond's good friend
director-composer Dimitri Mitropoulos, whom Carson had met earlier with
Diamond. She told Diamond that it was wonderful to be with him again,
and also with Mitropoulos, whom she admired and loved.

Once home in Columbus, Carson found her father's condition much
as she had expected. Although he was greatly depressed by the war and his
own poor health, he still had not consented to see a doctor. Carson wrote
to Newton Arvin that he had been drinking almost a quart and a half of
liquor every day for months. Lamar Smith still managed to go to work regularly, but he apparently sustained no real interest in the store. He was
still an able watch repairman, however, and his drinking had little effect
on his ability to function well at his craft. His assistant, Martha Hogan,
tended largely to the managing of the store, waited on customers, kept
the books, and did all she could to help, but the jewelry stock had gotten
low. He had not been making his customary buying trips to Atlanta for
some time.

More immediately unsettling to Carson than her father's health,
however, was an anonymous letter which came in the mail the morning
after her arrival home. There were several fan letters relative to *The Ballad of the Sad Café* and on the whole her readers seemed to like it. But
among the batch was one letter, a single paragraph, unsigned except for
the phrase "An American." It was handwritten on 6-inch by 8-inch stationery with a patriotic letterhead of red, white, and blue and a picture of
a formation of bombers in the sky against an American flag unfurled,
with the phrase "Keep 'Em Flying" underneath. It read:

> To the distinguished young writer whose story I started to read but
> at the bottom of the second page you poke fun at the Jew. After see-
> ing who the publisher is it is no wonder such a story goes on. Why
> don't you leave race alone and stop and look around and see who the
> big crooked polititions [*sic*] are and heads of the money corporations.
> Your friends Mr. Lewis and Hitler perhaps too. Will certainly pan

Harper's Bazaar until you and your kind learn to be human like the Jews are.

The reference to which the letter writer took offense read as follows:

> At last one of the twins said: "I'll be damned if he [the hunchback] ain't a regular Morris Finestein."
> Everyone nodded and agreed, for that is an expression having a certain special meaning. But the hunchback cried louder because he could not know what they were talking about. Morris Finestein was a person who had lived in the town years before. He was only a quick, skipping little Jew who cried if you called him Christkiller, and ate light bread and canned salmon every day. A calamity had come over him and he had moved away to Society City. But since then if a man were prissy in any way, or if a man ever wept, he was known as a Morris Finestein.[9]

Carson found the accusation incredulous, and since it was not signed, she was frustrated because she could not respond to it directly. Instead, her whole being was thrown out of kilter. She wrote many frantic letters seeking advice. First she wrote to Newton Arvin, reminding him that he had read the manuscript and had seen no cause for offense. She told him that Philip Rahv, a Russian-American Jew, had read it the preceding summer, too, and had found nothing objectionable. Carson wrote next to Alfred Kazin, also Jewish, to learn his response. Certainly no one hated prejudice and cruelty any more than she did, Carson insisted, but she wondered if one who did not know her and saw the reference to the Jew might rightfully find it offensive. It was agonizing for her to think that anyone could have misunderstood her story. She had ridiculed or made light of not only the Jew, but everyone else in the novel as well. She explained in each letter that the book was her fairy tale—all in the manner of satire and the style of that particular work. The whole story was laid against a background of neglect, narrowness, meanness, and barbarity, but the sadness and grief in the tale were due to her awareness of the cruelty inherent in everyone. Carson sent the anonymous letter to Kazin and asked him to read it and see what he thought, then to keep it so that she herself would not have to see it again.[10] To Kazin, "it was a tempest in a teapot," and he wrote back reassuringly for her to ignore it.[11]

In the meantime, Carson prepared in her defense an "Open Letter" which she planned to ask Carmel Snow and Mary Lou Aswell to run in the December issue of *Harper's Bazaar*. In it, she explained that when one is insensitive to irony or misunderstands it, it is difficult for the author to rationalize the point intended. *The Ballad of the Sad Café* was a light tale, told in a jesting manner, but beneath its simple narrowness were purposeful and bitter implications. The Jew, said Carson, was treated in the traditional and light way that she handled all of her characters. There was no intent to poke fun at the Jewish people. It was a tale of menacing tragedy indicting not the Jew, but the society which allowed such degradations to occur. For Carson to have to defend her work, when those who had read her writings knew of her loathing for the Fascist elements in her country and her hatred of discrimination against any minority group—especially the undemocratic principles which she felt extant in her southern region —all seemed to Carson a grotesque joke. Yet she could not rest so long as anyone misunderstood her.

Carson's "Open Letter" was a brilliant one, but it remained unpublished. Mary Lou Aswell, who had succeeded George Davis as literary editor of *Harper's Bazaar*, wanted to run it, but the Hearst office refused permission. Mrs. Aswell had "pushed" to publish *The Ballad of the Sad Café* complete in one issue, and now she suffered with Carson over the "absurd accusation."[12] Carson was finally reconciled to believe that there was no reason to defend what had never occurred to anyone else, especially to anyone who understood her intent in the story; yet during her agonizing turmoil, she wrote five letters to Alfred Kazin, three to Diamond, four to Arvin, and other assorted missives relative to the matter to George Davis, Mary Lou Aswell, and to countless others, begging each one to please get in touch with someone else who might also be able to advise her, pleading for a telephone call or wire advising her as to how he felt. In the meantime, she mailed copies of her "Open Letter" to Kazin, to Diamond, and to the magazine. For a week Carson lived in an eerie world, unable to believe that this strange accusation had actually happened to her. It had challenged her whole sense of good and evil and was alien to her very soul. She told Kazin that it was as though one of her favorite stories by Chekhov, "Rothschild's Fiddle," had been interpreted as an anti-Semitic story, or that a reader of "A Modest Proposal" had accused Swift of actually cooking the babies. Soon she had telegrams from Kazin, *Harper's Bazaar*, and George Davis and phone calls from Diamond and Arvin. She had blown the whole affair out of proportion, they assured her, and she must forget it. It was almost the end of August before Carson could think about writing again, but finally, with rest and reassurance from her friends, she returned to her typewriter.

In September 1943 there was new anguish. Her father collapsed and at last allowed his family to send for a doctor. The first thing to cope with, the doctor said, was the alcohol. Carson stayed by her father's side, kept the liquor, and doled it out, drink by drink, until in less than a week he was able to do without it completely, and eventually, to go back to work. The doctor found no sign of the cancer Lamar Smith feared, but his heart had been seriously damaged. Lamar very much needed the attention, love, and empathy he got from Carson that summer, and to her, it was one of the most meaningful times of their entire relationship as father and daughter. He had felt estranged from his family for a long time, but especially after his older daughter had gained fame as a writer. In spite of how much Carson appeared to rely upon others for decision making and her emotional well-being, she was the one who was looked to by Marguerite for advice about things pertaining to the family. "Let's ask Sister," Marguerite responded if a problem came up that might normally be discussed and settled only by her and her husband. But now, since his illness, Lamar Smith had become much more important in the eyes of his family.

In late September, Reeves was sent to Fort Dix, New Jersey, his staging area for going overseas. He and Carson had corresponded often since their reconciliation, and he had recently begun to write, also, to David Diamond. Reeves took a two-day pass into New York City the first of October and tried unsuccessfully to see his old friend. Disappointed, he wrote Diamond later that he hoped to be back in the city one more time before leaving and asked if they could meet for dinner and drinks. He told his friend, too, of his new strength and sense of purpose since his reconciliation with Carson. He said that having everything all right between them made him complete, but that having the affection and respect of the admirable men in his company made him a man. When he and Carson were not on good terms he felt scattered, crazy, unable to function, like gears that would not mesh; but now he felt that they were synchronized and would always be. He lamented the fact, however, that it took a catastrophe, a war, to strengthen him and give him a meaningful goal. Reeves was almost euphoric in his praise of his outfit. He had never known such dedicated, brave, and faithful men. They were trained to kill the enemy, but they were not ruthless. They were sensitive human beings, whom he loved and respected.[13]

On October 21, Carson wrote similar letters to both David Diamond and Newton Arvin in which she told them that she expected to leave the next day for Fort Dix to join Reeves for his few remaining days in the United States. She said, too, that she had written to Reeves to propose a remarriage. She did not think he would suggest it himself. Their being reunited would be a talisman for him, she decided. He would know a new sense of peace and confidence before going into battle, and if he were wounded or killed she would suffer as much as any wife would who deeply loved her husband, regardless of a legal paper to bind them. She felt that for Reeves the actual ceremony would be reassuring and spine-stiffening. Carson asked Arvin for his blessing, yet observed that most of their friends would think a remarriage imprudent. In her heart, however, she was sure it was right. Carson told Diamond much the same thing, but she cautioned him to please keep their marriage plans a secret. She wanted their ceremony to be very personal and quiet. Reeves was on maneuvers and communications were difficult, she said, but she expected him to have two or three days of leave.

After Carson wrote to Reeves, and then to Arvin and Diamond before leaving Georgia, she spent many hours thinking and rationalizing on the long train trip North regarding the wisdom of such an abrupt remarriage. Certainly he would be no safer in the adventurous Rangers simply because of a marriage ceremony, and she had to admit that they knew they got along much better as devoted friends than as husband and wife. Once together again, Carson and Reeves knew that they loved each other as much as they ever had loved; but as they talked, they realized that a remarriage then would have its roots in desperation and an attempt to prove their love. Instead, to leave things as they were seemed a wiser decision. Each had striven for a sense of individual wholeness and personal freedom at great anguish and expense. Such wholeness was the core of their tender friendship.

Carson stayed a week at the Officers' Club at Fort Dix. Seeing Reeves with his men, visiting in his tent in the field, meeting and loving his fellow Rangers who seemed to exude love, trust, and admiration for their company commander—all greatly impressed Carson and filled her with awe and pride for the man she loved. They were also able to have two days together in New York City. They saw David Diamond and one night went out to George Davis' house in Brooklyn Heights for a reunion and farewell dinner in Reeves's honor. Alfred Kantorowicz joined them, too, for Carson was anxious that he and Reeves should get to know each other. She had written to Kantorowicz earlier that she thought the two of them would get on well together. Her trouble with Reeves had been brought on *only* by sex, she added, not by any difference in more fundamental concerns.[14] By this admission, it was evident that Carson had put out of her mind completely the other factors which ostensibly had contributed to their divorce. On October 30, Carson called Diamond to say that Reeves had decided that they not remarry; she then arranged for them to meet Diamond the next day in the city. Diamond's diary entry that night revealed that his relationship with both of them, again, was firmly rooted:

October 31, 1943: Reeves called at 5. Met him with Carson at the Buckingham Crown Cafe. I arrived a few minutes before they did, and I was nervous. But once they were seated and we were drinking our whiskies, I felt better. I had resolved before to not let Reeves know that I still felt anything for him . . . but by the end of the evening, after several drinks, a visit to Kay Boyle's at the Sevilla, dinner at the Russian Tea Room, I knew Reeves still cared. In the taxi en route to Brooklyn he took my hand, and held it so tenderly.

And all the pain that remained after these two years disappeared for
good. I came back emotionally exhausted. Reeves will try to see me
before he sails.[15]

Later, after her return to Columbus, Carson wrote to Newton Arvin to
explain that a remarriage would have been a mistake. When Reeves returned from the war, they would reassess their destinies and take one thing
at a time, she said.

Carson returned to Columbus in early November with a new sense
of dedication to both her work and life style as an artist and a person.
Each day she expected to get word that Reeves had left, but he did not
ship out until the twenty-third, the day before Thanksgiving. Rumors
abounded regarding their destination, but by then most of the men guessed
that they were going to England. There they would join other combat
forces for the great invasion that lay ahead. Reeves's Second Ranger
Battalion joined the Fifth, which stormed Omaha Beach on D-day, June
6, 1944. But in the meantime, over six months of further training was in
store for his outfit. Part of this time Reeves attended an intensive intelligence school in London. Every spare moment seemed golden and
valuable, for there was almost no time off. He rarely wrote to anyone except Carson, and occasionally to his mother, who now lived in Baltimore.

In February, Reeves had an accident, fracturing his left wrist in a
fall from his motorcycle. Removed from line duty, he was forced to assume
a staff position until he could get out of his cast some two and a half
months later. When Carson heard of the injury, she prayed for a thorough
but slow recovery. If only she were a sorcerer who could conjure up a
spell, she would keep the bones from knitting until time for him to come
home, she said.

After the first of the year, the war intensified with more and more
American troops pushing into Europe. Carefully she listened to every
news report on the radio and avidly read the newspapers for any mention
of Rangers in action. On January 22, 1944, three Ranger battalions made
a perfect, silent, unopposed landing directly in the harbor of Anzio, Italy.
The rest became bloody history. For sixty-seven days the First, Third, and
Fourth Ranger battalions held the Anzio beachhead at great personal expense. On March 11, Carson heard that nine hundred Rangers had been
killed or captured on the Anzio beachhead, and for days she did not
know whether Reeves's battalion had been involved. She had a horror
of learning that he might be wounded or dead and buried in some un-
marked grave in a foreign country. Her dreams were nightmares. Sometimes she dreamed that the letters kept coming after his death, but she
would not know it and all along think him safe. If only she knew that

she could die at the same time he did, it would be some solace—then she might face her present existence more bravely. To live in the United States, where there was so little deprivation, seemed grotesque in view of the holocaust elsewhere. It was hard to realize the terrors and agonies of war when the American people at home had only to put up with blackouts, a shortage of gasoline, and ration stamps for food and miscellany. Carson could no longer imagine life without Reeves—it would have no dimension, only nothingness, an awful blackness, death itself. She had suffered Annemarie's death deeply, and it had grieved her that she had not been able to recall what she had been doing at the precise hour and day that Annemarie had died, that she had not known until weeks later that her beloved friend was dead. She felt she could not take such a loss twice. Reeves was everything to her now. Although their marriage may have been a mistake, their love was not. With a concrete plan for a way of life after the war that they could both embrace, that would not threaten the identity and mental well-being of the other, that would not prostitute one's values or aspirations, or make a martyr of either of them, Carson knew that they could again have a life together more dear to them than they had known before. With a new, strong sense of purpose, she believed now that she could finish her *Bride* manuscript and possibly be able to hand it to Reeves as a gift of herself by spring—if only he might be safe at home by then.

Carson had been reading at home that spring a new translation of Karl von Clausewitz's *Principles of War*, which presented the fundamental concepts of the art of waging war. Written by a Prussian army officer and published in three volumes in 1833, it was considered basic reading for all officers and others concerned with the conduct of war. Carson thrived on it and anything else factual concerning tactical warfare that she could locate. It was a way of sharing vicariously Reeves's wartime experiences, and she felt closer to him as a result of it. (At Yaddo in 1944 she had surprised listeners by her ability to handle abstract intellect in a way that most of them had not guessed possible.)

In April, Carson learned that Reeves's unit had not been a part of the Anzio siege. After heavy casualties, the survivors of the three Ranger battalions involved were brought home to the United States or transferred to a crack Canadian-American Special Service Brigade which had formed in Great Britain. Reeves's Second Battalion and the Fifth still were Rangers and allowed to wear their Ranger patches into action, but their official headquarters unit now was the combined Canadian-American Special Service Force.

Attached to the 116th Infantry, 29th Division, the Second and Fifth Ranger battalions landed at Omaha Beach and accomplished their mission of capturing the Pointe du Hoe German coastal batteries after spearhead-

28 Carson with her thermos of sherry (or hot sherry tea), which she frequently carried about with her on the Yaddo grounds, July 1941.

29   Carson with Newton Arvin and friend, Quebec, August 1940.

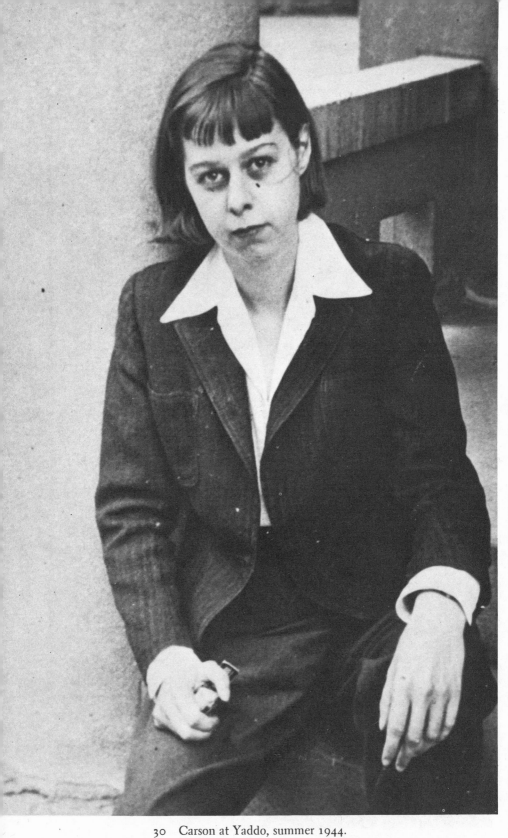

30 Carson at Yaddo, summer 1944.

31 ABOVE:
Lamar Smith, Jr., Carson's brother,
in uniform with the United States Seabees,
shortly before going overseas, 1942.

32 LEFT:
Carson's mother, shortly after the
death of her husband and her move
to Nyack, New York, 1945.

33 FACING PAGE:
Carson's sister, Margarita Gachet Smith,
on the porch of the Smith home
at 129 South Broadway, Nyack, New York.

34 Carson at 1519 Starke Avenue, Columbus, Georgia, at work on *The Member of the Wedding*, August 1943.

35 Tennessee Williams and Pancho Rodriguez, New Orleans, 1946, a few months before Williams invited Carson to spend the summer with them at Nantucket.

36 Carson in Central Park, April 1941. Said Louise Dahl-Wolfe (the photographer):
"Carson was so shy when I first photographed her [October 1940], she would blink
every time I clicked the shutter. I had to talk to her like a magpie to make her forget
herself and her fright."

ing the Normandy invasion by scaling towering cliffs and knocking out the shore batteries. Then they moved on to assist in the capture of Grandcamp and the destroying of scattered enemy opposition between Grandcamp and Isigny. Reeves was wounded on the initial day of the assault. Carson heard his name mentioned in an Associated Press report, along with other Ranger casualties, but she did not believe that the report specifically stated that Reeves himself was wounded. It was weeks before she heard anything definite, and she was almost out of her mind. Reeves, however, had recovered quickly and was back with his outfit in time to participate in the Bay of Brest siege, in which a chain of enemy forts had to be captured. In September his unit, attached to Task Force Sugar of the 29th Division, drove through numerous outpost strong points to reach the German main line of resistance. Then came the fierce encounter at the Le Conquet Peninsula, in which Reeves's Second Battalion assisted in breaking into 280mm gun positions and forcing the surrender of the Le Conquet garrison commander. For two months he fought on German soil, interrupted only for a brief respite in Luxembourg, and earlier, a single day in liberated Paris.

Then, on December 2, 1944, Reeves was sent to a rest hospital in Belgium. He had been on the front for twelve days in the cold and rain. That week he wrote to Alfred Kantorowicz that his commanding officer had sent him to the hospital for a day or two of rest. The bad weather and exposure had activated rheumatism in his hips, he said, but warmth and a little bed care had made him fit again and he was looking forward to rejoining his men at the front.[16]

Reeves wrote at least five letters while he was in the hospital in Belgium: to Carson, to his mother, to Edwin Peacock, who had returned to the United States for an early discharge from the Navy because of a hearing disability, to Vincent Adams, and to Kantorowicz. In his letter to Peacock he said that he was physically rested and mentally ready to go back to the fighting. It seemed to him, however, that he had used up all of his luck for he had already been hit three times. What happened next was up to God or chance or geometric design, he admitted. The fighting in Germany was bitter, much worse than in the Pacific, according to the men who had been in both places. Reeves confided to Peacock that he sometimes felt he was on the brink of a breakdown, but that the thought of his superb men and how much they depended on him and trusted him kept him pushing on. In fact, they cheered each other; sometime at the darkest moment some ribbon clerk or farmer would make a crack that brightened the whole place, he said.[17]

In his letter to Kantorowicz, Reeves said that, like it or not, the German people would have a winter war waged throughout their homeland. Although the average German citizen might never want to make war upon his neighbor again, it would be a lesson at great cost, but a lesson their psychopathic leader deserved to be taught. Reeves and Kantorowicz had talked at length at 7 Middagh Street one evening when he was on leave in New York City with Carson just before he went overseas, and it was his German friend's opinion then that the German soldier would not strongly resist if he were backed up to his own borders. Reeves told him now, however, that he had fought for two months on the soil of the Great Fatherland, yet the morale, mortar, and artillery had shown no sign of weakening. At times Hitler's pitchfork-and-youth Army seemed almost a joke, Reeves said. Often they got scared and ran. He related that one day his men captured two little boys, aged ten and twelve, trying to operate a mortar. Reeves marveled that they were not blown up in the process. Later, they turned the mortar upon a German position and showed the boys how it should work. To Reeves, the war was won, but the Infantry still had a great deal more slugging, fighting, and dying to do. Mortar and artillery were their enemies, and not even the good Lord or the greatest general could help them just then, said Reeves. The fighting men of the U.S. forces were desperately tired and longed for the end of the war, but not so tired that they could not endure much longer, if necessary.[18]

Three days after this letter to Kantorowicz Reeves was wounded again, this time with numerous shrapnel wounds in the body and a badly fractured hand. He had returned on December 4 to the front in Rötgen, Germany. This time, it was the end of his fighting career. When Reeves returned to the States on February 24, 1945, he was a highly decorated combat veteran lucky to be alive. Although neither Silver nor Bronze stars were given out freely to Rangers, who were in an outfit in which every man was expected to be gutsy and a hero, Reeves received four battlefield commendations—the coveted Silver Star and three Bronze stars—as well as a Presidential Unit Citation, various campaign ribbons, his combat infantry badge—of which he was especially proud—and a Purple Heart. To Carson, he was the most decorated hero who ever lived.

In the meantime, Carson stayed busy during Reeves's absence, traveling frequently back and forth between Columbus, New York City, and Yaddo, sometimes writing well and other times suffering such impasses that she wondered if she ever could complete a work again. She remained in Columbus throughout the winter of 1943–44, wanting to stay near her mother and father. Granting an interview with Mary McMurria of the Columbus *Ledger*, Carson told her that she spent her time that winter writing on her new novel and making fruitcakes, which she "sent to friends all over the world." It was her first public statement of such culinary arts or interests, and doubtless an exaggerated one. Relatives in Columbus conceded that she may have turned out *one* to *two* under the tutelage of her mother, who made marvelous fruitcakes.[19]

Carson was also pursued that winter by Columbusites who wanted to entertain for her so that they might see for themselves what kind of young woman their "little Lula Carson" had grown up to be. At one of the parties she consented to attend, she was asked about *Reflections in a Golden Eye*. Abruptly Carson dismissed her questioner with the comment: "I'm not interested in that book—I'm writing another." Then, although all the guests had not yet arrived, she announced to her escort: "I'm ready to leave." En route home, the gentleman volunteered that he was sorry she was not feeling well, to which she replied, "Well, I've been living on gin and cigarettes for the last two months."[20] Worried about Reeves, she neither slept well nor wrote well. She did not hear often from Reeves, although he wrote when he could. In the spring when most of the Ranger forces were being devastated on the Anzio beachhead, she had been frantic with worry. In March, she suffered another queer nervous attack which made her quite ill. The nervous problem occurred simultaneously with the news that nine hundred Rangers had been lost at Anzio, and that her application for overseas work as a foreign correspondent had been rejected. Having received earlier encouragement that she would get the job, Carson considered it a personal affront to be turned down. She had not been accustomed to being told *no* about anything, and it was a blow to her pride as well. For days she was nervous and tremulous, could not write, ate little, and suffered from a skin eruption similar to hives. She wrote to both David Diamond and Edwin Peacock of her new disorder and prayed to God she would soon get over it.

Carson's sister, Rita, had been home in Georgia since her graduation from the University of Miami the end of May 1943. Rita, too, showed promise of being a successful writer. According to her brother, Lamar, in her senior year Rita had won a *Mademoiselle* story-writing contest and had her story published by the magazine. When the *O'Henry Memorial Award Prize Stories of 1943* appeared, there were two stories authored by sisters: Rita's prize-winning story, "White for the Living," and Carson's "A Tree. A Rock. A Cloud." By March of 1944, Rita, wanting desperately to move to New York, was determined to put it off no longer. She had hoped that Carson would go up with her so that they might be in the city together and share an apartment. Carson, however, was apprehensive about living in the city again so soon, where her difficulties of working had been all too plain in the past. She felt that it would be best if she either stayed in Columbus or returned again directly to Yaddo. By mid-March, Rita— whom Carson now referred to in letters as "Skeet"—went on alone to New York City and took an apartment on Bleecker Street. Carson wrote friends that spring that Rita was happily considering a choice of editorial positions, that George Davis had been looking out for her, and that she had an opportunity of working either with *Mademoiselle* or *Harper's Bazaar*.

In the meantime, Carson settled down to work after getting over her disabling nervous attack. By April her father's health had improved tremendously. Dedicated once more to his work at the store, Lamar Smith also took cheer and pride in being the head of the household—perhaps for the first time in his life, or so he felt. Lamar and his wife enjoyed a much closer and more harmonious relationship now than they had known in years. By late spring, Carson felt that if there were anyone to worry about besides Reeves, it was her mother, who looked thin and unwell, she told Edwin Peacock, who had always taken a special interest in Marguerite and loved her as though she were his own mother.[21]

Carson also was much concerned about Mrs. Ames's health, even more so than she was about her friend's sick sister. In a letter to Arvin, Carson proposed that perhaps just the three of them—Mrs. Ames, Arvin, and she—could go to the seashore for a few days. She had once suggested it to Mrs. Ames herself, who replied that she "would love to if it should prove practical." Carson realized that she simply would have to be at Yaddo herself to assess the situation and then take Mrs. Ames with her if she felt that she could get away.

In early May, Robert Linscott wrote Carson that he was coming South and wanted to stop off in Columbus for several days and visit her. Linscott had recently left Houghton Mifflin and moved to Random House. Carson had once indicated that she was interested in a possible change of publishers, but Linscott did not push it. Lambert Davis, with Harcourt Brace, also came to Columbus to see Carson that spring, but at the time of both his and Linscott's visits, she was feeling not only concern, but alarm, even, over her seeming inability to finish *The Bride*. She had almost decided to put it away for a while and write short pieces, instead, until she felt sufficiently illuminated to return to her book-length manuscript. Carson had wanted to show Linscott some one hundred salvable pages of the work she had now begun to call *The Member of the Wedding*, but instead, she allowed him to leave without his seeing a single page. She felt like F. Jasmine Addams, who wanted so badly to tell her brother and his bride that they were her we of me and that she must accompany them on their honeymoon since they belonged together; yet after the wedding ceremony, F. Jasmine had only choked up and said nothing. If only she had read Linscott those two good chapters, Carson lamented; she was sure he had gone away disappointed in her.

Immediately Carson wrote Linscott a touching letter of apology for not sharing more openly with him. She felt, however, that she had been honest in her assessment of her creative disorder, which she attributed largely to the chaotic world conditions, her anxiety over Reeves and the hundreds of thousands like him, and to her own youth. Pleading with Linscott for patience, she said that she, too, needed patience—that, plus work, would be the combination necessary for a successful novel. She could do it, she knew—it was all a matter of time.

On May 9, Linscott responded with a reassuring letter:

> There are a few things in this unstable world of which I'm certain, and one of these is your future as a writer. Please don't worry about the lag in production. My own feeling is that you should go ahead with the short stories and novelettes that you have in mind and not attempt a full-length novel until it begins naturally to take shape in your mind. If, meanwhile, it would conceivably help for me to read all or part of *The Member of the Wedding*, please send it along.[22]

Carson, in her encapsuled environment in the South, had been worrying, also, about the business details of her future work, the status of her present royalties, and other financial arrangements. She had no ability at handling figures, particularly where money was concerned, she told Linscott, and she did not want to come up short as she had two years earlier when she learned that the six thousand dollars she had earned the preceding year had mysteriously disappeared. Linscott agreed to meet with Carson's new agent, Ann Watkins, upon his return to New York City to discuss the financial aspect of her career, but he assured her that there was actually no need to concern themselves with a problem that did not exist. To Carson, anything could be a problem once embedded in her mind, no matter what it was in actuality.

Soon after Linscott's departure, she became ill again. This time her doctor feared it was diabetes, but later the disorder appeared to be a kidney infection, from which it took several weeks to recover. She also was much depressed by the death of the little boy next door, Robin Mullin. Robin had visited frequently and freely in the Smith home, eating treats and sitting about the kitchen with Marguerite, Carson, and a servant, Vannie Copland Jackson, who worked for both families. Robin's father had lived next door to them on Starke Avenue since Carson was a little girl, and Carson had been a friend of Robin, Sr., and his wife, Josephine. Much earlier, another young child in the neighborhood had died, too, Dudley Spain, Jr., to whom Carson was also devoted. Doubtless, these two children contributed much to Carson's conception of John Henry West, Frankie's five-year-old cousin who was in and out of the Addams household until his death near the end of *The Member of the Wedding*. Carson's tender note to Robin Mullin's parents after the child's death revealed much of her feelings and empathy for the little boy's family.[23]

In the meantime, Carson had no word for over two months from Reeves. Finally a cablegram arrived on June 1. It was a loving message with no special news—only Reeves's reaffirmation of his love and his desire to be able to give to Carson selflessly, if only he were blessed to come out of the war alive. Reeves knew that they would push off any day for the Normandy invasion, and he wanted his message to get to her quickly, no matter what might befall him in the battle. Five days later Carson heard the news of the Omaha landings and Reeves's name again among the wounded. By then the Georgia heat had become unbearable. She stayed at home only long enough to be assured that Reeves's injuries were not serious. With her nerves almost gone and still weakened by her recent physical and emotional disabilities, she felt that she must once more seek out Yaddo as her refuge. This time, her mother decided to return to New York with her, feeling that her husband was well enough now to do without her for a few days, and wanting, also, to see her daughter, Rita, who had gone to work with *Mademoiselle* as assistant fiction editor under Carson's friend, managing editor Cyrilly Abels. Carson had promised her mother, too, that she at last could meet David Diamond, who had become almost a legend in the Smith household. On June 14, Diamond gave a party for Carson, Rita, and their mother; then the next day, Carson left for Yaddo.

In contrast to Carson's earlier summers there, almost no one else was in residence the summer of 1944. Since the war years were also lean years financially, and most of the men who had been guests of the artists' colony in the past were overseas, the mansion was not even kept open that year. Carson asked if she might have the Pine Tree studio again. It was there that she had had word of Annemarie's death almost two years earlier, and she had the feeling now that a second catastrophe would not occur in the same place. This time the only ones in residence besides Elizabeth Ames, her ailing sister, the caretaker, and the cook, were Carson, Gerald Ehrlich and his wife, Sophie, who had served for two summers as a substitute secretary for the Yaddo office, and the Ehrlichs' baby daughter, Marianne; Agnes Smedley, who had become something of a permanent resident until she could eventually return to China to live; and Helen Eustis, whom Carson had seen occasionally in New York.

Carson was visited at Yaddo in 1944 by Reeves's brother Tommy, who had just arrived from a brief tour of duty in England with the U. S. Air Corps. Tommy McCullers had been sent home early with a nervous condition and given a medical discharge. But before he left England, he had seen Reeves and promised him that the first thing he would do in the United States would be to go see Carson. She was devoted to Tommy, whom Reeves loved and worried over like a distraught father. Tommy was the youngest of the four McCullers offspring, a tall, handsome, personable young man who had told his brother that he felt a lack of strong sexual identity. Upon Tommy's return, Rita Smith had taken him to meet David Diamond, who also lived on Bleecker Street. According to Diamond, "Tommy was miserably unhappy when I met him, in love with a very silly but pretty boy, loaded with guilt; and knowing of my relationship with Reeves, he counted on me for advice about himself, not wanting Reeves to know of his own homosexual affairs—although Reeves *did* know."[24]

Again, Carson's writing began to flow well at Yaddo, for here she had greater peace of mind than she had known for some time in Georgia. The geographic proximity of Saratoga Springs to Europe also seemed to make Carson feel closer to Reeves than when she was South. Living once more in the Pine Tree studio lulled her into a sense of complacency and well-being, too; yet in spite of what she thought of as her superstitious stratagem, calamity again struck. On August 1, 1944, Carson's father died of an acute coronary attack. His body was discovered early that evening by a patrolman, who in checking doors in the downtown area found the jewelry shop unlocked and the light on. Lamar Smith had slumped to the floor, his hat, *The New Yorker,* and the *Nation* nearby, ready for him to pick up on his way home.

The next morning Carson left Yaddo, met Rita in the city, and together they traveled by train to Columbus. Edwin Peacock, who had been home in Thomasville, Georgia, on leave from the Navy when Marguerite called him to come, was at the station to meet them. None of the men of the family were even in the United States at the time—Lamar, Jr., was with the Seabees in the Pacific, Marguerite's sister's son and the men her daughters had married were away in the service, and no one else close to the family except Peacock was nearby. Lamar's death was a shock to everyone who knew him. To his family, his health had been better that summer than it had been for several years. The town, too, seemed saddened by his death. Many people came to the funeral whom the family did not know. Loved and respected for his integrity, honesty, and skill as a craftsman, Lamar Smith had a host of friends and no enemies—except, perhaps, as some people said, himself. Carson's response to her father's death was a dreadful mixture of guilt and grief. Never before had she realized just how deeply she loved her father and what he had meant to her.[25] Reeves's comment later in a letter to Edwin Peacock was a fitting eulogy. He said that they would all miss Carson's father very much. To Reeves, Lamar Smith loved his family more than any other father he knew. Although at times he seemed terribly displaced and frustrated, he was scrupulously honest and candid in all his relationships with people. Reeves told Peacock that he was immensely fond of Lamar Smith, who was always a good person.[26]

The next days were difficult ones for Carson. After the funeral her mother collapsed and had to be hospitalized.[27] Marguerite refused to go back into the house on Starke Avenue—would never go back, she vowed. Instead, she stayed in the hospital, and then at the home of her sister, Mrs.

C. Graham Johnson. Rita had had to return to her job with *Mademoiselle*, but Carson stayed on to take care of her mother and to help settle the family's affairs so that they could proceed with plans to move North together. On September 14, Carson wrote to Newton Arvin from her family's new location in Nyack, New York, telling him that the past six weeks had been the most nerve-racking and disordered of her entire life. Not only had she *not* anticipated the grief she herself felt, but she had no idea how to cope with the myriad details. While her mother was in the hospital, Carson worked alone as best she could. Marguerite's lawyer handled the legal affairs, the settling of the estate, the sale of the shop, and the paying off of the mortgage on the Starke Avenue house with Lamar's insurance money. (The shop was sold to Lawrence Holzman of Atlanta, who bought the jewelry stock, kept the store, and retained the services of Lamar's employee, Martha Hogan.) According to Lamar's will, dated September 24, 1924, all property was bequeathed to his wife, who was also named sole executrix.

Carson found that washing woodwork, hauling out trash, disposing of personal items no longer needed, occupying herself with other manual chores, and consulting with her mother on which pieces of furniture and other household goods to ship North—all comforted her in a way she had not thought possible. She told Robert Linscott that she was reminded of Emily Dickinson's poem:

> *The bustle in the house*
> *the morning after death . . .*

Turning to Linscott for help, she asked if he could find an inexpensive place in the country or near the ocean where she, her mother, and sister could live which would not be far from New York City. They wanted to buy or rent a house but could pay no more than seventy or eighty dollars a month, she said. Carson was convinced that since Columbus was an army town spiraling with inflation, they could not reasonably afford to continue living there.[28] That was not the real reason, of course. Carson knew that there was no reason at all for them to continue living in the South. Marguerite wanted to be where her daughters were. Both of them were brilliant, she was now convinced, and with Rita also bent on a literary career, Marguerite wanted to be where she could take care of them, could cook and keep house for them, and once more have a happy home which the three of them could share.

Linscott's response was that it would be almost impossible for them to rent or buy a house in a desirable location for the money they wanted to pay. Although Carson had indicated their willingness to go to some remote village, Linscott insisted that such a place would be too harsh and isolated as a winter residence for Carson's delicate health and would, no doubt, be too far for Rita to live with them and commute. Rita and Linscott consulted in the city, too, and made plans to search together for an appropriate location and house. In the meantime, he urged Carson and her mother to remain in Columbus until the first of October. By then they would surely have located something. Army post or no post, Columbus had no corner on rising prices, said Linscott. The suburbs north of New York City would be every bit as high as real estate in Georgia, he assured her.[29]

Carson and her mother, however, were anxious to get settled elsewhere, away from memories and the old environment. By the first of September they had rented the house on Starke Avenue and were on their way North. Carson had already asked a friend to be on the lookout for a place in the Nyack-New City area in the vicinity of Rockland County, New York, for she had always loved the little village of Nyack on the western shore of the Hudson River, some twenty-five miles north of New York City and directly across the river from Tarrytown and Washington Irving's Sleepy Hollow. Upon their arrival, the friend took them to meet Helena Clay, who owned a large, rambling four-story apartment house, Graycourt Manor, located two blocks from the downtown main street on South Broadway, the north-south artery connecting several towns along the Hudson. When Mrs. Clay showed them the spacious, main-floor apartment—one of twenty-four in the building—they immediately took it. Although it had only one large bedroom, there was a huge living room and large kitchen and bath. They regretted that it did not have another bedroom, but they decided that they could double up and manage anyway. Rita would be at home relatively little since she would be commuting to the city and in Nyack only for sleeping and weekends. Carson felt that she would have as much privacy as needed for her own work, and soon she had settled down and was writing again.

Marguerite loved Nyack and its small-town atmosphere. It seemed almost southern in its tempo and friendliness of the people. To her, a stranger was strange only until she had introduced herself, whether he was the pharmacist or her seat companion on a bus. She chatted loquaciously, the conversation usually centering upon her two brilliant daughters and the challenge it was to bring them up. Rita was no less difficult to rear than Carson, only different, she said. Marguerite quickly made friends with her neighbors in the apartment house, the tradesmen, merchants, and civil servants of the community. But most of all, she enjoyed relaxing at home with her daughters, talking, reading, drinking sherry, and listening to good music. Carson missed her piano, but she had left it behind in Columbus to be sold.

The Nyack Library was across the street and down a block, and Marguerite went frequently to select books. She especially liked murder mysteries and detective stories, checking them out by the armsful. For a change of pace, Carson, too, enjoyed similar reading. She would not read a "who done it," but preferred, instead, the true and grotesque accounts by William Roughead, who wrote of crime in Great Britain. Roughead came up with a new volume almost every year, and between the two women, they read them all. *Mainly Murder, The Seamy Side, Rascals Revised,* and *Reprobates Reviewed* were a few of the recent ones, and Carson and Marguerite felt that they knew intimately each character depicted. That fall in Nyack Carson also rediscovered Henry James, whom Newton Arvin recommended to her. In several of her letters to friends written at that time Carson told of her admiration for James's *The American* and the intriguing "The Beast of the Jungle." Reading the latter, she said, made her feel like a child gawking at the freaks at the circus. She wrote Reeves that she wanted to read it with him when he got home, for she knew that he, too, would like it immensely.

Writing to Arvin, Carson lamented especially that they did not have enough bedroom space for him to come and stay with them. She missed him terribly, she said, and wanted him to visit her in Nyack and, at last, meet her mother. Since he could not come soon, Carson decided to go again to Saratoga Springs for a few days. Perhaps he could at least get over there. She also longed to see Elizabeth Ames and share with her the most recent version of *The Member of the Wedding,* although it was still by no means near completion. Newton Arvin came to Yaddo from Smith for two days, and it was a joyous reunion for the three of them. By mid-November Carson was back in Nyack. She wrote Reeves that as soon as she got home, the first snow of the season fell, which reminded her of their first snowfall at the McKethans on North Cool Spring Street, where they had lived in Fayetteville. They had both loved the snow, she reminisced, just as did every major adolescent character Carson created. She remembered how they had walked about in the cemetery and read the gravestones, then later drove into the country, parked, drank beer, and watched the falling snow. Their first snows had always been occasions for quiet festivity, she recalled.[30]

On December 9, Carson was shocked by a telegram from the War Department. It caused only momentary alarm, however. Upon hearing that Reeves had been only slightly wounded, she immediately prayed that he was injured badly enough not to have to go back on the line—particularly in view of the heavy Allied winter offensive—yet also not enough to permanently disable him. Carson was worried, but somehow she knew in her heart that he would be home soon. No direct word followed until January 7, 1945, when Reeves was able to write from a British hospital. Carson cabled a loving message in reply. She also said that Kay Boyle was en route to England and would visit him in the hospital the middle of January. Carson's next word was a cable saying that he expected to be home soon. She was ecstatic.

A few days later, Carson returned again to Yaddo to spend Christmas with Elizabeth Ames, barely getting through to Saratoga Springs because of the heavy snowfall. For Carson, it was an exhilarating vacation. She wrote Newton Arvin that she had gone skiing one day with David Aiken, a young Harvard professor, in 20-below weather. It felt wonderful, she said, and just then she was preparing to catch the station wagon into town to see if she could exchange a Christmas present from her mother, a cardigan sweater for a pullover, at a local shop.

As Carson reflected at Yaddo upon the year's end, counting her blessings, she recalled that there had been only one note of sadness in her personal relationships with people that year—other than the death of her father, of course. When Martha Foley's *Best American Short Stories* appeared for 1944, *The Ballad of the Sad Café* had been included. It was with mixed emotions, however, that Carson had allowed its publication. Her friend Mary Lou Aswell had originally asked if she might publish it in an anthology she was editing, but Carson's agent, Ann Watkins, advised her not to release it yet for an anthology. Then, when Martha Foley asked later if she could have it for her book, which Houghton Mifflin published annually, Miss Watkins thought it would be a good thing. Carson felt bad about having earlier turned down Mary Lou Aswell, who had originally published the story in *Harper's Bazaar*—and at great personal distress when she had insisted on running it complete in one issue. Carson apologized profusely for her apparent inconsistency, but Mrs. Aswell assured her that there had been no breach in their friendship and that she must not trouble herself about it. Carson did worry, however, for she wanted everything to be well between her and everyone with whom she shared a kinship.[31]

In early January, Carson returned to Nyack. Although she did not know just when Reeves would arrive, she wanted to be home herself and waiting for him. Uppermost in her thoughts was the fact that Reeves was coming *home*. There was no question in her mind where *home* was. It was with Reeves, no matter where. In February, when Marguerite received nine thousand dollars from the sale of the property on Starke Avenue in Columbus, she was anxious to invest it in another house of her own.[32] Through her friend and landlady, Helena Clay, Marguerite found that the house right next to Graycourt Manor, where the Smiths had been living on South Broadway, was for sale. A handsome, white, Victorian-styled clapboard home of ante-bellum vintage, three stories high with wide porches, a sun deck, and beautiful view overlooking the Hudson, it would be just the house for all of her children, and for Reeves, too, when he came home from the war. On May 15, 1945, Mrs. Smith purchased 131 South Broadway for nine thousand dollars.[33]

In early February, Reeves cabled Carson that he was leaving England and was on his way home. He said that there would be weeks of hospitalization and treatment ahead for him, and he joked that he almost clanked with a body full of shrapnel. On February 24, Carson met his ship in New York, and three weeks later they remarried. As she explained it to Newton Arvin, as though to justify the action, the legal part of the ceremony did not really matter, except that it would be more convenient since Reeves was still in the Army. There would be certain benefits, of course, but the important thing was their spiritual union. She and Reeves had known each other by then for ten years, and even during the sad and anguished times when she had wanted and tried to put him from her mind, she could not. They realized that they were irrevocably bound to each other, no matter what. The war itself, the hell, had added years to his face, Carson thought, but the gentleness, the tenderness, were still there. The old Reeves, the good Reeves, was also a more settled and sure Reeves now. On March 19, 1945, they appeared before County Judge John A. McKenna, who, dressed in his black robe, married them in his private office of the Rockland County Courthouse in New City, New York. The ceremony was witnessed only by Ann Hofstatter of Nyack and Margaret Stanley of Piermont.

Afterward, Carson and Reeves drove first to share the news with two dear friends, who lived nearby. "Why, Reeves, why did you marry Carson again when you both went through such hell before?" they asked that afternoon in a quiet moment alone with Reeves.

There was a pause, and then came his enigmatic answer: "Because I think we are all drones—and Carson is the queen bee." It was a foreboding answer, and one that belied Reeves's apparent joy and optimism on his wedding day. There was no doubt that he loved Carson and was irrevocably committed to her, but he also knew that he was risking his newly earned identity. Although submerged again in Carson, he hoped that their legal bond and oneness would not mean destructive capitulation.

Chapter Nine

NYACK AND PARIS, 1945 – 47

*R*eeves *had been ordered directly to a military hospital in Utica, New* York, upon his return to the United States. There the doctors decided he could no longer climb down nets in amphibious landings or be a combat soldier, for his badly smashed wrist bones had not mended properly. His left hand and wrist still weak and inflexible, the doctors considered a bone graft. More distressing to Reeves than the injury, however, was that his service career seemed in jeopardy. It was not that he necessarily wanted to be a twenty-year man, but he would have liked to dictate his own terms, getting out of the Army when he himself was ready. A dedicated soldier, he would doubtless have had an outstanding military career. The Army needed successful officers like Reeves, who led his men well and instilled in them pride in their outfit and fierce loyalty to one another. To Reeves, it seemed an irony of fate that he was thwarted in pursuing what gave him the greatest and most singular identity he had known. Today, he was First Lieutenant James Reeves McCullers, Jr., serial number 0-1301851. In any other environment, he might again become merely Carson McCullers' husband.

There was pleasure, of course, in sharing Carson's identity. He recalled an incident in France in which, after nineteen days of heavy fighting during the siege of Brest, he captured a German naval officer. When the prisoner heard Reeves's name, his face brightened and he asked if his captor were the author of *The Heart Is a Lonely Hunter*. The prisoner had found an English edition of the book in France and had read and greatly admired it. When Reeves told him who he was, they talked for a while as though they were old friends. Then, just before being taken back to the prisoners' pen, the German captive went to his sea chest and took out a bolt of beautiful cloth. "Please send this to your wife, the author of that remarkable book," he said. Carson was touched by Reeves's story. It reminded her of the stranger in the wine shop in Charlotte, North Carolina, who had pressed the money back into Reeves's hand when she and Reeves had purchased—from a very thin wallet—a particularly fine bottle of wine after thoughtfully and appreciatively savoring a number of them.

Although Reeves's postwar plans had been, of necessity, vague while he was in action, the European people and the countryside—particularly of Brittany—had gotten under his skin. Of all the places he had been, he felt more at home in Luxembourg than anywhere else. The people there seemed hard working and gracious in spite of a war, he observed. In letters written to both Edwin Peacock and Alfred Kantorowicz while in Belgium the preceding winter a few days before he was injured, he said that he wanted to return to Europe after the war when he had had a chance to readjust himself personally. He conceded that he had grown sick of Europe then, of course, but it was a fascinating region. He felt a kinship with the people and the land that surprised and touched him.[1]

Once again in the United States, Reeves spent much of his first six weeks traveling back and forth between Utica, Nyack, Baltimore, and Washington, D.C. He was granted weekend passes from the hospital to stay with Carson and her family in their apartment at Graycourt Manor in Nyack. Then, accompanied by Carson, he took a short leave to visit his mother in Baltimore. For a week Carson stayed at Reeves's bedside in Utica while he underwent extensive analysis and treatment for his injured wrist and hand. By late March the doctors still had not decided whether to perform a bone graft.

Reeves, in the meantime, made up his mind that if he could not be a combat soldier, he would like to get into the American Military Government. After seeing his mother in Maryland, he and Carson went to Washington for an interview with the colonel in charge. He had seen how the AMG worked in France and Germany while he was overseas, and although he thought AMG had made some terrible mistakes, especially in Germany, he believed that with the right intelligence, a superior job could be done. He decided that he, too, could be a vital part of that intelligence. With the surrender of Germany expected any day, he was sure that many new men would be needed for overseas assignments.

The colonel seemed impressed by Reeves, but told him that the quota for the European theater was filled. There would be an excellent possibility, however, for him to receive an assignment in the Pacific within the next five months. Reeves learned, also, that a college baccalaureate degree and a degree in law were the usual requirements, but that the examining and screening board for AMG sometimes waived them for men with exceptional combat records. If he could get assurance from his doctors that he was fit for administrative work overseas, his chances of being accepted were good.[2] After the European armistice, the AMG men would be able to have their families with them, too. Reeves would not have consented to go anywhere again where Carson could not accompany him. Even if he should be admitted to the program and assigned to the Pacific, he felt certain that he could soon wangle a European assignment.

The second week of July 1945, Reeves appeared before a disposition board of the Utica hospital. He had been permanently disabled, they decided. The doctors might still operate at a later date on his injured wrist, but in the meantime they recommended him for "permanent limited service." Immediately he was ordered to Camp Wheeler, Georgia, outside Macon, and given two days to get there. Resentful and unhappy about his new assignment, Reeves wrote to his old army friend and roommate of the 1930s, Vincent Adams, who also had returned to the military and was now a major stationed in the Washington, D.C. area. After identifying his location as three miles from hell, Reeves registered his anger and indignation in a profane outburst about being sent back to the region he had spent twenty years trying to leave. Although a medical board at the hospital he had left recommended him for a medical discharge with a pension, he said that he blamed Washington for trying to squeeze a turnip which had already been bled almost to death. He had rather be in the Pacific than on a southern base trying to make fighting men out of misfits whom the Army had classified as 4-Fs for years. But his days of volunteering for Uncle Sam were over.

Reeves also asked Vincent Adams to check with AMG headquarters from time to time to see if the board were accepting any more applications for Europe. He had completely given up the possibility of an assignment to the Pacific, he said. The only thing he liked about the Orient was rice about once a week, and only then if it were served with beef roast gravy, he added. He said that a friend of his who was very close to Senator Wagner of New York and another who was a close personal friend of the commandant of the AMG School in Virginia could apply some pressure, perhaps, but he did not want help unless it were needed. In the meantime, he did not want to jeopardize in any way his captaincy which was coming up.[3]

About ten days before Reeves left for the South, Carson had a surging impulse to return to Yaddo and stay until she finished what she now referred to as her "cursed book." She had hoped to be able to "deliver" it to Reeves by March 15—as though it were the fruit of her womb—but it had been impossible and the end still was not in sight. If she had the discipline and quietude of Yaddo, she told Reeves, she was certain she could finish it in two months. This time she simply wired Elizabeth Ames that she was on her way and would arrive on June 26.

As in 1944, the artists' colony had very few guests in 1945, even though the group was slightly larger than it had been during the past two summers. Yaddo was still operating on a wartime basis, with food supplies—especially meats—difficult to get in quantities. The mansion remained closed that summer, and everyone dined in the garage and lived in the outlying buildings. Eleanor Clark, Carson's acquaintance from early 7 Middagh Street days, was there, and Agnes Smedley continued in residence at Yaddo for another year except for occasional lecture tours throughout the country. Home from the war and back at the artists' colony, too, was writer Leonard Erhlich—to whom Elizabeth Ames was devoted—joined once more by his brother Gerald, Gerald's wife, and their year-old daughter. Other guests included Howard Doughty, Jr., Eitaro and Harv Ishigaki, Jerre Mangione, Kappo Phelan, Hobson Pittman, Esther Rolick, Klane Blazek, Alexei Haieff, and Ruth Domino.

Writer Jerre Mangione, a newcomer to Yaddo, was greeted upon his arrival by Carson, who had delegated herself to show him his room and the Yaddo grounds. "She looked something like a farm boy in her jeans," said Mangione, yet he found her quite feminine in her manner. "Because of her long legs I could not help likening her to one of those boudoir dolls seated on a chest of drawers that I've occasionally seen in French movies— a loose-jointed rag doll, I would say."[4]

It was this year at Yaddo that Eleanor Clark saw the facet of Carson she admired most: her sense of anguish and personal integrity in dedication to her art. Several times that summer Miss Clark observed Carson struggling and suffering with her family of characters as though she, too, were shut up in the hot, bright kitchen in which Frankie and John Henry made queer drawings on the walls. She was Frankie, too, "an unjoined person" who could no longer stand under the arbor and pick scuppernongs like the other children. On the other hand, Miss Clark occasionally became exasperated with Carson, who at times "could be one hell of a childish liar" in much the same manner that Edward Newhouse recalled Carson's proclivity for fantasy foisted off as truth when he first met her at Yaddo in 1941.

The trait was not one that Carson outgrew. One story she told Eleanor Clark that summer was of an incident in which she purportedly had been in a small boat crossing the Hudson River near the George Washington Bridge, accompanied by Reeves and another man. Suddenly, halfway across the river, Carson decided to jump into the water and swim to the New Jersey shore, whereupon she arrived "at a dock amid huge water rats." It was an impressive tale and one which Miss Clark tended to believe until she saw for herself Carson's performance in the water. One hot August afternoon the two of them decided to go swimming at Saratoga Lake. To Miss Clark's astonishment, it turned out that Carson could hardly swim at all. "She could barely struggle to the dock from a few yards out," said Miss Clark.[5]

Regardless of the Hudson River water rats story or Carson's floundering at Saratoga Lake, the truth seems to be that at one time she did swim well. As an adolescent and high school student, she frequently swam in pools and natural lakes around Columbus and in the Fort Benning Officers' Club pool as the guest of Colonel and Mrs. Tucker. Also, several of Carson's girlhood friends remembered that Carson enjoyed swimming so much that had there been a high school swimming team, she probably would have been on it. Yet, undoubtedly, it suited Carson *not* to be a good swimmer at Yaddo. Again and again she played the role of a wounded sparrow. If someone were around who might sympathize or take an interest in her because of her weaknesses, she sometimes tucked in her wings and fluttered feebly from her nest. This pose was by no means limited to her later years after she had become infirm from her various illnesses and strokes.

By the end of August 1945, Carson had sweated over, suffered, and written almost seven different versions of *The Member of the Wedding*— and Elizabeth Ames had read every one of them. One night around eight o'clock, Yaddo's executive director was sitting alone in Pine Garde, her home, when she heard a knock at the door. It was Carson. "Here is the manuscript, Elizabeth—I have finished it. . . . No, I am not going to stay," she whispered, rushing off into the night. Her voice was barely audible, to Mrs. Ames reminiscent of their first meeting in New York when the young author, in her timidity, had been struck speechless.

Mrs. Ames immediately took up the manuscript and began to read. At 2:30 A.M. she wearily put it aside, knowing at last "that it was perfect."[6] When she walked over for breakfast that morning, she tucked the manuscript inside her bag. It was an occasion Mrs. Ames never forgot:

> Carson was watching for me to come into the dining room. At the time her nerves were so bad that her hand shook when she held a cup of coffee. I walked up behind her as she sipped her coffee, the cup rattling when she attempted to put it down. "You have done it, my dear," I said, handing her back the manuscript. As I spoke, she tipped over her glass of water and laid her head down upon the table with a great sigh. It was all over. Her child, in a sense, had been born.[7]

The next day Carson sent the manuscript to her agent, Ann Watkins. It was almost impossible for her to believe that the work was finished. She also was anxious for others to read it, to tell her that it was good. Carson needed applause. She planned to send it—or take it—to Reeves later, but first she wanted critical responses from friends in the literary world. When she left Yaddo the last day of August 1945, she had the greatest feeling of accomplishment she had known, as well as the most acute sense of emotional relief she had yet experienced relative to her writing. As Carson embraced Elizabeth Ames good-by, both shed quiet tears. Carson had written the book for herself—and she had savored it, loved it, anguished over it more than over anything else she had done or would do—and she intended to present it now to Reeves as a token of her love. Yet Mrs. Ames had shared her soul in its creation, had served devotedly as critic and friend. Although Carson chose not to tell her then, she had known for some time that the dedication of the book would be to Elizabeth Ames. Had it not been for Mrs. Ames, Carson felt that *The Member of the Wedding* might never have been finished.

The first person to share her manuscript after Elizabeth Ames approved it was Kay Boyle. Carson called her from Yaddo to tell her that the book was ready and that she was leaving immediately for the city. Miss Boyle insisted on meeting Carson at Grand Central Station. She wanted to see the manuscript and take it home to read. Carson told Newton Arvin later that Kay Boyle wrote her the next day that she loved the book, but had one objection: in one particular episode Carson as author had deliberately turned her face away. The part involving the soldier seemed evasive, suggested Miss Boyle.[8] Disturbed now and uncertain about what to do, Carson wired Ann Watkins to return the manuscript. She did not want it to go to the publisher until she was certain in her own mind that it needed no further revision. Miss Watkins replied that she thought the book superb as it was, but that she would send it back with reluctance if Carson insisted.

With the two copies of the manuscript again in her possession, Carson began to share the book with other close friends. Its most youthful reader and critic was Truman Capote, then not quite twenty-one. Agreeing with Carson that the soldier was brought into the novel and used in just the right proportions, remaining—in a sense—on the outward fringes of a dream, Capote believed that the whole story would have been off balance if the soldier had been brought into sharper focus. According to Carson, the book impressed the young author more than any other work he had read in years.[9] Although she agreed to some extent with Kay Boyle's criticism, Carson felt that compassion—which Miss Boyle had apparently found lacking—in a work of fiction was sometimes artistically wrong, and that this was one of those times.

On September 24, 1945, having decided to keep the manuscript as it was, Carson lunched in New York City with Harwick Mosely and Ann Watkins. Mosely, who had prevailed upon her to change the title of her first novel from *The Mute* to *The Heart Is a Lonely Hunter*, was Houghton Mifflin's sales manager and a director of the firm. Although not an editor, he had been performing as editor to some of the company's most prestigious authors.[10] He would add Carson to his list of authors with pleasure, he said. It had been a shock to Houghton Mifflin when Robert Linscott moved to Random House in 1944 after forty years with Houghton Mifflin. Moreover, Linscott had taken a number of his best authors with him. He had hoped that Random House could publish *The Member of the Wedding*, but Carson decided to stay with Houghton Mifflin. When she signed the contract a few days later, she felt a twinge of remorse, she admitted. Writing to Linscott on September 30, Carson apologized to him and acknowledged that he had helped her in immeasurable ways. She hoped that he would forgive her. They had talked earlier by telephone when she called to tell him of her decision, and Linscott assured her that her staying with Houghton Mifflin for the publication of *The Member of the Wedding* would not affect their friendship and love one whit. But Carson wanted to put her apology in writing, too. There was something hallowed about writing, she thought. Writing something made it true—no matter what it was—just as truth could be more wholly accepted in fiction than if it had been bared in factual exposition.

She also wrote to tell Linscott about her young friend Truman Capote, whose story "Miriam" had been published two years earlier by her sister, Rita. As fiction editor of *Mademoiselle*, Rita Smith had, in a sense, discovered Capote. He had just turned twenty-one, said Carson, and Random House would do well to acquire him now as their author. Capote's stories had delicacy and beauty, and she was convinced of his ability and promise as a writer. Recommending him to Random House would assuage her own feelings about disappointing Linscott. If she could not give Linscott her book, she would offer Truman Capote in its place. Linscott followed up Carson's advice, and years later he was one of three editors Capote credited with helping him most when he first began to publish. Not only did Linscott, Rita Smith, and Mary Lou Aswell buy his work, but they also "were very generous with advice," Capote said.[11] Never before had Carson been so enthusiastic about promoting another young writer, who looked more like a prankish little schoolboy than a promising creative genius. She was able to identify completely at this time with her young friend, who many people thought served as a model for her final concept of John Henry West in *The Member of the Wedding*.

Soon after Carson's return to Nyack upon finishing the book, Reeves, on leave from Camp Wheeler, joined her. A few days later his mother, his brother, Tommy, and his sister Wylie Mae gathered in Nyack for a family reunion. Reeves's other sister, Marguerite Lee, home in Jesup, Georgia, had been too sick to come. Almost immediately after Jessie McCullers and Wylie Mae returned to Baltimore, they received word from Marguerite Lee's husband that his wife was desperately ill and he was taking her at once to Johns Hopkins Hospital. En route to Camp Wheeler, Reeves took time to spend a few hours with his ailing sister. He had felt a special kinship with his older sister over the years because they had been farmed out together during much of their youth. Reeves loved his family, but in actuality did not know them very well, having grown up largely away from home. There had seldom been a home to which he might return. Like Carson, Reeves felt displaced, although the circumstances had been quite different. The South was fraught with unpleasant memories for them both.

In spite of the confusion caused by a household revolving around house guests and Carson's tension over her manuscript, its possible revision, and plans for publication, she resolved to put off no longer an article promised to George Davis for the November issue of *Mademoiselle*. She removed herself psychically from the disorder at home, then wrote "Our Heads Are Bowed" in a mood of apparent serenity and peace. It was Carson's Thanksgiving message to the American people, a feature which struck a universal note reminiscent of her "Letter from a War Wife." This time she wrote of her gratitude and rejoicing for those who lived in a recuperating world no longer ravaged by war. Yet it was a quiet and grave celebration, she said, because of the blemishes and scars left on almost every family. "Our Heads Are Bowed" was also her prayer for wisdom and guidance for all Americans, who bowed in humility and strength before what she identified as a power mightier than themselves.[12]

Hers was a poignant message, and the editors at *Mademoiselle* liked it. Carson herself was elated, for—as she wrote to Newton Arvin later—she received five hundred dollars for an article only four paragraphs long. With the money, she planned to repay her mother for having had a bathroom installed in the third-floor attic quarters, which Marguerite was preparing to rent to Carson and Reeves as a separate apartment.

Marguerite would have liked to have all her children stay with her in Nyack. In the fall of 1945, she excitedly awaited the arrival of Lamar, Jr., who was to be discharged in October. After rejoining his wife in Columbus, he would bring her to Nyack for a Smith family reunion. Marguerite also urged Edwin Peacock to come. He, too, was one of her "boys"—as she had said many times—and she hoped that with her family around her once more they might recapture the old spirit of home. To her, Lamar, Jr., in spite of his tall, strapping build, would always be her "little boy," her Brother-Man. Even though many people in Columbus outside the family thought of her son as having grown up largely on his own, Lamar thought nothing of the kind. He felt a warm bond of closeness between himself and his mother. If he had seemed like a Huck Finn character to others, it did not matter to him, for he had always known that he was much loved and very special to her. He not only loved his mother, but also admired her immensely. For her to have coped with three very different—and difficult—children and to have emerged with relatively few scars while maintaining an incongruous mixture of old world sophistication and new world naiveté amazed those who knew Marguerite well. In a sense, she "made" her children what they were, and her husband looked on in wonderment that he had sired three such remarkable children.[13]

It had been over a year since his father's death, but Lamar, who had not been able to leave his combat area to attend the funeral, remembered his father with a clarity and love as though they had said good-by at the station only yesterday as he headed for the Pacific early in the war. Lamar's outfit had been frogmen, underwater demolition experts, whose missions included the dismantling of mines in Japanese waters. For Lamar, the extra energy required to return safely from a harrowing mission was frequently the simple and warming thought of being able to go aboard his ship and stir his coffee with the silver spoon and drink from the china cup and saucer that his father had sent him overseas. "No son of mine is going to drink out of a tin cup if I can help it," Lamar, Sr., had said. Nor did the young Seabee mind the ribbings from his fellow men as he luxuriated with his bone china amid a war flacking about him.

It was a good reunion for Lamar, Jr., and his wife, Virginia, in Nyack that fall as they reminisced, yet made plans for the future. Marguerite Smith had anticipated for weeks before her son's arrival a special homecoming gift. She intended to buy him his first Brooks Brothers suit, in which she was sure he would look like a young executive and be ready for anything, she said proudly. Lamar told his family that he had bought some acreage in South Georgia which he thought he might like to farm someday, or perhaps he would go into industry. He simply did not know at this point; but whatever it was, he told them he would remain in the South.

Reeves, in the meantime, could hardly wait to relocate permanently in the North, or go overseas. He did not get back to Nyack until just before Christmas, but he was granted a terminal leave and was able to stay. The army doctors having chosen not to do the bone graft and thus perhaps enable him to be made combat fit again, Reeves decided that after four months of life at Camp Wheeler he wanted nothing more to do with the Army if it had to be in the capacity in which he was now working. In February, his promotion to captain came through, which Carson referred to as his posthumous award since it was only a matter of weeks before he would be discharged from active service. Reeves wrote Vincent Adams that getting the extra brass meant little, but the money felt good. Although he would not be officially discharged until March 16, 1946, Reeves began to cast out feelers for a civilian occupation soon after the first of the year. He also made one last trip to AMG headquarters in December on his way North from Camp Wheeler. This time he learned that only specialists in limited areas, such as chemistry and structural and electrical engineering, were being accepted for overseas AMG work. He would have to think wholly along civilian lines, he resolved.

Vincent Adams had heard about a position for a New York territorial sales manager with the Wilcox-Gay Corporation, manufacturers of recording equipment, and had recommended Reeves for the job. The firm's executive director was a friend of Adams'. The new territory had failed to expand as predicted, however, and Reeves's application was put into a *hold* file. He wrote his friend a few days later that he was getting a bit anxious about just what he would be doing. Carson had been bothered that winter by what the doctors diagnosed as neuritic rheumatism, and Reeves now felt keenly his psychological need to be a wage earner himself. In the back of his mind, he was still optimistic that something with AMG would break by late spring. He felt relief that the job with Wilcox-Gay did not materialize. Moreover, the United States Department of State had announced that it would soon take over administrative details in much of Europe and Africa. Besides that, Reeves reasoned that there were some three hundred thousand Americans overseas who wanted to come back home. There would be a place for him overseas somewhere, he assured Carson. The United Nations Relief Agency was a possibility, too, he thought.

Another career lurking in Reeves's mind was medicine. As AMG possibilities became increasingly remote, Carson began to encourage her husband to return to school and take advantage of the new GI Bill. He had always wanted to go back to college, she reminded him, and now was the perfect opportunity. He was entitled to forty-eight months of tuition under the GI Bill and would get an additional ninety-five dollars a month subsistence under the present allowance. With the recent sale of *The Member of the Wedding*, an advance, and good royalties anticipated, Carson was confident that she would have the money to see him through his schooling after the GI Bill ran out.

Reeves wrote Adams that the field of psychiatry interested him especially and that he hoped to get into a good school and pursue it. If that did not materialize, he would go into some other medical field, he resolved. Seemingly committed, Carson and Reeves set out to get him admitted to Harvard for the February 1946 term. Almost frantically they prepared, as though they might change their minds if they stopped for a deep breath. Reeves missed the February admission date for Harvard, however, and they considered Amherst, which was located just eight miles from Newton Arvin's home in Northampton. Carson became suddenly taken by the idea that the three of them could be together while Reeves studied, Arvin taught, and Carson wrote. It would be another we of me. Reeves and Arvin had not met, and she was anxious for them to know each other. Arvin, too, wrote encouraging letters to Reeves and invited him to come up and stay with him, visit the campus, and have an interview with the Amherst dean. In the meantime, Reeves applied for admission and began to review mathematics and history. He wrote Vincent Adams that he would enter Amherst in June and had been cramming ten hours a day to pass the matriculation examination.

In early February, Reeves visited Arvin and the Amherst campus. Even though he liked Newton Arvin and was impressed by the college, Harvard still interested him more. In an appreciative letter to Arvin after his return from Northampton, Reeves said that he was especially pleased that he, like Carson, could count Arvin as his dear friend. He told him that the new relationship filled a void and that he hoped the three of them would allow neither time nor location to deprive them of many joyous moments together in the future.

The first of March, having received an encouraging letter from the dean of Harvard, Reeves went to Cambridge to see for himself what the situation was there. He found the aura of Harvard exciting, and he liked what he saw. The veterans' adviser pointed out a number of fringe benefits at Harvard which seemed more bountiful than benefits noted at other schools to which Reeves had made inquiries. Another thing in Harvard's favor was that the school had a free tutorial service for veterans. Reeves's meeting with two of the deans in the School of Medicine, however, ended on a more disappointing note. They pointed out that even though he probably would be admitted to medical school, he would not be certain of it until he completed almost three more years of undergraduate work. Then he would still have four years of medical school and another two or three years of internship. Thirty-one now, Reeves would be forty before he could qualify to practice. To them, he would simply be too old. They encouraged him, instead, to consider going into labor management relations or a related field in which he also acknowledged interest. He could take a special matriculation test in March to qualify for a June admission. With his goal of a medical career now as elusive as AMG, Reeves returned to Nyack more sober and wise than when he had departed, but determined, nevertheless, to prove himself a man and a fit, competent, and worthy husband. He would take the tests and enroll in Harvard in June, he resolved.

During Reeves's several trips about the countryside, Carson, too, was struck with wanderlust. The thought occurred to her that she would like to go South again—not to Columbus, but to Charleston, where Edwin Peacock lived. Peacock had recently opened a bookshop with John Zeigler, a friend with whom he had served in the Navy. The opening had been scheduled for Carson's birthday, a date Peacock chose especially for her. The gesture touched her, just as little unexpected things had always thrilled her when she was honored in some special way. Unable to come just then, however, Carson wrote a note of appreciation and said that she and her family had gathered and drunk a toast to the success of the venture. It would suit her better to come in March, she said, while Reeves was at Harvard taking his matriculation examination. She would accompany him to Boston, then go by ship to Charleston. Reeves could join them after his test and return to Harvard in time for the June term. In fact, Marguerite might come, too, Reeves added in a note of his own.

Carson intended to stay on in the South for a few weeks and write.

Peacock and Zeigler's bookshop was in the basement of a spacious three-story, ante-bellum home owned by Zeigler's aunt. The three of them shared the home, and Carson longed to visit Peacock there and quietly steep herself in his warmth and friendship. He was her and Reeves's dearest friend, she assured Peacock, and she wanted him to know that she loved him as though he were her own brother.[14] As a writer, Carson felt that she needed to bask in the South again, to replenish her stock of southern mystique. The old bitterness of the South as a place to "renew her sense of horror" had eased, and she thought of it kindly now, almost with affection.

The birthday toast which Marguerite, Rita, Reeves, and she drank in honor of the Book Basement proved to be a prophetic one, for Peacock and Zeigler shared their shop with Charleston readers for over twenty-five years. Located across the street from the campus of the College of Charleston, the Book Basement very quickly became one of the most popular bookstores in the city, exuding an old-style European flavor combined with the graciousness of its genial southern hosts.[15] Peacock responded to Carson's request to visit with an enthusiastic invitation. They would be delighted to have Carson, Reeves, and her mother whenever it suited them. To Carson, March seemed a perfect month because *The Member of the Wedding* was due to be released then. She fantasized that with her new book she doubtless would become the most sought-after writer in the country. Charleston would be a fit haven to retreat to from reviews, requests for interviews, and the hubbub of the city. By all means, she should come then, Peacock urged.

The Member of the Wedding, originally scheduled to be released in February, was delayed until March 19. For the most part, immediate reviews in the United States were favorable. Orville Prescott, Lewis Gannett, Richard Match, Isa Kapp, George Dangerfield—all praised it. British critics treated the book somewhat less kindly than they had Carson's earlier works, about which they had been largely enthusiastic, but she attributed their judgment now to a lack of feeling and appreciation for the nuances and rhythms of southern speech. Only Edmund Wilson in America responded with a wholly negative appraisal. He found nothing redeemable about the novel. Furthermore, he attacked it for its lack of a sense of drama, which he reminded his readers was necessary to any good story.[16]

Instead of going to Charleston after accompanying Reeves to Boston for his matriculation examination at Harvard, Carson decided to go directly to Yaddo. *The Member of the Wedding* had been dedicated to Elizabeth Ames, and Carson felt now the need for security in the seclusion of Yaddo, which would be even more private for her than Charleston. Although the first reviews had been good, she looked forward to facing the critics—or retreating from them—at Yaddo, with Mrs. Ames at her side.

Carson arrived at the artists' colony on March 23, 1946, four days after the first reviews. It was a week later that she heard news of Edmund Wilson's review and experienced new trauma. She had become increasingly nervous that year and was subject to sudden attacks in which she became dizzy, short of breath, and possessed by an overwhelming fear that she would black out on the street or elsewhere in public. She could feel the awful blackness rolling up in great surges from her feet, legs, heart, and chest, accompanied by a sense of being lost or abandoned.

Carson saw Newton Arvin at Yaddo when she first arrived. She told him later that she had gained strength and solace from him, but that she was greatly saddened that he could stay only a few days, for she needed him, she said. As soon as Carson saw him off on the bus in Saratoga Springs, an attack immediately came over her and she barely managed to cross the street and make it to Hewett's drugstore, where she had arranged to meet Agnes Smedley.[17] The terror of fainting in public had become almost an obsession with Carson. It was with the greatest physical exertion imaginable, she explained to Arvin, that she had propped herself upon a soda fountain stool and held onto the counter to await her friend. When Mrs. Smedley arrived, she found Carson ill and unable to speak. Finally she managed to get her home in a taxi and arranged for fellow artist Howard Doughty to stay with her. Doughty fixed hot soup for her and told her amusing anecdotes until she began to feel almost normal again. Such quirks were frightening, Carson told Arvin, for she was reminded of her strange paralysis at the Bedford Hotel in 1941 when she was unable to sign her name. Carson marveled that simply by writing Newton Arvin's name on the page and then smoking and drinking tea as she related her tale to him, she received immediate psychic and physical relief. She found it even curiously amusing that in taking a kind of backhanded pleasure in telling Arvin of her miseries and thus being cured, she had demonstrated that there could not be very much wrong with her after all.

Arvin was her most precious friend, she assured him now; she would always treasure their friendship. Most of all, she was happy that he and Reeves had met that spring, for she felt it necessary that Reeves, too, know that he was included in her relationship with Arvin. She said she had known that Arvin and Reeves would love each other and become great friends because there was such tenderness and loyalty in each. No one else was more capable of exquisite friendship than these two men whom she loved above all others.[18]

The very afternoon of her letter to Newton Arvin, Carson was shaken again. It was the day after Edmund Wilson's review appeared, but no one in Saratoga Springs had seen it yet. Marguerite Smith read the review first, and in an effort to shield her daughter from the impact, called her at Yaddo to urge her to ignore it. Until now, Carson had coped rather capably with her critics in print. Through the years that she had been in the public eye she had been able for the most part to disregard or discount the judgment of unfavorable reviewers. Even though the attack on *The Ballad of the Sad Café* in 1943 had greatly unsettled her, the fact that the letter writer hid behind a mask of anonymity convinced her that his charges of her having ridiculed Jewishness were unfounded. But for Edmund Wilson to have missed the mark in *The New Yorker*, in which she herself had been published, and which was now being seen by thousands of readers, was devastating. To be sure, through the years Carson became increasingly vulnerable, an oyster without a shell, susceptible to hurts both real and imagined—which, in the final analysis, were all the same.

Unfortunately, the afternoon of her mother's call, Carson was expected at a cocktail party given by fellow artist Howard Doughty, who was entertaining for Granville and Dorothy Hicks's newly married daughter, Stephanie. The Hickses had driven up from Grafton, New York, for the affair, and most of the guests from Yaddo had been invited as well as a number of others from Saratoga Springs. Everyone else was there, yet Carson did not appear or send word of her delay. Time passed, and still there was no Carson. Her absence became increasingly noticed and talked about, for the group knew that it was not like her to miss a party. Besides, she, too, was being honored, and they wanted to drink to her success with her new book.

When she finally arrived, it was obvious that she had been crying. Caroline Slade, wife of John Slade—president of the Yaddo board of directors and a Saratoga Springs lawyer—went over to console Carson, for they had become especially close over the Yaddo summers. Immediately the wounded and distraught author dissolved into tears in her comforter's arms and sobbed uncontrollably. It was many minutes later—and with great effort—that she was able to recover enough to tell the group hovered about her of her mother's phone call and Wilson's review. Both infuriated and desolate over *The New Yorker* piece, as well as embarrassed by her own actions and vulnerability, she vowed never to read another review of her works.[19]

A few weeks later, Carson related the incident to Marguerite Young, a distinguished and promising writer and poet who was at Yaddo in 1946 for the first time. When she told Miss Young that she would read no more reviews of her books, Miss Young did not comment, but she sensed that someday she, too, would write about *The Member of the Wedding*, and she believed that her review might be one Carson would want to read.[20]

Indeed, a year later, Marguerite Young wrote the first and what has stood as the most perceptive and appreciative depth study of *The Member of the Wedding* perhaps ever written, a work entitled "Metaphysical Fiction," published in the *Kenyon Review* in the winter issue, 1947.

Reeves came twice to Yaddo that spring to be with Carson, although spouses did not usually stay unless they were invited as guest artists in their own right. But Reeves had been up once the summer before, and Elizabeth Ames believed that it would mean a great deal to Carson to have him there at this particular time. The 1946 group was still small and there was ample room. Although Carson had arrived earlier than most of the other artists, some dozen others were there before she left on May 31. Still in school, Newton Arvin spent only intermittent weekends at Yaddo until his summer vacation began, when he came for six weeks. Carson was pleased to see young Truman Capote at the artists' colony. Capote, at work on his first novel, was housed from early May until mid-July in the atmospheric tower room, a haven of lacy woodwork, gothic spires, monastic white walls, and high ceilings which overlooked the great lawn in front of the mansion. The tower room, which had been founder Lady Katrina Trask's hideaway where she retreated to write poetry, was now an apt setting for the writing of Capote's book, which proved to be rich in gothic trappings when published two years later by Random House as *Other Voices, Other Rooms*.[21]

Others in the group that spring during Carson's stay included her old friend, the talented writer, biographer, and patron of the arts, Leo Lerman, whom she and Reeves had known since their early days on West Eleventh Street when Lerman lived across the street from them. Lerman became one of her close companions. Jerre Mangione was back, too, for a three-month stay. Fond of Mangione, Carson enjoyed strolling over the Yaddo grounds with him and having long private talks in the rose garden. She also invited him to accompany her and several of the others into the black district of Saratoga Springs for a round of the more atmospheric night spots. At Jimmy's on Congress Street, Carson proudly elaborated how she and Langston Hughes had spent many profitable evenings at craps during his two summers there. Also back at Yaddo for a second summer were Leonard Erhlich and artist Esther Rolick. As newcomers, there were only Jean Garrigue, Ralph Bates, Paolo Milano, Richard Plant, and Clara Stillman.

It was a compatible group. More play and frivolity abounded in 1946 than during the wartime years, stimulated this year frequently by newcomer Truman Capote, whose practical jokes on various members of the staff sometimes proved embarrassing to his victims. Carson began drinking more heavily this spring, too, than she had during previous Yaddo stays, having progressed from caching stores of wine by the gallon during the early 1940s to whiskey by the case in 1946. Sometimes there was dancing in the music room while the group awaited dinner. One evening a number of guests responded to the music of Stravinsky's "Rite of Spring" with various antics and impromptu swayings of the body, both individually and as couples. Carson danced with Mangione with an abandonment he never forgot. Although she obviously had danced little and was awkward in her movements, she seemed enchanted by the idea of moving her body to the rhythm of the music. It was as though she had never imagined or experienced how beautifully free the body could be.[22]

On April 15, 1946, Carson received word that she had been awarded a second fellowship by the John Simon Guggenheim Memorial Foundation. This time the citation read "for the continuation of creative writing in the field of fiction."[23] Although the New York *Times* reported that she had been invited again to spend the 1946 summer season at Yaddo, Carson had difficulty making up her mind what to do. She would stay on at Yaddo at least until the end of May, she decided; then she would go either to Charleston or return home to Nyack. Reeves, in the meantime, had not entered Harvard. Whether he had not performed well on the matriculation examination or simply had second thoughts about committing himself to an academic life for the next nine or ten years—a routine incompatible with Carson's life style as an artist—is unknown. Most of all, he wanted to return to Europe. In the back of Carson's mind, too, were thoughts of going abroad, and if Reeves were free to travel, she conjectured they could take her Guggenheim money and live in Paris more cheaply than in the United States.

On May 31, Carson told her cronies—as she called them—at Yaddo good-by. Then Leo Lerman, Marguerite Young, Truman Capote, and Esther Rolick saw her off at the station. Carson had been "poor-mouthing" her financial situation for several weeks that summer, and although Lerman sympathized with her, he found it incredible that she could be out of money. He was fond of Carson and usually amused by her antics, but sometimes he saw through the fantasies she foisted off as truths and called her hand. This time he accidentally discovered her fantasy of being almost penniless as he hauled her luggage onto the platform and prepared to put her aboard the train for New York City. Lerman noticed that her shirt seemed unusually bulgy. Unaccustomed to seeing anything resembling a bosom on Carson's thin frame, he said, "My God, Carson, what is that at your chest?"

"Oh," she replied demurely, "those are my royalty checks pinned to my brassiere. I wouldn't dare trust them to banks again." With that she blew a kiss and gaily waved good-by to the crowd.[24]

Several days after Carson's return to New York City from Yaddo, she was off again, this time to Nantucket Island as the guest of playwright

Tennessee Williams. Williams, thirty-four, arrived in New York City in mid-May from the Vieux Carré of New Orleans while his first successful play, *The Glass Menagerie*, was still on Broadway. While trying to decide where to go for a quiet vacation retreat in the East, he and his companion Pancho Rodriguez, a young Texan of Spanish descent, were the guests of Miss Elisabeth Curtis, a wealthy artist spinster, in her palatial apartment on East Seventy-second Street off Fifth Avenue. One night during their stay with Miss Curtis, Williams began reading a novel by a fellow Southerner whose works he had never seen before. It was *The Member of the Wedding*, and he sat up most of the night to read it, stopping only intermittently to wipe his eyes—for he had cried through much of it, he admitted—and to reflect upon the remarkable compassion inherent in the book. The playwright instantly recognized its author as a kindred soul and believed, moreover, that she possibly was the greatest novelist then alive in America. Unable to sleep, he got up, threw on a dressing robe, and wrote what became his first fan letter. He told Carson that she was an author he greatly admired and that he would like very much to meet her. Several days later, Williams saw his good friend Paul Bigelow and Carson's cousin Jordan Massee, who had come to New York from Macon, Georgia, for a brief holiday. When he found that they knew Carson personally and that Massee was her cousin, he told them that he had just written her an extraordinary letter of admiration. Confident that the two of them would get on well, Bigelow suggested that after Williams got settled at Nantucket, he might write to Carson and invite her to visit him on the island.

The playwright had been ill that spring, and when he arrived at Nantucket in late May, he found the dismal and chilling air disturbing to his psyche. Then the rains came, and for days afterward the atmosphere was heavy and depressing. Williams worried now about inexplicable heart pains and palpitations, which he assigned to the young heroine he was creating at the moment, Alma Winemiller, in his new play *Summer and Smoke*. Filled with the romantic notion that he was dying, he wrote to Carson that before he completely "gave up the ghost," he would like to spend a few days with the remarkable young writer whose book he had just read. Curiously flattered by Williams' strange invitation and pleased to be sought out, Carson readily accepted. She had not seen *The Glass Menagerie*—in fact, had seen no more than a handful of plays in her entire life—but she sensed in his letter their kinship in sensitivity to human relationships and their ambivalent feelings toward the South. For the young playwright from Columbus, Mississippi, as well as for his new friend from Columbus, Georgia, the South, admittedly, was a storehouse of painful memories from which they alternately withdrew and returned.

As Williams and his companion waited for the 1:00 P.M. Hyannis ferry bearing Carson to Nantucket a few days later, the playwright was filled with second thoughts: "My God, what am I going to do with this

perfect stranger for a whole week? And what if I don't die as I promised
I would?" Pancho Rodriguez had his own mental picture of Carson—a
tall, imperial-looking woman dressed in tweedy clothes, or a sophisticated
glamorous type—perhaps even mannish.[25] Neither of them had any idea
what the young author looked like or how she would act, and they were
apprehensive that she might in some way interrupt their casual life style
on the island that summer. They could not have been more wrong.

As the ferry docked and the passengers disembarked, they scrutinized
them all, guessing which one she might be. "Oh, that's she in the blue
dress," suggested Williams.

"No, it's that one in the white shorts," countered Rodriguez.

After all the passengers had apparently alighted and no one had looked
like their version of Carson McCullers, the two men started up the gangplank to see if anyone else might be aboard. Just then a tall, slim figure
wearing faded blue dungarees, white moccasins, a man's shirt, and a wide-
brimmed straw hat timidly approached them carrying two battered suitcases. "Are you Tennessee and Pancho?" she whispered.[26] Just as she had
been unable to face Elizabeth Ames at their first meeting in New York
when she aspired to be a Yaddo guest for the first time, so, too, had Carson hidden herself away until her hosts came looking for her. Had she only
realized how much in awe of her they were, she would not have worried.
Rodriguez recalled his reaction:

> Here before us stood the Genius. Sparkling eyes, the softest South-
> ern voice I had ever heard, shy and almost trembling. She couldn't
> talk. Tennessee embraced her and I kissed her and immediately
> we knew we were going to like each other. She was so plain and
> unassuming, yet warmth and affection oozed out of her as if from
> an inexhaustible fountain.

As they walked arm in arm away from the ferry, Carson was suddenly
reminded of Hart Crane's "Voyages," long a favorite poem. Uninhibitedly
she began to recite the beginning of Part II:

> —And yet this great wink of eternity,
> Of rimless floods, unfettered leewardings,
> Samite sheeted and processioned where
> Her undinal vast belly moonward bends,
> Laughing the wrapt inflections of our love;
>
> Take this Sea, whose diapason knells
> On scrolls of silver snowy sentences,
> . . . .

Amazed, Williams turned and looked at his new companion with affection. What would he do with her for a week, he had asked. What a foolish

worry, he knew now as he joined Carson in the recitation. Hart Crane was his favorite poet, too, one who had known a tragic and tumultuous visceral life, who had committed suicide in the sea on a last Caribbean voyage, who had loved unconventionally and dared to live honestly in an insensitive world. There already were facets of Crane's life and poetry in Williams' plays because they were so like his own—and they were embedded again and again in almost every play he wrote.

Carson loved at sight the old gray frame, two-story house at 31 Pine Street which leaned lopsidedly into the northern winds. There was no longer a question as to how long she would stay. Williams had rented the house for the summer, and he urged her to remain with him and Rodriguez as long as she wished. Two earlier house guests, an opera starlet and a female artist—who specialized in painting and arranging dried sea refuse —departed the morning of Carson's arrival, occasioned not so much by the intrusion of a newcomer to the household as by the storm that had blown in two nights before. A great wind had shattered all the upstairs windows on the north side, causing the women to seek refuge downstairs in Williams' working quarters. To cap the night's activities, a pregnant cat had slipped unbidden into the house and given birth to a half-dozen kittens on the bed downstairs.

Undisturbed by the clutter in the house which greeted her, Carson volunteered that she would be very comfortable sharing the bed with the litter of kittens. Williams and Rodriguez consolidated their personal belongings into the single upstairs sleeping quarters which still had windows, then helped Carson settle into the downstairs bedroom. Almost miraculously the sun came out, warm winds wafted up from the South, and soon the ocean was calm and warm enough for swimming.

Carson suggested that they go out immediately and rent bicycles so that they might ride to the beach and stores. Soon they were cycling about the island shopping for food, liquor, and flowers. Carson also bought flowered paper curtains for the windows, a red-and-white-checkered oilcloth and candles for the table. "We're going to eat fancy," she said. If Carson had ever played the role of kitchen prima donna in the past, it was abandoned that night and for the duration of her stay. She cooked more during her month at Nantucket than she had cooked since the early days of her marriage. Among her culinary skills that summer were homemade mayonnaise, which she admitted was really her mother's speciality, clam chowder, canned green pea soup enlivened with small chunks of wieners, and a unique dish which she labeled "spuds Carson," made with creamed potatoes, ripe olives, minced onions, and grated cheese.

Her first night in the kitchen Carson prepared what Rodriguez described as "a delicious meal which we ate by candlelight. She also magically transformed every room in the house through her warm, womanly touch."[27] Later, she saw that fresh flowers were brought in daily for the house and that the fireplace was kept filled with beautiful blue and white hydrangea cuttings. The next day they bought an old windup Victrola so that they could play some newly discovered records found stored in one of the unoccupied rooms. "For some reason," said Rodriguez, "the 'Santiago Waltz' was our favorite piece."

At night Carson played Bach, Schubert, and other favorite composers on the ancient upright piano in the living room. Sometimes she played popular songs and they sang. Carson amazed Williams—just as she had Edwin Peacock many years earlier—with her ability to sing both soprano and alto. Often they read poems by Hart Crane aloud to each other from a book Williams admitted he had taken from the St. Louis Public Library as a boy. Some nights they sat around the living room drinking hot rum and tea while the playwright reminisced and talked about Laurette Taylor's life in the theatre and the people whose lives she had touched. Laurette Taylor, who had played the role of Amanda in Williams' *The Glass Menagerie* for over six hundred performances, learned that summer that she was dying, and when word reached the playwright, he was grief-stricken. Miss Taylor had come out of retirement to play the mother in Williams' play. Of all the friends Williams had made in the theatre, she was his favorite. It was more than simply being close friends; he loved her deeply. Miss Taylor had given his play her all, he said. She was a gallant lady and one of the finest actresses in the American theatre.

Carson and Williams spoke often of death that summer, a romantic notion that Williams eventually relinquished after his depressed spirits were lifted by Carson and what he described as her "radiant, crooked-toothed smile. She did have very bad teeth, you know."[28] He decided that he had no business dying after all. His heart now seemed stronger and the strange palpitations much more infrequent. Williams and Carson talked, too, of their feelings regarding God and immortality, which he said were mutual. According to Williams, Carson did not believe in God in the conventional sense, nor did he ever know her to read the Bible. "We also agreed that no sane person could believe in the immortality of a soul, regardless of how attractive the thought might be. After death, there was nothing. Carson had a presentiment that she, herself, would die young."[29]

After a discussion of the theatre one night, Williams suggested to Carson that she should try to write drama. By this time he was convinced that all of Carson's works would make "strong theatre." Encouraged by his enthusiasm, as well as goaded by Edmund Wilson's remarks that *The Member of the Wedding* was static and lacked a sense of drama, Carson decided to begin work immediately on a dramatic adaptation of the book. The next morning Williams acquired a portable typewriter for her. Then they positioned themselves at opposite ends of the long dining-room table and began to write. Sometimes they worked into the afternoon, a bottle of whiskey between them, which they passed back and forth. *Summer and Smoke* had become something of an impasse for Williams, but with Carson in the house and working, too, the play came alive again and he knew that now he could bring it to a satisfactory conclusion. There were elements of himself in John Buchanan, the young doctor in his play, who knew his anatomy charts, but even more important to his identity, dared to live them. His reticent young heroine, Miss Alma, shared qualities of both Carson and the playwright. Miss Alma could well stand a lesson or two from the doctor's charts. They were adversaries, but they were lovers in a sense, too, although their relationship was never physically consummated.

When Carson began to function that day as a playwright, she and Williams worked separately, yet together. "She was the only person I have ever been able to work in the same room with, and we got along beautifully," said Williams. To Rodriguez, Williams seemed to be Carson's guiding spirit, and she, an attentive, adoring disciple. But that was not the case, said Williams:

> In no sense of the word was I Carson's mentor. If she wanted to ask me something or read some lines aloud for my reaction, she would. But that was rare. Carson accepted almost no advice about how to adapt *The Member of the Wedding*. I did not suggest lines to her more than once or twice, and then she would usually have her own ideas and say, "Tenn, honey, thank you, but I know all I need to know." I was busy with my own script, and we sat there working very independently, you know. It was not until after Carson came to the island that I suggested she adapt her book as a play. And she pretty much finished the whole script while she was there.[30]

The two playwrights worked hard every morning and swam in the ocean and stretched lazily on the sand in the afternoons. With Rodriguez they bicycled to the beach and frequently rode about the island. They swam almost daily that summer, but Carson found that she could not keep up with Williams' exercise pace, nor could she swim particularly well, Williams recalled. "But we had a marvelous time, and we played all afternoon. Carson and Pancho got on well together, although he tended to get angry with me when he had had very much to drink, which was often back then," Williams added.

At night they sometimes went out to eat, for Williams was generous in spelling Carson from the kitchen, although he himself did not care to take her place. When they both were feeling lazy, they simply opened a can of tomato soup. "We ate a lot of soup together," he said. Occasionally the three of them went to parties given by others on the island. In fact, a number of people were at Nantucket that summer whom Carson and the playwright had already met. Her former housemate from 7 Middagh Street, artist and set designer Oliver Smith was on the island and visited them often at 31 Pine Street. They also saw a good bit of actress Rita Gam, who was part of the cast of the Straight Wharf Theatre, and director and choreographer Jerry Robbins. To Carson and Rodriguez, Miss Gam was one of the most beautiful women they had ever known.

Early in Carson's stay, they met a charming couple from Connecticut at a party given by friends of Elisabeth Curtis. Infatuated immediately by the two of them, Carson proceeded to "moon for days over the woman, especially," said Rodriguez: "The husband was quiet and observant and the wife beautiful and all smiles. Carson went wild and raved about her beauty, poise, and elegance. Although they visited us twice at 31 Pine, the beauty stayed away from Carson and was more interested in Tennessee. How this shattered the beautiful fragile magnolia from Columbus, Georgia!"[31]

According to Williams, Carson made no effort to get over her infatuation that summer:

> Instead, she would go out and buy a fifth of Johnny Walker, then sit drinking at the foot of the stairs, perched on a step or in a straight-back chair nearby in which she sat to "punish" herself. There she would remain for most of the night—or until the bottle was empty. When I got ready to retire for the night, I would step around her, pat her fondly good night, remind her to put the cats in or out— wherever they needed to be—and went up the stairs to bed. Sometimes she sat fantasizing for half the night about a romance that went on only in her head. Finally Carson began to keep company with a baroness. Then there was no more mooning over her unrequiting lover.[32]

Carson's new companion was a wealthy German who vacationed at Nantucket regularly with her husband, a European automobile magnate. Carson had met her earlier through Annemarie Clarac-Schwarzenbach, but she considered her then a rival for the affections of Annemarie and had taken no interest in her personally. Now, however, the two women spent much time together. The baroness was a superb cook, whereupon Carson's interest in recipes was again stimulated. She yearned to emulate her European friend in the kitchen; thus occasionally Williams and Rodriguez were subjected to what they considered "strange dishes Carson concocted."

The new infatuation of Carson's might have run a still longer course, said Williams, had the baroness left at home her entourage of chow dogs which accompanied her almost everywhere about the island. After she and the baron departed from 31 Pine Street one evening with dogs in tow, Carson discovered that one of the chows had killed one of the little kittens she had adopted. Hurt and upset by such a wanton act, Carson, in retaliation, invited the playwright to accompany her on a late night mission to the baroness' compound. With a quart of scotch in her arms, Carson walked up to the baroness' pig trough and emptied the bottle, then invited Williams to stretch out on the grass beside her and watch the results. "We had more fun seeing those sows get drunk as they rooted up to drink than almost anything else we did that summer," recalled Williams. "They would fall into the trough and tumble all over themselves. It was an expensive amusement—all that scotch—but we both felt better afterwards."[32]

On June 29, 1946, Carson left Nantucket and returned to Nyack for a few days. On her arrival, she wrote to Newton Arvin that she had just returned from a very pleasant vacation on Fire Island, where she had become dazed and roasted in the sun. Whether she had not wanted to tell Arvin of her new relationship with Tennessee Williams, another sensitive person she now loved and admired—reluctant to risk any feelings of jealousy that might ensue—or if she, indeed, had stopped at Fire Island, but chose not to comment to Arvin on her Nantucket experience, is unknown; whatever the reason, however, she failed to mention to Newton Arvin at this time the important basis of what later proved to be one of the most enduring friendships and loves she was ever to experience with a fellow artist.

Over the Fourth of July weekend, Reeves and Carson went together to Nantucket. Reeves had stayed in Nyack while Carson was there the first time. He could not help being jealous when she was off having a good time and working away from him, but it no longer seemed prudent to question her comings and goings. He simply was grateful when she included him in her activities. While she was gone this time he had helped Carson's mother paint and redecorate the house and had done odd jobs about the property. He was not working elsewhere, but Carson urged him not to worry. They would manage at present on her income and his army disability payments. (She told Tennessee Williams that summer that Reeves had received two thousand dollars from the Army.)[34] When they finally got to Europe, Reeves reasoned, he would surely be able to get on with UNRA, the State Department, or perhaps even on a newspaper as an American correspondent.

In midsummer, the first draft of her play finished, Carson prepared to leave the island. Reeves had remained at Nantucket only a few days, then returned later to accompany Carson home. The plan was for them to go to Martha's Vineyard with Williams, who wanted to talk with

Katharine Cornell about the role of Alma Winemiller, the heroine of his play *Summer and Smoke*. Reeves waited in the village for them while Carson and Williams went on to Miss Cornell's home, where they were expected. As soon as they arrived, Carson rushed up to her hostess and announced "rather indecorously," said Williams, that she "needed a sanitary napkin and would Miss Cornell please get her one."

"My dear, I'm through with all that," the actress replied. Nevertheless, Miss Cornell "marched off with Carson and somehow took care of things," recalled Williams. Then he added, "You know, somehow I never thought of Carson doing things like that."

Miss Cornell's companion and friend, Gertrude Macy, remembered well the visit by Williams and Carson that summer, but she admitted that her reminiscences were "not too flattering":

> Tennessee wanted to talk to Miss Cornell about doing a play he had just finished. So in order to leave them free to read and discuss the script, I took Carson over to my beach house. Both Tennessee and Carson arrived from the long trip by boat quite under the weather and were very frank about the amount they had consumed on the trip. Tennessee seemed to show it less than Carson. She adored Miss Cornell's house and wanted to find a place just like it, or rather just like my so-called "shack" on the beach. She thought it would be conducive to her writing and was very complimentary. . . . I took her back to Miss Cornell's house in time for them to leave on the late afternoon boat.[35]

"The part of Alma Winemiller was not right for Katharine Cornell," said Williams, "a fact we both readily acknowledged that day we met and talked about the script. When it opened in October of 1948, Margaret Phillips had the lead."

Williams had begun to feel very ill by the time he and Carson met Reeves in the village to catch the ferry. He was going to return alone to Nantucket, but Carson persuaded him to go home with them to Nyack, where she promised he could rest, have medical care, if necessary, and recuperate in the privacy of their home. Besides, Carson wanted her mother to get to know her new, dear friend. She was sure that Marguerite would love him, too.

Although the playwright volunteered that summer to introduce Carson to Audrey Wood, his agent and friend who had helped him get started in the theatre, and offered to take Carson's new play to Miss Wood for a reading and promotion, Carson declined. She felt that she should stay with Ann Watkins, who had been her agent since 1943. Eventually Audrey Wood did get the play, but not for another two years. By then Carson had suffered two severe strokes—one of them crippling—and great trauma over the work before it finally was produced and became a hit on Broadway.

Near the end of the summer of 1946, Carson gave *The Member of the Wedding* to Ann Watkins with instructions to find a Broadway producer. Then, once again she was caught up in dreams to go to Europe. All thoughts of Reeves returning to college were abandoned, for he, too, wanted more than anything else in the world to live in France. With her new Guggenheim money to launch them, along with early royalties from the book *The Member of the Wedding*, the two of them prepared to sail for Paris on the *Île de France* on November 22, 1946.

Arrangements tumbled pell-mell as Carson's emotions skittered from ebullience to trepidation. Amazed at the complexity of getting ready, she found the whole process of passports, visas, inoculations, packing and wondering what to pack, arrangements for housing—all beyond her ken. Reeves, as usual, took the lead where practicalities were concerned, pleased to have the opportunity of playing the cavalier.

They made trips to the dentist, contended with typhus and typhoid shots—to which they responded with fever, aches, and what Carson referred to as her grandstand act, fainting in public—and went on shopping sprees at grocery stores and delicatessens. They learned that food prices in postwar Paris were exorbitant and many foods were scarce, but they were told that they could carry into the country 240 pounds of foodstuffs between them. Carefully Reeves selected staples, cooking oils, dried and canned meats and fish, pickled tomatoes and okra, beets, artichoke relish, and other vegetables and fresh fruits which Carson's mother began putting up for them. Carson insisted, also, on taking aboard a jug or two of scuppernong wine, regardless of assurances that they were going to the wine capital of the world.

Most indecisive of all were they about their plans for prospective lodgings, although neither of them worried openly. One simply did not go to Paris without knowing where he was going to stay, a well-meaning friend confided to Marguerite, who already was bereft at the thought of her "children" leaving her once again and for what threatened to be an interminable time. Marguerite had had a "sinking spell" in early October when she first learned of their impending departure, but she had rallied and now assumed a brave and buoyant countenance.

More to please her mother than to alleviate her own fears, she said, Carson hastily sought out everyone she knew who had been to Paris since the war or had some remote connection there. Her friend George Davis promised to help, for he knew a number of people who had lived in Paris or were living there then. One of his acts of kindness was to introduce Carson to Ira and Edita Morris, both successful writers who had been established in France for many years. The Morrises were living temporarily that fall in New York City. Delighted by Carson, they assured George Davis that they would be in Paris themselves shortly and would personally look out for her. They frequently vacated their own château in the country for months at a time, and there was a possibility that Carson and Reeves might even stay in their home, Morris volunteered.

Carson also lunched with John Lackey Brown, whom she had met earlier as an editor with Houghton Mifflin, along with his charming French wife, Simone. Brown, now European editor for his publishing house, was correspondent for the Sunday edition of the New York *Times*, as well. He, too, would be back in Paris in a few weeks and promised to meet them at the station upon their arrival. He also would reserve for them a hotel room or apartment until they could choose for themselves more fitting quarters. Briefing them on Paris life, Brown warned them, however, that living conditions were still very difficult and that they must not expect the comforts and conveniences to which they were accustomed in the United States.

When Carson wrote to Newton Arvin on October 26, 1946, to apprise him of her latest flurry of activities—following a dearth of correspondence between them that had extended for many weeks—she told him how helpful people had been. She spoke of her friend Henri Cartier-Bresson, who had recently photographed her with George Davis, and visited in Nyack with her and her family. He told Carson that in Paris she must meet his sister Nicole, whom she would love, and that he was recommending her and Reeves to his family, whom he had asked to take them in until they might find permanent quarters elsewhere. If that anticipated hospitality should inadvertently not materialize, Cartier-Bresson urged Carson in his warm, breezy manner that she and Reeves should simply move in upon his good friend writer Claude Roy.

To appear at someone's door uninvited and walk in with luggage in tow, however, was not quite what Carson had in mind as a triumphant entry into Paris, although she had never in her entire life failed to do exactly what she wanted to do if it were physically possible. Later, she had no more qualms about descending uninvited upon the country estates of Elizabeth Bowen or Dame Edith Sitwell—although she always telephoned or telegraphed that she was en route—than she had had about her earlier calls upon Greta Garbo, Klaus and Erika Mann, and others when she first came to New York.

In her mind's eye now, Carson pictured a red carpet being stretched from the gangplank of the *Île de France* to the Hôtel Continental—or the Ritz—and on to Maxim's—while a lovely French child greeted her with an armful of fresh flowers and delivered in flawless English a proclamation of welcome on behalf of France, followed by the mayor's presentation of the keys to the city. She saw throngs of Frenchmen—and beautiful, voluptuous French ladies—kissing her on both cheeks, Left Bank Americans inviting her into their smoke-filled, aromatic, cognac-laden dens of creativity, and the French literary coterie led by André Malraux, François Mauriac, and Jean Paul Sartre seating her as guest of honor at their table at El Café Flore, greeting her intuitively as a kindred spirit. On the other hand, the naive, insecure side of Carson sometimes nudged aside such fantasies and prompted a self-portrait of her and Reeves sheepishly unrolling sleeping bags in Luxembourg Gardens under a cloak of dusk and anonymity.

The American good-bys were real enough. There were festive parties given by two of her most recent Yaddo cohorts, Leo Lerman and Marguerite Young, a near endless stream of visitors who had heard the news of their imminent journey and wanted to ascertain for themselves that it was true, a quiet luncheon with Elizabeth Ames in the city, and countless telephone calls and hurried letters to special friends who lived outside the New York area. Truman Capote, who had been Rita Smith's good friend since the "Miriam" days of 1944, and now was also Carson and Reeves's, appointed himself personal ambassador to help get the young couple off and stayed several days and nights in Nyack to help tend to last-minute details. "Our friends must be awfully glad to be rid of us—they've been so gay and helpful," Carson remarked to her next-door neighbor, Helena Clay.

On November 22, the day of departure, Capote, Marguerite Young, Carson's sister, and her mother accompanied the pair to the ship. To Miss Young, who liked Reeves and knew him well, he seemed to be "the happy troubadour come back to life."[36] "This is no ordinary bus ride," Reeves sang out exuberantly. "This is the bus that is taking us to Europe." Nor were Carson and Reeves "ordinary" passengers. The young author walked up the gangplank of the *Ile de France* wearing a bushy squirrel hat, lumber jacket, and blue jeans, looking every bit like a triumphant Daniel Boone emerging from the wilderness.

Six days later, the couple descended upon Paris, the lanky, twenty-nine-year-old author resembling a bewildered, nervous prep-school girl who had been launched on her great European tour without quite being *finished*, and squired by a handsome, adoring husband whom she treated as her "cavalier-savant."[37] According to Janet Flanner, "Carson burst like a tiny bottle of glass on Paris—melodramatic, a genius."[38] Indeed, literary Paris heralded Carson's coming, although somewhat short of the flourishing trappings of her imagination. Her arrival had been preceded earlier that year by the French translations of *The Heart Is a Lonely Hunter* and *Reflections in a Golden Eye*, with *The Ballad of the Sad Café* having just appeared in a French anthology. These works prompted literary Parisians —and many others who were discovering her for the first time—to recog-

nize her as one of America's foremost female writers, one who had dared
to expose sensitively and artistically the nerve endings of a South she both
loved and hated.[39]

John Brown met Carson and Reeves at the Gare Saint Lazare when
they arrived on the boat train and took them to the Hôtel Cayré on the
Boulevard Raspail on the Left Bank, where he had reserved a room for
them. As quickly as possible Brown arranged meetings for Carson with
several French publishers and other literary people who were anxious to
meet her: editor André Bay, at Stock, who later adapted *The Member
of the Wedding* for presentation in the theatre of the Alliance Française
on the Boulevard Raspail; Belgium critic René Lalou, of *Les Nouvelles
Littéraires*; Jean Blanzat, who had written the preface to the French
translation of *Reflections in a Golden Eye*, and was now at Grasset; and
translator Hélène Bokanowski, who later published an article on Carson
in *L'Arch* in May 1947. The impressionable young American writer was
given an enthusiastic welcome by those in the French publishing world,
who soon made everyone else in French letters aware that she was in
town.

A few days later, Carson and Reeves spent a week with the Cartier-
Bresson family in Sologne, and then took more permanent quarters at
the Hôtel de France et Choiseul on the Rue du Faubourg Saint Hônoré
near the Place Vendôme. It was a small, old hotel, formerly a convent,
with a lovely courtyard, old-fashioned rooms, and little attic apartments.
Here Kay Boyle, her husband, and six children—one of them Carson's
namesake, Faith Carson—also lived. Miss Boyle had secured for them a
charming three-room attic apartment, which Carson loved with its view
of the city, its ancient French furnishings, open fireplace, and wallpaper
of cabbage roses. Carson could not have been happier than she was,
living in such close proximity to Kay Boyle, whom she considered now
one of her dearest confidantes.[40] She also saw others she had admired
since her 7 Middagh Street days: Janet Flanner, Eleanor Clark, and
Richard Wright (who had been lionized by the French). Carson was
also quickly sought out and photographed by Louise Dahl-Wolfe, her
good friend from Frenchtown, New Jersey, an excellent professional
photographer who had taken pictures of her in Central Park in 1941 and
now was living in Paris. Reportedly much taken by Carson, too, was
Henri Cartier-Bresson's lovely sister Nicole, who went frequently with her
about the city. Carson never outgrew being impressed by beautiful women,
particularly those who loved or admired her inordinately.

Very quickly through John Brown, Kay Boyle, Janet Flanner (the
name *Genêt* opened "any literary door," said Carson), Ira and Edita
Morris, and Richard Wright, Carson and Reeves found themselves moving freely among the Paris and American literati. Gertrude Stein had

died following a cancer operation the summer before their arrival, and although Alice B. Toklas continued to live in the apartment she and Miss Stein had shared on the Rue Christine for many years—the second of their famous addresses—most of the Americans, no longer called expatriates, were scattered over the Left Bank of Montparnasse, the Latin Quarter, and the St. Germain-des-Prés. Here, James Baldwin, William Saroyan, James Thurber, William Burroughs, James Jones, Sherwood Anderson—who still came occasionally to Paris—David McDowell, a bright young Ph.D. candidate in comparative literature at the Sorbonne whom Tennessee Williams had recommended Carson meet, and a number of other American students and budding writers—all met Carson that winter or spring. A frequent visitor to the apartment at the France et Choiseul was Monica Sterling, correspondent for the *Atlantic Monthly*, and an author and biographer of Ouida, whom Carson met through Natalia Danesi Murray and Janet Flanner. (Miss Sterling's father was director of the English theatre in Paris, and through the two of them Carson was put in touch with many people she perhaps would not otherwise have met.)

A host of French authors and playwrights also took her into their hallowed circles. She met such writers as Madame Colette, André Malraux, François Mauriac, Jean Paul Sartre, Simone de Beauvoir, Claudet-Edmonde Magny, Albert Camus, David Rousset, André Gide, Jean Anouilh, Samuel Beckett, Jean Cocteau, Andrée Chedid, and the poets Saint-Jean Perse and the youthful Anne Marie Cazalis. Most of the French writers did not get to know Carson well. She was handicapped by not knowing their language; moreover, she made no attempt to learn it. Madame de Beauvoir remembered meeting Carson with Richard Wright at a party in her (Madame de Beauvoir's) apartment on Montparnasse, along with a great many other guests. Although Madame de Beauvoir said that she greatly admired Carson for *The Member of the Wedding*, their friendship never developed.[41] Nevertheless, Carson felt that she was well known and accepted by the French writers. And it was so—she had made an indelible mark upon Paris.

Writing to their friend Edwin Peacock in the spring of 1947, Reeves spoke somewhat modestly of Carson's success in France. He said that Carson had taken a vacation from her literary and social doings in Paris and had gone to the Italian Tyrol with friends. He had talked with her by telephone just the day before. She was well, eating heartily, and having a marvelous time. She would stay on another three weeks; then he would go and get her. They would remain in Paris for perhaps another year or two, Reeves told Peacock. Carson had made a hit with the literary set, including Sartre, he said, yet she was still modest in spite of her fame.

Reeves's statement that literary Paris had fallen at Carson's feet was an "inflated one and should be modified," said John Brown, who saw her and Reeves frequently in Paris: "Carson's contacts were in general limited to those French literary people who were interested in American literature and those who were able to speak English, since neither Carson nor Reeves could carry on an extended conversation in French. When she came to France, however, she had a high reputation there as an 'original' and had been recognized as an impeccable craftsman."[42]

As had been the case with countless other authors, Carson soon found it almost impossible to write in Paris. Nor did Reeves settle down to finding a job. In no way was life normal for them. There was too much exuberance in Paris to be taken in, to be lived, they felt. There simply was not enough time—enough of themselves, in fact—to do all that they wished. Reeves wrote Edwin Peacock that coming to Europe after the war was almost like being born anew. When he had been in England, France, Belgium, Luxembourg, and Germany before, his life had been totally unreal. He had known fear then, wondering when a German might come up from the other side of a hill and take his life. Although there was still abject poverty and misery among many of the people, he found it wonderful and exciting to be a part of the European scene once again. Reeves acknowledged, too, that he had hoped to be working by now, but that he kept missing opportunities and simply was not at the right place at the propitious moment. He had not given up trying to be hired by UNESCO or the United Nations, he told Peacock, and he hoped to have a firm offer soon. General Motors and American Aid to France had offered him a job, Reeves added, but he had declined because both required traveling and he did not want to leave Paris.

According to John Brown, however, Reeves doubtless was fantasizing regarding his job prospects: "Reeves and Carson both were given to daydreaming and the making of plans that had little basis in reality. Reeves had no background of education or experience to fit him for a job in the United Nations, though he might have been hired by UNESCO, then being set up in Paris, had he tried. They *talked* a great deal about Reeves's getting a job, but nothing much was ever done about it on the practical level."[43] Reeves would admit to no one that it rankled his manhood that he was spending money, but not contributing to the larder; yet his not working was a thorn between them that they both did their best not to embed more deeply.

To Reeves, neither God nor man could have created a more perfect place for anyone to live than Paris. The winter months were difficult for them both—rainy, cold, and, at times, depressing—but Carson's health in general was good, and with the atmosphere of spring, life became much more pleasurable. The people, the gardens, the parks, the architecture—

all took on a marvelous new hue. Together he and Carson explored the curio shops and bookstores along the Left Bank from the Rue des Saints-Pères to the Rue de Seine, bought cut flowers from the pushcarts, and watched the beautiful, full-bosomed Parisian women who moved sensuously among them. They sat in the sidewalk cafés along the Champs Élysées and never ceased to be amazed at the glaziers who went along the boulevard hawking window panes. They liked to walk through the flea markets and sometimes strolled for hours through the Marché aux Puces. They marveled, too, at the oystermen, the seafood women, the pretty prostitutes, the genuinely nice people they met in bars with whom they freely exchanged drinks and pleasantries, the Seine fishermen who seemed to sit for hours along the quays without a catch—as though part of the landscape—the Seine itself with its dozens of bridges, and the indescribable streets of Paris. Reeves wrote Peacock that he had walked every street in Paris and that there was not a boring one in the lot. He added that he did not even mind the insane traffic, since he himself never drove. In Paris in 1946–47, the motorist was always right. Cars passed either on the right or the left, with traffic entering from the side streets having the right of way over the mainline traffic. Reeves loved to play the game of getting across the street safely, although Carson often got panicky.

She frequently went out without Reeves, either by herself or in the company of others. During the daytime she liked to sit in the sidewalk cafés and watch the other patrons, the sidewalk artists, and the subjects of their art. She met the surrealist André Breton, who held forth regularly at Des Deux-Magots on St. Germain, next door to her favorite café of them all, De Flore, where the tenets of French existentialism were still being expounded by Sartre and Madame de Beauvoir, and where Camus stopped in frequently. Another arena of existentialism was Café Le Tabou, but for Carson and Reeves, it lacked the electric atmosphere of De Flore. Pablo Picasso, Henri Matisse, and André Minaux also were painting in Paris in 1947, and occasionally Carson and Reeves found themselves within hand-shaking or elbow-bending range of these august artists. Each time they withdrew, however, without seeking proper introductions.

The cafés stayed open until 2:00 A.M. and some bistros all night. The night life in "The City of Light" was fascinating to Carson, who enjoyed the cafés far more than she did private parties among the more elite sybarites. She usually preferred the cafés on the Left Bank, although on one occasion she asked Reeves to take her to the Casbah and then to Lido, a Champs Élysées cabaret. Edith Piaf was singing there that winter, and later Marian Anderson came, two great singers Carson admired immensely and whom she would not have dreamed of missing. The Left Bank district of Montparnasse had been Hemingway's realm, and although he was never in Paris when Carson and Reeves were there, they sometimes went into his favorite retreat, La Closerie des Lilas on Rue Montaigne, and then to nearby La Coupole. Invariably they heard snatches of reminiscences about "Papa" Hemingway by the many Frenchmen and Americans who spoke of him still as though he had just dropped in yesterday. Often they were among the last to leave the Left Bank cafés, and before going home to the France et Choiseul, would stop at Harry's Bar up the street for a nightcap.

The fact that prices were high for dining out deterred Carson and Reeves very little. At Maxim's a bottle of champagne alone cost fifteen hundred francs, and an average meal without wine (which during the early months of their stay would have been inconceivable) in only a good, medium-priced restaurant came close to six hundred to eight hundred francs apiece. In the winter of 1946–47, a thousand francs amounted to about eight or nine dollars, but Reeves always dealt with the money-changers, and Carson had no idea what anything cost.

Theirs was a euphoric existence in the spring of 1947 before Carson left for the Italian Tyrol—on a skiing expedition, she called it—excited by the prospects of being high in the mountains and in deep snow. She was going with a Russian couple, Monique Kotlenko and her husband, refugees living in Paris, both doctors, and one of them also a writer. Carson admitted to a crush on the woman and was thrilled to be included in their vacation plans. As usual, she had no second thoughts about leaving Reeves to his own resources.

Carson would have said "Oui" to almost anything suggested to her that spring. One afternoon someone very formally telephoned her and made what seemed a simple request: that he be allowed to call upon her that afternoon. Handicapped by the language—but not very, since she usually smiled and said "Oui" to everything she was asked or offered when Reeves was not at hand to translate through his aberrations of the French language—Carson was aware that she was consenting to something, but had no idea just what. Context or demonstration usually filled her in on necessary details. Had it been an offer of a drink, an invitation to dinner or the theatre, she would have recognized the gestures and responded accordingly. But this time she was baffled. As she told someone later, "It is much easier in any language to say *yes*, rather than *no*." At any rate, it gave her pleasure when the young man visited her that afternoon, shook her hand cordially upon leaving, and said enthusiastically, "Oh, bon, Madame—merci, merci." This pantomine was repeated on two later occasions, yet still without further enlightenment on Carson's part except that she recognized that the titles of her novels translated into French had been mentioned.

A few days later, Kay Boyle reportedly ascended to Carson's apartment with a printed card in hand and asked her what she was up to "now." Carson tried to recall what new indiscretion she might have committed, then looked at the card: "The Sorbonne of The University of Paris is honored to announce that Carson McCullers, American novelist, will speak on the comparison of American and French literature at the LaSalle Richelieu . . ." Horror would be an understatement of Carson's immediate response. Her platform debut was to be three days hence. Since she knew practically nothing about contemporary French literature, let alone the language in which she would have to speak, she was appalled at how such a dilemma could have happened. Surely it was all a dreadful mistake. Indeed it was, but it was not difficult for anyone who knew Carson to imagine her allowing it to happen. It was only then that she remembered the little man with the attaché case who had pumped her hand so heartily as he backed out of her apartment with bows and "mercis."

In desperation, Carson tried to think of a way out short of leaving the country. If she were not ill because of it, there was no doubt that she could arrange to be. Finally she called her doctor at the American Hospital, who only laughed. Then she turned to her friend John Brown and pleaded seriously for help. Brown laughed, too, but after discarding rapidly the alternates, which included Carson's doing the can-can—she volunteered to do it, but acknowledged that she was no more adept at dancing than she was with the French language—he proposed a solution. He would ask his friend Professor René Lalou to lecture on French literature, and Brown, himself a professor of comparative literature, would speak on American literature. A stage craftsman as well, Brown visualized immediately the scene: the three of them would sit onstage, with Carson in the middle listening intently and "doing her best to look intelligent," while the two men beside her delivered *her* lecture.[44]

But Carson, too, should perform, Brown concluded. Perhaps she could be like Robert Browning, who once chose to speak in trochees, a metrical form the poet used only in a very special love poem for his wife; or Dante, who painted for Beatrice a picture of an angel instead of writing another sonnet; or Raphael, who wrote a "century of sonnets" for his beloved in lieu of painting another madonna. There was the answer: Carson, the prose fictionist, would move outside her medium, too, for the people she loved, and like Salene—who showed the other side of her moon only to Endymion—recite *in English* one of her poems. It was a good ruse, and it worked.

Something else Carson could hardly wait to do that spring was to go with Reeves to an old-fashioned one-ring circus, the pride of Paris. They were both enchanted as they watched the greatest clown in all France, Francesco Fratellini, the star of the Cirque Médrano. Another night they went to Paris' other great circus, D'Hiver. Here, Zavatta was featured, a clown younger than Fratellini and thoroughly delightful.

The French people were wonderful circus enthusiasts, and Carson had been struck by the close-knit families who made circusing not only an art but also an enviable way of life. These were not George Davis' freaks of his photograph collection or the Pin Head and Rubber Man troupe of the Chattahoochee Valley Fair who had fascinated but repelled Carson as a frightened nine-year-old. These were the true artists—the aerialists, animal trainers, and clowns that only the Old World produced.

Carson was happy in the spring as she walked the streets of Paris thinking of Proust and Baudelaire, sitting alone in the sidewalk cafés, watching, dreaming, drinking. Life was good, but there were problems, for both her and Reeves, that had been further stimulated by their life together in France. They were both drinking more heavily than ever before. Just as Jack London had attributed many of his ills—and other peoples'—to "John Barleycorn," many people in Paris attributed to "Jacques Cognac" most of Carson and Reeves's problems. In retrospect, many who knew Carson in Paris felt that it was a great shame, a pity, in fact, that she had ever come to France. In the strange environment of postwar Paris, lacking discipline, inordinately vain, ignorant of practicalities, the value of money, or the relative exchange between American dollars and French francs, she found it both inviting and inevitable that she abandon restraints.

Going to bed with Reeves, for instance, had not interested her in some time, and after nights and nights of heavy drinking, neither of them was awakened sexually by the other. Chronically, however, Carson had misgivings and felt that she was not treating Reeves well. In Paris one evening she found herself away from the crowd and having dinner alone with Eleanor Clark. According to Miss Clark, "Carson told me about her hatred of sexual intercourse with men, including Reeves, yet she didn't like Reeves sleeping with cheap women; she wished he would sleep with a nice girl like me."[45] To Eleanor Clark, it was "really quite a fantastic suggestion." She said that she had always found Reeves quite appealing, "but totally uninteresting in other ways."

In April when Carson was in Italy, she stopped in Rome after her skiing expedition with the Kotlenkos to visit Natalia Danesi Murray, her Italian friend she had met through Janet Flanner in New York in 1941. Mrs. Murray was an executive with Arnoldo Mondadori Editore, which had just published the Italian translation of *Reflections in a Golden Eye*. "Carson was somehow different that spring," said Mrs. Murray. "I will never forget that visit. I gave her a party because *Reflections in a Golden Eye* had just been translated into Italian and everyone wanted to meet Carson. She was welcomed by Alberto Moravia, Irene Brin, her translator, Gianna Manzini, and all of the major literary figures and newspapermen of Rome at the time. She was drinking very heavily then and was rather short tempered, but everyone loved her anyway and said that she must come back when she could stay."[46]

Mrs. Murray's favorite recollection, however, of Carson's visit to Rome that spring was an excursion to her tailor to order for Carson a pants suit:

> I had this marvelous tailor, Ciro Giuliano, who had made me a beautifully tailored pants suit. He was a great tailor in Rome for men's fashions. When Carson saw my suit she said that she must have one, too. So I said, "Come with me and we'll speak to Mr. Guiliano." At that moment, Carson was wearing what she had come down in from the mountains—her famous old blue coat that I used to see her wear in New York—rather like a sailor's navy jacket—and she had on boots that looked absolutely awful (certainly not those marvelous snow boots that most people wear when they have been in the mountains), and a funny little blue knitted cap that she liked to wear, with a visor, like a military working cap. And, of course, she had that stringy hair coming out from under it. Well, the weather was beautiful—almost like a sunny, summer day—and we went together into this very fashionable tailor shop; or rather, I walked ahead, because I knew the way, and Carson followed rather slowly behind. My tailor turned and looked when he saw this creature behind me and suggested that I was being followed by a beggar, or by someone who might rob me. But I responded, "Oh, please, as you can see, she is a great American writer, and I want you to make her the most beautiful pants suit in the city."
>
> "How soon do you want it?" he asked, hardly able to believe what he saw, and Carson responded, "Immediately." I explained that she was leaving the city very soon, and he agreed to have it in forty-eight hours—which he would never ordinarily have done. We went back the very next day for her fitting, and she brought the Italian edition of *Reflections in a Golden Eye* with a special inscription in it for him. Well, never before had he made a suit in such a hurry, but he did for Carson McCullers, and it was the most beautiful pants suit she ever had in her entire life. Carson loved it. She wore it to my party, and she wore it the whole time until she left.[47]

The spring of 1947 was Carson's last season of good health for the rest of her life. When she returned from Italy, she and Reeves moved from the France et Choiseul to a little country château belonging to Ira and Edita Morris in Rosay-en-Brie, sixty kilometers east of Paris, while the Morrises were to be in India for the summer. According to Janet Flanner, there had been some question as to whether Kay Boyle and her family would move into the house, or Carson and Reeves, and in the process, Carson and Miss Boyle's friendship waned.[48] Carson's health worsened as she and Reeves continued to drink heavily. For Reeves, who had been alcoholic in the early 1940s, the problem was an acute one. The trouble for them both, thought observers, stemmed from their having switched from bourbon to brandy, which they found to be much cheaper in France. Whereas Carson and Reeves *each* could manage to drink a bottle of bourbon daily, almost no one, even the French, could manage a daily bottle of brandy, which has a very different and often devastating effect on its imbibers. Carson and Reeves were attempting the near impossible, said one friend, and *almost* getting away with it.

The self-destructive aspect of Carson's nature became more apparent that summer to those who knew her in Paris than even to those who had seen that side of her during her unhappy days in New York City in 1941. Carson's new acquaintances in Paris were gravely upset by what they thought of as sadomasochistic tendencies and an irascible, aggressive personality. She and Reeves bickered frequently over trivialities and became violent over petty irritations that someone else would have tossed off with a glass of wine. Arguments often ended with Reeves storming out into the night while Carson cried and berated him in an alcoholic harangue.

By the time they sat down to an evening meal now, they had consumed so much liquor that dinner wines were out, and by midsummer they were doing very little entertaining at home. Also, people stopped entertaining for them. Natalia Murray, who had enjoyed hostessing Carson in Rome that spring, found that by summer when she saw her in Paris Carson was a difficult person to be around for any period of time. She remembered Carson's inviting her to dinner one night at the château belonging to the Morrises, but finally having to go away hungry:

> It was something of a riot that evening, since we never did eat.
> We were very convivial, at any rate. I remember Carson's saying that
> she wasn't drinking at the time, but, of course, she seemed to be
> drinking it through a funnel. She said that it was tea. Nine o'clock
> came, then nine-thirty, and ten, and everyone was very hungry—for
> there were other guests, also—and finally the cook came out of the
> kitchen to join us, and we discovered that she was drunk, too, and
> that the dinner had been burned to pieces.[49]

It was in August 1947 in the little château of the Morrises that Carson suffered what doctors later called her second stroke. As she explained it to Richard Wright, who came to see her in the hospital, she was at home alone while Reeves had gone to be treated at the American Hospital in Neuilly for an infected leg.[50] Carson told Wright that she had awakened in the middle of the night, felt parched and thirsty, and got out of bed to get a glass of water. After moving only several steps into the room, she fell to the floor in what seemed to be a paralyzed condition. Not once did she lose consciousness, but for eight hours she lay alone on the floor, terrified and unable to move or call out for help. Finally Reeves returned and found her. For Carson, most of the remaining months in Paris were a nightmare.[51]

She lost the lateral vision of her right eye, the whole right side of her face was numb, and the left side of her body was partially paralyzed. After weeks in the hospital, she was released with the injunction that she must drink no more. Such directives fell upon deaf ears, however, or a body incapable of responding. At best, she shifted to beer in the afternoon—as many beers as she wanted—and then to cognac for the cocktail hour and the evening. A few weeks later, in early November, she was seriously ill and in the American Hospital once more. By this time she and Reeves had leased Richard Wright's apartment when Wright moved his family to a luxurious seven-room apartment on Rue Monsieur-le-Prince. She wrote to friends that a Madame Lieutier had graciously lent them some silver flatware, linens, and the use of her maid for a few weeks. Carson's stroke in August had not made her think seriously about returning to the United States and the sanctuary of home with her mother; instead, she was determined to be close to her doctors at the American Hospital and to settle down and work when she was better. They signed a six-month lease for Wright's apartment and intended to stay on through the winter, at least.

Part of Carson's illness was perhaps unfairly attributed to the creative impasse she was then experiencing. Although she was in Paris on a second Guggenheim Fellowship, the year had not been a creatively productive one. Only the short story, "The Sojourner," published in May of 1950 in *Mademoiselle*, was written against a backdrop of Paris, but it was a memory story, largely, involving the South and New York City, with much of it taking place in an airplane as the protagonist flew between Paris and America. In no way was "The Sojourner" directly connected with her life in France, nor was it written there, although it doubtless would not have evolved had it not been for her unique experience abroad. Carson hoped later that she might be able to renew her Guggenheim Fellowship, for she rationalized that she had been unable to produce that year because of her illnesses and strokes. Her third application, however, was turned down.

Besides the fact that Carson drank excessively and did not take good care of herself physically, another factor that may have contributed to her various illnesses was her distress over what had happened to her play *The Member of the Wedding*. It was a good play. Williams himself had told her so. But Ann Watkins wrote Carson that she had been unable to find a producer for it in its present form. Finally the Theatre Guild agreed to produce it, said Miss Watkins, if Carson would consent to letting an experienced playwright collaborate and revise the script. In a moment of weakness, she agreed and signed a contract with Greer Johnson, who had been recommended to be her cowriter.

Unfortunately, Carson was grossly disappointed when she finally read the revised script during the fall of 1947. She wrote to friends that she liked nothing about the new manuscript, could in no way see it as an improvement over her own singular efforts, and acknowledged that she should never have consented to a collaborator in the first place since no one knew better than she how closed-minded she usually was to suggestions for revisions of any kind on her manuscripts, once completed. Coincidental with her reading of the Johnson script, Carson was stricken with a serious kidney infection. The next day she suffered a third stroke. Her doctors concluded that several severe vascular spasms had resulted in a hemorrhage to the right side of the brain, thus closing off the circulation and causing varying degrees of paralysis to a large portion of the left side of the body. The major contributing cause was a damaged rheumatic heart that had not been diagnosed during Carson's early years in Columbus.[52]

For three weeks following Carson's latest stroke she lay in bed in the American Hospital while her chief physician, Dr. Robert Myers, worked ceaselessly to relieve the pain and reduce the paralysis. When it was considered safe for her to travel, the medical decision was made to transfer her to the Neurological Institute at Columbia Presbyterian Hospital in New York City. Reeves, too, was seriously ill. On December 1, Marguerite Smith met the plane at New York International Airport with two ambulances which whisked the invalids away before the customs officials could even look under the covers. "These are my children coming home to their mother," Marguerite cried out to no one in particular as one stretcher was borne down the steps carrying Carson, and then another one bearing Reeves, who suffered from delirium tremens and had had a convulsive attack on the plane en route home.

Had Marguerite herself been in Paris all year, she could not have shielded her children from the "ungentle winds" which had boiled up this time to hurricane velocity, but she would have tried. To Marguerite, her children could do no wrong. Some observers over the years who knew Carson, Reeves, and her mother expressed the thought that if Marguerite had turned her daughter over her knee as a child and spanked her a few times and had otherwise been less permissive—and if Reeves had done something equally fitting—Carson and Reeves might have been spared many of the physical and psychic ills that ensued. Doubtless far more accurate and important in any final analysis, however, is the opinion of Carson's cousin Jordan Massee, whose understanding of Carson and her mother during the period that Marguerite Smith was alive was second to no one's. According to Massee:

> Second only to being born Carson, her greatest gift from the gods was having Bebe [Marguerite] for a mother. Without that particular mother she would never have survived. Think how precarious at best was the continued existence of that strange, fragile spirit that the world knows as Carson McCullers. We speak jokingly of Carson being indestructible, and so at times she seemed to all of us who stood between her and the outside world, against which she had no other protection. Hers was a vulnerability without defenses against the forces of destruction that singled her out or to which she was especially susceptible. There was iron in Carson, but it was all within; she had none of that protective coating that the rest of us acquire and wear like a suit of armor.
>
> How can people say that Bebe was overly protective when Carson's existence was utterly dependent on protective assistance, which when it was not available from Bebe was required of other people. It is a dependence not uncharacteristic of all physically handicapped children, and all genius aspires and seeks by any means to realize its fulfillment.
>
> The same people who insist on the extremely delicate nature of Carson's health and personality, to the point of deeming it freakish, then turn around and criticize Bebe as though she were the mother of a "normal," robust child. Without an acceptance of Carson's dependence there can be no understanding of her relationships to Bebe and others. I do not say we must completely *understand* the dependence. . . . Carson's own view of her mother was inconsistent, as would be expected. . . . In any final analysis of the relationship of Carson to her mother, one must realize that Bebe was a remarkable woman who produced and sustained a genius, allowing that genius to flower in its own particular fashion, and in response to its own nature, not, as is usually the case with the mothers of great artists, as a fulfillment of their own creative frustrations.[53]

Chapter Ten

GLOOM AND ELATION:
NYACK AND BROADWAY, 1948 – 50

The winter and spring of 1947–48 were the most abysmally depressing months of Carson's life. She remained at the Neurological Institute of Columbia Presbyterian Hospital for most of December, then returned home to Nyack just before Christmas for weeks more of bed rest. In the meantime, Reeves, in his own debilitated state, was gradually weaned from alcohol and tenderly nursed at home by Marguerite as though he were her own son. Somehow, Reeves was responsible, she felt, for her daughter's dreadful condition now, but unless Carson herself indicted him, Marguerite, too, would remain loyal. Gradually Reeves improved and by mid-January was out looking for a job, but not until he had suffered two more frightening convulsive attacks before Christmas.

Marguerite did her best to promote holiday cheer and to draw her little family protectively around her on Christmas Day. Dozens of gaily wrapped presents, telephone calls from well wishers, and greeting cards helped offset the gloom of sadness and illness. Several of Carson's close friends were allowed brief visits, but the doctors—and Marguerite—still considered their patient dangerously ill and insisted that she be kept as quiet as possible. Any compassionate expression of love or sympathy provoked Carson to tears. Never had Marguerite seen her daughter looking so wretched or touched by such sorrow. Marguerite regretted that Brother-Man and his wife could not be with them, too. Rita Smith had been living in the city to be close to her work, but she found herself commuting to Nyack almost daily to help at home and relieve her mother of some of the cooking and caring for her two invalid siblings.

New literary recognition came Carson's way in December, but what normally would have been received by her with jubilation and great personal satisfaction this time brought only a faint smile. On December 17, *Quick,* a weekly news magazine, announced that Carson McCullers was one of the six "best postwar writers in America." She had been selected by Edward Weeks of the *Atlantic Monthly,* David Dempsy of the New

York *Times,* John K. Hutchens of the New York *Herald Tribune,* Joseph Henry Jackson of the San Francisco *Chronicle,* and Frederick Babcock of the Chicago *Tribune.*[1] On Christmas Day, the New York papers announced still another award. Carson was cited by *Mademoiselle* magazine for "outstanding achievement by a young person in literature for the year 1947." She was officially recognized in the January 1948 issue by Betsy Talbot Blackwell, editor in chief, who presented the *Mademoiselle* Annual Merit Award to the ten most deserving young women in the United States in all areas and genres of service and talent during the current year.[2]

In spite of Reeves's pride over his wife's accomplishments, it was recognition such as this that contributed to their tenuous marital relationship. To be the husband of Carson McCullers was sometimes devastating to his sense of manhood, a situation he had feared since their first days together in New York City. It had become apparent even earlier, in fact, in North Carolina when he wrote Vincent Adams that his wife was writing a novel that could well be a best seller, and that he would have to shelve his own literary aspirations for a while.[3] Eventually they had both known that it would be she who would always do the writing in the family, who would win acclaim with her novels, stories, poetry, nonfiction, and now, even plays. Reeves, the writer, was dead—and had been—once he consented to move into the shadow of his wife's genius. Now, parched and aching in his own thirst to be somebody, feeling acutely his fallen state, faking often, exuding bravado and a charm that frequently smacked of insincerity, he struggled to survive on his own terms. The tragedy of Reeves's life, and the pity of it, was what he had feared in the spring of 1945 upon his remarriage to Carson, in a sense, his capitulation, and then his compulsory disability discharge from the United States Army—that he could not always be a leader of men, a professional soldier, the head of a household, a man's man.

Therein lay another problem, too. Not strongly identified in his own sexuality—a condition which many of Reeves and Carson's friends increasingly recognized in the last ten or twelve years of his life—having sexual problems himself which he could not resolve, Reeves was incapable of coping with his wife's sexual inclinations or of helping her to become more heterosexually oriented. Carson was completely open to her friends about her tremendous enjoyment in being physically close to attractive women. She was as frank and open about this aspect of her nature as a child would be in choosing which toy he most wanted to play with. She was always more physically attracted to women than to men.

Carson wanted and needed warmth and tenderness. It could simply be the warmth of a touch, either a man's or a woman's—and she had to be touching always, sometimes to the disquietude of her female companions—whether it was the brush of a hand, the pat of a knee, an embrace

on the cheek, or eyes communicating a closeness that denied actual
physical touching, yet mirrored in one's pupils the exchange of souls.
She always looked intently at a person she loved—and she loved many
people—her eyes taking in every plane of the face, each line and texture
of nose, cheekbone, brow, ear lobe, lips, teeth. The eyes, above all, she
gazed fixedly into, and then at the hands, which she felt the good Lord
had made especially for her. She observed the length and shape of the
fingers, their curves in repose, the character of the nails, the smooth cuti-
cles, the veins that made small ridges upon the back of the hand and
seemed to swell from wrist to finger joints. She liked looking at rings on
fingers, too. They enhanced the beauty of the hand; there was a quality
of oneness about them which implied reciprocity. She herself usually
wore a plain wide wedding band which Reeves had given her, and then
later, a jade and emerald ring which was a gift from Tennessee Williams,
a ring that had once belonged to his sister, Rose. She liked to clasp a
person's hand also. It somehow made it seem more hers. Even better, she
liked for her hand to be tucked into someone else's. She loved being
snuggled up to, held, kissed, stroked on the forehead and through the
hair, caressed on the neck, the arms. She wanted as much closeness as
she could get from a beloved, but consummation rarely was a part of it—
would, in fact, have threatened her serenity and security. With homosexual men, she was always more at ease for they posed no threat to her
sexuality, nor she to theirs. Moreover, they knew how to treat a woman,
how to give her pleasure, how to make her feel womanly, for they could
identify with her.

James Joyce could no more have created Molly Bloom in all her
womanly fullness than Carson could have created Biff Brannon, Miss
Amelia, or Captain Penderton had the authors not had the capacity to
love bisexually, had Carson not also been a woman's woman. Her brother
once commented that he thought of his sister as being *asexual*.[4] But
Lamar, Jr., had no way of fully understanding the sexuality of his sister's
nature. To anyone who knew Carson well outside of the South, she was
a highly sensuous, sexual person. Not to be interested in sex with men—
even though there were sexual experiences, of course—was as much a part
of her physiological make-up as having two legs, arms, a heart, and a
brain. Moreover, Carson's internal chemistry was the fulcrum of her
existence as an artist, her creative hallmark, the product of inner conflicts.
She would have no more consented to a psychiatrist's attempting to
change her psychic chemistry than to a surgeon's changing her sex.

Carson's despair over her ill health and her situation with Reeves
began to set in more deeply in mid-January 1948, when the worst blizzard
New York had experienced in sixty years struck the area. As soon as roads
were passable, Reeves left Nyack and went into the city to look for a job.

He needed to work, to stop drinking completely, to regain his sense of manhood and prove that he could sustain himself as a personality independent of his wife. For two months he went intermittently into the city, but the longer he went without work, the more impossible seemed his chances for a compatible and halfway normal life with Carson again. By the spring they were heavily in debt at home, and there still were bills incurred in Paris to be paid. At last they decided to separate, Reeves feeling less and less welcome under his mother-in-law's roof and increasingly estranged from his wife. The end of February he moved into New York City and took an apartment.

Positions to which Reeves was inclined were scarce, and until May he did not work—had not worked, in fact, since the war—had been on no one's payroll but the government's since his re-enlistment in the Army in 1942. His only income since his discharge in 1946, except for Carson's money—which he had always freely spent—had been his disability pension. He was determined now not to go back into credit work, either in the office or as an investigator. The idea of photography appealed to him, for he had played with it as a hobby while in high school in Wetumpka, Alabama. Reeves had resented the requirement that his class travel to Montgomery to have senior pictures taken for the yearbook; therefore, he had photographed himself, then developed and printed the pictures. His was the only homemade picture in the lot, but it was good. Even as a youngster, Reeves could not be pushed. He would do what he pleased, and to *hell* with the consequences. His attitude toward work was the same. Deciding to look into professional photography that spring, Reeves was referred to someone in the New York Police Department Photo Lab, and then to a photo school, but no one wanted to hire him with his limited experience or seemed willing to train him.[5]

In the meantime for Carson the winter days crawled unbroken one into another, the snowy landscape of the village of Nyack and the Hudson River with its chunks of ice floes no longer a pretty Currier and Ives print on which she looked out daily, but a depressing *mise en scène*. She had succeeded in detaching herself completely from the routine of the household, finding a kind of morbid satisfaction in her withdrawal into her "inner room," broken psychically as well as physically by her cerebral vascular accident and living as though the sword of Damocles hung above her head. Terrified that she might experience still another severe stroke and suffer alone as she had in Paris, Carson existed from day to day almost unaware, not daring to hope for a tomorrow less dismal than the day before.

One reason for Carson's depression was what she decided later was the mistaken notion that she was in love with her doctor in Paris, Robert Myers. He had finally written her a personal note some six weeks after she left Paris; in the meantime, she suffered woefully in her role as un-requited lover. On Valentine's Day, however, she received a letter from Tennessee Williams telling her that he had met Myers and did not care for him one bit. Immediately Carson decided that her infatuation was but a by-product of her own terrible physical condition, and that it was absurd for her to continue pining. Williams was in Naples when he wrote. She told him now that she imagined their swimming together in the Mediterranean and that he played the lead in her fantasy life. Were it not for that, she might go beserk, she said. Nyack was just emerging from a three-week blizzard, and her doctor and friend William Mayer had been unable to visit her. He would be able to come that afternoon, however; surely the playwright's letter, and now, Mayer's visit, were good omens, but her pain, she admitted, was devastating. She was seldom free from it.[6]

In a letter to Paul Bigelow dated February 18, 1948, Williams wrote from Rome:

> Carson and I are exchanging letters by almost every post between the continents. She says she is "unable to eat or sleep" and is in pain. She had two unhappy loves in Europe—neither consummated, I take it— and Reeves caused her a great deal of anguish with what she says was deliberate and cunning persecution. I am relieved to learn, from her last letter, that he is now living in New York City and that she rarely sees him. One must not accept too literally Carson's account of things now. She is in a state of highly inflamed sensibilities. Reeves is also a sick person and a very painfully maladjusted one who needs help, too. When Carson is better she hopes to join me in Europe and I am also hoping that this could be accomplished. My life is empty except for the "trapeze of flesh" as Crane called it, and it might do me good to have to devote myself to someone who needed and deserved so much care. On the other hand, I wonder if I would be good for her, or would the irregularities of my life and nature—which I know I would not give up—add to her unhappiness? I have talked this over with her in my latest letter. Of course it is very questionable whether she will be able to travel any time soon.

Another source of her wretchedness was the further disposition of her play, *The Member of the Wedding*. Carson's collaborator, Greer Johnson, was now threatening to sue her since she had refused to allow the Theatre Guild to go ahead with the production of their joint script.[7] Carson explained her dilemma to a new friend, a young psychiatrist she had recently begun to correspond with, but had not yet met in person.[8] She said that she was so frightened after hearing from Johnson's three lawyers that she childishly pulled the sheet over her head and wailed, certain that the prison wagon would scream up any minute to take her away. She told her new friend that the Theatre Guild was on her side, however, and had called in its own lawyer, who assured the Guild that Johnson had insufficient grounds for his suit. Carson acknowledged then that signing her name to certain documents in good faith had been her weakness for many years and had gotten her into more trouble than anything else in her life.

Carson's friendship with the young psychiatrist became an important psychic perch on which she rested and derived solace for the next two difficult years. Sparking their relationship was a fan letter from the doctor similar to the one she had received two years earlier from Tennessee Williams, which had launched their unique friendship and love. The letter arrived at a particularly fortuitous moment, for if Carson ever needed esteem, reassurance, and appreciation, it was during the spring of 1948.

Her new admirer was an intern at the Medical College of Virginia in Richmond. He had been well acquainted with Carson's works for years, he assured her, ever since one of his professors, Dr. Hervey M. Cleckley, had recommended that his students at the University of Georgia Medical School not expect to glean all of their psychology from the classroom, textbooks, and laboratory, but should read also the fiction of some of the world's greatest authors. Cleckley had recommended especially a fellow Southerner, Carson McCullers. Although he did not know Carson personally, he knew through her fiction that she spoke the truth and had deep, intuitive insight into the so-called aberrant relationships and needs of men and women.

What provoked the young man's accolades to Carson at this particular time was a letter she wrote to the editor of *Life* magazine. Carson thanked the editor for presenting a rare and sensitive portrait of Tennessee Williams, who was not only an artist and genius, but also one of the most wholly beautiful human beings she had ever known.[9] The feature article to which she referred (*Life*, February 16, 1948) was Lincoln Barnett's "Tennessee Williams: A dreamy young man with an unconquerable compulsion to write finds himself at 33 the most important new playwright in U.S. theater." Barnett had captured Williams' life and success, particularly as marked now by A *Streetcar Named Desire*, which had opened on Broadway December 3, 1947, and was still playing to large, enthusiastic audiences. Talk abounded in theatre circles that a Pulitzer prize for its young playwright was imminent.

The doctor saw Carson's letter in *Life* and immediately wrote to tell her that he appreciated her comments on Tennessee Williams and that he loved and respected *her* work also. He thought that Williams and she were akin in their compassionate treatment of psychic disorders and fights for survival by the sensitive souls who were threatened on all sides—as was Blanche in A *Streetcar Named Desire*—by a crass society and the Stanley Kowalskis of the world.

Coming when it did from someone of such apparent depth and sensitivity, Carson likened her new friend's letter to a handclasp in the dark. On March 9, she responded with a special delivery letter of her own. Candidly she told him of her many months of illness, her collapse in Paris, and her present despair. She said that for months she felt like a broken doll that a spoiled child had cast into a closet, but that now she had been gently lifted from the darkness by his wonderful and illuminating letter. In fact, just being noticed and hearing from someone who beautifully expressed his belief in her as an artist made her feel better immediately. She would send his letter along to Tennessee Williams, she said, who would find it enormously pleasing too, because of the things that had been said about both of them. But would he please write her another letter to replace it and tell her more about himself, she pleaded. Carson also recounted to the doctor much of her Nantucket summer with Williams, whom she likened to a much-loved brother, and sometimes, even a mother, she added.

Williams, too, responded to Carson's letter in *Life*. The clipping had been sent to him by a friend, Paul Moore. Williams wrote Carson from Rome that he was much touched by her tribute. He also sent new accolades her way: "For three nights last week I read *The Ballad of the Sad Café* and they were the loveliest nights I have had in Europe. The story of Miss Amelia and the hunchback is in my opinion the most beautiful story in all American fiction."[10] It was Williams' first reading of *The Ballad of the Sad Café*, which had been published in *Harper's Bazaar* back in 1943 but did not come out in hardback in a collection of her own until 1951. Carson had sent the story to him when he mentioned that he had never read it.

Then followed almost a month during which Carson wrote no more letters to Tennessee Williams, her psychiatrist friend, or to anyone. Both Williams and the young doctor had written her, but she could not answer. A few days after her initial letter, in a temporary fit of melancholy —as she called it later—Carson was hospitalized at the Payne Whitney Psychiatric Clinic in Manhattan. She told her new friend that she had slashed her left wrist and been committed to the psychiatric clinic for her own protection and for treatment. Fearful of not doing the right thing, Marguerite had reluctantly agreed with her daughter's medical doctor's decision that she should be hospitalized. Carson herself was in no condition to prove that some other course of action might have been more prudent, nor was Reeves on hand to consult or help make the decision.

For three weeks Carson remained at Payne Whitney. Never before had she felt such utter helplessness and abandonment. Perhaps worst of all, she acknowledged, was the feeling that her mother had used trickery in effecting her confinement. Nothing seemed more devastating to her than that. Encapsuled, it seemed, in a vacuum, unable to try to help herself or to read or write undisturbed, allowed no veil of privacy, she felt stripped bare, defenseless, exposed to the marrow. She wrote her psychiatrist friend later that she knew exactly how Franz Kafka must have felt in his suffering; but even worse, she added, was that she lacked his hope of ultimate redemption.

Knowing the misery her daughter was experiencing, grieved by her own part in it, and fearful that permanent psychic damage might result from Carson's incarceration, Marguerite urged Carson's friend, Dr. William Mayer—who was not on the case, but had been what Carson considered her protective angel for ten years—to help get her out. Together they decided that it might be more injurious than healing for Carson to be hospitalized in such a place any longer. When the doctors at Payne Whitney would not authorize Carson's dismissal, Marguerite took her home anyway.

Hurt and embittered, Carson sought solace again in her new psychiatrist friend and tried to speculate what it must be like to be in his profession. It seemed ironic to her that she had railed against psychiatry in the form to which she had been exposed to it at the clinic, yet she loved and respected William Mayer, whom she thought to be of a different breed: a sensitive, imaginative, and creative person, a musician as well as a psychiatrist. And now there was her new friend, whom she knew she would love also as the days passed. She told him that there had been one kind doctor in the hospital in whom she had confidence, but that most of those she saw seemed like peasants totally devoid of insight. Carson said that she had developed such an antipathy to her chief doctor that she dreaded to see him walk into her room.

Apologizing for burdening him, but pouring heart and soul out to her new friend whom she still had not met in person, Carson attempted to describe what she thought was her psychic condition while in the hospital, as well as the way the doctors there seemed to respond to it. She realized that she lacked their perspective but thought that she could still describe the encounter objectively. She told her friend that her doctor criticized her for not facing her ill health, then questioned her about her defenses. When she replied that writing was her bastion, he insisted that work was not enough, that writing in itself was a form of neurosis. Yet to Carson, the act of artistic creation was the prime expression of health, as well as the only conceivable hope for solace and salvation.

She acknowledged to her friend, also, the tremendous sense of responsibility a psychiatrist must feel in working with a person and attempting to improve his psychic health. She wondered if psychotherapy could ever be the answer for creative people, who needed their internal chemistry intact regardless of the suffering that might ensue because of such chemistry. Carson concluded that she must maintain her fragile grasp of whatever soul she had, despite the cost, as long as she had life. To her, the psychiatrist and the writer were concerned with the same subject: man in his relation to the human condition. But whereas the psychiatrist was forced to regard anxiety as an individual, neurotic problem, the true artist regarded anxiety as an essential, basic aspect of human existence. She felt that man alone knew and feared the acknowledgment of finity, yet it was his very acknowledgment of the finite that enabled him to face life fully and to get as much from it as possible, realizing that he was responsible to himself, and to himself only, for his physical actions and psychic life. To Carson, the artist matured as he acknowledged and accepted the agon of the human condition, rather than through a denial of his sufferings, as her doctor seemed to suggest that she should. When she maintained to her doctor that she was well and sane, even though she suffered, he replied: "How can you tell me you are not sick when there are tears in your eyes right now?"

Even more indicative to Carson of her Payne Whitney psychiatrist's inability to understand or reach into the particular recesses of her mind was his response to a poem she recited to him which she said she had recently written[11]:

When we are lost what image tells?
Nothing resembles nothing. Yet nothing
Is not blank. It is configured Hell:
Of noticed clocks on winter afternoons, malignant stars,
Demanding furniture. All unrelated
And with air between.

The terror. Is it of Space, of Time?
Or the joined trickery of both conceptions?
To the lost, transfixed among the self-inflicted ruins,
All that is non-air (if this indeed is not deception)
Is agony immobilized. While Time,
The endless idiot, runs screaming round the world.

"Do you have moods like that often?" he asked.

Carson explained to her new friend her abortive suicide attempt. As she saw it, she simply had become so emotionally unhinged that she did not know what she was doing; she was certain, however, that she had no true suicidal tendencies. Nor would she ever hurt herself again, she vowed. It was only that having lost almost all hope of good health, she had be-

come overstrained and fearful that she might become permanently paralyzed. Carson acknowledged, also, that she was separated from her husband and no longer married except legally. She thought that part of her
temporary breakdown was due to the prolonged anguish she had suffered
in her relationship with Reeves. Nothing was more saddening, she conceded, than the inch-by-inch disintegration of a marriage or the death of
love.

Carson speculated that spring that her entire condition might be
called a psychosomatic state, yet she felt that her emotional attitude could
not possibly have brought on the vascular attacks she suffered in Paris or
the spasms she had intermittently felt since; nor could it alter them now.
From time to time in the future, a number of persons who knew Carson
well—including those with sound medical backgrounds, as well as hyp-
notists, quacks, and laymen—speculated on whether her condition might
have been attributable, in part, to some kind of hysterical paralysis, particularly in view of her sudden attacks of hysteria and difficulty in speaking, writing, walking, breathing—even the very act of remaining conscious
at times—all things she had experienced in the past. Some who knew
Carson suspected that her paralysis was psychosomatic because there were
times when they saw her relax her maimed arm and hand and use it to
some degree. Later, however, as various physicians and surgeons with their
many advances in the theory and practice of science and medicine entered the case to work with Carson over the remaining years of her life,
there was no medical doubt that she was, indeed, severely handicapped
by the sequelae of a serious cerebral vascular accident suffered in 1947,
which had caused permanent damage and paralysis, a gradual deterioration of the body, and eventually, after another massive stroke, her death.

Carson wrote to her young psychiatrist almost immediately upon her
return from Payne Whitney the second week of April. The very next day
she heard from him by special delivery and concluded before opening the
letter that it was his kind attempt to allay any escaped-lunatic notions she
might be harboring after hearing of her unauthorized departure from the
hospital. But their letters had crossed. He had not had time to receive
news of her recent incarceration. Instead, he was writing to invite her to
attend a meeting of the American Psychiatric Association in Washington, D.C., the middle of May. It would not only be their first opportunity
to know each other personally, but he also wanted her to meet some of
his fellow psychiatrists, whom he was sure Carson would like. He was
especially anxious for her to know his former medical school professor
Hervey Cleckley, and Cleckley's wife, Louise. (Cleckley, who was to
present a paper at the meeting, soon gained recognition and fame
along with his colleague Dr. Corbett H. Thigpen, for their case study of
schizophrenia which resulted in the book, The Three Faces of Eve.[12])

Carson was beside herself with amusement and pleasure that she had been invited to be a guest at a national meeting of psychiatrists when she herself had just been a patient in a psychiatric clinic, had been declared incapable of rationality and an ordered creative experience, and had made an unauthorized departure. Now she would be attending the meeting with august psychiatrists because of the very capabilities that others in the profession said she lacked. Furthermore, she told her friend that she felt a childish and inexplicable sense of justification as well. She could hardly wait to know the young psychiatrist in person. Before the meeting, he sent her a snapshot of himself so that she would have no difficulty in recognizing him. Many times Carson had pictured her friend in her mind and imagined him to be somewhat ugly, she admitted later, to help make up for his other qualities. It was obliging of the Lord to have made him handsome when he was also such a good person, she told him, for it seemed logical for the Lord to have shaped him carelessly to compensate.

With new incentives brought on by her evolving friendship with the young doctor, Carson experienced renewed hope for recovery of her maimed limbs. She wrote him that he had restored her faltering self-confidence and was a source of strength and happiness for her. Carson began now to eat hugely and to exercise daily to get into shape for the trip. She even returned to the piano and managed to struggle through little Schubert and Bach pieces which had simple left-hand parts. Carson had no piano in Nyack, having sold hers when she and her mother left Columbus for good, but she made a point now of going into the homes of friends nearby who did have pianos. Gradually she began to see people again and to feel almost like her old self. Presently she began to walk much better, too, although her left leg had been seriously affected by the stroke, and even her left hand became more adroit. Impatient for good health, however, Carson longed for greater bodily vitality and confidence, and for a doctor who could cure her mysterious ailment.

Most important, she began to write again. Her first project was a complete revision of her play, *The Member of the Wedding*, which she dictated from her bed to a part-time secretary. Although Carson had mobility in her left hand, there was not enough strength in her fingers to type. It bothered her only momentarily not to see the typed words in front of her. The play was her story, her life. With a keen sense of the dramatic and a superb ear for rhythm, she had only to open her big-toothed, generous mouth and the dialogue poured out like thick brown molasses. She seemed only half there, reliving her Georgia girlhood, becoming alternately Frankie, John Henry, and Berenice, talking softly in her inimitable southern voice, eyes glowing, smiling. When Carson finished the play this time—in scarcely two months—she got in touch with

Tennessee Williams' agent, Audrey Wood, whom he had recommended to her two years earlier. Since the break with Greer Johnson, it seemed no longer to be in Carson's best interest to continue working with Ann Watkins, who was also Johnson's agent. According to Carson, Audrey Wood was more than willing to take her on as a writer, but after reading the revised script Miss Wood thought that it needed more work. Carson had already asked Joshua Logan to direct the play and had sent him the new script. Logan was in Europe at the time after directing the successful opening of *Mister Roberts,* which he had coauthored with Thomas Heggen. Carson said that Logan read the revised script, then met with Tennessee Williams in Rome to talk over its possibilities. According to Logan, it was not Carson who first approached him, but Robert Whitehead; nor was it the *revised* script he read first, but the collaboration.[13] After Williams read the revised script, he wired Carson a congratulatory message: "SCRIPT A THOUSAND TIMES BETTER." Well attuned to the master craftsman and artist, however, Carson knew that her friend would not have used a comparative expression—regardless of the degree—if he had thought the play truly finished and ready for production. Seeking more help now from Williams than she had been receptive to at Nantucket, Carson wrote that she looked forward to receiving his detailed suggestions about the script.

Eager for production of her play and knowing that there was money to be had on Broadway—but never dreaming how much—Carson was preoccupied for months writing letters about the play and talking with producers. When she visited Cheryl Crawford in Connecticut in early May 1948, she hoped that Miss Crawford herself might see fit to produce her play. (Many people thought that Cheryl Crawford had a knack for turning a sow's ear into a silk purse, although that thought had not occurred to Carson in relationship to *her* play.) Even though Carson told her young psychiatrist friend just before their Washington, D.C., meeting that Cheryl Crawford had been reading *The Member of the Wedding* and giving her valuable advice about directors, casting, and lighting, Miss Crawford apparently had no intention of producing it herself. Later she reportedly explicitly declined Carson's invitation to produce her play, which quickly put a quietus on their friendship. (Robert Whitehead, who eventually produced the play, recalled that Cheryl Crawford suggested that Carson "throw it in an ash can."[14]) For a while she thought that Oliver Smith would produce it. It was another year before Robert Whitehead and Oliver Rea agreed—in spite of misgivings—to produce *The Member of the Wedding,* knowing that it would be a high risk for its backers.

In the spring of 1948, Carson was optimistic. She was not only feeling better and writing, but also playing the piano and seeing new people.

The weekend she visited Cheryl Crawford, she told friends, the two of them had gone to Mary Martin's to spend several days in Miss Martin's lovely home in Connecticut. Since Carson thrived on exaggeration and fantasy, one might more readily accept Miss Martin's recollection of the incident: that they had met, instead, one lazy summer afternoon at Cheryl Crawford's home in Connecticut, "with my singing songs Carson liked—and my liking singing for *her*."15 Carson loved Mary Martin's warm effervescence, identified with her gamine personality, and was thrilled to have a private sharing of a voice that charmed audiences all over the country.

Although Carson had no more stories published in *The New Yorker*, she told friends that spring that the magazine had bought another story from her which would be published later in the year. She said that they were not only paying her one thousand dollars, including a bonus, but had offered her an attractive contract for future stories as well, for which there would be bonuses that would nearly double the original payment. She had a whole series of stories planned, she said, and hoped to have some money to jingle before long. Such monetary rewards were especially appreciated now, she said, for her illness and other financial responsibilities had again left her penniless and in debt to her mother.

Except for her psychiatrist friend whom she still had not met, there were no men in Carson's life at present who were close at hand. Usually Carson never lacked devoted attention and love by at least one person other than her mother, and she longed now for a more immediate and meaningful personal relationship. More than anyone, she missed Tennessee Williams who was still in Europe. She also resumed her correspondence with Newton Arvin, whom she took pleasure in telling about her invitation to a convention by psychiatrists who loved and respected her work—all in contrast to her earlier tale of woe in which she recounted her Payne Whitney ordeal; however, she and Arvin were never again as close as they had been during the war when they were seeing each other frequently at Yaddo and writing to one another while she was at home in Columbus. She had not seen Arvin since her return from Paris, nor had she been well enough to see much of Williams, either, before he left for Europe. She and Reeves had come home the first of December 1947, Williams' play had opened on the third, and then the playwright had gone to Italy soon afterward, visiting Carson at her bedside only briefly before his departure. They had written often, however, and in March 1948 he invited her to join him in Rome. Again, the old wanderlust struck Carson, but she knew that she had to be much better physically than she was at present before she could leave home—and her doctors—again.

For a long time Carson had not written to Williams about her emotional disturbance or hospitalization. It was not that she wanted to keep anything from him or doubted for a moment his perfect understanding—in fact, their *mutual* understanding, which, to Carson had been complete and unblemished since their first meeting—but that she simply did not want to add to his worries. Seldom was Carson that altruistic, but she knew that his sister, his beloved Rose, had been the sorrow of his life for the past ten years, having been mentally ill and in an institution since 1938. Rose Williams had had a frontal lobotomy—one of the earliest performed in the United States—over her brother's objections; but the doctors had prevailed upon his mother to allow the operation, and now his only sister could never be quite the same again. Carson had been unwilling to burden Williams with the knowledge of her own psychic illness, for she was certain that he believed his sister and her to be spiritually related. In May, however, when Carson began to feel well and in command of herself again, it preyed upon her mind that Williams might hear of her illness through someone else. When finally she wrote of it to him and assured him that she was quite all right now, he replied that in Rome he had seen Janet Flanner, who had heard of her illness and told him that Carson was psychically disturbed. Indeed, Williams had worried.

He also suggested to Carson that when he returned to New York, perhaps they could move West together or take a ranch in Mexico, where they might live and work in seclusion—in "adjoining trances"—as he phrased it. He wondered, too, if they might consider having his sister with them. She was in a hospital but improving daily, Williams reported. Carson had met Rose Williams in 1946 before she went to Europe, and she yearned now to share with him the responsibility of his sister's care and happiness. Miss Williams' illness had weighed upon her brother long and painfully and he wanted to be able to help her in a more meaningful way. Perhaps she might approach a normal life if she could live with two people who dearly loved her and had no restraints in tenderly expressing it, Williams suggested. Carefully Carson explained the situation to her young psychiatrist friend and informed him that she was aware that any decision on her and Williams' part would have to be made with expert professional guidance. For years Rose Williams had suffered from the delusion—as Carson called it—that her brother Tennessee had set himself against God and was writing plays against Him. It would be conceivable, said Carson, that they, with their good intentions, might contribute to a relapse or new grief and disappointment for her if they isolated her with them while they continued to write as they must— regardless of Rose Williams' inability to understand or accept it.

Williams and Carson were never to take his sister with them and go West. Carson's health would not permit her to be that independent again —even if it had been a good thing for Williams' sister—but the playwright,

over the years of their love and friendship, was always deeply grateful
for Carson's concern for his sister's comfort and happiness and for the
love that Carson very openly gave to her. The two women eventually
became good friends, chatting almost as children together—or housewives
—talking about food, recipes, small-town stories, people in the theatre,
and other celebrities whom Miss Williams had met or heard of. They
shared, also, an empathy for wounded and fragile things, for birds, for
certain animals, for delicate flowers. Frequently, when they were both
well enough, Rose Williams spent weekends with Carson in Nyack. The
playwright brought her down from Ossining on the Hudson, where she
lived in a small private sanitarium. Sometimes he and Carson visited her
in her "apartment" in Ossining.

There was no doubt in Carson's mind that she shared some kind of
extrasensory perception with the people she loved. Even with her young
psychiatrist friend before they met, she felt a oneness that she could explain in no other way. One illuminating incident that particularly struck
her was that she had written him a letter that spring in what she identified
as the tone and semantics of a hurt, offended child—something doubtless
provoked by her Payne Whitney experience, she conceded—to which he
responded with brilliance, wisdom, and calm reassurance. He comforted
her not only with his own warm words, but also with the poetry of
A. E. Housman and a passage from Thomas Mann. The remarkable
aspect of the incident was that Carson herself had checked a collection
of Housman's poetry out of the Nyack library just the week before, and
the very lines which her friend quoted to her now came from a poem
she had read only two nights earlier—when he doubtless had been writing them in the letter itself. She was sure that there was some sort of
inexplicable telepathy between persons whose spirits were analogous.
The passage he quoted to her from Mann was also something she had
read earlier, she said, and when she looked at it now, coming from him,
she had a much clearer and dearer perception of the lines than she had
ever had before.

Finally the day arrived when Carson and her psychiatrist friend were
to meet in person. Although the original plan had been for her to be
accompanied by her mother to Washington, they decided at the last
moment that Carson was well and strong enough to go alone. Marguerite put her on the train May 19, and in Washington she was met by her
friend and taken to the Statler Hotel, where the official meetings of the
psychiatric convention were held, and where they, too, would be staying.
Whereas Carson frequently avoided a situation that might shatter some
preconceived image and destroy the goodness of the fantasy, she felt
intuitively that there was no cause for worry about her meeting with her

new friend. Indeed, she found him everything she had imagined him to be.

They had warm, intimate talks, attended together many of the readings and discussion groups of the psychiatric association, heard Cleckley deliver his paper, and spent much of her two evenings in Washington with the Cleckleys and with two or three other young psychiatrists who were special friends of her companion. During their brief hours together, Carson told her friend a great deal more about Reeves. Although they were still separated, she said that he had gained control of himself again in what seemed to her to be a near miraculous way. Whereas she had told her friend earlier that Reeves had been alcoholic, morally sick, and grossly unhappy, she said that he now had a job, his first since the war, and that he seemed a different person. He was an accountant with radio station WOR in New York City, where he was like a youngster in his pride about his job, Carson said. Reeves had visited her in Nyack a few days before her trip to Washington to tell her about his work. Then he had called later to share his delight in now having a dictaphone and a private secretary.

It was not only difficult for Carson to forgive someone who had hurt her, taken advantage of her, failed to be completely honest with her, or had proved to be as undependable as Reeves had been at times, but it also was impossible for her to forget an offense and willingly start over again without reference to the past. Yet with Reeves, she was different. She always seemed willing to take him back under her wing, given sufficient time to believe that some change for the better had occurred. His well-being had always been greatly important to her even when they were not living together. In 1941 and 1942 after they were divorced and Carson was living at home with her parents, or at Yaddo, she still had been deeply concerned about Reeves. Of course she never concealed the fact, either, that he could also be a "real sonovabitch."

Carson related candidly to her friend in Washington that spring a number of tales about her husband's weaknesses and their relationship that she said later she wished she had not shared, for during the summer Reeves began to return to Nyack regularly on the weekends, and once again she found him to be the gentle, delicate, and endlessly generous and considerate person he had been when they first married. Moreover, he brought her money now and helped pay off her considerable debts, including what she had borrowed from her mother. Later, Carson wrote her psychiatrist friend that Reeves, in coming back into her life—in a cured state from his alcoholism, drinking neither beer nor wine—was now an abiding and real comfort to her. She also regretted having talked about him as she had, for she hoped that soon Reeves and her new friend would meet and she wanted them to be fond of each other. It was important for Carson when she and Reeves were reconciled that people whom she loved should also love him. But when they were apart, it did not matter what people thought of him. If anything, she wanted them to know what a scoundrel he had been and how badly she had been treated and taken advantage of.

By midsummer, Reeves was accepted again as a bona fide member of the family. Although he kept his apartment in the city, he came home weekends and frequently at midweek, sharing with his wife a new spirit of communion. In August, however, Carson's health suddenly worsened. She began to walk very badly, her left leg ached and was stiff and her arm began to draw up. In one letter Carson drew a little stick figure for her young psychiatrist friend to show him how her arm behaved now.

She told him, too, how discouraged she had become in her writing and that she was disappointed in *The New Yorker*'s reception of a new story she had believed in and worked hard on. Carson could not understand why she was more ill now than she had been in the spring, for nothing of note had occurred physiologically which might account for the change. She wrote friends that she longed for physical strength and had begun dreaming again, as had her youthful protagonists in her fiction, of skiing in the Alps.

In August 1948, Carson was cheered by Tennessee Williams' return to the United States. He was ready to get *Summer and Smoke* into production, which he told Carson he was dedicating to her. The play premièred in Dallas, produced by Margo Jones at her own theatre there; then, on October 6, it opened on Broadway. Williams was worried about how his play would go in New York, for it was not the immediate box office success that *A Streetcar Named Desire* had been, nor were the critics by any means unanimous in their praise. Many felt that it had opened too close on the heels of his Pulitzer Prize winner and thus suffered by the immediacy of the comparison.

Carson, in the meantime, had her own worries regarding the theatre, but they took time to console each other. Since she had balked at allowing the production by the Theatre Guild of the several joint scripts of *The*

Member of the Wedding, which had been written originally by Carson and then rewritten by her collaborator, Greer Johnson, and had attempted to break her contract, she was notified of the impending lawsuit. Tennessee Williams spoke of the suit in a letter to Paul Bigelow, dated October 27, 1948: "Carson goes to court Friday. She is being sued for $50,000 by her alleged collaborator, who claims that their joint work would have been that profitable to him personally. I have to testify." Instead of going to court, however—Carson had threatened a counter-suit—both parties were advised to submit the case to the American Arbitration Association for settlement. According to a "Submission Agreement" dated September 27, 1948 (file ⸶8489), Carson and her collaborator agreed to stand by the judgment of the American Arbitration Association. The "statement of controversy" read: "Percentage of royalties due for dramatization of a novel entitled 'The Member of the Wedding.'" On November 8, the decision was made: "Contract for dramatization of the novel is in full force and effect until November 1, 1949—subject to the assumption that the Theatre Guild, if it produces the play, will use the several scripts prepared by both parties."[16]

The arbitration settlement was disturbing to Carson, who had hoped to go scot free. She did not want her play tied up for a year and not be able to have it produced elsewhere. Although the Theatre Guild had a year's option to dramatize the play, it would have to use the collaborated scripts; but if the Guild should choose not to exercise its option—a course Carson strongly advised—she would then be free to negotiate with another producer based on her own revised script she had completed that spring.

When Carson had been dictating her revised script, utilizing freely the changes Tennessee Williams suggested, she had hardly missed her typewriter. It had given her little difficulty to dictate a play that she already knew well, had anguished over in its novel form for five and a half years, and had been at work on the play script for almost two years, but it was quite another thing to dictate a story from the very beginning, to visualize the words on a blank page in her mind—which was never blank —to write and revise mentally only, and then to say aloud her thoughts and see them in someone else's hand and, eventually, on the typed page. In September, before the lawsuit and arbitration developed, Reeves bought Carson an electric typewriter to supplant the old manual portable which had become almost useless to her. With practice she found that she could operate the new machine, for it required only an ounce of pressure from the crippled fingers of her left hand. Although her hand tired easily, she was able now to work at her typewriter intermittently for several hours a day. Once again she renewed her correspondence with friends and began working on manuscripts.

Carson had had no fiction published in magazines since her novella

The Ballad of the Sad Café, appeared in *Harper's Bazaar* in August 1943, nor had there been a prose essay since her Thanksgiving message, "Our Heads Are Bowed," in *Mademoiselle* in November 1945. Anxious to keep her name in front of her reading public, as well as to receive the immediate cash of a magazine sale, she found *Mademoiselle* to be a perfect vehicle for the stories and articles she had begun to write again. In the fall, her sister was promoted from assistant fiction editor to fiction editor of *Mademoiselle*, and with Rita Smith and George Davis both on the masthead, Carson was encouraged to submit her manuscripts first to *Mademoiselle*.[17]

In September, *Mademoiselle* published "How I Began to Write," a nostalgic piece that poured forth when she put herself back in time and place and depicted her formative, creative years in her family's old Georgia home. She told of the plays she had written and then directed in their "double living rooms," in which sliding doors between the two rooms served as a curtain. The plays had starred Baby Sister and Brother-Man. She wrote of her difficulties in being "custodian, the counter of the cakes, the boss of all our shows."[18] She told, too, of her discipleship of O'Neill and Nietzsche, of her wanderlust for New York City, skyscrapers, and snow, of her discovery of Dostoevski, Chekhov, and Tolstoy, and of her "intimations of an unsuspected region equidistant from New York, Old Russia, and our Georgia rooms, the marvelous solitary region of simple stories and the inward mind."

In September, Carson had two poems published in *New Directions*, her first poetry to appear since "The Twisted Trinity" in *Decision* in 1941. One of the poems was "When We Are Lost," which she had recited for her Payne Whitney doctor, and the other, "The Mortgaged Heart," she had also written earlier that year. Carson took demonic pleasure in sending a tear sheet of her poems to the Payne Whitney psychiatrist who had uncomprehendingly asked her if she had moods like that often. "Yes, thank God," she might add now.

Tennessee Williams had invited her to return to Europe with him after his play *Summer and Smoke* opened. He wanted her to go with him to Italy, he said. As the fall advanced, however, she feared that she had suffered another major reversal. Walking had again become difficult, and her arm was even more spastic and drawn than before. She could go nowhere at present, she told Williams, adding that she had changed doctors and gone to a new hospital for treatment. Again she was deeply discouraged and wondered if she would ever be supple and well as before. No one had an answer that could satisfy her.

Williams also asked her if she would like to go to Key West with him in late October, for he now had a winter home there. For a while the prospect buoyed her. She wrote to Edwin Peacock and John Zeigler that she planned to drive south in Williams' car, stop in Charleston for a day or two, and be gone a week in all. She wrote to her psychiatrist friend, too, that they would visit him en route at Fort Belvoir, Virginia, where he had gone upon signing a contract with the Army for a portion of his internship. Almost at the last minute, however, they decided not to go—or perhaps they had never really intended to. Carson wrote the friends whom she had planned to visit that Williams had been very nervous lately and she was reluctant to be on the road with him in his present condition. It did not occur to her that Williams might also hesitate to assume the responsibility for her in her weakened and unpredictable state. Instead of going to Key West with Carson, Williams decided to fly to North Africa with Paul Bowles, who had settled in Morocco with his wife, Jane. He invited Carson to go to North Africa with him, too, but she declined. She said that she longed, instead, to return to her old milieu and talk with Southerners once again. Her work demanded that she go back from time to time, just as she had told Eleanor Clark at Yaddo a few years earlier that she must periodically return to the South to renew her "sense of horror." Since Carson's young psychiatrist friend was from Atlanta, she decided that she would ask him to take her with him the next time he went home.

Carson was not so wrapped up in self, however, that she could not cast about and see what was going on in the world around her. In October, she joined a group of twenty-seven leading American writers, headed by Nobel Prize winner Sinclair Lewis, in support of the candidacy of President Harry S Truman. Also signing the statement were five Pulitzer Prize winners (Conrad Aiken, Archibald MacLeish, Arthur Schlesinger, Jr., Bernard De Voto, and Robert E. Sherwood) and a number of other writers who had achieved outstanding critical acclaim, including her friends Newton Arvin, Granville Hicks, Lillian Smith, Marguerite Young, and Truman Capote. Their message read in part:

> We will not vote for what has traditionally been the party of reaction, nor will we contribute to the victory of that party by voting for minor candidates whose campaigns are quixotic or worse. . . .
> We believe that the Democratic party offers the only practical hope for a liberal tradition abroad. Harry Truman's stand in favor of civil rights, his constant advocacy of aid to Europe, his effective resistance to totalitarianism abroad and at home, his veto of the Taft-Hartley Act, his fight for price control, his efforts on behalf of the preservation of national resources. These are services to democracy that entitle him to the support of every liberal.[19]

Many persons who knew Carson and Reeves over the years felt that it was Reeves who provoked most of his wife's liberal stands on issues. To know Carson well, however, was to know that even though Reeves may have stirred her liberal fires in the mid-thirties, the issues themselves and Carson's humanitarian principles and sensitivity in empathizing with those less fortunate than herself whose views she supported were impetus enough. On February 28, 1948, for example, when she and Reeves were estranged from one another and Carson herself was ill, she dictated a letter to the editor of the Columbus *Ledger-Enquirer* of her hometown. It was prompted, she said, not only by her intense interest in the welfare of the Columbus Public Library, but also by important moral issues central to her personal ideology. First she acknowledged her significant debt to the library, which had nurtured her as a child and had been her spiritual home during her formative years. Then she revealed that she had heard that use of the *new* Columbus public library (later called the W. C. Bradley Memorial Library) had been restricted to the white populace of the community. Although she said that she might not understand the concrete issues, she knew too well the abstract ones. It was intolerable to her as an author represented in the Columbus library that blacks were not granted the same intellectual privileges accorded to white citizens. On behalf of herself, as well as others to whom she was inestimably indebted—such as Tolstoy, Chekhov, Lincoln, and Paine—she urged the library to grant freely to all citizens the right to read the works of those who had helped mold the conscience of world civilization. It was still several years later before the civic fathers of Columbus saw fit to integrate the library, but her letter was published in the newspaper and a copy of it sent to the library. Carson felt good about having registered her indignation and gone on record for her convictions. Already she had another novel boiling in her mind that had begun to simmer years earlier in a homeland she both loved and hated. Although it was not published for another thirteen years, the fuel for *Clock Without Hands* was readily available, both in her psyche and in the land a stone's throw below the Mason-Dixon line.

In February, Reeves wrote to Edwin Peacock to ask if Carson could go to Charleston for a few weeks to write and to visit him and John Ziegler. He said that she had a story in mind that she was ready to begin as a novel. It had been four years since she had been South and it was time now for her to get back and renew and sharpen her feelings and sensitivities regarding her roots.[20] Reeves assured Peacock that Carson's needs were simple and few and that she would be an easy guest to have around. He even suggested she would be an asset to his, or any, household, as though she were applying for a position as governess or housekeeper. Reeves asked, however, that his friend employ a servant at least part time to handle the cooking and housecleaning chores. They considered it a necessary expense and one that he and Carson could afford. Any other expenses incurred by her visit would also be taken care of if they agreed to have her, said Reeves. Carson added her own postscript in a separate letter enclosed with Reeves's, saying that she longed to be back with them in Charleston for she loved and missed them, but that they must be frank and admit if her visit might work a hardship on them. She assured them that she was no invalid, but almost well. Reeves and Carson both had a knack for saying just the right thing when an invitation to visit was the issue. One could hardly turn them down even if he wanted to. Peacock and Zeigler responded that they looked forward to having Carson anytime she could come. It would never have occurred to them to reply otherwise.

Carson and Reeves had spent most of January in Reeves's bachelor apartment in what she identified as "Little Italy," a few blocks below Washington Square. Their address was 105 Thompson Street, apartment #20. Reeves had made their three rooms, which rented for eighteen dollars a month, quite comfortable, she told Tennessee Williams in a letter addressed to him in Rome that winter. In her hand-written missive she drew for Williams the layout of the apartment and even the arrangement of furniture, just as she had done earlier for Janet Flanner and Newton Arvin when she sketched her Starke Avenue bedroom in Columbus to illustrate how happily she was situated there. Carson always enjoyed sharing as graphically as possible her physical situation, as well as her psychic state, when she was writing to those closest to her. She also thanked the playwright for the ring he had sent her. Williams had asked his friend Donald Wyndham to take it to Carson after his departure for Europe. It was his sister Rose's ring, and he wanted her to have it as a special bond between them. With Carson wearing it, he said that he somehow felt that his sister might soon recover. She would wear it and treasure it always, Carson told him, or until their beloved Rose was well once more.

Carson stayed with Reeves in the city until just before her birthday. Her mother had hoped that she would come home for it, for the family had always hugely celebrated Carson's birthday. Except for their stay in Paris, Carson and Reeves's cohabitation this winter in New York City marked their first time alone for any extended period since their early days in the city in 1940. They discovered, happily, that they were almost as compatible as they longed to be. Carson wrote Tennessee Williams that Reeves took beautiful care of her. He cooked for them, came home at lunchtime, kept the apartment spotless, and was kind and tender with her in every way. The only disadvantage she could think of was that the apartment was on the fifth floor and she could not go out unattended. Yet she was working rather well at present, she acknowledged. Her play, *The Member of the Wedding*, was in a state of limbo for the moment, she said. Oliver Smith was most enthusiastic about it and wanted to produce it as soon as he could find the right director, she told Williams; in the meantime, she was continuing with some other pieces. She had just sold two short stories to *Mademoiselle*, "Art and Mr. Mahoney" and "The Sojourner," she added modestly.[21]

Happy again with Reeves, Carson began to dream once more of how good life might be if the two of them could retreat to a farm in the country. They would have an apple orchard, some animals, perhaps, and an old homey farmhouse with a special room always in readiness for Tennessee Williams, Carson promised, which they would call the 10 *room*. She told the playwright that he was to come and stay with them any time the city got too much for him. They would probably spend two or three months each year in Europe, she said . . . and the dream went on and on.

Carson needed to get away from her mother occasionally, and spending a few weeks in the city with Reeves accomplished that end, too. There were times when she felt that her mother tended to smother her, encouraged her childlike dependence, and helped preserve her as the precocious little girl she had been at age twelve and thirteen, like Mick Kelley and Frankie Addams, who wavered uncertainly on the brink of puberty. Carson loved her mother, but found at times that it was difficult to *like* her. Some who knew Carson well believed that she was unaware of her own ambivalent love-hatred which she inadvertently felt toward her mother. In spite of her best efforts, Marguerite did not—could not—always fulfill the mother role which Carson craved, any more adequately than did the mothers in Carson's fiction who failed to meet the psychic needs of their daughters. Carson did not even give Frankie Addams a mother, but instead, had her die in childbirth; nor was Frankie's surrogate mother, the black cook Berenice, a completely satisfactory substitute. According to Lamar, Jr., his sister did not depict a meaningful mother-daughter relationship in her fiction because she did not want to strip herself that bare and show the utter dependency that she felt for her mother. Carson's brother understood all too well his sister's vulnerabilities and her unwillingness to show that particular side of herself to her readers.[22]

Carson was not overcome by people, but by things. Although physically weak, she was overbearing and powerful, a far stronger person than her mother or Reeves. She usually was in control of the situation where people were concerned. In the city with Reeves that winter, she had grown restless and could not work as she had hoped, just as Manhattan had always affected her except when she was very young and single. When Reeves wrote Edwin Peacock that Carson felt cramped in New York and needed to breathe country air and be near burgeoning green things, Peacock's reply was an enthusiastic *yes*. He had been disappointed

in her not coming in 1946 to Charleston, where she had planned to hide
away upon the publication of *The Member of the Wedding*. They
would love to have her for as long as Carson cared to stay, he assured
them; nor was she to worry about the financial aspects of her visit—she
was to be their guest. After all, that was what friends were for. Instead of
going directly to Charleston, however, Carson and Reeves decided that
she would go first to her hometown in Georgia and start there in the re-
experiencing of her southern milieu by visiting again the old places she
had known when growing up. Then, over "a little sippin' whiskey," she
looked forward to what she called "sweet talks" with old friends and family with the southern fondness for storytelling which had nourished so
much of her fiction. She wrote Edwin Peacock that she would also go to
Macon, Georgia, where she would visit her cousin Jordan Massee before
coming on to Charleston.

Marguerite soon decided that she, too, wanted to visit in Columbus,
to be with her sister Mattie again for a few days, and to see the friends
she had left behind upon moving to Nyack (with her daughters in 1944
after her husband's death). The main reason, of course, was that she was
reluctant for Carson to make the long trip South alone. She would go
with Carson, also, to Macon and Charleston, for both Jordan Massee and
Edwin Peacock had made the invitation explicit for her, as well, as soon
as they learned that she, too, was coming South. Marguerite planned to
take a side trip alone to visit Brother-Man and Virginia, who now had a
baby and were living in Brunswick, Georgia.[23]

Soon the whole itinerary was arranged. They would travel by Pullman, leaving on Sunday, March 13, for Columbus, where they would
stay with Carson's good friend Kathleen Woodruff. Just as Reeves had
written Edwin Peacock, so too had Carson told Jordan Massee and
Kathleen Woodruff that she needed to return home to renew her sense
of the past and to steep herself again in talk with fellow Southerners.
Once in Columbus, however, Carson exhibited little interest in her external surroundings. Mrs. Woodruff had looked forward to driving Carson around the old Fifth Avenue neighborhood in which she had been
reared, down the main street, Broad—now renamed Broadway—past the
site of Twelfth Street where her father had had his shop, past the
mill and the old library, and then down the old brick street beside the
river and over to Phenix City, where Carson and her father had had
some of their best walks and talks together. But upon her arrival in mid-
March of 1949, thirty-two years after her birth, Carson discovered that
she had no enthusiasm for seeing the old verities of her youth, that things
had changed in actuality and had been irrevocably lost except in the
imagination and the memory.

She did concede to Kathleen Woodruff that there was one thing she wanted to do more than anything else in Columbus, and that was to visit the old Sam Slate home on Oak Avenue where she had played as a child. Mrs. Woodruff quickly arranged for the visit, delighted that Carson showed an interest in something concrete. Jeanette and Jack Key, who had bought the Slate home, assured Mrs. Woodruff that they would be most pleased to have such a famous author as their guest and looked forward to taking Carson through the house. Once there, however, Carson was bored and listless. She not only would not go into the house; she did not even want to walk through the garden, which now was a show place with azaleas and other spring-flowering shrubs at their zenith. One or two other guests had also been invited to "drop in" for tea and join them. Carson, poorly groomed and dressed in faded bluejeans, sat outside with them in sullen silence, contributing no word to the conversation. To Kathleen Woodruff, Carson looked as though she were thinking, "Why on earth do I *have* to be here?"—as though she had been hogtied and dragged there. The explanation for her rudeness was simply that she had been ready to turn around and leave as soon as they had driven up to the house. Again, to Carson the imagined and remembered image was far more gratifying and useful to her than the real thing. Like Henry James's artist who threatened to destroy himself when he attempted to paint "the real thing," Carson had almost had enough of Columbus as soon as she and her mother stepped off the train.[24]

Of course the idea of the "tea party" had also offended her. She much preferred an Old-fashioned glass of straight bourbon, a habit which sometimes shocked people. When Carson's former next-door neighbor on Starke Avenue, Mildred Miller Fort, stopped in for a visit with her and her mother in Columbus that spring, Mrs. Fort assumed that Carson was drinking sherry in an Old-fashioned glass until she went into the kitchen to fix her own drink and to give Carson a refill. "But it was straight bourbon," said Mrs. Fort.[25]

Carson was drinking heavily in Columbus when she was Kathleen Woodruff's guest in 1949, but no more so than she had been for the past three years. It simply took more alcohol to enable her to start her day and function on a normal keel than most people might consume in an evening. She never appeared *drunk*. Her speech did not thicken, nor did she slur her words any more after considerable alcoholic consumption than she did when she first woke up. If there was any change, it was for the better. Moreover, she usually verbalized slowly, speaking with long pauses between clauses or sentences. Often in response to a question, she waited for more than a minute and appeared not to notice that she had even been addressed. Then she gave a slow, but lucid answer, or none at all if she chose to ignore the question. On the other hand, she responded immediately if she wished to and engaged in an animated conversation in spite of her slow cadence. Carson was a great poseur when it suited her, assuming a mask as a part of her cultivated enigma.

To her, the most satisfying aspects of her four days in Columbus were her long conversations with Kathleen Woodruff and her rereading of Baudelaire's *Flowers of Evil* (in translation) and Isak Dinesen's *Out of Africa*, which she had read every year of her life since 1937. Perhaps Carson's most precious memory of her stay, however, was an outing she and Mrs. Woodruff took the day before her departure. Mrs. Woodruff put her in the car and they drove a few miles out of town to Oak Mountain. When Carson asked why she was being taken to that particular spot, her friend responded: "There's a lovely little snow-white house on the edge of the mountain where an old colored family lives. Since you've always been interested in colored people and how they live, I want you to see it." Mrs. Woodruff had been on the site before with her husband, and she knew the family, from whom cooks and servants had come through the years to old Columbus families.

Carson was fascinated by the house, which had been brightly white-washed and put in good repair. The spry old grandmother and grandfather came out and greeted their unexpected guests warmly, inviting them in. Immediately, Carson's eyes were caught by a handsome organ which appeared to be brand new. "Where did you get this, may I ask, please?" probed Carson sensitively.

"I bought it thirty years ago, hoping somebody would play it. But nobody ever has," the old man answered.

"May I play it?" she asked. Gingerly she sat down and stroked the keys. Then she played something from Bach, her left hand responding to the music in her soul.

When she had finished, he sat there for a moment and looked at her. Then, with warm, brown eyes aglow, he said, "Well, it was worth it."[26]

The next morning, through some inexplicable divination, Carson got it into her head that she wanted a home permanent, the new rage, an "hour Toni," which her friend "Baby Chile" Mullin had given to several friends with great success. Baby Chile's Tonis were the talk of Columbus— or so it seemed to Carson—and Carson decided that she, too, should have one. "But, Sister, you've never had a permanent," her mother wailed apprehensively. True, she had never had any curl in her hair except as a toddler when her mother had rolled it in rags.

"Yes, but Baby Chile has bought all the equipment," Carson countered as she rationalized why she should go through with it. Soon her well-meaning friend had cut, rolled, and immersed her with the magic chemicals that Madison Avenue promised would turn her into a new woman within the hour. Some two hours later, with Mrs. Woodruff, her mother, and

Baby Chile looking on admiringly, Carson gazed at herself in the mirror and responded with a sickly smile. She restrained herself from saying what she really thought, then demurely thanked Baby Chile, adding faintly that she guessed her new hairdo would take a little getting used to. A few moments later, however, Carson's face broke out in ugly red splotches and began to swell. Blaming the permanent, she cried and railed against her new condition, but before anyone could think of an antidote, her cousin Jordan Massee arrived with his sister Emily and their father to take her and Marguerite to Macon.

What Kathleen Woodruff had planned as a happy bon voyage luncheon for the group was now transmogrified into a strained affair, an atmosphere set by Carson's embarrassed silence over her hapless appearance and Marguerite's prattle as she reminisced and recaptured a bit of her lost youth and personality of thirty-five years earlier when she had first met and been charmed by Massee, Sr. That evening young Massee recorded in his diary impressions of the afternoon:

> March 17, 1949: . . . I was shocked at Bebe's appearance. She shows
> the effects of the terrible strain under which she has lived these last
> two years. Carson looked better than I had anticipated, despite the
> fact that her hair had been cut and subjected to a "Toni" by
> some friend of Kathleen's. She was very much upset at meeting some
> of the members of my family for the first time with her hair in such
> an unnatural state, and with her face badly swollen with hives—the
> result, I believe, of nervous strain, although it may be an allergic re-
> action to the hair preparation.[27]

En route home, they had a flat tire, which Massee, Jr., changed while Carson squatted beside him and handed him a tool now and then. Jordan's diary entry continued:

> Most of the way, I sat on the back seat with Carson and Bebe,
> talking. Conversation with Daddy was difficult since he couldn't hear
> above the noise of the motor and the wind, but he talked a great
> deal, mostly of his years of affluence. He seemed to be under some sort
> of compulsion, with Bebe, to live up to the image of the dashing
> young man who was a legend in her family as far back as she could
> remember, to justify the promise by presenting himself at the peak
> of his achievement.

Massee, Sr., was amazed when he saw Marguerite this time. She looked exactly as he remembered her mother when he was in his twenties. The elder Massee was a legend in the Smith family because he had once courted Marguerite's first cousin Mabel Carson, her uncle Alphonso's daughter. However, Massee was a distant cousin of the Carson family, who disapproved of the match and insisted that she marry someone else. Several years later, wed to a new suitor, Mabel Carson died in childbirth. Massee, Sr., reportedly grieved openly and enormously at her funeral in the First Baptist Church of Columbus. It was a story Carson loved to tell, which she enhanced with various embellishments.

Marguerite told young Massee that her son and younger daughter "belonged to the Smith clan" in personality and looks but that Sister and Massee, Jr., were Carsons as surely as she was. She also decided that Carson and her young cousin looked like his mother; therefore, they undoubtedly were double cousins, she declared. Carson herself thoroughly enjoyed the fantasy and listened now with rapt attention to fresh legends of the family, repetition of the old ones, and sundry other small-town tales. To Carson, her relationship with Jordan Massee, Jr., was "fore-ordained." Although they had almost lost touch with each other during the war years, for Carson was either in Columbus or Saratoga Springs most of the time that Massee was in New York, they renewed their ties in 1946. Then, he and his friend Paul Bigelow moved to Macon, preparing to settle in for a four-year stay "under the mistaken impression that my father needed me," said Massee.

Upon their arrival in Macon March 17, Carson and Marguerite were totally unprepared for what awaited them at 556½ Mulberry Street, the old brownstone residence of Massee and Bigelow. It seemed to them that they had never before seen such splendor in a private home anywhere. Massee had leased what was known locally as the old Emerson house, named after a Dr. Emerson who had built it when he moved to Macon from New Hampshire in 1853. Emerson had commissioned an eastern architect for the job, Ayers, who had come to Macon to build the Johnson-Felton-Hayes house—now a museum—and was able to use the same Italian workmen imported by Ayers for the Hayes house. Both structures were early symmetrical Victorian in the Italian style, with the Hayes house reportedly the finest example of that style anywhere in the United States. The house on Mulberry Street had remained vacant, however, for ninety years until Massee envisioned its restored beauty and elegance, leased it, and set about almost single-handedly to make the dream a reality. The magnificence of the old home, its handsome staircase, gigantic casement windows across the front, and splendorous interior—all rendered the two women speechless, a rarity for Marguerite under any circumstance. Even though Carson eventually visited much grander establishments, such as the country estates of Elizabeth Bowen and John Huston in Ireland and Dame Edith Sitwell's town house in London, she told Massee later that never in her lifetime had she seen any place with which she had been more enthralled, or which had had a more profound effect upon her.

Massee had named his house on Mulberry Street "The House of the

322   *The Lonely Hunter*

Salutation," a name he took from "The Salutation," a story by Sylvia Townsend Warner. That it was his favorite story was a closely guarded fact, for Massee was afraid he might someday let it slip out to Carson, who would have considered it a betrayal and been jealous and hurt. But Carson too, who knew the story and loved it, understood well why the house had become its namesake. In fact, if one is to begin to understand the relationship that flowered that spring between the two cousins in The House of the Salutation, he must first read "The Salutation," for it was here that Carson and Massee came together as brother and sister in spirit, cementing the bond that remained unbroken for the remaining eighteen years of Carson's life (except for a brief rift over mistaken loyalty, a separation that caused her to strike him from her will and then inadvertently fail to reinstate him). No one in her entire experience—not Marguerite or Mary Tucker or Reeves or Annemarie Clarac-Schwarzenbach or Edwin Peacock or David Diamond or Tennessee Williams—approached the relationship that was uniquely theirs until Mary Mercer came into her life ten years before Carson's death.

The evening of their arrival at Mulberry Street, Massee's servant Isaac prepared a simple, but delicious, typical southern meal for them: a steaming, deep dish meat pie, green salad, and tapioca pudding. They were joined at dinner by Massee's mother, whom Carson was meeting for the first time, and his father. Massee, Jr., knew Carson's propensity for startling statements which frequently shocked conventional ears—no matter whose they were—but the evening went nicely and there were no unseemly remarks. The elder Massees retired early, and after driving them home Massee, Jr., bought Carson what she called her "bedtime beer," then picked up his younger sister, Martha, and brought her to Mulberry Street to meet her cousins. That part of the evening went well, too, except for an unquotable remark by Carson, which was fielded in the most honorable southern manner. Massee's sister never changed her expression, and Massee, Jr., avoided Bigelow's glance.[28]

Carson was late in retiring that first evening. Before Massee's sister departed, Nonie Morgan, a journalist with the Macon *News*, dropped in after her rehearsal at the Little Theatre to meet Carson and interview her for the paper. Massee was not certain how physically equal his frail guest was to meeting all the people that Bigelow, especially, had proposed, but Carson surprised even herself at how nice she was to all of their friends. Miss Morgan had been at Fort Benning in November 1941 when *Reflections in a Golden Eye* had gone on sale at the Post Exchange in its first installment in *Harper's Bazaar*. She recalled that the harassed PX officer had finally inquired what it was all about when the exchange was besieged for copies of the magazine. Carson's picture (by Richard Avedon), looking like a teen-ager, had been in it, too, and Miss Morgan recalled that she wondered at the time how a young girl could have written such a magnificent piece of fiction. "And how I'd like to meet her," she sighed.

Now at last she had, and Miss Morgan found her "still the same young strangely disturbing child whose face looked out at me from the jacket of *The Heart Is a Lonely Hunter* . . . and her other writings." In her article published the next day, Nonie Morgan continued:

> The bangs and the long bob which have distinguished her are gone. Carson has cut her hair and given it a very slight wave. It is brushed back from her childlike brow, and gives her the look somehow of a young knight. She has been ill, very ill, and her pallor enhances the intense darkness of her wonderful eyes. She is a tall, thin girl, as simple and direct and without pretense as her writing.[29]

Indeed, by the time Carson met Miss Morgan that evening, she had washed as much of "the slight wave" out of her hair as was possible.

The days flashed by quickly for Carson and her mother in Macon. Her hives disappeared after two days, the swelling in her face receded, and she began to feel good for the first time in over a year. Carson had come to imbibe the South, yet she never dreamed that her deepest inhalations would come from the Massee family itself. Massee, Sr., was a beautiful repository of southern manners, morality, legend, and life. In Macon to gather substance and shadow for her new novel, Carson found it inevitable that she invest in her fictional octogenarian, Judge Fox Clane, some of the senior Massee's attributes, although exaggerated almost beyond recognition. It was not that there was a one-to-one relationship between Massee, Sr., and the old judge, but that Carson used many of his stories and drew from his broad canvas the fictional character she wanted. The only thing that bothered the elder Massee after *Clock Without Hands* was published twelve years later was that his young cousin had not used the stories just as he had told them to her.

Carson met four women in Macon who helped her considerably as she researched the psyche and pulse of the deep South as she encountered it in Macon. Perhaps the one who contributed most was Susan Myrick, who had been an editor on the Macon *Telegraph* for years. An amusing and highly intelligent woman, well read, and a close friend of Flannery O'Connor and Margaret Mitchell, Miss Myrick had been a long-time confidante of Massee, Jr.

Another friend of Massee's, also with the Macon *Telegraph*, was Margaret Leonard Long. Invited for breakfast at Mulberry Street one morning, Miss Long was told that Carson had come South to inspect the region for a new novel. She was alarmed, however, that Carson was seeing the South through a telescope, as it were, and told her so. She said that she was seeing, for instance, the Bibb Manufacturing Company through "the hospitality of the crown prince of the cotton mill, as well as other aspects of southern change through the eyes of the smallest and most privileged group of people in Macon."[30] To counteract the affluence through which Carson was viewing the South, Miss Long offered to take her to meet millhands on strike, labor leaders, local blacks who were re-organizing their regional NAACP, and the various black and white "do-gooders" on the Macon Council on Human Relations. Although Carson was vitally interested in these aspects of southern life, she left Macon abruptly after trouble erupted at Yaddo involving Elizabeth Ames and did not get to tour the town with Margaret Long as they had planned.

One of Miss Long's most vivid memories of the visiting author in-volved her own willing sacrifice of garters so that Carson could be well dressed at a Sunday dinner in the home of Massee's parents. Because of Carson's "mysterious and creeping ailment," as Miss Long called it, which caused her "to walk with difficulty and favor her left arm and leg," she and some of the other women to whom Carson had been introduced came in to assist with several ordinary chores such as dressing. Marguerite, of course, was usually there to help, but she had gone to Brunswick for the weekend to see Brother-Man. Thus Miss Long was accorded the "privi-lege of ironing her black skirt and white blouse," although she readily admitted that she would have found washing them better suited to her talents. Then, in the process of helping Carson dress, she discovered that her young celebrity had no garters for her stockings. Immediately taking off her own "disreputably old and twisted ones (the kind that hold the stockings up just above the knee)," Margaret Long recalled that, finally, "we got her dressed properly enough for a nice Sunday dinner in a big house in Macon."[31] As she walked home later with her own stockings in her pocketbook, she felt that in having helped prepare their "hallowed girl for dinner," she had rendered up her "inadequate all to hold Carson's stockings up." The truth of the matter was that Carson had no garters because she almost never wore stockings. When she decided that she must have them on that special occasion, it still did not occur to her that she needed some accouterments for them, nor would she have dreamed of wearing a girdle.

There were others who came to see Carson in Macon, too, by whom she was much taken, such as Otis and Sara Knight, whom Jordan in-troduced as "two of God's archangels," and Kit Birdsey, whom he re-ferred to as Macon's only truly "sophisticated and worldly woman." The two women shared an immediate rapport. Miss Birdsey's impressions of people, memories, and life in the South were not simply black or white, but of the subtlest hues. As was the case with Massee, Carson loved Miss Birdsey for her charm and honesty.[32]

Although Carson thrived on her new friendships and the storehouse of materials she was mentally collecting, she liked especially the quiet evenings in The House of the Salutation when there were only the four of them—Jordan Massee, Paul Bigelow, herself, and her mother. They talked late into the night, listened to music, and sometimes read. Marguerite usually retired early. "Carson was a demanding companion, whether guest or hostess," said Massee. He looked forward to a respite in the midafternoon when his guests lay down to rest or nap. As soon as they closed their door, Massee sat down with his journal and recorded the events of the preceding day, trying to set down the facts, at least, hopefully to be elaborated on at a later date. Once up, the women were again bright and chatty. They both started their drinking day on dry California sherry, which they insisted on buying for themselves in gallon jugs. They kept a supply both in their room and in the kitchen. "There were so many bottles and so cheap—$1.98 a gallon—that I was embarrassed to set them out on the street early for the garbage collection," said Massee. Instead, he subtly kept one eye on his watch and an ear cocked toward the front windows; when he heard the truck he bounded down the long flight of steps with sherry jugs in tow as though he had just remembered them. Marguerite rarely drank hard liquor, but she got herself into a state of euphoria on sherry without ever getting drunk. "Like most things that are cheap, the sherry was, fortunately, weak," recalled Jordan. There was never any speech hesitation or slurring by Marguerite. She simply reached a calm, happy state, taking sherry or wine "like many people took Miltown."

When Marguerite went to Brunswick to be with her son and daughter-in-law and to see her new grandchild, Massee drove her on Saturday morning to the train station, then picked her up Sunday night. It was while Marguerite was away that the two cousins revealed the innermost secrets of their hearts and arrived at a knowledge of each other which complemented the love that had preceded it. Carson also talked to Massee at length about Reeves and shared a letter from him she had received a few days after her arrival. In it Reeves told her about several southern senators who had voted against a plan of the President's, an act which he said smacked of bigotry and regionalism. Reeves was always good about calling various events of national and world significance to Carson's attention, although he was strongly prejudiced. Frequently he suggested something newsworthy that might be useful to her fiction. He was particularly alert to news that came out of their native South. That night Carson told her cousin that Reeves was vital to her existence and that she loved him very much.

She told Massee, also, about her need for a woman's love and companionship, about Annemarie Clarac-Schwarzenbach and the grief and happiness that had accompanied her sexual ambivalence. In one sense, she felt that she had the best of two worlds. They spoke also of God. She said that she believed in God and felt blessed and filled with a religious spirit that did not depend upon dogma or ritual or whether she went to church. Carson did go to church occasionally over the years of her adulthood, but she never felt compelled to go. She told Massee that she loved the Bible, especially the Psalms. One evening she recited her favorite psalm: "The Lord is my shepherd, I shall not want . . ." When she finished, she was in tears. According to Massee, anytime Carson recited or heard the Twenty-third Psalm, she cried. Fittingly, years later, it was read at her funeral.

On March 21, Paul Bigelow, who worked for the Middle Georgia Broadcasting Company, WBML, went to Dayton, Ohio, on business, but before he left, he interviewed Carson in their living room for his broadcast. Together the next night, the three of them hovered about the radio listening to the transcription. Carson had never been on the radio before nor heard her voice on a recording. After the first several minutes of near disbelief, she became convinced that it was, after all, *her* voice, her slow, soft-spoken southern drawl, her pauses, her almost inaudible responses at times. How good that she could at least write, she quipped. It was almost another ten years, however, before she put herself into that position again, when she read from her books and poems on an MGM recording for commercial distribution.[33]

That same day, sudden and jolting news reached Carson apprising her of a plot to discredit Elizabeth Ames. Alfred Kazin wrote Carson that a group of four writers—reportedly led by poet Robert Lowell—had spearheaded a drive accusing Yaddo's executive director of being mysteriously connected with the Communist party, charges which apparently stemmed from Mrs. Ames's friendship with Agnes Smedley, an avowed supporter of the Chinese Communists, who had been allowed to remain at Yaddo from the summer of 1943 through 1946. The accusing group demanded that the executive director be fired immediately, whereupon the board of directors called a meeting to decide the situation. Carson responded to the attack quickly and passionately. She cried, made phone calls, wrote furious letters, and finally decided that she should be in New York and at Elizabeth Ames's side. Reluctantly, Massee put Carson and her mother on the train, bound first for Atlanta, where she was to meet briefly with Ralph McGill of the Atlanta *Constitution* while she changed trains, and then on to New York City.

Carson arrived the day of the directors' meeting and learned that Mrs. Ames had been exonerated and given a vote of confidence.[34] When she wrote to Massee and Bigelow upon her return to Nyack, she said that she had talked with Elizabeth Ames on the telephone, but decided not to go on to Yaddo since the whole matter was now settled. Although

Mrs. Ames was a woman of great fortitude, she admitted to Carson that she had suffered a great strain because of the accusation and the divided loyalties that ensued among people she thought of as her friends. According to Alfred Kazin, said Carson, Robert Lowell had acted in an uncharitable and intolerant manner, which she thought to be a lovely understatement. She was pleased to hear that Katherine Anne Porter had behaved well. Miss Porter had wired and written in Mrs. Ames's defense. Disappointed in Newton Arvin, however, Carson found his attitude oblique. It would take awhile for Yaddo's executive director to recover from her hurt, Carson knew, but Mrs. Ames was tough, and erratic personalities and a vicious personal attack would not keep her down for long. Although Carson hoped that she might go back to Yaddo to work on her new novel that summer, she did not return until 1954.

Carson longed to complete the last leg of her tour in the South which had been recently aborted. She had called Edwin Peacock from Macon to explain about Elizabeth Ames's predicament and to cancel her Charleston trip, but she wrote her friend now that when Reeves's vacation began on May 13, they would come down together. Reeves had worked for over a year at radio station WOR, steadily and with success. He had kept his same apartment in the city, joined AA (Alcoholics Anonymous), and for many months touched nothing alcoholic. Then he began to drink again, but tried—though often unsuccessfully—to keep it under control. For the most part, Carson and Reeves were compatible during the spring of 1949. They came and went as they chose.

Carson suggested to Jordan Massee that she and Reeves go to Macon for the first two days of his vacation, then take Massee and Paul Bigelow with them to Charleston. More than anything else now, she wanted Edwin Peacock and her cousin from Macon to know each other, to comprise another we of me relationship with her at center. Massee had no real intention of going, but he agreed for the moment because she was so insistent. Secretly, however, Massee was tired and longed to be alone. Although Carson's visit to Mulberry Street remained one of the most remarkable events of his life, it had also been exhausting. To Massee, "the part that was meaningful was *not* tiring; but housing a great celebrity, guarding my family, and contending with small-town rivalries were."[35] Since he did not know Carson's Charleston friends, but knew that they meant a great deal to her, it seemed better to him to plan only on seeing her next in Nyack, regardless of what he had led her to believe.

Carson and Reeves arrived in Charleston May 13 with typewriter in tow, intending to stay two full weeks together. Carson would stay on longer and write if she chose to, and if it were agreeable to her hosts. Their time was spent both at 9 College Avenue, the large ante-bellum home belonging to John Zeigler's Aunt Detie (Marie Alicia Elfe), and on Sullivan's Island in the beach cabin he and Edwin Peacock rented every summer. Carson loved the atmosphere in both households. The house in town teemed with people. Another of Zeigler's aunts, Mrs. Harry L. Erchmann, lived elsewhere but maintained the old home and employed a cook to come in daily to prepare the evening meal for both households. Zeigler's mother came frequently, too, along with his sister Virginia and her two children. Another woman came in regularly to clean. Reeves realized now why Peacock had said that there was no need to hire anyone part time on Carson's behalf. There was always a houseful of potential attendants. While together in Charleston, Reeves performed all of the personal chores necessary for Carson and insisted in helping in other ways when he could.

It was quieter at Sullivan's Island, where they retreated for complete relaxation, although Carson enjoyed the hubbub of the big household and the southern talk that flowed. Peacock invited their old friends Robert Walden and Edward Newberry, whom Carson had not seen since their camaraderie in Columbus during the summer of 1942 when Walden had been stationed at Fort Benning. Walden, now a banker, and Newberry, an architect, shared a home in Charlotte, North Carolina, where they moved soon after the war. Both had kept in touch with Edwin Peacock and John Zeigler over the years, along with another mutual friend from Charlotte, Harrell Woolfolk, who came to Sullivan's Island with them now to meet Carson. It was Walden's first meeting with Reeves, whom he liked immensely. To the group in Charleston that spring, Carson and Reeves seemed very much in love. Reeves had stopped drinking again and was kind, gentle, and attentive to Carson's every need. One night he attended an AA meeting in Charleston, and Carson spoke proudly of how well he was doing. She thoroughly enjoyed the all-male household on the island, a situation in which she had always been comfortable. She and the others were simply chums together, eating, drinking, smoking, swapping yarns, swimming, and lying about lazily in the sun. Although the ocean was chilly, she insisted on swimming each time the men went in. Then shortly, she would come out of the surf and pull on an old sweater or army jacket of Reeves's until she felt warm again. The sun and fresh salt air seemed wonderfully good for her weakened limbs, and Carson thought that if she could stay on indefinitely, she might eventually recover completely. Her damaged arm seemed more supple than it had in months. The excitement of the weekend was a telegram she received from New York acknowledging that her play definitely would be produced the next season. The group toasted with great joviality to Carson's future success and agreed that each would be in the audience when *The Member of the Wedding* opened on Broadway.

Soon, however, Carson blamed the ocean breezes for her next illness. Suddenly she had become dazed and weakened, her condition aggravated by pain and fever. Rather than risk treatment by a local doctor who did not know her case history and its many tangents, she and Reeves decided to return to Nyack for medical attention from her friend Dr. William Mayer, who diagnosed her ailment as flu. It had settled in the kidneys, but it was nothing serious and would pass, he assured her. When she felt well enough to write a letter again, her first missive was to Jordan Massee, this time not only to apprise him of recent developments and her untimely departure from Charleston, but also to console him, for he had learned that someone he dearly loved had just died. Massee's grief reminded her anew of her own sense of loss of Annemarie Clarac-Schwarzenbach, grief freshened now not only by her cousin's desolation, but also by news she had read in the paper only the day before: that her friend Klaus Mann had committed suicide in Nice, France. It was Mann who had relayed the news of Annemarie's death to her that winter in Yaddo. Again, the past became the present for Carson.

Many years later, after Carson's death, Massee attempted to explain the nature of his relationship with his cousin, "cemented that momentous spring of 1949, conjoined first in 'The House of the Salutation' and made irrevocably fast by our sense of oneness and the similarity of our individual responses to situations." As Massee saw it,

The bond, the strength of the bond, had to do more with *the similarity of our individual response to situations* than to the similarity of the situations, although there was a striking resemblance there, too. This is an important distinction. I think, perhaps, that neither of us ever knew anyone else whose response to certain situations, most particularly to the commitment of love and friendship, so resembled our own. We actually had few intellectual interests in common. But we had a profound understanding of each other and I think it was based on this recognition of identical emotional response and commitment. Where we differed on this point was invariably the result of Carson's struggle to survive and my tendency to self-sacrifice (a quality the Freudians rather quaintly call masochism). In me, the difference was largely a matter of degree; whereas the difference in Carson was, no doubt, an aspect of her genius.

How ironic that in our physical—or should I say "actual" since I don't mean sexual?—relationship, Carson held on to me in desperation, as she did to all of those people who were actually necessary to her physical survival; whereas I as often as not struggled to avoid her in my own subordinate struggle to survive (subordinate, that is, to me, to other and stronger motivations; to her, subordinate to her own struggle, although never lacking in sympathy for mine). None of this must be confused with the struggle to maintain identity, a quality neither of us *ever* experienced, a quality we could comprehend when we encountered it in others only intellectually.[36]

While Carson was still recuperating in Nyack that spring from what she identified to friends as her "nasty grippe," she read the galley proofs of Tennessee Williams' preface to a new edition of *Reflections in a Golden Eye*, soon to be published by New Directions.[37] Several weeks later Carson wrote Williams a deeply apologetic letter for having crossed out a paragraph in his preface. She said that she was influenced both by her poor state of health at the time and her sister's comment that the sentences in question (about a bawdy house) were too personal. Now that her mind was clear and she was no longer feverish, she said that she regretted her action and wondered if the deletion had thrown the piece off balance. It was presumptuous of her to have altered his writing in any way, she apologized, and begged him to ignore the notation. Carson's editor and Williams decided to retain the changes, however.

In June, once well, Carson set heart and soul on seeing her play through to production. Although the Theatre Guild had received considerable publicity over the past year that it would produce *The Member of the Wedding* from a script prepared by both Carson and her collaborator, the Guild made little headway in actually mounting the play. Earlier, the theatre group had asked Ethel Waters to read the script and play Berenice Sadie Brown, but she turned it down. It was a "dirty play," said the actress, and she did not like her role. The cook was a bitter woman, a chain smoker, a heavy drinker, in short, a sordid, ugly creature who had lost her faith in God, Miss Waters concluded.[38] Although she admitted that she was down on her luck, both professionally and emotionally, she said she was not "*that* down."

When it was apparent that the Theatre Guild would not exercise its option, producer Robert Whitehead became seriously interested in *The Member of the Wedding*. He read the revised script late that spring when Audrey Wood came to him with it, and he bought it on the first submission.[39] Miss Wood was convinced that the play still needed extensive revision, but Whitehead believed that it had excellent possibilities as it was. Before he sailed to Europe in early June, he discussed the script with Carson over the telephone. Still in bed recuperating from her flu and kidney infection, she was cheered by Whitehead's optimism.

In May, Whitehead asked Ethel Waters about playing the role of Berenice, but her reply again had been less than enthusiastic. On June 28, Whitehead wrote to Carson from Rome to apprise her of developments:

> There seems to have been some small misunderstanding between
> Audrey Wood and myself regarding the submitting of your play to
> Ethel Waters—I was under the impression that I had told Audrey

that we would send a script to Miss Waters if her response to my
letter written in May was enthusiastic. I am, of course, dreadfully sorry
if this has been a tactical error but am naturally anxious to bring her
in on our plans as soon as possible so that we can count on her
availability. Though we have all agreed to withhold rewrite plans
till Harold Clurman returns, I still think, as I told you on the phone,
that the play does not need any large scale revision, particularly in
the case of "Berenice" who seems to me already drawn with great
substance.

Though Ethel Waters' reaction to playing the part was disappointing, I have not given up hope about her at all. I think she would
be making a tremendous mistake in refusing the part and hope she
will seriously reconsider after we have had a chance to discuss it with
her ourselves.

Whitehead said that he would be back in New York July 26 and looked
forward to meeting with Carson as soon as possible.

In the meantime, Joshua Logan also became seriously involved with
The Member of the Wedding, so much so that many people were surprised when Harold Clurman emerged as director. According to Logan,

I first read Carson's collaboration with Greer Johnson, and even
that had enough of the book in it to appeal to me greatly. Later, I
met Mrs. McCullers and she brought me her script, which I liked
even better; however, I did not like the scene where Frankie had her
near-affair with the young soldier in the hotel room. Somehow, I did
not feel that in the play it earned its way. The scene itself was not as
moving as the scenes back in the house with the little boy and the
old colored woman. When I left the play, however, it was still in the
script. I am sure that it would have been eliminated had I gone on
directing, just as it was when Harold Clurman took over.

My not directing *The Member of the Wedding* had nothing to
do with "having time" or "liking the script." I loved it in all forms,
and I had an open season in my schedule. But an Act of God prevented my continuing with McCullers:

Mary MacArthur, the lovely daughter of Charles MacArthur and
Helen Hayes, died of polio. I had directed Mary in her first play, *A
Kiss for Cinderella,* two seasons before; and I had directed Helen
Hayes the year before in *Happy Birthday.* Charles MacArthur called
me and said that unless Helen worked immediately she was headed
for a mental collapse. He insisted that the only thing she would be
willing to do was the southern play I had sketched to her once, based
on *The Cherry Orchard.*

I told him how much I was involved in *Member,* but he was

so eloquent in his plea for Helen's "sanity" and was so effusive
about her love for me and this idea I had had that he persuaded me
to call off my participation in *Member*, much as I loved it, and go
to work on my own play, *The Wisteria Trees*, which I rewrote under
great pressure and put on the boards as a gesture to Helen and the
memory of Mary. I always will regret giving up *Member*, even
though I am very proud of *The Wisteria Trees*. Somehow, I feel one
of them could have been postponed, making way for the other.[40]

Clurman, in Israel at the time Robert Whitehead sent him the script,
was not readily available. Then, after reading Carson's play, he did not
know if he wanted to be available. Whitehead acknowledged frankly that
he, too, was worried about the play. Those who had turned it down had
said that it was not a play, that it had no regard for theatrical conven-
tions, that it had little plot and no big climaxes or sweeping movement.
Clurman was even more dubious. He did not think the public would like
it, nor was it Broadway material, he added. He was on the verge of rejecting it, succumbing "to a kind of highbrow jaundice which bitterly sup-
poses that truly unusual forms of the theatre are only jeopardized by
production on Broadway," he explained later, but he agreed to at least
talk to the playwright.[41] Upon his return, Clurman met with Carson and
asked her, "What is your play all about?"

"Togetherness," she replied. Clurman told her that he understood
her play, but did not think the public would. Yet the fact that *he* did gave
Carson confidence, and she clasped his hands in an attitude of grateful
recognition.[42] Yes, he would do it, Clurman agreed, half suspecting that
this, his fiftieth production, would result in one of his greatest failures.
Later, his wife said that she was going to invest in the show. "You're dead
wrong," he told her. "Don't do it." Clurman's wife invested anyway, ig-
noring her husband's advice. "I was glad, of course, later, when we saw
that it was a hit," Clurman recalled.

Whitehead's next step was to convince Ethel Waters to play Berenice Sadie Brown. In late July he flew to Chicago with the script and met
with her. Again Miss Waters read it and shook her head. Although it was
Carson's revised script—not the one Miss Waters read when the Theatre
Guild courted her—she still did not like it. "There is no God in this
play," she told the producer confronting her now. She could not be in a
godless play, even though she needed the money, as well as the job.
"I'm ten thousand dollars in debt," she told Whitehead. If she got to
New York, however, she would at least talk with the playwright, she
promised. Whitehead departed, still without a star. In a few weeks, Miss
Waters, accompanied by Whitehead, appeared in Carson's living room in
Nyack. No, she would not play Berenice as the playwright had drawn her,

she argued, but if they would let her change a few lines, interpret the role herself—in a sense do her own directing—she would consent. Finally, Whitehead and Carson agreed to Miss Waters' demands, although they knew that it would mean additional headaches for Harold Clurman. (In 1952 another director had difficulty with Miss Waters in her starring role of Berenice, too. According to Fred Zinnemann, who directed the movie version of *The Member of the Wedding,* "Ethel Waters clung to the play . . . and it was at times difficult to get her to change or to unlearn some of her lines and stage movements. She was very amiable, but she did have very crystallized ideas of her own. I remember that on several occasions when she disagreed with the directions I was giving her, she would look up to heaven and say: 'God is my director.' You can imagine that it wasn't easy to find a comeback to that kind of remark.")[43]

In August 1949, a twenty-three-year-old actress from Grosse Pointe, Michigan, Julie Harris, was signed to play the title role of the sensitive, twelve-year-old Frankie Addams, who wanted desperately to be "a member of the wedding." Miss Harris had made her Broadway debut five years earlier, appearing with Burgess Meredith in Synge's *The Playboy of the Western World,* but her Broadway roles had been minor, and many of the plays unsuccessful. The critics had begun to notice her, however, and for Julie Harris now, Carson's play was a chance at stardom. She was asked to take the part even without auditioning, Carson having seen her in Nyack that summer in Helen Hayes's production of *The Glass Menagerie.* Carson told Clurman that Miss Harris would be perfect for the part. Clurman and Whitehead, independent of each other, had also hit upon Julie Harris to play Frankie. It was only a matter of waiting until she was available to take the role. During the interim, the search continued for a suitable John Henry West, Frankie's seven-year-old cousin.

One of the chief problems lay in getting backers, but finally a handful was found who agreed to become partners in the venture. The chief investors were producers Robert Whitehead and Oliver Rea, although the latter had little to do with the actual mounting of the play. Sculptor Stanley Martineau, functioning as assistant producer, also backed the show, along with Whitehead's wife, Virginia Bolen, Barry Hyams, the publicity man, and Lester Polakov, whose job was sets, costumes, and lighting.

The play was destined to open on a shoestring budget. Even in 1950 a twelve-hundred-dollar allowance for costumes was unheard of for a show that aspired to Broadway, but Polakov and his assistant, Eddie Cook, were told that they could spend not a penny more. Instead of having costumes made, they scavenged the shops on Seventh Avenue for bargains. One such "find" was Frankie's garish orange silk evening dress which she selected to wear to her brother's wedding. Miss Harris, in fact, required two of them, which Polakov found on two different shopping sprees. The niggardly budget extended to staging and lighting as well. As a further saving, Polakov himself handled the souvenir book for the show, for which they quickly sold advertising in time for the New York opening after the Philadelphia tryouts had given them reason to hope for a hit.

The Member of the Wedding was scheduled to go into rehearsal on October 28, but by that date there was still no one to play seven-year-old John Henry. (In the movie version, he was six years old.) Virginia Bolen had already toured the East looking for him, then, practically on the eve of rehearsals, returned unsuccessfully from a southern tour. Every other role had been cast, but nowhere had a child turned up who seemed properly plaintive, curious, and impressionable—or as Harold Clurman specified—"someone who would melt your heart." Everyone connected with the show was asked to be on the alert for the kind of child they were seeking, but they found no one. Then one of the group suddenly looked at Fritz de Wilde, who had been cast as Jarvis, the bridegroom. "Fritz, you've got a kid, haven't you?"

"Yes, but my boy's never acted before. Why, he can't even read," De Wilde responded.

"Get him down here—let's give him a try," Whitehead urged.

Once they saw young Brandon de Wilde, they liked everything about him. Immediately afterward the De Wildes drove South to a wedding, and en route, they read the play to their son so that he could learn his lines. By the time they got back, the youngster knew not only his lines, but every line in the play.[44]

When the play went into rehearsal, the greatest problem lay in the veteran actress Ethel Waters. Unable to direct his star, Clurman found that handling her was more like "training a bear," he said, a mental image which set Carson into amused convulsions whenever it came to mind.[45] Miss Waters had a difficult time coordinating actions with words, as well as learning her lines. Part of the success of the play lay in Whitehead and Clurman's decision to treat "the child like a veteran, and the veteran like a child," said Polakov. At first, young Brandon prompted Miss Waters on her lines, and she flashed him an embarrassed smile. But the prodding soon got on her nerves, and she finally frowned fiercely at him and said, "Now, honey, I don't want you to bother me any more." The child held his tongue, and Miss Waters continued to stumble through her lines and bumble around the stage until opening night in Philadelphia. "The boy, by contrast, performed beautifully from the beginning," said Polakov. "His timing was excellent, and he learned with great rapidity."

The night of the Philadelphia opening, Clurman noticed that Miss Waters was more agitated than usual. Everyone knew that she still did not know her lines. Aware of her state and eager to console her, Clurman said, "You're only nervous, Ethel. You'll be wonderful tonight—just don't you worry about a thing."

"You're very reassuring, Mr. Clurman, but I'm not reassured," she countered. She had terrible cramps, she told him; then she went on to explain that when a black actress faced an audience, her responsibility was greater than that of a white actress. She had to succeed, and, indeed, she was nervous, she admitted.

A few months later, when Miss Waters wrote her autobiography for Doubleday, she expressed her appreciation for the extraordinary way Clurman had directed such a fragile play. Then she added that "even though Mr. Clurman had been an actor at one time, during rehearsals I did not feel so strongly his sympathy and understanding. But the sympathy and understanding were there. His way of telling you when you are good is to say nothing."[46] The night they opened in Philadelphia, Miss Waters recalled that she said her prayers as usual and then told herself: "I'm gonna walk out there and say everything just the way I feel it." Ethel Waters did just that, and according to the out-of-town critics, she gave a superb performance.

Carson, in the meantime, was interested in every aspect of the forthcoming production. When she met Polakov at Whitehead's house for the first time, she said: "I don't know what to say to you. I don't know anything about the theatre." She said that she had seen only six plays in her life and that most of them had been on her high school stage. Then Carson asked: "What about the set?"

"Don't worry," he said. "We'll work it out."

A few weeks later, they met again in Nyack. Miss Waters was entertaining at a party in Carson's home, and she had brought Fletcher Henderson along to play for Carson. Polakov arrived with his sketch of the set as he now envisioned it and showed it to her. He explained that he had tried to catch in his set what he thought of as his personal metaphor for *The Member of the Wedding*, the "sense of isolation, the vaporization of human experience so soon lost, the green summer."[47] Its hues were misty, soft greens and blues, the whole set exuding a feeling not only of closeness in the kitchen, in which most of the action was to take place, but also of openness—gained by the two great trees painted behind and beside the house on the flats, the gate opening to the neighbor's yard, the grape arbor, the porch and the room in which the wedding would take place off from the kitchen, the open door—all open to the view so that one would have the sense of belonging at the same time to the house and to the yard as he sat in the theatre. "It's just beautiful, Lester," Carson responded.

Afterward, Carson gave much thought to the set, and several weeks

later—one week prior to the Philadelphia opening—she saw Whitehead's
wife and told her that she had some new ideas for the set, some changes,
possibly. Virginia Bolen then showed her what had already been done
and explained how involved the making of a set was—the blueprints,
fourteen sketches, light plots, cues, the actual construction, painting, and
the like. Amazed, Carson said that she had had no idea of the complexi-
ties. She thought that the set involved simply a painted background with
a few loosely arranged pieces of furniture. Her earlier plays had all been
given in the back yard or the living room, she said. She had no concept
about lumber, carpenters, technical plans, or what went on backstage,
that there were a wardrobe mistress, a master carpenter, ten stagehands,
a master prop man and six assistants, a master electrician, an assistant
electrician—all of whom had to be contracted for the opening in Philadelphia and were a part of the "traveling company." Then there were the
many additional people furnished by the theatre itself. Miss Bolen explained that the cast required five understudies, a general manager, a
stage manager, an assistant stage manager, an assistant to him—and the
list went on and on. Carson's head whirled. "I had no idea," she repeated.

It was not until November 28 that the entire cast sat for an initial
reading of the play. At Whitehead's invitation, Carson attended too, and
nervously welcomed and thanked them for consenting to help make her
play a reality. "Do I need to be at rehearsals every day?" Carson asked
Clurman.

"No, but we want you to feel free to come whenever you'd like," he
responded warmly.

The first few days, she dropped in regularly, always accompanied by
Reeves, who was fascinated by the whole procedure. Carson, however, was
bothered by aspects of the theatre she did not understand, and she sometimes thought it best to stay away. Occasionally she ventured a suggestion to Clurman about something she wanted him to try. There were
two scenes in the play, for instance, which called for music to be heard
coming from a neighbor's house—notes made by a piano tuner. Carson
was adamant with Clurman and Whitehead that the notes from the piano come from a piece by Bach, for that was the way she remembered it
actually happening in her childhood. Clurman thought it was a bad idea
and told her so, but he let it ride until late in rehearsals. Then they tried
it one day when Carson was in the theatre. As though she were the first
to realize that the music sounded staged, out of place, she quickly volunteered, "Fakey. Forget it." Another time, she saw Julie Harris using Clurman's briefcase for Frankie's suitcase, but knowing nothing about props,
she was much concerned. "But, Lester, that's too small, that briefcase,"
Carson protested. "It was a *suitcase* Frankie packed." Patiently, Polakov

explained that it was simply a substitute for the real thing, which he assured her they would have on opening night.

Carson loved, especially, to watch Julie Harris in her role as Frankie. At one rehearsal, Carson arrived just before the knife-throwing incident. Miss Harris had been somewhat apprehensive about the way the script called for her to handle the knife and angrily throw it into the door, but she had practiced until she was able to do it repeatedly with perfection. Carson's line in the script read: "I'm the best knife thrower in town." But this time the young actress missed. Changing her expression, she also adapted the line to the situation without missing a beat. "I'm *almost* the best knife thrower in town," she said. Carson loved it. Thereafter, it did not matter if Julie Harris hit or missed—she always had the right line. Later, the word *almost* became a part of the published version of the play, Carson assuming that without Miss Harris in the role, there were bound to be more misses than hits.

The playwright also knew that *her* Frankie had short hair—had chopped it off herself, in fact—and she wondered how Miss Harris, whose long reddish-blond hair was the admiration of all who knew her, would become transformed into a crew-cut Frankie. Soon the New York *Times* (October 27) carried a story pertaining to that very problem:

> Tomorrow morning Carson McCullers' *The Member of the Wedding* goes into rehearsal, and tomorrow morning, too, one of the town's most important tonsorial artists with one of those long French names will try giving Julie Harris a haircut that won't look like a haircut. Just how the tonsorial artist is squaring this with his artistic conscience, this corner does not know, but it is entirely necessary in the name of art, anyway.

The operation was not a success the first time, however, and just before opening night, Polakov said to her, "Cut it *all* off, Julie, like Frankie did." "All of it?" she asked.

"All of it," he repeated.

When Julie Harris came back this time, she had lost the last remaining inches of measurable hair. "Oh, you *are* my Frankie," Carson cried when she saw her now.

On December 22, 1949, the play—dedicated to Reeves—opened at the Walnut Theatre in Philadelphia. A week earlier, the cast traveled by train in special cars, along with the sets. Carson and Reeves went down the day before. It was a cold, gray, winter afternoon when a handful of staunch supporters met at Pennsylvania Station and set out for the City of Brotherly Love, only to find it even grayer. In the group were Jordan Massee and Paul Bigelow, who had come up from Macon just before the Philadelphia première; Carson's good friend Emanuel Romano, who had recently been painting and sketching her; Romano's brother-in-law Hugo Dreyfuss; and their mutual good friends, Nancy Ferguson and Yetta Arenstein, who were both connected with the theatre. At Miss Ferguson's home many writers, editors, playwrights, and other artists frequently gathered, and Carson was fond of both women. Carson had met Romano through David McDowell, whom she had known earlier in Paris and now saw occasionally at Nancy Ferguson's. According to Romano:

> One morning McDowell came with a lady to my studio. She looked pale in her countenance; she had a body impairment and moved with great effort. She told me she had hemiplegia. Half of her body was paralyzed, but she tried courageously to hide her handicapped limbs. I was immediately attracted by the sensitivity of her personality and asked her to pose for a portrait, to which she immediately agreed. With pride she showed me the shirt she wore and the gray-green slacks—her man's shirt, a dark blue plaid with emerald green stripes, had been a present from Tennessee Williams, from Milano. From time to time I would ask if she wanted to rest, but she would say, "No, I can sit some more." But she wanted to have a cup of very hot black coffee and a smoke. She smoked continuously.
> The next day she came with a bouquet of tiger-lilies and a package; it was the French version of *The Heart Is a Lonely Hunter*, inscribed to my mother. Usually she came in the morning and went to rehearsals of *The Member of the Wedding* in the afternoon.

After the opening of the play, Romano did another oil of Carson and a series of drawings. (In October of 1968, Romano showed his paintings and sketches of Carson at the Gotham Book Mart.)[48]

The New York delegation arrived in Philadelphia to find Carson distraught and nervous, drinking one glass of whiskey after another in desperation. She had been told that Ethel Waters was still bumbling her lines at the last rehearsal. Carson was sure that the play could not survive. She would have been even more upset had she been aware of the problems backstage at that very moment. In addition to Miss Waters' "cramps," young Brandon de Wilde had peeked out from the edge of the curtain and become terror-struck by the noise and sea of murmuring faces. In rehearsals, there had been only a handful of people out front, most of whom had looked friendly and smiled at him, talked to him later, and given him candy bars. What the boy saw before him now caused him to falter, panic, and sob uncontrollably. Clurman reached his side first, knelt beside him, and said stalwartly: "Now, Brandon, this is your first play. You go out there now, and someday I'll do *King Lear* with you." Still the tears rolled, and Clurman called for the boy's father. The senior De Wilde had been relieved of his role of Jarvis in the play—a minor one compared to the

37 LEFT:
Carson and Reeves
in Paris, 1946.

38 BELOW:
Carson and Reeves
in Paris, 1947.

39 Carson in her back yard at 131 South Broadway, Nyack, New York, 1947.

40 Carson with her sister, Margarita Gachet Smith, New York City, 1949.

41 Carson at a first reading of the play *The Member of the Wedding*. Left to right: Julie Harris, Ethel Waters, producers Stanley Martineau and Robert Whitehead, director Harold Clurman, Carson McCullers, and stage manager Frederic (Fritz) de Wilde.

42 ABOVE: Carson and Reeves at Sullivan's Island, off the coast of Charleston, South Carolina, May 1949.

43 BELOW: Carson McCullers looking over the script of *The Member of the Wedding* with director Harold Clurman, 1949.

44   ABOVE: A scene from The Member of the Wedding; left to right: Brandon de Wilde, Janet De Gore, Julie Harris, James Holden, Ethel Waters, William Hansen.

45   BELOW: Set of The Member of the Wedding, designed by Lester Polakov.

46   A scene from *The Member of the Wedding* with Brandon de Wilde, Julie Harris,
Ethel Waters, January 1950.

47 LEFT: Carson and Reeves at Castelgandolfo, near Rome, spring 1952.

48 BELOW: Carson is greatly disappointed as, one by one, her prospective travel companions back out of their planned trip to Vienna. Left to right: Valentine Sherrif, Carson, Rowland E. (Jack) Fullilove, Reeves; Thanksgiving 1952, Paris.

49 LEFT: Carson McCullers, winter 1952, Bachvillers, France.
Like the adolescents in her fiction,
Carson had always longed
to live in a snowy land.

50 BELOW: Carson with her boxer pup in the orchard behind her Bachvillers home outside Paris, spring 1953.

stardom of his son—and "promoted" to stage manager, replacing Polakov, who earlier had been assigned that job, too, because of their minuscule budget. Whatever De Wilde told his son, it was the magic word, for immediately the curtain opened upon the barefooted John Henry West—wearing gold-rimmed spectacles and a skimpy sun suit—picking scuppernongs from the grape arbor in the yard of the Addams family. Nearby were his cousins Frankie and Jarvis; Janice, the bride-to-be; and his widower uncle, Mr. Addams. In the center of the stage, working in the kitchen, was Berenice Sadie Brown. Throughout the evening no one missed a line, the three protagonists performing in perfect harmony with fugue-like precision.

Of the Philadelphia opening, Romano said, "Waters was sublime as a good old colored 'nanny' and Julie Harris seemed to dance, so sprite a spirit was she. Brandon de Wilde, the little boy with eyeglasses and wings, was surely an original angel." During the intermission, the group from New York moved into the lobby to watch the faces and listen to responses. There they found Carson and Reeves standing near the front door, "so intoxicated that they could barely stay upright," said Romano. They had been across the street drinking, waiting for the intermission. "No matter how we encouraged them now, there was still great fear and anxiety up to the very end of the performance," recalled Romano.[49]

After the play, Tennessee Williams, who arrived separately from the New York delegation, having been urged by Carson to come from Key West for the opening, went backstage and asked Ethel Waters for her autograph. She demurred, adding that it was she who should be getting his, instead. Williams protested, and finally Miss Waters said, "Honey, I'm not from the South, but I can keep this up as long as you can."[50] After the play, the visitors from New York returned to the city. "We were glad it was over, the way one feels after a difficult examination," said Romano, but they sensed that everyone had passed.[51]

The play ran four hours in its initial form—much too long for a Broadway audience—and now the producers, the director, the other partners in the venture, Carson, Jordan Massee, and Oliver Smith, Carson's friend from 7 Middagh Street who also had an interest in the show, met late into the night discussing the problem. The cast had performed beautifully and there was nothing wrong with the lines or timing, they agreed, but, obviously, changes and cuts were in order. Carson had a great deal to say about the cuts. It was *her* play they were getting ready to operate on, and after her last experience with a script doctor, she was zealous in guarding her offspring. According to Jordan Massee, "Oliver Smith practically took over the doctoring session. It seemed to me that he would have had the entire play rewritten if he had had his way."

Finally the group decided to delete the whole barroom scene, for which an entire separate set had been built. Every other scene was the same—the kitchen and the Addams' back yard. It was a difficult change for Carson to agree to, for it was the scene that Tennessee Williams had helped her with in the revision of the play. To leave it out now seemed to be the ultimate betrayal. To Clurman, however, it was the only thing that kept the play from "working," that broke the mood, and was not a part of its organic unity. Although they worried about the transition, they decided to try it, to go simply from one scene to the next and skip the barroom scene without any bridge. This major cut was precisely what the play needed. Clurman was overjoyed by the decision. It also meant deleting the role of the soldier who attempted to pick Frankie up in the bar, thus dashing the hopes of a young actor, John Fielder, for a run on Broadway. Four others who appeared only in that scene were also out of the play, but it could not be helped. Almost immediately, Clurman and Whitehead knew that they had a hit. Only minor changes were made from then on during its nine-day run in Philadelphia. The day before Christmas, the New York *Times* carried "A Reporter's Gleans":

> The Philadelphia critical fraternity was impressed on Thursday night by Carson McCullers' *The Member of the Wedding*, now en route to Broadway. The *Bulletin* appraiser described it as an interesting and stimulating play while the *Inquirer* reported that it would very likely be that play you wait for all season. The *Daily News*'s comment pointed out that it proved a perceptive story of adolescence . . . given theatrical validity.

Each of the Philadelphia papers also zeroed in on the play's weakness. Henry Murdock, writing for the *Inquirer*, said:

> It is long and its physical maneuvering is clumsy. It has impressive, atmospheric settings, but they are by no means flexible. Not for a play that requires eight scenes to tell its story.

After complimenting the three principals of the cast, Jerry Gaghan said in the *Daily News* that

> The trio are on stage virtually the whole evening, and seldom permit their characterizations to lag in interest—a remarkable accomplishment considering that the final curtain didn't ring down until 11:30, which is long even for a musical. . . . Like most novels transcribed for the stage, it requires too many scene changes and stage halts.

The *Bulletin*'s reviewer was more taken by Julie Harris than by any other single facet of *The Member of the Wedding*, but he also lauded all the principals and said that the first performance of the play, "barring some tardy scene changes," might have been the one hundredth. Of the play-wright, he added:

> Miss McCullers made the play from her own novel and has been more successful in characterization and striking incidents than in con-structing a unified drama. However, she shows herself a mistress of true talk and literate writing as well as having a flair for moving climaxes to the eight scenes in the three acts of her play.

Upon her return from Philadelphia the end of December, Carson granted an old friend with the New York *Times* an interview to talk about her play. It was Harvey Breit, whom she had known at Yaddo in 1941. Breit described her now as one who moved with the "awkward hesitancy of a shy, wise, overgrown child, and who in her ways and looks perhaps resembles Frankie most of all." Breit said she told him that "the play (it's the same as the novel) is about adolescence, but that's not really what it's about. It's a play about identity and the will to belong."[52] Breit found her speech "hushed and soft as a languorous wind. She lingers over parts of a word and flees over others: 'ah-den-t-tee,' she said. 'Everybody wants to be a member of something. The little boy, John Henry, wants to be a member of the kitchen, he wants to belong to the kitchen. Berenice—Ethel Waters—is the president of the kitchen. Frankie wants to belong to the world, by means of the wedding.'"

And how had she conceived the idea of the play, Breit asked. "Any creative thing," she responded, "is so mysterious that it's impossible to remember the source—if there were a traceable source. But I do think the idea of wanting to belong haunts every child. And not only children. I think it is the primary question: 'Who am I? What am I? Or, where do I belong? And where can I belong?' But childhood or adolescence is a time of crisis, and such questions are more haunting, more immediate, then."

She acknowledged, too, the problems of creating a play out of a novel. She simply had to forget the novel, for "it all had to spring from another medium. It was fascinating. The play has to be direct. The inner monologue has to become the spoken word. It has to be more naked emotionally, too." Perhaps the most thrilling part of the whole creation, said Carson, was participating with the producers, the director, the cast, and others connected with the play during the Philadelphia tryout. She, too, had become "a member," the one thing that young Frankie had longed to do, but could not.

Soon after her interview with Breit, Carson was hospitalized. She had not felt well in Philadelphia, but attributed it to the strain of the production as well as to her own chronic ill health. She suspected now that the trouble was wholly unrelated to her other problems. The doctors quickly confirmed it: She was pregnant. To go through a full-term pregnancy and delivery, however, was an unwise and dangerous risk, a threat to her life, they told her. It was not a matter of whether Carson wanted an abortion; the medical advice was that she must have one.

In an interview several months later with critic Ward Morehouse, Carson said that her hospitalization after the Philadelphia tryout was for the purpose of tests and new treatments for her mysterious malady. She made no reference to the medically aborted pregnancy.[53] The news had been kept even from Carson's brother. Marguerite had been visiting Brother-Man and Virginia Smith, her son and daughter-in-law, in the South just before Carson went into the hospital, but when she received word of the impending surgery she rushed to New York to be at her daughter's bedside. She told her daughter-in-law the reason for her sudden departure, but not her son. After all, women did not discuss such things with men, she reflected. In fact, it was one of those social taboos that would not have even occurred to Marguerite to breach. Nor did Virginia Smith tell her husband of it, either. Not until a biographer asked about "the miscarriage" some twenty years later did Lamar's wife acknowledge that it was so.[54] To "busy her mind," Marguerite bought a "mess of turnip greens" en route from Nyack to the hospital, which she and her daughter Rita boiled at Rita's apartment while the surgery was in progress. "Sister loves turnip greens," said Marguerite, who planned to take a dish of them to Carson at the hospital.[55] Although Carson was out of the hospital in time for the Broadway première of her play at the Empire Theatre on January 5, her doctors advised that she not undergo the excitement and crowds of an opening night. Only when she was told that she could go to the producers' party afterward did she reluctantly consent to stay away from the theatre.

Articles had appeared in the New York papers almost daily since the first of January alerting the theatregoing public to expect a new Broadway hit. On December 29, the New York *Times* carried a story that *The Member of the Wedding* had been selected by the Show of the Month Club as its January "bonus" production, which meant that its members would attend the preview performance on January 4. The company itself did not arrive from Philadelphia until the first day of the new year, a fact which rated still another story. On January 5, Louis Calta emphasized in his New York *Times* article that the play opening that night was "the entire handiwork of Mrs. McCullers," and that the Theatre Guild, which had "contemplated producing" an adaptation of the novel by the playwright and Greer Johnson, had nothing to do with this production by Whitehead, Rea, and Martineau.

From the moment the curtain opened on the full house of first nighters, there was no doubt that *The Member of the Wedding* would be a runaway at the box office. After the final curtain, people threw their programs and hats into the air and gave a standing ovation and loud cheers for Ethel Waters, Julie Harris, and the little boy who almost stole the show, Brandon de Wilde. The next day long lines formed at the box office, and before long the house was a sellout for weeks, and then months in advance. But in spite of how enthusiastically the crowds acted at the performance on opening night, it was the critics who set the pace and measured the longevity of the run.

During the play, Carson waited with Virginia Bolen and Florence Martineau, the wives of her producers, for the party that would follow at the Martineaus' apartment. The cast was exuberant as they came in, with Carson now on center stage, kissing and embracing and being embraced, the crowd caught up in nervous excitement in anticipation of the drama critics' cogent remarks that would soon be on the streets. The playwright drank champagne with her fellow "members of the wedding" while everyone waited, toasted, and was toasted. Even Ethel Waters, who normally would not touch alcohol, joined them now. Carson posed for pictures, snuggled up beside Miss Waters on the sofa, and sat for a moment on her lap as Frankie had done in the play.

That Reeves was not at Carson's side at the producers' party surprised many who had seen him often at rehearsals. Instead, he was at her sister's apartment, where another celebration was in progress. Rita Smith was entertaining at a still larger party than the producers' for their more intimate friends and others of the theatre, literary, and musical world that Carson's sister was a part of too. One of Rita Smith's guests was Helen Jackson, Carson's girlhood friend from Columbus. Carson and Helen had not seen each other or communicated for many years, but just before Christmas Carson had called Helen on the telephone and said: "Helen, I have a play that's opening in New York in a few days, and I have reserved a box for you and some of your friends. Please come." Deeply touched, and delighted that her friend—who, indeed, had found the fame she sought—remembered her and wanted her to see her play, Helen Jackson took the train to New York and invited seven of her friends to go with her.

Another guest was David Diamond, who had been in Europe and had not seen Carson for over a year. Diamond had come to New York for the opening and then to Rita's afterward. He and Rita had become good friends since her move to New York in 1944, and he had seen even more of her in recent years than he had of Carson. Tennessee Williams had gone first to the producers' party, and then to Rita's. Williams had recently become acquainted with Diamond and was much impressed by his work and the new honors he had won. That night they talked about Williams' new play, *The Rose Tattoo,* and Williams invited him to do the music when it opened in Chicago the end of the year. Everyone at Rita's thought it was a wonderful party Carson was missing, and they felt certain that she could not be having as good a time as they were.

Marguerite Smith had also gone to her daughter's party, although she thought it would have been nice to be with Carson at the producers' party, where she could bask further in the reflection of Carson's newest achievement and glory. Marguerite reasoned, however, that her "place" was at Rita's, where she could help, and where she knew most of the guests and would be more comfortable. She was delighted to see Helen Jackson again, who had seemed like a member of the family for many years, and her "boys," Edwin Peacock and John Zeigler. At Rita's she also was assured of being treated royally as a kind of "Queen Mother." Marguerite loved parties and was entertaining in her own right. Good-humored, loquacious, she was knowledgeable on many topics, although people noticed that she usually saw to it that the conversation circled back to Carson. Marguerite was naive, sometimes to the point of absurdity, it seemed to some who knew her. She had a marvelous sense of humor, yet she frequently did not know when she herself was being funny. Most people who knew Carson's mother well, genuinely liked her. There were a few, such as Janet Flanner, who thought her "an abysmal mother."[56] Carson had come honestly by her sense of independence in dress as well as in other things, for Marguerite would be dictated to by no one. She dressed to suit herself. When a well-meaning woman asked her at a small, preopening party when it was almost time to leave for the theatre if she would like to change in her room, Marguerite, wearing what her friend described as a tam and a crumpled, dowdy-looking coat suit, replied with surprise: "Change? Why I'm ready now, aren't you?"

At both parties, exhilaration mounted as the moment approached for the early morning reviews. At the producers' party the first paper to arrive was the New York *Herald Tribune.* As Howard Barnes's cryptic, negative review was read to the group, Carson nearly fainted. Barnes complained that the play lacked structure and a sense of the dramatic, though he praised the acting. Not since Edmund Wilson's damning review of her book *The Member of the Wedding* had Carson felt so personally insulted as an artist. Then the New York *Times* arrived, bearing Brooks Atkinson's praise. He conceded that although there was practically no dramatic movement in the play, the fact seemed unimportant. "It may not be a play, but it is art." To Atkinson, the play had "incomparable insight, grace, and beauty."[57] Jubilant, Carson knew now that everything would be all right.

Other papers soon arrived to support the *Times's* reviewer. William Hawkins reported in the New York *World Telegram:* "I have never before heard what happened last night at the curtain calls . . . when hundreds cried out as if with one voice for Ethel Waters and Julie Harris." John Chapman's plaudits in the New York *Daily News* heralded the end of the theatrical drought: "A new play . . . came to the Empire Theatre last night, and at the fall of the third-act curtain a play-parched audience gave voice to its relief with loud, honest cheers." Robert Coleman in the New York *Daily Mirror* lauded it as a mood play rather than the conventional "well-made" one; it was a mood which "held an audience spellbound. . . . So fascinated by the McCullers characterizations were first-nighters that they threw their yardsticks away and enjoyed themselves immensely."

When it came time for theatre awards in the spring of 1950, *The Member of the Wedding* swept the field. On April 5, the New York drama critics met to cast their ballots for what they considered the top honors for American theatre, the New York Drama Critics' Circle Awards. Carson's drama received seventeen of a possible twenty-five votes, making it the best American play of the year for the period April 1, 1949, through March 31, 1950.[58] The following weekend, Carson and her producers—along with other recipients—received scrolls at a special awards ceremony. Highlights of each winning production were dramatized for the radio audience and the entire program carried live over ABC.

Other honors soon came Carson's way too. While the critics were speculating to whom the coveted Pulitzer prizes and Donaldson awards would go, the Theatre Club, Inc., announced that it would give its gold medal of the year to Carson McCullers for "the best play by an American author produced during the year." Jean Miller, president of the Theatre Club, presented the medal to Carson at the club's annual luncheon meeting April 25. Carson hardly dared hope that she would win a Pulitzer, for its rules stated that the prize must go to the playwright of "the original American play performed in New York which shall best represent the educational value and power of the stage." Although the *original* restriction had been broken twice in the past, the word "original" kept *The Member of the Wedding*, as well as several other top plays, out of contention in 1950. In a New York *Times* article entitled "Second-Hand Drama," Brooks Atkinson acknowledged that only three notable plays written directly for the stage had been produced during the current theatre season. Of the three that took the Drama Critics' Circle Awards, reviewers suggested that *The Member of the Wedding* would come closest to Pulitzer prize specifications since both its playwright and setting were American. The Pulitzer, however, went to *South Pacific*.[59]

The annual Donaldson awards, presented now for the seventh year, were announced May 1 during a coast-to-coast ABC broadcast. Once again, Carson's play took the principal honors, receiving awards both for "best play of last season" and "best first play by an author to be produced on Broadway." Others involved in the play also received individual honors. The Donaldson "best director" award went to Harold Clurman, the "best supporting performance" by an actor to young Brandon de Wilde. Ethel Waters was edged out by Shirley Booth as "best female performer" of the season, Miss Booth having costarred in *Come Back, Little Sheba.*

Later in the year, *The Member of the Wedding* received still another honor when it was selected one of the top ten plays of the year for inclusion in *The Burns Mantle Best Plays of 1949-1950*, edited by drama critic John Chapman.[60] In Chapman's introduction, the play's uncertain history with its seemingly insurmountable odds was recounted. Chapman cited the reservations to which countless critics had clung—including his own—that *The Member of the Wedding* was not *exactly* a play. Then he quoted what Carson herself had said about the matter. Carson had been invited by *Theatre Arts* to share her vision and experience in writing her play, and she responded:

> *The Member of the Wedding* is unconventional because it is not a *literal* kind of play. It is an inward play and the conflicts are inward conflicts. The antagonist is not personified, but is a human condition of life: the sense of moral isolation. In this respect *The Member of the Wedding* has an affinity with classical plays—which we are not used to in the modern theatre where the protagonist and antagonist are present in palpable conflict on the stage. The play has other abstract values; it is concerned with the weight of time, the hazard of human existence, bolts of chance. The reaction of the characters to these abstract phenomena projects the movement of the play. Some observers who failed to apprehend this modus operandi felt the play to be fragmentary because they did not account for this aesthetic concept. . . . Some observers have wondered if any drama as unconventional as this should be called a play. I cannot comment on that. I only know that *The Member of the Wedding* is a vision that a number of artists have realized with fidelity and love.[61]

Harold Clurman wrote for *New Republic* his own defense of the play several weeks after it opened:

> I am convinced that Ethel Waters, Julie Harris, Brandon de Wilde and the other actors of "The Member of the Wedding," following the line of action I sensed in it as a director, have made a play of "The Member of the Wedding" because it was a play to begin with—albeit of a different kind than any other we had previously done. Ibsen once said of his "Brand" and "Peer Gynt": "If these weren't poetry before, they have become poetry now." The

same may be said of "The Member of the Wedding" in regard to its status as a play. The proof is in the doing of it.[62]

Then he went on to explain the source of the action and how every character struggled in some way. His job as director was to find "a physical or visual equivalent for every emotion that is the concomitant of the action." Clurman also gave Robert Whitehead and his associates credit for their vision in seeing the potential in *The Member of the Wedding* as a box office success; they were "eager to face real theatrical problems because they think of them not primarily in the light of 'investments' but as objects of their love."

According to Lewis Gannett, the novice playwright was "properly speechless" over the new honors accorded her.[63] Carson told people that she had seen only two Broadway plays in her life and that each had won a Drama Critics' Circle Award as the best American play of the year. One had been written by her favorite artist of them all, Tennessee Williams, whose *Streetcar Named Desire* had won in 1948. The other was Arthur Miller's *Death of a Salesman*, which had received the award the year before. Carson never forgot the Miller play, not only for its great dramaturgy, but also for her mother's unabashed demonstration in the theatre as she empathized with the plight of Willy Loman. Immediately upon hearing the lines by Willy's wife (played by Mildred Dunnock) in which she tells her son that "a small man can be just as exhausted as a great man," that his tragedy can be just as enormous, Marguerite leaped to her feet and shouted and clapped a resounding "Bravo!" Although others in the party shifted uneasily with amused embarrassment, Carson's mother was not at all reproachable—her philosophy had always been "If you feel something strongly about a person—or a thing—let it be known."

The night that the Drama Critics' Circle Awards were made public, the cast and production crew of *The Member of the Wedding* celebrated with an informal party backstage. They knew well that in light of past history, the prize meant immediate additional advance sales of at least $150,000.[64] Before the play closed on March 17, 1951, after 501 performances, it had grossed over $1,112,000 for its Broadway run alone. A long, successful road tour followed. A month after its Broadway closing, New Directions published the play, whereupon it became the April selection of the Fireside Theatre, which sent plays out monthly to over ten thousand subscribers. Carson was beginning to realize more money than she had ever envisioned in her life. Indeed, she had more than a "few pennies" in her pocket at last.

With more money coming in, Ethel Waters reportedly wanted more, too. Miss Waters had been a great star, the only star in the company when the play opened, and stars do not forget their stature no matter how dark the periods between their successes. The playwright took Miss Waters' demands as a personal offense. As she saw it, if Miss Waters got more money, she, Carson, would get less. To Carson, it was like taking money out of her own pocket and giving it to Miss Waters. The playwright disapproved heartily and let her star know it, an attitude which contributed toward a temporary estrangement between the two women. Miss Waters, however, stayed with the play, got more money, and signed a contract—along with Julie Harris and Brandon de Wilde—to continue with the show until July 1, 1951. To be sure, Miss Waters was temperamental. Some connected with the play felt that as she gained confidence in herself, she became arrogant and attempted to upstage the others. In the past, each night after the curtain calls, Lester Polakov waited just offstage and kissed her as she came off. At the opening in Philadelphia Miss Waters' cheeks were wet with tears when he kissed her, and he had known then that they had a hit. She had *become* Berenice at last, an organic part of the close-knit little group that revolved about her in the kitchen. But later, as the play got well into its long Broadway run, Polakov and she had a tiff during what he called one of her "haughty moments," and he stopped kissing her. To Polakov, she seemed changed—"remarkable, of course, in the role, but different as a person."

Indeed, *The Member of the Wedding* had been a success for every participant. Just as each character within the fiction had been affected and changed that "green crazy summer" in some unique, irrevocable way, so too had each person connected with the production been spun together, forged into something new, and then flung out with great force in new directions, each having profited enormously by the "wedding." The show was a coup not only for its playwright, but also for every principal involved. Carson proved that she could overcome great physical adversity, mental depression, and the advice of obdurate, seasoned producers and agents who told her that her play would never survive a fickle Broadway public, even if she succeeded in getting it mounted. Julie Harris became a star at last. (Later, Miss Harris wrote to Carson: "I remember so well—the first time I met you at your house with Bessie [Breuer]. You made me terribly happy. Frankie changed my whole life."[65]) Ethel Waters at age fifty made a remarkable comeback in the role that made her famous to a whole generation that was not old enough to remember the international triumphs of the jazz singer whose name was close to that of Bessie Smith, or the subsequent triumphs on Broadway in musical comedy, or even the singer turned actress who made theatrical history with her performance in *Mamba's Daughters*. Miss Waters returned to a glittering entertainment world in which she stayed active for another twenty years. Young Brandon de Wilde was launched on a successful theatrical career, both on Broadway and in Hollywood, and later as a folk singer, which was cut short by a fatal automobile accident in 1972. (His father continued for over twenty-five years as Robert Whitehead's stage manager.) And Harold Clurman was able to count his fiftieth assignment as a director one of the top three or four plays he ever directed.[66]

To Carson, the play had other far-reaching consequences, too. Perhaps its most meaningful ramification was the reunion that ensued between her and Mary Tucker, who was more responsible for *The Member of the Wedding* than anyone except Carson herself. She was the fulcrum of Carson's adolescent existence, the centrifugal force that spun her loose from the South and propelled her toward a literary career instead of a musical one. They had been estranged for over fifteen years, the long silent spaces wide and deep. But in February, a few weeks after the opening of the play, a letter came to Carson from her beloved music teacher. Her whole psyche had been attuned to expect it. When Marguerite asked her daughter that morning to make three guesses as to who had just written her, she knew immediately. The most important four years of Carson's adolescent life flooded over her with Proustian fidelity in a kaleidoscope of Bach, Beethoven, flowers, and artichokes, the strange and marvelous and everyday.

Mary Tucker, living in Virginia then, wrote to congratulate Carson on both the overwhelming success of her play and novels and her whole career as an artist, and to convey, at last, the love and hurt that she, too, had felt. Carson responded that afternoon with an exuberant, eight-page, handwritten letter in which she recalled those magic and fatalistic moments. She explained to Mary Tucker why she had been unable to communicate in the past. She loved her so much that she could neither understand nor cope with her strange emotions, she said. Mrs. Tucker was both Beethoven and Mozart to her. Although she worshiped at her shrine, in the past she was unable to express her love openly; thus she responded only with the music Mary Tucker taught her. Carson spoke of her shame and the sense of failure she felt during their last year together when she had pneumonia and could perform well neither technically nor emotionally for her mentor. Then the Tuckers went away. Carson said that she had never realized that Mrs. Tucker, too, had been upset by the strange turn of events until the letter arrived that very morning. She told Mrs. Tucker now that she thought only she, Carson, had been emotionally unhinged by the break and had not been able to cut through her own feelings of sorrow and shame and understand that she, too, had been much loved and needed.

Carson told Mrs. Tucker in her letter how right it had been that she had not persisted in her dream to be a concert pianist, that she would never have had the temperament, and that her talents were creative, not interpretative. She explained, too, about her mysterious and paralyzing illness. She could barely play chopsticks now, she rued, but she was grateful that her creative life had not been seriously impaired. To Carson, Mary Tucker was the flesh and blood music which she craved, and she urged her and her husband to come to New York to visit and to see the play as her guests. Carson told her, too, that had it not been for the Tuckers, *The Member of the Wedding* would not have been written. She was sure that when they saw it, it would tell them something that she could not have conveyed any other way.

In April, the Tuckers came to New York. Carson was staying in the city with Reeves at the time, having recently moved into Cheryl Crawford's East River apartment for several weeks. "Cheryl Crawford went South and asked us to come live here," Carson told Ward Morehouse in an interview for the *Atlanta Journal Magazine*.[67] When the Tuckers arrived on April 24, they had lunch and later spent two afternoons together, but Carson was not able to articulate to her friend as directly in person as she had in her one, all-revealing letter. Nevertheless, there was now an irrevocable, spiritual communion from which they continued to draw sustenance for the rest of Carson's life.

When Ward Morehouse came to interview Carson, he found her wearing gray slacks, bedroom slippers, and a beige cowboy blouse. Her hair was short, and she said that, like Frankie, she cut it herself. She told him about her sickness and that she planned to go to Ireland for her health. She would visit Elizabeth Bowen and then go to France to meet with Robert Whitehead and Harold Clurman to discuss possible production plans for the play in England, France, Italy, and Switzerland. (Whitehead said later that there were never any plans as far as he was concerned to arrange for *The Member of the Wedding* to be produced abroad; it was a "perfectly logical thing" for Carson to have dreamed up, however, he conceded.) Soon the New York papers picked up stories of the impending trips, and Carson announced that she would sail on May 20 for Ireland where she intended to resume work on her latest novel, *Clock Without Hands*, at Miss Bowen's fabulous manor in County Cork. She and Miss Bowen had met a few weeks earlier through Stuart Preston, art critic for the New York *Times*, with whom Miss Bowen was staying during a brief visit to America.

Carson, deciding one evening that she should confirm her plans with Miss Bowen, put in a transatlantic telephone call so that they could "have a little talk" before she came. It never occurred to Carson that there would be much difference between life at "Bowen's Court" and life at 131 South Broadway. Nor did she think about any time differential when she placed the call, even though she, too, had lived in Europe. When a butler answered the telephone, she said: "This is Carson McCullers calling from New York. I would like to speak to Miss Bowen."

The response was a dry "Madam, it is four o'clock in the morning. I suggest you call again later."

The incident struck Carson as being hilariously funny and became one of her favorite stories. She was not embarrassed, nor did she apologize for the inconvenience or her thoughtlessness; she simply thought it was a great joke and could hardly wait to size up the butler in person. Carson was happier now than she had been in years. With Mary Tucker back in her life, a new star glittering in her crown from her recent Broadway triumph, an impending trip to unexplored lands in castles with other literary giants, the dream loomed large and shimmery. It was almost as though she were going around the world with Frances Addams and Mary Littlejohn.[68]

Chapter Eleven

FAME AND DISILLUSIONMENT,

1950 – 53

*A*fter a brief interlude in Cheryl Crawford's apartment, Carson and Reeves moved during the spring of 1950 to the fashionable Dakota at 72nd Street and Central Park West. Audrey Wood had been able to arrange a sublet for them so that Carson might remain in the city a few more weeks. She loved having people around her, and until she got down to serious writing again had no intention of limiting herself to the reclusive life of her mother's Nyack home. She would stay in the city until she left for Europe, she decided.

In spite of her exuberance over the unbounded success of *The Member of the Wedding*, the deep satisfaction of knowing that the Tucker family again were her we of me, and her excitement over the anticipated trip to Bowen's Court, Carson still had many bad moments. Besides the physical pain which seemed a constant reminder of her maimed body, she found it unbearable psychically to be left by herself. Reeves, to whom it was almost equally difficult if he were forced to stay cooped up in the apartment alone with her for long spells, grasped every opportunity to get out and be with other people. Restless and impatient, he sometimes arranged to have visitors come to pay court to Carson—if there were none already expected—so that he might slip out for a few hours and do exactly as he chose. Often, regardless of the time of day or night, he would take a crosstown bus to see Paul Bigelow.

One night Reeves made his "escape" very late after Carson's bedtime, and once at Bigelow's apartment, decided he would like to have a little talk with Tennessee Williams, who was in Key West. The playwright had long been asleep, but was awakened by the ring and filled with apprehension. Finally he got to the telephone and heard a friendly voice say: "Hello? Tenn? This is Reeves."

There was a pause while Williams pushed back sleep. At last he replied with great concern: "Why, hello, Reeves—what's the matter?"

After another pause, Reeves answered stoutly: "Why, nothing's the matter, Tenn. I just thought I'd call you."

A still longer silence ensued while Williams waited for an explanation. Finally, he asked, "How is Carson?"

The next pause, a long, *long* one, was followed by a deep intake of air, then Reeves's resolute answer: "Indestructible!"

Marguerite Smith worried about her frail daughter going off again alone—regardless of Reeves's recent appraisal of her—but Carson assured her mother that she needed to get away, to write, to travel by herself, and that she wanted no encumbrances. At Bowen's Court she would rest first, for she was weary; then, if she felt like beginning serious work on her next novel, she would. It occurred to her, also, that she might write some poetry. Having money at last to do with as she wished, Carson answered Reeves and her mother's queries that she had no idea when she would return home. To travel freely in Europe without a time schedule or extraneous demands was a part of her grand scheme; nor did she care whether it suited anyone else or not. That his wife was leaving him again to jaunt off God knows where did not particularly disturb Reeves this time. In the past, he might have been deeply resentful, he conceded, but he was used to her sudden departures and inexplicable whims and agreed now that a temporary separation might be good for them both. Yet in spite of Reeves's protestations to the contrary, there was still a twinge of envy, a sense of apprehension, perhaps even panic, at the thought of being left alone.

On May 20, 1950, Carson sailed for Dublin, the port from which her maternal Carson ancestors had emigrated almost two hundred years earlier. That it was James Joyce's Dublin stimulated a double fascination for her. Once there, she took the Cork-Dublin train to Mallow in southern Eire, where she was met by car for the half hour's drive to Bowen's Court. Carson could no more have imagined what Elizabeth Bowen's grand mansion would be like than she had guessed beforehand the splendor of Jordan Massee's House of the Salutation in Macon, Georgia, a spring earlier. Isolated in what seemed to be boundless tracts of emptiness, Miss Bowen's stately limestone manor was located in lonely country remote from village or other habitation. When the car swung off the Dublin-Killarney-through route and up the long, private road toward the great, square house of many windows, Carson was ecstatic.

The mansion had been built in 1775 by Miss Bowen's ancestor Henry Bowen III, and his descendants had lived there ever since. Whereas the house had once been maintained by landowning gentry who administered property, farmed hundreds of acres, and drew rents from the rest, Miss Bowen explained to Carson that she maintained Bowen's Court solely as a place in which to write and to entertain her friends. Counting the basement, the house had four stories, and Carson explored them all—

including the enormous, bat-filled attic. From its front windows, looking south, she could see only trees, grassland, heather, and bogs. No roads or other dwellings were visible. Woods framed the sides of the mansion, and mountains, the rear. There also were lovely flower gardens and a three-acre vegetable garden—which was walled from view—as was everything utilitarian. Stables and a stable yard were in the rear, with the front of the house eminently social.[1] Inside, on the ground floor, were four living rooms—all the same size—a library, drawing room, dining room, kitchen, and a handsome gallery from which guests ascended two massive side flights of stairs to the second floor. Large square bedrooms and dressing rooms filled this floor. A gigantic "Long Room"—once intended as a ballroom—dominated the third level. It ran the depth of the house, with three bedrooms on each side opening upon it. Here, in one of the little bedrooms, Carson stayed.

Enchanted by the elegant surroundings, yet amazed that within them Miss Bowen led a relatively simple and quiet life, Carson immediately began to convey—with a delicious and subtle humor—her impressions in letters to friends at home. To her cousin Jordan Massee she added immodestly that she had made a *hit* at formal Bowen's Court wearing her faded bluejeans and "coat of many colors"—actually an old jacket—in which she attired herself much of the time. To Mary Tucker and her husband "Tuck"—as Carson now addressed Colonel Tucker—she exuded wonderment at living near the castle in which Edmund Spenser had written many cantos of his *Faerie Queen*. She, too, would write some verses of her own while there, she promised. In fact, she had already written several poems on the ship coming over, copying them out laboriously in longhand while still at sea, revising them only slightly once she had committed her images and thoughts to paper. Carson was able to work out most of her lines mentally before she even picked up a pencil. She told several friends at home that she would send them copies of her poems just as soon as Miss Bowen's accountant typed them out for her.

Except for poetry, however, Carson could not seem to get down to the business of writing. Instead, she wandered about the gardens, poked around the stables, and watched herds of sheep graze docilely on the vast expanse of lawn that rolled down from the front of the house to the distant roadway. After the first few days Bowen's Court was almost too quiet for her. She read avidly, choosing books from the enormous library of her hostess, but she did not care to be left alone as much as she had been—almost ignored, she felt—for she was accustomed to being entertained when she was in someone else's home. Frequently she committed the sin unpardonable to a fellow writer, that of finding some little excuse to break in upon Miss Bowen at her work, which seemed to go on interminably. Always Carson was impatient for the late afternoons and evenings when Miss Bowen stopped writing and began entertaining countless visitors from neighboring estates or distant cities. The group generally gathered in the library by the "public fireplace"—as Carson described it—for drinks, conversation, and storytelling.

One afternoon writer Frank O'Connor, a consummate teller of Irish folk tales, held court in the library while Carson listened enthralled to his stories of what Miss Bowen described as "the magnificence of the Midnight Court, poetry and bawdry of an Ireland before the potato had struck root."[2] Suddenly Miss Bowen's cousin, Dudley Colley, a racing ace and representative of "New Eire" rushed in. Fascinated now even more by the new guest and his Frazer-Nash automobile than she had been by O'Connor, Carson leaped into the driver's seat of Colley's car and cried, "I'm off!" The car did not move, explained Miss Bowen, but Carson's face "grew tense with the thought of speed." Watching the spectacle, Miss Bowen felt that her young friend's imagination and the visionary force were so strong that "the stationary car seemed to roar and devour space . . . veritably her hair streamed back from her forehead."

Such exciting diversion was rare, however, for Carson at Bowen's Court. By early June she was intensely nervous and was making her hostess edgy, too. Although there were frequent visitors in the afternoons and evenings, Carson wanted to have Miss Bowen more to herself. Unable to write, she was bored much of the day; consequently, she drank more whiskey than usual—a considerable amount, certainly—for sedate Bowen's Court.

Carson's boredom and restlessness were entirely the result of her inability to penetrate the barrier that Miss Bowen placed between them. It was a barrier erected not simply for the occasion; rather, it was an essential part of Miss Bowen's own unapproachable self—developed through generations of courtly manners. Carson had gone to Ireland as a starstruck devotee of Miss Bowen, Great Britain's leading contemporary female novelist and short story writer, and she expected comparable homage in return. Moreover, Carson was infatuated with Miss Bowen as a person, and she wanted to be in her presence constantly. To the American author, they had much in common. Miss Bowen, too, wrote about impoverished or unrequited love and the problems of the child and adolescent as he hovered on the brink of maturity or some initiatory experience. Two of Miss Bowen's novels, *The House in Paris* and *The Death of the Heart* involved youth, and her other novels and collections of short stories abounded with characters and situations with which Carson identified, although largely only through fantasy. In 1948, Miss Bowen was honored by the Irish people as a "Companion of the Order of the British Empire." And if a "companion" to the Anglo-Irish people, then why was she not *more* of a companion to her, Carson, within the confines of Bowen's

Court, she wondered. In actuality, it is doubtful that any two people could have been more dissimilar.

"Carson was a welcome visitor, but I must say a terrible 'handful,' to use that old-fashioned expression, once she'd arrived," her hostess admitted later.[3] Finally, disillusioned by the contrast between anticipation and reality, Carson wired Reeves that she was ready to leave Ireland and wanted him to meet her in London. She missed him, loved him, and needed him, she declared. Moreover, she would like to stay abroad for a while, she said, and possibly settle permanently in France. Reeves, overjoyed at having an excuse to leave what he considered a dull, routine accountant's job at WOR, packed their trunks for an extended stay, bid farewell to his mother-in-law, and booked the next flight for England. Carson then notified John and Simone Brown that they would soon leave for Paris. Once again, Carson asked Brown to reserve rooms for them, this time at the Hôtel de l'Université, where they had stayed once or twice in the past.

Reeves, too, loved being back in Paris. Quickly Carson saw to it that word circulated that they had arrived, and soon they were seeing old literary friends and making the rounds of cafés and night clubs—although their pace was slower now than it had been during their Paris days and nights of 1946–47.

Tennessee Williams, too, was in Paris, but he did not see as much of Carson and Reeves as they might have liked. On June 7, 1950, the playwright described in a letter to Paul Bigelow an afternoon they spent together. Referring to Carson as "Sister Woman"—a name he made up to match her brother Lamar's nickname of Brother-Man—he said that she had returned from Ireland on schedule and that apparently Elizabeth Bowen had hosted Carson and Reeves with "amazing grace" and considerable tact. The letter continued:

> Of course Carson is talking of flying to London to join her [Miss Bowen] there, but it is only talk so far. She and Reeves came over to our little left-bank hotel the other day and spent the entire afternoon. Jane and Paul Bowles were also present. . . . Sister Woman and Reeves kept the chamber-maid hopping between our rooms and the wine-shop.

Williams then related that a long-distance call had interrupted their "happy occasion." It was "America calling Carson," the playwright told Bigelow. Someone had called to inform her that —— had "fallen off the wagon" and that advice and instructions were urgently needed. Williams continued: " 'Get Marty Mann!' cried Carson. Carson was then asked if Reeves had stayed, or gotten back, on the wagon. She said, 'Reeves is just drinking wine!' And here was Reeves reeling about the room like a storm-wracked schooner. 'Get Marty Mann! Tell her to get Marty Mann!'[4] Reeves shouted. Then both started babbling maudlinly into the phone at once. . . ." Williams quoted to Bigelow a little more of Carson and Reeves's conversation, then commented:

> It must have been the longest and most intense transcontinental phone call since the war ended, and the McCullerses looked really happy and satisfied when they hung up and immediately sent out for another bottle of wine. Reeves called this morning, and I asked if they had had any further conversation with —— and Reeves said, No, we just sent a cable confirming the talk on the phone!
>
> So you see, Paris is not really so far from New York, after all. I wonder if Rome will be any further? When I said we were getting an apartment in Rome (we hoped) Reeves immediately said, How many rooms? Oh, one and a half! I answered without a moment's reflection. There was a slight suggestion that Frank [Merlo] and I, being rather small people, might be able to occupy the "half" until I remembered that the "half" room was really only a sort of a vestibule. Carson said, Oh, how lovely! I bet it's like Mrs. Spring's apartment in Rome, which I think was a slightly confused reference to my novel, the one that contained that extremely felicitous line about "amethyst dust." . . .[5]
>
> The meeting between Reeves and Paul Bowles was not a happy one. Reeves said, Well, son, how does it feel to be a published writer? Bowles looked like a Moroccan camel with a mouthful of the spiniest and most indigestible plant that grows on the desert. But the McCullerses were so entranced over the good news about —— that every response to their benign gestures struck them as expressing the most suitable gratitude and delight. Carson told me three times, by careful reckoning, that I did not like her play. If she had told me once more I would have agreed with her, but luckily my final response was peculiarly inspired. When have I ever *not* liked anything you have ever done? For this I received a tender kiss on the lips. Paul Bowles was accorded the same tribute when their hosts came to take them away. Paul is terribly squeamish about any physical contact . . . and he looked more like a camel with something suddenly impossible to get down his throat than ever.
>
> I am sorry to devote so much space to a really American topic but nothing has yet happened of a strictly European character that is worth noting. There is a vast and dreadful crowd of tourists here and we don't know where, how far South or East, it will be necessary to go to feel we have really left New York. But the Bowleses are a pure delight as ever and, all in all, one might say the same for the McCullerses, although quite naturally in a dissimilar fashion.

A few days later, Williams and Frank Merlo left for Rome.

Carson wrote friends later that she was especially pleased to be staying at the Hôtel de l'Université because Jane and Paul Bowles were there, too. She had been fond of the Bowleses since they had first met at 7 Middagh Street in Brooklyn Heights, where they had both lived. The Bowleses were good friends of Tennessee Williams, and their home in Morocco was often a stopping point for Williams and many other creative artists whom Carson, too, knew and took an interest in. She thrived on humorous anecdotes and enjoyed hearing tales about such people as Truman Capote and Gore Vidal, who were friends of the Bowleses and frequent visitors to Morocco. Williams once told Carson that her eyes were like Vidal's. The remark pleased her, for she was fascinated by Vidal's almost unbelievably good looks. She was fond of Vidal during the days of his early success, even though she was put off by his ego. It never occurred to her that he, too, was put off by hers.

After a few days of hotel living in Paris—which she inevitably found tiresome—Carson and Reeves moved in with the Browns. In 1950, John Brown had gone into United States Government service and was now attached to the American embassy under the Marshall Plan as director of information. Carson found the fanfare of embassy life with the Browns exciting, particularly after the hauntingly isolated chambers of Bowen's Court, but she quickly tired of the endless stream of parties and long, six-course dinners. Although she admitted that she adored the Browns, she was bored by having to look at food for hours and sitting on indefinitely at the table. Also, she missed being the center of attention. Although Simone Brown was attentive and also very sympathetic to Carson's needs, she had her *own* children to look after. If only they could find a suitable house of their own in France, Carson lamented.

Finally she conceived a plan that she proposed to Mary Tucker. She asked Mrs. Tucker to please try to locate for her either a cook who was single or a black couple from the South who might be willing to come to France and live with them. Carson acknowledged that with her physical infirmities and writing demands she would always need good household help, but that it was impossible for her to communicate effectively with a servant in French. Almost none were bilingual, she complained. Even worse, she said, was the fact that servants who did not speak French, spoke Spanish or Basque, which was even more foreign to her. If she could have a native of her own South as her cook and housekeeper, it would all be so simple, she figured. First, they would locate a suitable house in which to live, for she would hate to put servants up at a hotel, she said. She would send passage to whomever the Tuckers might hire for them.

As soon as possible Carson and Reeves arranged to be driven about the countryside outside of Paris to look at farmhouses and little country cottages where expenses would be considerably less than in the city. Some of Reeves's happiest moments of youth had been spent on his grandfather's farm in Georgia and his uncle's plantation in Alabama, and both he and Carson dreamed of having a farm someday. As they looked into the situation in France, however, and the idyllic image gave way to reality, the problems of coping with the physical inconveniences of life in a remote country home seemed overwhelming. Poor heating, plumbing, and lighting, inadequate cooking facilities—all were the accepted norm outside of the city, and Carson feared that they would suffer from the raw, cold winters. Even if they should find suitable English-speaking domestic help, they would still experience a language barrier in communicating outside of the home. Too, they would have to be close enough to Paris and the American Hospital for Carson to receive medical treatment when necessary. To fend for themselves in the country would be an abrupt change from their accustomed way of life, and perhaps they should think about it awhile longer, they decided.

It was at this point that Mary Tucker suggested to Carson that they consider, instead, returning to America and settling in the South. They could take a well-equipped place in the country near Lexington, Virginia, have modern conveniences, and live close to the Tuckers. Carson replied enthusiastically to the new scheme and was filled with wondrous imaginings of how marvelous and exciting it would be to live again—after all these years—near her precious friends. By all means, the Tuckers should be on the lookout for a home for them and a housekeeper and cook, Carson urged, promising that they would be in Virginia soon.

Before leaving Europe, she wanted Reeves to accompany her back to Bowen's Court. Whether Miss Bowen liked it or not, Carson persisted in thinking of the Irish writer as another great love in her life, and she wanted Reeves to participate with her in a new we of me relationship. Carson wrote to inform her hostess that they were on the way—Miss Bowen having extended a courteous "you must come back any time" invitation—and by the last week of July they were ensconced at Bowen's Court. Again, Miss Bowen graciously received Carson, but this time she had another house guest, her good friend, British writer Rosamond Lehmann. (Both Carson and Reeves were much taken by Miss Lehmann, whom they visited the following summer at her country home near Oxford, when Carson was introduced to the British literati.) Miss Bowen became fond of Reeves during their few days together in Ireland and felt a little sorry for him. She could see that his relationship with Carson was a difficult one, and that to maintain it required a delicate balance. Later, she was grieved by his death, for she understood something of the destructive forces at work in his life. In retrospect, Miss Bowen concluded:

> I always felt Carson was a destroyer; for which reason I chose never to be closely involved with her. Affection for her I *did* feel, and she also gave off an aura of genius—unmistakable—which one had to respect. Possibly, some of the company she kept did her no good. . . . Therefore, hers and mine could not be described as a "close friendship"—in the sense that I rejoice in having a close friendship with that other great Deep-Southerner, Eudora Welty. . . . Carson remains in my mind as a child genius, though her art, as we know, was great, sombre, and above all, extremely mature. I remember her face, her being, her bearing with a pang of affection—and always shall.[6]

During Carson's second stay at Bowen's Court, her nerves were raw and on edge. She felt psychically disturbed and physically unwell. After a visit with Miss Bowen of less than a week, Carson announced that she and Reeves were departing immediately for home. She took time only to write Mary Tucker that they would arrive in New York August 2, and that before long they would join the Tucker family in Virginia. When Carson was at odds with Reeves, as she was now for he had been drinking excessively again, she often made enormous declarations of affection for others. Just as she used to tell David Diamond and Newton Arvin how much she loved them in larger outpourings than usual when things were amiss between her and her husband—scrawling hearts and dozens of x's beside and under her signature—so, too, did Carson posit once more her great love for the Tucker family.

For a month after her return home, however, she did not write to Mrs. Tucker. It was shame, she finally admited, as well as illness, that kept her from writing. She had been reluctant to tell Mary Tucker that a Lexington farm and the trip South with Reeves were off, but finally she wrote and apologized for putting the Tuckers to the trouble of trying to find a house and servants for them. They were not only not coming, said Carson, but a divorce was imminent. They probably would separate again and Reeves would possibly go back into the Army, she acknowledged. It was the death of her marriage and she was saddened by it, said Carson, but she now accepted it with tranquillity and prayed that Reeves might find some semblance of happiness without her. In not succeeding in her marriage, she reasoned that she had also failed in her relationship with the Tuckers, and she deeply regretted having to tell them.

During the month that Carson did not write to the Tuckers, she was trying to find herself and some semblance of an acceptable way of life. While in Europe she had begun to feel persecuted by Reeves and others whom she had formerly held dear. Tennessee Williams, in fact, wrote a hasty note to Paul Bigelow the day after Carson's return to New York City, saying, "Senta, per favore! Not a word to Sister Woman about my letter describing her phone conversation with ——! She is already inclined to list me among her persecutors, I am afraid. Hope she arrived in good condition . . ."

Once in New York, Carson went directly to the home of friends, rather than to Nyack and her mother, and Reeves took an apartment in the city. For a while Carson stayed with Florence and Stanley Martineau in Glen Cove, New York. The Martineaus had become close friends of Carson's through his work as assistant producer of *The Member of the Wedding* and were intimately involved with all facets of the production. They had given the cast party in their New York apartment after the opening night's performance and believed in the play's aesthetics and its promise of success.[7] As for Carson personally, both were immensely kind and patient with her in her dependencies, for they loved her and respected her great artistry. Earlier, it had been Carson's habit to call Florence Martineau on the telephone many times daily—and often through the night—to confide in her the various anxieties, yearnings, and trivia of daily life which Carson felt the urge to share. Once again Carson urgently needed the Martineaus' friendship, and they responded with loving concern.

Another haven for Carson upon her return from Bowen's Court in August was the home of Marty Mann and Priscilla Peck, who maintained a summer place on Fire Island. Both women were active in AA and had gotten Reeves interested in it in 1948 shortly after the four of them had met through Cheryl Crawford. Miss Mann was the founder of the National Council on Alcoholism in 1944 and served as its executive director. Through her help, Reeves had reached "Twelfth Step Work." "He was a difficult person to help, however," conceded Miss Mann, for "Reeves was always on again, off again." Miss Mann viewed Carson during this period as "a lovely and lovable person, but also a very helpless one—both about Reeves and about her own crippled condition."[8] The two women welcomed Carson in their home whenever she felt the need to get away from Nyack or simply wanted a place to stay in the city, where they also had an apartment. Carson kept most of her music there after Miss Peck began encouraging her to play the piano and exercise her left arm and finger joints. Priscilla Peck was art editor of *Vogue*, and when she was away at the office, Carson occasionally sat at the piano alone and struggled to play. If the pieces were very simple she could play a few of the notes and chords with her left hand; more often, she played with her good right hand. It was cheering for Carson to be with them that summer for a few days, and then again later, in the fall. In the home of Marty Mann and Priscilla Peck Carson also began to write poetry again. She was at work on a cycle of poems, published eventually under the title "The Dual Angel: A Meditation on Origin and Choice."[9]

When Carson finally was able to write to Mary Tucker and tell her about her separation from Reeves, she said that her intentions were to stay at home in Nyack with her mother, who could give her the solace and care that she needed. She acknowledged, also, that she had had a new illumination of her novel and now felt very close to God. Mrs. Tucker had worried about Carson during the few weeks that she had not heard from her, and she responded at once with an invitation for Carson to join her and Colonel Tucker in Lexington. They wanted her to rest there, and to work, too, if she chose; but most of all, they wanted her to feel that "Tuckaway" was her second home and that she was welcome to come and stay as long as she wished. Although Carson had barely gotten settled in Nyack with her mother after her visits with the Stanley Martineaus and Marty Mann and Priscilla Peck, she was ready to pack again and take the very next train south. Once more Marguerite Smith helped get her daughter ready for her next trip, exuberant for Carson's sake, but saddened, also, that there was so little time for just the two of them to be together. Marguerite missed Carson dreadfully whenever they were apart, but each time another separation was imminent she maintained a cheerful façade and bravely sent her on her way.

To be with her "other family," as she referred to the Tuckers, was the fulfillment of a dream Carson had hardly dared to imagine. She had no intention of working in Virginia; rather, she wanted to take into every pore of her being the spirit and presence of Mary Tucker, to rejoice in the great waves of emotion that overcame her just visualizing the reunion and the marvelous music they would share once again. In the Tucker home at last, Carson sat enchanted as she listened to her beloved friend play Bach fugues on the piano for her, and both women thrilled as before to their favorite recordings of Mozart, Beethoven, Schubert, and Liszt, which they had listened to many times in the past. Although Carson's inability to play the piano had been a *fact* for several years, she felt an overwhelming and sudden sense of bereftness that she could never again play for her august teacher and that the musical part of her life as a performing artist was forever over. Yet they both knew that the inward sharing, the empathy, the love, the communion they now had was greater than anything they had known together before. Nor did they feel that it would ever elude them again. When they were not listening to music or talking recipes in the kitchen, they laughed and fondly reminisced the life they had shared in the old Tucker home on Austin Loop at Fort Benning. The spend-the-night weekends with Gin, the Tuckers' daughter who had become Carson's best friend, the two girls' zany emulations of Isadora Duncan, the crazy impossible tricks that Gin's brother had pulled on them, the piano lessons, theory, and listening sessions that Carson and Mrs. Tucker had shared, the fragrant blossoms beside the front drive, the savory kitchen aromas, even the old illnesses and sick-room smells—all came back to Carson with vivid fidelity.

Her two-week stay in Virginia with the Tucker family—who clasped her to them now in a way she had never before experienced—was the most idyllic interlude of her middle years. A heightened sense of release had come about through Mary Tucker and their new spirit of communion, and Carson knew that she could return to New York and write again. Most of her problems with Reeves had stemmed from his excessive drinking, she told Mrs. Tucker. Once he began to drink, he could not stop, and he often drank himself ill. Mary Tucker was saddened to hear of her young friend's trouble-ridden life, and she was distressed to know that Carson and Reeves felt that they could no longer live together harmoniously. Mrs. Tucker did not know Reeves well, having met him only a few months earlier when she and Colonel Tucker had gone to New York to see Carson's play, but she had liked him, at any rate. She yearned for Carson to find happiness with Reeves, for she felt that her friend would always need a strong man in her life regardless of her emotional needs for others. Mrs. Tucker also worried about her friend's physical health. Carson looked too thin, but Mrs. Tucker avoided making explicit suggestions. A few days after arriving home, Carson wrote to the Tuckers expressing pleasure that she had already cut down considerably on her smoking and drinking and had gained three whole pounds—to her, the grandest feat of all.

She was back at work, she said, and the writing was going well. Moreover, she had become somewhat reconciled with Reeves, who had volunteered again for treatment through AA and was much improved. She said that when they had gotten back together again, both realized that regardless of their hostilities, they knew that they still loved each other. Carson felt that if only he could control his drinking—and his fierce temper which erupted when he drank—they might get along together once more. She resolved that she would try again to live compatibly with her husband if he would do everything he could to keep from drinking. On October 21, 1950, Jordan Massee recorded in his journal a weekend visit to Nyack:

> . . . Reeves is reinstated. He comes out every weekend. Carson looks very well. She stays in bed a great deal of the time. After supper she recited some new poems, one of which, certainly, is marvelous. I enjoyed being there, even though Carson is more demanding than anyone else I have ever known.
>
> There was an unpleasant argument after dinner. Finally, Carson

was sent to her room to be quiet before retiring. I was allowed to sit with her. She wouldn't let me leave her, despite Bebe's protests, but clung to me, literally, in a kind of pathetic desperation.

Part of Carson's unrest was attributed to a tale a friend had told her. A mutual friend of hers and Jordan Massee's had supposedly said to another mutual friend: "Eventually everyone will leave Carson, everyone except Jordan, who is her cousin and loves her. He'll never see her as others do." Although Massee soothed and assured her that the tale was not so, that it had been twisted beyond any resemblance of truth, Carson was grievously troubled that people she loved sometimes said things facetiously and thoughtlessly which invariably hurt others. Massee's journal entry continued:

> Later when I sat with Carson she told me that we should have been married, that we would have understood each other and been happy. And she was sure that if we had met sooner, before Reeves, we would have married. I was embarrassed because I knew what a bad idea that would have been, but she was so pleased with the idea that I left it at that.

By early December 1950, Carson told a number of friends that Reeves was completely over his trouble with alcohol and was not even drinking beer or wine. He also was on the verge of a good, respectable job, she declared, something equally important to his self-respect. The day after Christmas, Reeves went to work for Banker's Trust Company in New York City, where he envisioned that he would soon be made an officer. Earlier, before Reeves had taken his job with radio station WOR, he had seriously considered going back on active duty with the Army. Carson wrote Tennessee Williams that the idea appealed to them, but it would mean Reeves giving up his $2,000-a-year retirement money. They reasoned, however, that as a captain he would make an adequate salary and have enough leisure time to do the things he wanted. She told Williams that army posts always had good libraries and swimming pools, which would appeal to the playwright, too. Carson visualized a house on the post, a car, and a maid. But most important, she said, would be a room just for him, and she hoped he would make their army home his headquarters.[10] It was another dream, but it sustained Carson when she needed sustenance. On a rational basis, the idea could not have been seriously entertained for long.

The greatest boost to Carson's spirits that winter was recognition and praise from someone she eminently respected in the world of letters: Dr. Edith Sitwell. In the fall, England's great lady, Dame Edith, arrived in New York City with her brother Sir Osbert on the first leg of a world lecture tour. On October 31, Tennessee Williams gave a party for her, inviting Carson, her mother, sister, Jordan Massee, Gore Vidal, Leo Lerman, and a number of other friends mutual to Carson and himself. Carson knew well Dr. Sitwell's enormous reputation, both as a poet and as an extraordinary and flamboyant woman, and she yearned now to know her in person. Jordan Massee described the encounter in his journal the night of the party:

> Dr. Sitwell arrived very dignified and very grand but with a natural grand manner, like genuine royalty, not a pose. Very grand and yet very simple, and that in spite of a topaz ring the size of a hen's egg. She wore a huge gold bracelet, oriental, I think; English walking shoes with low heels; a long black dress and a long black cape, both to the floor, which she kept on, and a rather peculiar hat. She took her seat in the center of the sofa and we were presented. She was completely at ease and put us at ease immediately with her quiet charm and amusing stories. I had expected a kind of exotic *epater le bourgeoise,* but I think she simply dares be herself.
>
> Carson sat with Dr. Sitwell on the sofa and they talked for a long time. Dr. Sitwell treated her as gently as one treats a small nervous child and told Carson that when she returned to England she would send her all her volumes of poetry and would even copy out those poems that have not yet been published. Carson asked if she might send Dr. Sitwell some of her poems, and she replied, "My dear, I hope you will. How nice that would be."

Dr. Sitwell invited Carson and Massee to attend a rehearsal of a recital of scenes from Shakespeare's *Macbeth,* to be presented at the Museum of Modern Art November 16. Appearing with her in the title role was Glenway Wescott. Carson and her cousin accepted with delight. Immediately after the performance she wrote Dame Edith a letter expressing her enormous admiration and gratitude for her new friend and sent with it two of her novels. On November 21, the British poet replied:

> I am deeply grateful to you for having sent me *The Heart Is a Lonely Hunter* and *The Member of the Wedding.* You are a transcendental writer. There cannot be the slightest doubt of that. I am most truly overcome by both of these books.
>
> *The Heart Is a Lonely Hunter* stabbed my heart and my conscience as nothing has done for many years. The part about those three children on a burning summer day with the pavement scorching Bubba's bare feet, the poor little baby's cap that was too small but was put on him to give him face, the part about the change in Bubba so that nobody ever called him Bubba again, the part about Bubba's

bicycle, all the parts about Dr. Copeland and the terrible passages about Willie's feet, the beauty of character and loneliness of Singer— the book is a masterpiece of compassion, of understanding, of writing. What a born writer you are. Only a born writer could have made Singer and his friend see the mad dog at a corner and not on a straight road, thus making the hazards of faith more appalling. I read that part when I was very feverish from an inoculation against typhoid, and I saw that mad dog running and biting all night.

As for *The Member of the Wedding,* the beauty of it is so great that I am living in the summer of that book. One lives in it from the first page with those trees of a bright dizzy green. I had just finished reading *The Member of the Wedding* and was now looking for that wonderful passage about the moths, one of the loveliest in the book, but as I am going to read the book straight through again, I shall soon find it. What a great poet's mind and eye and senses you have, together with a great pure writer's mind, sense of construction and character. What would a poet not give to have written "the long gold sun slanted down on them and made their skin look golden," also "the long gold sun." I have not been so excited by any books as by these for years. In fact, I am so excited by them that I find it impossible to write coherently. I should have written this days ago but I was made ill by an inoculation and was then seized by the doctor and put to bed because my vocal chords are swollen and I have to make gramophone records, hence the delay.

I am sending you by the same post my "Canticle of the Rose." Please read the later poems first and *Poet's Notebook,* and tomorrow I shall copy out two new poems for you and send them. I do hope to see you again very soon. We start on our terrible tour on Tuesday. We shall be back for a fortnight at the beginning of March, and I will, if I may, write to you beforehand, and suggest times for meeting. May I send you love, which indeed I do, and my deepest admiration.

Yours,

Edith Sitwell

According to Jordan Massee, Carson would rather have received that letter than "to have taken Quebec."[11] On November 26, Carson wrote to Dr. Sitwell a four-page reply to that first letter. She said that she felt both proud and humble at praise from such a great poet and that her letter was, indeed, generous and beautiful. It brought tears to her eyes and made her very happy. Assuring Dame Edith that she already knew well "The Canticle of the Rose," Carson praised her poetry for its combination of lyricism and intellect. Then she compared Edith Sitwell with Milton and Shakespeare, adding that she wished T. S. Eliot had been capable of such development. Overjoyed, too, that Dr. Sitwell was sending her some new, unpublished poems, Carson said that she eagerly awaited both the poems and her visit. She would keep the entire first fortnight of March open, she promised, for she would rather talk with Dame Edith than with anyone else in the world. Never before had Carson been so thrilled by an artist's praise. To her, Edith Sitwell was the greatest poet on earth. To be sure, Carson and Dame Edith's initial meeting and these two letters exemplify the immediacy and completeness of the response of genius to genius.

Carson also invited Dame Edith and her brother Sir Osbert to accompany her to the production of *The Member of the Wedding*. The play had been going beautifully, and every indication was that it would run for more than a year. In August 1950, Robert Whitehead flew to the West Coast to discuss with independent motion picture firms the sale of the play's screen rights, and in September, Brooks Atkinson wrote in the New York *Times* that even though a war had broken out in Korea and the country was "riding a whirlwind again," *The Member of the Wedding* remained "constant and intact at the Empire Theatre." Carson's writing, Harold Clurman's directing, and the acting grace of Ethel Waters, Julie Harris, and Brandon de Wilde—all had made the play "an intensely personal work of art and the chief literary treasure of this year in the theatre," said Atkinson.[12] By now, backers received another dividend, distribution of an additional $15,000 profit, making a total of $112,500 paid out to the investors of the play in less than nine months. In February 1951, Whitehead returned to Hollywood, this time to conclude negotiations with independent producer Stanley Kramer. According to the Kramer Company, the screen rights were bought for $75,000 plus 10 per cent of the profits. Carson's share as playwright was approximately 60 per cent of the sale. Unfortunately, however, according to Kramer, no profits were made on the movie; thus the playwright participated in no additional royalties.[13] By early summer Ethel Waters, Julie Harris, and Brandon de Wilde had been signed to repeat their stage roles for the screen.

The play ran on Broadway for fourteen and a half months, closing March 17, 1951. Only *South Pacific* had had a longer concurrent run. The troupe took a week off, then began its tour of major northern American and Canadian cities, opening March 26 at the Colonial Theatre in Boston. Most of its original cast stayed with the show.[14] Early in the tour there had been a personality clash, with Ethel Waters tending to overplay her role, both on and off the stage. After various members of the cast complained that she was attempting to "take over," she was told that she must settle down. An out-of-town reviewer also stoked the coals when he said of Miss Waters: "This was not the performance we saw in New York." According to Harold Clurman, "Miss Waters became angry, but soon settled down and played the role to perfection. Julie Harris was perfect all along."[15] Later, for the road company tour, Miss Harris was replaced by Betty Lou Holland, and another child replaced Brandon de Wilde.

The Member of the Wedding had only two weeks more to run on Broadway when Edith Sitwell returned from her world tour, but there was no time for Carson to take her to see her play. The two women exchanged several letters during the interim, however, and by the time they met again in the spring when Carson and Jordan Massee attended her reading at the YM-YWHA (Young Men's and Young Women's Hebrew Association), the two women knew that they shared a special kinship. In an anguished outburst written just before Christmas 1950, Carson had told Dame Edith that she had seen a new doctor on whom she had very much counted to treat and cure her, possibly, of her mysterious paralysis. Instead, he told her that there was absolutely no hope that she would regain free movement of her arm, hand, and left leg, and that her illness suffered three years ago in Paris stemmed from a hemorrhage that had destroyed certain motor nerves that could never be restored. The verdict greatly saddened her, Carson admitted, but only confirmed what she had suspected and secretly accepted for a long time. Dr. Sitwell responded in a long, handwritten letter to Carson in which she expressed enormous feeling and sympathy. The letter read, in part:

> Jan. 2, 1951, Mexico City
>
> . . . Dear, what can I say in answer to what you told me in your letter. There is no sympathy that wouldn't seem futile,—indeed, I think, impertinent. One can only hope, from the depth of one's spirit and the bottom of one's heart, that the doctor may yet prove to be wrong. Such things have happened. Oh, I pray it may be so. . . . It is unbelievably wicked that such a thing could happen to you, of all people. That it should happen, and that you should be in such pain. . . . I only tell you this to show that I know and understand such suffering—though it is a different kind of suffering. . . . Oh, I've seen so much, these last 5 years. . . . People—foolish people —say that pain ennobles. It only doesn't debase a nature when it is a nature as noble as yours. . . . What can I say to you of the New Year? Only that I *hope*.
>
> My love to you, dear Carson—
>
> EDITH

Upon receiving this letter, there was no doubt in Carson's mind that in Dame Edith she had found a spiritual companion and champion. Carson resolved now to visit the poet in England just as soon as she was able. In March 1951, when they met again, Dr. Sitwell extended the invitation. But first there was new literary recognition for Carson by her American contemporaries. In the April 15, 1951, issue of *Vogue*, she and Tennessee Williams were featured with full-page photographs and cut lines as "Incessant Prize-Winners." Williams had recently won laurels with his newest Broadway success, *The Rose Tattoo*, and Carson was being heralded for her past literary successes and phenomenal Broadway success, as well as for the forthcoming omnibus publication of her collected works. Entitled *The Ballad of the Sad Café and Other Works*, the collection included *The Heart Is a Lonely Hunter*, *Reflections in a Golden Eye*, *The Member of the Wedding*, and five of her published short stories: "Wunderkind," "The Jockey," "Madame Zilensky and the King of Finland," "A Tree. A Rock. A Cloud." and "The Sojourner." There was also a new story, "A Domestic Dilemma," a poignant piece very close to Carson personally that had not been published elsewhere.

"A Domestic Dilemma" mirrored several facets of Carson's troubled life with Reeves and her mother at home in Nyack. Its tone was strangely reminiscent of an earlier story, the then unpublished "The Instant of the Hour After," written during the author's study with Sylvia Chatfield Bates at Columbia University, before she and Reeves had married the first time. In the person of Emily Meadows, the sherry-tippling housewife who precipitated "the domestic dilemma," were elements not only of Carson and Reeves, but of Carson's mother as well. The setting, unnamed, was doubtless Nyack; the cottage overlooked the Hudson much as Carson's own house did at 131 South Broadway. In the story, Emily's husband, Martin Meadows, whose job had wrenched them from the South, tried to analyze the source of his wife's problem:

> The change from Alabama to New York had somehow disturbed her; accustomed to the idle warmth of a small Southern town . . . she had failed to accommodate herself to the stricter, lonelier mores of the North. The duties of motherhood and housekeeping were onerous to her. Homesick for Paris City, she had made no friends in the suburban town. She read only magazines and murder books. Her interior life was insufficient without the artifice of alcohol.[16]

Angered, however, by Emily's furtive drinking and fearful for the safety of their two small children when she proved incapable of caring for them on the maid's half day off, Meadows ambivalently both loved and hated his wife. He had come home that day from work as a commuter from New York City and found his wife drunk in their bedroom, the children unsupervised, and his six-year-old son complaining of the "hot toast," which Meadows discovered had been sprinkled with cayenne instead of cinnamon. A year earlier his baby daughter had been hurt in a more serious accident because of his wife's drinking. Now, after a drunken scene in front of the children, Meadows put his wife to bed. Later, he bathed his young son and daughter with great tenderness and love, tucked them in for the night, and returned to the living room to read. Angry, unhappy, wrapped in self-pity, he finally climbed the stairs to bed, undressed silently, and watched his sleeping wife. Mysteriously, however, the anger and sorrow abated as "all thoughts of blame and blemish" left him and he reached for "the adjacent flesh," while sorrow paralleled "desire in the immense complexity of love."

When the omnibus collection appeared on May 24, 1951, it received excellent reviews and sold well. Charles Poore, writing for the New York *Times*, lamented that America no longer had anything resembling Hawthorne's Concord literati, but rejoiced that it at least had Carson McCullers and William Faulkner:

> On the contrary, we have a funereally flourishing school of hand-
> wringers that you might call the Discord literati. . . . The All-Is-
> Lost Generation decidedly does not include Carson McCullers,
> whose new book, *The Ballad of the Sad Café and Other Works*
> would probably impress even the melancholy Hawthorne. For she is
> at once too young and too wise to bog down among the all-is-losters.
> Like Faulkner, she speaks for the human spirit—undefeated, undefeat-
> able.[17]

Others reviewers singled out "A Domestic Dilemma" and "The Sojourner," written only slightly earlier and published in the May 1950 issue of *Mademoiselle*, as two of her finest short works to date. Not only did her earlier published works hold up well under new critical examination, but there was no doubt in the minds of people very close to the author personally that she had in no way lost any of her creative powers during the last two years because of physical handicaps. On September 16, 1951, "A Domestic Dilemma" was again published, this time in the New York *Post Magazine Section*, where thousands of readers saw it and were introduced to its author for the first time.

Throughout 1951 Carson continued to form many new relationships in the theatrical and literary world, secure now and touted as a renowned author and playwright both in America and abroad. Her new friends did not have to be famous; they had only to admire her inordinately. Because she was infirm much of the time, her intense pain increasingly troublesome, she was accustomed to having people come to her in Nyack to pay homage. Carson went out relatively little at this time; yet when she was not actually with people, or working, she was frequently on the telephone. With money coming in regularly—as well as devotees—she lacked incentive to work.

The old friends, however, she was still partial to as long as there were no estranging incidents. Tennessee Williams returned to New York the first of the year for the production of *The Rose Tattoo*, and Carson was overjoyed when he came up to Nyack to visit, along with his sister, Rose, and Frank Merlo, Williams' friend and traveling companion, of whom Carson, also, was very fond. When *The Rose Tattoo* premièred on Broadway February 3 at the Martin Beck Theatre—it had opened in Chicago on December 29—Carson and Reeves were in the audience as the playwright's guests. It was a superb opening, said the critics, and Carson reveled in the excitement shared with other prominent first-nighters, including David Diamond, who composed the music for the play.

Carson and Reeves had seen little of Diamond since their remarriage. It had been almost ten years since the three of them had first become entangled, and although Diamond was delighted to see them now, he was nonetheless hesitant to throw himself wholeheartedly into a repetition of their former relationship. That evening David Diamond wrote in his diary his impressions of the evening:

> February 3, 1951—Saturday: To see Carson and Reeves tonight was not at all painful. Only Carson's very ill appearance pained me. They both want me to come back to Nyack with them Monday. But I will not go—not that I am afraid. But that I feel they may still be able to *force* me to accept *their* helplessness and loneliness as a part of my own. . . .[18]

Carson and Reeves sent Diamond a congratulatory message after the première, saying, "Overjoyed to hear some Diamond music. Want to see you soon." A week later, Reeves telephoned to ask him out to Nyack for the weekend. Again, Diamond was reluctant; yet he felt that after all the intervening years he should be able to see Carson and Reeves "without the old pain and remorse returning." To him, the important thing was that they *wanted* to see him again.[19] But he did not accept this invitation either. Perhaps after he returned from Boston he would go, he rationalized. Two months went by, and again Diamond received a telephone call from Nyack. This time it was Carson, thanking him for T. S. Eliot's "Lines for an Old Man," which Diamond had set to music and dedicated to her. Once more she urged him to come to Nyack for the weekend: "You will have a room all to yourself," she promised. Diamond thought he wanted to go, yet ambivalated. That night (April 10) he wrote in his diary: "I *think* I *should* be able to see both Carson and Reeves now, with no pain. So, in the near future, I may go to pay them a visit. . . ." Again, however, he was unwilling to test or expose his vulnerability. He knew that they could never be a trio in the old way, nor would he risk a dual alliance now even if one were possible.

Yet still the "courtship" continued. On June 25, Diamond received another wire from Carson, this time an invitation to a supper party the next evening. In response, he called her and was told that she was having "a fair-sized crowd"—that included Lillian Hellman, Henry Varnum Poor, Cheryl Crawford, actresses Ruth Norman and Zita Johann, her cousin Jordan Massee, her sister, Rita, and her mother. "Dear David, please come and spend the night with us, also," she urged. At last Diamond assented. There was a certain safety in numbers, he felt.

That night after the party (June 26), Diamond recorded pertinent events of the afternoon and evening:

> . . . Met Reeves, a pleasant ferry crossing and train trip to Nyack.
> When I came into the house, Carson was seated in the living room,
> of course sipping, as tho' it were sugar water, a whiskey highball. She
> kissed me tenderly and showed great pleasure to see me, as did "Bebe"
> and Rita. Carson had never looked so ill, so fragile, so remote and
> anguished. The partial paralysis of her left arm and leg is not as
> disabling as I had expected. I think the steady consumption of so
> much alcohol per day (she has several highballs daily before dinner
> and a bottle or two of wine after) does more harm. Reeves is so much
> better since joining Alcoholics Anonymous, and "Bebe" does not
> drink any more. This means there is peace between them. Had Reeves
> and I avoided so much drinking when we were together, we might
> have worked our problems out.
>
> The party pleasant. Cheryl and Ruth, Bessie Breuer (chattering
> mercilessly on and on—a somewhat amusing hysteria apparent as in
> some zany comedian's antics), Zita Johann whom I was much taken
> with and talked to for hours. . . . More tomorrow . . .

After the crowd dispersed, Diamond, Miss Hellman, Carson, and Reeves sat chatting amiably for several more hours, Miss Hellman having been invited, also, to spend the night. The next day, Diamond's diary continued:

> . . . After Lillian retired to the third floor to sleep, Carson, Reeves,
> and I sat up 'til 3:30 A.M. talking over the past and the violences
> in our relationship when we first met. We agreed our youth, our
> ambivalences, our confused seeking for happiness and security was
> based not on reality but falsely directed by too much alcohol and
> not facing the homosexual question tolerantly. . . .

Carson and Reeves urged him to stay on still another day, and on June 28, Diamond's diary entry read:

Last night, Reeves confided that never had he come closer to loving a man as he did me. But his misery, having left Carson to come to Rochester, after forging checks, the guilty feelings developing there, all contributed to his undoing, and in turn I was almost dragged down with him. While his war experience embittered him and gave him severe shock, it acted as a kind of catharsis, and really saved his life. . . . But love me he did. It is good to know this now. Now that the pain is gone forever and the hold he had on me is released.

As for Carson—I still feel that as long as she lives in the alcoholic haze so much of the time (and she does not realize it!), it will be impossible to *really* have a healthy, mutually gratifying relationship. She can *take* only. Reeves now gives and takes. They want me to consider their house *my* house; and to come whenever I want to, even when they are away. Carson's new novel will be tremendous. Reeves read several extended sections to me and I was overwhelmed.

Carson could now legally refer to 131 South Broadway in Nyack as *her* house, and *theirs*, for on March 8, 1951, she purchased it from her mother. Marguerite Smith had almost run out of her own money, and out of Carson's percentage of the sale of screen rights for *The Member of the Wedding*—some forty thousand dollars—Carson bought the house with the understanding that it would always be her mother's as well.[20]

The "alcoholic haze" in which Carson reportedly had been living much of the time proved even more distressing to Lillian Hellman, her other house guest the night of the dinner party. Carson and Reeves met Miss Hellman in March after her play *The Autumn Garden* opened on Broadway. Soon after the initial meeting Carson bought a car—another cash purchase with her "movie money"—so that Reeves could run errands and drive them to parties and plays in the city, to the hospital for checkups and treatments, and out into the countryside for visits with their suburban friends. One of the earliest excursions was a drive up to Pleasantville, New York, where Miss Hellman had a farm. They were much taken by the plight of the playwright's good friend and companion, writer Dashiell Hammett. Hammett and two other trustees of the bail bond fund of the Civil Rights Congress had refused to reveal the names of the fund's contributors, and now faced a jail sentence. Moreover, according to Miss Hellman, he did not even know the names. Carson and Reeves were sympathetic to Hammett's situation and wanted to talk about it with Miss Hellman. It was another cause in which Carson could become

emotionally involved without expending any undue intellectual energies
or becoming physically involved in actually doing anything.

At a second meeting, recalled Miss Hellman, "Reeves very generously
offered some money for bail to help Dash. I didn't accept it, but I was
impressed that Reeves offered it. Carson didn't say anything, but she
didn't object to it, either."[21] In the months that followed, Miss Hellman
was frequently struck by the contrast between Reeves's spirit of generosity
and Carson's penuriousness, as she saw it. Ironically, as most people realized, it was Carson's money with which Reeves was munificent.

It was a few weeks later that Miss Hellman was invited to Carson's
supper party in Nyack, after which she and David Diamond spent the
night:

> I was to have stayed for more than one night, but I was uneasy there.
> The whole atmosphere of the house was oppressive and made me
> nervous. I didn't sleep that night, and when I got up the next morn-
> ing early—around six—I went into the kitchen and there was Carson's
> mother, roaring drunk. I left that morning without seeing Carson,
> leaving her a note instead.[22]

According to Diamond, "tho Bebe had said she drank no more, she
was 'tight' the next morning, and sobering up (!) on beer."[23] Miss Hellman continued to see Carson and Reeves occasionally over the next two
years, but she chose not to become involved with them. "Carson bur-
dened everyone who got close to her. If you wanted burdens, liked burdens, you accepted Carson and her affection. I don't like such burdens,"
said Miss Hellman.

The drinking problem depicted by Carson in "A Domestic Dilemma"
was, as she saw it, more her husband's problem and her mother's than her
own. Although Reeves had stopped drinking from October of 1950
through the following June, he began to imbibe heavily a few days after
Carson's supper party that summer. On July 12, he left his job with Banker's Trust Company, ill and depressed, both from too much alcohol and
disappointed at not having been made a bank officer as he had expected.
Once more through the encouragement of Marty Mann, Reeves volunteered for treatment and committed himself, this time to Doctors Hospital in New York City for another drying-out period. Carson, in the meantime, decided to leave as soon as possible, alone, for England. On June
28, she sailed aboard the *Queen Elizabeth*.

As the time approached for her departure, it occurred to Carson's
mother that the least Reeves might do for his wife would be to check
himself out of the hospital for the day to take Sister to the ship and help
get her aboard with her luggage. "Sister hates to ride the bus, for people always stare at her so much," Marguerite Smith rationalized to a

friend. Then she asked her other daughter to serve as emissary for the quest.[24] Rita Smith, who lived only a few doors from Doctors Hospital, decided to invite Andrew Lyndon—who knew Reeves and Carson and also lived in the vicinity—to come to dinner at her apartment and then share with her the hospital mission. Reeves happily welcomed his guests from his hospital bed, for he loved Carson's sister and they had remained close through the years. After they were seated, Reeves brought out beer, which he explained a nurse had slipped to him the second day of his incarceration, and chatted gaily about how well he was feeling. When his sister-in-law proposed that he chauffeur his wife to the ship, however, Reeves vehemently declined. According to Andrew Lyndon, Reeves's reply went something like this:

> I always do the *big thing* by Carson—my coming here, getting the cure, taking care of her—but I'm not going to get myself out of here on her account now. Carson will just have to make good her own way.[25]

True to his word, Reeves did not take Carson to the ship—but he did leave the hospital and take *himself* there. When the *Queen Elizabeth* sailed on July 28, not only Carson was aboard, but Reeves as well. Having neither money, wallet, nor passport with him, he stole aboard as a stowaway. Several times Carson thought she caught a glimpse of Reeves aboard, but in each instance passed it off as an impossibility. A few weeks later, in London, she told Lillian Hellman the incredible story of their transatlantic crossing. By this time, the tale had become increasingly amusing in the retelling and a favorite of Carson's. She was sitting on deck the first day out, she declared, when she looked off in the distance and glimpsed a strangely familiar figure. "That sure looks like Reeves," she thought. The next day she saw the figure again. "That sure looks even more like Reeves," she repeated. "But of course it couldn't be." The third day it happened once more, prompting Carson to check with the captain to see if a James Reeves McCullers could possibly be on the passenger list. Finally, having tired of the charade, having no place to eat or sleep, snacking off leftover trays found outside cabin doors, and sleeping in deck chairs pulled into obscure corners, Reeves decided to seek deliverance. "Dear Carson, I'm aboard, too," said the scrawled note handed her by a cabin boy who waited for an answer.

Amused and intrigued by her husband's antics, Carson sent an amiable note in return: "That's nice. Are you free for lunch, by chance?"[26] The rest of the voyage was fairly pleasant for them both, although upon their arrival in England Carson resented having to pay for Reeves's passage for the *entire* trip. Nonetheless, she felt a pang of sympathy when he was unable to convince the immigration authorities to allow him to debark without a passport. To the rescue came British poet David Gascoyne, who was to host Carson during most of her stay in England this trip. Gascoyne met the ship in Southampton and spoke up in Reeves's behalf when he discovered his plight. The passenger in question was, indeed, the husband of England's prominent literary visitor from America, he told them; moreover, he was a decorated war hero and a Ranger who had trained on Her Majesty's soil. He must be given sanctuary. Finally, an appeal was made to the American ambassador in London, whereupon Reeves was allowed to leave the ship provided his passport could be forwarded to them before the ship sailed. Reeves stayed for two weeks, then flew home, but it was not a particularly happy time for him.

Upon his return, he wrote to David Diamond that he had just arrived a few days earlier and found Diamond's card awaiting him. He said that Carson was in London and would stay on several more weeks. As for him, he had taken ill and returned early. He also needed to get back to work, he added. As for Carson, he did not know what her travel plans were regarding the rest of Europe.[27] Reeves, as usual, had gilded the lily. True, he had been sick, but he also had resumed his drinking. An anecdote involving Reeves and his alcoholism which Carson relished in telling later involved a small party at Dr. Edith Sitwell's that summer. Carson said that while Reeves was sitting in the drawing room imbibing freely and listening to her and Dame Edith expound on multitudinous topics, he suddenly slid to the floor, where he lay for another hour—while the conversation continued uninterrupted and the distinguished poet revealed not the slightest notice. Although Reeves's intentions to return to work may have been sincere, Banker's Trust Company did not rehire him. Nor was there any other job awaiting him in New York City. Reeves simply went home to Nyack, kept his mother-in-law company, and awaited his wife's return.

Carson herself remained almost three months in England, moving in on different literary acquaintances who seemed delighted and honored to have her *temporarily* as a house guest. Dennis Cohen, a rich and pleasant man who owned Cresset Press—which had published all of the British editions of her novels—gave a large reception in Carson's honor early in her stay in London. Most of the leading British literati of the day came out to meet her, and a number of smaller parties ensued. The people of London whom Carson met that summer seemed genuinely fond of her and were anxious to entertain for her. They were much taken by her rather droll sense of humor, her soft, slow, southern talk, the long pauses which demanded attentive listening, her poetic speech with its often dignified and almost cadenced rhythms. They also were admiring and sympathetic because she had overcome the adversities of paralysis and pain and continued to write.

Writer David Garnett, one of the few survivors of the Bloomsbury group, proclaimed Carson the only American author for whom he had any respect. She was one of my "Best Things," he recalled later. "It was at the very worst time in the last war, when I thought we were doomed and nobody would ever do anything that I cared about again. I read *Reflections in a Golden Eye*, and everything changed."[28] He told friends later that he had been on the brink of suicide, but that *Reflections in a Golden Eye* had saved him.[29] Garnett and Carson met in America after the war, and he told her the story. He was delighted to see her again now in England.

Another prominent British writer who admired Carson's work, John Lehmann, saw her several times that summer and one evening gave a small dinner party for her, David Gascoyne, and Tennessee Williams, who had just arrived in London in time to be captured by Carson and carried off to dinner. In his published memoirs later, Lehmann recalled his impressions of that visit:

> . . . As usual, Carson and David talked across one another, and at
> one moment I rather rudely told him to shut up, as I wanted so much
> to hear what she was saying. He jumped up and made off, and I had
> to wheedle him back from the front door and ask his forgiveness. I
> was particularly struck by the tender and affectionate consideration
> Tennessee showed Carson. He knew exactly how to handle his er-
> ratic and brilliant friend, and revealed an impressive side to his char-
> actor of which I had, I confess, not been fully aware before. After-
> wards, we all jumped into the car, and drove round and over the
> bridges to see the lights of the Festival of Britain and the Fun Fair
> in Battersea Park.[30]

Reeves had already left for America before Lehmann's dinner party; therefore, they did not meet, but Lehmann was struck by Carson's insistence at the dinner table in describing Reeves "without any reticence, as an 'alcoholic epileptoid.' "[31] Nor was Lehmann the first one to whom Carson described Reeves's condition as epileptic.[32] Reeves had no medical record of such a malady, however.

He had not wanted to leave Carson in England and return home alone, but he felt that he had little choice. It was obvious to everyone that Carson preferred that he not be there. Once back in Nyack the end of August, he worried exceedingly about her. He could tell by Carson's behavior before he left London that she was embarking on another round of parties, heavy drinking, personal involvements, and infatuations—all of which he was sure would lead to exhaustion, despair, and, possibly new illness. Yet with his own psychic and physical health precarious, he felt powerless to cope with Carson's problems.

For three weeks after his return, Reeves received no word from his wife; then, finally, there was a brief note and an accompanying letter from John Lehmann's sister, Rosamond, with whom Carson was then staying. Reeves and Carson had met Miss Lehmann at Bowen's Court the previous summer and had seen her again in London in the apartment of David Gascoyne. An accurate diagnostician, Reeves's foreboding apparently had come to pass, as Miss Lehmann's letter confirmed. She wrote that Carson had been hospitalized for a few days at St. George's in London in a state of near collapse, having become "exhausted from seeing too many people, drinking too much, and thrashing about in a welter of plans and projects with which she could not cope."[33]

Although Carson's home base throughout her ten-week stay in London was with David Gascoyne at Grosvenor House, 25 St. Leonard's Terrace, where Gascoyne had a large, luxury flat, the two of them traipsed about London and the countryside for weeks without rest. Gascoyne had a wide assortment of friends, and he was either entertaining for Carson at home or they were off together at teas, cocktail parties, luncheons, formal dinners, and overnight visits with sundry other poets, writers, artists, and *artistes*. If Carson's visit were an extended one, however, the host or hostess invariably found her a demanding guest, welcome upon arrival—as Elizabeth Bowen had discovered—but once ensconced, "a terrible handful."

One day Carson announced to Gascoyne that she would like to give a party for Dr. Edith Sitwell—who had already entertained for her several times at the Sesame Club, Dame Edith's London home—and asked if he would like to cohost the party with her. Carefully they made up the guest list and included everyone who had invited them to parties since Carson's arrival, as well as others from the literary world who were friends of Dame Edith's or those whom Carson decided upon on her own that she wanted to meet. Carson thought the party a great success, except that to her chagrin, several of the guests appeared more interested in fellow guest Dylan Thomas than they were in their eminent guest of honor, Dr. Sitwell, or their American cohostess.

A few days later, Gascoyne and Carson drove fifty miles northwest into the countryside near Oxford to the estate of Rosamond Lehmann, who had invited them to spend several days. "Carson had a curious way of invading people's auras, so to speak, and drawing on them," recalled Miss Lehmann many years later. "I found her fascinating and lovable, but at the same time a terrific psychic drain. She made enormous emotional demands; besides that, as you must know, her drinking habits made her a very difficult guest."[34] Interestingly, Gascoyne, who was touchy and temperamental, seemed to enjoy having Carson under his wing. To him, she was a kindred spirit. Sometimes gruff with her, he did not cater to her whims. Their parries and thrusts with each other were stimulating, with each sensing when to press and when to hold.

Among the guests of David Gascoyne at Grosvenor House one evening was the beautiful and charming wife of Carson's British publisher, Katherine Hammond Cohen. An American by birth, Dr. Cohen was now a practicing psychiatrist and lived in London with her husband. She had come late to her profession, having been a medical student in the United States while in her early thirties during World War II. Dr. Cohen had a relatively young and flourishing practice. Sensitive at once to the frail, young writer's physical infirmities and needs, she took a professional interest in Carson and extended warmly her friendship and affection. As had been Carson's wont for many years, she often presented herself to a prospective and vulnerable devotee as the "wounded sparrow." Now, pressing her maimed left arm pathetically to her side, turning her dark eyes shyly away from her new friend, Carson announced unhappily, "My case has been abandoned as hopeless." Such a comment was certain to elicit pity and prompt an immediate pledge of assistance. So, too, responded Dr. Cohen. Unwilling to accept the conclusions of Carson's earlier doctors and anxious to help, Katherine Cohen asked if *she* might examine and treat her. She explained that she had been working successfully through hypnosis with a number of patients whose problems appeared similar to Carson's.

The idea of hypnosis intrigued Carson. Her reaction to her potential deliverer was not only admiration and trust, but rapt passion and infatuation. Body and soul she dedicated to her new doctor to do with as she wished, for Dr. Cohen—in her eyes—could do no wrong. Immediately the two women became almost constant companions, but before the actual treatments began, Carson already had pushed herself to the point of exhaustion. Quickly Dr. Cohen arranged for her patient's hospitalization at St. George's. Then, during the week-long rest and recuperation that followed, Dr. Cohen performed a series of tests to determine the nature of Carson's paralysis. At last she reached a decision. There was no organic reason for the paralysis, she affirmed. Instead of having suffered from a hemorrhaged vessel in the brain, Carson was experiencing a "conversion reaction," or "hysterical paralysis." The symptoms were the same, explained Dr. Cohen, whether the malady stemmed from a stroke or was a conversion reaction, but the latter could be treated and cured. With Carson's permission, she would treat her through hypnosis—and was almost certain of success, she encouraged.

It was at this point that Rosamond Lehmann wrote to Reeves to apprise him of Carson's hospitalization and the projected treatments. His response was relief, enthusiasm, and hope. He said that he was much encouraged by Miss Lehmann's assessment of the situation and of Dr. Cohen's ability to bring about Carson's recovery. He had been reading that very day about some of Freud's early cases in which remarkable cures were effected through hypnosis. It had set him to thinking about the practicality of having Carson undergo hypnosis, not knowing that such treatment was already under consideration. Reeves told Miss Lehmann that he was sure that his wife would react well to the psychiatric sessions because of her love and trust in Dr. Cohen. He had worried about his wife while he was in London and was certain that she was headed for trouble, he said, but he would have rested more easily if he had known that Miss Lehmann had remained close at hand. He knew that he had presented himself in the most unattractive light to Miss Lehmann, both earlier in Ireland, and then in London, but he told her that he sensed her awareness that he was a better person than his actions revealed. He hoped that they would meet again soon and that he would have a chance to redeem himself.[35]

Two days after Reeves's letter to Miss Lehmann, Carson wired that she was well, happy, and furiously at work on her poem. Addressing Reeves as "Precious," and signing the cable "Your own Carson," she was in love again not only with her husband, but with Katherine Hammond Cohen and the whole world.

The long poem at which Carson had been at work intermittently for the past year was "The Dual Angel: A Meditation on Origin and Choice," which she hoped to finish that winter in time to send mimeographed copies as Christmas presents to various friends around the world. She was unable to complete the poem in England as she had hoped, however, for early in October her psyche took a sharp, downward spiral. She had been staying at what she identified in her wire to Reeves as a "wonderful club in the country," where Dr. Cohen was attempting her treatments—the theory being that alternating periods of rest, hypnosis, exercise, and work would relieve the atrophied muscles and eventually make Carson whole again. Yet in spite of Carson's desire to co-operate—too strong-willed herself—she inadvertently could not respond satisfactorily to the mesmeric powers of someone else. Neither Dr. Cohen nor another psychiatrist called in to assist on the case could effect a successful hypnotic trance. Discouraged, her patient found that her arm and fingers seemed even more taut than before and her lame leg more painful than ever. Even harder for Carson to accept was her doctor's reluctance to become more emotionally entangled with her than she already was. The professional distance between them was, to Carson, an unbearable barrier. Feeling a new sense of rejection and deeply hurt, reliving again the role of the unrequited lover being put off with great finality, Carson wired

Reeves that she was still ill, that there had been no cure, and that she was coming home.

The end of October, she was back in Nyack, pouring out her heart and disappointment to her sympathetic husband. A few weeks later, Reeves summarized to Rosamond Lehmann the events of the past month. He said that Carson was quite ill when she returned from England and that they had gone to New Orleans in an attempt to shake off her various problems. Although she managed to get over her emotional entanglement with Dr. Cohen, he said she caught a dangerous virus which attacked her respiratory system and caused her temperature to shoot up to 105 degrees. Once back in Nyack she was hospitalized for bronchial pneumonia and pleurisy. The so-called miracle drugs did their part, said Reeves, but if he had ever doubted Carson's indestructibility, he was convinced of it now. Their domestic life was tranquil once more. They were living in Nyack with Carson's mother; they had found a cook and housekeeper who pleased them; Carson was completing the long poem that she had labored over for months; and Reeves was working in New York City and commuting at a job he did not identify. They would stay put in America for a few years, he predicted, but he hoped that Miss Lehmann would see fit to visit them in Nyack before long.[36]

Barely three weeks passed, however, before both became restless again and completely reversed their plans. In a letter to David Diamond on December 18—Diamond having left for Rome the end of September —Reeves announced that whereas they had tentatively expected to stay in Nyack for the next two years, they now had a better plan. They would rent the house, pack up a few belongings, and move to Europe for a year or two. As they visualized it, they would make either Paris or Italy their headquarters. They would spend the warm months near Paris and the winters in Italy. Extending their dream, they thought that they might spend two or three months in Austria. Neither of them had been to Austria, but the country appealed to their romantic natures. But for now, Reeves asked Diamond to begin looking for a three- or four-room apartment for them in Rome. He, too, would begin writing again, he announced. It seemed impossible to find the quietude and peace of mind that they both required by staying on in America, he told Diamond, but they were confident that it could be found in Europe.

Nyack, London, New York, or Paris—nowhere had Carson found the peace she sought; yet once more she experienced through Reeves a renewed sense of hope, strength, and security. She did not want to put her faith in doctors or psychiatrists again, having learned a bitter lesson from her London involvement with her female psychiatrist friend. Next time she would not be so vulnerable, she vowed. Besides, she had become rather accustomed to her black, silver-beaded cane, which she fondled now as a child might caress a favorite doll or savor an all-day sucker. She was grateful for what she had—and to hell with the rest.

In the fall before Carson's return home, her name had again appeared in the theatrical column of the New York *Times*. Robert Whitehead told a reporter that he had recently read the first draft of an original, still untitled play written by Carson McCullers in two and a half weeks. Set in a suburb of New York City, the play dealt with a child, his mother, stepfather, and father. The columnist urged readers not to look for its production this season, however, because the playwright reportedly was still trying to complete a new novel, *Clock Without Hands*.[37] Carson's new play was destined not to be produced for another six years, during which time it underwent more than a dozen revisions and was staged finally as *The Square Root of Wonderful*. Nor was *Clock Without Hands* finished first. It was almost ten years later that her fifth novel was published. But she was certain that she would write again—and well—if she and Reeves could go off to a new environment together.

There was no doubt in the minds of the most important people in the realm of American arts and letters in 1951 that Carson McCullers deserved a permanent place in American culture. On January 15 of the new year, Carson made the New York *Times* headlines as one of fourteen to win new lifetime admission to the National Institute of Arts and Letters. Her letter that day from playwright Marc Connelly, secretary of the Institute, informed her that she had been one of eight elected to the Institute's eminent Department of Literature. Carson was delighted to learn that her good friends Tennessee Williams and Newton Arvin were also selected, along with novelist and short-story writer Eudora Welty, poet Louise Bogan, biographer Jacques Barzun, historian Henry Steele Commager, and novelist Waldo Frank. Named to the other departments were one musician and five artists. With the membership of the Institute limited to 250 living members, the elections of 1952 brought the roster only eight short of a full roll.

The formal induction at the Public Ceremonial was to take place May 28 at the Academy Auditorium, but Carson wrote a letter (January 16) of regret to Marc Connelly that she would not be present because she would be leaving soon for Europe. She requested, however, that her friend Floria Lasky might attend in her behalf and receive the diploma for her. Later, the 1952 NIAL–AAAL Ceremonial Program carried the following citation:

> Carson McCullers, *novelist and playwright*, born in Columbus,
> Georgia, 1917. A deeply penetrating yet compassionate observation

of human behavior has marked all of Mrs. McCullers' work. Beginning with her memorable first novel *The Heart Is a Lonely Hunter*, she has unfailingly displayed a unique talent for lyrical narrative. Her transference of many delicately achieved values in her novel *The Member of the Wedding* to the stage revealed her rare talent as a dramatist.[38]

When the announcement of Carson's election to the National Institute of Arts and Letters arrived, she and Reeves were busily preparing for the next important step in their lives—a move to Europe, complete with car, trunks, and Kristin, their boxer. Natalia Danesi Murray, with whom Carson and Reeves had stayed in 1946 on their first visit to Italy, was now in New York and met them for lunch one day to talk over their plans. Mrs. Murray advised them to make reservations at a good hotel before their arrival—Rome being filled with tourists during the late winter and spring—and recommended the Hotel Inghilterra, which for generations had catered to British and American writers. Again Carson enlisted the aid of David Diamond. She had already urged him to be on the lookout for suitable permanent quarters, but she asked now that he reserve a double room with bath at the Hotel Inghilterra for them. They were to sail on January 30 for Naples aboard the *Constitution* and planned to drive to Rome upon their arrival February 6. According to Reeves, they would stay in Italy during the rest of the cold winter months, then go to Paris in the spring.

Carson's election to America's highest and most elite organization for creative artists was a timely entrée into the Italian world of arts and letters. Before her departure she received several dozen letters and cards from the Roman intelligentsia after word circulated that she was soon to be a guest in their city. Among them was a letter from Princess Marguerite Catani de Sermoneta, editor of the leading literary magazine of Rome, *Botteghe Oscure*, which published articles in Italian, English, and French. Princess Caetani was also the cousin of T. S. Eliot, an American heiress, and the wife of an Italian duke, Roffredo Caetani, a distinguished musician and composer.

Carson and Reeves sailed second class to Italy, Carson observing that there was no need to spend money where it did not show. Not at all interested in her surroundings aboard ship, she read Proust and daydreamed of her grand entry into Rome, infatuated once again with grandeur and enamored of people who courted her favor, especially those with prestige and money. One afternoon while seated in her deck chair, her lap filled with papers, Carson spied Marguerite Young nearby, who also was en route to Rome, and invited her to join them. "Reeves and I were just counting our letters and cards of the writers we have been invited to see in Rome, Marguerite," said Carson. "How many cards do you have?" Miss Young made no pretense of Rome's falling at *her* feet, and gave an honest reply. "Well, I am sure we will see you at some of the affairs, anyway," said Carson with exaggerated magnanimity.[39]

Upon their arrival in Naples, Miss Young was invited to ride with Carson and Reeves in their automobile to Rome, whereupon they checked into the same hotel, the Inghilterra. The next afternoon, after Carson and Reeves decided to move to what they considered a first-class, luxury hotel, Miss Young called to Carson's attention a plaque in the room which had escaped Carson's eye earlier. "And to think that I have just slept in the same bed that Lord Byron did," Carson responded gaily. But what was good enough for Lord Byron would have no effect on her own decision to live elsewhere, she said. Her move would simply be the Inghilterra's loss, Carson declared as she continued to pack up her things.[40]

In the meantime, ever since Carson's first letter in December apprising David Diamond of their impending visit, Diamond had alerted a number of his friends to be on the lookout for suitable quarters for them. (Reeves had written that they hoped to "get by" on his retirement pension of almost $350 a month. If there were additional expenses, they would be met by the monthly "allowance" which Carson's lawyer, Floria Lasky, had established for her from the proceeds of the sale of the movie rights of *The Member of the Wedding*, Carson's largest source of income.) Two of Diamond's friends, George and Tina Lang, Americans in Rome who knew the nearby towns well and were great admirers of Carson's works, volunteered to find an apartment for the McCullerses and to make all the necessary arrangements. The Langs called upon Carson and Reeves in their hotel to tell them that they had located what they considered ideal quarters in Villini-Castelgandolfo, thirteen miles from Rome on the road to Naples. A village castle high in the mountains overlooking Lake Albano, Castelgandolfo had long been known as the summer residence of the pope. In the winter, Castelgandolfo was a beautiful ski resort.

It was not until their fourth day in Rome that Carson and Reeves saw David Diamond. He had had no word from them since their arrival, nor had he sent any, but on February 10, Diamond opened the door of his apartment and discovered Carson and Reeves smiling at him. They had both been there before, for the apartment was Natalia Danesi Murray's (※9, Via Piemonte), which she had sublet to Diamond before his departure for Italy (arranged through the intervention of Cheryl Crawford). They had already gotten settled in their apartment in Castelgandolfo that the Langs had found for them, Carson said, proud of having managed on their own, but she admitted their disappointment that Diamond had not immediately come to the hotel to welcome them. She was not especially pleased with the apartment. "There are such horrid decorations on the fireplace," she complained. Nevertheless, they urged Diamond and his new friend, Ciro Cuomo—a young Italian who was Diamond's companion-secretary during the 1950s (and became his inseparable, devoted friend for more than twenty-three years)—to go out with them to Castelgandolfo the next morning and spend the day.

Diamond's diary entry that evening revealed as never before the extent to which his old affection for Carson and Reeves had abated. It was obvious now to Diamond that the love and triangle relationship they had once shared would never be recaptured:

Sunday, February 10, 1952: Carson and Reeves walk right in on us this afternoon! Carson obviously happy to see me. Reeves, I notice, keeps observing Ciro, and I could swear I heard him thinking: "At last David has what I could not give him." In no time at all I could see that Carson was itching for a drink. She managed to down the remaining half bottle of Gordon's gin . . . and when I said I had no more hard liquor in the house, that we drank fire-water rarely, she sulked and showed such an obvious irritability I could not wait to see her go. I felt sorry only for Reeves who must put up with her nonsense still! . . .

The next day, Reeves and Carson, along with their dog Kristin, picked up Diamond and his companion to take them to Castelgandolfo. For Diamond, it was a wearing experience. By late evening he had become completely disillusioned by Carson and Reeves as he found them now. That night he wrote in his diary:

Monday, February 11, 1952: . . . all day Carson groans, and sips highballs. Only during the late evening does she relax when I remind her of the early days we knew each other in New York. . . . But she grumbles again and again about the apartment (and it is a fine modern one) and perhaps leaving for France; Italy does not please her; and she has seen nothing of Italy!!! Reeves drives us back at midnight. Can this still sullen fellow be the reason I once was near collapse?!

Through mutual, though unspoken consent, the three of them saw little of each other after that. The last time David Diamond saw Carson after she left Italy was at a Christmas party given by director Lee Strasberg several years later, Diamond having returned home in December 1956 to be with his mother, who was dying of cancer. When he saw Carson sitting on a footstool talking with Franchot Tone, he quickly approached her and they embraced. Then she asked, "David, how are you? Are you happy?" He replied that he had never been happier in his life. According to Diamond, "Carson's face froze. She glowered at me a moment, then turned her back and resumed her conversation with Tone. It was as though she were saying, 'You've no right to be happy without me. If you're happy now, then I don't want anything more to do with you.' And she didn't. She could not bear to think that she had been replaced."[41]

To Jordan Massee, Carson's reported reaction to the situation involving Diamond was "completely out of character."

> I'm not saying that it could not have happened, but Carson was usually just the opposite when it involved her friends' falling in love. Usually she would try to get into the act herself, transferring to the other person the affection she felt for her friend. Now, if she thought her friend may have been lying to her about his blissful state, then she would have seen through it and reacted in that fashion.[42]

What Massee perhaps failed to take into consideration, however, was that Carson at this point knew that it was completely unlikely she could ever become a part of Diamond's relationship with his Italian friend.

Carson no doubt realized in Rome in 1952 that there could be no we of me with Diamond again, and it was pointless to attempt to recapture the former rapport; thus she willingly let go of the relationship and made no more overtures. She was much more interested in her involvement in Rome's social scene and the countless literary figures and newspapermen who were clamoring to entertain her. Foremost was Rome's leading lady of letters, Princess Marguerite Caetani de Sermoneta. Very quickly Carson was introduced to Alberto Moravia, Gianna Manzini, Elio Vittorini, Carlo Levi, Ignazio Silone, and a host of other major Italian writers. She also met for the first time and was charmed by her Italian translator, Irene Brin, whose conversion of *Reflections in a Golden Eye* into Italian in 1946 made Carson the most sought-after American writer in Rome. Miss Brin and her husband, Gaspero del Corso, were directors of l'Obelisco Galleria d'Arte. Their meeting was at the Hotel Santa Chiara in Rome, a strange background for the occasion, recalled Del Corso. A very old hotel situated near the Pantheon, the Santa Chiara was cherished mostly by priests and cardinals.[43]

There were a number of literary Americans in Rome that winter and spring, yet few with whom Carson cared to spend her time. Truman Capote, Wystan Auden, and Gore Vidal were there, and Marguerite Young stayed on at the Inghilterra for several months, but Carson saw little of them. Auden had little interest in Carson then, and Capote was a better friend of Reeves than of Carson. She and Capote frequently feuded, although their banter was light and fairly unscathing. As for Vidal, he reportedly cared for Carson not at all; she was far too egocentric for his taste. Carson, of course, felt the same about him. Richard

51 RIGHT: Gypsy Rose Lee, pictured with her self-portrait collage, 1953.

52 BELOW: Carson with Edwin Peacock (center) and John Zeigler, her good friends from Charleston, South Carolina, in the garden of their home, spring 1954.

53   Carson at home in Nyack, New York, 1957.

54 ABOVE: Carson with her cousins from Macon, Jordan Massee, Sr. and Jr., at Rhinebeck, New York, 1959.

55 RIGHT: Carson with Dr. Mary Mercer, New York City, 1959.

56 ABOVE: Carson hostessed a champagne luncheon in Nyack in honor of Isak Dinesen.
Seated, left to right: Marilyn Monroe, Isak Dinesen, Carson; standing, left to right: Arthur Miller, Felicia Geffen, Jordan Massee, Clara Svendson; May 1959.

57 BELOW: Carson with Isak Dinesen, Nyack, May 1959.

58 Carson on her porch in Nyack.

59 A publicity photograph of Carson for the dust jacket of *Clock Without Hands*, Nyack, 1961. Said Louise Dahl-Wolfe (the photographer): "She was so stooped from the strokes that I had to put her in this chair to help hold her neck up to a more normal position."

60   Carson's home in Nyack, 131 South
Broadway, until her death in 1967.

61   RIGHT: Fashion fabric designer
Marielle Bancou, Carson's French friend,
who made her home in Nyack and later
in New York City.

62   BELOW: Carson on the porch of her
Nyack home, 1965.

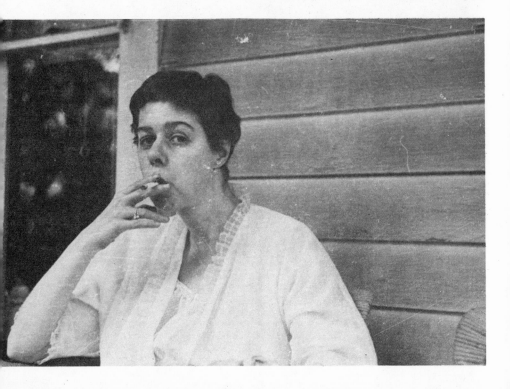

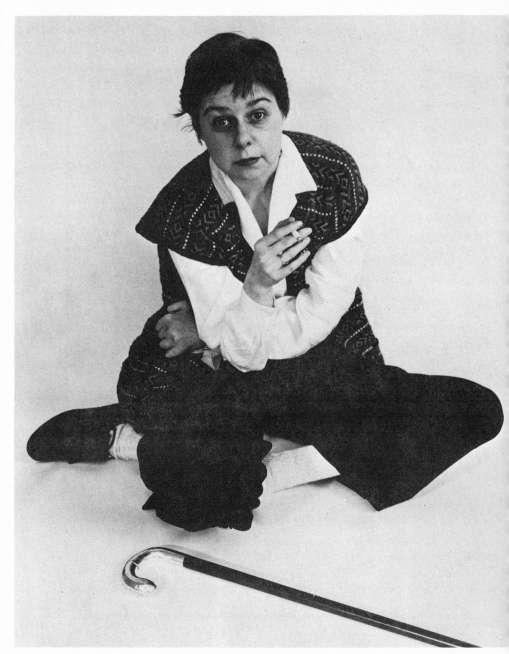

63   Carson in New York City, 1956.

Gibson, a young black writer and newspaperman, gave a party one evening for Carson to which he invited most of the American artists and writers presently in Rome. Marguerite Young recalled that Carson failed to invite Reeves to accompany her—an omission she frequently made feeling that *she* was the artist and her husband had no place there. More often, she did not reason at all; she simply went wherever and with whomever she chose. Once again Reeves had no real identity. Those who knew the couple well during their stay in Italy thought that Carson was insensitively abusive of her husband, and they sympathized with him. According to Marguerite Young, "Many of us saw Reeves as a beautiful human being, kind and generous—a kind of cavalier savant who waited on his lady hand and foot."[44]

Princess Marguerite Caetani entertained lavishly for Carson in her twin palazzos in Rome, then invited her to spend several days in her eleventh-century castle Ninfe, located out from Rome on the road to Naples. When Princess Caetani told Carson that she would like to publish something of hers in *Botteghe Oscure,* Carson showed her the poem she had completed in Nyack in December: "The Dual Angel: A Meditation on Origin and Choice." She said that her "Dual Angel" was very close to her personally and that she wanted it published now more than anything else.

It was a long poem divided into five parts: "Incantation to Lucifer," "Hymen, O Hymen," "Love and the Rind of Time," "The Dual Angel," and "Father, Upon Thy Image We Are Spanned." Each one probed some aspect of man's search for self, his struggle between good and evil, and his attempt to acknowledge and accept his ambivalent nature. The final poem was a synthesis of the others: Man's dual nature is attributed to a union between Lucifer and God. Caught between the polarities of faith and disbelief, good and evil, selfishness and altruism, one cannot break out of his duality but must work toward some semblance of harmony within the paradox. To cope with his ambivalence, he must compose himself contrapuntally and accept what he cannot resolve.

Carson's lyricism and poetic diction were reminiscent of the seventeenth-century metaphysical poets, particularly John Donne and George Herbert. The editor of *Botteghe Oscure* was delighted by Carson's poem and was sure that her readers would be, too. Princess Caetani made space for "The Dual Angel" in the next issue, placing it beside a new series of poems by E. E. Cummings.[45] Publication of this particular work gave Carson tremendous personal satisfaction. She had written the poem not only for herself, but also for Dame Edith Sitwell, whom she adored and considered her spiritual mentor in the realm of poetry.

In early April of 1952, Carson decided that she and Reeves should leave Castelgandolfo and stay in Rome. It not only was too far out, she complained, but the apartment was cold and drafty and it was impossible to stay warm there. They had few visitors and Carson wanted to be in the center of things, with social activities and literary gatherings pivoting around her. She also was bothered by pleurisy again and blamed it on coming home late into a chilled apartment. Reeves, too, was out of sorts, having nursed a peptic ulcer almost since his arrival. It flared up with his heavy imbibing—although he was drinking no more than Carson— and both were irascible and quarrelsome with each other.

Just before Easter they moved into the Hotel Eden in Rome, but their departure from Castelgandolfo caused new estrangement from David Diamond. Carson reportedly balked at paying the last month's rent for the apartment since they were breaking the lease and leaving early. Finally, Diamond and George Lang chose to settle the account themselves for her rather than haggle. By now, Carson and Reeves's caustic attacks upon one another were more frequent. Reeves's temper was violent. Although over the years Reeves maintained that he never physically hurt or attacked his wife, he did admit that he shook her occasionally. As he commented to friends, Carson's manner alternated between tiresome sulks and a vitriolic tongue. She drove him to extreme behavior, he said, which was almost uncontrollable at times. Later, Carson related her own tales of his abuse. She said that he once threatened to throw her out of a window while they were in Rome, and in another incident he threatened to jump from an upper story of the Hotel Eden and carry her with him if she did not change her ways and become at least civil to him. Doubtless, fantasy and fact were so interwoven that neither Reeves nor Carson was certain of actuality. They made little attempt to confine their quarrels to the privacy of their own quarters, and many friends witnessed unpleasant scenes during their turbulent months in Italy and, later, in France. Such onlookers were reluctant to be quoted, but the consensus was that life during Carson and Reeves's last year and a half together was "pure hell" for each of them. There were devastating arguments and scenes about the apartment or room, with Reeves occasionally breaking panes, splintering doors, knocking furniture about, and then storming out into the night. Extravagant apologies and countless reconciliations followed.

By the end of April both decided that a change of scene was in order. Tired of Italy, restless to get settled in a home of their own—which they envisioned hopefully to be a panacea since all else had failed— Carson and Reeves set out with their boxer, suitcases, and trunks to motor through northern Italy and the rest of southern Europe en route to France. In Milano, Carson met Leo Longanesi, director of Longanesi & Company, which later published an Italian translation of *The Heart Is a Lonely Hunter*. According to Mario Monti, who first recommended

Carson's works to Longanesi and served as an interpreter for Carson and her Italian publisher: "Leo Longanesi had been one of the strongest personalities in our field in Italy, and I noticed that Miss McCullers was very strong, indeed, too. It was her first visit to Milano, and she was very curious about everything. Nor will I forget the white socks she wore."[46] Carson wrote to her friends at home that she had been invited to lecture at Salzburg, Austria, at a seminar sponsored by Harvard University, but that she had not yet decided to accept. Instead, they chose to go directly to Paris. In spite of their tempestuous relationship that spring, Carson and Reeves managed to write cheerful cards and letters to their friends back home. Reeves usually was the letter writer for the two of them, Carson's cursive writing having become so poor that she seldom attempted letters in longhand any more.

Upon arrival in Paris, Carson and Reeves went out to Brunoy to stay with John and Simone Brown for more than a month while Reeves looked for a house. Carson tried to work on her novel while they were with the Browns, but her efforts were sporadic. Her hands were trembly, and she typed laboriously. Yet it was easier for her to work alone than to dictate to Reeves. He tried to sit patiently and type what she directed, but her thoughts and words were marked by such great pauses that he fidgeted restlessly. As had been her habit for years, Carson read aloud to Reeves, then invited his reaction; he found now, however, that his suggestions frequently antagonized her.

Simone Brown, like so many others who hosted Carson at length, found her a difficult house guest and a taxing person with whom to maintain a close relationship:

> Carson was writing *Clock Without Hands* at the time she and Reeves lived with us. She was a terror. Reeves would come downstairs and say, "Christ, I have wife-itis. Now she wants *scrambled* eggs" (instead of what he had brought her). Reeves swore like a trooper. He was not an intellectual, but he had a powerful personality. Carson would make appointments to see people, but often she would be gone and not show up until hours later. Embarrassed, Reeves would get drunk and say, "Simone, you know Carson won't show up—why does she do this to us?"
> What Reeves did for Carson was beyond human endurance. He loved her too much—just as we all did. Carson had a terrible power of destruction. She destroyed everything around her—everything she loved. Yet she also wanted to give. It was a viperish thing—all involved in a rather unusual cycle of love. One can see it in her works. Certainly *The Ballad of the Sad Café* illustrates that power of destruction. Poor Reeves. He was a nice guy through it all. I sympathized with him.[47]

John Brown's comments of Carson during this period were even more stringent and damning:

> She was cannibalistic, a vampire. She was never an intellectual; she only felt. She was a child—an affected, naive image. After Paris, I knew nothing of her to speak of. Sick and tired of Carson's shenanigans, I dropped her completely before she left.[48]

According to Jordan Massee, however, who well understood Carson and Reeves's inner conflicts and dilemmas:

> If Carson were carnivorous, if she tended to devour people, it was due only to her overwhelming, insatiable craving and need for love and affection. To be sure, those she loved had to rest periodically from her demands, which threatened to overcome them. Reeves, on the other hand, destroyed out of great bitterness.[49]

In June, Carson and Reeves found a comfortable, old house in the town of Bachvillers, about an hour's drive north of Paris in the Oise Valley. Known locally as l'Ancienne Presbytère, the house was once a vicarage. Unlike most of the other cottages in rural France, l'Ancienne Presbytère had central heating, fireplaces in each room, fully equipped plumbing in bathroom and kitchen, and screens on all the windows—a rarity anywhere in Europe. The house had thick walls, which helped keep it cool in the summer and warm in the winter, and its floors were of tile, heavily sanded and polished. Although l'Ancienne Presbytère was in the village next door to the church to which it had once belonged, it was situated on an acre of land surrounded by a low, stone wall and heavily planted with apple, peach, quince, and pear trees. The whole farm—with its house, orchard, barn, and outside "studio"—was purchased for less than five thousand dollars.

Bachvillers was a tiny village with scarcely 150 inhabitants. No one in the vicinity spoke English, and the two of them were the only Americans for forty kilometers around. Carson settled in to write while Reeves began to make repairs on the house and make it more cozy and livable. Once again he found a task he could cope with and perform well. Handy with a hammer and saw, Reeves had a deft decorating touch. He was sensitive and imaginative to color and form. Reeves particularly loved working outdoors, and soon he had a vegetable garden swollen with lettuce, beets, pole beans, squash, carrots, and tomatoes. Before long there were also great beds of flowers in bloom. Kristin, the boxer, played at his heels and Carson usually made a turn about the acreage two or three times a day, then sat in the crook of a pear tree, ruminated, and watched her husband at work.

Their entire life style now vastly different from what they had experienced in Italy, Carson and Reeves found themselves drinking far less than before. For a time they were remarkably happy. Life was fairly tranquil and uncomplicated and they seemed to enjoy each other's company once again. They felt completely isolated from the world, yet marveled that they were still only an hour's ride from the heart of Paris. They went into the city infrequently. Carson was still sought after at dinners and cocktail parties, to which Reeves drove her, then left her—although for a time he attended a number of functions with her—but more often, Carson preferred that people come out to Bachvillers to see her. She felt more "special" that way. One of her first visitors at Bachvillers was Tennessee Williams, who came in mid-June with his friend Frank Merlo en route to Rome. The playwright had come to Paris to see Anna Magnani, who expressed interest in making a movie of *The Rose Tattoo*. Devoted to Miss Magnani, Williams introduced her to Carson and Reeves and entertained the three of them for several evenings in a round of sidewalk cafés, restaurants, and night clubs throughout the city.

Reeves frequently went in alone to Paris to shop at the post exchange and commissary at the government facility, where they purchased all of their food except fresh bread, which they bought in their tiny village, and the vegetables and fruits which they grew themselves. When Reeves wrote to Edwin Peacock and John Zeigler that fall to urge them to come visit them in France, he said that they were living in Bachvillers for a third less than their living costs had been in the United States. Since there were no state or federal taxes to pay, explained Reeves, their food alone cost them about half what they would normally pay in their own country.[50]

Several weeks after their move into the country, Carson received word that her mother had suffered a severe heart attack and fall and had fractured six ribs. Immediately she and Reeves flew home to Nyack and stayed until Marguerite was out of danger. When they left, they said that they would send for her to come to Bachvillers just as soon as she was strong enough to travel. Later in the summer, Marguerite became gravely ill once more, this time suffering from a pulmonary embolism, and again Carson flew home—this time without Reeves—to comfort her mother and to help get her located where she could recuperate without anxiety, yet be assured of constant care. Marguerite pined and did not take good care of herself when her children were away. Her daughter Rita came to see her on weekends and sometimes Marguerite stayed with her in the city, but Marguerite was lonely and unhappy in Nyack without Carson and Reeves.

Carson's brother, Lamar, and his wife, Virginia, at last decided that the situation involving their mother might best be remedied if they themselves returned to their former hometown and had their mother come South to live with them. There she could also be with her sister, nieces, and other family, as well as with old friends who loved her and would welcome her back. Lamar Smith gave up his job in Brunswick, Georgia, where he had lived since 1945, and moved his family back to Columbus. Soon he had rented a house in the Smith family's old neighborhood and was working as a tool- and diemaker with a surgical manufacturing company. Marguerite loved being "home" again with her son and daughter-in-law, who lovingly cared for her and attended to her every physical need. Perhaps some of the most pleasurable moments in Marguerite's life came once more in Georgia during the next year and a half as she got to know her only grandchild. Daily she held three-year-old Bill on her lap for hours, reading to him and cuddling him fondly. Throughout her stay in Georgia, however, Marguerite lived most of all for the infrequent mail that came for her from Carson and Reeves. With each missive she prayed that it would be *the* letter inviting her to Paris, but the summons never came. Not being sent for was a disappointment from which Marguerite never quite recovered.

During Marguerite's illness and absence from Nyack, Reeves's mother acted as landlady for 131 South Broadway. Jessie McCullers had purchased a paint store in Nyack for Reeves's sister, Wiley Mae, which she operated with her husband, Sam Altschuler. Mrs. McCullers alternated her time between Nyack, assisting her daughter and son-in-law in the paint and decorating business, and Greenwich Village, where her son Tommy lived. When construction began on the Tappan Zee Bridge, hundreds of laborers poured into Nyack and sought temporary quarters, whereupon Mrs. McCullers rented all the available rooms at 131 South Broadway to the bridge workers.

In September, Carson and Reeves returned to Rome, where she had been invited by David Selznick to work on a movie script, *Terminal Station*. It was a tension-filled month for them both, and the venture ended in failure. Carson wrote her young intern friend from the American Hospital, Jack Fullilove, a long letter at the end of her first week there to explain their difficulties. She said that the calm scene around her as she wrote belied her inner turmoil. It was a Sunday morning and church bells were sounding throughout the city. From the balcony of the Hotel Eden where they were staying, she could see the monks walking in the garden across the way. The walls outside were colored golden by an early sun, and life in Rome seemed beautiful and peaceful. But her heart was heavy and she felt constant tension and anxiety because of her work and Reeves, who was not well, she admitted. In Paris, Reeves had been taking Antabuse, a drug prescribed for him so that he would not drink. If he should try to combine it with alcohol, he would become violently ill. He went off the drug shortly before their departure for Rome, however, and began to drink on the plane. The first two days in Rome he was in terrible shape, Carson reported; then, for several days he recovered enough to type her dictation of some of the script. Now he had begun taking sleeping pills during the day and staying out most of the night. She was beside herself with anxiety, she told Fullilove. The night before, Reeves had come in late and begun to talk of suicide. He told her that life had no meaning for him any more and that death would be a sweet relief. Carson felt deeply sorry for her husband, but the constant worry and psychic pain were almost more than she now could bear. The job itself of writing a movie script was difficult and alien, she admitted. She had been working the exhausting schedule of thirteen hours a day for all the preceding week, and she told Fullilove that she must work that day—Sunday—as well. In Selznick's absence she had been working closely with Wolfgang Reinhart, whom she liked and appreciated because of his intelligence and thoughtfulness, but it was Selznick whom she would ultimately have to satisfy, and she was dubious. After the first week's work the script was sent off to Selznick in Paris. He had not returned to Rome with it, but if he did not like it, she would be fired, Carson told Fullilove.

When Selznick finally arrived the end of September, life became even more chaotic, and for a time Reeves felt as harried as Carson. On September 25, he typed a brief note to Jack Fullilove, complaining of the numerous script changes required after Selznick galloped into town and trampled over people like a herd of stampeding animals. He had succeeded in thoroughly confusing everyone, said Reeves. The middle of October after their return to Paris, Reeves glossed over the venture in a more controlled statement to Edwin Peacock and John Zeigler: It was a hectic month, he admitted, but they worked industriously and did their job. Not satisfied, however, Selznick decided to rewrite the script himself. He and Carson left on good terms with everyone, said Reeves. There were disappointments, of course, but they had learned much about the wiles of Hollywood. No matter what else had happened, they accomplished their main purpose: to make money. That, they did quite nicely, he added.

Before Carson and Reeves left Rome, fired at last by Selznick, she retreated to the Salvador Mundi Clinic in Rome—a hospital run by nuns—in a state of near collapse and exhaustion. Here she stayed for almost a week and pulled herself together enough to cope with the trip back to France. When they returned to Paris in late October, they discovered that their temperamental Turkish housekeeper had—in Reeves's words—"gone quite mad," as had Kristin, who suffered from eclampsia after giving birth to six purebred puppies. Reeves wrote Edwin Peacock that they had been forced to turn their housekeeper, who claimed to be a direct descendant of Genghis Khan, loose on the streets of Paris, but that Kristin had recovered and become a fit mother for her litter. Soon Reeves was able to locate a local country woman who came in to cook and take care of things. The new housekeeper spoke no English, and Carson and Reeves still knew little French, but the mood of the house was tranquil once more, at least as far as domestic chores were concerned.

Inwardly, Carson knew little peace. She suffered not only from a sense of physical isolation living in the remote village of Bachvillers, but from spiritual isolation as well—no matter how glowingly she spoke of her contentment in letters to friends at home. People rarely visited them at Bachvillers. She felt set apart from both Paris and her American friends nearby, who found it easier to avoid her than to make excuses for not going to see her. Even Tennessee Williams, during the two or three additional trips he made to Paris while Carson was living in the country, seemed reluctant to visit her. The playwright had met Fullilove that fall at the American Hospital, where he was treated for a heart condition, and later Carson urged Fullilove to bring Williams to Bachvillers the next time he came. But to be with Carson and Reeves now was depressing to Williams, and he preferred not to go. Carson also urged Richard Wright to come to Bachvillers, yet he, too, was hesitant. Wright had become disillusioned by her—as well as by Reeves—in 1947 in Paris, and although he sympathized with their situation, he had no interest in renewing the friendship. Nor did Kay Boyle, who also was in Paris in 1952–53, remember her relationship with Carson and Reeves during this period with any degree of pleasure.

Janet Flanner continued to maintain good relations with Carson and Reeves, having known them since the old 7 Middagh Street days in Brooklyn Heights, but she had no illusions about them, either. Carson and Reeves admired Miss Flanner and respected her reputation, her "Genêt" column in *The New Yorker* having endeared her to readers on both sides of the Atlantic since 1925 and made her the best known American in Paris. The columnist, however, actually saw little of Carson during this period. She was incredulous, even, that one might suppose she had ever been Carson's house guest in the country: "Visit her? My dear, I am much too old and much too experienced to be anyone's house guest."[51] She conceded, however, that she had made an outing to Bachvillers one afternoon, her chief memory of the occasion being Reeves's frequent trips to the well for "cool spring water," which, in reality, was straight gin. "He was becoming more refreshed by the moment and, of course, fooling no one," Miss Flanner added. "I was very fond of Reeves," she continued:

> Of course, he was a liar and thief, unreliable—especially a liar. And with my brief relations with him there was nothing he should lie about. But he literally went out of his way to lie. He was rather a

predatory liar—he stole the truth, and then he lied about that. And he didn't have to steal the truth at all—because it was of no consequence to anyone except himself.

And Carson? Ah, she was a sharp persuader if ever I met one. One couldn't possibly know Carson and not realize that she also created her own truths. Part of her fictions became part of her truths. Reeves was a storyteller, too, but he was not gifted. And that was the great difference . . . one of the many great differences between them that was apparent. Yet Reeves was a very courageous man, a very brave man. And he was simply splendid when he went overseas to serve his country during the war—the country that he so loved. But together they were not good for each other.

The French took much more kindly to Carson during both of her visits to Paris than did the Americans who were there. In 1946, John L. Brown had introduced Carson to a number of the French literati and promoted her work in a variety of ways. It was through Brown that André Bay, literary editor of Stock Editions, met Carson and bought up French rights to everything that she had then produced. The French edition of *The Heart Is a Lonely Hunter* was published in 1947 and *The Member of the Wedding* in 1949. By 1952, Carson's literary reputation in France was considerable and secure. Bay himself had "fallen much in love with Carson's work," but when they met in 1946 he had been somewhat "frightened" by her having received him in her hotel room at 1:00 P.M. wearing only a nightgown and holding a glass of cognac and whiskey in each hand. In 1952, they renewed their acquaintance and had a more satisfactory relationship. He found Carson in a better state of mind and health now than before her strokes, when she seemed more psychically ill. Although she was obviously in much pain when he saw her in 1952–53, it seemed to Bay that she complained little and that she and Reeves again had the will to work and to find some degree of equilibrium and peace in their country cottage. Through Bay, Carson met William Hope, a young American theatre producer and writer who had been working and living in Paris for several years. Together Bay and Hope prevailed upon Carson to be allowed to write and produce a French adaptation of *The Member of the Wedding*. The work, however, was not presented on the stage in Paris for another six years.

Bay and his wife also visited Carson and Reeves in Bachvillers, bringing with them one afternoon a new and promising French writer, Andrée Chèdid, who greatly admired *The Heart Is a Lonely Hunter* and wanted to meet its author. Fond of Carson at their initial meeting, Miss Chèdid later invited her and Reeves to lunch with her in Paris. They were joined by Miss Chèdid's husband and the Bays. "We all spoke English that day," said Miss Chèdid. "I was impressed by Mrs. McCullers' personality.

She was very still, on account of a sort of paralysis, I think, but she had the most extraordinary eyes. There was something harmful in the depth of those eyes, yet at the same time something so open, warm, and friendly."[52]

Jack Fullilove, the handsome young bachelor from the American Hospital whom Carson had met in July and corresponded with while she was in Italy, saw more of her and Reeves than anyone else during the winter and spring of 1952–53. Frequently it was at the hospital, where Carson went periodically for checkups. She loved to go to the hospital and stay for a few days, for there she basked in the attention of the American doctors and enjoyed the American food. To Carson, food was always better when she was surprised by it on her tray. She liked to be made over when she was served and to have people around her while she ate, with whom she could talk about the food and to speculate on how it was prepared. Fullilove remembered how Carson loved to eat. "She often wore an expensive, green silk, coolie-type coat and pants outfit which hid her large, flatulent stomach. Her appetite for both food and drink was huge at that time," he said. "Carson also liked going to the American Hospital because she knew and saw more people there who were warm and friendly to her than anywhere else in Paris during 1952–53."[53] Dr. Robert Myers, with whom she became infatuated when he was her physician in 1947 upon her first hospitalization in Paris with her stroke, kept watch over her now, along with her internal medicine specialist, Dr. Neal Rogers, a private physician with a large prestigious practice which included the Duchess of Windsor. Rogers, Myers, and Fullilove were good friends of one another, too, and also very fond of Carson and Reeves personally. The three men sometimes drove up to Bachvillers for Sunday lunch and got together with Carson and Reeves on holidays and other special occasions. Most people, however, preferred to see Carson in Paris—if, indeed, they saw her at all. According to Fullilove, who went often to Bachvillers, "Most people thought she lived too far out and didn't want to go. I also don't think she was a very gracious hostess— except when she wanted to be."[54]

Fullilove remembered the time that an old schoolmate from Carson's hometown visited her at Bachvillers, bringing with him a female reporter: "For some reason Carson became irritated with her old chum and at lunch sat sullenly, barely communicative. It was an ugly interview, and I felt sorry for the girl."[55] Through the Bachvillers period, Fullilove felt that Carson was "such a leaner on people that they stayed away rather than get into that position":

> I had the feeling that most people were avoiding her. . . . I remember that Robert Whitehead came to Paris and she had me try to locate him since she knew he was there but didn't know which hotel,

and she wanted to see him. I called fifteen hotels at least, trying to locate him, and did at last—but he never went to see her, and she only talked with him on the phone. And regardless of what T. Williams is writing now about his love for her, he avoided coming to Bachvillers to see her—and this kinda hurt her. Actually I suppose the reason she liked me so much was that there was no one else around who "idolized" her, and I must say that during that time I was completely mouth-hanging-open about her—never having gotten over *The Heart Is a Lonely Hunter*, and then to be so close to her was hard for me to believe. But the "idols" do indeed have clay feet, and we came apart after about a year and a half.[56]

On Thanksgiving Day, 1952, Carson had all of Fullilove's friends from the hospital at "l'Ancienne Presbytère" for an American-style dinner. Fullilove was deeply touched that she had invited only his friends —and hers and Reeves through the hospital—and none of her literary friends, in whom she might have been more interested. For Christmas, she chose to go to the American Hospital as Fullilove's guest. She and Reeves stayed several days in Fullilove's staff quarters apartment. She was feeling quite well then, recalled Fullilove, and they decided to attend a showing of *Gone With the Wind* together. Back home in the apartment afterward, Carson, in a sudden, impulsive moment, invited her young host—she was ten years Fullilove's senior—to go to bed with her and Reeves. "Let's all sleep together," she enjoined.

"Carson and Reeves frequently addressed each other as 'Brother' and 'Sister'—they simply didn't act like husband and wife," recalled Fullilove. At Bachvillers, Carson sometimes got up and begged Fullilove to dance with her. A poor dancer, she moved awkwardly because of her lame leg, but Fullilove usually complied and made a few turns about the living room with her while Reeves looked on appreciatively. Then Carson frequently would say: "Now you and Reeves dance together, too, Jack." To Fullilove, it seemed that since Carson could not dance well herself, she took vicarious delight in seeing two others whom she loved share a physical experience. Again, it was a way of projecting her we of me relationship upon other people. Such complicity did little, however, to encourage Reeves's sexual identity as a man. There were times when Reeves, too, prompted Carson to participate in a triangle relationship that was physical. In 1949, for instance, when Carson and Reeves spent a few days on Sullivan's Island off the coast of Charleston, South Carolina, with Edwin Peacock and a handful of young men friends, Reeves astonished everyone when he spoke up before the assemblage to Harrell Woolfolk: "Come on, Harry, how would you like to sleep with Carson and me tonight?" Woolfolk declined, but the invitation had been a little unsettling to their easy rapport that weekend. Woolfolk did not quite know how to "take it," he said, for to him, an invitation to bed meant sex.[57]

In Paris in 1952, Carson encouraged still another combination. She sometimes invited Fullilove and their good friend Valentine Sherriff to sleep with her. According to Fullilove, the relationship seemed to stem from Carson's desire to be physically close to people, yet not to participate in a fully realized sexual experience. Miss Sherriff was a wealthy Russian who came to Paris by way of Shanghai, then California and New Orleans, where she had found herself a rich, Louisiana-born husband. Now a divorcee and admittedly addicted to drugs, she was also a very warm, gentle, and generous person. Miss Sherriff was a cosmopolite the likes of which Carson had never known before, and Carson was intrigued by her. A friend, also, of Tennessee Williams, she traveled in an orbit of upper-Parisian society and introduced Carson and Reeves to a strange and sometimes motley assortment of Europeans and Americans. During the winter, Miss Sherriff proposed a trip to Vienna, a city Carson had long dreamed of visiting, but one by one the prospective travelers fell away and the plans were abandoned. Carson's disappointment matched in full that of her fictional counterpart, Frankie Addams, who cried bitterly when she was denied a place on the honeymoon trip with the bride and groom in *The Member of the Wedding*.

Occasionally Carson's advances toward Fullilove seemed more amorous than he appreciated. More than once when she and Reeves spent the night in his apartment at the American Hospital, Carson left the bedroom she shared with Reeves—after he had fallen into a deep, alcoholic sleep—and felt her way down the darkened hall to the bedroom of her host. "Jack, are you in there?" she whispered. Feigning sleep and not interested in a clandestine meeting in bed with Carson—particularly with a husband in such close proximity—Fullilove looked up to see her thin shadowy figure coming in the door and moving quietly to his bedside. "No, don't get up . . . I just want to be with you . . . I got lonely," she said. According to Fullilove, Carson was not interested in sex per se; she simply wanted to lie next to him, tell him how much he meant to her, and *be*. Recalling later such incidents, Fullilove added:

> Carson made me right nervous coming into bed with me as she did. I wouldn't have wanted Reeves to have found us like that no matter what we were doing. Carson didn't want sexual intercourse, but I've never felt a body temperature as feverish as hers was on anyone who was not violently ill. She would trace my facial features with her hand, put her arms around me, and kiss me occasionally—rather wet, sloppy kisses—but as quickly as I could, I would get her back into her own bedroom.[58]

In December, Jewish refugee Otto Frank requested an appointment with Carson to talk about his deceased daughter Anne and the famous diary she kept during World War II. According to a letter Carson wrote Mary Tucker that month, Cheryl Crawford planned to produce the book as a play and asked Carson to work on it. At Carson's first meeting with Frank at the Hotel Continental in Paris, he gave her the book to read—which she had not previously seen—and told her that she was the one he most wanted to make a play of it. Carson accepted the book and said she would read it and think about it; in the process, however, her hands and feet broke out in a red, splotchy rash, and she feared that if she proceeded, the emotional involvement would be too much for her. When Otto Frank came out to Bachvillers a week later and stayed several days, Carson decided that she would have to tell him *no*—that her other responsibilities and tensions prohibited her from doing it. Moreover, she explained that she had not fully recovered from her "folly" in Rome. Later, Carson related that because of her disappointment and chagrin, she felt that she should not see the superb dramatization of the book done by Frances Goodrich and Albert Hackett. Never had she met a man who radiated such pure goodness of soul and intellect as Otto Frank, she marveled.[59]

Early in the new year, 1953, a storm moved in from the North Sea, and Carson and Reeves were snowbound for two weeks. The idyllic interlude was good for them both. She worked on her *Clock Without Hands* manuscript with little interruption, Reeves helped her by typing, and they both wrote letters and read. Reeves told Edwin Peacock that they had been snowed in since New Year's Day, but had not minded it one bit. They had a seemingly endless supply of firewood, food, and wine and were happy in their encapsulated mode of existence. Their only lament was that Peacock was not there to share in the music and games. The dog had had puppies, said Reeves, and they had kept two of them, Nicky and Autonne. The other four had been sold for enough money to pay Kristin's expenses for another year. Reeves added that in December he had returned to his strict ulcer diet and now felt better than he had in months. They were optimistic that the new year held much promise for them.

In the spring of 1953, as the snow melted and the bulbs bloomed, Carson was overcome by a flood of desolation. She wrote Jordan Massee on April 5 a tearful letter in which she enclosed a forget-me-not blossom and told him that he was her dearest friend and that she loved him deeply. She had written infrequently to her cousin since her departure for Europe, but she now felt an overwhelming need of him. The letter she had just received from him had reached her when she needed it most, she explained, for she was ill, distraught and oppressed with a terrible sense of loneliness. If he could only come to her, she pleaded, they could be marvelously happy together. He would love the orchard, with its apple trees, quince, pears, and peaches in flower, and the garden in brilliant bloom. Reeves now left her alone often, she complained. He stayed in town throughout the week, supposedly job hunting, but also drinking heavily, seeing other women, and going on and off Antabuse, depending on his mood.

During the summer Reeves became more suicidal than ever before. He talked frequently of taking his own life, but he also felt that if he died, Carson would have no one to take care of her. The best thing would be for her to die with him, he concluded. One day Reeves made a serious suicide attempt by hanging himself from a pear tree in their orchard. Even that he did not do well, said Carson to friends later. The limb broke under his weight and she went out to investigate the cracking noise, the thud, and Reeves's cry for help. After she cut him loose, she reportedly admonished him: "Please, Reeves, if you *must* commit suicide, do it somewhere else. Just look what you did to my favorite pear tree."

Another time he invited Carson to walk out to the barn with him because he wanted to show her something. As they stood there, he picked up a length of rope, pointed to a beam overhead, and said: "See that rafter, Sister. It's a good sturdy one. You know what we're going to do? Hang ourselves from it. I tell you, it's the best thing for us both." According to Tennessee Williams, to whom she told her tale later, Carson thought that she had finally talked Reeves out of a double suicide, that she had convinced him that it was unnecessary, for they would both feel better in time. A few days later, however, in the early fall they were en route to Paris and the American Hospital for a checkup. She became curious when she noticed that they were taking what appeared to be an indirect route into the city. When she asked him about it, he was noncommittal. Then she looked down on the floorboard and noticed two lengths of coiled rope. "Tenn, honey, that made me right nervous looking down at that rope," Carson related to her friend later.

Finally Reeves volunteered his plans. "You're right, Sister. This isn't the way to the hospital. We are going out into the forest, Sister, and hang ourselves. But first, we'll stop and buy a bottle of brandy. We'll drink it for old times' sake . . . our one last fling." Reeves stopped the car a few minutes later and went inside a roadside tavern to buy the liquor. "You stay here," he demanded. Carson waited until he got out of sight, then fled from the car and hailed a ride with a passing truck. Terrified and almost speechless, she attempted to communicate with the French driver that she needed to get to the American Hospital immediately. Then she decided that she should not go there, for Reeves would surely follow her. Instead, she found refuge with friends elsewhere and immediately made arrangements to leave the country. "That was the last time Carson ever saw Reeves," said Tennessee Williams. "She left Bachvillers with the clothes on her back and never returned."[60] Those closest to Carson and Reeves in Paris at the time, who understood Reeves's terrible psychic dilemma, considered him temporarily deranged and believed that it was exceedingly dangerous then for her to be around him. Carson wired Robert Whitehead that she was en route home and desperately needed him to meet her plane at La Guardia. She also wired her sister of her impending arrival, as well as her mother in Columbus. To Carson, once on the plane, a terrible, frightening part of her life was over. She would do her best to blot it out, never to think of her past with Reeves again. He was "dead" to her now, and she never wanted to see him or hear his name spoken. Immediately Marguerite Smith flew north to get the house in Nyack ready for her daughter's homecoming.

A contributing factor to Reeves's problems before their final break in France was what some observers referred to as Carson's "increasing penuriousness." She told friends that she simply was not going to allow Reeves to "go through her money" in the manner he was now attempting. He had bled her enough, she said, and she had taken as much of his shenanigans as she could stand. According to Carson, they were living on seven hundred dollars a month, which normally would have been more than ample in France in 1953 when they were growing most of their own food. She complained that Reeves frequently made extravagant purchases and gave no accounting of large sums of money. When she refused to give him an unlimited supply from her own funds, he once again resorted to what she called "his old trick" which had estranged them in 1941 and led to their divorce—forgery. At first in Paris, he forged her name to a number of small checks, which Carson made good when she learned about them. Then he forged a very large check that he gave to the Russian money-changer in Paris in exchange for francs. A friend of many Americans, the Russian gentleman took their United States currency to Switzerland, where he converted it at 490 to 500 francs to the dollar instead of the 340 francs available on the open exchange, and in the process made a 10 per cent profit. When Carson found out about Reeves's exorbitant check to the money-changer, she angrily placed a stop payment on it at her bank. The money-changer, however, had already given Reeves the francs for it, and he was left only with the bad check that the bank would not honor. This act led to a final estrangement between Carson and a number of her American friends in Paris, as well as between her and Princess Marguerite Caetani, who had introduced her and Reeves to the money-changer and now bitterly resented her act since an innocent person was the real victim. Several of Carson's friends in Paris helped make good Reeves's debt, but they never felt the same toward Carson, whom they blamed. As one former friend from the Paris days—who preferred to remain anonymous—expressed it: "I hate mean people, and Carson was mean."

A few days after Carson's departure, Fullilove drove to Bachvillers with Valentine Sherriff to check on Reeves, whom they found in a state of acute depression. His eyes were vacant, he was slow-moving, and he had barely eaten since Carson had left. Fullilove realized, looking at Reeves then, that he had lost some thirty pounds since they met the preceding summer. With Fullilove's help, Miss Sherriff moved Reeves to the Hôtel Chateau-Frontenac on rue Pierre Charron in Paris. She told the hotel that she would assume full financial responsibility for him. Reeves still had Carson's car, but he was without money. According to friends, the police were on his trail because of additional bad checks which had shown up. By now, few people who knew Carson and Reeves well in Paris blamed him for the forgeries. As Janet Flanner explained it, "Reeves was simply trying to survive, for Carson had abandoned him without money."[61]

On November 18, Reeves called Simone Brown and told her that he was "going west." "Don't do it, Reeves," she pleaded, knowing that his intentions were suicide. He also called his doctor at the American Hospital, Robert Myers, and gave him the same message. Then he called Jack Fullilove and asked him to eat dinner with him that evening. Fullilove, on twenty-four-hour call at the hospital, could not leave until the next day. "Let's make it tomorrow night, Reeves," he replied. But Reeves was insistent. "No, that will be too late—I am going west tomorrow."

At the time, Fullilove was unaware of the meaning of the phrase "going west." The saying had come into vogue during World War I. If a man felt that his death was imminent, he said that he was "going west." Finally, Reeves sent a telegram to Carson in Nyack: "Going west— trunks on the way." Then he sent similar messages to John and Simone Brown and to Janet Flanner.

That week Reeves also sent Janet Flanner what she described as "the most incredible bouquets of flowers I have ever received in the world—bouquets as large as this," she said, making a great sweeping gesture with both arms extended in a wide circle:

> The flowers he sent that last week were the most beautiful flowers I
> ever received, accompanied by the most elaborate, almost tender mes-
> sages, which had no authority at all. There was nothing true about

them. It was as if he had just pinned them—*pinned* himself—on to me. The last message I had from him was very characteristic and very curious and very interesting. It came with another incredible bouquet the day after Reeves's death. It said, "From the man across the Styx."

His body was found on November 19, 1953, at the Hôtel Chateau-Frontenac. Fullilove had gone to Reeves's room in hopes of being able to make the dinner date he had been unable to keep the night before, but when he arrived, the Paris police answered his knock. The body had been taken to the morgue, but the authorities were waiting for someone to confirm the identification. A note found nearby requested that his friend and doctor Robert Myers close his eyes.[62]

Reeves's death was attributed to various causes. The New York *Times* obituary that followed more than a week later carried this statement: "Several weeks ago, Mr. McCullers suffered severe injuries in an automobile accident. It has not been determined if the accident was the cause of his death."[63] True, there had been an automobile accident in which Reeves had wrecked Carson's car, but he had not been seriously hurt and had been hospitalized only for observation. According to the Veterans Administration records, Reeves's death was due to "natural causes." The affidavit was signed by the Secretary of the Army, with no further explanation appearing in his file.[64] Some who knew Reeves well in Paris and saw him shortly before his death said that he had been on Antabuse again and that a fifth of liquor taken in combination with the drug had killed him. According to Jack Fullilove, however, "Reeves had been on Antabuse for five or six months before his suicide, but he was not on it when he killed himself. I had been with him for a couple of weeks off and on before his suicide, and he was drinking with me and Valentine. You cannot drink and take Antabuse. He had taken a large amount of barbiturates on top of the liquor, and this is what killed him. Actually, he threw up and choked to death."[65]

Perhaps Tennessee Williams' compassionate understanding of the entire situation, however, enabled him to cut to the core and come closest to the truth, even though his statement, to some, seemed oversimplified: "Reeves died, ultimately, out of great love for Carson. His was a desperate loneliness. Without her, he was an empty shell."[66]

Chapter Twelve

EMERGENCE
FROM THE CHRYSALIS,
1953 – 55

When word came of Reeves's death, Carson was in Clayton, Georgia, visiting novelist Lillian Smith and Miss Smith's friend and literary associate, Paula Snelling. Carson and Miss Smith had become friends in New York soon after the Broadway success of *The Member of the Wedding,* and she was anxious to renew the acquaintance. She also had been commissioned by *Holiday* magazine—for fifteen hundred dollars— to write a feature on Georgia. Miss Smith's novel *Strange Fruit,* along with her keen sense of social justice and protest of black-white inequities inherent in her southern region, now firmly allied the two writers. Carson planned to use Miss Smith as a fulcrum for her article. She would steep herself in north Georgia lore and southern social consciousness through Lillian Smith and Paula Snelling in their rustic mountain haven high atop "Old Screecher" at the tip end of the southern Appalachians.

Carson asked her agent to call Miss Smith and announce that she was already on her way, then prepared to depart by train for the South. The Clayton novelist herself, however, was tired and ill, having just finished her autobiographical *The Journey,* and she was recuperating from recent radical surgery for breast cancer. It did not suit her to have a house guest at this time, but the prospective visitor could not be reached to postpone the trip. "It was not easy to change Carson's plans once her mind was made up," recalled Paula Snelling.[1] Carson arrived the next afternoon, surprised to find her hostess much frailer than she. Yet they sat up late that evening, talking energetically, catching up on the last several years since they had been together, and laughing over the curious and bizarre happenings of their lives. The women spoke of their books, and then, intimately, of their feelings and attitudes—about loneliness, unhappiness, love, hatred, perversion, lust, estrangement, suicide, and death. Carson referred bitterly to Reeves and told what seemed to Miss Snelling to be "ghastly tales" of his suicidal and homicidal nature, of her fear of his psychopathic traits, and of her sudden flight from Paris. She told Lillian Smith of Reeves's affairs in Paris their last year together and of how he had stayed away from Bachvillers for days at a time during the spring and summer of 1953, ostensibly to look for a job. She resented his absences and was jealous of his attentions elsewhere. He also had kept the car in the city with him, and she felt helpless and abandoned, she complained.

She said that Reeves himself had sometimes sought advice for his troubled state of affairs. Carson learned that one night in Paris after she and Reeves had had dinner with Lillian Hellman, he later called Miss Hellman and awakened her with an urgent request. According to Miss Hellman, "Reeves said that he had to come back to talk with me and asked if I would let him in. He was in 'terrible, terrible trouble,' he complained. When he came he said he had fallen in love with a girl and wanted to leave Carson—which surprised me, for I had the impression that Reeves was homosexual. He was upset and very tight. I really could not help him or offer any advice. He must have been in worse shape than I knew that night because not long afterwards he committed suicide."[2]

Reeves was no longer her husband, Carson announced to her friends in the South the night of her arrival. Her doctor in Paris urged her to leave him and return to America, she said—even before the frightening rope incident in the car when he intended to carry out the double suicide—and she swore anew that she would have no more to do with him. To Carson's mother, the tragic turn of events was grievous. To know that Carson had lived those last few weeks in Bachvillers in fear of her life caused Marguerite Smith to repudiate again her son-in-law and to urge Carson to divorce him immediately. Her daughter initiated no legal proceedings against him, however, for to her, Reeves was already dead.

The night of November 19 the telephone rang very late in Lillian Smith's mountainside home, interrupting Carson's diatribe. It was Rita Smith, calling from New York. She did not want to talk to Carson, but instead, quickly told Lillian Smith that Reeves had committed suicide. She asked that Miss Smith convey the news to her sister. The Clayton novelist did not identify her caller, but appeared to accept casually the information while Carson sat nearby. In response to the question, "When will you tell her," Miss Smith nonchalantly answered: "In the morning." The conversation was soon terminated and Miss Smith calmly turned her attention to her guest. Now, however, Carson's abusive and vitriolic tirade against Reeves was almost more than her already ill hostess could bear. Finally, at about eleven o'clock—having drunk much whiskey and obviously mentally and physically exhausted—Carson was tactfully shuttled off to bed. Lillian Smith then told Paula Snelling of Reeves's suicide, and the decision was made that Miss Snelling should be the one to break the news the next morning after breakfast. "The ordeal, together with the late evening, had drained Lillian, who was far weaker than Carson," said Miss Snelling.

The next morning the unsuspecting guest novelist ate a huge breakfast and felt marvelous, she said, as she viewed enchantedly Old Screecher in its late autumnal colors through the thirty-five-foot glass wall of the great room. Afterward, Miss Snelling drew up her chair close to Carson and calmly told her of Reeves's death. For a few moments Carson appeared stunned; then she asked for a drink. For the rest of the day, she wavered between a façade of helplessness and an astute ability to perceive keenly what must be done and then to act quickly and efficiently. She also struggled to control her anguish and horror of the whole affair. It was one thing to have considered Reeves dead to her, but quite another to know that it was an actuality to himself and the world as well.

Carson made some twenty telephone calls to various people throughout the day. She spoke with her lawyer, agent, mother, sister, brother, cousin, and a number of other friends to get their thinking on what kind of funeral arrangements should be made. Sometimes she directed Lillian Smith to talk for her. At other times she abruptly took the telephone away from her hostess if she did not quite agree with the way the message was being conveyed or if she wanted to tell it herself. According to Paula Snelling, it was during these moments of trauma and stress that Carson seemed to forget completely about her maimed arm and hand. She reached for the telephone or door almost as readily with one arm as the other. Her hostesses noted that her helpless "wounded sparrow" dependency seemed suddenly to vanish, then startlingly reappeared. Often Carson waited at the heavy outside doors for Lillian Smith to come open them for her, yet at other times she boldly pushed them ajar herself.

As the day wore on, Reeves's funeral plans largely were completed by telephone. It was a trying experience for Carson, even though deep personal grief was not involved. She resented his suicide, and now it was putting many people to a great deal of trouble. Although Carson's hostesses noted that she consumed a fifth of whiskey that day, she nevertheless retained remarkable control of herself. Even the weather was unsettling and depressing to Carson. The winter rains had set in heavily by midmorning, and dark clouds and fog obscured the mountains. Carson told them that bad weather always upset her, and in her struggle now to maintain equilibrium she was filled with dread and needless fears. Perhaps the telephone would stop working and there would be no communication with the outside. Or the roads might become impassable and she would be unable to leave the mountain. Although she had no intention of returning at once to New York, she did not want to stay where she was any longer, either. Lillian Smith felt that her guest might want to remain on their mountain in seclusion for a few days, but Carson became adamant about leaving. Finally she said that she believed she would go to Augusta, Georgia—some one hundred miles away—and stay a few days with Dr. Hervey M. Cleckley and his wife, Louise, to whom she had become attached when they met in Washington in 1948 at the meeting of the American Psychiatric Association. To Lillian Smith, the Augusta visit seemed like a good idea, for Carson might well be in need of psychiatric counseling without being aware of it herself.

The second morning of Carson's stay, Paula Snelling drove her down off the mountain into the little town of Clayton and put her on the bus for Augusta. As Miss Snelling installed Carson in the seat behind the driver, she asked him to be very careful with his "fragile charge" for she had just had a terrible shock. Miss Snelling regretted later, however, that she had not thought to send along a little whiskey "to help stave off the shakes," which would have done more good. Lillian Smith, in the meantime, called the Cleckleys and explained Carson's situation. Their response was enthusiastic; they would be happy to have her, they said, and thought it wise that she have some tranquil moments in a stable situation before her return North with friends and family with whom she would become emotionally embroiled once more.

Carson's four-day stay in Augusta provided a much needed cushion from the shock of Reeves's death. She also found it to her liking to be in a warm, new atmosphere with two people she now attached herself to as old friends. Demonstrative in her affection for the Cleckleys, she also was candid about the love she said she felt for the young psychiatrist who introduced her to them. Cleckley said that although they talked about Reeves and the circumstances surrounding his death, he did not get the impression that she was in deep grief. "Nor did I get the impression that she particularly blamed herself for her husband's suicide," he added.[3] Carson showed much greater interest in the work Cleckley was doing in psychopathology than in herself. She reread his published study of psychopathic behavior, The Mask of Sanity, wherein she felt she recognized many of Reeves's characteristics. Too, she was much struck by the case history of schizophrenia on which he and his colleague Dr. Corbett Thigpen were at work, which resulted in their impressive and incredible book, The Three Faces of Eve.

By November 25, Carson felt strong enough to cope with a return to Nyack. The next day Reeves's obituary appeared in the New York Times. Immediately Carson's friends began to call, send messages, and come by. Although they offered condolences, a number who knew Reeves well expressed relief over his death and felt that Carson could enter now into a new phase of her physical, psychic, and creative life with fresh promise and buoyancy. When actress Helen Hayes arrived to pay her respects—she lived a few blocks away on South Broadway and they had been close friends for many years—she was met at the door by Marguerite, who told her that Carson was in bed resting. Miss Hayes kissed Carson's mother on both cheeks, then reportedly confided: "I'm not going to say I'm sorry, Bebe, because I don't think I am."

Marguerite Smith was deeply affected by her son-in-law's death, but her public attitude was that it was "for the best." She called Edwin Peacock in Charleston while Carson was still away, and loving Peacock as though he were her own son and knowing, too, that he was Reeves's closest friend, she tried to cushion the news by telling him: "Please try to accept it, Edwin, and know that it is for the best." Marguerite's reaction was an attitude that had its roots in the mores of her class and served her well time and time again. In the face of Reeves's death, that attitude helped to quell her own doubts and overcome her personal grief.

According to Jordan Massee:

> In the period when I knew Reeves he loved Bebe as devotedly as any son—more, I believe, than he loved anyone else at that time, excepting only Carson.
>
> It is not true that Bebe turned against Reeves when Carson did. The choice she *seemed* to make in favor of Carson was like the choice she *seemed* to make at times between Carson and Rita. To her it was not a question of choice, only a need for immediate action. She *acted* in behalf of Carson, and if it seemed to Reeves, or to Rita, that her actions indicated a withdrawal of love, it was not so. Even in the face of the only evidence she had concerning how Reeves had treated Carson in France she continued, as did Rita, to express and, I am sure, to feel genuine love and compassion for Reeves. Her grief over his death was deep and very real. In those dark days in Nyack after Reeves's death and Carson's return from the South, only Jack Dobbin and I were there to observe, first hand, apart from Rita and Carson herself, neither of whom was in any condition to observe what Bebe felt or how she reacted. Some of the many friends arriving brought their understanding with them—Henry Varnum Poor was an unforgettable example. More brought with them preconceived notions or their own characteristic myopia.[4]

Carson, having accepted his death before the actuality, suffered less from Reeves's death than did her mother or sister. For Carson, there was too much to forget before she could forgive. It was not the time for either. Instead of being left to her own thoughts and the quiet assurance of loved ones, she was almost immediately placed on the defensive by rumors and half truths, even by what Jordan Massee referred to as "downright

EMERGENCE FROM THE CHRYSALIS

lies," some of them from the most unexpected sources. Few people knew much about the months in France before Carson left Reeves, and almost no one in the United States had accurate information at the time on how Reeves died. Many were all too willing to believe anything detrimental to Carson. All the accumulated resentment felt by various members of Reeves's family found ready expression and willing acceptance. Even friends of long standing reacted to hearsay in the absence of facts. There were many who were genuinely grieved over Reeves's death. Most of them had known him long, long before, or were witness to his final disintegration, but not to the traumatic experience Carson had endured. Some were puzzled as well as grieved, and if they turned to Carson for enlightenment they were offered little that did not add to their confusion.

Even those who regarded Reeves's death as the inevitable result of his own tragic flaws found it difficult to accept what appeared to be callous indifference on Carson's part. Her refusal to go through the motions of the grieving widow served to outrage their sense of propriety. Even among those who were appreciative of Carson's deep hurt, some would have welcomed a token acknowledgment of "what was expected."

According to Tennessee Williams, "The only thing Carson ever did that I did not like was casting off Reeves as she did and showing no feeling for him or his memory after he was dead. She spoke of him in the most unkind terms, and it always upset me. Reeves died for her, yet she refused to admit it."[5] To be sure, Carson's "terms" for Reeves were unfavorable, but they were true. They were tactless, but the last thing that people ever expected—or wanted—from Carson was tact. "For one to expect compassion from Carson at that moment revealed, also, a lack of compassion for *her*," said Jordan Massee. At best, those who knew the situation had compassion for both Carson and Reeves, but not for one at the expense of the other. Although many people felt little sympathy for Reeves, they did feel compassion for him in spite of the way he had treated Carson. They felt compassion for him because of his pathetic vulnerability.

Others who expressed sympathy to Carson were concerned not so much with the fact that her husband had died, but with how she would fare in the years ahead without Reeves, who—as they saw it—had performed superhuman tasks in coping with an impossible wife. To John Vincent Adams, who had known Reeves since their army days in the early 1930s and had met Carson long before their marriage:

Carson needed Reeves and she knew it. Perhaps that is why she gave the poor soul such a hard time, and I mean hard! . . . Reeves was the best thing that ever happened to her. He was a completely normal, extremely intelligent, empathetic and kindly soul with a delightful sense of humor. Extremely handsome, and with his talents and other attributes, he could have been an exceptional actor, but he took life too seriously to consider this as a career. He liked people and had the rare faculty of bringing out the best in you. He could probe deeply with his endless searching questions, and force out answers from you that you were not aware you were capable of. His acceptance or agreement with your profound answers served as an additional reward. He made you feel capable and important to yourself. He was a serious thinker and troubled with the inequities of the world and times. He did aspire to a writing career and had the potentiality in scope and depth of becoming an important writer. In time this would have been realized, but he didn't get around to doing it.

Partly, but primarily, he didn't want to compete with Carson. He loved her too much and knew her ambitions and was aware of her weaknesses. Partly, because he was too busy in the early years in making a prosaic living, so that Carson would be free to do her writing. Partly, because Carson always had to be taken care of as a child in practically all living activities, cooking, housekeeping and all. She was constantly absorbed in her creative efforts and he encouraged her. Partly, because in addition to the burden of ordinary household chores after his regular work day, there were her emotional problems to be coped with. Partly, because he was too busy maturing himself and soaking up life, so that eventually he could write about it with authenticity and the dignity it deserved. Partly, because of his unusually unfortunate war experiences that had such a devastating effect upon him in both mind and body. There were other factors as well; he had so many disparaging problems of life affecting those around him. He told me only bits and I never pressed him for more, but he did have a disproportionate share of unsettling problems over which he had no control.

Carson was the most troubled of all, and the mental anguish she inflicted upon him is positively unbelievable. Any lesser man could not have been able to take it, and I don't know how he did. Yet he loved her deeply and believed that with his strength he could help her overcome her problems, but at the end she won and he lost out. I'm certain that it was this final realization, plus his war wounds along with his generally unhappy life experiences, that triggered his final action. Until this happened he took all things stoically and it did not shake his confidence in mankind or his stability of character. Just the opposite—he gave of himself in love, hope, inspiration and his quiet strength. . . .

We all have our weaknesses and strengths. We are here for such a short time and what we do, is *it*, and a matter only of record. Carson accomplished a great deal under enormous hardships of her own making, but she was not alone. She was blessed with the support, encouragement, and contributions of a selfless, loyal and utterly devoted partner, whose only aim was the dedication to her happiness. Carson lived a great love story that few women have ever experienced, and *that* she may not have even realized. It belied her self-inflicted miseries that caused them both to pay such a tragic cost.[6]

Adams, however, had no knowledge of Carson and Reeves's relationship in Italy and Paris during 1952–53. There was no correspondence between them during the last two years of Reeves's life.

Anyone seeking to understand the relationship between Carson and Reeves must first examine each separately in terms of his basic personality and needs. For all of Carson's dependence on Reeves, he was never completely necessary to her fulfillment as a person/artist, terms synonymous in Carson's case. When Reeves was not there, Carson found others to help meet her needs. On the other hand, the need that Reeves had of Carson was of a very different nature—and absolute. When his presence had become a hindrance rather than a necessity, as well as a direct threat to her life, Carson left him. Once she had left him, his end was, in a sense, inevitable. Carson had a will to survive, a will to realize itself that took what it needed and sacrificed whatever obstructed it; whereas Reeves, if not recklessly bent on self-destruction, destroyed as he went along because he never found anything or anyone, other than Carson, who even vicariously fulfilled his insatiable need for identity and fulfillment. Why his needs were what they were and why they could not be fulfilled is difficult to assess, but it is unlikely that his sexual ambivalence was the basic cause.

The funeral was not held until some ten days after Reeves's death. Excessive red tape was involved, both because Reeves was an American military veteran dying on foreign soil and because the cause of death was ambiguous. There were also unnecessary delays. According to Reeves's friends in Paris, Carson changed her mind several times about the funeral arrangements. She had first planned to have the body returned to the United States for burial. Then it was rumored that she had decided against it after learning how costly it would be to ship a body commercially by air freight. Next, she considered having the body cremated and the cremains flown home; but she learned that that, too, would be expensive. In New York it was reported that friends of Reeves—aggravated by what seemed Carson's inexplicable penuriousness—started a telephone campaign to raise money to have his remains flown back to the United States, where they believed that Reeves, himself, would like to have been buried.

Lillian Hellman recalled having been telephoned by Cheryl Crawford, who said that she and a few others were contributing to a fund to
have Reeves brought home. "I asked Cheryl why we were paying for
the funeral when surely Carson had more money than most of us—certainly a great deal of money then. Cheryl said she was furious with Carson
over her stinginess, but there was nothing to be done about it. I told her
I would contribute, but I didn't like it."[7] Unfortunately, Reeves left no
insurance, having let his National Service Life Insurance policy lapse a
few months prior to his death.[8]

In the meantime, Carson decided that a military burial in France
would be most fitting of all, that Reeves should be cremated and his
cremains interred in the adopted country he loved—France—in the cemetery for the American dead who had given their lives in World Wars I
and II. According to Jordan Massee, "In actuality, Carson had decided
soon after hearing of Reeves's death that he should be buried in France.
It was not a question of expense—but of distance. It was only when his
family insisted on having the body returned to the United States and at
her expense that she refused to accept the responsibility."[9]

Reeves's mother and the rest of his family appealed to Carson to
have his body brought home for burial in the South and would not accept
her refusal to accept any responsibility in the matter. That Carson would
not relent resulted in permanent estrangement from all the McCullers
family except Reeves's nephew, young Stanton Lee, Jr., the only child
of Reeves's sister Marguerite. Carson saw very little of the McCullers
family after that. Later she learned that each of Reeves's siblings had
committed suicide as well.[10] Carson eventually came to believe that the
tragic motives which prompted Reeves's suicide had possibly been germane
to the McCullers family.

Perhaps no one in Paris knew Reeves as well as John and Simone
Brown. Mrs. Brown knew all too well Reeves's suicidal nature—in fact,
she had begged him on several occasions during the last months of his
life not to kill himself in her home when his threats and the apparent
seriousness of his intent became increasingly frequent and alarming. Carson wanted John Brown to conduct the funeral service, which she hoped
could be arranged to be held in the American Church on the Left Bank
of Paris. To her, a preacher and a sermon would have been a travesty of
Reeves's mode of thought and way of life, but she knew that their friend
Brown could *talk* about him, at least, in a meaningful and dignified manner. Carson had no intention of flying to France herself for the interment
and requested that Janet Flanner attend in her place. Like Brown, Miss
Flanner agreed to do her part. In fact, "Genêt" was surprised that although
Reeves had "left enormous butcher bills for the meat that those cursed,

tiresome dogs had eaten, he had conscientiously paid his dues and kept up his connection with the American Legion."[11]

John Brown arranged for Reeves a veteran's military funeral with full honors. Later, Miss Flanner wrote Carson a detailed report of the funeral, but more recently she recalled vividly many events of that bleak November day:

> I went out to the crematorium that morning, and there was a woman waiting there, an American writer and friend of Reeves, Monica Sterling. I did not wait for the entire cremation—one doesn't—but later we gathered at the American Church, where John Brown gave a little talk. Then several of us went on to the cemetery. It was a very solemn and impressive ceremony. The American Legion commander came in bearing the American flag, and someone carried Reeves's ashes in a little box. A half dozen chaps in uniform followed—there was a drummer and a bugler. After the benediction, the firing party fired three volleys and the bugler sounded taps.
>
> John Brown spoke of Reeves's bravery and courage. He told of how splendid Reeves had been in the military, how he had landed in France on D-Day as an American Army Ranger, shooting his attaching hooks high above the side of the giant cliffs his men were to scale, and then leading his soldiers, raising himself arm over arm, looking absolutely fearless. It was a splendid muscular performance. He was wounded that day, but returned to France to fight again and to help liberate the country he loved. The French have a saying for someone who dies courageously: "*Il est mort stoiquement.*" Then, as I stood there, I took this beautiful red rose which I held in my hand, kissed it, and said: "Carson said, 'Good-by, Reeves darling.'" Then I dropped the rose down the aperture which led to the urn with the ashes.[12]

Only a handful of Reeves's friends attended the funeral services: Monique Kotlenko, the Russian doctor with whom Carson had gone to Italy in 1946; Monica Sterling, who had been a friend to both Carson and Reeves since 1946; the two doctors from the American Hospital, Robert Myers and Jack Fullilove; an unidentified French woman; and writer Truman Capote. Reeves and Capote had become very close over the years and had seen much of each other in Italy and France. At the cemetery, Mrs. Kotlenko and Capote reportedly broke down in tears, and Capote cried out in anguish, "My youth is gone."[13] The night of the funeral Fullilove encountered Capote at the Ritz bar in Paris, where he was still obviously shaken and bereft over Reeves's death, which to Capote seemed such a useless and tragic waste. Fullilove, too, was much upset.

His idealistic love of Carson had gradually diminished over the months, and his final disillusionment had come with her handling of the bad check to the money-changer. When Carson left Paris a few weeks before Reeves's death, it had been a permanent break—both physically and psychically—from most of the friends she had made there. The house in Bachvillers eventually was sold—as were the two boxer puppies, Nicky and Autonne—but Kristin, the mother dog, was sent home to Nyack.

Once back in Nyack and the furor had settled involving the funeral, Carson was eager to regain her old social rapport with various literary and theatre friends in New York and Nyack. Some, however, were reluctant to renew the relationship. Carson turned now more and more to her mother, her sister, her cousin Jordan Massee, to her friends in the South, Edwin Peacock and John Zeigler, and to others such as her young psychiatrist friend, who soon would be opening an office for private practice in Georgia. The day after her return from Augusta, Carson wired her friend an affectionate message. She made no reference to Reeves's death, but volunteered, instead, that she had just spent several days with the Cleckleys and that they had talked constantly of their mutual friend with great love. She urged the young doctor to write or phone her immediately, and to come to Nyack as soon as possible. She told her mother that she was ready to resume work on the *Holiday* article she had begun and that she wished to return South. On December 3, Marguerite Smith wrote a note to Lillian Smith and Paula Snelling to thank them for their love and care of Carson during her recent visit with them. She also asked them to let her know the amount of the charges for the various long-distance telephone calls Carson had made from their phone (which Miss Smith had no intention of doing). Marguerite said that Carson was leaving that night for other points in the South so that she could continue her article. Even though Carson had left the house in Nyack that very day to go into the city to catch her plane, Marguerite said that already she missed her very much and that the downstairs seemed empty with only Kristin to keep her company.

There was not the slightest doubt in anyone's mind now as to who would look after Carson, wait on her, and do all of the physical and secretarial chores for her that were possible. It would be Rita Smith, her sister. Carson's mother was no longer a well or strong woman herself, but so long as there was life she was determined to dedicate it, as always, to her older daughter. Her closeness to Carson became greater upon Reeves's death than it had ever been previously. When her son-in-law was on the scene in Nyack, and he and Carson appeared relatively happy and secure, Marguerite was more preoccupied with her daughter Rita, with whom she frequently stayed in the city. But with Reeves gone, Marguerite wanted to be constantly at Carson's side to protect her, shield her from unkindnesses, and minister to her every need.

Carson once again focused her emotional and physical dependency on her mother, who accepted unquestioningly everything Carson did. Never could Marguerite conceive of Sister's doing anything that might be considered unworthy, unfair, unethical, unacceptable, spiteful, malevolent, or gross. Although many persons over the years thought that Carson committed a number of small-minded, mean, or vindictive acts with only imagined provocation, there were far more who knew her intimately who defended most of her actions. Some spoke out boldly, as did Whit Burnett, who knew her well during a wide span of her New York life: "With Carson, compassion transcended talent. Her creative and life drives were based on compassion. She never took advantage of anyone—or anything."14 There were those, too, from the Paris years, such as Francis Price, who was in Doubleday's Paris office and knew Carson and Reeves well. According to Price, "Most people who knew Carson *well* loved her until the day she died, and love her still."15 Although Jordan Massee could write at length about the "goodness" of Carson, he also recognized and sometimes suffered from her inordinate demands. Perhaps Terry Murray, a men's toiletries merchant in New York City who also was a talented pianist and saw much of Carson during the last third of her life, expressed himself on this facet of Carson's personality more succinctly than anyone else: "Carson never did anyone 'dirty.' She had a reason for anything she did."16

Marguerite Smith was a strong ally, not only of Carson, but of her daughter Rita as well. To have come from a solid, upper middle-class, genteel southern family governed by conventional mores, Marguerite was an exceptionally broad-minded mother in her attitude toward the life styles of her daughters. Whatever they did was perfectly all right with her. She supported them 100 per cent. Yet if it were a matter of priorities, Carson came first. Carson's attitude that nothing could be more important than her own wishes or determinations came to her honestly, for they had been imposed upon her since birth and encouraged by a devoted mother. It was a foregone conclusion in the Smith household that anything Carson set out to get, she got. Many people believed that what had begun in the old maternal homestead on Fifth Avenue in downtown Columbus as sibling rivalry between young Lula Carson and "Little Pretty," her sister—who, indeed, was the prettier and more sophisticated of the two—evolved through the years into an ambivalent relationship of love and hatred with painful ramifications. To be sure, the sisters felt great love for each other, but Carson always needed Rita Smith more than her sister gave evidence of needing her. Rita was more than dedicated in her service to Carson, even when the demands often were not to her liking and fulfilled with few thanks or rewards in the process; rather, she was heroic. Yet there were conflicts because both were strong-willed women. Just as Carson had contributed to Reeves's self-destruction, so, too, were others in danger of being consumed and destroyed by too close an alliance with her unless they were phenomenally strong. Even though Carson's infirmities made her a weak person physically, she was far stronger in psyche and personality than the people around her. Her mother could handle Carson through gentle words, tact, and indirection in a way that sheer will and negative responses could never have achieved.

Rita Smith was not as strong as her sister, but she gained a large measure of strength and independence by living a few miles from Carson and their mother and maintaining her own apartment in New York City. She also created as much as possible an identity of her own. Just as Reeves had lacked a sense of personal identity by being known too often simply as the husband of Carson McCullers, so, too, did Rita find it difficult to have a meaningful literary career in New York without feeling that she was in the shadow of her more famous sister. Rita Smith herself was a very talented writer. Her stories had appeared in *Mademoiselle* before she joined the staff, and she had an outstanding career with *Mademoiselle* for sixteen years as assistant fiction editor and then as fiction editor. In 1960, she moved to *Redbook* magazine, where she was fiction editor, and later, contributing fiction editor. At the same time she had an outstanding career as a conductor of short story workshops at the New School for Social Research in New York City and at Columbia University. She also was a guest lecturer and summer school instructor at a number of eastern colleges and universities. But throughout Carson's lifetime—and even after her death—Carson continued to be a weighty shadow with which her sister reckoned.[17]

Carson's own mode of life after Reeves's death can best be understood if one realizes first that she was completely unwilling to assume any guilt or sense of responsibility for her husband's death. To Carson, Reeves's suicide was an act of ultimate rejection of his role, and one of her means of coping with that rejection was to cast him off first, to deny his existence. An important aspect of her ambivalent attitude was a sense of resentment, antagonism, and hostility felt at times toward people on whom she was forced to be dependent, instead of demonstrative appreciation for them. Now, through a transfer of her dependency from Reeves to her mother, Carson inadvertently renewed the hostility she had felt in childhood toward a parent who had pushed and, in a sense, exploited her in her efforts to create a genius. And now Carson *was* a genius, no matter what the measurable, inherited intelligence genes might indicate. She apparently was never given a bona fide I.Q. test, but she did take the

Rorschach test when she was living in Brooklyn Heights in 1941, administered by Dr. William Murphy, said Jordan Massee, who took it with her. According to Massee, Murphy told Carson: "Your mind would be the joy of any psychoanalyst in the world, and it would be a life work." But he also told Carson that if she underwent psychoanalysis, it would be to her detriment as a writer. "When they got through with you, you would never write again," he concluded.[18]

During the winter of 1953–54 after Reeves's death, Carson became increasingly unhappy as her dependency upon her mother grew. As a result, she resented Marguerite's yoke and threw it off rather vigorously at times. Interestingly, never in Carson's creative life did she present a happy, secure mother-daughter relationship in her published fiction. Her brother Lamar once tried to explain why it was that she did not honor their mother in her writings in any attractive, revealing mother-daughter relationship. His conclusion was that Carson had been "so utterly dependent upon Mother throughout her lifetime that she would not have dared strip herself that bare in her writing."[19] To Lamar Smith, Carson would not have wanted to expose her vulnerability and dependence on her mother to her readers. Therefore she went out of her way to make her fictional mothers die in childbirth, become preoccupied with running a house, or perhaps attempt suicide—as the mother does in her short story "The Haunted Boy"—rather than allow them to have a strong, viable love with a daughter or son.

"The Haunted Boy" germinated, in part, from Carson's psychic concern in 1954. The tale was not published until a little more than a year later, some five months after her mother's death; when the story actually was written is unknown, but its seeds lay both in her feelings about Reeves's death by suicide and her worry and ambivalent attitude toward her mother, who died in June 1955 from, reportedly, a bleeding ulcer. In "The Haunted Boy," a youngster who was very dependent upon his mother had once found her lying in the bathroom in a pool of blood after an unsuccessful suicide attempt. Although his mother recovered, after being committed to a psychiatric hospital, the boy lived in constant fear that the incident would repeat itself, and that this time she would succeed. The story is told from the "haunted boy's" point of view, in which there is one line which reveals a basic truth found frequently in Carson's fiction: "He [the "haunted boy"] hated John, as you hate people you have to need so badly."[20] Later in the story, the child asked his mother why she had done it. Misunderstanding the question, she replied:

> "The first warm day I just suddenly decided to buy myself some new clothes."
>
> But he was not talking about clothes; he was thinking about "the

other time" and the grudge that had started when he saw the blood
and horror and felt *why did she do this to me*. He thought of the
grudge against the mother he loved the most in the world. All those
last months the anger had bounced against the love with guilt between.

There was little doubt in the minds of those who knew Carson and her
mother well that in "The Haunted Boy," she was reacting to a severe
love-hatred-and-guilt relationship which she tried, unsuccessfully, to sup-
press, while at the same time, to hide from her mother.

The thought of death also loomed large again in Carson's mind in
December 1954 when, on her return South, her mother's single surviving
sister, Mrs. C. Graham Johnson, died suddenly. Carson's "Aunt Mattie"
was her favorite aunt, and she was deeply grieved by this loss of a blood
tie that had been very close. Although she had often poked fun in her
fiction of excessive deference to one's ancestors and loved to hear tales
that alternately violated and reinforced family ties, she felt a strong
attachment and devotion to her own living kin. Moreover, she had maintained a close rapport with her aunt and Columbus cousins since early
childhood. Carson worried about how her aunt's death would affect her
mother and immediately flew home to Nyack to break the sad news in
person. It was feared that the shock of a second death in her family—so
close to Reeves's death—might be too much for Marguerite's weakened
heart and other chronic conditions of poor health to bear. Carson realized,
too, that her mother had felt more keenly the loss of Reeves than she
dared express.

In her attempt to comfort her mother now, Carson realized anew,
as did Marguerite, how transitory life was. Neither of them believed in
an eternal hereafter. Marguerite could not help imagining her own death
and feared especially for Carson's survival without her. Carson, too, pictured what it might be like to live without her mother. It was not a
pleasant image, so she pushed the thought to the recesses of her consciousness. Carson's relationship with Marguerite was, in a sense, like a second
marriage. She was pinned securely to her mother's apron, just as she had
felt helplessly ensnared in the net of a troubled, tragic marriage that she
herself had helped weave. She needed her mother desperately, but—as
with Reeves—she resented and sometimes even hated the umbilical cord
which bound them.

There was still another facet of the author's relationship with her
mother of which Carson herself was perhaps not fully aware. In childhood, she had created and staged original plays in her living room and
back yard, but the audience and applause had always been stimulated by
her mother. Marguerite Smith herself was both an actress and puppeteer,

but she always deferred to her older daughter and worked deftly and un-obtrusively behind the scenes to detract in no way from the importance of Carson herself. This selfless characteristic continued to manifest itself over the years. Often in Nyack—both before and after Reeves's death—Carson performed best when entertaining a small group of friends. Ear-lier, there had been Reeves, who also was good at role playing, her mother, sister, one or two other women, and a single man, perhaps, to appreciate her performance. Somehow their dialogue and antics over the course of the evening, with sherry and whiskey flowing, assumed the dimensions of an absurd, grotesque play. Perfectly normal situations took on a hysterical tone. It was as though the little group was living a zany Broadway show with hilarious, fantastic things happening, yet every one of them rooted in real life. The action was quick, twisted, ludicrous. It also was every bit as fantastic as some of the grotesquely absurd hap-penings in Carson's own fiction. The remarkable fact was that Carson contributed in no way to the antics. She merely sat on the sidelines snick-ering, watching askance through half-closed eyes, sometimes emitting great spasmodic laughs, and being very much aware that it was her mother who was causing it all. Marguerite Smith had the uncanny knack of pull-ing everything normal apart, creating madcap situations out of real life, then putting them back together completely askew, whereas Carson par-ticipated vicariously in the action, then transformed it immediately into imaginative fiction. Many of Carson's tales rendered as pure fact bore almost no resemblance to their actual counterparts, yet they became a vital part of her oral repertoire which she relished in the telling. Carson's twistings to create fantasy frequently found their way into her published fiction through a technique amazingly like her mother's fantastic scenes, which actually had been enacted.

Carson had absorbed into her pores since childhood the nuances of the South, and she exuded at will with great fidelity—as well as through purposeful distortion—her youth and life in Georgia. Whereas she used to feel that she had to go back periodically to freshen her ambivalent feel-ings about the South, the imagined grotesqueries were always more real to her than the actual. Her mother had a way of keeping the South—with its absurdities and incongruities—in front of Carson far more effectively than Carson did through actual visits. Carson realized during her last trip to Georgia in December 1953—as other southern writers similarly dis-covered—that she could accomplish nothing further by going home again. Although she returned twice to Charleston, and once more to Charlotte, she never again saw her home state, nor felt that it was necessary.

Carson's desire not to be confronted by the "real thing" is illustrated by two anecdotes shared by George Lang, whom she met in Rome in 1952 when he helped David Diamond acquire an apartment for her and

Reeves in Castelgandolfo. The single characteristic which stood out in Lang's mind later was the "feverishly exaggerated expectations about imagined wonders, which invariably ended up in dismay and disappointment":

> One afternoon, for instance, I came to visit with Carson and Reeves and mentioned that I had seen some marvelous white Sicilian rugs in a little shop somewhere in Rome. Suddenly her eyes lit up and she queried me about them for half an hour. She was not well enough to go to Rome, and for weeks she kept talking, thinking, and dreaming about the white Sicilian rugs. Finally one day she went to Rome. Then, a little later with great sadness in her voice she said to me: "They weren't really what I thought. . . ."[21]

Another incident Lang recalled concerned what he called the "case of the flowering tree":

> At the time I had a scholarship in the Academia Santa Cecilia and went to the master class of Professor Corti twice a week from Castelgandolfo to Rome. One early spring day I saw a huge bunch of flowering almond tree branches near the school and bought the whole bunch, leaving barely enough money to get home. Holding the bulky package way above my head, hanging on for dear life on the Rome trams leading to the railroad station, after a pretty rough time, I got onto the train going to Villini (the actual stop next to Castelgandolfo) and—through all kinds of difficulties—I arrived at the station. There is a series of steps leading up to the level where their apartment house was located, amounting to about ten stories, I guess. Panting, I opened her door. Carson was lying in bed and I stood in the doorway with my flowering branches, hoping to give her a little bit of pleasure. Carson looked at it, and with an infinite sigh she closed her eyes and said: "Oh, but this is not like our flowering peach trees used to be in Georgia. . . ."[22]

Another time Lang remembered how Carson had not had an opportunity to be confronted with the actual object of her fancy and thus to be disillusioned by it. In Rome he once mentioned to her that he had seen strange little teacups in which each cup had three tiny legs to stand on. She talked on and off about the unusual cups for weeks, thought of what a lovely idea it was, and wondered where she could get one. Yet Lang had the definite feeling that she was secretly hoping "*not* to get one so that she could dream about it undisturbed." Nor did she.[23] This characteristic of Carson's was exactly what Reeves discovered early in their marriage when he invited her to attend a deaf-mute convention in Macon, Georgia, at the time she was creating the character of John Singer for

The Heart Is a Lonely Hunter. She could not bear to risk jarring the imagined image, which, to her, was much truer than "the real thing."

When Carson prepared to leave Nyack in early December 1953 and return South again, she preferred once more to go alone. Although Marguerite Smith would love to have gone with her daughter to Columbus, there simply was no question of it—Carson chose not to invite her. Still pursuing mood and facts for her *Holiday* article, Carson flew to Atlanta, where she was met at the airport by Ralph McGill, the astute, social-reforming editor of the Atlanta *Constitution* who had become an aggressive, inspiring spokesman for the New South, and Celestine Sibley, feature writer for McGill's paper.[24] Carson had met McGill in 1949 and they shared an affinity in their compassionate protest against the injustices of the South. She told McGill and Miss Sibley about her new book, *Clock Without Hands,* which she said she began serious work on in France. It would not be ready for another three or four years at least, for "I work very slowly," she explained to Miss Sibley. Carson also told her about her Georgia article for *Holiday* magazine which she hoped to finish soon. She acknowledged, too, that a new nonfiction piece had just appeared in the December 1953 issue of *Mademoiselle*—a nostalgic, autobiographical story about her early childhood in Columbus, especially her illumination at age five of the real nature of Christmas. It was called "The Discovery of Christmas." Her discovery was that not only was Christmas "parents," but that her baby sister was someone dear to love and accept. The most exciting thing she had done lately, she told Miss Sibley, was a television play. She had adapted her short story "The Sojourner," published in 1950, into the television play "The Invisible Wall." It would be presented live on the Ford Theatre "Omnibus" December 27.

On December 10, Carson left Atlanta and arrived in the hometown she had not visited in almost five years. This time the Columbus-born novelist was the guest of her mother's closest friend from their early girlhood, Mrs. George Swift, Sr. Carson was fond of Mrs. Swift—whom her mother deeply loved—and she tried now more than ever before to be sociable for interviews and parties given in her honor. Yet it was hard for Carson, for she was no more inclined now to be gay and charming in Columbus than she was during the twenty-odd years she had lived there. It also rather irked her that some of the people who were so nice to her now would not have even given a "weather report" of her "rarefied atmosphere" fifteen years earlier. She did consent to meet Constance Pilkinton for an interview at Mrs. Swift's one day for the newspaper on which she herself worked some twenty years earlier. Unfortunately for Miss Pilkinton, it was perhaps the most difficult interview the reporter ever had. Carson gazed off disinterestedly from her questioner and allowed such long pauses between answers that Miss Pilkinton was certain that the novelist either had not heard, or simply had no intention of answering. Just as Miss Pilkinton came in with a new question, Carson haltingly and tenuously answered the preceding one—unless she chose to ignore it completely.[25] As in the past, Carson was obviously impatient to get the necessary encounters with outsiders over with as soon as possible, then retreat into seclusion.

In spite of Carson's unwillingness to see people, Mrs. Swift recalled that she was a pleasant house guest: "She was very sensitive, very sweet. Carson could not have been more considerate or thoughtful of my husband and me. Of course, my husband was never as fond of Carson as I was. We talked some about her writing, and I remember her saying: " 'I wouldn't want to live if I couldn't write, Miss Helen. I simply couldn't live.' "[26]

Carson's nonfiction feature on Georgia never came off successfully. Even though she worked on it intermittently for four months—and then rewrote it at *Holiday*'s request—her editor objected that she put too much of Lillian Smith and Miss Smith's social consciousness into an article that was meant to publicize Georgia and attract people to the state as a vacationland. Most of the blame lay, however, thought Carson, on a prejudiced southern editor who refused to see the South as it was. Later, Carson suggested to Miss Smith that perhaps she had written too feelingly and lovingly about her as a person.[27] Whatever the reason, she was not accustomed to failure. Just as she had returned to Bachvillers from Rome after her unsuccessful venture into screen writing, rationalizing that she was not only coping with Reeves's illness at the time, but also with a temperamental, unpredictable director, so, too, had she had too much to contend with now because of Reeves's recent suicide, her aunt's death, and her mother's bereavement; these reasons, plus the fact that she was reaching again outside of her usual medium in which memory, imagination, and distortion were vital—all rendered her impotent for straight, objective reporting. Although she painted wonderfully realistic character sketches of Georgia backwoods people and vivid descriptions of the scenery, she failed to create an organic work of art. She was paid for the article, thanked by *Holiday*'s editors for her efforts, then informed that the piece was not suitable for their present needs. Carson's attitude was a shrug of the shoulder and a conviction that the decision was *their* loss, as well as that of their readers.

By now she had again been soundly applauded as the writer of a new medium, television drama. Carson was paid fifteen hundred dollars—plus an additional one thousand dollars for one-time broadcast rights—for her script "The Invisible Wall," presented live at 5:00 P.M., December 27, 1953, on the TV-Radio Workshop, a program created by the Ford Foundation, entitled "Omnibus." Carson had been requested by the Ford Foundation to make the adaptation back in midsummer when she was still in France, but she delayed the work until she returned to America and gained some semblance of peace of mind in the early fall. By mid-October the script was completed. Staged by Mel Ferrer and directed by Robert Ellis Miller, who later directed the screen version of *The Heart Is a Lonely Hunter*, the television play starred David Wayne as John Ferris, Rex Thompson as Valentin, Frances Starr as Mother, Neva Patterson as Elizabeth, Lorne Greene as Ed Bailey, and Johnny Klein as Billy Bailey.[28]

With money coming in once again, not only from book royalties, foreign editions, new magazine publications, and enterprises such as the recent television script, Carson was also receiving a regular "allowance" from proceeds of the sale of the screen rights of *The Member of the Wedding*. Everyone who knew Carson's lawyer, Floria Lasky, gave her credit for being an astute financial manager who carefully doled out money to Carson so that she might continue to live well. Miss Lasky had wisely invested the money from the movie rights of Carson's play, but even though Carson received periodic financial statements, she was never sure what they meant. It was much easier to call her friend on the telephone and ask such questions as "Please tell me, Floria, if I have enough money to subscribe to *Vogue* magazine." As Jordan Massee saw it, "Carson was shrewd about money, but just could not cope physically with the problem of handling it." Carson once had Miss Lasky figure out how much she had earned by the hour since writing *The Heart Is a Lonely Hunter*. "It came out to approximately thirty-two cents an hour," Carson told her cousin. "I could have done a lot better as a plumber."[29] Carson's brother, too, was generous in his appreciation of Miss Lasky's handling of Carson's money: "Carson would have gone through it many times over—not to mention what Reeves might have done had he lived longer—had it not been for Floria."[30]

Whose idea it originally was is unknown now, but in the spring of 1954 a new money-making venture was conceived for Carson. Although she admitted that the idea of talking to large groups of people terrified her, she agreed to begin a series of lectures, or "conversations," at various colleges and fine arts halls in the East. Many people in the past had asked her in interviews and personal conversations about her creative process and what she meant by her "illuminations" and the "flowering dream." Carson received considerable advance publicity and a banner headline in the *Goucher Weekly* for her Isabelle Kellogg Thomas lecture scheduled for Goucher College in Towson, Maryland, February 16. Hers was to be a full two days of activities. She was to appear the afternoon before the lecture as the honored guest at an English Department tea for faculty and English majors; then, on the following day, she was to hold two in-

formal conferences open to all members of the Goucher College community, one in the morning on fiction writing, the other in the afternoon
on drama.[31] Carson was such a success that she gained new confidence
and accepted invitations to talk at Columbia University, the Poetry Center in New York City, and the Philadelphia Fine Arts Association. As
she explained later to Newton Arvin—having written to see if Smith
College would be interested in her coming up there—she simply talked
about the kind of things that the two of them had shared, and that she
had been concerned with for over twenty years. She told Arvin that she
thought she would die when she first began lecturing, but that now everyone seemed to enjoy her little talks.[32]

While Carson was as far south as Baltimore for her Goucher appearance, it seemed to her a good idea to continue on to Charleston.
She wanted to get away and relax with friends whom she felt loved her
and accepted her for exactly what she was. When she told Edwin Peacock
and John Zeigler that she was almost in their territory, they urged her
to come *farther* South and have a little vacation with them. Carson went,
and was more relaxed this visit than she ever had been before. She looked
better than she had in years, it seemed to Peacock, and her personality was
more radiant than it had been in 1949 when she and Reeves had been in
Charleston together. According to Peacock,

> Although Carson was always somewhat ill when she visited us, she
> enjoyed the atmosphere of a house in the South and she loved atten-
> tion. She also loved to sit in the little kitchen of the Book Basement
> and read by the hour. The people she met, the evening meals,
> and the whiskey highballs which she sipped—all gave her pleasure.
> Charleston as a city did not particularly interest her, though she did
> seem to like the place. Perhaps getting away from New York was
> what pleased her most. She *disliked* Columbus, but she brought it
> fame, just as Tennessee Williams brought fame to Columbus, Mis-
> sissippi.[33]

Peacock and Zeigler's bookshop was in the basement of the enormous
ante-bellum home into which they had moved with Zeigler's widowed
aunt. Carson said that she had been in no home in the South that was
as elegant and stately, and she fed now on the many stories that her
friends told her about it.[34]

Peacock again had called Robert Walden and Edward Newberry to
come to Charleston for the weekend to be with Carson, whom they had
not seen since their trip to New York for the opening of *The Member of
the Wedding*. Walden, in turn, urged Carson to come to Charlotte and
stay with him and Newberry for a month or so, assuring her that she
could have long uninterrupted blocks of writing time while they were at
work. She was not ready to go to Charlotte or anywhere else for a while,

however; she wanted only to relax and to work on *Clock Without Hands* if she felt like it. The novel had taken on the characteristics of a much-loved stepchild, carted about, but at the same time ignored as much as possible. The first chapter of it had been published simultaneously the preceding summer in *Botteghe Oscure* in Italy, and in *Mademoiselle*.[35] Although Carson worked on it fairly often, she could not seem to sustain a long-term drive on the novel. She also carried with her to Edwin Peacock's a couple of drafts of her new play, *The Square Root of Wonderful*, plus an idea in the back of her mind that *The Ballad of the Sad Café* could be adapted into a musical ballad. Prior to Carson's visit South, Walden had blocked out—in rough outline—*The Ballad of the Sad Café* as a play, envisioning it as a ballet, which seemed to him an apt medium for presenting Cousin Lymon, the transition between the "happy" and "sad" café, the grotesqueness of the fight, and the coda of the "Twelve Mortal Men" and their song. In sharing his ideas with her now, Walden found Carson not only receptive, but enthusiastic.

Once again Carson consented to a photographic session and interview, this time with the Charleston *News and Courier*. She insisted on being pictured with her hosts, Zeigler and Peacock. It would be good publicity for the Book Basement, as well as for her own books, she volunteered. During this visit Peacock and Zeigler prevailed upon Carson to let them give her a small garden party. When she complained that she had no shoes for a dress-up affair, the men went out and returned with a pair of gold slippers just in time for her to put them on before the guests arrived. A *grande dame* of Charleston who came to the house that evening was a Miss Bragg, but Carson appeared not to be impressed and she resumed her usual noncommunicative, petulant "party manner." Another guest was Hilda Marks, an attractive and scintillating German refugee married to a brilliant, prolific nonfiction writer and Ph.D. graduate in political and social science, Robert Marks, a native of Charleston who had been a long-time friend of Peacock and Zeigler. During the course of the party while most of the guests were in the garden, Hilda Marks noticed that Carson was sitting in a chair off by herself, wearing a "sour, mean expression on her face. I went over to talk with her, but she was very unresponsive and obviously irritated by having someone seek her out as I had," recalled Mrs. Marks later. "But the next day I saw Carson again, and she was a different person. By now she had decided that she liked me, and she apologized for the way she had acted.

" 'You see, it was really Edwin's fault,' Carson explained. 'He went out and bought me some new slippers, but he put them on the wrong feet. I'm afraid I was terribly bitchy because my feet hurt.' "[36]

A few days later, Carson decided to accept the invitation by Walden and Newberry to fly to Charlotte from Charleston the last weekend in March. Newberry, an architect, had designed and built the new house they were in, and Carson was intrigued by it even before she saw it. She was afraid to see it—"it couldn't be true," she told them. It was almost a one-room house, large and sprawling, with a huge living room and stone fireplace, a bedroom alcove and library—which was not a separate room, but a part of the living room—a kitchen and eating area off in another alcove, and finally, the only single room with a separate door on it, the bathroom. Radiant heat came up from slate floors to heat the house, an engineering feat that Carson found fascinating. When the house was first described to her, she decided almost on the spot that the young protagonist in her play, *The Square Root of Wonderful*, would be an architect and that the house he would design would have many of the characteristics that Newberry's house had.

Carson lived with Walden and Newberry as though they were three chaps sharing bachelor quarters. She wore men's pajamas and slept on a day bed beside the fireplace in the living room while the two men shared the bedroom alcove. The house was cheerful and bright, with wide expanses of glass throughout. Carson enjoyed puttering about during the daytime doing exactly as she chose. A great deal of the time she sat in front of the fire, feeding it logs, ruminating, and reading from her hosts' extensive library. A new book she found particularly gripping was William March's *The Bad Seed*. She told her Charlotte friends that it was "marvelously creepy," and that she would have given anything to have written it herself. Then she sat down to write the author and tell him so.

In the evening when the men came home, they sat and talked, drank, and told tall tales. Sometimes they found Carson very amusing and gay; yet more often, she seemed unhappy. Regardless of their attempts to lift her spirits, she frequently became sullen and morose. The housekeeper, whom the men employed during the day so that Carson would not be left alone, apprised the men that their guest did little writing, but rather, sat for hours staring into the fire.

A number of friends of Walden and Newberry expressed interest in entertaining for Carson, as did the men themselves in an effort to cheer her. Also, it was not often that such a celebrity visited in the Piedmont area, and the townspeople themselves wanted to be entertained by the celebrated novelist. Carson was not interested in the slightest in a party, but finally she consented to meet a few people for cocktails in the home of Mr. and Mrs. Martin Cannon, Jr., of Cannon towel fame. According to Harrell Woolfolk, who lived next door to Walden and Newberry and had enjoyed seeing Carson in Charleston, the affair was disappointing. Said Woolfolk:

> Carson attended, wearing her bedroom slippers. As a celebrity, the guest of honor was expected to converse with the other guests and

be normally agreeable, but they apparently had never reckoned
with the likes of Carson McCullers before. She said absolutely nothing to anyone, was exceedingly tiresome in her behavior, and was
ready to go home before the party had hardly begun. It would be
an understatement to say that everyone took a hearty dislike to her.[37]

Woolfolk was aware that he, too, had alienated Carson that visit. He believed that she was faking some of her physical dependency, for he said
that there were times when she waved her bad arm around when she did
not seem aware of it. Finally he was goaded into saying: "You are a very
sinister person, Carson—you really don't need that walking stick after all."
Her reply was "very sharp and unladylike," said Woolfolk. "I regretted
having offended her."

Later, when asked about Woolfolk's version of the party and
Carson's behavior, Walden disagreed. At no time during his acquaintance
with Carson did he find her "tiresome" or "uncommunicative," he said.
As Walden saw it,

> Whether there was one or two of us, or a group, she was ever alert
> and interested, drawing out everyone so that all gatherings had a
> specialness. Only afterward were you aware that she was the catalysis,
> not the primary contributor to the conversation—normally she would
> concentrate this focus on one person who, in turn and unknowing,
> became the one "on." I think that this delayed realization of what
> had happened disappointed people who accepted her genius as a
> writer and had anticipated a conversational style equal to her writing.
> There were the same rhythms and premises in her statements as in
> writing, but here the gambit was to let others make conclusions, her
> interest not to impose hers, which she reserved and/or refined those
> of others. I am not sure that this was done knowingly, only that the
> result on others was great and that the consternation over one's own
> actions and thoughts were often misattributed to Carson.[38]

According to Walden regarding the Cannon party, "It being a work day,
Martin Cannon said that he would pick Carson up and we could come
straight from work. The maid was not there and she could not find her
clothes—which were in a hall closet except for a few things—so Marion
Cannon supplied shoes, make-up, etc. When we arrived, Carson regaled
us with the tale and was completely charming during the entire evening,
all present knowing her work and captivated by her personally upon
meeting her."[39]

An ancedote Carson later loved to tell involved her and a fellow
guest of the Cannon party, Elisabeth Holt, who owned one of Charlotte's
leading bookshops and was Woolfolk's employer. Much taken by Carson,

Mrs. Holt reportedly said to her when she rose to go: "You are not at all the way I thought you would be, Carson" (which seemed to Walden a typically southern effusiveness).

"Carson recognized the remark for just that," said Walden, and perhaps having dispensed enough sweetness and light for one evening, she smiled one of her crooked little smiles and responded:

"And what did you think I would be, a sonuvabitch?"

According to Walden, "Both women instantly realized the reasons for the other's remarks, whereupon they embraced, sat down, and then began a truly meaningful conversation."[40]

Although both Carson and Walden had been excited at first over the possibilities of working together on the musical adaptation of *The Ballad of the Sad Café,* eventually their enthusiasm faded as they discovered that he could not help her in the creative process—her province alone—and that her concentration for sustained work was not sufficient at that time. She did work on it occasionally during the mornings when she felt well, and at night her first week there she read to Walden what she had written and invited his suggestions. To Walden, the whole tempo of *The Ballad of the Sad Café,* its narrative tradition, poetic qualities, fuguelike structure, framework, musical coda at the end—all were eminently suited to a musical rendition, and he hoped that she would not drop the idea completely. At night they also reread aloud much of the novel to each other.

Although Carson read very poorly, slowly and haltingly with enormous pauses between phrases and sentences, she loved an audience and expressed herself with great feeling. When she attempted to read from the coda at the end, about the "twelve mortal men . . . who are together," her voice usually broke and she gently cried. While in Charlotte, Carson autographed Walden's copy of *The Ballad of the Sad Café* on the page containing her famous thesis about love and the relationship between the lover and the beloved. She also wrote a special message pertaining to the passage. She told him that her thesis was unadulterated truth only when a person was *not* in love. Under other circumstances, it was to be interpreted differently. The inscription was dated March 8, 1954.

Another aspect of Carson which surprised Walden that spring was her interest in the Bible. At night they frequently read aloud passages to one another from the King James version. Carson usually chose her lines from her favorite books of the Bible, Psalms, Proverbs, and Ecclesiastes. Walden was impressed that Carson knew the Bible as well as she did: "She knew exactly where the passages were about music and love." Yet regardless of how fond Walden was of his famous house guest and how much he respected her attributes, he hoped she would not be "depicted biographically for posterity cloaked in white or wearing a halo. She was a bitch, and I don't want her coming out looking like an angel. Although what *she* wanted to be was always most important to her, she also could be exactly what *you* wanted her to be. If she wanted to please you, she would suddenly decide 'I'm going to be charming,' and charming she was —like a princess. But she was still a bitch."[41]

During Carson's third week in Charlotte, she received in the mail the register book from Reeves's funeral and a number of letters forwarded to her by Robert Myers, their friend from the American Hospital. "The visual reminders of Reeves's death had a deeply depressing effect on her," said Walden. "Although she did not discuss with us her feelings or share any of the documents, it was obvious that Carson was experiencing significant and devastating inner turmoil." When her hosts returned home that particular evening, they found her distraught and drinking heavily, characteristics unprecedented during the first part of her visit. According to Walden, Carson seemed obsessed with the disposition of the house in Bachvillers. It was as though Reeves had died and been buried on that particular April day, 1954, four and a half months later than actuality, said Walden:

> Carson made many long distance calls at this time to her lawyer, agent, friends; she was preoccupied with the garden tools, a certain tree which she wanted bagged and sent over, with why certain people had attended the funeral, etc.—all incoherent, not from the drinking we think as much as it was a kind of rebellion in her spirit. We seemed of no help, although I stayed out one day from work and both of us went to lunch with her when we could. Finally we came to a resolution that we could not help, let alone cope. I'm afraid my hospitality, patience, and endurance had been stretched almost to the breaking point. Finally, I wrote Rita—explaining—and asked her to call Carson and find some ruse by which she might get her to return home early, which she did. And we put Carson on a train and out of our lives. I think that Rita never told her, for there were subsequent letters, but none tinged by those short disastrous days. Whether by a feeling of guilt or inadequacy, we never again were close, except by memory and infrequent crossing of paths.
>
> We think the friendship a rare and good one:—treasure it, and let it go at that. . . . She was at once complete and incomplete, complex and simple, and on occasion our dear friend.[42]

On April 19, Carson left for New York City. Before her departure, she insisted upon her hosts taking her to a nursery to buy a flowering shrub, a purple leaf plum which she sentimentally renamed "the Carson tree" and often inquired about in subsequent years—as though she had left a little touch of herself in Charlotte, too.[43]

Whatever arrangements had been made—Walden never sought the

details—Carson was invited by Elizabeth Ames to work again at Yaddo and she proceeded immediately to Saratoga Springs. Carson had not seen Mrs. Ames since before her paralyzing stroke and subsequent illnesses over the past seven years. Although Mrs. Ames expected her to have aged somewhat, knowing that she had suffered excruciating pain and heartache during the interim years, she was in no way prepared for the spectral writer who greeted her now. "Her physical appearance alone was shocking," said Mrs. Ames.

> Her face was pale and pasty-looking. She had a kind of bloated look as well. I was sure it was because of her heavy drinking, which was even more profuse than before. She also smoked so furiously that I was half afraid she would set the whole place on fire. She made me very nervous while she was here. I don't believe she worked much— her heart wasn't in it. She had changed, of course, because of the stroke. It had affected not only her brain, it seemed, but her personality as well. Her temperament was more irascible. I didn't see this so much in her relationship with me, for she continued to be very sweet to me and we always got along well together, but I could see how she was with others. She was much less tolerant, especially when she had been drinking, and she was more liable to make an unpleasant remark about someone at the dinner table, or goad someone in an irritating manner. She was very lame then and depended heavily upon her cane. Her hand seemed withered and her speech thick when she had been drinking, nor could she control her tongue. I attributed much of that to the stroke. I am afraid she was a terrible handful. It was no wonder that Rita had become so tired of having the responsibility of Carson that she was anxious to have her return to Yaddo that spring.[44]

Carson was at Yaddo only a few weeks when her mother suffered another fall, this time a broken hip. The accident occurred at a particularly inopportune time, for the home at 131 South Broadway had been in a state of turmoil for days. Its tenants were being shunted from room to room while the interior was painted and new bathroom plumbing and kitchen facilities installed to help make full apartments out of some of the existing rooms and porches. Carson again rushed home to be with her mother, and this time she and her sister persuaded Marguerite to move from the Nyack General Hospital into a nursing home nearby where she would be assured of constant care. Carson had no intention of remaining in Nyack and living at home alone, however. After her mother recuperated enough to oversee the running of a household again, then she, too, would return. In an attempt to apprise friends of her present situation and also elicit pity, Carson described her plight now as one who was forced to wander forlornly among friends.

Carson was encouraged in the spring of 1954 to resume her lecture series, having received many compliments on her talk at Goucher College a few weeks earlier. She was also appreciative of the honorarium. One of the most prestigious and popular centers at which fiction and nonfiction writers, poets, playwrights, and actors—both American and foreign—appeared for readings and discussions about their work was the Poetry Center of the 92nd Street YM-YWHA. Almost before she realized it, she said, her name was placed on the program, but as the date approached, she pleaded stage fright. At the last moment she arranged for Tennessee Williams to appear with her. Admittedly a very poor speaker and stupefied by large audiences, she insisted to Williams that she could not go on without him. If he would at least come and read for her, she would get by, she conceded. Her talk had been publicized as "Twenty Years of Writing," just as it had appeared on the Goucher program. But with advertisements appearing in the Sunday New York *Times* and the *Village Voice*, word quickly spread that Tennessee Williams, too, would be on the program. Privately, Williams agreed to the stint only if a pitcher of martinis on the table might be substituted for water—a suggestion to which Carson readily concurred.

As the 850 seats in the Kaufman Auditorium on Lexington Avenue began to fill up, so, too, did the featured artists. When it was finally time for Carson to speak, after a lengthy introduction by poet John Malcolm Brinnin, in charge of the Poetry Center that year, she got to her feet unsteadily—as usual, aided by her cane—and solemnly faced a fidgety audience, made nervous now because their featured speaker stood there before them for what seemed like five minutes, looking out over the audience and saying nothing. Then, as though she had had a sudden illumination, Carson McCullers began to talk. Her voice was soft, low, and intimate, her words sometimes almost inarticulate and indiscernible because of her deeply southern enunciation. She spoke, however, directly to the enormous group with a visual contact and rapport that cut through all extraneous claptrap and protocol and revealed a sensitive inner soul with no façade or reserves. Although there were still long pauses intermittently in her speech rhythms—as was her custom, having nothing to do with the alcohol she had consumed—she cut deftly through to her core of meaning to expose the heart of the matter.

Carson spoke of the genesis of creation as she had experienced it in her various works, even as far back as her juvenile pieces and sometimes aborted story writings, closet dramas, and back-yard plays. When she came to a particular passage in one of the stories or novels from which she wanted to cite to illustrate her narrative, she turned to Tennessee Williams at her side and asked him to read from the specific passage in question. After the talk and the readings, as was usual, there was a period

for questions and answers. Some listeners queried Carson on plot questions, such as "Why was it necessary for John Henry to die?" Regarding
the play, *The Member of the Wedding,* it was more a question of mechanics, answered Carson. She said that she simply wanted Ethel Waters
at the end to be alone on the stage. She also answered questions about
her personal life and the career in music she had given up for writing. But
she had not abandoned music, she insisted; music and writing had been
contrapuntal most of her life, and the music she loved so deeply continued to be an integral part of her fiction. Occasionally Williams, too, was
asked a question about something that concerned them both, and in answer the two *playwrights* created a little impromptu dialogue together.

When Carson finally returned to her seat, the applause was deafen-
ing. Most of the audience joined them afterward in the reception room
to speak with them personally and to ask for autographs.[45] It was very
late before the two of them could leave. Carson had been staying since
her return from Yaddo with the couple she had met in Charleston earlier that spring—Hilda and Robert Marks—who lived in an old brownstone on Madison Avenue in midtown. When Carson arrived at the
Marks's apartment, accompanied by Williams, she volunteered with great
relish, "Well, I certainly hypnotized Truman tonight." Then she explained what *to her* seemed to be the situation: Looking out over the audience at the Poetry Center that evening, she suddenly caught the
eye of Truman Capote in the audience, whose presence there surprised
her, she said. By now, Carson had become very sensitive and resentful
that someone whom she felt she had aided in his climb to literary success
might have misused her in the process. She was obsessed by the thought
that certain passages in Capote's novels—*Other Voices, Other Rooms* and
The Grass Harp—were plagiarisms from her own writings. She thought
that one passage in particular in *The Grass Harp* had a striking affinity in
meaning, imagery, and syntax to her own "A Tree. A Rock. A Cloud."
When Carson spotted who she thought was Capote in the audience, she
turned suddenly to Williams and asked him to read the speech by the old
tramp in her story, which she believed supported her conviction. It was
Carson's way of indirectly saying to Capote: "I know what you've done,
and now you know that I know, and what I think of it." Most people who
knew Carson's feelings about Capote and the alleged plagiarism felt the
whole thing absurd, however. Even Carson's phrase "A Tree. A Rock.
A Cloud." was taken from Thomas Wolfe's "A Leaf, A Stone, A Door,"
whether consciously or unconsciously. It was fairly ridiculous, people
thought, that she reacted so strongly to someone's "poaching" from her
—even if he had—when she herself had borrowed.

If, indeed, Capote was in Carson's audience May 8, 1954, he had no
recollection of the incident later; in fact, he was certain that he attended
no such reading. Nor from his point of view had he and Carson ever

"fallen out," regardless of the rumors she perpetrated. Capote agreed that they did not see much of each other during Carson's last years, but certainly there was no professional jealousy on his part. They were always "friendly," he maintained; moreover, he recalled that only "a few months before her death she wrote me, out of the blue, a very affectionate letter."[46] According to friends, however, who knew them both well, Capote simply refused to "pay lip service to Carson and make over her inordinately when he had more interesting and sincere friends" with whom he preferred to spend his time. It was not that he lacked gratitude for favors or encouragement that she had given him in the past; it was that their lives at present touched very little, nor was there any occasion for them to come together again until her funeral.

Carson never quite relinquished the idea that Capote had been more than casually imitative of her works. Some nine years after the reading at the Poetry Center, she requested of Oliver Evans, who had a critical biography of Carson in progress, that he point out in scholarly fashion that Capote had, indeed, plagiarized from her works.[47] Carson herself never directly accused the younger writer, and even though Evans noted in his book that there were similarities in the imagery and syntax between the two writers in certain passages, he refrained from explicit accusation.[48]

Later, Carson not only suspected Capote of too closely emulating her, but she also expressed resentment, criticism, or jealousy of those whom she thought to be descendants of her school or who showed other stylistic similarities. In the same letter in which she asked Oliver Evans to point out Capote's imitation, she noted that she was irritated by fellow southerner Harper Lee for the same reasons; therefore she no longer read her.[49] To Jordan Massee, who once asked Carson what she thought of Harper Lee, the reply was only slightly reproachful: "Well, honey, one thing we know is that she's been poaching on my literary preserves."[50] Another day, Massee was interested in finding by Carson's bedside a copy of a new collection of short stories by a fellow Georgia writer, Flannery O'Connor. "Oh, I see you've been reading Flannery O'Connor," said Massee, fond of Miss O'Connor's work himself and curious to see what his cousin's reaction would be.

"Well, Boots, I started it—but I didn't finish it. I did read enough, though, to know what 'school' she attended, and I believe she learned her lesson well." To Carson, Miss O'Connor, too, was a deft imitator, but she was to be commended for what she did well. Much later, in the early 1960s, Miss O'Connor commented on several recent books she had read. In response to her advance copy of *Clock Without Hands*, she said that it was absolutely the worst book she had ever read. To her, the novel represented total disintegration.[51] Miss O'Connor's comment, however, was simply an objective aesthetic judgment. She had never felt that there was any reason for a comparison between the two authors, their techniques, or modes of thought. They were contemporaries who had been born and lived much of their lives in the same state less than two hundred miles apart. But it would never have occurred to Miss O'Connor to resent or be jealous of Carson McCullers, or anyone else, for that matter.

Even with Tennessee Williams, about whom it was often said that he and Carson never fell out with one another over anything, there was still, admittedly, on Carson's part, some professional jealousy. Williams' attitude was that Carson was a wonderful writer, but not really a dramatist. He thought one contemporary female writer surpassed Carson as a dramatist. "Jane Bowles's *In The Summer House* is perhaps better than anything Carson ever wrote. But, of course, I would never have admitted that to Carson," Williams added.[52] Although Carson was prouder of her intimate rapport with Tennessee Williams than with any other great artist or celebrity, her professional jealousy sometimes revealed itself in such offhand comments as "Now why should *A Streetcar Named Desire* make over a million dollars when *The Member of the Wedding* didn't make that much?"[53]

Occasionally it was obvious to friends that Carson and Williams were engaged not only in friendly rivalry as writers, but also in the telling of their own "tall tales"—even to the point of trying to outdo the other in their experiences in psychoanalysis or therapy. Dr. Ernst Hammerschlag, a New York psychiatrist, recalled recently the luncheon date he once had in New York City with Carson and Williams. He found their vying at tale telling "extremely interesting" facets of their personalities. "It is a strange fact that people who gather with psychiatrists have the impression that they have to unload all their personal hidden problems, and this lunch was for me an almost historical event because both tried to outdo each other in this respect," he acknowledged.[54] Although Hammerschlag was the personal psychiatrist of neither, he found that they created and performed their own group encounter that day. Hammerschlag knew Carson well during the mid-1950s and continued to see her occasionally thereafter; he was one of the few who felt that she was riddled by guilt feelings over Reeves's suicide in spite of her vehement denials. Her protestations resembled those of the Queen in *Hamlet*, who announced to her son during the "play within the play": "The lady doth protest too much, methinks."

Carson exhibited no apparent jealousy of great writers or poets if they maintained considerable physical remoteness from each other or wrote in quite different genres or languages. She had already revealed great affection and admiration for the Irish writer Elizabeth Bowen, for Great Britain's Dame Edith Sitwell, and for Denmark's Isak Dinesen—although she did not meet the Danish writer in person until the spring of 1959—but an ocean, as well as an entirely different life style and mode

64 Tennessee Williams, New Orleans, 1972.

65 One of several publicity pictures taken by Werner J. Kuhn for the publication of the play *The Square Root of Wonderful*, New York City, 1958.

66 Carson at Yaddo, Saratoga Springs, New York; her last visit as a working artist, with both *Clock Without Hands* and *The Square Root of Wonderful* in progress, June 1954. Window seat, left to right: John Thomas, Clifford Wright, Harold Lazarus, Jacob Lawrence, Carson McCullers, Leon Edel, Rosemarie Beck Harvey Fite, Walter Aschaffenburg, Parker Tyler; front, left to right: Margaret Lowery, Jerome Greenfield, George Reavey, Pat Haley, Anne Walters, Philip Murray.

67 Katherine Anne Porter at North Farm, Yaddo, January 1941.

68 LEFT: Composer David Diamond at the time he met Carson and Reeves McCullers, 1941.

69 BELOW: John Zeigler, Carson, Reeves, and Edwin Peacock at Sullivan's Island, South Carolina, May 1949.

70 Ethel Waters, Carson McCullers, and Julie Harris at the party after the New York première of *The Member of the Wedding*, at producer Robert Whitehead's apartment.

71 Yaddo's artists during the summer of 1943. Standing, left to right: Kappo Phelan, Elizabeth Ames, Rebecca Pitts, Paul Zucker, Hans Sahl, Langston Hughes; seated, left to right: Isabella Howland, Margaret Walker, Jean Stafford, Harold Shapiro, unidentified, Agnes Smedley, unidentified, Carson McCullers, Alfred Kantorowicz.

72 The group at Yaddo in August 1942. Standing, left to right: Newton Arvin, Nicholas Marsicano, Nathan Asch, Philip Rahv, Michael Seide, Karol Rathaus, Carson McCullers, Malcolm Cowley, Karnig Nalbandian, Langston Hughes, Kenneth Fearing, unidentified, Leonard Ehrlich, Jean Liberte; seated, left to right: Carol Asch, Frances Mingorance, Merle Marsicano, Katherine Anne Porter, Helena Kuo, Juan Mingorance, Nathalie Rahv, Elizabeth Ames.

73   LEFT: Carson with her
good friend, novelist
Peter Feibleman,
Columbia University, 1964.

74   BELOW: Producer John
Huston greets his house-
guest good morning at
his palatial estate in
Galway, Ireland,
April 1967.

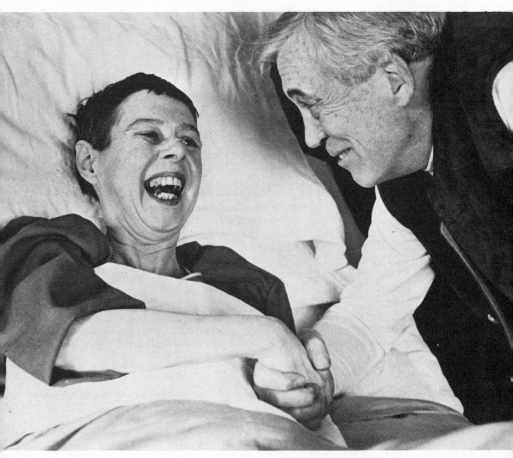

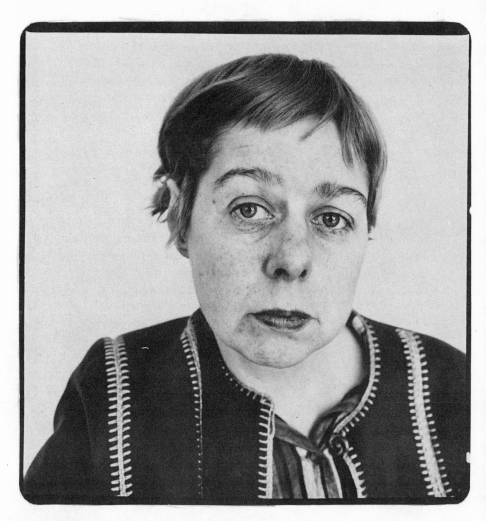

75   Richard Avedon who took this picture in June 1958 says, "This sitting was done with natural light on the porch of Carson's house in Nyack. I remember her saying to me, 'I just want to look like Greta Garbo.' Even though she was in pain, she couldn't have been more giving of herself. She had complete understanding of the complexity and complicity between the sitter and the photographer and the fact that a portrait has nothing to do with the truth."

of thought and writing usually provided the necessary distance to make jealousy or friction unlikely. By the same token, Carson doubtless could not have continued to love or remain passionately attached to her beautiful young Swiss friend, Annemarie Clarac-Schwarzenbach, had the Alps, European culture, and different writing genres of the two women not imposed a basic demarcation. Their intimate relationship had been interrupted, of course, by the Swiss author's death scarcely three years after they met.

Later, in August 1954, a new dimension in affection and art between Carson and still another female writer evolved. She was invited to Roslyn Harbor, Long Island, to meet Gabriela Mistral, the Chilean poet whose "poems of love dedicated to death," said Langston Hughes—who had arranged the meeting—won for her the Nobel Prize for literature in 1945. Even though Miss Mistral did not read English well, she knew of Carson's writings and hoped that they would be translated into Spanish. She herself never wrote in English, but she made an effort to learn the language and haltingly spoke it since it was the tongue of what she called her "newly adopted country." (In 1953, Miss Mistral was made a permanent honorary consul to the United States and lived on Long Island until her death.) Gabriela Mistral felt that she and Carson shared a deep affinity in spite of the generation that separated them. While still a young woman, Miss Mistral had been devastated when the man she loved shot himself. Upon his death, however, the bereaved woman began to express in beautiful, lyric poetry the deep springs within. Through her *Sonetos de la Muerte*, Gabriela Mistral evolved from a quiet, unassuming provincial schoolteacher in rural Chile into a poet known as the "spiritual queen of all Latin America."[55]

Although Miss Mistral was not translated into English until after her death in 1957, Carson had read much about the Chilean poet and knew well her reputation. She also knew intuitively that she would love this now tranquil, older woman who had suffered great anguish and pain, yet had endured and achieved profound artistic and intellectual attainment and recognition for her humanitarian spirit. Carson idealized, too, the thought that she shared with Gabriela Mistral an instinctive maternal love for children. Miss Mistral had never married or had children of her own, but she became known throughout Latin America as Chile's "poet of motherhood." Carson had no comparable honor, but she adored the *idea* of children. Her devotion, however, was directed toward children in the abstract instead of those with skinned knees, peanut butter sandwiches, and other physical needs to be attended to. She was always closely observant of children, but preferred to render them impressionistically— elfin, mischievous, with bold exaggerated strokes of childlike grotesqueness. (A few years later Carson wrote and dedicated a collection of children's verse, *Sweet as a Pickle and Clean as a Pig*, to Emily and Dara Altman, the children of her friend and lawyer, Floria Lasky, and to her agent's son, Tony Lantz.)[56]

Novelist and short story writer Hortense Calisher was surprised once by a question Carson put to her without apparent provocation: "Hortense, did you want yo' chil'drun?" Miss Calisher's answer was strongly affirmative, whereupon Carson responded: "Ah diddun want any. Ah always felt they would innafere with my woik."[57] Although Carson claimed to like children, and wanted them near her, she frequently frightened or alarmed them. If they were in the room she wanted to hold them on her lap or clasp them tightly to her side. Often the children she approached did not know her well, and their responses were frantic looks at their parents as though to say, "Help me—this lady scares me—I don't think I like her." Carson was doubtless aware that she did not naturally attract children any more than she herself had been drawn to adults as a little child. But when a child's rebuff was particularly noticeable, she was reminded afresh of her physical infirmities and resented and hated her strained-looking and sagging facial features, her frail arms and thinning legs, all of which contributed to a somewhat spectral appearance. Yet through it all, Carson retained her own qualities of childhood, sometimes amazingly childish, yet more often simply naive, honest, and childlike.

That day on Long Island Gabriela Mistral saw and liked the childlike quality in Carson McCullers and identified with her deep personal suffering—both psychic and physical—as an adult. She yearned that this great American writer who sat timidly with her in her living room now, who transcended southern regionalism and Americanism and was a spokesman for the lonely and alienated peoples of the world, should also have greater universal recognition. Gabriela Mistral resolved at that moment to do something about it. On August 15, 1954, Carson wrote to Newton Arvin at Smith College to tell him a wonderful secret she wished to share with him: Gabriela Mistral reportedly had written Stockholm to nominate her for a Nobel Prize for literature. The honor was both frightening and overwhelming; there were too many others who were more deserving, she said modestly, thinking of such literary giants as E. M. Forster, Edith Sitwell, and André Malraux. She assured Arvin that it embarrassed her even to think of being the recipient of such a prize when she was certain that her best work had not yet been written. Carson took pleasure in sharing her secret with others, as well, about her day with Gabriela Mistral and the great international honor she might receive. Although they had spoken few words directly to one another, the visiting novelist felt that they empathized in the things that mattered—the sensitive feelings of love, understanding, and compassion. It had never bothered Carson in the past to sit with others for long periods of time saying nothing;

she herself had been comfortable, but she often suspected that her companions were ill at ease, wondering, perhaps, if she were being bored by them. But now the situation was reversed, and Carson hoped desperately that what had been unsaid between her and Miss Mistral was in itself a form of communion. Later, Carson was puzzled about the nomination for the Nobel Prize which Miss Mistral had indicated that she was making, for the Georgia-born novelist never heard officially that she had been a Nobel nominee or runner-up. Recently, however, a Nobel committee confirmed that Gabriela Mistral did not nominate Carson McCullers for a Nobel Prize in literature, nor did anyone else.[58] The illusion, however, sustained Carson, and she never knew otherwise.

Carson had returned to Yaddo a few days after her talk at the Poetry Center that spring. This time she stayed until July 3. The group during the spring and summer of 1954 was not nearly so interesting to Carson as groups had been in the past. There were some twenty guests at the artists' colony this time, but Leon Edel—who became Henry James's official biographer—was the only writer of stature whom she found personally appealing, nor did she develop interesting relationships with any of the other Yaddo guests.[59] The rest of the group consisted simply of faces she saw at the dinner table or occasionally joined in town for drinks. Carson introduced some of her new acquaintances to the more disreputable clubs on Congress Street, including the clubs in the all-black section of town, which they usually found more to their liking than the respectable New Worden. They were careful, of course, to avoid mentioning their itinerary to director Elizabeth Ames, who still kept close watch over her charges.

Most of the Yaddo artists that spring looked upon Carson with sympathy. They felt that she was not there as a working artist, but rather, as Elizabeth Ames's guest who was being helped through a difficult period. This time Carson stayed in Pine Garde, Mrs. Ames's personal residence, an accommodation which Yaddo's executive director rarely extended to anyone. Elizabeth Ames was exceptionally good to Carson that summer and handled her well. She knew that her young friend had been through a difficult period over the interim eight years since she had last been at Yaddo. Extremely debilitated, Carson was trying simply to exist, to learn to cope with herself as a person again, to live with her own poor health, yet to keep on writing and to re-establish herself as a working author. She realized that the fact that she had published a few things in the early 1950s, in addition to having produced a great Broadway success, was no guarantee that she could continue to produce publishable and artistically good literature.

Leon Edel found Carson very interesting that summer for what he referred to as "her curious way" and the strange fantasy life she seemed

The Lonely Hunter

to lead, which was a mixture of the nightmare of *The Ballad of the Sad Café* and the wonder of the little girl in *The Member of the Wedding.*" To Edel,

> Carson had a great deal of warmth, and a picturesque mind—a mind in which its fancies leaped and plunged and offered always the unexpected. She was already in poor health then; and at the end of the day found solace at the cocktail hour: it was a way, apparently, of banishing the nightmares. One never knew whether she talked out of fancy or out of reality. She read us poems newly written that had in them tender feeling and much of the childish wonder that she had kept intact within her; and she could be, in a group, very lively and witty. But also like the little girl she could be attention-demanding, and there was a certain pathos in her pleading look, those large liquid eyes that asked the world for love and in the way of the little girl in *The Member of the Wedding,* found such fanciful logic in the asking. I did not get to know her well, but I remember her making some rude remarks one day and then realizing what she had done, apologizing—this was at a cocktail party—and with a gesture that was, I felt, completely involuntary, dropping a little-girl curtsy in the process. . . . I do remember that her inventions were always startling and often delightful, like some surrealist painting. . . .
>
> I valued knowing her, even so briefly. I saw in her always a parade of the grotesque, the morbid, the joyous and the free, and I suspect it is the merging of these opposites that gives her work its peculiar color and its eerie fascination. One always felt the burden she carried—a kind of sense of doom which she eased with the comedy of her mind and her devotion to her art. She shaped and reshaped her fancies, and her "case"—a little case—is poignant in its accomplishment, in the face of her life-denying demons.[60]

Granville Hicks remembered having seen Carson very briefly in 1954 when he and his wife, Dorothy, went up to Saratoga Springs from Grafton for the weekend. In no way did Carson resemble the puckish girl who had accompanied Newton Arvin, their daughter Stephanie, and themselves to Quebec in 1941. Her body was now but a frail container for what seemed to house little soul. Hicks would not have guessed that she could live more than a few months.[61]

Composer Walter Aschaffenburg recalled, also, that Carson seemed quite ill while at Yaddo this time:

> I did not see her very much as she kept to her room a good deal. As I remember, she wore no make-up, her hair was usually in disarray, and she seemed to favor a cotton dress or housecoat. I do believe she

drooled a good deal and that she was suffering from a speech impediment. . . . I remember, too, that Elizabeth Ames was most solicitous of Mrs. McCullers.[62]

Carson was not as seriously ill as Hicks and Aschaffenburg believed. Although she withered considerably during the next four years, Hicks, especially, was mistaken in his prognosis. Later, in 1958, Carson's psychic and physical health took a significant turn for the better and she lived almost ten years longer. No one referred to her again, as Reeves had, as "indestructible," but she had far more life then—and continued to have —than anyone properly gave her credit for. If there was any truth in the statement that many people made over the years that Carson was her own worst enemy as far as her health was concerned, it was true, also, that she was her own closest strong ally.

When she returned to New York City from Yaddo over the Fourth of July weekend, her mother was still recuperating from her broken hip in a rest home in Nyack. It was with some relief that Carson felt she did not have to join her mother in a restrictive invalid's existence in their South Broadway home. A black servant, Suzie Belle, was employed to come in regularly to keep the house open and clean so that Carson could come to Nyack when she chose, could see her mother, and stay at home as much or as little as she wished. She found it much more exciting, however, to remain in the city as much as possible.

Occasionally Carson stayed in Tennessee Williams' comfortable apartment on East Fifty-eighth Street, which he had sublet from a friend, Buffie Johnson. In and out of town, Williams generously invited friends to stay in the apartment in his absence. Sometimes to his embarrassment, however, he occasionally forgot that he had scheduled two people to occupy it at the same time. One such occasion was the summer of 1954 while Carson was in it. He had earlier promised his good friend British actress Maria Britneva (the Lady Maria St. Just) the apartment for a few weeks; then, when he realized the conflict, he worried about how to get Carson to move out and not be offended. Finally Jordan Massee solved the problem by convincing his cousin that she would be happier at the Gladstone Hotel, where the apartments were "better," and where there were full services, including domestic help and prepared food, which was not the case at Williams' place. Moreover, Audrey Wood would be paying the bill "out of Tennessee's pocket," said Massee, since Miss Britneva had come to America to star in one of Williams' plays. Carson decided that the move at her friend's expense was a great idea. She was even more pleased after she met Marilyn Monroe at the Gladstone, where Miss Monroe, too, was a guest. According to Carson, Miss Monroe had wonderfully admirable attributes and she was delighted to get to know her.

By now, Carson also had developed a close friendship with Hilda and

Robert Marks, whom she had met earlier that year in Charleston. She thought she had discovered in the Markses another we of me relationship. For Carson, the relationship seemed perfect. If Robert Marks were at home, too, she loved being with him; and if only Mrs. Marks were there, that, too, was perfect for she was much taken by her, as well. Robert Marks was fond of Carson during the first five or six years of friendship, but later his admiration waned. "Carson's mind was alert when we first met," he recalled, and he found her quite charming:

> Carson could talk beautifully in the early days. Even though she did not understand deep concepts and abstracts, she was in love with the idea of analyzation—not a psychological analysis—but she was very excited about the implications of words and theories. We could talk about astronomy, the modern philosophy of science, the theory of relativity. It was not so much that she really could talk astronomy, but she was interested in it and could ask the right questions. These were not so much her self-centered days, which came later.
>
> She talked about her writing, yes. She was working then on *The Square Root of Wonderful,* her next play, and she was very much taken by the phrase of the title. It was a nice phrase that she had thought up, but it didn't quite fit. What she really wanted was the nth power of wonderful, not the square root. Carson got hooked up on the music of words and phrases; and with the "square root of wonderful," she just liked the phrase.[63]

Writer Vance Bourjaily found Carson similarly enamored of the title of her play when he found himself seated next to her at a dinner given by novelist Hortense Calisher. By this time the play was in rehearsal and Carson began to tell him about it. "She was quite frail, a wraith almost, though I found her an appealing one. What I recall best is a fragile hand on my arm, and a husky, drifting voice saying that pretty phrase over several times: 'It's called, listen: . . .' [She would pause very briefly and then speak it solemnly as a child would with an important, memorized message] '*The Square Root of Wonderful!* Don't you see? *The Square Root of Wonderful.'* "[64]

Hilda Marks found her relationship with Carson quite different from that of her husband's. Quickly Mrs. Marks became one of Carson's dearest friends:

> We had what I call a girlie-girlie relationship. I used to love to cook, and Carson liked to stay at our apartment and eat my cooking. I kept gourmet magazines, which she would read, and we would pick out things for me to make. Sometimes she went on dreadful diets, however—like once she just wanted to eat tamales, all the time, no

matter what. Her cravings for food were whimish. She really liked
recipes more than she did the food that evolved from them.

Carson and I talked about everything—books, recipes, cooking,
men, sex. It was like we were young teen-agers, the kind of relationship that girls have when they are about fourteen or sixteen. Ours was
a very warm rapport and an unintellectual friendship—unlike hers
with Robert. We were very honest with each other. She was very
curious about sex, as though she were naive, yet Robert and I knew
that she wasn't. She also was very open about her exploits, including
her bisexuality. We used to get into long discussions about her attempts—and ability—to seduce people. All except Arnold Saint
Subber. She really thought she was in love with Saint and talked
about how much she wanted to marry him. It even reached the New
York gossip columns once, but I really think that Saint was petrified
of Carson sexually. She used to scheme about how she might get him
to marry her.[65]

Occasionally when friends stopped in at the Gladstone to see Carson
during her temporary stay there, they saw Arnold Saint Subber coming
out, "looking as though he were pursued," said Massee. "Carson is so
beautiful—she overwhelms me. I have to go home to rest," he told Massee
one day.

According to Hilda Marks:

Carson's motto was "Anything a man can do, I can do better." She
had no secrets, but there again, you never knew how much she was
fantasizing and what was the real thing. Of course, to her, it all was
real. Soon after Carson first came to stay with us—as she did often
for the rest of her life—Robert went to Spain for the summer. She
used to beg me to leave Robert and go to Nyack and live with her;
yet at other times she simply wanted to be a part of our marriage
and thought that the three of us could live happily together forever
after. She used to wear Robert's pajamas when he was gone and
play the man of the house. She didn't act very infirm then. Later,
Robert saw Carson as a threat and was jealous of her, but I never
gave in to Carson or took her game seriously. You know, it really was
a game, and I indulged her.[66]

When Robert Marks returned from Spain the summer of 1954, he
resented finding Carson comfortably ensconced in his home. Later, he began to find the "threesome" relationship a strain:

If Carson did not get sufficient attention from me, she would ask
terribly embarrassing questions. More and more our conversations
became strained—not really conversations at all. We would sit in *my*

living room in the later years, with Carson leaning on her cane, non-communicative, head bowed, her responses nonexistent or in mono-syllables. I would be increasingly uncomfortable, a stranger in my own house. Then Hilda would come into the room, and Carson was transformed as though into a new person. She was alive, animated, and appeared to worship Hilda. When my wife was not around, I wanted to tell Carson to snap out of her self-indulgent egotism and think of someone else for a change, but I didn't. Carson could look at me, though, as if she knew exactly what I was thinking. It was a bit eerie. Her looks would sometimes tell me to drop dead.[67]

Fortunately for Marks, producer Arnold Saint Subber came into Carson's life at this time. Saint Subber, too, had been staying at the Gladstone at the time Carson was there. (The Gladstone was not far from the Marks's apartment on Madison Avenue, and Carson came and went frequently.) She had met Saint Subber soon after publicity began about her new play, *The Square Root of Wonderful*. On April 8, 1955, the New York *Times* announced that Carson was working diligently on three different projects: the dramatization of her novella, *The Ballad of the Sad Café*—begun in Charlotte, North Carolina, under the impetus of Robert Walden's encouragement the preceding spring; an unidentified original drama, the rough draft of which had been finished the preceding October (*The Square Root of Wonderful*, which she admitted later having worked on at Yaddo that summer); and third, her novel *Clock Without Hands*. Although Saint Subber did not become intimately involved at this time in working with Carson on *The Square Root of Wonderful*, they did begin now to see each other socially.

Robert and Hilda Marks rented a car every summer so that they could escape the heat of the city, and in 1955 they drove frequently to Nyack and began to see even more of Carson. Just as Carson had called dozens of other friends over the years and awakened them late at night to ask about a triviality that might best have remained unsaid, or could have waited until morning, so, too, did she begin to insist on an almost twenty-four-hour relationship with Hilda Marks. Although Robert Marks said later that he would have appreciated it if his wife had not gone up to Nyack almost every weekend over the next twelve years, she went often, joined frequently by her husband. Each time Mrs. Marks took soup or some delicacy which she knew would be especially pleasing to Carson or her mother.

In the fall of 1954, Marguerite Smith had returned home to 131 South Broadway after recuperating from her broken hip in a nursing home in Nyack, but she was left alone frequently while Carson spent days, and sometimes weeks, at a time in New York City. A black housekeeper, Ida Reeder, had been hired to stay during the day, but Marguerite usually had no one in the house with her at night. Her daughter Rita came home many nights to be with her mother when Carson was not there, but it was tiring for her to try to commute daily from her job at *Mademoiselle*. Although Rita Smith did not complain, many people who knew the situation wondered how she could avoid bearing some resentment or antipathy toward her sister for what seemed to be Carson's careless abandonment of their mother.

During the winter and spring of 1955, while she was still spending much time in the city, Carson began to see more of Tennessee Williams. To her friends now, she presented the image of a strong, buoyant young widow, crippled physically, but suffering none of the psychically impairing qualities that had been so much a part of her psychological make-up in the past. A few days before Easter, Williams invited her to accompany him to Key West. It would have to be a working trip, he cautioned, for he was rushing to meet a deadline for the publication of *Cat on a Hot Tin Roof*, which he was revising extensively from the Broadway version. Carson accepted, announcing that she would work on the projects to which she had already given publicity. They agreed, however, that if there was time they would play for a few days in Havana. Hemingway was there, and they wanted to meet him.

The week-long trip to Key West was another highlight in Carson's relationship with the famous playwright. This time, Frank Merlo, Williams' companion, joined them. Carson was fond of Merlo and they got along well. In the mornings both she and Williams worked, but in the afternoons the three of them swam, drank, and socialized, beginning at two o'clock, the hour which the playwright felt had been designed by the devil alone. "Nothing could come from the hours of 2:00 to 5:00 P.M. except boredom, evil, swimming, and then, alcoholic conviviality," said Williams. To Carson, the week was almost as idyllic as their stay on Nantucket.

Françoise Sagan came to Key West that spring to visit Tennessee Williams and to meet Carson, whose works she much admired. Miss Sagan's novel *Bonjour Tristesse*, published in 1954, had leaped to the top of the American best-seller list, as it had in France, and its young author was something of a celebrity in the United States. The women appeared to become fond of each other, said Williams. Miss Sagan liked to swim, go deep-sea fishing, and drive the playwright's car at high speeds, and the three of them spent many recreational hours together. Later, Williams wrote for *Harper's Bazaar* of his week in Key West and his meeting and impressions of Miss Sagan. He said that he and Carson liked her very much. He felt that Miss Sagan had great promise as a writer: "Perhaps she doesn't have, now, at this moment in her development, the alarming, deeply disturbing, visionary quality of her literary idol, Raymond Radiguet, who died so young after a little great work, nor has she yet written anything comparable to Carson McCullers' *Ballad of the Sad Café*, but I have a feeling that if I had met Mme. Colette at twenty I would have noticed about her the same cool detachment and warm sensibility that I observed in the gold-freckled eyes of Mlle. Sagan."[68]

It had been almost nine years since Carson and Williams had first met at Nantucket, and although their love had flowered instantly, the relationship they shared now, seasoned by the years of joy and heartache between them, was more meaningful than ever before. At the end of the week, accompanied by Merlo, they flew to Havana. Hemingway, however, failed to answer Williams' telegram that they were coming to Cuba and would like to see him—a slight that Williams laid to Mary Hemingway, who he thought was obsessed by a spirit of overprotectiveness of her husband. Nevertheless, the visitors from Key West were offended and found little about the island that pleased them except Havana's atmospheric bars. The trip to Cuba was brief and disappointing for them. With Tennessee Williams, as with Carson, the anticipation had been more pleasurable than the real thing.

There was a prime facet of real life, however, that had sustained Carson over the years far more than she dared acknowledge to anyone: her mother. Other loves and nourishments had come and gone, but her mother was always there. The sudden death of Marguerite Smith on June 10, 1955, only a few weeks after Carson's return from Key West, had more painful ramifications for the artist—her life and work—than anything else that had previously touched her. With the death of her mother, Carson lost the prop and impetus for creativity on which she had depended since infancy.

In spite of her good intentions to work on the various manuscripts she had taken with her to Key West, in actuality Carson had accomplished little. Upon her return North, she continued to spend as much time as possible in the city. Once again she made the apartment of Hilda and Robert Marks her home base, but this time she became increasingly involved in a working relationship, as well as a social one, with producer Arnold Saint Subber. She went home infrequently to see her mother. It was enough to know that her mother was there when she needed her.

Ida Reeder took good care of Marguerite. Kind and gentle with her mistress, she was relentlessly insistent that Marguerite take her medicine, cut down on her sherry, and do the other things her doctor deemed consistent with good health. Ida was especially valuable to the household in establishing some semblance of a routine, serving regular meals, and encouraging Marguerite to eat. Friends who had known Marguerite in the South during the early years, and then saw her in Nyack in the 1950s, were appalled by her emaciated condition. Bleeding ulcers and a bad heart had hastened her failing health, but Marguerite also suffered from malnutrition and had even been hospitalized for it.

It was seldom that Carson's mother took to her bed, but on the morning of June 10, she told Ida that she was "feeling poorly" and would not try to get up at all that day. Several hours later, her good friend from Columbus, Helen Swift, called from the city to say that she was nearby and wanted to come to see her. Ida at first told Mrs. Swift that her patient was too ill to see or talk with anyone, but when Marguerite learned that it was her "good friend from home" calling, she insisted on talking from the bedside phone. "Oh, Helen, please come anyway," Marguerite said, her voice barely audible. "It would do me so much good just to see you now." When Helen Swift arrived at the house by taxi less than an hour later, she was met, not by Ida, but a young police officer. The premonition Mrs. Swift experienced en route seemed confirmed now by an ambulance parked at the curb. "I am sorry, but you can't see Mrs. Smith just now," said the officer gently, stepping outside to speak quietly to Helen Swift. "She died about ten minutes ago."[69]

Later, Carson, her sister, Rita, and Lamar heard the full story as Ida reconstructed it. Their mother had called the housekeeper into the room a few moments after Mrs. Swift's telephone call and told her that she felt strange and that she thought she was dying. Terrified, Ida reportedly called everyone she could think of who might help in an emergency: the police, the doctor, the hospital, an ambulance, and the home of Hilda and Robert Marks, where she knew that Sister could be reached. Carson, however, was at Saint Subber's apartment, working with him as had been her habit for several weeks, on the revisions and new drafts of the play. Ida's first message to Hilda Marks was that Carson's mother had just had some kind of terrible attack and could Carson please be contacted. A few moments later Ida called back to say that Marguerite was dead. A policeman had arrived first from among the emergency crew summoned, and he was with her when she died. Frightened, Ida had hovered in and out of the room available to help if need be, but anxious to greet the various emergency vehicles as they arrived.

It was Jordan Massee who broke the news to Carson of her mother's death, and then Rita and Lamar were notified. Carson's sister was in the hospital at the time recuperating from an appendectomy. Even though Rita was desperate to leave her hospital bed and rush to the funeral home, she was in no condition to be dismissed. Outwardly far more distraught than Carson, Rita was frantic as she thought of her mother lying in the mortuary alone with no daughter or son to stand vigil. The next several days were spent in stunned shock by those closest to Marguerite Smith. To Carson, Reeves's death had been impersonal and remote, for with Reeves, the psychic tie had already been severed. But the bond between her and her mother had remained intact regardless of hurtful stress in times past, and Carson was almost devastated now by her sudden loss. Her sister was unable to leave the hospital immediately, and her brother had not yet arrived, but Carson could not bear the thought of returning "alone"—even with friends—to Nyack to cope in person with funeral arrangements. To accept the reality that her mother had ceased to be was a role she could not play. To her, after death there was nothing, and she did not want to see or think of her mother as a cipher. Carson's fear resembled that of the little boy's in her fiction, "The Haunted Boy," who did not want to go upstairs to the bathroom to know for certain at that moment whether or not his mother was lying on the floor dead.

Carson pleaded many excuses to keep from returning to Nyack at once. She and Hilda Marks could plan the whole funeral from the Marks's apartment, she rationalized. She had arranged for Reeves's funeral without actually being there, and she could do the same now, she pleaded. They would select the Psalms which were her mother's favorites, plan the service, choose the music, ask an Episcopalian minister to officiate, do all of the necessary mechanical chores—but she recoiled from all suggestions and urgings by the Markses and others that she return to the house in Nyack or go to the mortuary herself. Instead, Rita checked out of the hospital before she was supposed to and went immediately to the funeral home and then to Oak Hill Cemetery in Nyack to select the grave site.

Carson's physical response to her mother's death was similar to her mother's actions upon the death of Lamar Smith, Sr., eleven years earlier. Marguerite had refused to return to the family homestead on Starke Avenue after her husband died, and Carson and her mother's sister had attended to the necessary details. Nor did Marguerite go back into her home in Columbus, but moved North with her daughters instead. In time, of course, Carson did return to the house in Nyack, but she had much emotional duress to overcome before she could move into the downstairs bedroom that had always been her mother's and feel comfortable in the house that now was *completely* hers—in spite of the fact that she had legally owned it for several years.

The day before the funeral—after her brother arrived from Cherry Lake, Florida, Carson was persuaded to return home.[70] The service and burial were remembered vividly by Hilda and Robert Marks, Hilda for her role in helping plan the arrangements, and Robert for his physical bearing of the burden:

> Carson had wanted to have quite a few honorary pallbearers, and the list had been chiefly drawn up by her. Since she had been working closely with Saint Subber on *The Square Root of Wonderful*, there were Saint, Tennessee Williams, of course, and Jordan Massee, Paul Bigelow, Floria Lasky's husband, David Altman, myself, and several others. There also was to be a host of regular pallbearers. There was no problem at the service in the funeral home, which was very nice, but not everyone went to the cemetery, and it was there where

the sheep were separated from the pallbearers. Rita had selected a
beautiful site high on the side of a mountain, from which there was
a lovely view of the Hudson. But there were no access roads up
which we could drive. As we were all assembled at the foot of the
mountain—both the regular and honorary pallbearers—the *real* pallbearers discovered that they had bad backs, and among the
honoraries, only Floria Lasky's husband and I admitted to good backs
at all. Of course it took seeing the mountainside and imagining the
long trudge uphill before the other gentlemen became completely
incapacitated. We finally were forced to wait until "ringers" could be
brought in from other funerals to assist us.

How I loved Bebe, but if ever there was a labor of love, it was
that one. My God, that casket was heavy—Altman and I were carrying most of it—but during our ascent, there was a kind of rapport
between the casket and me, the transcended Bebe and me as
we moved to the top. And the service truly was beautiful. It was at
sunset, with the top of the mountain reflected in the Hudson, and a
nice Episcopalian minister to read the service. The poetry in the
Psalms that Carson and Hilda had picked out made a good deal of
sense. Carson was totally nonreligious, but she had a poetic feeling of
something omniscient. It was not that she believed in the existence
of a real God, though.[71]

Hortense Calisher, who had known Carson and her mother for many
years, drove Carson to the cemetery, where she was joined by Saint Subber. Rita was dressed in black and Carson in white. Saint Subber, too,
arrived dressed in white. As they walked up the hill—Carson and Saint
Subber arm in arm—some onlookers thought that they looked like a
wedding pair, a likeness which Carson, too, remarked on later. About her
mother, Carson reportedly said after the funeral: "Now I'll always know
where she is."

A convivial postburial "wake" was staged the night of the funeral at
131 South Broadway, with the guests drinking many times to Marguerite,
whom they felt would remain the underlying spirit of life in the old home
no matter who came and went in the future. They believed that Marguerite, too, would have approved, for no one loved a good party more
than their beloved master showman whom they had buried that day.

Upon the reading of the will a day or so later, however, there was
less cause for conviviality. Marguerite Smith's last will and testament had
been drawn up on September 30, 1949, and it was at a time when she
believed that none of her children had money to spare. Lamar and Rita
Smith had good jobs, were able-bodied, and were reasonably expected always to have some means of earning an income. Carson, on the other
hand, had been exceedingly ill, gave every indication of needing medical

treatment and someone to care for her physically for the rest of her life, had a psychically dependent husband, and as yet had not made her fortune—which was to come during the next two years with the production of *The Member of the Wedding* on Broadway and the sale of its screen rights. In an effort to be fair to all of her children in her will— knowing that she had shown partiality to her oldest child in actuality during her lifetime—Marguerite had bequeathed her house, furniture, and the rest of the estate (except for jewelry and silverware, which the daughters alone were to share) to her three children to be divided equally. If her son should predecease her, his wife, Virginia, was to have his portion. The house, however, had later been purchased by Carson from her mother, and now a major portion of the intended bequest was no longer a part of the estate.

According to Carson's friends who preferred to be identified only as "onlookers," perhaps the most serious dissension that ever arose among the three children after their mother's death stemmed from Rita and Lamar's alleged feelings that their more affluent sister—who was in a better position financially in 1955 than they—should be willing to take less of the estate than her assigned portion, particularly since Carson now owned the house outright and had expended relatively little in the care of her mother compared to the efforts of her brother and sister. Carson was ever a businesswoman, however, and even though she did not understand the mechanics of things, she understood principles and saw no reason now to relinquish anything that was rightfully hers. According to "onlookers," there were heated words before Carson threatened to have her brother and sister physically evicted from *her* premises if they did not quietly leave on their own.

Soon after the funeral Lamar Smith returned South, destined to see very little of his sister Carson over the remaining years of her life. Rita Smith returned to her apartment in Greenwich Village, and in time the breach healed and life became sweet for the three of them again in their relationship as a family. But Carson realized now that she would have to make her way the rest of her life with far greater reliance upon inner resources and shrewd ingenuities than she had ever been forced to call up before. She would always need people—and she would have them—but at age thirty-eight she began to emerge from the fragile chrysalis that had protected her for so long and to become a kind of "iron butterfly."

Chapter Thirteen

THE LAST YEARS:
DISSOLUTION AND REGENERATION

*I*t was largely as the iron butterfly that Carson experienced the most intensely consuming involvement of her life. At the same time she encountered also her only significant brush with professional failure. Just as
friends at Marguerite Smith's funeral had wryly observed that Carson and
Arnold Saint Subber dramatically conveyed the impression of being bride
and groom, so, too, did Saint Subber himself conceive of his relationship
with Carson as a connubial state: "My life with her was, for three years,
to the exclusion of absolutely everything else, a kind of marriage. I have
never been so scarred—scarred beautifully, and also maimed—as I was
then."[1] Officially, their alliance continued as that of producer and writer
of her ill-fated play *The Square Root of Wonderful*, which opened on
Broadway October 30, 1957, some three years after their liaison began.
Many persons close to the play's source thought it should never have
opened. Most of the critics concurred.

The night before the romantic tragi-comedy began its three-day pre-
Broadway engagement in Princeton, New Jersey, Carson sat in her room
in the Princeton Inn and reviewed the play's troubled history. Exceedingly apprehensive, she realized that the very life of her creative offspring
was hanging precariously in the balance. Yet her foreboding spirit had not
anticipated how completely her play would be altered at the hands of the
many script doctors who worked over it before its move to the National
Theatre on Broadway. Carson revealed some of her pangs and the play's
evolvement for an article published in the Philadelphia *Inquirer* several
days later, when the drama began its two-week run in Philadelphia. Hopefully, there the rest of the kinks of the production could be worked out.[2]

For the interview, Carson looked back that night with nostalgia and
recalled the day in 1954 when Saint Subber telephoned her from New
York and asked if he could come to Nyack to see her, having heard of
what she termed the "seedling version" of the play she had first drafted
in 1952. She was not particularly cordial to the producer at the time, for
she had been immersed in other work and had let her play lie fallow for

many months. Upon his insistence, she showed it to him with diffidence, knowing that it was not good. When he read the play, Saint Subber agreed, but told Carson that he believed it could be a great play if she would rewrite it. She acknowledged then only that she would think about it. In the night, her thoughts were lured to the fantasy world of Mollie and Phillip Lovejoy, and in a moment of illumination the entire opening scene came to her. When Saint Subber returned to Nyack the next day, she greeted him enthusiastically and said that she was ready to resume work on *The Square Root of Wonderful* if he would work with her. The fascinating yet enervating personal rapport that followed aptly supported what Carson had espoused earlier in her poem "The Dual Angel"—the thesis that man's nature derived from a consummation of God and Lucifer. To Carson, her "saint" had seemed, over their long road together, both archangel and Satan, mirroring identical facets of her own ambivalent nature. He was charming, enthusiastic, and bright, yet his charisma both attracted and repelled her. He also was full of love, affection, and dedication to Carson as a writer, working indefatigably to extract the play and to effect its transition from playwright to stage.

From the beginning of their association—and more intensely after her mother's death—until the disastrous closing of the play when they parted as "bad friends," according to Saint Subber, the two of them worked, quarreled, cursed, ate, and loved voraciously, their tempers and passions flaying one another in enormous measure, only to be followed by a volley of affectionate and gentle gestures. "In a sense, I almost lived in Nyack with Carson, commuting seven days a week," he explained. "Of the eight hours I was in my apartment in the city, usually four of them were spent on the telephone with her, sharing little details we had forgotten to say only minutes earlier before parting."

Indeed, Carson was fascinated by Saint Subber. "It was an odd infatuation," recalled Robert Marks, for Saint Subber was very pleased with himself and his life style as a bachelor. "But Carson thought that she had converted him. She would say, 'I'm in love with Saint, and he's in love with me. We're going to be married.' She would sit with his picture on her lap and hold it like an ikon before her."[3]

It seemed to Saint Subber that during their three years together they scarcely withdrew from each other for a minute's privacy:

> To know Carson well, as a friend, was an occupation that took 100 per cent of your time. Even going to the bathroom was something you shared with her, as you did every intimate detail. You shared not only what was on your mind, but also what you were thinking, all your fantasies. Carson lived 100 per cent on so many different levels. And the fantasy world and friends were as important to her as

the real ones. She was as considerate of her fantasy friends, and as vicious or voracious with them, as she was with her real ones.

Saint Subber maintained that there was no one, dead or alive, closer to him than Carson:

Although dissimilar, we also were desperately alike. We were born on the same day, were the same age, were the same everything.[4] Yet we battled such as no two people had before. Maybe that's what kept her alive—as it did me—for it was a terribly depressing period in both of our lives. I also was forever comparing myself and being compared to Reeves. There was not one trick I didn't use, or that Carson didn't use, to make a point. I know as many twists and turns of hers as anyone, yet I dare say there were that many more in re-serve. There is nothing I could say about her that someone else could not contradict and also be true. Carson was the most innocent angel in the entire world and also the reddest, most bitchy devil. She was the most sweet-mouthed person in the entire world, yet no sailor could curse as she did, and no degenerate descend to her low level. No two people ever gulped life as we did, ever ate as much as we did together, smoked as much, cursed as much, believed in God as much, read the Bible as much as we did together. She was a contradiction and an absolute perversion of beauty, yet she was beautiful. She clung to life and believed only in one thing: life. She always said that death meant only one billion zillion dead people who never re-turn.

There is no person, dead or alive, in my walk through life—and I have walked through many famous people—who has come any-where near her. When people say, "I knew Carson McCullers," and they don't dare say it to me—not even people like Rex Reed—I say nobody *knew* Carson McCullers. You have to live with her for three years on the level I did even to say you were acquainted with her. And I believe I was better acquainted with her than almost anyone. You use the word *facet*. That was Carson's word. You could take a diamond and put it into the sunlight, and it would reveal a billion facets. That's Carson. Does one ever take her under his wing? Was she the wounded sparrow? Horse manure! My wing is very strong, but it's nothing compared to Carson's. She was a powerhouse. There was nobody stronger in the world. She was enormous. She staggered the imagination. She was the iron butterfly. Yet, Carson was both the giver and receiver. One could not tolerate it if she were just a taker. She enriched my life, beautifully enriched it. *The Square Root of Wonderful* was not only my biggest failure, but also my greatest suc-cess.[5]

On the eve of its opening October 10 at the McCarter Theatre in Princeton, Carson acknowledged that perhaps the chief difficulty as far as she was concerned was in handling tragedy and comedy "almost simultaneously." She wrote in her article: "If there is a funny scene or love scene in the face of sickness or ruin, it is offensive unless it is handled with the proper emotional progression."[6]

For others connected with the play, the troubles sprang from an assortment of causes. Anne Baxter, who played the lead, Mollie Lovejoy, loved the script, but it seemed to her that no one else—except Carson—understood it. The play also suffered from what Miss Baxter called Carson's "inability to rewrite."[7] To her, the story of the production of *The Square Root of Wonderful* was "a very sad one":

> When I accepted the script, I was in London for a movie. Robbie Lantz had sent me the script, and after reading ten pages I cabled him "yes" in great excitement for I was mad about Mollie and the play. It had everything—love, tragedy, bitterness, humor. It also seemed to be just the vehicle to get me back on Broadway. I felt like women do before childbirth. It was all very terrifying. I didn't know any of the people directly connected with the play, but José Quintero was to direct it and he was then extremely well known because he had just done *Long Day's Journey Into Night*. And, of course, Carson was a goddess of mine and I happen still to be one of her greatest fans. I believe she wrote in the script of one of her characters being skinless. She herself was skinless. It was very hard on her as a human being, but it made her the brilliant writer she was, for she was able to receive direct impressions from other human beings—even to the point of destroying herself.
>
> When I arrived in New York just before the play went into rehearsal, I went from the airport directly to the Drake Hotel, where I met Carson, Saint Subber, Quintero, Robbie Lantz, and several others connected with the play. Carson's sister was there, and Tennessee Williams. Why Tennessee was there I don't know, but he had some peculiar connection with her, both jealous and loving. They had just read the first act and were all in tears when I walked in. They were a very strange and unique group of people. Carson herself was a hysteric paralytic, you know. Her arm did not work and it was slowly atrophying. She was a very sick woman. I should have said "no" to the play right then, but what I didn't know was that she couldn't rewrite. For this reason there were many different versions of the play. In rehearsal, as the problems of the play mounted, Saint Subber would dig in her trunk, as he called it, for another version, and then they would fiddle around and try to insert something that she had written earlier.[8]

Albert Marre, Carson's first director for the play—who preceded Quintero—disagrees with Anne Baxter that Carson could not rewrite:

> That's not quite fair to Carson. She could rewrite, but she was not able to do the kind of square, so-called theatrical craftsman writing they tried to require of her; instead, she would go off on tangents of her own which actually were much more engaging and amusing. I thought that that was the way the play really ought to have been done. Her versions were much more comedic than what was finally produced.[9]

Marre, thirty-one, was a brilliant director with an M.A. degree from Harvard and a number of successful plays that he directed to his credit, including *Kismet* and *Saint Joan*. In the early summer of 1956, *The Chalk Garden*, which he directed, having closed in March, Marre was asked by Saint Subber to direct "a play that Carson McCullers was still writing." What followed was a close association between playwright and director, with Marre working with Carson through six different scripts. Several of the earlier scripts Carson called *Who Has Seen the Wind?* Early in 1956 she rewrote one of them as a short story, changed the plot somewhat, and sent it to *Mademoiselle*, where it was published under that title the following September.[10]

In spite of Saint Subber's recollection of his consuming relationship with Carson, according to Marre, "The degree of Saint's involvement with her lessened dramatically after they had a director; although Saint did work off and on, sporadically, it was not on the constant basis that I did for a whole season, from the summer of 1956 until the next. We'd all meet, of course, when we had a new revision ready. We never got a script to Carson's satisfaction, I might add." Marre knew, too, that she was attempting a play "which, in a weird way, was ahead of its time":

> The versions I have are glowing and fun, but they also are black comedy. She was doing the play in a grotesque kind of way. I remember I wanted to have Carol Channing play the part of Mollie Lovejoy, rather than someone like Anne Baxter, who is a very square lady, although a wonderfully fine actress. Carson and I had once talked with Miss Channing about the role.[11]

Marre had no intention of leaving *The Square Root of Wonderful*, but he was in California during the summer of 1957 doing a play he himself owned, Anouilh's *Time Remembered*, when Saint Subber announced that Carson's script was ready. "To me, it was not, but Saint didn't want to wait, and he had already booked the theatres," said Marre. "Also, *Time Remembered* had to go into production first—everything was ready —and I couldn't leave. I really hated to give up Carson's play, but they wouldn't wait for me and I had to bow out. Carson was a wonderful person to work with, and I liked her enormously. She always behaved impeccably with me. I found her amenable, charming, and complicated, with a genuine grace and a large, keen sense of humor."[12]

Marre remembered her broad humor on one occasion, especially, when she felt she had put something over on Saint Subber. It was in 1956 in the Doctors Hospital, where she retreated at the insistence of her producer. Saint Subber said she needed a long rest and a change of environment before beginning the intensive work with her new director. Carson reluctantly agreed, but wanted it clearly understood that she was not going in as a patient for what might be misconstrued as an alcoholic cure (Doctors Hospital was where Reeves had gone for occasional drying-out periods), but only for a rest. Moreover, she insisted that she intended to take a drink in the hospital whenever she wished. "Of course," Saint Subber assured her, and off she went with childlike faith that all would be well. A few days later, Marre visited Carson in the hospital:

> There she was, sitting up in bed with a tumbler full of bourbon. In spite of the talk that had always abounded about Carson and her drinking during most of her lifetime, I knew that she was doing relatively little of it then. She wouldn't start drinking until five or six in the evening, and she wouldn't drink at all during the day. Of course, she could polish off a whole bottle of sherry in the evening, but she was no kind of alcoholic. It was early in the day when I saw Carson, and I said to her: "What in the hell is that?"
>
> "Oh, it's a riot," she said. "The people here think I'm some sort of wild drinker, and so they bring me a drink at nine in the morning, and then again at two and at six—and I'm getting absolutely stoned, sipping like this. But if you dare tell Saint Subber, I'll kill you." She was mad at Saint Subber for arranging the whole thing, and she was going to get even. It amused her that her "rest" was at his expense.[13]

Although Carson was fond of Albert Marre and affectionately applied the epithet "my black swan" to him, she was unhappy that he saw fit to leave the play. According to John Leggett, her New York editor with Houghton Mifflin for *The Square Root of Wonderful* who met her at about this time:

> She was furious about the first director who had just quit. What angered her most was not his misconstruing her play, though she thought he was guilty of that, but that she had given him a rug in the peak of earlier enthusiasms. She kept pointing at the bare place on the floor where it had lain, and saying he refused to return the rug since it was a gift.[14]

People close to Carson, however, said that it was not Marre to whom she had given the small, oriental rug, but José Quintero, Marre's successor. Marre, too, said that he received no such gift from Carson.[15]

The play suffered from a series of directors and theatrical craftsmen before the Broadway launching. Quintero did not come into the play until late summer, and very quickly Carson transferred her affections from Marre to him. She was fascinated by his personality, his handsome Latin features and accent, his dark, brooding eyes, his quiet though sometimes volatile manner. She fantasized, also, that they were "twin brother and sister." Quintero, too, loved Carson, but he began to drink rather heavily —according to observers—after the play went into rehearsal. He seemed to consume more and more as rehearsals progressed and problems encountered in the production mounted, and to assume less and less responsibility for the play's success. Those close to the play who knew the situation well, however, felt that his drinking was simply his way of coping with seeing Carson's beloved creation crumble while being unable to do anything about it. Recalling the devastation of the Princeton opening, Anne Baxter said:

> Quintero knew that the play was sliding down the drain, but he was powerless to save it. He could not rewrite, and he knew that Carson couldn't either. He couldn't cope with what was wrong. He simply ran away. I remember throwing my arms around him in Princeton that afternoon, crying to him: "Jose, Jose, none of them understand about a man and a woman," and I wept. But he didn't understand either.[16]

Yet Carson forgave Quintero for his abandonment of the play with a more generous heart than she had reacted to Marre's departure. Many years later Quintero professed a great and enduring love for the playwright and appreciated the fact that she was sympathetic and understanding of his dilemma at the time.[17]

Carson and Quintero remained on good terms, although they seldom saw each other after he left the play. In 1959, according to a New York Times article, Quintero entered into negotiations to purchase the screen rights of The Heart Is a Lonely Hunter, having decided to branch out into movie productions as well, but the plans eventually were dropped and Carson sold them, instead, to Thomas Ryan.

One day while she and Quintero were having lunch together in a New York restaurant, they saw Carlotta O'Neill, the famed playwright's last wife. Quintero, who had directed Long Day's Journey Into Night earlier and The Iceman Cometh, was now the only one allowed to direct O'Neill's works. Since the O'Neill plays had catapulted him into fame, he and Mrs. O'Neill shared a warm rapport. Approaching the table, Mrs. O'Neill spoke graciously to Quintero, was introduced to Carson, then departed. As soon as she could get to a telephone, however, she called the director away from his lunch. "May I please come back to your table and join you?" she asked. "I would like so much to know Carson McCullers better."

Carson was flattered and pleased to sit at the elbow of one who had been married to her childhood writing idol (to whom she had even sent one of her early manuscripts), and she encouraged Mrs. O'Neill to talk about her late husband. One anecdote the woman told, however, curdled Carson's meal. Mrs. O'Neill told of a night they had been in Boston together when he had come home alone in a snowstorm very late and very drunk. He rang the doorbell and then pounded upon the door, but could get no response from his wife; yet she had been watching his assault from a window. Finally he moved away from the door, struggled a few feet through the deep snow, then collapsed and lay still. Mrs. O'Neill looked on while the snowflakes swirled down upon him. When he was completely buried, she went out into the snow and dragged his nearly frozen body into the house.

Made almost ill by the horrendous tale, Carson hurried to her cousin's apartment to tell him the story. "I don't think I ever want to see that woman again, Boots," she declared to Jordan Massee with finality. To be sure, the infliction of cruelty, humiliation, and injustice to others, or being cheated or lied to—all made Carson react with indignation, sadness, irritation, or anger more easily than anything else in her human relationships.

The afternoon that Quintero left the play in Princeton, Carson went onstage to address the crestfallen cast: "I have never directed a play, and I have never seen anyone direct a play, but I wrote this play, and I know what the characters are and what I want them to be. You can go home if you want, but if you'd like to stay, I'll take over and do the best I can."[18]

No one left. "We want you," they assured her. "We'll stay." According to Miss Baxter:

> The child, Carson's play, was dying, and she knew it. It was pathetic. She loved the child, but there was no one who knew what was really wrong with it. Nor did Carson have the emotional, mental, or physical strength to take over herself. Joseph L. Mankiewicz took charge and began rewriting the script until George Keathley could arrive, a director secured through Tennessee Williams. But neither of them knew how to fix it either. They somehow didn't put the things back in that shouldn't have been taken out in the first place. I can't blame Saint

either. You see, the play is about love and its opposite. The square
root of wonderful is love, and the square root of evil is the murder
of the heart, humiliation—or what the young kids call now the
"complete put-down." It was a very delicate play, a cobweb. There
were lovely things that happened, such as lovely things lighting up because of love, literally lighting up because of Mollie's childlike imagination. The whole world lit up—which was also one of the problems.
With due respect for Jo Mielziner—who is a fine designer—but
as one of the reviewers said, it looked as if somebody was about
to come in with a brace of rabbits. Also, the set was too real. It
should have been impressionistic, as light as a feather, like a fine,
strong, elegant fishbone. But instead, it turned out to be veal
knuckles. For anyone to try to rewrite Carson was like replacing fish-
bones with veal knuckles.

Princeton was bad enough with its reviews, but Philadelphia
was excoriating. Carson realized she was facing disaster, and it was
like watching a child die of lobar pneumonia with no sulfa. Saint
was doing *Dark at the Top of the Stairs* at the same time and rushing back and forth to New York, and Jo was trying desperately to
glue everything together. There was a point before we opened on
Broadway when I could have left the show—and should have. It
would have been better for Carson, better for the play, better for
me. But I thought I would be running out on the others. Years later
I talked to Phil Abbott, who played the role of the young architect
who loved Mollie. He told me that everyone was praying that I
would leave, but, of course, I thought if I did, I would be letting
them down. I should learn to live by my instincts. When they started
to kill the child, patching it up piecemeal, I should have believed my
inner voice. Yet if I could do the play again as Carson conceived it, I
would. I'll never forget the line in which Mollie is sitting all alone
on the stage and she says, "It's so awful when you're an adult and
you don't have adult companionship," tears streaming down her
face.[19]

While the play was in Philadelphia, theatre readers in New York
City heard rumblings of the difficulties. On October 23, the New York
Times carried a tidy paragraph:

To have everything as perfect as possible for next Wednesday night's
première at the National, a new third act went into *The Square
Root of Wonderful* last night in Philadelphia. Since the Carson
McCullers play, starring Anne Baxter, started its pre-Broadway trip

October 10 in Princeton, alterations also have been made in the
first and second acts. The new director is George Keathley, who was
called in when Jose Quintero resigned.

The play opened in New York on Halloween Eve, and reviewers treated
it as a disastrous *Walpurgisnacht*. Of the seven New York dailies, only
Frank Aston of the *World-Telegram and Sun* gave it a nod. The headline
declared that the play was "like magic," but Aston's text complimented it
only as a "sturdy entertainment."

Glenway Wescott, who was not well acquainted with Carson personally but had known her primarily through the National Institute of Arts
and Letters, was much interested in the play and had attended several rehearsals and an out-of-town preview. "I was deeply concerned," he said
later, "that it was not going well despite certain moving scenes and excellent acting." After attending the New York première, Wescott wrote
Carson a six-page letter of criticism offering concrete suggestions, a letter
which he said later was doubtless "fatuous."[20] Even though some of his
ideas were implemented, the production by then was not salvable.

Wescott was only one of several who offered suggestions to her in
writing over the years concerning *The Square Root of Wonderful*.
Knowing that much about the theatre was beyond her ken, Carson usually took such criticism appreciatively. As early as November 25, 1955, she
wrote a grateful letter to playwright John van Druten, thanking him for
being such an inspired artist. She said that she had read carefully his notes
on *The Square Root of Wonderful* and that they were sound and beautiful. He had pointed out ways to heighten the poetry and drama of the
play, and she promised to work toward them. She still had not digested
them thoroughly, she said, for it would take several days, as well as nights
to work them over in her sleep. Carson urged him to come visit her in
Nyack, where he would find books, music, and a garden. But he replied
that he must seclude himself in "Purdah" for a while longer. Carson
grieved when Van Druten died in December 1957, a few days after her
play closed. Although they never became well acquainted personally, they
knew and admired each other's works and shared a profound affinity.

Robert Lantz, who gave up his literary agency in 1957 to go into producing, coproducing with Saint Subber *The Square Root of Wonderful*
as an executive of Figaro, Inc., was quoted two years later (after a second
failure) regarding the need for more revision of most Broadway plays
when they go into production: "I feel that if I had had *The Square Root
of Wonderful* to work on from the beginning—which I didn't—it would
have been a much better play. I came in on that too late, and it taught
me a lesson."[21]

The play taught Carson a lesson, too, so much so that she never wanted to do anything again for the stage. Tennessee Williams had once told her: "It takes a tough old bird to work in the theatre." Much concerned for his friend's well-being, Williams had stayed with Carson during many difficult moments, smoothing her feathers as best he could from the time the play went into rehearsal until after its demise and she could find other interests. Carson said in her Philadelphia *Inquirer* article that the "picayune last-minute changes" were "irritating but important" because every weakness was magnified on the stage. She wrote that she had learned through her long experience in writing books that one works "out of abundance and strength," and that deadlines are a terrible hindrance: "But in the theatre, deadlines are necessary and often the abundance and strength flickers, but the author works on." Once *The Square Root of Wonderful* opened, however, Carson could cope no longer. Whereas her health had been relatively good during the two years after her mother's death and before the opening of the play—Marre recalled that throughout his long association with her she moved well and never used a cane, with only her arm apparently giving her any trouble—she now appeared to be completely spent. As Anne Baxter recalled,

> The play had gone too far on the wrong road, and I myself didn't have the self-confidence to really help either, except to play Mollie as I believed Carson wanted her. I felt in awe of all those so-called geniuses around me. Oh, that play taught me a lot. There had been enormous advance sales because of Carson's name—and some because of mine—and we had to play what was no longer her play for eight dreadful weeks. We had theatre parties, and they came and went out like the tide. I don't remember the two lines now, but I remember that after one, I'd get them back, and then with the other one I would lose them again. It was a terrible thing. Carson realized that her play had been destroyed, and I remember her saying that it would never be published that way. I don't know how much money the backers lost—I was the only really expensive actor—but we had some $180,000, which in those days was an enormous amount for a straight play that was a one-set show.[22]

Working later with John Leggett to get the play ready for publication by Houghton Mifflin, Carson was deeply resentful of the rewrites that had been made in the acting version without her permission. "She was angry then," said Leggett. "In working with her over the Houghton Mifflin edition, I made some proposals and she nodded, saying 'Yes, that's fine. Put it in like that.' When I protested that these were *my* words, that I didn't presume to write the play for her, she said ruefully, 'Why not, Jack? Everybody else has.'"[23]

Leggett remembered how ill Carson looked the week of the play's Broadway première:

> I saw her in a stunning dress she was being fitted for, made of that heavy Indian silk that has a homespun look. She was trying very hard to be gay and attractive when I took her out to dinner, but she was far too sick to be able. The night of the opening she was a wraith, green-white in color and so thin and tiny she seemed made of sticks.

Upon publication in July 1958, *The Square Root of Wonderful* was accompanied by a carefully worded personal preface by its author:

> I have learned this in my work in the theatre: the author must work alone until the intentions of his play are fulfilled—until the play is as finished as the author can make it. Once a play is in rehearsal a playwright must write under unaccustomed pressure, and alas, what he has in mind is often compromised. This may be due to the actors, the producer, the director—the whole prism of the theatrical production.
> And so begins a transmutation that sometimes to the author's dismay ends in the play being almost unrecognizable to the creator.
> That is why of the five or six evolutions this play went through I prefer to publish the one which follows. It is the last one I wrote before the production was set in motion and is the most nearly the truth of what I want to say in *The Square Root of Wonderful*.[24]

More than a curtain dropped when the play died on December 7, 1957, after forty-five performances on Broadway. Its playwright had also tried to work out in fantasy her ambivalent feelings regarding her deceased husband and mother; but unlike *The Member of the Wedding*, which had given Carson the psychic release she craved as well as great critical and popular success, *The Square Root of Wonderful* had failed and become its opposite—"the square root of humiliation."[25] The iron butterfly had been buffeted by strong winds, her fragile wings bent, the butterfly dust smudged. She fluttered desolately now, with no honeysuckle in sight.

For solace Carson turned to those she had most relied upon in the past: Hilda and Robert Marks, Jordan Massee, her sister, Rita, and a number of others she had been close to over the years. After the death of her mother Carson was too busy to grieve deeply, she explained, caught up as she was in work on *The Square Root of Wonderful*. But now that the play had failed, she found herself weeping uncontrollably, often going into shattering hysterical laughter. She seemed to need people around her now more than ever, yet even with friends there were long spells of glowering silence. Her fantasy world salved her little, for she had reached an impasse in her creativity and could no longer work out her inner life in fiction. Increasingly despondent, unable to write, she questioned if there were any reason to live. More and more Carson revealed her vulnerability. British photographer Sir Cecil Beaton not only caught that vulnerability in a picture a few months earlier, but aptly described her in words, as well:

> Today, Carson McCullers' appearance has been softened by the dignity of suffering. She is no longer a ragamuffin with lank hair, but a woman of moving spiritual stature. Her air is still remote, intensely shy, and strange. Defensively, she will offer you a smile which is more like a frightening leer. Her eyes are like those of some wild forest creature—a lynx or an ocelot. The somewhat puffy cheeks and vulnerable mouth and chin complete the impression of a sick wildcat caught in a parlor.[26]

To others, she seemed an oyster without a shell, skinless, in a sense— as Anne Baxter had perceived—or as the writer herself expressed it through Frankie in *The Member of the Wedding*, "I feel just exactly like somebody has peeled all the skin off me."

Those who knew Carson well loved her and saw her frequently during this period; they also worried increasingly about her psychic health and tried to divert her in every imaginable way. Her friends sent her funny cards and notes of love, then came to call bearing small gifts—a cigarette lighter, book, nightgown, or a new recipe or "food toys," as Hilda Marks referred to the tiny gift dishes with which she surprised Carson. The ailing writer whose fictional specialty for over twenty years had been loneliness, isolation, and estrangement was cheered and temporarily forgot her unhappy predicament when a friend arrived with a recipe for some unusual or exotic dish. Not so much interested in *reading* about its preparation as *hearing*, she would demand an imaginatively detailed description: "Tell me about it—describe it to me—how do you serve it?" According to Massee, "Even during Carson's sickest spells when she didn't care to eat anything, she never stopped loving hearing people talk about food. She couldn't boil an egg, but she knew how everything was cooked. If she learned that a dish was prepared with chopped almonds or a seldom-used condiment, she would make a mental note of it for a discussion with Ida."[27]

Most of Carson's guests thought Ida Reeder a competent cook who did all she could to stimulate her appetite, whether it was with an old-fashioned southern dish or a complicated continental recipe. Occasionally a friend came in on Ida's day off with plans and ingredients for a festive meal and urged Carson to join him in the kitchen if she felt up to it. One such concerned and good-natured culinary artist was Dr. Ernst Hammerschlag, a psychiatrist Carson had met a few years earlier through Natalia Danesi Murray. "We were ambitious cooks," said Hammerschlag, who recalled preparing with Carson a particularly intriguing lamb and vegetable dish which they playfully called "Racatouille à la McErnst." "We enjoyed it very much," he added.[28] Getting her into a particularly gay mood one evening, Hammerschlag, an amateur photographer as well, took several delightfully natural pictures of Carson in color which were among the best that anyone took during the last ten years of her life.

Carson's hair was red in these pictures, or as one visitor described it, "pale orange." An old friend of Carson's who was a house guest for several days in mid-August 1958 painted a less flattering verbal picture of Carson and the aura surrounding her as he saw her then. His journal entry for August 10, 1958, read in part:

> The rambling old white house on South Broadway is the same as I have remembered it during past visits—the dining room crowded with a big marble-topped table, the living room with its anonymous, late Victorian furniture, and, across the entrance hall, Carson's bedroom with its incredible disorder of medicines, tranquilizers, sleep masks, lights, ash tray overflowing with scarcely smoked cigarette butts. Carson herself is virtually untouched by time, neither more or less ruined than when I was here a year ago. She's had her hair cut shorter and dyed a pale orange. She smokes endlessly and steadily sips a tumbler of *vin rouge*. She is still pale, partly paralyzed, and so incredibly thin that she reminds one of prisoners of Dachau: pipestem legs, skeletal arms, the fingers of the paralyzed left hand clutched coldly together like a dead bird's claw. And she *would* wear shorts, like a Hindu holy man deliberately exposing all the defiant misery of his body. Evenings for dinner she affects frilly, pink nylon, nearly transparent negligees.[29]

Edward Newhouse, fellow writer and friend over the years from early Yaddo days, recalled a similar picture of Carson and her whim for skimpy and unusual garments at this time:

> One day she called and said, "Eddie, I am permitted by the doctor to leave the house now. Will you take me for a walk?" It was summertime, and when I arrived, I found her dressed in what seemed to be a homemade bikini made from three large handkerchiefs tied in knots. Here she was with her poor shrunken leg, no muscles or flesh over her body, carrying her walking stick, and announcing: "I wish to go to the five and dime." She looked like an apparition. We went

—and children in the neighborhood followed us. With Carson, it was impossible to blend in with the landscape. The walk was considerable, but fortunately she got very tired and we returned home before reaching the dime store.[30]

A successful and happy diversion in which Carson's guests engaged was the telling of flavorful small-town stories or humorous anecdotes about people she knew. She always enjoyed a hearty laugh, often to the point of hysteria, and it would be several moments before she could speak again. Carson liked jokes, but never off-color ones. According to Massee,

> She was too high-minded for low jokes and too childlike for sophisticated ones. One had to be careful around her, in fact, not to be too sophisticated in one's humor. If he were, she would fail to see the point and take it seriously. There were whole areas of things humorous to many people that Carson didn't think funny at all. Black humor, for instance, she had no appreciation of, even though some of her own humor was close to it. A "cruelty joke," such as "Apart from that, Mrs. Lincoln, how did you like the performance?" she would not have cared for either.[31]

Leo Lerman, who saw her during this period, found her wit excessive as always, but a wit that could be turned on one very suddenly. To Lerman, her humor was "a kind of deadpan wit that was very sharp tongued. Sensitive people found it troublemaking."[32]

Lerman had always thought Carson vain, too, but to him, it seemed that her real egocentricity came with her sickness. "She could be destructive. You sometimes could see sheer meanness inside coming through. Yet there was always something likable about Carson, and I felt sorry for her," he added. Just as Lillian Hellman acknowledged earlier, so, too, said Lerman: "You had to like burdens to *love* Carson, and many of us could not afford her emotionally or economically. We had our own needs."

It was during this despondent period in Carson's life that through Robert Marks she met Thomas Ryan, a reporter for *Collier's* magazine. When Ryan learned that Carson was a close friend of Hilda Marks, he spoke of his great admiration for Carson's works. Quickly Mrs. Marks arranged a small dinner party in her apartment, hoping that Carson's spirits would be lifted by a new devotee. Ryan, twenty-three, had no idea then that he would go into the filmmaking industry as an associate of Otto Preminger with the independent Landau Company four years later and be able to buy the screen rights of *The Heart Is a Lonely Hunter*. Soon he would be writing, directing, and producing his own interpretation of the novel as a motion picture. Ryan's memory of Carson at their first meeting was vivid:

> She was dressed very simply—a plain black dress, if memory serves. She wore absolutely no make-up, and in fact, gave the impression that to her, her body was just an envelope she used to carry her mind around in. Her hair, extremely fine, like a young child's, and gleamingly clean, was cut as you can see it in all her later photographs: as if it were done at home with an inverted bowl.
>
> My first impression of her was that she resembled a wounded deer, or a frightened bird. This was not due to her physical condition as much as to something in her attitude. She sat well back in her chair, as though removing herself as far as possible from harm's way. Her play *The Square Root of Wonderful* had just been done in New York and had failed. She seemed, at the beginning of the evening, whether due to this or some other reason I cannot say, to feel herself slightly passé, and was deeply grateful that someone as young as I knew her work and loved it. . . . But as she talked, particularly of writing—her own and others—she seemed almost to grow. I suppose some people might think Carson was egotistical. I didn't. She talked a great deal about herself, of course, and was not the least bit shy about making it clear that she had a very high regard for her work. Yet when she spoke of her work, it was as though she were talking about someone else's. I must add that she had, in my opinion, an excellent critical sense.[33]

Nor did Ryan forget a remark by his new friend that evening involving two of her contemporaries in the world of letters: "I have *more* to say than Hemingway, and God knows, I say it *better* than Faulkner." In retrospect, however, Ryan felt it important to note that both men were alive and working at the time: "Carson was not trying to pre-empt the judgment of history; rather, she was merely making a comparison between her own work and that of the two most widely regarded competitors in her own field."[34]

As fond of Ryan as he was of her, respectful of his considerable talents, and immensely pleased by his attentions, Carson saw the young writer occasionally later in her home in Nyack. Ryan recalled that one day he and Hilda Marks drove up to have lunch with her but that she had forgotten they were coming: "Ida had to make do with canned chili and pineapple and cottage cheese salad. Carson could be quite scatter-brained about things which did not relate to her work." Later, he realized that the period then was one of great depression and introspection for the frail artist, and he was no more able to minister to her psychic needs than were most of the others who yearned to help.

According to Hilda Marks, "Everyone was on the lookout for an analyst for Carson. We wanted to find someone in Nyack, if possible, who always would be accessible."[35] Finally, Carson's friend Hammerschlag came forward with the name of a doctor he had located who might be the very one to help. Her name was Mary Mercer, and she was a specialist in child psychiatry with a private practice in Nyack. Recalling the situation, Hammerschlag commented:

Although I was not quite officially Carson's doctor, she showed always great confidence in me and my advice. I had switched from internal medicine to psychiatry and analysis, and as her many complaints were often of a psychosomatic, somatic and psychological nature I was able to assist her in many quite critical situations. I remember that she was once hospitalized because of an assumed cardiac condition and I was able to convey to her the psychological roots of this incident. I was, too, the one who established contact between her and Dr. Mercer, for I was now convinced that she needed more organized psychiatric help and inquired about a psychotherapist in or near Nyack and so found Dr. Mercer.[36]

A Connecticut native, Mary Mercer had graduated from Simmons College in Boston, received her M.D. from the University of Colorado, interned in pediatrics in New York Hospital, had been a commonwealth fellow in psychiatry at Payne Whitney Clinic at the time Carson herself had been a patient there in 1948, and had been in private practice in Nyack since 1953. A brilliant doctor with outstanding professional credentials, Dr. Mercer was also a handsome, charming, and gracious lady. Five years Carson's senior, she had married at age forty Dr. Ray E. Trussell, an epidemiologist and assistant dean of the College of Physicians and Surgeons at Columbia University. They had no children, although he had three by a previous marriage. Dr. Mercer and her husband lived in an impressive-looking modern house overlooking the Hudson River Palisades a mile or two south of 131 South Broadway. However, she had never heard of Carson McCullers.

Ernst Hammerschlag told Dr. Mercer about Carson and arranged for their first meeting. He also recommended that she begin reading the novelist's works so that she might learn as much as possible about her patient before attempting treatment. According to Hammerschlag, "Carson told me that for a while after the start of therapy she was doubtful about Dr. Mercer's ability to help her as she did not know her work. It turned out, however, that it was not even so important to know her work—to know her was good enough to learn to understand her." Later, Carson admitted to Dame Edith Sitwell that at first she had been terrified at the thought of therapy, but that her doubts soon vanished once she and her doctor began to see each other regularly. Whereas formerly she had sat in her living room for weeks staring out of the window like a resigned Elizabeth Barrett before her future husband came into view, she told Dame Edith that through Mary Mercer she had again found "livingness"—a word Carson recently had coined, that she would also use in *Clock Without Hands* to describe the search of her dying druggist, Malone.[37]

According to Thomas Ryan, who was one of the first of Carson's friends to meet Mary Mercer, "Carson said to me in Dr. Mercer's presence, 'She saved me. She saved my life.' Dr. Mercer pooh-poohed this idea, saying that Carson had never been in that much trouble, that all she needed was a little straightening out, and that whatever the treatment had consisted of, it was certainly not psychoanalysis, but more in the line of guidance."[38] Dr. Mercer reportedly dismissed Carson after their third therapeutic hour, telling her that she did not need psychotherapy. Ironically, however, such assurance was devastating to the patient, who felt that the cord which had so newly connected her in a relationship of enormous love and nurture was now being severed (she had telephoned many friends during her first visits with her psychiatrist and announced candidly: "I'm in love"). Although she had tried to say good-by to Dr. Mercer in a state of outward calm, Carson was grievously anguished. Climbing heavily a flight of stairs upon her departure from Dr. Mercer's office in the basement of her home, she walked into an icy winter's wind and stepped forlornly into a waiting taxi. Almost immediately she was overcome by excruciating pain, suffering from what seemed to be a severe cardiac failure. Rushed to the hospital, she was placed in an oxygen tent for several days, her condition termed serious. During the examination and treatment which followed, cardiologists and other specialists completely reassessed her physical condition. Their findings were that Carson had suffered since childhood from chronic rheumatic heart disease and that her strokes were the result of emboli from her damaged heart rather than a congenital anomalogy of the cerebral blood vessels, as had been diagnosed earlier. A number of Carson's friends, however, knowing the great personal attachment she had formed for her doctor, believed her heart attack to have been precipitated in part, at least, by her sudden sense of fear and loss.

Dr. Mercer had no intention of abandoning Carson. Fond of her, she had not meant to abort the total relationship—only the formal alliance of patient-psychiatrist. Quickly reassured, Carson found Dr. Mercer at her hospital bedside daily, overseeing her treatment and arranging examinations by the best specialists in the New York area. What Carson considered one of the miraculous by-products of the whole agonizing experience was the discovery that surgery could help her damaged arm and leg.

A series of four operations by Dr. F. Randolph Bailey of Columbia-Presbyterian Hospital were then scheduled, with two of them to be performed within the year. First Carson's left elbow was successfully operated on so that she could lower the arm to her waist and let it drop almost to her side. Then Dr. Bailey worked on the left wrist so that the stiffened hand could have some degree of mobility. Later, Carson described the process to friends as "nicking the tendons" of her arm and wrist, which, in turn, relieved the spasms that had caused her joints to atrophy.

The following year Carson wrote to Dame Edith Sitwell an enthusiastic letter about her new physical and mental health. She was so elated upon receiving a letter from Dame Edith that she said she had mentally hugged her, thrown her above her head, caught her and kissed her, then kissed her once more. After the next two operations she would be able to engage in such play literally as well, she vowed. Whereas Dame Edith wrote that she had found salvation through the church, Carson replied that her salvation had come through the wonderful doctor who had healed her maimed soul. She had finished her analysis, Carson announced, and she and Dr. Mercer were very close friends. Having been made physically well, she told Dame Edith that she now spent hour after hour with Mary Mercer, and that through her she had been able to approach truth and God again and to realize at last a spiritual radiance that she feared she had lost forever. In April 1959, Carson had written Dame Edith that she was writing again and had completed half of her novel; now, in September, she said that she was almost through with Chapter Ten (which meant that she had four more to go).[39] Several years later Carson told a reporter that writing was a great deal more to her than a mere profession. She said that it was not only how she earned her living, but also how she earned her soul.[40]

Not only did Carson feel warmly embraced by Dr. Mercer, she told her friends, but by Ray Trussell, Dr. Mercer's husband, as well. In a letter to Dame Edith, she said that Trussell deserved his wife's love, and that Dr. Mercer truly loved him. Carson said that she loved him, too. Dame Edith could well imagine the difference between the way Carson used to act—lying in bed and sitting diffidently in a chair—and now, communing and doing things with a family she loved, who had "adopted" her, she told her British friend. One evening Carson called Jordan Massee in an effervescent mood of accomplishment: "We have been building a brick wall, Boots." According to her cousin,

> Carson had been helping Trussell lay the bricks, apply the mortar, scrape, and whatever else was involved. She spoke of it as "our wall." Of course, she probably only laid two or three bricks, but that didn't take anything away from her feeling that she was also a brick mason now and that they had had a special "connection"—as she

called it—together. The Trussells were her new we of me, and just as she had welcomed triangles before, her love for Mary embraced Trussell as well.[41]

Ray Trussell, too, spoke warmly of Carson:

Carson, indeed, became very much a member of the family and loved to be included in everything that was being done. . . . I am a "do-it-yourself" man and I'm always building or painting. During the time that Carson was around, I was either putting up stone walls or laying a brick terrace, and she, indeed, might put down a few patches of mortar as a form of participation in which she drew great glee. More often, we cast her in the role of supervisor and let her sit in a chair with a drink and observe and comment; she was too frail to take any active part in any construction.

She also wrote a good deal of her last book in our living room. Her ability to concentrate was fantastic. One could walk into the living room and find her staring at the one page she had punched out with one finger during the day and she would never know you had walked through.

Carson was a very gracious and warm person who loved her friends dearly. Some of them misunderstood the reason for her drinking as much as she seemed to at times. She was not really an alcoholic; she was in continuous pain and sometimes drank in an effort to get some sleep. That problem pretty well disappeared with the reconstructive surgery which she should have had years before.[42]

In the same autumnal letter to Dr. Sitwell in which Carson had spoken of Trussell, she announced that if Mohammed would not come to her, the mountain would have to go to Mohammed. She longed to take the Trussells to Europe, she said, so that they could meet Dame Edith and love her as she did. Carson's threesome, however, as often was the case in her fictional triangles, was destined to be short-lived. Mary Mercer and Ray Trussell were divorced in 1961, and Trussell remarried that same year. Regardless of talk to the contrary, those who knew Carson and Dr. Mercer well felt that the novelist had little to do with the breakup of a marriage that doubtless had already begun to disintegrate before she came into the picture.[43]

Before Carson's surgery—during 1958 and 1959, as well as intermittently for the rest of her life—she often was in excruciating pain; yet she complained little and managed to get about in the city during the next four or five years with relatively good mobility. She walked with a cane to the car, could climb a few steps—in fact, managed a whole flight during her frequent visits to the Markses' Madison Avenue brownstone—and went into New York City every few weeks. Occasionally she saw Cyrilly

Abels, managing editor of *Mademoiselle*, whom she had known since 1943 when Miss Abels was with *Harper's Bazaar* and had published *The Ballad of the Sad Café*. Carson would meet Miss Abels for drinks or dinner, along with Miss Abel's husband, Jerome Weinstein. "She had spells of calling frequently," recalled Miss Abels, "but one night after I'd telephoned her in Nyack I was brought up short when I detected in her voice a slight quaver. 'What's the matter, Carson?' I asked, and I can still hear her voice":

> "Oh, Cyrilly, I am in such pain I can hardly talk, and it never stops," said Carson. She regained control almost instantly, but it was the only time in our long friendship that I ever heard her talk about pain. It was only then that I realized how truly gallant she was, and how amazing her iron will.[44]

Another infrequent time when Carson spoke of her pain was when she asked her friend writer Dorothy Salisbury Davis if she believed in God. When Miss Davis replied that she did not, Carson said, "I don't either, or I could say, 'God, take this pain away,' and if he did exist, I think he would do it."[45]

It was at about this time while Carson was still getting about the city with some mobility, although obviously in frail health and frequently in pain, that Paul Bowles last talked to her. He ran into her in a New York bar, sitting with Cyrilly Abels, Sir Osbert Sitwell, Tennessee Williams, Gore Vidal, and Carson's sister, Rita. Bowles had not seen Carson in almost eight years, and he was surprised to find her in such a debilitated state, particularly in contrast to the days in the early 1940s when he had known her at 7 Middagh Street in Brooklyn Heights. Even now, he could not help seeing her as "the essentially childlike woman she had been all her life." Yet it seemed to Bowles that with "this exaggerated simplicity went a total devotion to writing and subjugation to it of all other facets of her existence. This undeviating seriousness did not give her the air of an adult, but rather that of a prodigious and slightly abnormal child who refused to go out and play because she was busy writing in her notebook."[46]

In 1958, little by little, Carson regained her interest in writing. One of the first things she wrote after meeting Dr. Mary Mercer was a manuscript she entitled "The Flowering Dream." Several versions of it are extant, although Carson reportedly destroyed others. She told Thomas Ryan that this particular manuscript dealt rather exclusively with a portion of her life following the failure of *The Square Root of Wonderful* and before she had resumed serious work on her novel. According to Ryan, "From other things Carson said, I had the feeling that the manuscript dealt with what she considered to be painful but very successful psychotherapy."

On one occasion she said to Ryan that she was unhappy with it as a piece of writing; another day, she told him: "I felt it was too personal, so I fed it to the flames."[47]

One "Flowering Dream" manuscript that survived was dated August 23, 1958. This piece, revised and shortened, was published a year later in the December issue of *Esquire* with the subtitle "Notes on Writing."[48] Although autobiographical to some extent, the published piece was more a descriptive analysis of her creative process and a carefully controlled comment upon her childhood and the southern milieu out of which she evolved as an artist than it was a deeply personal statement of her inner life. Those who knew Carson well recognized that "The Flowering Dream" reflected the newly acquired confidence, radiance, and strength which the author happily attributed to her healer and spiritual mentor, Mary Mercer.

In the spring of 1958, after the therapy had successfully begun, Carson felt such renewal of body and spirit that she agreed to read some of her poetry and excerpts from her novels for an MGM recording. Jean Stein vanden Heuvel, who had interviewed Faulkner in France and New York City for George Plimpton's *Writers at Work: Paris Review Interviews*, hoped now to arrange recordings with Carson and Faulkner, both of whom she thought would have great appeal for a listening audience. Picking her frail author up one brisk spring morning at Jordan Massee's West End apartment where she frequently spent the night, Mrs. vanden Heuvel took Carson to the Manhattan MGM studio for a long recording session. "Working with Miss McCullers was a very moving experience," recalled Mrs. vanden Heuvel:

> She seemed tormented by the ordeal ahead, and I almost wished that I hadn't suggested the project to her. During the reading I felt that she could hardly bear to communicate with her unknown audience.
>
> Later on I spent hours and hours splicing the tapes, eliminating her long pauses . . . even pulling syllables together. Looking back now, I think that it was dishonest to distort the way in which she expressed herself. But there remains untouched one shattering moment in which Miss McCullers broke down sobbing as she read the part of Frankie in a passage from *The Member of the Wedding*: "I know that the bride and my brother are the 'we' of me. So I'm going with them, and joining with the wedding. This coming Sunday when my brother and the bride leave this town, I'm going with the two of them to Winter Hill. And after that to whatever place that they will ever go. I love the two of them so much and we belong to be together. I love the two of them so much because they are the *we* of me."[49]

Upon release, the album was reviewed by Thomas Lask of the New York *Times* on May 4, 1958, with Carson's record as one of four in the album. MGM was offering not only readings from Carson and Faulkner's works, but from Joseph Conrad's (read by Sir Ralph Richardson), and Jonathan Swift's (read by Sir Alec Guinness), as well. Lask found much to cherish in the collection, but conceded that the problems involved in making selections from larger works "have not been entirely overcome." Of Carson's record, he wrote:

> Mrs. McCullers' recording stands apart from the others, for it is not so much an introduction to her work as it is to the lady herself. Her occasional waywardness with the text, her emotional involvement in what she is reading, the break of her voice in certain passages—all these give this recording its own special quality, though it is not always a literary one. Mrs. McCullers reads from *The Member of the Wedding, The Heart Is a Lonely Hunter, The Ballad of the Sad Café*, and three of her poems. The poetry was a good idea since it is a side of her art not so well known.[50]

Actually, Carson was disquieted by the recording session, for she had forgotten to take copies of the poems to the studio with her. Instead, she did not *read* them, but presented them from memory. Returning to her cousin's apartment later, she said with much concern: "Boots, I forgot my poems, and I realize now that I left out two lines. What shall we do?" Knowing that the studio work had been difficult for her and reluctant to think of Carson's being subjected to it again, Massee suggested that they look at the poem together and see what had been omitted. He explained to Carson that the tape could easily be spliced and the lines inserted, but assured her that the poem made sense without them. Pleased and relieved, she agreed, adding that she thought it even better now without the omitted lines. (The record, unavailable now except through rare book dealers, soon became a collector's item.)

Another of Carson's ventures into the public's eye came that summer in the form of a television appearance. On August 19, she met before the cameras with N. Richard Nash, playwright, and Robert Seaver, of the Union Theological Seminary, on the program "Lamp Unto My Feet" to consider the place of drama in the religious and spiritual life of America. When the conversation turned to *The Member of the Wedding*, Carson volunteered an anecdote involving Ethel Waters which she thought appropriate to their discussion. She said that Miss Waters declined the role of Berenice when she was approached for the part on the grounds that there was no mention of God in the play and that it used foul language. When it was offered her again, she reconsidered, for the producer Robert Whitehead insisted that the play did have spiritual meaning. He agreed,

however, that if there were objectionable lines she could work that problem out with the director. He also assured her that the play would be a
great success at the box office and that she would be making a mistake if
she did not accept the role. Miss Waters was not convinced of the play's
spiritual qualities until she saw the profound impact it had upon its audiences, said Carson.

An unidentified reviewer of the program in Carson's hometown
newspaper registered his surprise that one whose speech habits were so
halting could be as expressive in writing as Carson was. His conclusion
was that "Mrs. McCullers still has the same difficulty talking she always
had—probably because of her innate shyness."[51] Although Carson had always spoken haltingly, her voice low, consonants softened, and final *g's*
sometimes dropped—even as a child she had been inarticulate, and *now*,
when she called someone on the telephone there was never any doubt as
to who was on the other end for there was always a great pause—she
could, nevertheless, express what she wished, whether vocally or in writing.
Yet anytime she articulated about *The Member of the Wedding*, she
was fraught with emotion. The birth of both the novel and the play had
been a painful and laborious process, layered by desolation and unhappy
memories almost too extreme to render in any form. Perhaps its chief
value to Carson lay in the reconciliation that took place between herself
and her past, and her beloved Mary Tucker. It was her financial salvation,
also, a fact Carson did not take lightly. Moreover, its continued success
touched her in a way that no other creative work of hers had. Seven years
had passed since the play closed on Broadway, yet it was still being staged
enthusiastically in theatres across the country. In 1970, it was revived
in Chicago with Ethel Waters in her original starring role. The play also
had crossed the ocean and premièred in London at the Royal Court
Theatre in February 1957.

The playwright was generally pleased by the British reviews and the
enthusiasm of London's audiences. For the British production, Geraldine
McEwan played Frankie; Bertice Reading, Berenice; and John Hall, John
Henry, who prompted reviewer J. C. Trewin of the *Illustrated London
Times* to say that young Hall had outstarred them all. Even though
Trewin suggested that in comparison to the novel, Carson's play lacked
solidity, that it was "too much the impression of the book," he still ranked
The Member of the Wedding, along with Arthur Miller's *The Crucible*,
as "the most considerable work the English Stage Company had done
during its up-and-down progress at the Royal Court."[52]

Almost two years after the London opening, in December 1958, the
play—translated into French—went onstage in Paris at the Alliance Française on the Boulevard Raspail, this time with far less success than its
British production. The adaptation was made by two of Carson's friends

from the publishing and theatrical world in Paris, Andrè Bay and William Hope. Although the French play ran only a month, it was, said Bay, a "success from the literary critics' view, but a financial disaster for its backers."[53] According to Bay, the producer had neglected to tell Hope that he could not keep the theatre after the first of January; thus the play closed prematurely, there being no available house to which it might move. Hope and Bay had secured Carson's approval to adapt her novel while she was still in Paris in 1953, but later she said that she did not like the French version and preferred that it not be produced. Finally persuaded by her New York advisers to grant permission, she reportedly was "not at all happy" with the production's untimely demise. Critics acknowledged that the uniquely southern flavor of Frankie's and Berenice's diction and syntax was difficult to translate into French, and in the process the play lost much of its poetic quality and nuance. "My rapport with Carson was spoiled after the play closed," added Bay, "but I always loved her and am still a great admirer of her works."

Another woman exceedingly important to Carson during the last decade of her life was a strikingly beautiful and charming young French woman who moved into 131 South Broadway in January 1959 and lived there for a year. The arrangement came about quite by accident. Carson had been awakened in the middle of the night by fire sirens screaming up to Graycourt, the large frame apartment building next door where she and her mother and sister had lived when they first moved to Nyack. Carson's bedroom windows on the north faced Graycourt, and looking out now, she watched with fear and horror as most of the twenty-nine tenants rushed pell-mell from the ancient house in their night clothes, their arms laden with precious possessions scooped from dresser top and drawers as they fled for their lives. Anxiously she scanned their faces until she saw her friend Marielle Bancou standing barefoot in the snow, dressed only in a red sweater and blue jeans. Snowflakes sifted down upon the disheveled group in the bitter cold of the early predawn hours while, vainly, the various families sought to account for each other. Throwing on a coat, Carson hurried outside to greet the distraught evacués and invite them into her own home. Soon, however, the firemen ordered the evacuation of 131 South Broadway as well, for there was danger of the flames spreading. By now, the three families who rented Carson's apartments were also on the street.

Never before had Carson been so close to alarm, fear, and the personal tragedy of others, but just as she had responded with composure and resolute action when her home in Georgia caught fire and she and her family were temporarily homeless, so, too, did she move among her neighbors now—most of whom she did not know—calming and allaying their fears. Three elderly women were missing, who, they discovered later, had perished in the blaze. That night Graycourt burned to the ground while hysterical tenants cried, cursed, and watched their life's belongings go up in flames. With the help of Miss Bancou, Carson supervised the making of pallets, coffee, and sandwiches for the homeless and assisted with their telephone arrangements to go elsewhere. Many evacués stayed at Carson's house through the night, as did Miss Bancou; nor did she leave the next day. Instead, she was urged to stay on as long as she wished.

They had already become good friends, having seen much of each other over the past two years. Marielle Bancou had taught French literature at Douglass College of Rutgers University before moving into Graycourt in 1953, but now she was an artist and fabric designer and had her own flourishing business in New York City. When she had first come to Nyack, she met Carson's mother, who showed her one of her own apartments, but Miss Bancou chose Graycourt. Marguerite Smith spoke glowingly of her famous daughter who was still in Paris, but the young French woman, like Mary Mercer, had never heard of Carson McCullers. In 1956, however, they met on a bus en route to the city, and a warm, easy rapport ensued. At work on *The Square Root of Wonderful* then, Carson talked at length about the characters in her play and their fantasy lives, especially Phillip Lovejoy, the young writer-husband who had married Mollie twice, failed as a novelist after his first successful venture, and now, a weak husband and father as well, committed suicide as the only positive act open to him. To Miss Bancou, Carson seemed almost obsessive at the time in her interest in death and how people died. Hearing more about the plot of her play, the artist related to Carson a favorite legend of which she was reminded—the story of Cleobis and Biton, sons of Cydippe, priestess of Hera at Argos: "According to legend," said Miss Bancou, "the priestess was supposed to ride to the temple each year during the festival in a chariot drawn by oxen. But one year the team was not at hand, and the boys told their mother not to worry, that they would drag the chariot themselves. After their mission was accomplished, the boys fell into a deep sleep, whereupon Cydippe prayed to Hera that her sons might be repaid for their courageous act of filial piety by some special boon. Hera responded with 'Thank the gods for you, and may the best be yours.' Her boon was to make both sons die a swift and painless death in their sleep." Intrigued by the Greek myth, Carson told her friend: "You French have such culture. I'm going to use this story in my play." Worried that she might not have rendered the tale accurately, Miss Bancou went to the Nyack Library to research it further. Upon her return, she told the playwright that she had erred; but waving aside the explanation, Carson interrupted: "Don't be so checky, darling." It was then that Miss Bancou began to realize something of how a writer utilizes her facts: "Her interpretation was more poetic than the legend."[54]

Similarly, Edward Newhouse was frequently reminded of Carson's disdain of fact. Several years earlier when Carson's mother was ill and Carson wanted to divert her, she called Newhouse on the phone and said, after a great pause: "Eddie, I would like for you to come over in your uniform." This was long after the war, said Newhouse, and he neither knew nor wished to know where, if anywhere, he had stored his uniform. But Carson would not take *no* for an answer: "I want Mother to see a general, Eddie."

"But, Carson, I wasn't a general."

"Then a colonel, Eddie."

"No."

"Well, I want you to come over and put on all of your ribbons for Mother to see, and wear your uniform." According to Newhouse, "Whatever I really had been could not matter less. She decided I was a highly decorated general of the Air Force, and that's all there was to it."

To be sure, Carson took great pleasure in creating stories about her *actual* friends, just as she had with Newhouse and Miss Bancou. Frequently she assigned them nicknames from fairy tales, ballets, and operas, or she simply made up names that sounded playful or teasing and connoted a unique relationship. (In Carson's unpublished *Holiday* article she conceded that Southerners were especially given to the tendency to nickname.) Just as she had almost always called her cousin "Boots," and Albert Marre "my black swan," so, too, did she have a name for Marielle Bancou. After the Graycourt fire, she often called her "Snowflakes," since their marvelous friendship had burgeoned when she saw Miss Bancou standing barefoot in the snow. Carson also went through a stage of referring to herself as "Snow White" and to dress predominantly in white. She sometimes asked, "Tell me, what is Snowflakes doing while Snow White is sleeping?" The fact that "Snow White" slept at all forever amazed her French friend, who never ceased to be reminded that Carson was an insomniac. According to Eric Preminger, Carson used the nickname "Junie Moon" for her physical therapist from Columbia-Presbyterian Hospital. Marjorie Kellogg, her therapist, discounted the tale, however, saying, "The name was my own invention. It had absolutely nothing to do with Carson and my book."[56] Miss Kellogg's best-selling book, *Tell Me That You Love Me, Junie Moon,* published in 1968, was likened by several critics to Carson's fiction in that both writers shared a similar vision through their psychically and physically maimed characters, who were distressingly alienated and lonely.

In contrast to Thomas Ryan's remark that Carson could be "quite scatterbrained about things that did not relate to her work," she could be totally single-minded about anything she wished. According to Jordan Massee, Carson had the most single-tracked mind of anyone he had ever known: "We didn't get off a subject until she was ready to get off it. *Nothing* could divert her. You cannot imagine how recklessly she could be in pursuit of something, whether it was a party or a present for Mary. You didn't dare bring up any irrelevancy, but just concentrated on that one thing."[57] Marielle Bancou knew, too, what it was like to be on the receiving end of Carson's steadfastness. Before the Graycourt fire and her move into Carson's house, Miss Bancou had been the recipient of numerous nocturnal telephone calls. When Carson had her night shade on, it was time for sleep; but so long as there were lights on in her house (as there always were), no matter what time it was, the telephone was fair game. "Oh, darling," she sometimes announced with great enthusiasm at 2:00 A.M.: "Listen, I have a perfectly wonderful sentence I *must* read to you." Then she would recite a line from *The Square Root of Wonderful*, or, later, *Clock Without Hands*. "Her lines from the play were little poems," recalled Miss Bancou.

It was at about this time that Carson became obsessively interested in the color white. "She loved for things to be in white—adored white nightgowns, wore white dressing robes, dresses, and even suggested that I redo my room in white," said Miss Bancou, who designed and made loose-fitting garments for Carson and tried to get her to begin wearing bright colors. Like Emily Dickinson, however, whose personality, ambiguous legend, and poetry intrigued her, Carson was reluctant to give up the image of whiteness and its ambivalent connotations. Soon she was granting interviews dressed in white nightgowns and tennis shoes.

Before Marielle Bancou moved into 131 South Broadway, she frequently spent her Sundays with Carson, for Sunday was the housekeeper Ida Reeder's day off, and the two of them would sit for hours together. Miss Bancou liked to mix her paints at Carson's dining-room table, where the light was true and she could look out over the Hudson and dream of her native France. Often interrupting her reverie, addressing her friend as "My little color combination," Carson begged Miss Bancou to talk about Seventh Avenue and the city. "Tell me about the outside world," she urged. "I know all about life on the sleepy Hudson." As with Jordan Massee, Carson wanted to hear the same stories again and again. Although Miss Bancou stayed at 131 South Broadway for over a year, she found it wearing to commute daily to the city as well as to give Carson the single-minded attention she craved. Finally, in the spring of 1960 she moved to a fashionable apartment house on East 33rd Street in Manhattan. By then, Dr. Mary Mercer had become such an integral part of Carson's life that there was little opportunity for Miss Bancou and Carson to enjoy the warm, sympathetic communion they had shared in the past.

Several years after Carson's death, Marielle Bancou summed up the nature and value of their relationship: "I owe to Carson most of the interesting people I know now, both in England and America. She touched my soul more than anyone else I know. Carson was my favorite American and the person I have known best. To me she was America."[58] The affection and admiration was mutual. To Carson, Marielle Bancou was France, just as Dame Edith Sitwell was England, Miss Bowen, Ireland, and Isak Dinesen—though Danish—was Africa. In 1964, when Carson made out her will, she chose to leave to her French friend her favorite portrait of herself, an 11-inch by 14-inch line drawing executed in 1946 in Italy by the Hungarian artist Vertès.

Perhaps Janet Flanner's comment is representative of the attitude of many of Carson's friends who had known her during the "pre-Mary Mercer days": "Few of us ever laid eyes on Dr. Mercer. I don't think she wanted to meet Carson's previous group of friends, or for Carson to have much to do with us any more."[59] Those who continued to see the frail author, however, particularly after she became a wheelchair invalid, and then a bed patient only—and also became well acquainted with Mary Mercer—gave "Carson's good doctor" much credit for her prolonged will to live. They may not have liked Dr. Mercer personally, but they readily admitted her role in Carson's survival. She brought order to Carson's life, which had been sorely lacking in the past, and saw to it that both the physical and psychic needs were consistently met until her death.[60]

Still another dimension in human relationships was also realized in 1959 when Carson's "African" heroine became a flesh-and-blood reality. On January 21, 1959, a joint meeting of the American Academy and National Institute of Arts and Letters provoked more excitement for Carson than any previous Academy or Institute function she had attended. Isak Dinesen had been made an honorary member and was to deliver the evening's address. For twenty years Carson had been entranced by the Danish writer and her ability to tell a tale, yet she was hesitant now to meet her, fearful that the imagined image might be destroyed or unsettled by the fleshly confrontation. Whatever the consequences, however, Carson decided that she simply had to be in the master storyteller's presence and know her in person. At the cocktail hour beforehand, she nervously approached Mark Van Doren, the Academy's president, and asked if she might be seated near the honored guest. To her delight, she learned that Miss Dinesen herself had already made a similar request. The place cards had been arranged, said Van Doren, and Carson and Baroness Karen Blixen-Finecke (Miss Dinesen) were to be seated together. Everyone in the auditorium seemed to fall in love with Isak Dinesen that night, but no one was more enthralled than Carson, whose imagined friend stood before her at last.

Miss Dinesen's talk after dinner was entitled "On Mottoes of My Life." She said that just as a man could be said to be as good as his *word*, so, too, was she as true as her *mottoes*, her word for the significant events and experiences of her life. Five had been paramount, she explained; and to Carson, each of Miss Dinesen's mottoes could also have been her own, especially the one the Danish writer phrased *"Pourquoi pas?"* (Why not?) For Miss Dinesen, the motto stood for all the books she had written. The *why* alone might have seemed a wail, a lament, she said, but coupled with the negative *not*, the question became an answer, a directive. So, too, had Carson's life been a cry for help, but also a cry which she herself could best answer. Miss Dinesen described her cry as the call of "wild hope."[61] So, too, had Carson sounded that call, as had most of the protagonists of her fiction. In her own first novel begun at age twenty, Carson embodied that cry in Mick, the young girl in *The Heart Is a Lonely Hunter*.

It was this same wild hope which continued to radiate from the Danish writer with whom Carson had fallen in love after reading *Out of Africa* so many years earlier. She had recognized it over the years in all of Miss Dinesen's works, knowing intuitively the affinity they shared. A mellower hope and radiance emanated now in profusion from the frail, wraithlike lady addressing an aggregate of America's most creative men and women of the century. When the honored guest finished her talk, Carson quavered with emotion as she stood with every member of the Academy and Institute who rose to applaud her—an ovation Carson had never seen extended before for an Academy's speaker. Three years later, upon Miss Dinesen's death, she recalled the experience in a special tribute to her friend:

> How can one think of a radiant being? I had only seen a picture of her when she was in her twenties: strong, live, wonderfully beautiful, and with one of her Scotch deerhounds in the shade of the African jungle. I had not thought visually about her person. When I met her, she was very, very frail and old but as she talked her face was lit like a candle in an old church. My heart trembled when I saw her fragility.[62]

During the dinner the baroness told Carson that before she left Europe she had four people in mind she most wanted to meet in America: Carson, Marilyn Monroe, E. E. Cummings, and Ernest Hemingway. It had been arranged for Cummings to escort her to the meeting, but Hemingway was out of the country and would not be back before Miss Dinesen would conclude her lecture tour. Carson replied that she could easily arrange a meeting with Marilyn Monroe, whom she said she knew quite well; her husband, Arthur Miller, was seated that moment at the next table. Immediately Carson introduced Miller to Miss Dinesen, then announced that she would give a luncheon and bring them together at her home as soon as it could be arranged.

When she learned from Miss Dinesen's secretary and companion, Clara Svendsen, that "Tanya"—the English name by which Carson was asked to call the Danish writer—ate only oysters and white grapes and drank only champagne, she had to send Ida Reeder scurrying around at the last minute trying to locate fresh oysters in quantity, grapes (in January), and champagne glasses, which she did not own. Finally everything was in readiness and photographers were at hand. Earlier, Carson had panicked temporarily and urged her friend Edward Newhouse to manage the affair for her ("Please, Eddie, I need you," she cried), but Newhouse declined and Jordan Massee and Marielle Bancou became her chief consultants. Other guests besides Miss Dinesen, Marilyn Monroe, and Arthur Miller (whom Carson knew only slightly, but enormously admired for his *Death of a Salesman*) were Jordan Massee, Felicia Geffen, executive secretary of the National Institute and National Academy of Arts and Letters, and Miss Svendsen.

Carson always performed best in small groups in which she could be assured control as the center of attention. Yet this day Carson happily relinquished the stage to her guest. She said later that everyone found Miss Dinesen "a magnificent conversationalist . . . talking with such warmth that the listeners didn't have to try to interrupt her marvelous conversation."[63] That day, Miss Dinesen told a tale that was published later as the title story of her collection *Shadows on the Grass* (Random House, 1961), about the killing of her first lion in Kenya and of sending the skin to the King of Denmark. The story symbolized for her what writing was, and what a story should be. Miss Dinesen's oral rendering of the tale and its printed version two years later were identical. According to Massee, not a word was changed. Miss Dinesen's tale telling was flawless, and when she concluded, no one spoke for a moment. Then Carson turned to her cousin and said, "Boots, honey, now *you* tell Karen [Miss Dinesen] about the Schofield girls," one of her favorite stories about Massee's maiden aunts. Gladys and Elizabeth Schofield and their mother were, in real life, "full-blown McCullers characters," said Massee. "They had, in a sense, already gone through the creative process. They were dead by this time, but Carson loved them, and loved to hear about them."[64] Massee, a connoisseur of the arts and a cosmopolite whose southern charm, genteel manner, and sense of decorum were never misplaced, looked at this moment as though he had been struck dumb. He could no more have followed the master craftsman, Miss Dinesen, and told his simple tale than he could have lectured on environmental and water resources engineering or life at Vassar. No amount of pleading on Carson's part or Miss Dinesen's polite entreaty could induce him to tell it, nor could Carson understand his silence. "Why didn't you tell Karen the story, Boots? She would have loved it," she admonished later.

Marilyn Monroe, who had a marvelous sense of humor and whom the guests found charming, entertained the group with an anecdote from her own kitchen. She told with much cleverness a tale on herself involving some homemade noodles she had tried to create one night for her husband like his mother used to make in the "old country." The conglomeration was such a failure that she was afraid she had lost not only a meal, but a husband, in the process. Miller aptly defended his wife for her other attributes, however, and assured the group that Miss Monroe's cooking was no problem to him. The talk then turned to recipes, and the playwright asked Miss Dinesen about her strange diet and the doctor who had put her on it.

"Oh, the doctors are horrified by it," Miss Dinesen replied, "but I love champagne and oysters, which is fortunate, since they agree with me. There's no problem—except when oysters are out of season. During those dreary months, I manage to eat asparagus." (Ironically, a few days after Carson's luncheon, Miss Dinesen was rushed to a New York hospital in a state of acute malnutrition. According to one of the doctors treating her, her symptoms were similar to those of prisoners rescued from the German concentration camps after World War II.)[65]

After the oysters and champagne—there had been soufflé for the others—Carson reportedly put music on the phonograph and invited Miss Monroe and Miss Dinesen to join her in dancing on the marble-topped dining-room table. Both Jordan Massee and Arthur Miller are certain, however, that such antics did not take place in *actuality*. "I cannot believe that either Carson or Miss Dinesen could have danced, given their physical condition, let alone on top of a table," said Miller.[66] Nevertheless, Carson cherished the tale and told it often. It had been years since she entertained with such frivolity or felt such childlike pleasure and wonderment at the love which her guests seemed to express that day for each other. Miss Dinesen also sought out Ida Reeder that afternoon. She had missed her black friends when she found it necessary to leave Africa permanently, and she was pleased to have an opportunity to talk with a black again. She sensed now in Carson's rapport with her black housekeeper and cook that Ida was a friend and confidante, as well. To her luncheon guests that day, Carson was a charming and modest hostess. She was accustomed to hearing her guests recount with great extravagance what a good time they had had, but never had the praise seemed more genuine than what she heard that day. To Carson, it was one of the best parties she had ever given. Although Arthur Miller was never to know Carson well, his memory of the luncheon remained vivid. Of Marilyn Monroe, who killed herself three years later (she and Miller were divorced in 1961), Miller said: "I do not know that Marilyn had ever read any of Carson's works, although she may well have seen her play *The Member of the Wedding*. However, at the luncheon there was certainly a sort of natural sympathy between the two women who lived close to death."[67]

Although Carson was physically infirm throughout 1959–60—frail, gaunt, her joints badly swollen, fingers unable to grasp a pencil firmly and write much more than a vaguely legible signature, arms too weak to hold a book or newspaper for any length of time, eyesight sometimes so poor that she had difficulty reading—her health, in general, remained relatively stable. After her first two operations, no more were to be scheduled until she finished her novel. Many people thought she would never live to complete *Clock Without Hands*, or that she would be able to create any major work again.

Carson, reportedly, had been unhappy with Houghton Mifflin since before the publication of *The Square Root of Wonderful* because she felt she was being neglected; and it occurred to her, whimsically perhaps, that she would like to move to Random House, where her former editor, Robert Linscott, had gone before the publication of *The Member of the Wedding*. Linscott had been anxious to have Carson as his author and to publish her book with Random House, but she had been loyal to her old company. Yet in the late 1950s when she seriously contemplated a move, she was no longer certain that Linscott wanted her. Several persons recalled that a meeting took place at Random House in the late 1950s with Robert Haas, one of the partners of the company, Linscott, and Carson's agent, whereupon negotiations for a Random House contract for *Clock Without Hands* were begun. Extant evidence of the intended move, however, is slight. According to David McDowell, formerly with Random House and later, editor at Crown Publishers, "It was Linscott who persuaded Haas that Carson's health was so poor that she would not live to complete the book."[68] Linscott's widow, however, maintained that Carson's health had nothing to do with her husband's interest in the book: "I am *sure* my husband did not fear for Carson's health. He read part, perhaps all of *Clock Without Hands, and did not like it*," she said.[69] When Albert Erskine was editor in chief at Random House, he said that "a secretary still with the company who had worked with Linscott remembers that the courtship took place, but not why it fell through."[70] Nor did Kenneth Lohf, curator of rare documents at Columbia University Library, in a search of the old Random House files turn up evidence of such negotiations.[71] Writer William Goyen, who was published by Random House during this period, said that he knew the story, but wanted to save it for his memoirs.[72] John Leggett, New York editor for Houghton Mifflin who worked with Carson on the publication of *The Square Root of Wonderful*—and then moved to Harper's later—added still another dimension to the tale: "I remember that Carson was interested in giving Harper's a crack at *Clock Without Hands*, but not why it never got to negotiation stage. Perhaps it was my own feeling that she was too sick to have a literary future," he conceded, "and Carson went a long way to prove me wrong."[73] According to Jordan Massee, a meeting was held at Random House in the office of Robert Haas, attended by Haas, McDowell, Carson, and himself, but it was only exploratory. "From time to time Carson became unhappy with her publisher and thought that he was not promoting her properly or doing something else that she thought he should, but it was usually just talk, and by the next day or so they would be as enamored of each other as ever," explained Massee.[74]

To be sure, Carson had published no major work since 1946 except her theatrical adaptation of *The Member of the Wedding*, the omnibus edition which included *The Ballad of the Sad Café* in hardback for the first time (and only one previously unpublished short story), and the play that failed, *The Square Root of Wonderful*. There had been little new in print for over ten years except a few short stories, two Christmas pieces and several other quasi-autobiographical writings, some poetry which the critics thought rather obscure, and the first chapter of her novel still in progress—all in periodicals. She had suffered from a variety of serious ailments before her writing career began, but nothing had daunted her seriously until the crippling stroke in 1947. From then on, grievously disturbed by an unhappy relationship with Reeves, harboring guilt and driven by ambivalent feelings of love, as well as hate, for those upon whom she had been dependent most of her adult life, alternately gratefully and lovingly embracing them and resentfully repulsing them, Carson found her physical and psychic life strung out between polarities of love and rejection, joy and despair, pleasure and pain, hope and disillusionment, success and failure. Yet through it all, she clung to life.

Whatever the true story was regarding her move to another publisher, Carson was determined to finish her novel as soon as humanly possible and prove her critics wrong. When she was not well enough to sit at an electric typewriter and physically press the keys herself, which she could do with a fair degree of rapidity and accuracy using her good right hand only, she dictated to one of several part-time secretaries. According to Carson's cousin, there were a series of "Salvation Army lassies" or girls from Nyack's Missionary College who came in two or three times a week and took dictation. Carson had almost total recall, and even though she became somewhat vague as the years of ill health progressed, her fantastic memory enabled her to cope with the physical and mechanical problems of writing. She composed much of her manuscript in her head, and when her "girl" arrived she dictated dozens of pages at a time, or as Massee said, "complete and total a whole chapter without changing a word or comma because the entire fiction had already been worked out and memorized. It was unbelievable to watch."

In 1959, when Carson's medical expenses began to spiral—as they continued to do over the remaining eight years of her life—she worried anew about money. She had always "paid attention" to it, as her friends termed it, often displaying penuriousness over petty things, but she had fears now that there would not be enough money to see herself comfortably through the rest of her life. One possibility she considered to help relieve her financial anxieties for the present, at least, was another writing grant. In 1958, Carson was invited to be a nominator in a program for creative writers administered by the Ford Foundation, but that year she suggested or sponsored no one. When she was asked to serve as a nominator in 1959, however, she was more interested in receiving a grant herself than in recommending someone else; besides, she said, she did not know anyone at the time talented enough who also needed nominating.

That summer Carson informed her good friend, writer and critic Carl Van Vechten—whom she had playfully nicknamed "Don Carlos"—that the Ford Foundation had written her of its desire to subsidize writers and poets who also were interested in the theatre. To Carson, her dramatization of *The Member of the Wedding*, together with the rest of her work, would doubtless qualify her for Ford money; as an added inducement, however, she planned to propose a grant based on her desire to dramatize *The Ballad of the Sad Café*. She hoped to secure a new Guggenheim, too, since it probably would take another year to finish *Clock Without Hands*, she told Van Vechten. By September 15 she confidently expected to be notified of the Ford grant, and in the spring, of the Guggenheim.[75]

In early April 1960, Van Vechten received from Carson a despondent letter. She said that the Guggenheim had been denied her on the technicality that she had already received two fellowships, thus was ineligible for a third grant. Carson was aware of the rule, but she had hoped that since she had suffered two strokes during her second fellowship and had had to abort her work, an exception could be made. The real cause of her distress, however, was that Van Vechten, whom she had asked to recommend her, had not written her his response to the first four chapters of *Clock Without Hands*, on which he was to have based his recommendation. If only she had sent in more material, she lamented, it might have made a difference. (She told Van Vechten that she had had ten chapters ready, but had not wanted to trouble her sponsors by asking them to read more.) Her friend's opinion would still mean a great deal to her, she pleaded, even though the fellowship was out.[76] Carson wrote an identical letter—except for the closing paragraph—to Newton Arvin, who had also agreed to sponsor her. Both men replied immediately that the Guggenheim people had not sent them any of her manuscript for reading, and that they had had no opportunity to support her application. Relieved, Carson wired each that it was not so much *not* getting the grant which had upset her, but the eerie feeling of having received no personal reaction to the manuscript from the friends she thought she could count on.[77]

Van Vechten was also an excellent photographer, and during the summer of 1959 Carson asked him to take pictures of Mary Mercer. Soon afterward, on a sweltering July weekend, the two women sat for more than a dozen photographs, both together and separately. The finished pictures were a great disappointment to Carson, although she assured Van Vechten that he was not to blame. The day of the photographic session had been Dr. Mercer's first free day in over a year of difficult hour-by-hour psychiatric consultation, Carson explained to Van Vechten. It was simply that she loved Mary Mercer so much, she continued, that she yearned to have a picture of her looking well rested and as radiant as she was in person. Dr. Mercer assured Van Vechten, however, that the picture Carson yearned for was impossible. In a Christmas note to the photographer in 1959, Dr. Mercer explained that Carson's vision and that which the camera revealed were quite different, but that she thought it better to bear with Carson and her fantasies.[78]

Carson continued to see Mary Mercer almost daily for the rest of her life. Usually they were not together on weekday mornings for Carson slept until ten or eleven o'clock, but there were frequent telephone conversations between appointments, and Dr. Mercer often saw her for lunch. In the late afternoon she stopped in again and listened to Carson relate the events of her day. Sometimes Carson read to Dr. Mercer parts of her manuscript and discussed with her what her various characters had done that day, too. There also was a full report by Carson of visitors, what she had eaten, the latest recipe she had acquired, perhaps a bit of news she had culled from the New York *Daily News* that she especially savored, and sundry conversations to quote from those she had had with various communicants. Carson sometimes asked "what was going on at the office" and probed gently for "grist for her fantasy mill," as one friend described Carson's creative process. According to Jordan Massee, "Although Dr. Mercer respected to the nth degree the confidence of her patients, there was an occasional anecdote she could share with Carson, who, in turn, twisted and used it later in some totally unrecognizable fashion."

An important ritual for Carson was reading the New York *Daily*

News, which she did voraciously, devouring the horrendous tales and picture coverage. "My God, this man murdered all three of his children with a butcher knife! Isn't that horrible," she would exclaim with relish. Although the New York Sunday *Times* came regularly into the house and showed vague signs of being read, or as Jordan Massee said, "mussed up a bit," she made no attempt to conceal her lack of interest in the writing of ordinary occurrences that made up the common practical and political aspects of life in the United States unless they somehow touched her. "You read the *Times*, and you don't know what's going on," said Carson, not intending to be facetious.

In 1960, she received an invitation to attend President John F. Kennedy's inauguration and reluctantly agreed to accept Mary Mercer's advice that the trip and activities would be too hard on her. "It would have been fun, Boots," she told her cousin, "but crowds terrify me, and I think it best that I stay at home where I know what is expected of me." Carson was invited, also, to President Lyndon B. Johnson's inauguration in 1964, but again she declined. A solid Democrat, however, she had spoken out on issues several times in the past to the White House. In 1948, she had wired her congratulations to President Harry S Truman for his courage in fighting inflation through governmental controls and expressed her gratitude and admiration for the President. Carson was disappointed when Adlai Stevenson did not win the Democratic nomination in 1960, but she was intrigued by the youthful charisma of John F. Kennedy and enthusiastically supported him.

Once Marielle Bancou moved into the city and Carson was staying alone again, everyone aware of the situation was concerned that Carson might have an accident during the night and no one would know it. She vowed that she could not bear again the agony of lying for hours on the floor alone, unable to move or call for help, as she had in France. Ida Reeder was never a sleep-in housekeeper or companion, but came and went by taxi daily to her house a few blocks away. Ida, who had a son at home, countless church activities, and her own home to keep up, was devoted to Carson, yet their relationship was always on a well-salaried basis. Friends tried to find someone else who might come in and live with Carson on the main floor. Elizabeth Bowen, who had come to Nyack when Marguerite Smith was alive and was well aware of Carson's physical dependency on someone, worried now about her, too. She had a young friend from the Midwest, she told Carson, who admired writers and wanted to live in New York. Nothing would please him more than to live with Carson and be on hand to help in any way. Carson agreed, and soon the gentleman arrived with much luggage in tow and moved into 131 South Broadway.

Less than a week later, Jordan Massee received a desperate call from

Carson. "Boots, come up here at once and save me from that man Elizabeth sent." Immediately her cousin went to Nyack to arrange for the visitor's departure. He had not expected Carson's guest to return—bag and baggage—to the city with him, however.

"Do not worry," said Miss Bowen's friend when Massee attempted to explain Carson's inability to keep him, "I adjust easily." Massee referred to him as " 'The man who came to dinner.' He played thirteen operas uninterrupted and kept my stereo going constantly. Yet once Carson was rid of him and he became ensconced with me, she thought the whole thing a marvelous joke." Finally Massee, too, was free of the visitor and someone conceived of a bell-pull system by which Carson could signal to Ruth Wells, a schoolteacher who rented the bedroom immediately above hers. Miss Wells also volunteered to check on Carson each night and see if there was anything she needed.

Nurtured and encouraged by Mary Mercer and other devotees interested in her physical and psychic well-being, Carson continued to work well on her novel, finally completing it the first week of December 1960. In July, *Harper's Bazaar* had published Chapter Three of *Clock Without Hands*, a piece Carson entitled "To Bear the Truth Alone." The announcement then was that the book would be out in September. Plans were already under way, too, for producer Kermit Bloomgarden to take the story to Broadway.[79] Actually, the book did not come out until the following September (1961).

She wrote Mary Tucker on December 3 that the book at last was finished and that it was beautiful. Already there was a sense of bereftness, as though she had been spiritually dispossessed, she confided. It had been almost twenty years since Jester Clane first claimed a fantasy life of his own, and Carson had created intermittently through the years with great pleasure the family and friends who had revolved around him. Now it was as though the family had grown up or away from her, with Sherman Pew and her druggist Malone dead and the old judge hopelessly and unhappily senile.

Carson had put her book down on numerous occasions, only to resurrect it when the characters made sufficient demands. It had been her major project in France in 1952–53, and she had worked on it again at Yaddo in 1954, after Reeves's death. Leon Edel recalled that at Yaddo she was at work first on a book with "the lugubrious theme" of a middle-aged man dying of cancer: "Along with these fantasies of death there would be interruptions in which her wit took over to restore a world of gaiety and joy. Nearly always this world was peopled with 'member of the wedding' material." Edel, to whom Carson sometimes read her material or verbally re-created for him some of the anecdotes of her fiction, remarked to her once that he found "her fancies about life much more appealing than her brooding on death." Later, he wondered whether his comment "did not have its effect":

> For she laid aside the clock-without-hands theme at Yaddo and started work on a very amusing play about a child, an architect father, I think, a divorce, something that had, at any rate, a very considerable amount of life in it. I gather this became her last play, and while it failed it must have been good for her to write it. Then she returned to the other theme. It was inescapable, I suppose, even though it was hardly tragic in substance.[80]

To be sure, Jester Clane, Malone, the old judge, Jester's black friend Sherman Pew, and the rest of her southern menagerie in the book evolved with unspeakable labor, single-mindedness, and genius through love, illness, pain, despair, and finally, "livingness" once again. *Clock Without Hands* was completed at great personal expense, but it also was Carson's salvation. Had she not finished it—as many had feared—friends felt that the psychic impasse might have killed her.

Once the manuscript was in and Carson felt free again, she and Mary Mercer planned a trip to Washington, D.C., where they were to be joined by Mary Tucker. For over two years Carson had wanted these particular friends to meet, and now she was thrilled by the anticipation that the three of them would come together at last. She loved the two of them so much, she said to each in a manner reminiscent of Frankie Addams' declaration for her brother and the bride in *The Member of the Wedding*. In a letter to Mary Tucker's daughter Gin upon their return, Carson said that Mary Mercer had been much impressed by Mary Tucker. Dr. Mercer had once had a close friend who had been an inspiration to her in much the same way that Mary Tucker had been to her, Carson, she explained.[81]

By the middle of January 1961, the galleys of the manuscript of the new novel were ready, and for the next five weeks Carson worked with Mary Mercer, Jordan Massee, and her secretary, Elzey Falk, weekend after weekend, laboriously correcting proofs. Massee, worried that all of Carson's sentences were not correctly punctuated, often said to her: "Now, Carson, a semicolon ought to go there instead of a comma." For a while she seemed to appreciate his grammatical prowess, but finally she bristled with irritation and accused him of "nit-picking":

"I'm not making any more changes, Boots. I don't want to hear any more about it."

According to Massee, the last fourth of the book was not as well edited as the rest of it, although eventually everything important did get changed. Once the galleys were read and corrected, he also worked with her on the dust jacket design, helped select quotations for the blurbs, and made up a special brochure to further publicize the novel. For the dust jacket Carson decided to ask Louise Dahl-Wolfe to take a new picture, Miss Dahl-Wolfe having photographed her on two earlier occasions. Miss Dahl-Wolfe had not seen Carson for several years, and when she went to Nyack to take the pictures she was distressed to find her friend in such a debilitated condition. "It was necessary to place Carson in a high-backed Victorian chair so that she would not have to hold her head erect by herself—she had such little strength in her neck," recalled Miss Dahl-Wolfe.[82] Soon both book and dust cover were ready, and by June 1961 advance copies of the novel had been sent out for review.

Carson enjoyed her new freedom, the work on her book over at last. She made occasional trips to the city, where she stayed overnight or for several days at a time with Tennessee Williams, Robert and Hilda Marks, or Jordan Massee, and received a number of invitations when people learned that she was in town. There were small, informal dinner parties, an occasional play, dinner meetings of the American Academy and National Institute of Arts and Letters, a birthday celebration, or simply a getting together with old friends in a New York bar.

She loved visiting Massee in his apartment on West End Avenue. It was filled with exquisite art objects, rare paintings and prints, pieces of Italian sculpture, beautiful American and European antiques, an enormous collection of operas and other rare recordings, and a grand piano. The apartment was usually shared by one or two other men and there were many visitors. Massee's friends for the most part were people connected with the arts, and soon his friends were also hers. She liked the way they dropped in at odd hours, often especially to see her, and enjoyed listening to their talk of "life in the outside world," as she called it, and to their day-to-day happenings, which she found fascinating.

Always insistent on sleeping in the tiny maid's room off the kitchen rather than allowing her cousin to give up his bedroom, Carson admitted that it was choice, not chivalry, which prompted her. In the "guest room"—as she called it—she would not miss out on anything, day or night, for the kitchen was the hub of the household activity. While Massee, an advertising executive, was at the office, she stayed in the little room by herself, reading, ruminating, or puttering about. Late in the day he usually rushed in, greeted her, and began preparing the evening meal. "What are we going to have for dinner?" she would ask with a note of urgency, as though she had thought about it all day. Massee told her and described in great detail the culinary processes he anticipated, knowing that such details would delight her. Once again he retreated to the kitchen to cook. After a brief silence, Carson would call out plaintively, "Boots, come talk to me."

"Well, I can't fix dinner and talk, too, Carson."

"We'll do both," she announced. "You come talk first, then we'll eat."

While Massee was cooking, having taken time out for more conversation, it was Carson's habit to call out again: "It's time for my other drink." When he picked up her glass and started with it back to the kitchen, however, she always said: "No, honey, just leave the glass there and bring the bottle." Just as she loved to hear good anecdotes repeated again and again, so, too, did she enjoy enacting an amusing real-life routine.

"Carson never trusted me to make her drinks," said Massee. "She'd laugh about it, too. My measurement was not the same as hers, and as I poured, she would say, 'Just keep on pouring, darling, I will tell you when to stop.' Of course, her idea of a drink in an Old-fashioned glass was some drink; and when Carson was told she could have only two, the jiggers got bigger and bigger. She took her bourbon with ice and just a touch of water. 'Don't drown it, darling,' she would tell me."

During the summer of 1961 Massee's father came to the city for an extended visit. The senior Massee had always liked Carson and was anxious to read Clock Without Hands and to see what use she had made of the stories he had told her during her last trip South. There were dozens of anecdotes in Carson's novel that either young Massee or his father had told her. When Massee, Sr., read an advance copy of the book, however, he was much put off by it. He objected to what he called Carson's "dirty words," but more than that, he took exception to the way she had used his stories. "She has ruined all my lovely stories by not telling them right. She has spoiled my story about Geraldine Farrow and the gooney bird in 'The Goose Girl.' Now I can never tell them again," he lamented.

Massee, Jr., on the other hand, was delighted to see how Carson had used the various tales. One anecdote Carson used to beg her cousin to tell again and again involved a prominent Macon woman who went to Washington to give a radio speech. Back home, her husband listened painfully to her initial remarks, then growled, "Shut up, Dollie," and twisted the knob. Carson had gone into hysterics over the story, and thirty minutes after hearing it had to be told it again: "Please, Boots, tell me about Mrs. Lamar and the speech." Later, after a mysterious transmogrifying creative process that only Carson could activate, the tale found its way into Clock Without Hands in the senile but lovable old judge's radio address against integration. In the book, Judge Clane pathetically took leave of his senses and began reciting the Gettysburg Address, then finally was cut off the air.[83] Carson also had consulted Massee many times for suggestions regarding the various situations in which her characters found themselves. "Sometimes they got her into a corner," said Massee, "and

Carson would tell me that she simply did not know what Jester would do next. Or she would admit that the old judge was cantankerous and bothering her just then. Of all the characters in her book, she loved Judge Fox Clane best, but she also admitted that she had secretly mistreated him and now felt sorry for him because he had 'gone wrong.'"

Massee had several touchy conversations with his father over *Clock Without Hands* that summer, but before the elderly gentleman departed for Macon, he was reconciled to Carson and the book. On August 12, Carson drove to the city in Mary Mercer's new Bentley to take the two Massees back to Nyack to spend the day and have dinner with them. In his diary entry that night, Massee recorded:

> And so today the hatchet was buried, and Carson will never know
> that Daddy disliked the book. He told her, "Honey, your book is like
> Ivory soap, 99 and 44/100 per cent pure." Mary's serene presence
> helped carry the day.

Massee was grateful that two of the people most precious to him also loved each other and had parted on good terms that day, for two months later, his father was dead.

Tennessee Williams also was unhappy over his advance copy of the book and wrote a letter begging Carson to hold up publication until she could rewrite Chapter Four, which he found especially objectionable. He felt that *Clock Without Hands* was not up to her usual high standards. He also was strenuously opposed to her portrait of the young black character, Sherman Pew. The playwright called Massee from Key West and urged him to stop publication. Carson, however, had gone into Harkness Pavilion for her third operation just before Williams' letter arrived. Intercepted, the letter was read by those who felt it would not be in Carson's best interests to be shaken by adverse criticism at present, and especially by someone whose opinion she revered. "Tennessee, you cannot do this to Carson—I simply won't allow it," countered Massee. "Whatever weaknesses there are in this novel, few people ever wrote a book under such obstacles. It means too much to have gotten this thing into print, and to stop her book after the critics have seen it and to withdraw it now would kill her, even if what you say is 100 per cent correct—and I don't even critically agree with what you are saying. Even assuming that Carson would agree—a most unlikely possibility—Robert Lantz says that it's too late."

The day the letter arrived, June 21, was a hectic one with endless telephone calls between Carson's lawyer, agent, and sister. It was finally decided that since the playwright himself was due in New York City three days later, they would wait and let him choose whether or not to give Carson his missive. Once Williams saw her, however, he readily gave in. He realized that his friend needed every possible confidence. A week after the book was officially out, *Saturday Review* carried a tribute by him and a favorable review by Granville Hicks. The article was a testament to her truth, courage, and achievement, rather than a strong literary endorsement of the novel's artistry. Yet Williams had in no way compromised himself in the process. His tribute is quoted here in full:

> Carson's strength is enormous but primarily exists in her spirit. From 1947 to the present year she has been, as many interested in American writing know, a gallant invalid. She has lived with that paralysis of the right arm and with an excruciating series of operations to correct it, yet all the while she has never surrendered to it. During those fourteen years she has kept on working steadily and with all the creative and personal distinction that makes her an inspiring figure to us relative weaklings. She has completed two plays of the most impressive quality, and at the same time she has given us stories and poems of the purest distinction.
>
> And all this time, these fourteen years, she has also been working on her fifth novel, *Clock Without Hands*.
>
> Before I went abroad last spring, she told me that she felt she couldn't complete it, that she had paid out all her strength. Then I reminded her of what she had told me, those fourteen years ago, that at the end, or near it, of a work to which the artist's heart is totally committed, he always feels that dread, that terror which is greater than the fear of death.
>
> When I returned from abroad, two and a half months later, an advance copy of the completed novel was waiting for me in Key West.
>
> If I hadn't known before that Carson is a worker of miracles, this work would surely have convinced me of it, for without any sign of the dreadful circumstances under which she accomplished it, this work was once again a thing set on paper as indelible as if it had been carved onto stone. Here was all the stature, nobility of spirit, and profound understanding of the lonely, searching heart that made her, in my opinion, the greatest writer of our country, if not of the world.[84]

On June 11, a few days before Carson's hospitalization, advance publicity on *Clock Without Hands* began in earnest. First, the New York *Times Magazine* section carried a blurb about the novel in a feature called "Authors Speak for Themselves," accompanied by one of Louise Dahl-Wolfe's new photographs. One of the first to request an interview was Nona Balakian, reviewer for the New York *Times*.

Carson arose from her wheelchair to greet Miss Balakian and sensed immediately that they would like each other. Carson was dressed simply, in white, as had been her habit for several years, and the reviewer noticed that she was wearing spotlessly clean white tennis shoes. Soon Ida appeared with a brightly decorated Guatemalan vest and slipped it on her. Over drinks, and later, an omelette lunch, the two women talked avidly. Unlike other interviews Carson had had with women, which often went poorly with her articulating very little, she found herself talking easily with Miss Balakian. She told her that she had written most of her new novel during the last year, typing one page a day with her good right hand. The fact that she had either body or soul at present she attributed to Mary Mercer. Carson also talked without restraint about her mother and husband and the kind of marriage she and Reeves had had. Hedging a little, however, she told Miss Balakian that her husband's death had been an accident, that he had died as the New York *Times* had reported it—the result of injuries suffered in an automobile accident. Perhaps by now Carson herself believed it. She also admitted that she felt betrayed when her mother "tricked" her into her confinement at Payne Whitney some thirteen years earlier. She thought she was going into a hotel, she said.

Becoming less articulate when asked about her work, she admitted that she had once written that "writing is a wandering, dreaming occupation"; yet she conceded that she had never learned to intellectualize her art. After Reeves died, Carson, in a sense, let go of her ability to grasp ideas, said Jordan Massee. Reeves had approached everything rationally all his life, and with Carson he had been insistent that she reason with him. Later, in the late 1950s and until her death, she preferred not to get involved in intellectual discussions about ideas. To Massee she once said, "Honey, you know everything, but let's not talk about it." As Massee saw it, "Carson arrived at her truths through intuitive genius, without reasoning. But she got there, and truths they were."

Carson was much more interested in people than in ideas, she told Nona Balakian. When she spoke of the people she had held dear over the years such as Tennessee Williams, Gypsy Rose Lee, Wystan Auden, and Henry Varnum Poor, her voice grew rich in timbre. She also spoke warmly of Ida Reeder, who, she said, had been invaluable. Later the talk turned to music. She had no regrets about losing music as the major dimension of her life, she explained, for she still listened and thrilled to it, even though she no longer played it herself. She especially loved Schubert, whom she called the most "heartful" of composers. She had worn out a record of "Winterreise" in one week, she added. According to Massee, Carson's response to music was on an emotional level only in the later years. He noticed that more and more she listened to the romantic composers—Chopin, Schubert, and Wagner—whose works she enjoyed identifying with emotionally. She kept a stereo console in her bedroom and listened to music for hours, both alone and with Mary Mercer, who also loved music and shared it with her.

When Miss Balakian asked Carson if she believed in fate, she replied *no*, but that she did believe in grace, which came only through effort, she explained. It was something that happened if one believed in people and in the soul. To her, grace and God and love were the same entity.

Then the interview turned to the locale of her latest novel. Carson commented that she had been watching the Freedom Riders on television and was optimistic of their success. "I believe in humanity," she said simply. She reflected then on earlier novels and noted that certain presentiments had been fulfilled. As early as *The Heart Is a Lonely Hunter*, for example, she said that Jake Blount planned to walk to Washington as a protest against social injustice. She said that Henry Miller had referred to her as a prophetess back in 1940 when he wrote her a congratulatory note. (Later Carson wrote a friend that the arguments presented by Jester's father, a lawyer in *Clock Without Hands* who had committed suicide when he could not cope with injustice, concerning the deplorable injustice to blacks, might well have been spoken by Robert Kennedy.)[85]

The South which Carson depicted in *Clock Without Hands*, as in her earlier works, was sadly lacking in the dimensions of justice and humanity. It was a South she had left but still viewed with the ambivalent feelings of affection and rancor. During the summer of 1958 when she again was grappling with the plot and characters of *Clock Without Hands*, myriad and sometimes distorted, exaggerated aspects of southern life and prejudice came back to her. She recalled that some months earlier the director of the Columbus public library had written to ask if she would consider donating some of her manuscripts to the library. Carson responded that to her delight she had a good-sized collection of manuscripts in her archives, but upon consideration of the request she decided that she could not, in good conscience, allow her loving works to repose where all peoples were not allowed an equal opportunity to enjoy them. If the library could assure her that it was, indeed, public, where men were treated equally in the manner that God intended, she would be happy to contribute her manuscripts to her hometown library. Director John Banister's answer did not suffice. He said that the W. C. Bradley Memorial Library, which had opened on October 21, 1950, now maintained a Fourth Avenue Library through the county Board of Education which served "as the main library for colored people," who could borrow on a day's notice anything available in the main library. But to Carson, the matter was closed.[86]

By the time *Clock Without Hands* was officially released September 18, 1961, it had already been on the best-seller list for a month and was ranked sixth in the nation. Such a feat was possible only because bookstores were free to sell copies in advance, the sole stipulation being that reviews would not appear before the announced publication date. For five months Carson's novel remained on the list; however, reviews were mixed, far more divided than those of any of her previous books. For fifteen years critics had waited for the novel which was to follow *The Member of the Wedding*. News of its progress had cropped up periodically, but most of the critics were aware of the series of physical and psychic misfortunes with which its author had been plagued since her critical stroke in 1947. Some reviewers were admittedly charitable because the book represented achievement in spite of great adversity. (Carson had once conceived of another book she intended to write, which she planned to entitle *In Spite Of*. It would be a collection of tales and jottings about the great artists and performers she especially admired who had achieved renown *in spite of* calamity or misfortune. She had planned to include such people as Sarah Bernhardt, Sergei Diaghilev, Waslaw Nijinsky, Hart Crane, and Isak Dinesen. None of the book was ever put on paper, however.)

Whereas the British critics were almost unanimous in their acclaim, London's Cresset Press having released the novel only a few days after the Houghton Mifflin edition, most of the American reviewers alternately praised and damned *Clock Without Hands* without restraint. If their reports were bad, Carson did not read them. Her attitude was simply that they did not know what they were talking about. She was disturbed only in the sense that someone had ignorantly insulted her or was rude to her. Carson became indignant when the good works of her friends were attacked, as well. She once became highly incensed by a review in the New York *Times* about Tennessee Williams and immediately wrote the editor a letter commenting upon what she thought was the "stupidity" of the reviewer.

During the fall and winter of 1961 people began to besiege the author for interviews. There were New York feature writers and reviewers from distant cities; college students, scholars, and professors at work on critical papers, doctoral dissertations, and books; foreign journalists to whom the name Carson McCullers had become a legend; and impressionable, smiling girls from the local high school or missionary college who merely wanted a glimpse of one of their town's most famous reclusive and eccentric artists.

After her illnesses and operations had drastically incapacitated Carson, she seldom appeared in public and was rarely seen except by appointment or special invitation. Her trips to New York City became less frequent. She did not like large crowds and seemed to grow even shyer to those who remained outside her close circle of friends and viewed her from afar. The one thing she continued to do that involved large numbers—besides an occasional première of a play—was to attend, when she felt up to it, the dinners and ceremonials of the National Institute of Arts and Letters. Babette Deutsch, who had first met Carson at Yaddo the spring after Reeves's death, recalled that probably the last time she saw Carson was in 1963 or 1964 at an NIAL meeting: "She was standing quite alone, shy and seemingly isolated from the writers, composers, and artists amiably chatting among themselves. One of the officers, noticing this, called it to our attention, and several of us went up to engage her in conversation; she was soon surrounded. At the time I was struck by her withdrawn appearance in the midst of her confrères."[87]

Carson's reputation for timidity, though genuinely earned, had nothing to do with a lack of self-confidence or sense of her own worth as an artist. Of that she had always had the highest regard, a fact drummed into her repeatedly without resistance since early childhood. But over the years, her shyness, fear of rejection, and rejection itself—whether real or imagined—had often caused extreme psychic reactions which, in turn, set off a variety of physical disorders: stammering, a tightening of the throat and an inability to talk, a hysterical paralysis for years before her bona fide strokes, which caused her hand and fingers to become so rigid that she sometimes could not write her name, or made her freeze on a crowded street, such as in Paris when she had frequently had to be carried bodily across busy intersections.

After the publication of Clock Without Hands, most visitors to Carson's house found her seated in an armchair in her favorite corner of the living room or, later, in bed—her left arm, hand, wrist, or leg often in a cast or splint. Weighing barely one hundred pounds, she looked tiny and doll-like in chair or bed, draped in a white nightgown or wrapped in a brilliantly colored Chinese robe. To Carson, it was wonderful to be noticed again and made over by an admiring public. Although her seclusion had been enforced by ill health, the image of "invalid" suited her perfectly. Ambivalently, she chafed at its painful reality; yet she loved "holding court" at 131 South Broadway, surrounded by an admiring retinue of friends and workers and receiving guests who paid homage with praise, gifts, and fidelity. Whenever possible, she turned every visit or special occasion into a party.

To people in the 1960s who met Carson for the first time, she had become her own fiction. Visitors were often told in advance by well-meaning friends or escorts "how to act" if they wanted to get along with the renowned artist. Houghton Mifflin's New York editor John Leggett recalled that when he first met Carson, he was taken to Nyack by Arnold Saint Subber, who told him "to expect anything, to behave naturally, and to speak bluntly and profanely." Following such a formula, Leggett would get along beautifully, he was assured. "After some early constraint (I was shocked at how ill she was), we got along fine," said the editor.[88]

One of the interviews that Carson enjoyed most was with Rex Reed in the fall after the book came out. When Reed had first arrived in New York City in 1950, he went at once to see *The Member of the Wedding*. Completely taken by it, he wrote the playwright a fan letter. Although she always answered personally her letters from enthusiasts, she found young Reed's note especially enchanting. Her answer went by return mail, written on what Reed described as "delicate parchment paper, in frail, lavender-pale ink." She told him that goodness and beauty were such precious truths that she was sending hers in return. They did not meet in person until 1961, however, and again, Reed was charmed. Carson was able to walk about then with some mobility, and she greeted him at the door dressed in a long cotton nightgown and white tennis shoes. She extended a glass of bourbon as he stepped inside and asked gaily, "A little toddy for the body?" She explained that the phrase had not only been a tradition in the South, but also had been her late-afternoon habit for years. Moving into the dining room, they sat for several hours at the marble-topped table which had become one of her favorite conversation pieces. The slab had been imported from Verona, Italy, purchased with movie-rights money from *The Member of the Wedding*. She explained that it had met recently with an accident, however, and had cracked when too many heavy books had been placed on it. Ida, especially, had grieved over the accident, said Carson, but she had consoled her: "It's only material, darling, and material things will outlive us." She told Reed that she had had everyone out searching for her marble slab for years before it was finally found; then it was placed on the handsomely carved legs and frame of an old flat-top piano.[89] Probably no one in New York wrote with a more acerbic tongue than did Rex Reed in the 1960s, but he never wrote an unkind word about Carson, whom he described as "a friend and an adviser whose personal courage was as inspirational to me as her literary output."[90] Six years after the *Clock Without Hands* interview, Reed spent another quiet afternoon with Carson, which was the last interview granted anyone, and, again, it resulted in one of the gentlest pieces he ever wrote.[91]

In addition to receiving journalists, unknown interviewers, and hosts of other well-wishers who came to call, Carson also attended several parties in her honor during the fall that her book appeared. The largest and most important to her professionally was Houghton Mifflin's party on

September 22, a sumptuous formal dinner at the fashionable Carlton Hotel to which dozens of celebrities from the New York world of arts and letters had been invited, along with many who simply were "Carson's friends" without any further claim to distinction. Closer to home, fellow writer and neighbor Bentz Plagemann arranged a joint reception at the Palisades Free Library in the community adjacent to Nyack in honor of Carson and two other local writers, Hortense Calisher and Polly Cameron. (Miss Calisher had recently published a new novel, *False Entry*, and Miss Cameron had released another children's book.) Afterward, Plagemann and his wife, Kitty, gave a small dinner party for the honorees, inviting, also, Mary Mercer, Miss Calisher's husband, Curtis Harnack (who became Elizabeth Ames's successor as executive director of Yaddo in 1972), and young Brandon de Wilde and his parents. The De Wildes were old friends of Plagemann, and Carson had loved young Brandon since 1949 when she first met him as seven-year-old John Henry West in *The Member of the Wedding*.

Plagemann had seen little of Carson since her mother's death, although he did see her and Marguerite Smith—as well as Reeves—frequently during the 1940s and early 1950s. They used to get together for lunch on Plagemann's back lawn, then go to an antique auction house nearby and "bid on bargains," as Marguerite referred to one of her favorite pastimes. Plagemann had never known just how "to take Carson," who seemed to find him something of a "square," he said. A favorite story of Plagemann's involved the two of them in 1958 when Carson was first considering surgery on her atrophied hand. Carson called to describe the proposed series of operations and to ask what he thought of one of the specialists who would be involved. Plagemann, having had an unpleasant experience with the very doctor in question, suggested that she not try to cope with him alone: "You must have someone with you, some 'square' who can handle the situation."

"What do you mean?" Carson asked.

"You know, a square—don't you know any squares?" persisted Plagemann.

"None but you, dear," she replied.

Plagemann knew well the adversity Carson had coped with in completing *Clock Without Hands*, and he wanted to do something especially nice for her in giving the dinner and arranging—as a board member of the library—the reception. But that evening was the last time he saw Carson, for he found himself purposely avoiding her during her last years:

> . . . I was a little afraid of Carson. She was, as you know very well, a very complicated person. There was a destructive quality in her, both self-directed and outer directed, which was, I suppose, the other side of her creative gift. My wife had a major stroke at the same time

Carson had her major stroke. They were both crippled in much the same manner, and the same physical therapist came to work with each. I can well remember how unhappy Miss O'Neill used to be when she came to our house, having been first to Carson, and been unable to work with her. Carson and I were also both involved, on separate projects, with the producer Saint Subber at the same time.

I once privately asked Saint Subber not to bring Carson to our house again. I am crippled from an attack of poliomyelitis during World War II; Saint Subber has a silver plate in his skull, or so he told me; my wife was still in bed much of the time, trying to recover from her stroke, and Carson walked with a very tall, silver-headed cane, with her paralyzed left hand in a sling. It was too much. And it saddened me to see her so indifferent to her own welfare, rushing toward, or so it seemed to me, her own self-destruction.[92]

When Carson died a few years later, Plagemann did not go to the funeral. As he explained it,

In our copy of *Clock Without Hands* she had written "Best love." When she died, and the memorial service was held at Campbell's, I told my wife Kitty that we wouldn't go—couldn't go—because I had not been a very good friend to her. I was awfully sad when she died.[93]

Just as Carson had responded to Plagemann with the tongue-in-cheek label of "square," and had begun her letter a few years back to the Columbus library in a light, disarming mood before saying *no* to its request for manuscripts and striking a solid blow for fair treatment to all, so, too, did she respond in a similar mood to a new request that winter. Her former writing instructor and editor of *Story* magazine asked permission to reprint "Wunderkind" in his new anthology, *Firsts of the Famous*. But it had always "stuck in Carson's craw," as a friend once remarked, that she had received such a paltry sum (twenty-five dollars) for her first story, which Burnett had published. Granting Burnett's request, Carson asked her agent Robert Lantz to state explicitly in the permission statement that she was thrilled to have been published in *Story*—and that she had been able to buy chocolate cake with the money they paid her.[94]

In spite of some of the disquieting facets of Carson's life in 1961, the holiday season with which it ended was one of her best, she acknowledged. There had been much to be grateful for: She had published the book she had anguished over for fourteen years; there had been more good reviews than bad ones; and the novel was still on the list of the top ten. She recently had written, also, another nostalgic Christmas piece, which was published in *Redbook*'s December 1961 issue. (Rita Smith, her sister, had moved recently from *Mademoiselle*, where she was fiction editor, to the same position at *Redbook*.) Comparable to the earlier *Made-*

moiselle piece, "The Discovery of Christmas," the new one, "A Child's View of Christmas," reminisced her childhood discovery of Santa Claus and the sudden illumination of why "bad rich children" got big presents and poor people got "useful clothes" or shoes. She told of how she had discovered the Christmas closet which she had been cautioned never to open, and of her discovery that as the eldest child there were certain privileges which accompanied being knowledgeable of the mysteries of Christmas: of staying up late on Christmas Eve and sometimes helping with Santa Claus's work, of receiving the chicken liver at dinner—an envied delicacy—and of being served a half glass of wine along with the *other* grownups.

For Carson, "A Child's View of Christmas" was a fitting piece with which to close out the year, especially when viewed in juxtaposition with *Clock Without Hands*, the novel of her druggist Malone, who finally could die after experiencing, at last, "livingness" and rebirth. The British critics had attacked Carson for her coined words in the novel, but Dr. Edith Sitwell defended her and told her not to despair: "Philistines! They killed Keats, and they'll kill you, too, if you listen." Unlike her dying druggist, however, who had found "livingness" through death, Carson found hers through her beloved friend Mary Mercer and life.

Another joy of the 1961 Christmas season for Carson—in addition to being invited to stay at 5 Tweed Boulevard as Mary Mercer's house guest for a week—was being able to attend the Broadway première of Tennessee Williams' new play, *The Night of the Iguana*. Invited to sit with the playwright and his mother, Carson was surrounded by such assorted celebrities and artists as Eleanor Roosevelt, Judy Garland, Helen Hayes, and Lillian Gish. Mrs. Roosevelt crossed the aisle before the curtain went up on the first act to talk with Carson, a tribute that meant more to her, she said, than if she had won a Pulitzer Prize. She had always greatly admired the President's lady and loved now what she described as Mrs. Roosevelt's remarkable natural charm and graciousness. Carson had not known Judy Garland before, but Miss Garland, too, came over to meet her. Also in their little "personal" group that evening were Jordan Massee, Williams' brother, Dakin—who usually appeared on opening nights but saw little of the playwright otherwise—Carson's sister, her friend and lawyer, Floria Lasky, Miss Lasky's husband, David Altman, and Jack Dobbin, Carson's neighbor and friend who handled all of her personal financial details not requiring the services of Miss Lasky. After the play, Williams took Rita Smith and Jordan Massee backstage to meet his stars, Bette Davis and Margaret Leighton; then there was a dinner party at Sardi's given by Miss Lasky and Altman. Later, the group went to Williams' apartment to wait for the reviews and rejoice in what proved to be another Broadway hit for the man most critics now hailed as the world's greatest living playwright. To Carson, however, he always remained her "beloved Tenn"—no more, no less.

Other good things happened to Carson in 1961. In addition to the publication of *Clock Without Hands*, it looked as though there would be other significant professional successes as well. In 1960, producer Kermit Bloomgarden had become much interested in *Clock Without Hands* as a play, having read the initial chapter of the novel when it was published many years earlier in the Italian publication *Botteghe Oscure*. Before Carson had even finished the book, Bloomgarden took an option on it for a theatrical adaptation, and the following March—while the novel was still in galley proofs—he went to Nyack to discuss it with her further. Accompanying Bloomgarden were writers Frances and Albert Hackett and director George Roy Hill. Carson was delighted by the prospects of the Hacketts writing the stage script, for she greatly admired their adaptation of *The Diary of Anne Frank*, which she, herself, had once considered doing. Whereas she had been grossly disappointed by previous efforts of others who had worked with her material, Carson was supremely optimistic that she would be *more* than satisfied with the Hacketts' script. She was told that the adaptation could probably be ready in six months, but unfortunately, the play never materialized. It was a disappointment about which Carson said little. According to Mrs. Hackett, "Neither Mr. Bloomgarden nor Mr. Hill was enthusiastic, so the project was dropped. We felt bitterly that we had failed so miserably, and we never again saw Mrs. McCullers."[95]

More solid groundwork for adaptations of two of Carson's other novels was laid in 1961 with far more satisfactory results. Not only had a promising young playwright named Edward Albee written her the preceding summer expressing his desire to adapt *The Ballad of the Sad Café*, but also Carson's young friend Thomas Ryan had purchased outright the screen rights of *The Heart Is a Lonely Hunter*. It was a long time, however, before these works evolved. Albee's play was three years in the making, and eventually proved to be another disappointment for Carson; the shooting of Ryan's movie did not even begin until two days after her death.

By 1960, Albee had written several one-act plays presented off Broadway, and his first long work, *Who's Afraid of Virginia Woolf?*, was in progress. The young playwright had been fascinated by Carson's novella since 1952, six years before he actually started writing for the theatre. It had struck him then that the book was visual and dramatic. "Someday," he said, "I will put that on the stage myself." When Albee first approached the author, she had been too busy finishing *Clock Without Hands* to get involved in a new venture, she said, but if he would write a first scene, she would be happy to talk with him about it later. In September 1960, Albee showed Carson enough script to convince her that he had the sensitivity and insight to render her story faithfully in dramatic form. From then on it was all his, she told friends; or as Albee expressed it, "Carson gave me carte blanche and was very pleased with the results that she read."[96]

Even though she agreed to interpose in no way with his adaptation, it was difficult for her to leave the young and relatively inexperienced playwright completely on his own. (She later told reporter Marjory Rutherford that she had felt like an "interested grandmother" and that it would not have been "courteous to interfere."[97]) In spite of their initial agreement that Albee would work alone, Carson was pleased when he proposed opportunities for their being together. Like a "grandmother," too, she at least wanted to look on during the "rearing" process. Although Albee discussed with her on several occasions the adaptation, he wanted, mainly, to get better acquainted with the author herself, to get into her mind, to think as she thought. Vital to his play, he told reporters later, was the technique of making it seem as though Carson herself had written the work for the stage: "I am using whatever craft I have to make the piece completely Carson McCullers. No one should realize where she stops and I begin."[98] One of his challenges was to create dialogue out of a book almost totally lacking in it, transferring the exposition revealed by the narrator—actually the voice of Carson herself—to the characters involved, and also using a "balladier" who retained much of the narration of the author's own words. It was once suggested that Carson herself act as balladier and read some of her passages from the novel intact, such as her memorable thesis on love and relationship of the lover and the beloved. The narration could be taped so that she would not have to be onstage in person. The plan was abandoned as unworkable, however, and actor Roscoe Lee Browne was selected to read the balladier's lines.

In the spring of 1961, Albee invited Carson and Mary Mercer to join him at Shelter Island (a part of Long Island) for a few days so that they might get better acquainted and talk further about the adaptation. They met the following spring, also, at the home of Mary Tucker in Lexington, Virginia, where the playwright was an Ellen Glasgow lecturer at Washington and Lee University. Again, in late summer 1962, Albee invited Carson and Dr. Mercer to be his guests at Water Island, a small community on the tip end of Fire Island. Here, in seven weeks—working four hours every morning—Albee was able to do the bulk of the actual writing. As the playwright attempted to explain to Thomas Lask a few days before the play's opening, "Seven weeks was a deceptive figure, for the play had gone through a great deal of rumination, most of it unconscious" before page one went into the typewriter. He had learned, in fact, to have much confidence in the "nonconscious" part of his mind.[99] Once Albee sat down to work, the composition went rapidly: a quick first draft, pencil corrections, a second draft, and then no more changes until the play was in rehearsal.

It was in the summer of 1962 when Carson was recuperating from a critical "double operation" at Harkness Pavilion that Albee read to her and Mary Mercer the first act of the play *The Ballad of the Sad Café*. Immensely pleased by his art, as well as charmed by the man himself, Carson wrote an appreciative tribute for *Harper's Bazaar* ("The Dark Brilliance of Edward Albee") in January 1963. Speaking admiringly of Albee's sensitivity, gentle dignity, and genius, she acknowledged that his personality, too, reflected enormous talent. She spoke of their holiday at Fire Island when they walked together on the beach and sat up most of the night. She said that he talked about the stars to her, and like a rapt child, she marveled at his great love of nature and his knowledge of cosmic beings.

The playwright, too, spoke glowingly of Carson in his own brief sketch in the same issue of *Harper's Bazaar*, published as a companion piece to her article. Referring to Carson as "the Curious Magician," he said: "Examine this: she is both Child and Sage: Pain and Joy. She has mastered the card tricks of both art and life, and she has seen equally clearly the sleight of hand of reality and the truth which resides in legerdemain. She is kind enough to call me her friend."

When Albee returned to his "isolated sand dune" at Fire Island during the summer of 1963, he applied the finishing touches to his play. Again Carson and Mary Mercer visited the playwright at Fire Island, this time for about a week. "I read the play to Carson, and we discussed it, but I can't remember making any changes as a result of our discussion," said Albee.[100] Here he worked without further distraction until Labor Day, when the cast went into rehearsal. Likening *The Ballad of the Sad Café* to a piece of music with one long movement, Albee acknowledged that one of his chief problems was to place the act breakdowns. Finally he decided to delete the intermission. His play would have no acts, he decided; this would not only help the organic unity of the play, but also enable theatregoers to catch their commuter trains fifteen minutes earlier.[101]

At the beginning of rehearsals, the play ran for over three hours, but Albee began to cut his script drastically and to reshape it until it was an hour shorter. Slightly behind schedule for its earlier announced opening of October 14, 1963, a date purposefully selected because it was the anniversary of the opening of *Who's Afraid of Virginia Woolf?*, the show premièred instead on October 30 at the Martin Beck Theatre. Instead of the conventional pre-Broadway tour, its producers decided to schedule two weeks of local tours and previews. Budgeted at $120,000, the play was produced by Lewis Allen and Ben Edwards and directed by Alan Schneider, who also directed *Who's Afraid of Virginia Woolf?* Edwards did the sets. Starring as the dwarfish Cousin Lymon was Michael Dunn; Miss Amelia was played by Colleen Dewhurst, who had just won an "Obie"—off-Broadway's top dramatic award for her role in a revival of *Desire Under the Elms;* and the third member of the trio, Miss Amelia's husband, Marvin Macy, was played by Lou Antonio.

Carson attended only two rehearsals, she told reporters later. Conceding that she had made one or two suggestions regarding the adaptation, she insisted, as she had in the past, that she had left the playwright quite free to create as he chose. "I believe his adaptation will be interesting and compelling and add a new and beautiful dimension to an already beautiful work," she added with an immodest air which reporter Marjory Rutherford found refreshing.[102] Carson responded with a similar sense of her own worth in an interview with a reporter from Lafayette College, Pennsylvania, who talked with her shortly before the play's opening for a feature in the college magazine, *The Marquis.*[103] When asked how she felt about people who try to *teach* her novels, she responded: "Well, I guess that would depend upon the pupils."

"And do you think that that can be worthwhile?" the reporter pushed.

"Well, I think my work is *very* worthwhile."

The play opened to fairly good reviews, with perhaps Howard Taubman's comments in the New York *Times* showing the greatest sensitivity and appreciation for the collaboration.[104]

Many of the reviewers showed more concern with "the terrible and dim face of a shattered, unnatural love"—as Taubman termed the heart of the story—than with the craft of Albee's writing or the directing or acting of the production, an attitude which caused lay critics to speak out in the New York *Times'* "Drama Mailbag" (December 29, 1963), as did Edith Dobell of New York City:

> I think it misleading of your reviewer to keep on apologizing for this strange love in *The Ballad of the Sad Café* when what strikes one is the utter naturalness of the attractions given a particular psychological bias of each of the central characters. It is really one of the strengths of Carson McCullers' creation, and thoroughly achieved by Edward Albee's adaptation, that she makes us look beyond the superficial deviations of the dwarf and the mannish woman to the universal lives and loves which animate them.

Carson herself attended opening night, along with a host of her friends from the South who joined her personally or sent their good wishes for a long run. In town for the play, too, was her brother, Lamar, and his wife, Virginia, of whom Carson had seen little since their mother's death eight years earlier. (She had not returned to Columbus since 1953; from then on, her vision of the South was gleaned exclusively through memory, one more trip to Charleston, South Carolina, and several to Lexington, Virginia.) According to those closest to Carson, she was not pleased by the production, although she tried to keep such feelings from the press. The cast had performed marvelously, but she simply was not happy with the craft of the play.

Unfortunately, the play ran only two and a half months, closing on February 15, 1964. Many of Carson's friends felt that she had become unhappy with the adaptation and disillusioned by Albee when she saw it in rehearsal, that she felt the story simply did not "work" as he had rendered it; others believed that Carson's resentment stemmed from jealousy, from the fact that *Who's Afraid of Virginia Woolf?* had opened a year earlier than *her* play, had won the New York Drama Critics' Circle Award and a Tony Award, and was *still* running, whereas *The Ballad of The Sad Café* had closed after 123 performances.[105]

Albee himself had left the country almost immediately after the play's opening to participate in a seven-week cultural Russian-American exchange program in Europe and Asia. Carson resented his going since it meant that he would not be on hand to help with any changes which might have revitalized the production. Nor did his flippant comment to a New York *Times* reporter after opening night endear him to her, either: "I'm relieved it's over. The show went well, the actors remembered their lines, and the scenery did not fall down," said Albee. "Carson was not amused when the play closed after some one hundred performances," concluded Albee succinctly, "but then, neither was I."[106] In her final interview with Rex Reed in 1967, she had still another word regarding Albee and *The Ballad of the Sad Café*:

> Edward Albee was very young when he came to me to ask permission
> to adapt my *Ballad of the Sad Café*. He rented a small cabin with
> no electricity on Water Island and I sat up all night on the beach
> while he read it to me. However, when I saw it on Broadway I was
> disappointed. Edward had his own genius and I thought he was just
> cooling his heels working on something of mine. He should've been
> working on his own plays. There was no dialogue and no action in
> my novella and I told him it could not be done. I don't know how
> he feels but I still think I was right.[107]

Unlike the emotional repercussions of all previous adaptations, there was no dissension, apparently, of any kind between Carson and the next adapter of her material, Thomas Ryan. Wisely, Ryan had purchased outright the screen rights of *The Heart Is a Lonely Hunter*. Planning to write the script himself, he knew that he must be absolutely free to do it his way. "My version was a long time a-borning," Ryan explained:

> I purchased the rights in February of 1961, and the film started shooting on October 2, 1967. And since I produced as well as wrote the film, my work was not finished until July of 1968 when the film was ready for release.
>
> Now to backtrack. . . . I had absolutely no contact with Carson during the writing of the screenplay. I had purchased the rights to the novel since I was aware that it had to be done right or not at all. I had never written a screenplay and therefore was reluctant to give her any approval over the finished script. This was largely due to the prolonged unpleasantness between Carson on one side and the Theatre Guild on the other over an adaptation of *Member of the Wedding* written by Greer Johnson. Here, Carson did have an approval, refused to grant it, and the whole thing went into arbitration. I therefore suggested that I give her instead an approval over the director of the film, pointing out that no reputable director would assist in the rape of a classic. This was acceptable to her. After she read the script, she delegated that approval of director to me.
>
> The script was finished [in 1963] and I had made a deal to do it with Montgomery Clift as Singer (this deal was later canceled due to the uninsurability of Clift). However, during the preparation period, rumors had drifted up to Nyack and Carson got curious. Once she had approved of the then director, Sidney Lumet, I had no objections to her reading it. However, she did not want to read it, she wanted it read to her. So up I went to Nyack on a hot August afternoon, and read it aloud to Carson and Mary Mercer. It was the most agonizing ordeal of my life. Only a writer can imagine the torture of reading his adaptation of her most autobiographical work to someone of Carson's standing.
>
> We had had lunch, and it was about three when I began to read. I had to read everything, the descriptions of sets and costumes and action as well as the dialogue. When I had finished, it was beginning to grow dark. Both women were crying, and I had the shakes. I didn't know whether she thought I had wrecked her book or was moved by the scenario. Finally she beckoned me over to her chair, embraced me, kissed me, and, still crying, said, "If I had had you with me to help me write the book, then it really would be as good as some people think it is." It's the greatest compliment I ever expect to receive.
>
> After that, everything was roses. She never mentioned to me the excision of Biff Brannon, nor any of the million other things that were changed from the book—two towns instead of one, the dropping

of Mick's older brother and two older sisters, the fact that it wasn't a boardinghouse, the fusing of Copeland's three sons and one daughter into a very different version of the daughter. In this latter regard, she was particularly taken with the drastic changes affecting this portion of the novel. I felt that she was particularly referring to this when she said it was better than the book. I had pointed out to her that all I had done was to try to do what she had done, some twenty years later in time.

About Biff, the question was one of time. The finished picture runs two hours and six minutes. More would have gotten too long, so something had to go. I felt Biff was the least dramatizable character in the book, particularly so in his never shown maternal feelings for Mick and so he was what went. I might add that it is my feeling that Carson was so generous in her praise of the adaptation not merely because she felt that the movie would say what the book had said, but also because by this time, having adapted *The Member of the Wedding*, she was aware of the necessity to change certain things and add and subtract others in order to translate the book to another medium. I was further helped by the fact that at the time of my reading, Edward Albee's adaptation of *The Ballad of the Sad Café* was going into rehearsal and *that* was an adaptation with which she was not happy.[108]

Ryan had been born and reared in New York City, as were both of his parents. Yet after Carson heard his script and loved it, she adopted the idea that Ryan, too, was southern. Robert Lantz, who became Carson's agent in the early 1960s, explained to Ryan that she felt a faithful adaptation of her work could only be made by a Southerner and that he had done so; therefore he was one. "No amount of argument on my part could shake her from this conviction," said Ryan. Again, a few months before her death, Carson avowed to Rex Reed that since the adapter of *The Heart Is a Lonely Hunter* was a fellow Southerner, Tom Ryan, his script had much of her original feeling in it. "I wouldn't trust a northern writer with it," she said.[109]

An option for still a third novel, *Reflections in a Golden Eye*, was taken in 1963 by producer Ray Stark, but as early as 1956 negotiations were begun with Harold Hecht and Burt Lancaster Productions. It was the hope of Hecht and Lancaster to acquire movie rights to the novel, to have Tennessee Williams write the screenplay, and Sir Carol Reed direct. Carson was skeptical, however, that the book could truthfully and artistically be transformed into a movie, and the matter was dropped. Years later, she was approached again, this time by John Huston. Perhaps the movie did have a chance if two outstanding directors wanted it, she replied. When Huston asked her if she preferred that the movie be an art film, or one with a prestigious cast, she chose the latter. She was sure that with the right cast, it could be both. Although casting was not completed and filming not begun until the fall of 1966, Carson kept in close touch with Ray Stark and John Huston, who apprised her fully of each major development. Tennessee Williams was never seriously approached to do the film script. Most of the writing was done by Huston's friend and long-time assistant, Gladys Hill. British novelist Chapman Mortimer coauthored the work.

Carson's last years were marked by a lack of the finite. There were unfinished stories, an unfinished musical version of *The Member of the Wedding* that she and Mary Rodgers worked on for almost three years, and an unfinished journal about her life, her works, and why she wrote them—a book she reportedly entitled *Illuminations and Night Glare*. These last years must be viewed against a backdrop of unspeakable pain, repeated hospitalizations for critical illnesses and surgery, and a body that had wasted away to a fragile container which housed little more than a soul. Sparking it all were enormous courage, a fantastic strength and will to hang on—which cannot be attributed to a fear of death but to an insatiable desire to live—and a love, nurture, and comfort such as she had never known before through her guardian spirit, Mary Mercer. Carson had said in the opening lines of *Clocks Without Hands* that "death is always the same, but each man dies in his own way." She, too, had died a little each day, but in the process—as Jordan Massee so aptly put it—"she gave her doctors one hell of a fight for survival."[110]

An overview of Carson's medical history during the 1960s alone is staggering. There were, of course, the two initial operations on her damaged arm in 1959 after her physical condition had been reassessed and it was determined that her maimed limbs could be helped by surgery. Two more operations followed in 1961 after the completion of her novel. In June 1962, there was a critical eight-hour "double operation" in which her cancerous right breast was removed, followed by the surgery originally scheduled for her left hand. (In the operating room after this ordeal Carson gave her doctors cause for alarm. Her blood pressure hovered dangerously close to shock level, and the next morning her nurse was unable to get a blood pressure reading. Carson herself called Mary Mercer that morning on the telephone to insist that she come immediately to the hospital. Later Dr. Mercer wrote Mary Tucker that she had not wanted to upset Mrs. Tucker unnecessarily, but that Carson's life had hung precariously for about twenty-four hours following the surgery.) In September 1963, Carson returned to Harkness Pavilion for still more surgery, this time on her aching and swollen crippled left leg.

Carson's most severe afflictions in 1964 were a broken hip and shattered elbow, the result of a fall when she had gotten up alone to go into the bathroom one night. It had been Carson's special arrangement with Dr. Mercer that she would telephone her friend if she were to get up in the night for any reason; then she was to call her again when she was safely in bed. This time Mary Mercer waited frantically for the return call, then rushed to the house to discover Carson lying on the bathroom floor. The accident resulted in critical surgery again, it being risky this time for Carson even to undergo anesthesia. A metal cap was inserted over the femur, and there were discomforting casts and bedsores to cope with later. Through it all, Carson withstood well the pain, but it was almost four months before she was able to walk again.

Later, from the spring of 1964 until July 1965, an excruciating ache in her hip became incessant, and doctors were at a loss to account for it. According to Jordan Massee, "The Nyack physicians who treated Carson had no real understanding of her pain, it seemed, and they thought it was psychosomatic. True, she may have invented many things for enjoyment, but pain was not one of them."[111] On July 14, 1965, Dr. F. Randolph Bailey of Columbia-Presbyterian Neurological Institute performed at Harkness Pavilion an exploratory operation and additional nerve surgery on every finger joint of her left hand. "This time the doctors discovered the real cause of Carson's pain. A pin had slipped from her hip after the earlier operation and was wandering around pinching her," said Massee. "Dr. Bailey said it was a miracle she came through it, or survived the next ten days. He also said that *miracle* was not a word he used very often." To Mary Mercer, it was not only a miracle, but also Carson's indomitable will which kept her alive.[112]

Carson spent the next three months on a flotation pad in a specially equipped motorized bed that rocked continuously from head to foot so that there would be less danger of fluids settling in her lungs or of blood clots forming. Throughout her long ordeal of great personal suffering, Carson required an inordinate amount of physical closeness of people she loved. When Jordan Massee came to see her in the hospital during this particular stay, she demanded that he get in bed with her so that they could be "close" and talk and rock in her moving bed together. Even when Carson was in an oxygen tent in the Nyack hospital after her heart attack in 1959, she wanted Massee to get inside the tent with her. Finally he put his head in, a gesture which appeased her.[113] Later, when Massee spent weekends at her house, she usually insisted that he bathe in her tiny bathtub off her bedroom so that she could come in and sit beside him during his ablution.

Once Carson was home again from the hospital, there were demanding hours of physiotherapy, spiritual solitude, and pain. If only she could believe in God as Mary Mercer and Mary Tucker did, she lamented from time to time, but she acknowledged that her loves, instead, had always been intensely personal, with human love at the center of every relationship. Mary Mercer continued to nurture and sustain Carson for the rest of her life. People who knew them both well—including Lamar, Carson's brother—gave Dr. Mercer full credit for giving Carson both a will and a way to live which prolonged her life by almost ten years. Carson loved her friend almost from the moment they first met. She also admired everything about her. Sometimes she would ask Jordan Massee if he did not agree that Mary Mercer was "sexy-looking." Massee, however, thought "there was more of Garbo than of Sophia Loren in that exquisite apparition. She was the only chic angel I ever encountered," he added. Massee was deeply devoted to Mary Mercer and grateful that Carson had her for a friend and healer. "Those who did not like Mary Mercer—and there were a few—could not bear her, but it was usually for some small and petty reason. Some people were jealous of their relationship, for they felt Mary was drawn to Carson only because of her fame and talent. Nothing could have been further from the truth," he said.[114]

During the 1960s, there was little physical difference between Carson's postoperative weakened condition and her so-called "normal" state, although her friends could tell when her *mind* was beginning to feel good once more. Massee noted that in about five days after Carson's critical "double operation" in 1962 she began to show something of her old vitality. When she began to pump her cousin for new tales and to tell him about funny encounters or conversations she had had with her nurses and doctors, he knew that she would recover.

In the hospital, and at home later during her various periods of recuperation, Carson was served appetizing meals, but no one stood over her and made her eat. Ida Reeder was more insistent, however, and achieved better results than anyone else. Massee, who tried to be with Carson at mealtime in the hospital as often as possible to encourage her to eat, saw to it that her trays usually were returned to the kitchen almost empty. "But I am afraid I ate much more of her food than she did. It was kind of a game with Carson. It was usually impossible to put anything over on Ida," said Massee, "but even in Nyack I frequently managed to eat for the two of us. During Carson's last years I was with her enough to know that she rarely consumed anything in quantity except bourbon and a chocolate bar of Ex-Lax nightly." To Massee, it seemed that Carson suffered from a chemical imbalance due to malnutrition. "Certainly she did not eat enough during her last years to stay alive, and no amount of pampering—mine or anyone else's—made Carson eat one bit more than she herself wanted." As with her friend Isak Dinesen, who suffered severely from malnutrition, the idea of food was always better than the real thing.

"She loved the idea of caviar, for example, but not the caviar itself," said Massee, "although there were times when she went on food binges and ate great quantities of certain dishes, such as boiled custard, artichoke relish, and oysters."

After the 1965 surgery, Massee recalled that Carson lamented that she had lost her taste for what she jokingly called her "beloved demon rum." And once or twice he found her drinking Coca-Colas. But at no time did Carson's doctors seriously attempt to eliminate alcohol from her diet or to insist that she stop smoking. According to Massee, "Mary Mercer would never have allowed it." Although many people over the years thought that Carson drank too much, her consumption during her last ten years—when she was most fragile—had no visible ill effects. "It was impossible for a visitor to tell whether she had had three drinks or none," said Massee.[115]

Perhaps one of the most difficult duties of a household attendant at night during the 1960s was to get Carson to be willing to go to sleep. It was usually several hours from the time she got up from her chair in the living room—that is, before she was bedridden during her last year—until she was actually ready to go to sleep. Carson had to have help dressing and undressing, for in spite of her surgical operations she could not lift her arm enough to pull a nightgown over her head by herself. Doubtless it was the liquor which made sleep possible at all, concluded Massee. In addition to wearing her night shade, as had been her habit for years, she required sleeping pills. Those who helped her at night always shuddered a little to see the assortment of pills and sleeping potions on her bedside table. Even though Ida put out the proper dosage in individual servers and specified which ones Carson was to take, and when, the bottles from which the pills came remained beside her. In spite of her pain and moments of despair over the last years, there was still a pervading confidence among her friends that she would never intentionally overdose herself. If cigarettes and alcohol soothed and helped her through the days and nights, such "addiction" was minor compared to her more serious afflictions. Carson was a chain performer rather than a chain smoker; smoking was simply a psychological necessity. Although she "smoked" a package of cigarettes every two hours, she never took more than three or four puffs off each cigarette before lighting another.

During her last several years there were only a few lighters Carson could manipulate, for she had little strength even in her good right hand. Finally, when butane lighters with their push-button mechanisms came on the market, she had no further problem. Keeping the flame on the highest setting, however, she alarmed her visitors, who feared that she might set herself, or her bed, on fire. One of Ida's chores over the years was to gather up Carson's old cigarette lighters and take them a few blocks down the street to Eli Avstreih, the druggist at Shea's Pharmacy in Nyack. Avstreih adjusted and repaired them or sent out new lighters for her to try. Fond of the frail, famous artist whose business he had had almost since her move to Nyack, he took pleasure in delivering drugs to her house and inquiring if there were any special service he might perform.[116]

Throughout these years Carson was surrounded by what one observer close to her called a "sickbed coterie." There was always a gentleman available for errands or to sit and read to her, or a "lady in waiting," workers who sincerely yearned to serve the living legend. Several women in the vicinity were exceedingly kind and generous to Carson during her last years, people like Dorothy Salisbury Davis, Jane Anderson, Betty Lee, and Ruth Wells, who came to see her often, and later, faithfully sat at her bedside in the hospital during the weeks of coma which followed her final stroke. There were also several friends who remained close to her throughout her adult life; among these was Henry Varnum Poor, who came to see her regularly. Once when Carson was recuperating from one of her serious surgeries, she went alone to a little art gallery-gift shop in Nyack that had been operated for years by her friends Margaret English and Virginia Johnston, to attend an exhibit of Poor's work. Miss English was impressed that Carson arrived unattended, by taxi. "She was walking with a cane and obviously very ill and in pain, but she wanted to show her great love for Henry Poor and her respect for his work," recalled Miss English. "Carson walked around slowly and carefully, then bought one or two of Mr. Poor's paintings."[117]

In addition to the workers and the sickbed coterie, there were also what some onlookers referred to as "the big names" and the "hangers-on." The former, however, were usually in the wings and rarely made an appearance. They might visit her in the hospital after seeing a sketchy news note that she was ill again, and they sent flowers and little gifts, but there was little personal contact. Frequently Carson's agent or a local devotee telephoned someone of importance from her literary past and said, "Carson loves you—please come see her." But they seldom came except on special occasions. Although the big names still admired her and some loved her, few could afford for long the emotional drain. On the other hand, to her intimate associates, it seemed that the hangers-on continued to sponge, soaking up hospitality and glimmers of glory. As David Diamond pointed out many years earlier, "Carson was never selective in her friends. They *selected* her, and if they paid the proper respect and adulation, they were her friends."[118]

Almost everyone who knew anything about Carson's habits and cared for her, knew when it was her birthday and made a point of calling on her with a present. The more thoughtful ones who were out of town and could not get to Nyack for the occasion called her on the telephone. To receive a greeting in the mail was usually a disappointment to Carson, for it meant that there would be no present. Cards were frequently put aside with "disgruntled appreciation," said Jordan Massee. Whereas she normally did not get up until about eleven o'clock, on her birthdays she was up and dressed by seven or eight o'clock, her hair combed, and she was sitting by the window waiting for the first visitor. Sometimes, in typically childlike manner, she ignored certain gifts that were handed her by friends coming to pay tribute and laid them aside so that she would have something to open later, after everyone had gone. Often she forgot about them temporarily, and when her guest prepared to leave she might ask expectantly, "But what did *you* bring me?"

Tennessee Williams always made a point to see Carson on her birthday if it were at all possible. He would frequently fly up from New Orleans or Key West just to spend a few hours with her. One birthday, however, he did not arrive until midafternoon, and Carson had been waiting impatiently for him all day. When he and his friend Frank Merlo finally walked into her living room and kissed her, they placed before her a bird cage containing two love birds. Williams was sure she would be charmed by such an unusual gift and think it marvelous. Carson eyed the cage suspiciously and was less than extravagant in her thanks. When Williams and Merlo got up to leave several hours later, they leaned over and kissed her, then started for the door. Carson called her old friend back and pointed to the cage. Smiling wryly, she said softly: "Tenn, honey, just take those ole birds back with you."[119]

Carson was almost as excited over Christmas as she was over birthdays, especially when it came to selecting gifts for Mary Mercer. She could seldom think of "just the right present," however, and would worry doggedly over it for weeks. Not being able to shop herself, she relied often on her cousin for suggestions and the final selection. One winter Paul Bigelow called Massee from Connecticut and told him about an exquisite blond mink stole which he had an opportunity to buy at a great savings. "Do you think Carson would like it for Mary?" asked Bigelow. Massee consulted her, believing it would be the perfect gift, and Carson was ecstatic. According to Massee, "She was also sure that Mary would be, too, but since it was impossible for her to keep a secret about anything, she hinted and hinted to Mary, then finally told her outright. Having no idea that the mink stole was a 'bargain,' however, and objecting strenuously to Carson's plan to 'spend that much money on her,' Mary decided that the best way to handle it would be to tell Carson that she simply did not want a blond mink stole and would not wear it." Crushed, Carson wanted to show it to Mary Mercer anyway in hopes that she would change her mind, but there was a complication which kept Bigelow from arriving with it when he had promised. Furious because she thought that Bigelow was "trying to put something over on her," Carson complained to Massee, who, in turn, tried to protect his friend—whom he considered the innocent victim in the intrigue—with a lie. "I should have known better, of course," said Massee, "for no one respected the truth more than Carson did, nor was anyone, inherently, more honest—in spite of her taletelling—but she at once saw through the story and was furious at my deception."[120]

Immediately Carson called Floria Lasky and instructed her to bring her will to the house. According to Massee, Carson had threatened to change her will on several other occasions when she became miffed at her sister, Ida, or one of the other heirs. Once she reportedly insisted on removing her sister from the will and another time threatened to leave the entire estate to Mary Mercer. But this time, with great relish she drew a line through her bequest to Jordan Massee and signed her name to the change. Although Massee's legacy was to have been only one thousand dollars, Rita Smith and Miss Lasky reportedly were horrified over Carson's drastic action and urged her to reinstate him, pointing out that he loved her and had served her long and well. After a few days of reflection on his misadventure, Carson thoroughly forgave Massee and reportedly asked that he "be put back in." Inadvertently, however, the change was never made. When Carson's will eventually was read, the major heirs were mortified that her loyal friend and cousin would not share in any way in the estate. At first, said Jordan Massee, they considered making up the portion out of their own inheritance and never letting him know otherwise, feeling that Carson would have wanted him to benefit as she had originally intended. Finally, it was agreed that he be told the truth; if not, they were afraid that someday a biographer would come along, see the will, and ask why Massee had been cut out of it (which, indeed, was the case).[121] Carson's cousin understood all too well the situation and was entirely forgiving; nor had he ever "served" Carson with the idea of there being any remuneration other than the spiritual and flesh-and-blood relationship itself.

Along with the myths and legends that abounded about Carson over the years—which bothered her not at all—to Carson's visitors during the 1960s, Ida Reeder became almost as much a legend as her mistress. Carson and Ida called each other "Sister," and it was obvious to all that their relationship was far more than employer-housekeeper. More also than a friend, companion, and confidante, Ida was indispensable to Carson's physical well-being. Large, gentle and kind, she was, as one friend observed, "Carson's arms and legs." Ida bathed and dressed her and took her to the bathroom, cooked her favorite dishes, cut up her meat, told her when to take her medicine, when to rest, and when it was time for guests to leave. Rex Reed remembered well Ida's interrupting him during a long interview, saying, "It's time for Sister to take her nap now."

"That, dear Rex," said Carson, "is orders from headquarters."[122]

According to many observers, Ida also performed all manner of non-personal tasks for the household at 131 South Broadway: cleaning woodwork, ironing curtains, making appointments, planning menus, buying groceries, running errands (by taxi), showing apartments, collecting rents —in short, being a shrewd businesswoman for her employer and an efficient housekeeper. From time to time she also wrote personal letters in longhand, which Carson dictated to her. Perhaps the most talked-about characteristic of Carson's ubiquitous companion, however—apart from her devotion to her mistress—was her dedication to her church. Ida took pride in being able to solicit more donations for the Pilgrim Baptist Church of Nyack than did any other member. There were times, even, when she reportedly raised more money than the rest of the congregation together. No one was more aware of Ida's devotion to the church dollar than Carson's guests. Because of her invalid state and sizable reputation, Carson doubtless had more people flow in and out of her living room or bedroom in an almost continuous stream during the 1960s than did any other single household in Nyack. If a visitor left 131 South Broadway without being approached for a solid donation, Ida either was ill or not on the premises. John Huston gave Ida one hundred dollars. Elizabeth Bowen was another generous giver, and there were countless other affluent visitors whom Ida habitually stopped on their way out, reminding them graciously that their gifts were tax deductible.

Ida had countless followers among the tenants at 131 South Broadway, tradespeople who dealt with her when she insisted that *she* was "the lady of the house," and visitors in general whom she met in the service of her mistress. To many, Ida was Carson's "unsung hero"; to others, she "got away with murder" and was well paid—extravagantly paid, said some —for every service performed. Ida could be "very demanding," said Ruth Wells, who lived in the house for a number of years. Once Ida *told* Carson that she wanted twenty-five dollars from her for an Easter hat, but Carson refused. "I've never hooded my own head, and I don't intend to help you hood yours," she replied.[123]

In November 1964, when Carson made out her will, Ida had been with her almost ten years. Many people who observed Ida's devotion and attention thought that she would be well remembered in Carson's will; a few skeptics believed that she would doubtless be left nothing. Knowing the author's affection and sense of fair-mindedness toward blacks and other minority groups, however, most people envisioned Ida's receiving a significant portion of the estate. It was shocking, therefore, when they heard that she had been left only twenty-five hundred dollars. To some, the bequest seemed "a betrayal of a devoted servant."[124] Others, who had observed the situation firsthand over the years, felt that Ida had been generously "given her due" during the author's lifetime and that there was no need for excessive further remuneration. Whatever the "right" or "wrong" of it may have seemed to others, the fact remained that Ida herself reportedly was grievously disappointed. (In other cash bequests, Carson left five thousand dollars each to the two children of Floria Lasky and David Altman; twenty-five hundred dollars to Jack Dobbin; one thousand dollars to her brother Lamar's son; one thousand dollars to Marielle Bancou's son, Pascal; and ten thousand dollars to Mary Mercer. The remainder of the estate was divided equally among her sister, brother, and Dr. Mercer, except for things that had belonged to Carson's mother—which were left to her sister—and the rest of her personal effects, dishes, furnishings, etc., which went to Dr. Mercer.)

Many people continued to find Carson less than generous during her last years. A few called her "downright stingy." But there was also a bountiful side to her nature. In 1962, when the Reverend Anthony McCombe, a black pastor who moved to Nyack as assistant minister of the Grace Episcopal Church, was unable to find a house or apartment anywhere in the vicinity into which he and his wife might move, someone suggested that he "try 131 South Broadway where there was a kind and liberal author who might take him in." Carson fixed up her tiny attic apartment for the couple and gave it to them for practically nothing. Another time she gave a job to an unmarried pregnant girl from the missionary college "because no one else seemed to want her."[125] When Kenneth French, a young librarian at the local high school who had rented Carson's basement apartment since 1961, prepared to go abroad one summer with little funds, Carson insisted that he keep the apartment during his absence and pay her no rent. They became good friends, and French helped her in the preparation of her book of children's rhymes. In the afternoon when he came in from school he read to her, and frequently they had a drink together in the evening. To French, except for her lack of munificence to Ida in the will, Carson was one of the most generous persons he had ever known.[126]

Another tenant at 131 South Broadway was Charles Cordova, an elderly gentleman who had moved into the apartment immediately above Carson's living room in 1962 and was still there ten years later. Pleased to be living in a celebrity's house, he had Carson autograph books for his granddaughter. "I did not see much of Mrs. McCullers," said Cordova, "for Ida always collected the rent. But Mrs. McCullers was friendly and kind when I used to see her before she got so sick. I do remember, though, that she didn't like to spend money on her property. Once I tried to get her to repair an old sink and drainboard which I had been putting up with for years, but she said that there was no money, so I spent $150 of my own and repaired it myself."[127]

Doubtless no one knew Carson during the 1960s as well as did Mary Mercer, who sometimes was put, inadvertently, into a position of explaining her to others. Carson and Mary Tucker had been reconciled since 1950 and were dearer to one another in the 1960s than ever before; yet there were times when Carson seemed to hurt Mrs. Tucker intentionally. In Lexington, Virginia, where she and Mary Mercer visited Mrs. Tucker a few months after Colonel Tucker's death, Carson could not seem to resist bringing up the painfully estranging circumstances that had wounded both of them deeply in the past. Hurt, Mrs. Tucker expressed herself on the subject to Mary Mercer, whom she now considered an ally and friend. There were times when each woman tried to explain Carson's enigmas to the other, but in this role Dr. Mercer was by far the more experienced one in coping with the many facets of Carson's genius and temperament. During the summer of 1962 Mary Mercer wrote several letters to Mary Tucker offering deep insight into Carson's ambivalent needs and desires. She said that in trying to minister to Carson's physical, emotional, and intellectual needs she was attempting a horrendous task, for Carson needed a troop of people twenty-four hours a day to absorb and react to her insatiable zest for life. Dr. Mercer explained to Mrs. Tucker how Carson was able to transfix and then resolve her emotional conflicts and tensions through her writing. Mary Mercer assured Mrs. Tucker once again that *The Member of the Wedding* would never have been created had Mrs. Tucker not left Columbus, and in Carson's eyes, abandoned *her*. Great art came out of the conflict, and then it was finished. The world was enriched by it, but that was secondary to the benefit which Carson derived personally from the writing itself. Although Carson identified indiscriminately with all humanity and was inconsistent to the nth degree, Dr. Mercer reminded Mrs. Tucker, she had the enduring quality of great compassion that came into play when it seemed that she had abandoned all else. No matter how persistently she might seem to harass her friend now, advised Dr. Mercer, Mary Tucker must know and be assured that Carson, indeed, loved her. Dr. Mercer suggested, however, that if Carson reproached Mrs. Tucker unduly, she should speak up to her and end the matter at once. Carson would respect that. With her, it was a kind of game. She meant to tease, rather than wound, said Dr. Mercer.[128]

Dr. Mercer and Mary Tucker continued their correspondence throughout most of the rest of Carson's life, and there were a number of visits over the years back and forth between "Tuckaway," Mrs. Tucker's Lexington country home, and Nyack. Whenever possible, Mary Mercer accompanied Carson on her trips. Carson traveled more during her last years than anyone thought possible. Only two months after her eight-hour double operation for breast cancer and hand surgery in 1962, she and Dr. Mercer spent a few days with Edward Albee on Fire Island—as they were to do each summer until *The Ballad of the Sad Café* was produced—and a few days after the Fire Island trip, she accompanied Major Simeon Smith (a West Point instructor and Ph.D. candidate from the University of Pennsylvania who was researching Carson's professional career for a dissertation) to the Academy for an afternoon and dinner meeting with William Faulkner and the cadets. Faulkner reportedly crossed the auditorium and walked up the aisle to greet her, whom he affectionately embraced and addressed as "my daughter." In the fall, she made a final pilgrimage to England to be a symposium guest on the "Sex in Literature" panel at the Cheltenham Literary Festival. Then she attended Dame Edith Sitwell's seventy-fifth birthday celebration and granted a BBC interview.

Carson's trip to England in 1962 was at the invitation of her friend British novelist Elizabeth Jane Howard, honorary artistic director of the Cheltenham Festival. It was a six-day affair, beginning on October 1 and featuring each day a different facet of the literary arts. Appearing on Carson's panel October 4—considered the "feature program"—were French writer and diplomat Romain Gary, British novelist Kingsley Amis (the husband of Miss Howard), and Brooklyn-born writer Joseph Heller. Before she left the United States, Carson told her friend Kenneth French that she had been asked to talk on love. "But what do I say to them, darling?" she asked him. "I don't have any more of it left." There was no problem, once she got there. She simply read from *The Ballad of the Sad Café* her love thesis involving the lover-beloved relationship and the coda of the chain gang. A reviewer described Carson as "speaking bravely despite illness . . . [who] deplored the tragedy of exclusive love."[129] She was also invited to present the literary prizes the last day of the festival.[130]

According to the reviewers, the festival was not a distinguished affair. Although the "Sex in Literature" symposium attracted the greatest public interest, several critics called it a "flop." Everyone spoke out against censorship. Joseph Heller volunteered that "so long as readers get excited about sex, it is unreasonable to expect novelists not to get excited about it as well." When asked what characters in contemporary fiction did not seem to get much pleasure from sex, Heller replied flippantly that in his novel *Catch 22*, "they had a hell of a good time." Kingsley Amis declared that he would rather write any scene than a sex scene: "Novelists are self-conscious people, and while they do not wish to appear genteel, they dislike displaying their hairy chests in public." Romain Gary suggested that there was something wrong with a society that allowed free expression to Fascists and Communists but worried about writers using four-letter words. To Gary, there were many things "dirtier" such as the hydrogen bomb that one should be concerned about. All the reviewers spoke kindly of Carson. Frank Tuohy, writing for *Spectator*, concluded that "there was the strange and suffering presence of Carson McCullers to remind us that the creation of art can still be a tragic and desperate endeavour, worthy of the last resources of the human spirit. At Cheltenham, an enjoyable British occasion, it was very easy to forget this."[131]

Joseph Heller recalled that "while Miss McCullers moved about London and Cheltenham with a great deal of mental zeal, particularly in the matter of shopping for antiques, she was accompanied by a nurse and was barely able to speak. I met her only twice: at a luncheon in London, where we sat apart, and at the symposium, where her remarks were brief, mainly of a perfunctory nature acknowledging her gratitude at being invited there, and uttered with very great difficulties, the vowel sounds long, the consonants muffled. It was, I recall, an occasion both depressing and inspiring—at least for me."[132]

The highlight of Carson's trip—and a greater motive for going abroad than the festival—was being with Dame Edith Sitwell again. Marielle Bancou was in Paris at the time, and when Carson arrived in London she called Miss Bancou and urged her to join Dame Edith and her for lunch. Immediately Miss Bancou flew to London. For her, it was a marvelous reunion with Carson, whom she had not seen in several months:

> The lunch lasted three hours, and I remember that Carson was
> dressed very crazily. She had gone over by herself—which impressed
> me—but she had an English nurse with her named Miss Fatwell, who
> gave Carson much to laugh about. It was marvelous watching
> Dame Edith and Carson attempt to outwit each other. Carson gave
> a champagne toast, saying: "To the true Queen of England," after
> which Edith returned the toast, saying: "To the First Lady of
> America." Then Dame Edith asked about the appropriate saluta-
> tion to the political First Lady of America. "Mrs. Kennedy,"
> Carson replied.
> "How dull!" retorted Edith.[133]

The official party for Dame Edith was a performance in the Royal Festival Hall in London. Dame Edith, dressed in scarlet and sitting in a wheelchair, read from her poetry. Then Peter Pears, Carson's former housemate from 7 Middagh Street, sang Benjamin Britten's arrangement of Dame Edith's "Still Falls the Rain." Another acquaintance of Carson's, Sir William Walton, conducted the English Chamber Orchestra, and the program was concluded by a performance of Dame Edith's musical drama, *Façade*. Afterward there was a party in Dame Edith's honor, where Carson met Graham Greene, whose work she admired.

Once again Carson was welcomed and acclaimed by many critics and friends she had met on her first visit to London during the height of her success.

Dame Edith died two years later, and in the memoirs written soon afterward by her secretary and companion, Elizabeth Salter, there was a description of Carson the day "she came to Greenhill to call on Dame Edith":

> About Carson herself she [Dame Edith] had a fund of stories, told with affection and exaggeration, from which I had built up a picture very different from Miss McCullers as she appeared that day. Very pale, wearing a fur coat and carpet slippers, she managed the walk down Edith's corridor with the help of a stick and the young nurse in attendance. Slim, younger looking than I had expected, she managed, in spite of the paralysed arm and the injured face muscles that could sustain a smile for a few seconds only, to convey the atmosphere of the perennial adolescent. Her attitude towards Edith was demonstrative, her southern drawl irresistibly reminiscent of dialogue written by her friend Tennessee Williams.[134]

Carson made one more trip to the deep South to see Edwin Peacock and John Zeigler. On April 12, 1963, she and Mary Mercer flew to Charleston for a four-day weekend, staying at the Hotel Fort Sumter instead of at Zeigler's ante-bellum mansion so that Carson would not have to climb stairs. Dr. Mercer had made it clear to their hosts that Carson would not be up to much frivolity and that her activities should be kept to a minimum. Carson was coming to see *them,* she emphasized. Dr. Mercer and Carson did, however, consent to attend one small party with Peacock and Zeigler in nearby Mount Pleasant, where they met Gordon Langley Hall, the adopted son of British actress Dame Margaret Rutherford, who had recently come to Charleston. Carson was intrigued by Hall, whom she later described as "a rather strange young British gentleman." Hall, twenty-six, was the author of a number of published biographies about famous American women, mainly wives of the Presidents. Always more an observer than a participant, Carson had little to say to Hall throughout the evening. But just as they were about to leave, she turned suddenly toward the young man and said, "I want to talk to the *child* [referring to Hall]. Please leave us together for a few minutes." Alone with the shy, rather diffident man who now sat beside her, Carson studied him closely without speaking. Then, with a bit of smile, she said gently, "You're really a little girl."

Hall looked at her, then nodded. Later, the young man reflected upon their "moment of truth," as he called it:

> Of course I knew the truth in Carson's words, but no one had ever seen that in me before. All my life I had tried to hide the fact

simply because a country midwife in England had wrongly registered
me as a boy. Years later—after Carson had "discovered" me—Dr. El-
liott Phipps, the eminent Harley Street gynecologist was to pronounce me as having always been a woman, wrongly sexed at birth,
and capable of having children. Carson, her senses sharpened by her
own affliction, saw me for what I was in a moment of truth and her
heart went out to me. I was a freak, yes, a freak, like one of her own
characters in *The Ballad of the Sad Café*. After that, we became
great friends, but she always worried because I had no intimate
friend, male or female.[135]

During the year that followed, Carson and her British friend corresponded frequently. When Hall was in the hospital undergoing what
he later termed "a prelude to the change," Carson sent him flowers with
a note expressing her love. Then in May 1963, he came to Nyack to
bring Carson a gift—an exquisite two-hundred-year-old Chinese robe he
had recently inherited from his cousin Isabel Lydia Whitney, America's
first woman fresco painter. Thrilled by Hall's generosity and the beauty of
the robe, Carson said that she would wear it to the opening of *The Ballad
of the Sad Café* that fall.

Several years later when Carson's sister, Rita Smith, was in Charleston, Peacock and Zeigler took her to a party at Hall's fashionable old
Society Street mansion. According to Peacock, a young Negro man
met them at the door, invited them in, mixed drinks, served them, and
then took his own off the tray and sat down to join in the conversation.
Amazed at the familiarity of the servant, Miss Smith reportedly could
hardly wait to tell Carson and Jordan Massee about the experience. It
seemed that Hall had fallen in love with young John-Paul Simmons, his
houseboy and chauffeur. Carson loved the story and delighted in hearing
further evidence that fact is often much better than fantasy, but seldom
believed unless cloaked in fiction.

Carson died before the next chapter in the ambivalent life of Gordon Hall could be recorded, however. Declared a transsexual, Hall underwent a series of operations at Johns Hopkins Hospital to complete his
transformation into a woman. Carson doubtless would have applauded all
facets of his unconventionality. In 1969, a few weeks after Gordon
Langley Hall was baptized Dawn Pepita Hall, she further defied Charleston society and became Mrs. John-Paul Simmons. In 1971, Mrs. Simmons
reportedly gave birth to a seven-pound daughter, Natasha.[136] She credited
Carson for stimulating in her the courage to dare to be herself, for
recognizing her as "a spirit kindred" to the lonely isolated creatures of
Carson's fiction, and helping her to relate to someone in a meaningful
human involvement.

Carson's fiction was her life, and even though she failed to publish a major work during her last six years, she tried and kept on trying. She wrote a little each day, or at least each day that she was not totally incapacitated. Even after her surgery in 1962 and 1963, she still typed with her good right hand. Unable to sustain prolonged sessions of writing, Carson found therapy and enjoyment in creating children's verses inspired mainly by incidents from her childhood. She was especially pleased to be writing poetry for the children of her lawyer, Floria Lasky. When Joyce Hartman, a Houghton Mifflin editor in New York, saw one or two of them, she asked to see the rest. The result was a slim volume released on May 10, 1964, entitled *Sweet as a Pickle and Clean as a Pig*. Carson insisted on calling her verses *rhymes*, not poems, for they bore no resemblance to her earlier published poetry. Reviewers of *Sweet as a Pickle and Clean as a Pig* found little cause to commend it to readers. The *Library Journal* described the poems as "contrived" and "unappealing" and criticized the "rather crude cartoon-like drawings" by Rolf Gerard. The book would be "suitable," however, for grades two through four, the reviewer conceded.[137] Walter Gibson in the New York *Times* acknowledged that "while it may seem slight and disappointing from so distinguished a pen," the space ships and slumber parties therein "will at least remind the children that poetry can speak for any world at all."[138] The *London Times Literary Supplement* said that the main interest in the volume is that it was by Carson McCullers, but "let not devotees think to find more than a grain or two of the novelist's dazzling idiosyncrasy in these musing, amusing, throw-away verses."[139]

Few other pieces of Carson's were published during her last years. One of her best was "Sucker," which appeared in *The Saturday Evening Post* in 1963, but it had been written at age seventeen before she left Columbus. Returned to her as "unpublishable" by her first literary agent who had sent it out to dozens of markets, the story lay fallow until it was discovered by Simeon Smith almost thirty years later when he was given permission to delve into her literary archives. The last short story published before Carson's death was "The March," a civil rights piece which she told John Huston she had sold to *Redbook* for four thousand dollars. "The March," finished in November, was the first of a trilogy of stories about blacks, she explained. By early January she was half through with "The Man Upstairs," the second tale, and in February she finished the last one, "Hush Little Baby." On February 13, 1967, she wrote Huston that Robert Lantz was especially pleased with the final story in her trilogy and thought it the best thing she had ever written. She loved these three stories very much, she said, and hoped that Huston would, too, when he read them.

When "The March" appeared, however, in the March 1967 issue of *Redbook*, most readers who knew her other works felt that it was only a token of her true genius. Her friends told her that they liked it, but many commented privately that it was not up to her former fiction. That she could write at all under the circumstances was a miracle, agreed those who knew her well.

Another late piece—the first posthumous publication—appeared in the December 1967 issue of *McCall's*. A poignant and sensitively written tale, "A Hospital Christmas Eve" told of a young woman she had met when they both were patients for physical therapy. Carson wrote admiringly of the woman's courage after having had both legs amputated and of her determination to walk on her new prosthetic legs at a Christmas Eve party.

There were times during Carson's last years when she would not trust her judgment concerning her own writing. In 1962, soon after her critical surgery at Harkness Pavilion, Carson wrote a story about a young music student in conflict with his mother and asked Massee to read the story aloud to a small bedside gathering. To Massee, it seemed as though it were "a case history lifted right out of Mary Mercer's files, though, of course, it could not have been. The group had been somewhat horrified by it, but Carson said that Mary had read it and accepted it as good. Then she wanted to know how I liked it. Rita and our friend Terry Murray did not have the heart to say that it was bad, but I certainly could not tell her that the thing was good. Finally I said: 'I don't like it, Carson. Put it aside for a while.' There was a long silence as though she were creating again in her mind, and then she said: 'All right. I'll do what you say, Boots.' She did not take offense, nor did she ever allow the story to be published."[140]

In spite of Carson's scanty creative output during these last years, there were occasional literary awards to remind her that she was still an important writer in the eyes of her public. In October 1965, she was the recipient of The Prize of the Young Generation, a German award given by *Die Welt*, a Hamburg newspaper. The citation commended her as "a distinguished novelist who, along with very few writers of our present day, speaks to this young generation and can expect a strong response."[141] In November 1966, the University of Mississippi awarded Carson a one-thousand-dollar Grant for the Humanities, and in April 1967 she received the 1966 Henry Bellamann Award, which also included a one-thousand-dollar grant. The accompanying certificate read: "In recognition of Mrs. McCullers' outstanding contribution to literature."

Another honor which Carson took a kind of secondhand pride in was that of runner-up for a ten-thousand-dollar International Publishers Prize in 1962. Normally she would have been annoyed at receiving secondary recognition, but this was an international prize in which thirteen countries participated: Great Britain, France, Holland, Italy, Germany,

Norway, Sweden, Denmark, Finland, Spain, Portugal, Canada and the United States. Each country was represented by one publishing house and a jury of a half dozen writers and critics. Carson was highly pleased when news of the contest appeared in the August 4, 1962, issue of *The New Yorker* in an article entitled "Our Far-Flung Correspondents: You Read Me and I'll Read You," by Alastair Reid.

Reid's story was an intriguing revelation of how the balloting was conducted. The prize was to go to the writer who had already made a notable reputation and still had a body of important work ahead of him. Lobbying went on by publishers, editors, and novelists, with each country armed with the names of a selective list of novels published in their country during the past three years. The balloting took place on Cape Formentor in Majorca, Spain, where during three days of intense debate the jurors substantiated their national choices and commented on the choices of others. To Reid, the most striking facet of the whole affair was the interest, good will, and humor of the proceedings in view of the many problems in determining a winner of books and manuscripts in languages that not all the jurors could read. The list included seventy-nine titles, with more than a third of them having been written by members of the juries. Since the Americans were "reticent to extol their own writers," said Reid, a Spanish critic delivered an "impassioned lecture on Christopher Isherwood, an Englishman of American nationality, and the French novelist Michel Mohrt waved the names of Saul Bellow and Carson McCullers in the air, with whisperings of why the Americans could be so modest" (Mohrt had recently published an article on Carson).[142] Angus Wilson declared that the conference was not "merely a battlefield between the Latins and the Anglo-Saxons." In the final voting, said Wilson, the United States "stood with France and Italy in defense of the German winner Uwe Johnson, and England stood with Spain in defense of the American writer Carson McCullers. And none of this was carved up in advance."[143]

Doubtless Mary Rodgers participated more actively in Carson's creative endeavors than did anyone else during Carson's last years. For three years off and on the two of them collaborated on a musical version of *The Member of the Wedding*.[144] Working with Mary Rodgers was "a real and thrilling collaboration," Carson told friends. The project of re-creating her childhood "memoirs" was more exciting to her than anything she had been involved in since *The Square Root of Wonderful*. The plan was for Carson to write the play and lyrics, and Mary Rodgers, the music. Carson intended to ask her old friend Oliver Smith to design the sets. According to Miss Rodgers, "Carson thought she could write the lyrics for the play herself, but she couldn't. I'm afraid she was an inept playwright as far as musicals go. She had seen only one or two on

Broadway in her entire life. Before her death, she said to me: 'Mary, I'll give you the rights to my play.' She thought she could, but she couldn't, for by now she apparently had lost all control over what was happening to her properties. Carson wrote a complete script for the musical, but it wasn't a very good one. She was too sick to work and really concentrate on it."[145] To Carson, however, the musical adaptation she had done of *The Member of the Wedding* was the most beautiful musical she had ever seen. She wrote John Huston in November 1966 that she was marvelously pleased with the whole thing and expected it to be on Broadway in 1967.

Before Carson's death the following September she had been talking for weeks about having her left leg amputated. For almost a year she had needed to have her leg elevated and held out straight if she were in a sitting position. She rarely sat, for she was more comfortable lying in bed. Circulatory problems had ensued after she broke her left hip and leg, and now she was almost never without excruciating pain in her left leg. If she were sitting in her wheelchair with people around her, she was tense and apprehensive that the leg might be patted, poked, or jarred in some way. At a crowded party one day, Dr. Mercer hit upon the idea of placing an end table over her outstretched leg to protect it, and Carson was able to relax and enjoy herself again.

"My leg gives me too much pain," she told people rather casually as she explained the possibility of amputation. "Besides, if Sarah Bernhardt could survive it, so can I." Carson had always been fascinated by the French actress' remarkable vitality and outrageous and magnificent spirit, and she had read and reread Cornelia Otis Skinner's recent biography, *Madame Sarah*, several times that year. Carson was reminded anew of the book she had wanted so badly to write—*In Spite Of*—which she conceived as a series of essays about those whose indomitable spirit had enabled them to survive and triumph despite great adversity. According to her friend Thomas Ryan, who saw Carson several times during the last months of her life while he shared with her his progress in getting ready for the filming of *The Heart Is a Lonely Hunter*, "Carson was told by her advisers that she would probably have to have her leg amputated, but it was my understanding that she was not told that the reason was bone cancer. The cancer was not very far advanced, and the operation was to arrest its spread. She was scheduled to have her leg removed on October 15."[146] Similarly, according to Gladys Hill, John Huston's assistant, "John and I thoroughly believed that Carson was to have her leg amputated. I think she gave us an exact date—like the nineteenth of October—and John promised that he would come to New York and be with her before, during, and after the operation."[147] Robert Lantz, Carson's agent, wrote John Huston on August 31, 1967, after Carson had suffered her final stroke, that if she should survive, she would probably be unable to talk, that her vision had apparently been seriously impaired, that she would be unable to use either arm, and that the necessity for amputation would doubtless be even more pressing. According to Dr. Mercer, however, there was never any medical plan to amputate the leg, nor was cancer involved in her last illness.[148]

"I remember," said Ryan, "Floria Lasky's saying to me that it was good that *Reflections in a Golden Eye* was being filmed and *The Heart Is a Lonely Hunter* in preparation (finally) because 'the problem is making her want to live, giving her something to live for.'" The most important "something" of her last year was her trip to St. Clerans, in Galway, Ireland, as the guest of her good and dear friend John Huston.

When Huston decided to do *Reflections in a Golden Eye*, he visited Carson several times in Nyack. Before the shooting began that fall, he took the script with him and read most of it aloud to her. A few days later she wrote a joint letter to Huston, Chapman Mortimer, and Gladys Hill. She said that she had just reread the script Huston had left with her and was overcome by its eerie power and splendor. Although *Reflections in a Golden Eye* contained little dialogue as a novel, the story and characterization had been beautifully re-created with clarity, truth, and powerful dialogue. Only she, as the original author, could fully appreciate what they had done, she told them, and she was deeply grateful. Carson also wrote a personal note to Huston the same day. She found it remarkable that they had not caviled over a single word or nuance in the script, and that nothing had marred their obvious enjoyment of each other. In October, after the shooting had gotten under way on Long Island, Huston visited Carson again. "How would you like to come to Ireland?" he asked.

"Are you serious?" she replied, finding the invitation incredible.

"Very serious," Huston assured her. "As soon as I finish *Reflections in a Golden Eye*—after we come back from Rome [where the bulk of the shooting was to take place]—you and Ida must come to Ireland."

"I'm almost pure Irish myself," Carson told him. "It would be marvelous to return to Ireland." And at once she began to plan her trip. When she told Ida that they were going to Galway, Ida said that she would much rather go to Hollywood and see the movie stars. In truth, Ida was thrilled over the impending trip because she knew what it would mean to Carson. Moreover, they had never traveled together any distance, and Ida had never crossed the ocean.

Every morning when Carson awoke, she thought about Ireland and how much she loved it. She reread Joyce's *The Dubliners*, wrote Huston that "The Dead," the last tale in *The Dubliners*, was her favorite of all stories, and played on her stereo over and over again *Tristan and Isolde*, which she cherished anew because of its Irish setting. Once she dreamed that she was riding to Ireland on a red pony given her by Huston. In her fantasy, her doctor had suddenly appeared and shouted to her that she must stop. She was unfit to travel because she had a patch on her lungs, he warned. But she and the red pony galloped on out of hearing and out of sight.[149]

Huston advised Carson that she must go into serious training so that she would be strong enough to make the long overseas flight. By return mail she assured him that she not only was eating enormously, sitting up more, and working hard with her therapist, but she had passed the first major hurdle: She had successfully given a large cocktail party at home for some forty-five guests. Her invitation list was a large one, for she wanted to include those who had been especially kind to her through her illness—and who had not been? she quipped—as well as old friends she had not seen for a long time. Carson told Houston later that the best part of the evening had been a presentation by her friend André Girard, whom she had invited to show his "Pictures in Motion," beautifully executed movies based on his own exquisite paintings. Her guests stayed late—much later than she usually entertained—and besieged her with telephone calls the next day to tell her what a marvelous party it had been.

Talk and preparations for the journey to Ireland extended almost five months. It took awhile for Carson's doctors and friends to realize that she was deadly serious about going, and even more important, that there was actually a possibility that she might go. They were accustomed to the fact that with Carson the anticipation of a pleasure was far more satisfying than the event itself. Finally, there was a round of trans-Atlantic telephone calls, telegrams, and letters to determine if, indeed, such a trip would be possible for her in her weakened state. (She told Huston that her 5-foot-8½-inch frame was draped with only seventy-five pounds of flesh.) During the current year she had seldom sat up more than a few moments at a time, even in her elevated hospital bed. At last with a new motivation to live, Carson began dictating letters to Huston three and four times a week. She even scribbled one note in longhand when no one was available to write for her, so anxious was she to get it into the mail. To Carson, Galway represented health, happiness, normalcy, and all other good things that seemed to elude her at home in Nyack. To make such a journey was the one experience that could transform her from an unhappy invalid to a joyous, normal being, she said.

At first Carson told Huston that her doctors surely must be conspiring against her going, that they feared she would be shipped home in a box if she undertook such an arduous trip. To be sure, Dr. Mercer and Dr. Glenn Patterson, her Nyack physician, were disturbed that she would be traveling such a distance in her precarious physical condition, yet it seemed best to acquiesce and share her enthusiasm. At the same time they were determined to do all they could to see that conditions were maximal for a safe trip. Finally it was agreed that Carson be allowed a trial run—to New York City and back—to see how she might hold up under the excitement and pressures of such a venture. In the meantime, she impatiently awaited John Huston's missive telling her just when it would be convenient for him to have her.

Robert Lantz flew to Rome on December 5 and spent a day at the studio with John Huston and Huston's wife. Greatly impressed, he reported to Carson that everything was going beautifully. She had received the stills from Huston that week and was excited about the possibility of a trip to Rome herself. At the same time, Carson recognized that such longing was a fantasy compared to her real goal: Ireland.

On Christmas Eve Huston returned to St. Clerans from Rome, the shooting completed, and on January 5 he wired her: "Carson dear, come as quickly as you can, and be sure I'll be here. Love, John." At first Carson had hoped that Huston would fly back to the United States and spend Christmas with her, but it was not possible. Yet that dream, too, sustained her. She also longed to go to Rome to watch the shooting. She asked Huston to tell the cast that she was with them in spirit and sent her love. Both Julie Harris and Marlon Brando wrote to her while they were on location. They told her how pleased they were to be a part of her magnificent work and that they thought she would be very happy with the results. Carson wrote Huston that Miss Harris was always superb, and that she was sure Brando was perfect in the role of the prissy, effete military officer. In an interview with the New York Times (October 17, 1966), while the Long Island shooting was in session, Brando was asked why he wanted to play the neurotic role of Penderton, the impotent husband of Elizabeth Taylor. He grinned and answered candidly: "Seven hundred fifty thousand dollars plus 7 and ½ per cent of the gross receipts if we break even. That's the main attraction . . . plus the fact that it's a book by Carson McCullers."

Others in the cast were Brian Keith, who played the adulterous Major Langdon; Robert Forster, the young atavistic soldier murdered by Penderton; and Zorro David, the spritelike Filipino devoted to the unhappy neglected wife Alison Langdon, played by Julie Harris. Carson was also impressed that the movie, filmed in color, required 650 background players, including several hundred men from the Rainbow Infantry Division of the Brooklyn National Guard and an army of uniformed extras from the Screen Actors Guild—all used during the shooting on Long Island.

Three different dates were set for the trip to the Plaza, where she would stay in New York, but each time it seemed prudent for various reasons to delay the trial run. In the meantime, John Huston sent round-trip tickets for Ida and Carson and urged them to come as soon as possible. He also sent pictures of his palatial home and told Carson just which room would be hers and how it was furnished. Carson promised that she would come as soon as she fulfilled the last stipulation of her doctors—that she weather well her sojourn at the Plaza. She had not the slightest doubt that she could manage it.

Carson had written Huston that winter that one of her very dearest friends did not want her to go to Ireland. It was Tennessee Williams, and she thought he was jealous, she explained. Williams had been teasing her about Ireland and comparing it unfavorably with Key West, which *he* loved. Actually, she could not stand Key West, Carson confided. She said she had spent several long stretches with the playwright, both in Key West and Cuba. During the visits she had begun to feel almost incarcerated, she continued, exaggerating further. Always she got homesick, yet was forced to stay longer than she wished. Carson told Huston that she was sure, nonetheless, that Williams loved her—and his sister, Rose— better than anyone else in the world. And in spite of his objections, real or otherwise, she was going to Ireland, and that was that. Actually, Williams was a great tease and flatterer. When he advised her that she should abandon her plans to attend the New York première of *Reflections in a Golden Eye*, set for the fall of 1967, he explained that it would be inappropriate since she would surely "steal the show." He teased her, also, about John Huston. One day when Carson had just finished a letter to the director, Williams penned his own note at the bottom: "Dear John— I have told Carson that you are a wild man who chases foxes, but she doesn't seem to mind. Love, Tennessee." Another time, Williams wrote her a note, saying: "Forget the Irishman in his bog and come to see me in good, old New Orleans."

Finally, the adjusted date of the trial run arrived. On March 3, 1967, accompanied by Ida, Carson traveled in an ambulance to New York City "to lie in state"—as one friend referred to the occasion—in a suite at the Plaza as the guest of Ray Stark. It was the most luxurious suite she had ever seen, she admitted. The management told her that it was the suite always reserved for Marlene Dietrich. Ida, too, was enthralled. Each woman had her separate room and bath within the suite and a beautiful connecting balcony, which seemed especially pleasing to Carson, who insisted on being carried outdoors on her stretcher so that she could examine her view. Immediately she and Ida began a steady stream of ordering from room service. As an entree before each meal, Carson ordered raw oysters, suggested doubtless by the memory of her Danish friend, Isak Dinesen, whose daily diet consisted chiefly of oysters and green grapes. Other dishes she chose that day were lobster thermidor, cold lobsters with chilled wine, and a special seafood casserole made with grapes. She also fell in love with two drinks she had never had before: a "Shirley Temple," a nonalcoholic concoction introduced to her by Floria Lasky's children, and sherbet laced with a generous portion of the potent French liqueur Grand Marnier. She wrote John Huston that she drank them continuously, and that she had never before had two such delightfully wild days.

To Carson, her stay at the Plaza was a marvelous stunt. Although she had made plans to stage a gala fiftieth birthday party there that year, her doctors felt it unwise for her to have such a big celebration with a more important trip pending. She was grossly disappointed, for she had wanted to outdo Truman Capote's recent extravaganza at the Plaza, but she was reconciled by the appeal that she must save her strength for Ireland. At the Plaza now, visitors streamed to her bedside as often as Ida allowed. Most of them brought gifts, sent flowers, and paid verbal tribute to her for her remarkable courage, cheer, and creative genius that had flourished in spite of devastating odds. To those who knew Carson well, her survival seemed superhuman. She loved the to-do of her Plaza extravaganza. It was like having two birthdays in one month, she told friends.

When Carson returned to Nyack, having successfully passed her last major trial, arrangements for the trip to Ireland were intensified. Since the first of the year Marielle Bancou had helped her get ready by designing and having made dozens of strikingly beautiful new outfits. To Carson, the colors and textures were ravishing. There were scarlets, purples, blues, and many subtle colors; there were sheer wools, rich velvets, and Siamese silks. Miss Bancou told Carson: "At Mr. Huston's they will change clothes twice a day—you will change *three* times." When Miss Bancou's mother heard of Carson's impending trip, she sent hand-embroidered garments from Lyons, France. Jordan Massee contributed to her wardrobe his sister Martha's flaming red Chinese robe, which Massee had been given upon his sister's death.

She could not resist telling John Huston every stage of her progress, often identifying things as "secrets" which she wanted to share only with him. Miss Bancou urged Carson not to tell Huston in advance about all of her new outfits, for she thought it would be fitting for him to think that Carson wore such clothes all the time. "What about your coquetry— it should be a surprise," she suggested.

"I'm less of a coquette than a croquette," Carson replied with a wry smile. Then she promptly wrote a letter to Huston telling all.

Throughout the month of March dozens of friends came to the house in Nyack with bon voyage presents. When Ken McCormick and Betty

Prashker of Doubleday came to see her, Carson called Ida into the bedroom to show them the gift she had selected for Huston—an exquisite silver goblet. Although it was beautifully wrapped and ready to present to her host, Carson insisted that Ida open it and show it to her visitors. Everyone exclaimed admiringly while Carson viewed her gift as though she were seeing it for the first time. To McCormick, she was like a child anticipating and then experiencing the joy that she knew would be Huston's when he opened it. McCormick had the feeling that Ida had been asked to unwrap—and then wrap—Huston's lovely goblet many times.[150] Carson told the editor that day that if it was not for her friends, the beauty and richness of life would be dreadfully distant.

For weeks Carson talked of little except her impending trip. Plans were discussed in great detail. She needed to know about each new development and phase of the journey so that she could anticipate it and share it with her visitors. Huston's assistant and long-time friend, Gladys Hill, handled most of the arrangements from the other end of the journey. Although Carson had requested that she be given a bedroom in the midst of the household's activities, Dr. Mercer was more explicit regarding her needs. She specified that his guest would require a hospital bed, much rest and privacy, a room nearby for Ida, and a bell or buzzer at her bedside. Carson would also need a bedside table on her right, a table equipped with cigarettes, lighter, an ash tray, tissues, her silver cup (which she would bring) for bourbon and water, and an occasional glass of Coca-Cola or fruit juice. Her medical record was also sent by her Nyack doctor to the local Loughrea physician, Martyn J. Dyar, in case difficulties should arise. But Carson, herself, had no worries.

A minor problem in logistics had to be worked out involving how to get her from the airport at Shannon, where she would land, to St. Clerans, Huston's home. By automobile, it was an hour-and-fifteen-minute drive. At first the plan was that Carson should be transported by Volkswagen bus so that she could travel in her wheelchair, remain in it during the bus ride, and then be conveyed in it into the house. That idea was aborted, however, before Carson's trip to the Plaza, which she intended also to make by Volkswagen bus. To sit upright for any distance in a moving vehicle would be entirely out of the question, her doctors agreed. Then arrangements were made for an ambulance. Immediately upon the heels of that solution, a friend of Huston's—a bone specialist— urged the film director not to allow Carson to make the long ride even lying down in an ambulance when a helicopter would be just the thing. When Carson got word that she would arrive on John Huston's expansive lawn in a helicopter, she was ecstatic. Imagine, riding in a helicopter, she exclaimed. No one she knew had ever ridden in a helicopter. It would be just like President and Mrs. Kennedy's arrivals at parties and summit meetings, she told Ida. And now a fresh detail of the trip could be relished with excitement and boundless anticipation.

Although Huston had tentatively arranged with the Irish Army to provide the helicopter service, an official finally had to regretfully announce that the Army would be unable to do so after all. Undaunted, Huston contacted a charter service. Indeed, their pilot would be most pleased to transport the famous American author from the Shannon Airport to the lawn of the Huston estate. Of course, it was a *little* helicopter, officials admitted when probed. They would have to convey her in a sling outside the craft, but it was just "the very thing," they insisted. After all, that was the way they took emergency maternity cases from the Aran Islands and other such places. "No thank you," replied Miss Hill, "I'm afraid we must make other arrangements." A few days later a series of bizarre events connected with the little craft gave cause for thanks that Carson had not been allowed to attempt the helicopter ride, in spite of her keen disappointment when she learned that she was again to be transported in routine fashion—by ambulance.

It seemed that the helicopter that would have carried Carson to St. Clerans was later engaged at the same time she would have used it to convey a casket from Shannon to the Aran Islands. The cargo contained the body of an islander who had died in the United States. Her last wish was that she be buried in her native soil. Now she was being flown there, while the whole family, the priest, and a host of friends awaited her arrival on Inishmore for the funeral and interment. Meanwhile, the helicopter's cable carrying the casket broke, dumping its load upon the town of Paradise. The remains were carefully gathered together, put into a second casket, and again placed in the sling, the cable now repaired. Shortly after the craft was airborne again, it dropped its burden once more, this time into the sea, from which it was never recovered.[151]

On April 2, at 8:30 A.M., Carson and Ida arrived at the Shannon Airport. After a warm greeting by Huston, she was transferred to a waiting ambulance. Then he and Ida led the way home, where Miss Hill and a houseful of other greeters nervously awaited them: Huston's two children, his estate manager, an art director, his secretary, sundry motion picture technicians and neighbors, and a staff of nine Irish men and women who kept the great home in operation. Other than a helicopter landing, nothing could have pleased Carson more than her grand entry that morning. The vehicle pulled up and she was conveyed by ambulance cot into the drawing room. Ida volunteered that Carson was extremely tired because of her uncomfortable flight, but Carson herself could not have been more marvelous, reported Miss Hill. The first flight plan called for the airline Aer Lingus to remove one seat in the bulkhead of the plane; in its place Carson was to sit in her wheelchair with her leg propped out straight. That scheme was abandoned, however, before her trip to the Plaza when it was decided that she had no business sitting up during the long flight. Next, the airline was to have removed a seat and concocted a bed on which she could lie flat, her leg elevated on pillows. Yet for some inexplicable reason, that arrangement did not materialize either. Carson sat up the entire trip, unable even to stretch her painful leg out into the aisle.

"Carson took everything in with those great eyes," observed Miss Hill. As soon as his guests arrived, Huston had champagne served. After a few moments of gay conversation Carson was carried upstairs to the "Grey Room," where she was put to bed to rest. She was determined to see all of the house and grounds that day, and "in our innocence," said Miss Hill, "we quite believed she might be capable of one brief look." She was brought down again in the afternoon, dressed in one of her Chinese robes, and placed in her wheelchair in the study. "When she kept slipping down in the chair, we began to realize that her expectations—and ours—exceeded her strength. She was taken back upstairs to her room and never left it again until her return to Shannon," Miss Hill lamented.

Word traveled quickly that one of America's foremost authors was the guest of John Huston, and by the next day flowers had arrived in profusion, along with dozens of notes and letters from admirers who simply left them in the hall outside her door without attempting to see her. "They just wanted her to know how pleased they were that she had come to Ireland," said Miss Hill. Ida, too, made a hit with Huston's household staff and others who met her. Blacks are rare in Ireland, and the children in the household—the head groom had seven—had never seen a black before. Of their parents they asked: "Does Ida's color come off when she bathes?" Ida loved her stay in Ireland. Never had she been in such a grand home. She ate at a big round table in the kitchen where the smaller children had their meals, watched television, slept in a room near Carson, listened for her bell, and took short walks about the estate when the bell was "covered" by someone else.

"We soon began to understand Carson," said Miss Hill:

> For example, at 11:00 A.M. she would ask for a bourbon and ice in her silver cup. This was brought. I then noticed that the cup barely touched her lips—the same for the Menthol cigarettes. Very little alcohol or nicotine was taken in. But after ten minutes or so, she would ask to have "another drink." I would carry the virtually untasted drink down to the bar, pop in another ice cube, and return.
>
> The same for food: Carson loved to talk about food, but she had little capacity for it. Mrs. Creagh prepared very small portions of ev-

erything for her and served the "meal" in a silver muffin dish with a lid. Carson became fond of that dish and John gave it to her.

She also began to love the room she was in—the Grey Room—a very large Georgian room with curving bay windows. She talked of having it reproduced in Nyack. . . . There were also fine Japanese screens and other art objects, which were to be—if not duplicated—reproduced in the same period and style.

A writer from the Dublin *Irish Times*, Terence De Vere White, came on the second day to interview Carson and John Huston and to take pictures. Huston said later that when White asked Carson what the meaning of writing was to her, she responded: "A search for God," whereupon a wooden Portuguese crucifix on the wall above her head moved slowly sideways on its hook.

Carson alarmed the entire household on the third day of her visit. Ida discovered her in a deep sleep and called to Huston and Miss Hill to look at her. They found her color bad, and she seemed to be in a coma. Dr. Martyn Dyar, who had been sent Carson's medical records, rushed to examine her and Dr. Mercer was telephoned. Mary Mercer, however, assured them that the sleep and the reaction to the long journey were normal and that they should not be alarmed. She would come out of it in a few days. "And she did," reported Miss Hill. "She 'woke up,' as it were, in a few days and was fine. She received us (the whole kit and caboodle) again and began dictating to Ida a story about her Irish visit." She also announced that she was starved.

When the doctor arrived to check on Carson—as he did daily—planning this time to give her a shot of penicillin, he found her sitting up in bed smoking and drinking. "The good doctor didn't know what we then knew," said Miss Hill, "that this was Carson's gallant salute to normal life." He gave her the shot, then took her temperature. "You'd be much better if you gave up smoking and drinking, Mrs. McCullers," he told her.

Carson indicated the crucifix behind her and responded: "I will when He comes down off that wall."

The doctor replied: "He has been known to do so."

There was a moment of silence before he walked quickly into the bathroom to rinse the thermometer.

Carson rallied quickly and began dictating to Ida "A Love Letter from Ireland," a four-page manuscript.[152] She held court at her bedside for another week, read Joyce, O'Casey, and Yeats when she was not being entertained, and schemed how she would copy every detail of the furnishings of the Grey Room for her own bedroom in Nyack. She especially admired a Jacob Epstein bronze, a portrait head of one of Epstein's grandchildren entitled "Peggy Jean Asleep."

Finally Carson announced that she was ready to go home. This time, to avoid the problems encountered on the trip over, Huston had his master carpenter, Brian Connolly, get the measurements of the plane's bulkhead. Then Connolly had a local seamstress make up an enormous hassock, which he filled with foam rubber. On April 18, Carson was conveyed by ambulance back to Shannon Airport and carried aboard the plane on a stretcher. Connolly had gone aboard first and wedged the hassock into place, creating a kind of chaise longue for her. The bed was then made up with embroidered Irish linen sheets, pillows, and a colorful Irish wool blanket. Once she was settled into place, Aer Lingus uncorked champagne for all of Carson's fellow passengers in the first-class section. Toasts went round the cabin in the gala impromptu *au revoir* celebration. Never had she felt so made over and loved.

A little over three months later, on July 31, 1967, Carson wrote her last letter to John Huston. She had become increasingly concerned that summer about the race riots going on in various parts of the country. To her, the riots, the looting, the killing—all seemed suicidal, with blacks even turning against blacks. Carson empathized with their plight. She told Huston that the blacks in America were tired of unfulfilled promises, gross unemployment, and shameful living conditions. She deplored the fact that Congress had recently defeated a rat control measure, and that the one solution—to rebuild the slums, which should have been done at least two decades earlier—still had not been put into effect. She found it intolerable that white men continued to have employment privileges over blacks even though their skills were inferior or equal. She also told Huston that she had again read and reread *The Dubliners* since coming home. To Carson, Joyce's theme of sterility and moral blindness in Dublin over fifty years earlier seemed so like the condition in the United States today.

Two weeks later, Huston received a terse wire from Robert Lantz. Carson had suffered a stroke on her right side and was unconscious. Whereas she had become somnolent in Ireland, it had caused only temporary panic and dismay before their fears were allayed. This time, however, the ramifications were tragic. For forty-seven days she lay in the Nyack Hospital in a coma while doctors examined her and friends kept a round-the-clock bedside vigil. They read to her, talked to her, and to one another. But from the beginning there was no meaningful response.

Almost daily Huston was apprised of Carson's condition, either through Robert Lantz, Dr. Mercer, Ida, or Carson's friend Marielle Bancou. On August 19, a tracheotomy was performed, but she remained unconscious, her condition unchanged. Her doctors felt the next day that there was some improvement, but on the twenty-first they began to fear that Carson now suffered permanent damage to her speech, and possibly to her sight. Occasionally those who came to her bedside felt that there was some flicker of recognition or reaction, but the longer she stayed unconscious the greater the chances seemed to be that she would never come out of it. For over six weeks her heart and lungs functioned well, her blood pressure, amazingly normal. On August 31, Robert Lantz wrote Huston that Carson was without pain, that her face was relaxed, and that she seemed at peace. It was a deeply touching letter, revealing Lantz's great love for his friend who had been far more to him than merely a client whose literary works he had tended carefully for over a decade. He explained that to hold out hope that Carson might survive now—to live without her mental and physical faculties—would be self-seeking only, cruel and unkind.

The days in September crawled by while hundreds of telegrams and letters of good wishes poured in as the world continued to learn of her condition. On September 8, Tennessee Williams, who loathed hospitals, came to her bedside. "She opened her eyes and looked at me and seemed to know me," he said. According to Robert Lantz, it was Dr. Mercer's opinion that Carson responded slightly to sound at that point, but had no real consciousness except for a few fleeting seconds. Any reaction on her part, any sensitivity to noise—such as the ringing of the telephone—was doubtless involuntary rather than deliberate.

On September 27, a deeply saddened Robert Lantz attended the Warner Brothers screening of *Reflections in a Golden Eye*, to be released October 11. The room was filled with priests and representatives from the National Legion of Decency. To Lantz and others who knew and loved Carson's novel, the movie was sensitively and beautifully acted and directed. Lantz wrote Huston later that he was most impressed by it, and that his only real criticism was of the young man Zorro David, a hair stylist, who played the fanciful Filipino servant, Anacleto. Although the film received the approval of the industry's self-regulatory body, the Production Code, it was soundly condemned by the National Catholic Office for Motion Pictures (formerly known as the National Legion of Decency), given a "C" rating, and released with the tag "For Mature Audiences."

Just as Carson's second novel had shocked and repulsed many of its readers in 1941 as an imaginative but sordid creation of an immature woman, so, too, did the motion picture of her book offend theatre viewers some twenty-five years later. As a movie, *Reflections in a Golden Eye* was censored for what critics called "its nudity, male and female, and almost no human insight." Had Carson lived to attend the première and become aware of such censorship and indictment, she doubtless would have remembered Tennessee Williams' advice to her many years earlier. "It takes a tough old bird to work in the theatre," he had warned her, and the same was true of any medium which pitted a sensitive creator against the masses. By the time Carson died she had gained a strange and comforting sense of serenity and well-being in spite of the physical and psychic forces which assailed her. Had she lived to hear once again the accusation that her work showed "almost no human insight," she doubtless would have clinched her fist a little tighter, drawn deeply on her menthol cigarette, exhaled a stream of smoke into her accuser's face, and smiled, saying: "Like I said before, darling, I bless the Latin poet Terence who said, 'Nothing human is alien to me.' "[153]

On September 29, 1967, two days after Lantz attended the screening of the film which had helped give Carson a will to live during her final difficult year, her weary heart simply stopped beating. America had lost its lonely hunter.

She was buried on October 3 beside her mother on a slope overlooking the Hudson River in Nyack's Oak Hill Cemetery. The Reverend Howard R. Moody of Judson Memorial Church in Greenwich Village—Rita Smith's pastor, who had been a comfort to Carson during several of her most difficult illnesses—officiated at a simple, private graveside service.

Earlier, a public service was held at St. James Episcopal Church on Madison Avenue, with the Reverend Frederick Hill officiating. There, mourners heard Carson's beloved Bach music, "Sheep May Safely Graze" and "Jesu, Joy of Man's Desiring," and her favorite Psalms. It was an extraordinary collection of people gathered that afternoon to tell Carson good-by. There were such old friends as Wystan Auden, Gypsy Rose Lee, Ethel Waters, Julie Harris, Harold Clurman, Janet Flanner, Truman Capote, Brooks Atkinson, Leonard Ehrlich, and countless others from the theatrical, literary, and artistic world who saw Carson intermittently over the years. There also was the handful of those who loved her deeply, Mary Mercer, her sister, Jordan Massee, Marielle Bancou, and others who had been with her on an almost daily basis for months, and some, for years. Ida Reeder, perhaps feeling as much a *sister* to Carson as Rita Smith herself, sat beside Lamar, Carson's brother. Friends from the South came, also, those who had known Carson's mother and husband, and those she had visited over the years in Columbus, Macon, Charleston, and Charlotte. There were people from all professions and conditions of life, perhaps a dozen blacks, the Italian vegetable man who stopped regularly at 131 South Broadway, the druggist, her tenants, her neighbors, her friends, her loved ones. At the funeral home the night before, hundreds came to call. Ida's son, Louis, paid tribute that evening without a word; he simply pulled a bud from the blanket of roses on her casket, tucked it into his lapel, and walked out into the night.

To Carson, the deepest feelings could never be articulated, but they could be written. One strove only to make some kind of meaningful human connection in *this* world, for there was none other. Tennessee Williams purposely stayed away from the church and cemetery that day. "It wasn't Carson," he said simply. "I saw her when she was alive. Funerals are for the dead and are terribly depressing. She lives on now only in her works and in the minds of those who knew her."[154] To Williams, Carson would always be the delicate youth of the poem he had dedicated to her a few years before her death[155]—the paradoxical child who rode her hobbyhorse freely between the mysterious worlds of adolescence and maturity, returning when she chose to her native South "in a single bound":

WHICH IS MY LITTLE BOY?
for Carson McCullers

Which is my little boy, which is he,
Jean qui pleure ou Jean qui rit?

Jean qui rit is my delicate John,
the one with the Chinese slippers on,

whose hobbyhorse in a single bound
carries me back to native ground.

But *Jean qui pleure* is *mysterieux*
with sorrows older than Naishapur,

with all the stars and all of the moons
mirrored in little silver spoons.

Which is my little boy, which is he,
Jean qui pleure ou Jean qui rit?

Notes

CHAPTER ONE

1 "The Flowering Dream," *Esquire*, December 1959, p. 163. See also Margarita G. Smith, ed., *The Mortgaged Heart*, Boston: Houghton Mifflin, 1971, p. 276.
2 Kenneth French to Virginia Spencer Carr (hereafter referred to as VSC), interview, Nyack, N.Y., December 17, 1970.
3 The *Enquirer-Sun*, Columbus, Ga., February 23, 1917.
4 Felda Gentry James to VSC, interview, Tuskegee, Ala., March 6, 1971.
5 Martha Kimbrough Hogan to VSC, interview, Columbus, Ga., October 13, 1970.
6 Lamar Smith, Jr., to VSC, interview, Perry, Fla., October 3, 1970.
7 Carson McCullers, "Loneliness . . . An American Malady," *This Week, Herald Tribune*, December 19, 1949, pp. 18–19. Also published in *Playbill*, January 1950, and Margarita G. Smith, ed., *The Mortgaged Heart*, op. cit., pp. 259–60.
8 "The Flowering Dream," *The Mortgaged Heart*, op. cit., p. 274.
9 See "The Discovery of Christmas," *Mademoiselle*, December 1953, p. 55; also, *The Mortgaged Heart*, op. cit., p. 238.
10 Ibid., p. 120 and p. 243.
11 Lamar Smith, Jr., to VSC, see above.
12 Margaret Long to VSC, Atlanta, February 7, 1972.
13 Lamar Smith, Jr., to VSC, see above.
14 *The Member of the Wedding*, Boston: Houghton Mifflin, 1946, p. 3.
15 Ida Thompson to VSC, interview, Columbus, Ga., February 10, 1971.
16 Ernst von Dohnanyi, Hungarian composer and pianist, who died in 1960.
17 "How I Began to Write," *Mademoiselle*, September 1948, pp. 191, 257–58; see also *The Mortgaged Heart*, op. cit., p. 249.
18 *Clock Without Hands*, Boston: Houghton Mifflin, 1961, pp. 9–10.
19 "The Russian Realists and Southern Literature," *Decision*, July 1941, p. 15; also, *The Mortgaged Heart*, op. cit., pp. 252–53.
20 "How I Began to Write," op. cit., p. 191f.; also, *The Mortgaged Heart*, op. cit., p. 250.
21 Unpublished radio interview with Tennessee Williams, 1952; from the Williams Collection, University of Texas Archives, Austin, Tex.
22 "How I Began to Write," op. cit., p. 193.
23 CMcC to Virginia ("Gin") Tucker, Columbus, Ga., ca. June 1936; from the Mary (Sames) Tucker Papers, Perkins Library, Duke University, Durham, N.C.

24 "Sucker," *The Saturday Evening Post*, September 28, 1963, pp. 69–71; also, *The Mortgaged Heart*, op. cit., pp. 9–19.

25 Ibid.

26 Ibid.

27 Edwin Peacock to VSC, interview, Charleston, S.C., August 30, 1972.

28 "How I Began to Write," op. cit., p. 257; also, *The Mortgaged Heart*, op. cit., p. 251.

CHAPTER TWO

1 Margarita G. Smith, ed., *The Mortgaged Heart*, Boston: Houghton Mifflin, 1971, pp. 20–29.

2 Ibid., pp. 25–26.

3 Mrs. Frederick Markloff to VSC, interview, New York City, May 5, 1971.

4 Edwin Peacock to VSC, interview, Charleston, S.C., August 30, 1972.

5 Edwin Peacock to VSC, interview, Charleston, S.C., November 4, 1972; also interview, Charleston, August 31, 1972.

6 Max Goodley to VSC, interview, Columbus, Ga., May 3, 1971.

7 Edwin Peacock to VSC, interview, Charleston, S.C., August 30, 1972. This early story was unpublished in Carson's lifetime, nor was it one which Margarita G. Smith, her sister, selected to include in the posthumous collection *The Mortgaged Heart*; however, several of Carson's friends recalled reading the story and liking it.

8 *The Mortgaged Heart*, op. cit., pp. 88–97.

9 Ibid., p. 89.

10 Ibid., p. 93.

11 Ibid., pp. 93–94.

12 Edwin Peacock to VSC, see above, November 4, 1972.

13 Ibid.

14 *The Mortgaged Heart*, op. cit., pp. 37–38.

15 Ibid., pp. 62–63.

16 Ibid., p. 40.

17 Ibid., p. 71.

18 Whit Burnett to VSC, interview, New York City, December 18, 1970.

19 In the published account of Carson's illumination of John Singer and the new direction of her novel, she said that she was walking across the road when it occurred. See "The Flowering Dream: Notes on Writing," *Esquire*, December 1959, pp. 162–64. This account of her pacing the hooked rug when the illumination occurred was found in an unpublished manuscript identified only as "A speech on her first public appearance." Oliver Evans Collection, Humanities Research Center Library, University of Texas, Austin, Tex.

20 *Esquire*, ibid. See also *The Mortgaged Heart*, op. cit., pp. 274–75.

21 John Vincent Adams to VSC, Sarasota, Fla., January 1, 1974.

22 John T. Winn to VSC, interview, Charlotte, N.C., May 9–10, 1971.

23 Mrs. George Woodruff to VSC, interview, Columbus, Ga., January 3, 1970.

CHAPTER THREE

1 CMcC to Virginia Tucker Melgaard, Charlotte, N.C., October 10, 1937; from the Mary (Sames) Tucker Papers, Perkins Library, Duke University, Durham, N.C.

2 J. T. Winn to VSC, interview, Charlotte, N.C., May 9–10, 1971.

3 *The Heart Is a Lonely Hunter*, Boston: Houghton Mifflin, 1940, p. 92.

4 Edwin Peacock to VSC, Charleston, S.C., May 31, 1972.

5 Edwin Peacock to VSC, interview, Charleston, S.C., November 4, 1972.

6 CMcC to Alfred Kantorowicz, Columbus, Ga., October 1943; also, Alfred Kantorowicz to VSC, Hamburg, Germany, July 13, 1972.

7 *The Mute*—the original title of *The Heart Is a Lonely Hunter*—was finally changed upon the persuasion of Carson's editor. It was a change she strongly resisted, and one of the few to which she finally consented. The new title came from a phrase in the poem "The Lonely Hunter" by William Sharp (Fiona MacLeod), in which this line occurs: "But my heart is a lonely hunter that hunts/on a lonely hill." See *Poems and Dramas* by Fiona MacLeod (William Sharp), New York: Duffield & Company, 1914, p. 27.

8 "The Flowering Dream," *The Mortgaged Heart*, Boston: Houghton Mifflin, 1971, p. 277.

9 Ibid., p. 29.

10 CMcC to Virginia Tucker Melgaard, see above.

11 Tennessee Williams and Carson McCullers typescript, unpublished interview; from the Carson McCullers Collection, University of Texas Humanities Research Center, Austin, Tex., n.d., p. 1.

12 "The Flowering Dream," op. cit., p. 280.

CHAPTER FOUR

1 Klaus Mann, *The Turning Point: Thirty-five Years in This Century*, New York: L. B. Fischer, 1942, pp. 331–32. The story to which Klaus Mann referred was "The Aliens," published in the posthumous *The Mortgaged Heart*. Carson's sister, Margarita Smith, editor, acknowledged three undated manuscripts of this story left in the literary estate. Miss Smith believed the work to have preceded *The Heart Is a Lonely Hunter* and to have been written when Carson was about nineteen. The Mann journal suggests that it had not been written before their July 1940 meeting, although Carson might well have told Mann something of the plot after she had already completed a draft or two.

2 Klaus Mann, ibid., pp. 151–52.

3 Dr. Suzanne Ohman, sister of Annemarie Clarac-Schwarzenbach, to Aimee Alexander, Meilen, Switzerland, February 24, 1971.

4 Ibid.

5 Ibid.

6 Annemarie Clarac-Schwarzenbach to Robert Linscott, Siasconset, Nantucket, Mass., August 23, 1940; from the Robert Newton Linscott Collection, Archives of Washington University Libraries, St. Louis, Mo.

7 Theodore Morrison to VSC, Ripton, Vt., August 8, 1972.

8 Wallace Stegner to VSC, Greensboro, Vt., August 14, 1972.

9 Brainard Cheney, a Georgia lumberman-turned-journalist, was with the Nashville *Banner* at the time he went to Bread Loaf. He had just published his first novel, *Lightwood* (1939), and a second one, *River Rogue*, was then in progress.

10 Ken McCormick to VSC, interview, New York City, September 5, 1972.

11 Louis Untermeyer to VSC, Newtown, Conn., October 1, 1971.

12 Ibid.

13 Brainard Cheney to VSC, Smyrna, Tenn., August 30, 1972.
14 Eudora Welty to VSC, Jackson, Miss., June 21, 1971.
15 John Ciardi to VSC, New York City, January 27, 1972.
16 Wallace Stegner to VSC, see above.
17 Theodore Morrison to VSC, Ripton, Vt., August 28, 1972.
18 Elizabeth Linscott to VSC, Sarasota, Fla., March 31, 1973.
19 CMcC to Louis Untermeyer, New York City, September 1940.

CHAPTER FIVE

1 See Carson's prose piece, "Brooklyn Is My Neighborhood," *Vogue*, March 1, 1941, pp. 62–63, 138, in which she further described her neighborhood and the strange and friendly people who inhabited it. See also Margarita G. Smith, ed., *The Mortgaged Heart*, Boston: Houghton Mifflin, 1971, pp. 216–20.
2 June Havoc to Aimee Alexander, New Orleans, La., November 28, 1970.
3 Louis Untermeyer to VSC, Newton, Conn., October 1, 1971.
4 Janet Flanner to VSC, interview, New York City, March 1, 1972.
5 W. H. Auden to VSC, Kirchstetten, Hinterholz, Austria, September 21, 1971; also interview, Hinterholz, Austria, September 14, 1973.
6 Preface, *Le Coeur est un Chasseur Solitaire*, Paris: Club des Librairies de France, 1946.
7 Paul Bowles to VSC, Tangier, Morocco, September 10, 1970.
8 Lotte Lenya and her husband Kurt Weill had been friends of Davis for many years, dating back to Europe in the 1930s. Weill died in 1950, whereupon Davis married Miss Lenya a few months later "out of kindness," she thought, for she "was so lost." Miss Lenya to VSC, interview, New York City, May 24, 1971.
9 *The Heart Is a Lonely Hunter*, Boston: Houghton Mifflin, 1940, pp. 17–18.
10 Richard Wright, "Review: *The Heart Is a Lonely Hunter*," *New Republic*, August 5, 1940, p. 195.
11 See Constance Webb, *Richard Wright, a Biography*, New York: Putnam, 1968, pp. 194–96, 269–73.
12 Anaïs Nin, *The Diary of Anaïs Nin, 1939–1944*, New York: Harcourt Brace and World, 1969, p. 270.
13 Anaïs Nin to VSC, New York City, August 21, 1970.
14 *The Diary of Anaïs Nin*, op. cit., pp. 270–71.
15 Eleanor Clark to Aimee Alexander, Fairfield, Conn., July 3, 1971; Eleanor Clark to VSC, Fairfield, Conn., October 15, 1973.
16 Golo Mann to Aimee Alexander, Zurich, Switzerland, October 13, 1970.
17 Paul Bowles to VSC, see above.
18 CMcC to Janet Flanner, fall 1940, New York City; from the papers of Janet Flanner and Solita Solano, Library of Congress, Washington, D.C.
19 "Look Homeward, Americans," *Vogue*, December 1, 1940, p. 74; see also *The Mortgaged Heart*, Boston: Houghton Mifflin, 1971, p. 209.
20 Ibid., *Vogue*, p. 75, *The Mortgaged Heart*, p. 213.
21 "Night Watch Over Freedom," *Vogue*, January 1, 1941, p. 29; see also *The Mortgaged Heart*, op. cit., p. 215.
22 "Brooklyn Is My Neighborhood," *Vogue*, March 1, 1941, pp. 62–63, 138; see also *The Mortgaged Heart*, op. cit., pp. 216–20.
23 Ibid.
24 Edward Weeks, *Atlantic Monthly*, April 1, 1941, p. xx.

25 In her essay "Books I Remember," published in *Harper's Bazaar*, April 1, 1941, Carson acknowledged her debt to the books of Dostoevski, who "opened the door to an immense and marvelous new world." In July 1941, Klaus Mann published her essay "The Russian Realists and Southern Literature," in *Decision*, which explored further relationships.

26 CMcC to Robert Linscott, Columbus, Ga., winter 1940–41; from the Robert Newton Linscott Collection, Washington University Libraries, St. Louis, Mo.

27 *The Heart Is a Lonely Hunter*, op. cit., pp. 269–70.

28 *The Ballad of the Sad Café and Collected Short Stories*, Boston: Houghton Mifflin, 1955 ed., p. 6.

CHAPTER SIX

1 Lincoln Kirstein to Aimee Alexander, New York City, October 14, 1970; Gore Vidal to Aimee Alexander, Rome, Italy, October 28, 1970.

2 David Diamond to VSC, interview, Rochester, N.Y., December 3, 1970.

3 Carson admired Miss Barnes's poetry and wanted to get to know her personally. Miss Barnes lived nearby in Patchin Place, and ate frequently at Rochambeau, a restaurant on Sixth Avenue and Eleventh Street, as did Carson. They sent Miss Barnes a bottle of champagne while she sat across from them at a table having dinner.

4 "Madame Zilensky and the King of Finland," *The New Yorker*, December 20, 1941, pp. 15–18.

5 David Diamond to VSC, see above.

6 Ibid.

7 Marjorie Peabody Waite, *Yaddo: Yesterday and Today*, New York: Saratoga Springs, 1933, p. 29.

8 Arriving with Carson at Yaddo in the first group in mid-June 1941 were painters Katya Albert, Jules Mervin, Karnig Nalbandian; sculptors José de Creeft, Eugenie Gershoy; writers Leslie Cameron, Ivan Goll and his wife, Robert Hivnor, Peter Martin, Clark Mills, B. K. Simkovitch, Gerald Sykes, Hilde Walter, Franz and Greta Weiskopf, Eudora Welty; and composer Colin McPhee.

9 Katherine Anne Porter to VSC, interview, College Park, Md., August 1, 1971.

10 Katherine Anne Porter's husband from 1938 to 1942 was Albert Russell Erskine, then a professor of English at Louisiana State University.

11 David Diamond to VSC, Rochester, N.Y., August 23, 1971.

12 Katherine Anne Porter to VSC, see above.

13 Eudora Welty to VSC, Jackson, Miss., September 27, 1971.

14 Katherine Anne Porter to VSC, see above.

15 Granville Hicks to VSC, interview, Grafton, N.Y., May 22, 1971.

16 Edward Newhouse to VSC, interview, Upper Nyack, N.Y., May 22, 1971.

17 Ibid.

18 Granville Hicks to VSC, see above.

19 Elizabeth Ames to VSC, interview, Yaddo, N.Y., May 21, 1971.

20 Edward Newhouse to VSC, see above.

21 "Correspondence," *The New Yorker*, February 7, 1942, pp. 36–39; published later in *The Mortgaged Heart*, Margarita G. Smith, ed., Boston: Houghton Mifflin, 1971, pp. 156–59.

22 Edward Newhouse to VSC, Upper Nyack, N.Y., August 28, 1973.

23 Alfred Kantorowicz to VSC, Hamburg, Germany, August 8, 1972.

[24] Edward Newhouse to VSC, September 29, 1971.

[25] Jordan Massee to VSC, interview, New York City, July 24, 1971.

[26] Ibid.

[27] Arriving at Yaddo in mid-July and early August 1941 were writers Harvey Breit, Bertha Egri, Elizabeth Herzog, C. P. Lee, Louise Ware; sculptor Miriam Cohen; painters Dorothy Gies, Grace Greenwood, Juan and Frances Mingorance; and composers Arthur Cohn and Nikolai Lopatnikoff.

[28] Nikolai Lopatnikoff to VSC, Pittsburgh, Pa., January 21, 1972.

[29] Elizabeth Ames to VSC, see above.

[30] Edward Newhouse to VSC, May 22, 1971.

[31] Edwin Peacock to VSC, interview, Charleston, S.C., October 3, 1970.

[32] Some twenty years later Carson expounded on her views concerning love and passion in her final novel, *Clock Without Hands* (Boston: Houghton Mifflin, 1961). The book became a kind of last will and testament of her feelings in her depiction of young Jester Clane's devotion to his black friend, Sherman Pew. See passages on pp. 81–82 and 135, especially.

[33] Jordan Massee to VSC, see above.

[34] CMcC to David Diamond, Yaddo, August 10, 1941.

[35] "Madame Zilensky and the King of Finland" and "Correspondence," op. cit.

[36] Diary entry by Granville Hicks, August 22, 1941; Hicks to VSC, interview, Grafton, N.Y., June 23, 1971.

[37] Granville Hicks to VSC, op. cit., interview, Grafton, N.Y., May 22, 1971.

[38] Ibid.

[39] Diary entry by Granville Hicks, see above; Hicks to VSC, June 23, 1971, see above.

[40] Ibid.

[41] Diary entry by Granville Hicks, August 30, 1941; Hicks to VSC, June 23, 1971, see above.

[42] Muriel Rukeyser, *Waterlily Fire*, poems, 1935–1962, New York: Macmillan, 1962, pp. 159–60; published originally in *Body of Waking*, 1958, pp. 28–29.

[43] CMcC to Newton Arvin, Wednesday (September 1941), Columbus, Ga.; from the Newton Arvin Collection, Rare Book Room, Smith College Library, Northampton, Mass.

[44] Rebecca Pitts to VSC, Indianapolis, Ind., August 10, 1972. See also CMcC to Newton Arvin, Sunday (October 1941), Columbus, Ga.; from Newton Arvin Collection, see above.

CHAPTER SEVEN

[1] Virginia Johnson Storey to VSC, interview, Columbus, Ga., May 19, 1970.

[2] Virginia Storey Reiney to VSC, interview, Columbus, Ga., October 1, 1972.

[3] Lamar Smith, Jr., to VSC, interview, Perry, Fla., October 3, 1970.

[4] After slight revision, the poem was published that winter in Klaus Mann's magazine, *Decision*, as "The Twisted Trinity"; *Decision*, II (November–December 1941), p. 30. The unpublished version, in Carson's handwriting, untitled and identified as AC14,103, is housed in the Library of Congress in a collection of Miss Flanner's papers and letters. It varies only slightly from the published version, in which Carson tightened syntax and pared her diction.

[5] Latimer Watson, Columbus *Enquirer*, Columbus, Ga., April 6, 1942.

[6] *The Member of the Wedding*, Boston: Houghton Mifflin, 1946, p. 105.

[7] Arnold Saint Subber to VSC, telephone interview, New York City, December 3, 1970.

[8] Eleanor Clark to Aimee Alexander, Fairfield, Conn., July 7, 1971; Eleanor Clark to VSC, Fairfield, Conn., October 15, 1973.

[9] CMcC to David Diamond, Columbus, Ga., February 11, 1942.

[10] "A Tree. A Rock. A Cloud." *Harper's Bazaar*, November 1942, pp. 96–99. Also published in *The Ballad of the Sad Café and Collected Short Stories*, Boston: Houghton Mifflin, 1955 ed., pp. 98–105.

[11] John K. Hutchens, "On the Author," New York *Herald Tribune Book Review*, June 17, 1951, p. 2.

[12] Carson had mentioned her desire to be a foreign correspondent in several letters and also was quoted to this effect by Frank K. Kelley in an interview for the New York *Times*, Sunday, November 16, 1941.

[13] The moth image which Carson used in describing Newton Arvin's treatment of Hawthorne was comparable to her description of actual moths on a summer night as she pictured them in what became the published version of *The Member of the Wedding*, op. cit., p. 12; thus Carson's moth imagery in the letter was no doubt prompted by the passage she had just written in "The Bride." Or possibly, "The Bride"'s lines owed their genesis to Carson's thoughts in her letter to Arvin, in which she complimented him on his Hawthorne biography, June 1942.

[14] Margaret F. Baseman, assistant registrar, University of Miami, to VSC, Miami, Fla., April 21, 1971.

[15] "Wunderkind," *Story*, December 1936, p. 64.

[16] *The Ballad of the Sad Café*, op. cit., p. 19.

[17] Yaddo artists in residence when Carson arrived in early July 1942 were Nathan Asch, Leonard Ehrlich, Benjamin Fagan, Alfred Fisher, Egon Hostovsky, Weldon Kees, Martha Levy, Alfred Kantorowicz, Michael Seide, Franz and Greta Weiskopf, Peter Busa, Eugenie Gershoy, Ruth Gikow, Merle and Nicholas Marsicano, and Burle Marx. Arriving with Carson—or a few days later—were Malcolm Cowley, Kenneth Fearing, Harry Granick, Langston Hughes, Laurette MacDuffie Knight, Nan Lurie, Edna Guck, Helena G. C. Kuo, C. Joan Liberte, Nathaniel Dett, Karnig Nalbandian, Frances and Juan Mingorance, Katherine Anne Porter, Nathalie and Philip Rahv, and Karol Rathaus.

[18] Elizabeth Ames to VSC, interview, Yaddo, May 21, 1971.

[19] Alfred Kantorowicz to VSC, Hamburg, Germany, July 13, 1972.

[20] Ruth Gikow to VSC, New York City, November 3, 1971.

[21] Leonard Ehrlich to VSC, Lido Beach, N.Y., January 15, 1973.

[22] CMcC to Newton Arvin, Yaddo, November 8, 1942. Miss Boyle named her daughter, born that winter, Faith Carson.

[23] Suzanne Ohman to VSC, Meilen, Switzerland, February 1, 1972.

[24] Suzanne Ohman to Aimee Alexander, Meilen, Switzerland, February 24, 1971, translated by James Chappell and Donald Spencer.

[25] CMcC to Klaus Mann, Yaddo, December 3, 1942; from the Erika Mann literary estate, Kilchberg Am Zurichsee, Switzerland.

CHAPTER EIGHT

[1] CMcC to Newton Arvin, Brooklyn, N.Y., February 1943; from the Newton Arvin Collection, Rare Book Room, Smith College Library, Northampton, Mass.

2 CMcC to Newton Arvin, Yaddo, June 1943.

3 Walter Damrosch, president of the American Academy of Arts and Letters, to CMcC, New York City, April 9, 1943.

4 CMcC to David Diamond, Brooklyn, N.Y., winter 1943.

5 CMcC to Klaus Mann, Columbus, Ga., September 5, 1943; from the Erika Mann literary estate, Kilchberg Am Zurichsee, Switzerland.

6 Alfred Kazin to Aimee Alexander, New York City, February 3, 1971; also Alfred Kazin to VSC, interview, New York City, May 23, 1971.

7 *The Member of the Wedding*, Boston: Houghton Mifflin, 1946, p. 30.

8 CMcC to Newton Arvin, Yaddo, August 5, 1943.

9 *The Ballad of the Sad Café and Collected Short Stories*, Boston: Houghton Mifflin, 1955 ed., p. 5.

10 CMcC to Alfred Kazin, Columbus, Ga., August 1943; Alfred Kazin to VSC, see above.

11 Alfred Kazin to VSC, see above.

12 Mary Lou Aswell to VSC, Santa Fe, N. Mex., April 9, 1972.

13 Reeves McCullers to David Diamond, Fort Dix, N.J., October 11, 1943.

14 CMcC to Alfred Kantorowicz, Columbus, Ga., October 1943.

15 David Diamond to VSC, Rochester, N.Y., August 23, 1971.

16 Reeves McCullers to Alfred Kantorowicz, Belgium, December 4, 1944.

17 Reeves McCullers to Edwin Peacock, Belgium, December 3, 1944.

18 Reeves McCullers to Alfred Kantorowicz, see above.

19 Mary McMurria to VSC, interview, Sarasota, Fla., November 3, 1972.

20 William Love to VSC, interview, Columbus, Ga., March 16, 1973.

21 CMcC to Edwin Peacock, Columbus, Ga., May 11, 1944.

22 Robert Linscott to CMcC, New York City, May 9, 1944; from the Robert Newton Linscott Collection, Washington University Libraries, St. Louis, Mo.

23 Mrs. Robin Mullin to VSC, interview, Columbus, Ga., November 10, 1971.

24 David Diamond to VSC, see above.

25 CMcC to Robert Linscott, Columbus, Ga., August 16, 1944; from the Robert Newton Linscott Collection, op. cit.

26 Reeves McCullers to Edwin Peacock, see above.

27 CMcC to Newton Arvin, Nyack, N.Y., September 14, 1944.

28 CMcC to Robert Linscott, Columbus, Ga., August 21, 1944; from the Robert Newton Linscott Collection, op. cit.

29 Robert Linscott to CMcC, New York City, August 21, 1944; from the Robert Newton Linscott Collection, op. cit.

30 CMcC to Reeves McCullers, Nyack, N.Y., November 21, 1944.

31 CMcC to Newton Arvin, Columbus, Ga., February 20, 1944.

32 Marguerite Smith to Edwin Peacock, Nyack, N.Y., February 3, 1945.

33 The deed to the purchase of 131 South Broadway is recorded in Liber 430, cp 298, with revenue stamps affixed in the amount of $9.90 ($1.10 per thousand), according to Mrs. McCall, deputy registrar of deeds, Rockland County, New York.

CHAPTER NINE

1 Reeves McCullers to Edwin Peacock, Belgium, December 3, 1944; to Alfred Kantorowicz, Belgium, December 4, 1944.

2 CMcC to Newton Arvin and to David Diamond, Nyack, N.Y., March 26, 1945.

3 Reeves McCullers to John Vincent Adams, Camp Wheeler, Ga., August 5, 1945.

4 Jerre Mangione to VSC, Philadelphia, December 8, 1972.
5 Eleanor Clark to Aimee Alexander, West Wardsboro, Vt., July 3, 1971.
6 Elizabeth Ames to VSC, interview, Yaddo, May 21, 1971.
7 Ibid.
8 CMcC to Newton Arvin, Nyack, N.Y., August 16, 1945.
9 CMcC to Newton Arvin, Nyack, N.Y., September 16, 1945.
10 John Leggett to VSC, Iowa City, Ia., April 3, 1972.
11 Truman Capote to Pati Hill, interview, in *Writers At Work: The Paris Review Interviews*, edited by Malcolm Cowley, New York: Viking Press, 1959, p. 290.
12 "Our Heads Are Bowed," *Mademoiselle*, November 1945, pp. 131, 229.
13 Lamar Smith, Jr., to VSC, interview, Perry, Fla., October 3, 1970.
14 Edwin Peacock to VSC, interview, Charleston, S.C., August 30, 1972.
15 The inventory of the Book Basement was sold in 1972 when Edwin Peacock and John Zeigler retired, and the building purchased by the College of Charleston to become a part of its campus. Edwin Peacock to VSC, interview, Charleston, S.C., August 30, 1972.
16 Orville Prescott, "Books of the Times," New York *Times*, March 19, 1946; Lewis Gannett, "Books and Things," Boston *Transcript*, March 20, 1946; Richard Match, "No Man's Land of Childhood," New York *Herald Tribune Weekly Book Review*, March 24, 1946; Isa Kapp, "One Summer: Three Lives," New York *Times Book Review*, March 24, 1946; George Dangerfield, "Books," *The Saturday Review of Literature*, March 30, 1946, p. 15; Edmund Wilson, *The New Yorker*, March 30, 1946, p. 87.
17 CMcC to Newton Arvin, Yaddo, March 31, 1946.
18 Ibid.
19 Granville Hicks to VSC, interview, Grafton, N.Y., May 22, 1971.
20 Marguerite Young to VSC, interview, New York City, December 14, 1970.
21 See *Life's* three-page spread about Yaddo and its guests who were in residence in June 1946, the first major pictorial publicity the artists' colony received: "*Life* Visits Yaddo," *Life*, July 15, 1946, pp. 110–13.
22 Jerre Mangione to VSC, see above.
23 New York *Times*, April 14, 1946.
24 Leo Lerman to VSC, interview, New York City, March 1, 1972.
25 Pancho Rodriguez to VSC, interview, New Orleans, December 13, 1971.
26 Pancho Rodriguez to VSC, New Orleans, November 23, 1971.
27 Pancho Rodriguez to VSC, December 13, 1971, see above.
28 Tennessee Williams to VSC, interview, New Orleans, January 30–31, 1972.
29 Ibid.
30 Pancho Rodriguez to VSC, November 23, 1971, see above; also, Tennessee Williams to VSC, see above.
31 Pancho Rodriguez to VSC, ibid.
32 Tennessee Williams to VSC, see above.
33 Ibid.
34 CMcC to Tennessee Williams, undated letter, Nyack, N.Y.
35 Gertrude Macy to VSC, New York City, July 1, 1972.
36 Marguerite Young to VSC, see above.
37 Ibid.
38 Janet Flanner to VSC, interview, New York City, March 3, 1972.
39 *Le Coeur est un Chasseur Solitaire*, translated by Jean Blanzat, Cleveland: World, 1946; *Reflets dans un Oeil d'or*, translated by Charles Cestre, preface by Jean Blanzat, Paris: Stock (Delamain et Boutelleau), 1946.

40 Miss Boyle had dedicated a long poem to Carson in 1944, which pleased her very much: *The American Citizen: Naturalized in Leadville, Colorado,* published by Simon & Schuster, which bore the inscription: "This poem is dedicated to Carson McCullers. Her husband, like mine, is serving overseas." Miss Boyle's poem was her expression of the meaning of her husband's fight against fascism overseas and what it meant to the wives at home. (At the time the poem was published, however, Carson and Reeves were divorced. Nor were they married when Reeves was serving overseas.)

41 Simone de Beauvoir to Aimee Alexander, Paris, May 10, 1972.

42 John Brown to VSC, Washington, D.C., January 9, 1973. See also René Micha, *Critique*, August–September 1973.

43 John Brown to VSC, ibid; also interview, Washington, D.C., March 4, 1972.

44 See John Brown's critical book on American literature, *Panorama de la Littérature Contemporaine Aux Etats-Unis,* published in Paris by Gallimard Press, 1954, in which he wrote about Carson McCullers. This work received the 1954 *Grand Prix de la critique,* one of Paris' major literary awards.

45 Eleanor Clark to Aimee Alexander, see above.

46 Natalia Danesi Murray to VSC, interview, New York City, March 2, 1972.

47 Ibid.

48 Janet Flanner to VSC, see above.

49 Natalia Danesi Murray to VSC, see above.

50 The American Hospital, operated since the French liberation as the U. S. Army's 365th General Hospital United, was returned to civilian status on January 31, 1946. Located in the suburb of Neuilly, outside Paris, it was a luxurious institution and the hospital where most Americans went for treatment.

51 Constance Webb, *Richard Wright: A Biography,* New York: Putnam, 1968, pp. 269–73. Also, Constance Webb to VSC, Los Angeles, June 3, 1971.

52 See various uncatalogued papers in the Oliver Evans Collection, Humanities Research Center Library, University of Texas, Austin, Tex., for a discussion of Carson McCullers' medical history.

53 Jordan Massee to VSC, New York City, July 17, 1973.

CHAPTER TEN

1 Other "best postwar writers" named by *Quick* magazine in 1947 were Norman Mailer, John Hersey, Arthur Schlesinger, Jr., Jean Stafford, and Peter Viereck. Runners-up included Tennessee Williams, Arthur Miller, and Truman Capote.

2 Others named for the *Mademoiselle* Annual Merit Award were Barbara Ann Scott, figure skater; Anahid Ajemian, violinist; Toni Owen, designer; Santha Rama Rau, writer; Elizabeth M. Ackermann, researcher; Mildred L. Lillie, judge; Shirley Adelson Siegel, housing director; Anne Waterman, university professor; and Elaine Whitelaw, polio foundation director. Mary Cantwell, managing editor, *Mademoiselle,* to Aimee Alexander, New York City, March 17, 1971; see also *Mademoiselle,* January 1948, pp. 118–19.

3 Reeves McCullers to John Vincent Adams, Charlotte, N.C., February 1938.

4 Lamar Smith, Jr., to VSC, interview, Perry, Fla., October 3, 1970.

[5] David Eisendrath to VSC, Brooklyn, N.Y., January 10, 1973.

[6] CMcC to Tennessee Williams, Nyack, February 14, 1948.

[7] Greer Johnson was unwilling to talk about the collaboration agreement or its ramifications for publication in this biography; Greer Johnson to VSC, May 5, 1971, February 17, 1972.

[8] The psychiatrist's identity has been withheld upon his request.

[9] "Letters to the Editor," *Life*, March 2, 1948.

[10] Tennessee Williams to CMcC, Rome, February 1948.

[11] This poem was published later that year in *New Directions*, X, 1948, 509, then in *Voices*, September–December 1952, p. 12. It also was recorded for MGM records, produced by Jean Stein vanden Heuvel under the title "When We Are Lost What Image Tells?" (Carson McCullers Reads from The Member of The Wedding and Other Works, E3619 ARC, 1958.) Most recently it was published in *The Mortgaged Heart*, Margarita G. Smith, ed., Boston: Houghton Mifflin, 1971, p. 287.

[12] Hervey M. Cleckley and Corbett H. Thigpen, *The Three Faces of Eve*, New York: McGraw-Hill, 1957.

[13] Joshua Logan to VSC, New York City, February 16, 1973.

[14] Robert Whitehead to VSC, interview, New York City, July 29, 1972.

[15] Mary Martin to VSC, Goiás, Brazil, February 1, 1972.

[16] American Arbitration Association to VSC, New York City, January 6, 1972.

[17] The contract with *The New Yorker* for "further stories," which Carson had mentioned earlier to her psychiatrist friend, had failed to materialize.

[18] "How I Began to Write," *Mademoiselle*, September 1948, p. 191; also, *The Mortgaged Heart*, op. cit., p. 249.

[19] New York *Times*, October 27, 1948.

[20] Reeves McCullers to Edwin Peacock, Nyack, N.Y., February 20, 1949.

[21] "Art and Mr. Mahoney" was published in the February 1949 issue of *Mademoiselle*, pp. 120, 184–86; "The Sojourner" appeared in *Mademoiselle* in May 1950, pp. 90, 160–66. "Art and Mr. Mahoney" was reprinted in *The Mortgaged Heart*, op. cit., pp. 160–63.

[22] Lamar Smith, Jr., to VSC, interview, Perry, Fla., June 3, 1969.

[23] CMcC to Jordan Massee, Nyack, N.Y., February 23, 1949.

[24] Kathleen Woodruff to VSC, interview, Columbus, Ga., January 3, 1971.

[25] Mildred Miller Fort to VSC, interview, Columbus, Ga., March 3, 1970.

[26] Kathleen Woodruff to VSC, see above.

[27] Jordan Massee's diary entry, Macon, Ga.; to VSC, interview, New York City, January 3, 1973.

[28] Ibid.

[29] Nonie Morgan, woman's editor, Macon *News*, "Carson McCullers, Distinguished Novelist, and Her Mother Visiting Here," March 18, 1949, p. 11.

[30] Margaret Leonard Long to VSC, Atlanta, February 7, 1972.

[31] Ibid.

[32] Jordan Massee to VSC, New York City, July 26, 1971.

[33] Ibid.

[34] CMcC to Edwin Peacock, New York City, March 1949; also, Alfred Kazin to VSC, interview, New York City, May 23, 1971.

[35] Jordan Massee to VSC, January 3, 1973, see above.

[36] Jordan Massee to VSC, New York City, July 26, 1971.

[37] *Reflections in a Golden Eye* with a preface by Tennessee Williams was

published by New Directions in 1950, followed by a Bantam edition with the preface in September of that year.

[38] Ethel Waters, *His Eye Is on the Sparrow*, New York: Doubleday, 1950, p. 263.

[39] Audrey Wood to VSC, New York City, March 19, 1973.

[40] Joshua Logan to VSC, see above.

[41] Harold Clurman, *Lies Like Truth*, New York: Macmillan, 1958, p. 64.

[42] Harold Clurman to VSC, interview, New York City, May 24, 1971.

[43] Fred Zinnemann to VSC, London, April 11, 1973.

[44] Lester Polakov to VSC, interview, New York City, May 20, 1971.

[45] Ibid.

[46] Ethel Waters, *His Eye Is on the Sparrow*, op. cit., p. 274.

[47] Lester Polakov to VSC, see above.

[48] Emanuel Romano to VSC, New York City, December 1, 1971; interview, March 1, 1972.

[49] Ibid.

[50] Jordan Massee to VSC, see above.

[51] Emanuel Romano to VSC, see above.

[52] Harvey Breit, "Behind The Wedding: Carson McCullers Discusses the Novel She Converted Into a Stage Play," *New York Times*, January 1, 1950.

[53] Ward Morehouse, "Georgia's Carson McCullers Writes Year's Best Play," *Atlanta Journal Magazine*, April 30, 1950, p. 5.

[54] Virginia Smith to VSC, interview, Perry, Fla., October 3, 1971.

[55] Jordan Massee to VSC, New York City, July 18, 1973.

[56] Janet Flanner to VSC, interview, New York City, March 3, 1972.

[57] See also Brooks Atkinson, "Three People: 'The Member of the Wedding' Superbly Acted by an Excellent Company," *New York Times*, January 15, 1950.

[58] Runner-up for the New York Drama Critics' Circle Award was William Inge's *Come Back, Little Sheba* with four votes. Gian-Carlo Menotti's *The Consul*, which received three votes for the award that Carson's play won, was named best musical of the year, and T. S. Eliot's *The Cocktail Party* was voted best foreign play.

[59] According to a New York *Times* article, *South Pacific* was ineligible for a Drama Critics' Circle Award because it had opened later than the specified award period, but it was eligible for the Pulitzer, which had a different cutoff period.

[60] John Chapman, ed., *Burns Mantle Best Plays of 1949–1950*, New York: Dodd, Mead, 1950.

[61] Carson McCullers, "The Vision Shared," *Theatre Arts*, April 1950, p. 30.

[62] Harold Clurman, "Theatre: From a Member," *New Republic*, January 30, 1950, p. 28.

[63] Lewis Gannett, "In Praise of 'Member,'" New York *Times*, April 9, 1950.

[64] Ibid.

[65] Julie Harris to CMcC, New York City, November 27, 1955; also Julie Harris to VSC, New York City, May 19, 1971.

[66] Harold Clurman to VSC, see above.

[67] Ward Morehouse, op. cit.

[68] At the end of *The Member of the Wedding*, Carson's autobiographical protagonist Frankie Addams knows that she can never literally be a

"member of the wedding," but already she is fantasizing a trip around the world with her new friend Mary Littlejohn, and life is bright and promising once more.

CHAPTER ELEVEN

[1] Elizabeth Bowen, "Bowen's Court," *Holiday*, December 1958, p. 86.

[2] Ibid., p. 191.

[3] Elizabeth Bowen to VSC, Kent, England, November 9, 1971.

[4] Marty Mann was active in AA and had helped Reeves previously; more about Miss Mann below.

[5] Tennessee Williams, *The Roman Spring of Mrs. Stone*, New York: New Directions, 1950.

[6] Elizabeth Bowen to VSC, see above.

[7] Stanley Martineau to VSC, telephone interview, New York City, February 17, 1973.

[8] Marty Mann to VSC, interview, New York City, March 3, 1972; letter, April 25, 1973.

[9] *Botteghe Oscure*, 1952, pp. 213–18; *Mademoiselle*, July 1952, pp. 54–55, 108.

[10] CMcC to Tennessee Williams, Nyack, N.Y., summer 1950.

[11] Jordan Massee to VSC, interview, New York City, July 25, 1971.

[12] Brooks Atkinson, New York *Times*, September 17, 1950, II, p. 1.

[13] Stanley Kramer to VSC, Burbank, Calif., February 22, 1973.

[14] After the Boston opening of *The Member of the Wedding*, the company played at the Royal Alexandra Theatre in Toronto, April 3; His Majesty's Theatre, Montreal, April 23; the Erlanger Theatre, Buffalo, May 7; the Rochester Auditorium, Rochester, May 11. In October, the regular road (national) company opened its schedule in Detroit; then followed Kansas City, Des Moines, Omaha, Denver, Los Angeles, San Francisco, Portland, Seattle, Spokane, St. Paul, Minneapolis, Milwaukee, Indianapolis, Columbus, Cincinnati, Cleveland, Pittsburgh, Baltimore, Philadelphia, Allentown, Reading, Hershey, Springfield, Hartford, and Providence, closing on April 28, 1952; the entire tour was considered by its producers a tremendous success.

[15] Harold Clurman to VSC, interview, New York City, May 24, 1971.

[16] "A Domestic Dilemma," in *The Ballad of the Sad Café and Collected Short Stories*, Boston: Houghton Mifflin, 1952, p. 92.

[17] Charles Poore, "Books of the Times," New York *Times*, May 24, 1951.

[18] Diary entry, David Diamond, New York City, February 3, 1951; to VSC, Rochester, N.Y., February 22, 1973.

[19] Diary entry, David Diamond, New York City, February 10, 1951; to VSC, ibid.

[20] The sale of 131 South Broadway, Nyack, New York, is recorded in the Rockland County Court House, Liber 524, page 329, March 13, 1951. The stamps affixed were in the amount of $12.10, indicating that the purchase price by Carson for her mother's house was $13,310, according to Mrs. McCall, deputy registrar of deeds.

[21] Lillian Hellman to VSC, telephone interview, New York City, March 2, 1972.

[22] Ibid.

[23] David Diamond to VSC, see above.

[24] Andrew Lyndon to VSC, telephone interview, Macon, Ga., January 8, 1971.

25 Ibid.
26 Lillian Hellman to VSC, see above.
27 Reeves McCullers to David Diamond, Nyack, N.Y., September 8, 1951.
28 David Garnett to Ruth Hall, interview for *The Times* of London, 1972; also David Garnett to VSC, Montcuq, France, January 17, 1973.
29 James Stern to VSC, interview, Tisbury, England, September 4, 1973.
30 John Lehmann, *In My Own Time, Memoirs of a Literary Life*, Boston: Little, Brown and Company, 1969, p. 468.
31 John Lehmann to VSC, London, England, February 28, 1973.
32 Andrew Lyndon to VSC, see above.
33 Rosamond Lehmann to Reeves McCullers, London, September 23, 1951, fragment of a letter; from the Oliver Evans Collection (uncatalogued material), Humanities Research Center Library, University of Texas, Austin, Tex. According to Mrs. Joan Gaskin, records department, St. George's Hospital, London, to VSC, April 9, 1973, Carson was admitted to the hospital on August 9, 1951, under the direction of a Dr. Gainsborough; her residence on admittance was listed as 25 St. Leonard's Terrace.
34 Rosamond Lehmann to Aimee Alexander, London, July 23, 1971.
35 Reeves McCullers to Rosamond Lehmann, Nyack, N.Y., September 27, 1951; from the archives of the Rosamond Lehmann Collection, King's College Library, Cambridge, England.
36 Reeves McCullers to Rosamond Lehmann, Nyack, N.Y., November 26, 1951; from the archives of the Rosamond Lehmann Collection, ibid.
37 New York *Times*, October 4, 1951.
38 Felicia Geffen, assistant to the president, AAAL, assistant secretary, NIAL, to VSC, January 17, 1972.
39 Marguerite Young to VSC, telephone interview, New York City, March 3, 1973.
40 Marguerite Young to VSC, interview, New York City, December 14, 1970.
41 David Diamond to VSC, interview, Rochester, N.Y., December 10, 1970.
42 Jordan Massee to VSC, interview, New York City, July 26, 1971.
43 Gaspero del Corso to VSC, Rome, February 23, 1973.
44 Marguerite Young to VSC, March 3, 1973, see above.
45 "The Dual Angel: A Meditation on Origin and Choice," *Botteghe Oscure*, IX (1952), pp. 213–18; the poem also appeared in *Mademoiselle*, XXXV (July 1952), pp. 54–55, 108.
46 Mario Monti to VSC, Milan, Italy, March 16, 1973.
47 Simone Brown to VSC, interview, Washington, D.C., August 1, 1971.
48 John L. Brown to VSC, interview, Washington, D.C., March 4, 1972.
49 Jordan Massee to VSC, interview, New York City, July 17, 1973.
50 Reeves McCullers to Edwin Peacock and John Zeigler, Bachvillers, France, November 3, 1952.
51 Janet Flanner to VSC, interview, New York City, March 3, 1972.
52 Andrée Chèdid to VSC, Paris, January 19, 1973; André Bay to VSC, Paris, February 4, 1972 and February 19, 1973.
53 Jack Fullilove to VSC, interview, Chapel Hill, N.C., December 18, 1970.
54 Jack Fullilove to VSC, Chapel Hill, N.C., April 19, 1972.
55 Jack Fullilove to VSC, December 18, 1970, see above.
56 Jack Fullilove to VSC, Chapel Hill, N.C., February 6, 1973.
57 Harrell Woolfolk to VSC, telephone interview, Charlotte, N.C., February 1, 1973.

[58] Jack Fullilove to VSC, December 18, 1970, see above.
[59] CMcC to Mary Tucker, Bachvillers, France, December 1952.
[60] Tennessee Williams to VSC, interview, New Orleans, January 30, 1972.
[61] Janet Flanner to VSC, see above.
[62] Reeves's death was also reported to have occurred on November 18, 1953, at the Hotel Pierre Ier de Serbie. However, according to Mary Ann Meysenburg, American vice consul, the American embassy in Paris, May 5, 1971, Reeves died on November 19, 1953, at the Hôtel Chateau-Frontenac, 54, rue Pierre Charron, Paris.
[63] "J. R. McCullers Jr. Dies; Husband of Novelist, Playwright, Succumbs in Paris at 40," New York *Times*, November 27, 1953.
[64] Edward P. O'Dell, chief, Contact Division, Veterans Administration Office, Washington, D.C. to VSC, February 22, 1971.
[65] Jack Fullilove to VSC, April 19, 1972, see above.
[66] Tennessee Williams to VSC, interview, New Orleans, January 31, 1972.

CHAPTER TWELVE

[1] Paula Snelling to VSC, interview, Clayton, Ga., October 19, 1970.
[2] Lillian Hellman to VSC, telephone interview, New York City, February 20, 1972.
[3] Dr. Hervey M. Cleckley to VSC, Augusta, Ga., October 5, 1970.
[4] Jordan Massee to VSC, New York City, July 17, 1973.
[5] Tennessee Williams to VSC, interview, New Orleans, January 31, 1972.
[6] John Vincent Adams to VSC, Westwood, N.J., November 16, 1970.
[7] Lillian Hellman to VSC, see above.
[8] Edward P. O'Dell, chief, Contact Division, Veterans Administration Office, to VSC, Washington, D.C., February 22, 1971.
[9] Jordan Massee to VSC, New York City, November 4, 1973.
[10] Reeves's brothers and sisters died in the order of their births: Marguerite McCullers Lee died, in 1946, at age thirty-two, from an overdose of sleeping pills. Carson and Reeves were in Paris and did not return for the funeral. Wiley Mae McCullers Altschuler took an overdose of prescription drugs in January 1961, reportedly as a result of her prolonged suffering over chronic ill health; she was forty-three. Tommy, the "baby"— whom Reeves had always worried about—hurled himself from an upper-story window in Greenwich Village in 1965. He, too, was forty-three. Both parents predeceased Tommy. James Reeves McCullers, Sr., Reeves's father, who had remarried, succumbed to a heart attack in Jesup, Ga., in 1955, and Jessie Winn McCullers, Reeves's mother, died of breast cancer in California in 1964.
[11] Janet Flanner to VSC, interview, New York City, March 3, 1972.
[12] Ibid.
[13] Ibid.
[14] Whit Burnett to VSC, telephone interview, New York City, December 15, 1970.
[15] Francis Price to VSC, East Quogue, N.Y., October 26, 1972.
[16] Terry Murray to VSC, telephone interview, New York City, December 15, 1970.
[17] Margarita G. Smith personally expressed none of these attitudes regarding her sister or herself to this biographer, nor did she contribute any factual or anecdotal material to this book. It was impossible, however, for Carson's friends and literary acquaintances to share the myriad facets of

the Carson McCullers they knew best without referring to the strong ties which linked her to the rest of her family. To have ignored them would have been a travesty in a depth biography of one whose creative art was so intricately linked with her life, both real and fantasy.

18 Jordan Massee to VSC, interview, New York City, July 10, 1973.

19 Lamar Smith, Jr., to VSC, interview, Perry, Fla., June 3, 1969.

20 "The Haunted Boy," *Mademoiselle*, XLII (November 1955), p. 154; reprinted in *The Ballad of the Sad Café and Collected Short Stories*, Boston: Houghton Mifflin, 1955 ed., p. 112.

21 George Lang to VSC, New York City, March 21, 1973.

22 Ibid.

23 Ibid.

24 Celestine Sibley to VSC, Atlanta, April 9, 1973.

25 Constance Pilkinton Johnson to VSC, interview, Columbus, Ga., December 23, 1970.

26 Mr. and Mrs. George Swift to VSC, interview, Columbus, Ga., September 29, 1970.

27 CMcC to Lillian Smith, Yaddo, May 29, 1954.

28 Danan Barnett, Robert Saudek Associates, to VSC, New York City, February 2, 1971.

29 Jordan Massee to VSC, interview, New York City, March 1, 1972.

30 Lamar Smith, Jr., to VSC, Perry, Fla., October 3, 1970.

31 "Carson McCullers Will Deliver Kellogg's Lecture," *Goucher Weekly*, Baltimore, February 12, 1954, p. 1.

32 CMcC to Newton Arvin, Nyack, N.Y., August 15, 1954.

33 Edwin Peacock to VSC, Charleston, S.C., November 4, 1972.

34 Ibid.

35 "The Pestle" (Part I of *Clock Without Hands*), *Botteghe Oscure*, XI (1953), pp. 226–46; *Mademoiselle*, XXXVII (July 1953), pp. 44–45, 114–18.

36 Hilda Marks to VSC, interview, New York City, March 24, 1971.

37 Harrell Woolfolk to VSC, telephone interview, Charlotte, N.C., February 1, 1973.

38 Robert Walden to VSC, Asheville, N.C., April 9, 1973.

39 Ibid.

40 Ibid.

41 Robert Walden to VSC, interview, Charlotte, N.C., May 11, 1971.

42 Robert Walden to VSC, April 9, 1973, see above; to VSC, May 11, 1971, ibid.

43 CMcC to Robert Walden and Edward Newberry, Yaddo, May 2, 1954.

44 Elizabeth Ames to VSC, interview, Yaddo, May 21, 1971.

45 Hilda Marks to VSC, interview, New York City, May 21, 1971; also, Tennessee Williams to VSC, interview, New Orleans, December 12, 1972; also, June Fortess, executive secretary, the Poetry Center, New York City, to VSC, January 29, 1973. In the archives of the Poetry Center is a tape of Mrs. McCullers' talk given at Kaufman Auditorium, May 8, 1954.

46 Truman Capote to VSC, Verbien, Switzerland, March 14, 1972.

47 CMcC to Oliver Evans, Nyack, N.Y., August 5 and August 8, 1963; from the Oliver Evans Collection, Humanities Research Center Library, University of Texas, Austin, Tex.

48 Oliver Evans, *The Ballad of Carson McCullers*, New York: Coward-McCann, 1966, p. 17.

49 CMcC to Oliver Evans, see above.
50 Jordan Massee to VSC, interview, New York City, July 24, 1971.
51 Flannery O'Connor to Tom Gossett, Milledgeville, Ga., August 22, 1961.
52 Tennessee Williams to VSC, interview, New York City, March 4, 1972.
53 Jordan Massee to VSC, see above.
54 Dr. Ernst Hammerschlag to VSC, New York City, January 4, 1973.
55 Gabriela Mistral abandoned her real name, Lucila Godoy Alcayaga, for her pseudonym upon the publication of her first book. See "Introduction," *Selected Poems of Gabriela Mistral*, introduction and translation by Langston Hughes, Bloomington: Indiana University Press, 1966.
56 *Sweet as a Pickle and Clean as a Pig*, illustrated by Rolf Gerard, Boston: Houghton Mifflin, 1964.
57 Hortense Calisher, *Herself—An Autobiographical Memoir*, New York: Arbor House, 1972, in which she tells this anecdote and renders Carson McCullers' pronunciation in the phonetic spelling given.
58 Mrs. Ulla Joyer, secretary for the Nobel Committee of the Swedish Academy, Stockholm, Sweden, to Aimee Alexander, December 3, 1971.
59 The working artists at Yaddo during the spring and summer of 1954 when Carson, too, was there were: Jeanette Andrew, Walter Aschaffenburg, Rosemarie Phelps Beck, Babette Deutsch, Leon Edel, Harvey Fite, Jerome Greenfield, Patience Haley, Jacob Lawrence, Margaret Lowery, Philip Murray, Charles Oscar, Simmons Persons, George Reavey, Isaac Rosenfeld, John Thomas, Parker Tyler, Mary Heaton Vorse, and Anne Walters.
60 Leon Edel to Aimee Alexander, Honolulu, Hawaii, May 28, 1971.
61 Granville Hicks to VSC, interview, Grafton, N.Y., May 24, 1971.
62 Walter Aschaffenburg to VSC, Oberlin, Ohio, April 10, 1973.
63 Robert Marks to VSC, interview, New York City, May 24, 1971.
64 Vance Bourjaily to VSC, Iowa City, Ia., September 21, 1973.
65 Hilda Marks to VSC, interview, New York City, May 24, 1971.
66 Ibid.
67 Robert Marks to VSC, interview, New York City, March 2, 1972.
68 Tennessee Williams, "On Meeting a Young Writer," *Harper's Bazaar*, August 1954.
69 Mrs. George Swift, Sr., to VSC, interview, Columbus, Ga., September 29, 1970.
70 According to the obituary of Marguerite Waters Smith in the Rockland County *Journal-News*, June 13, 1955, funeral services were held at the McCloskey Funeral Home at 3:00 P.M., June 14, with Reverend Harold B. Thelin, rector of Grace Episcopal Church, Nyack, officiating.
71 Robert Marks to VSC, May 24, 1971, see above.

CHAPTER THIRTEEN

1 Arnold Saint Subber to VSC, telephone interview, New York City, December 17, 1970.
2 "Playwright Tells of Pangs," Philadelphia *Inquirer*, October 13, 1957, section b, pp. 1, 5.
3 Robert Marks to VSC, interview, New York City, March 2, 1972.
4 According to *The Biographical Encyclopedia and Who's Who in the American Theatre*, Walter Rigdon, ed., New York: James E. Heineman, 1966, p. 798, Saint Subber was born February 18, 1918, which would make him a day and a year younger than Carson.
5 Arnold Saint Subber to VSC, see above.

[6] "Playwright Tells of Pangs," op. cit.

[7] Anne Baxter to VSC, interview, New York City, March 1, 1972.

[8] Ibid.

[9] Albert Marre to VSC, telephone interview, New York City, May 4, 1973.

[10] Carson McCullers, "Who Has Seen the Wind?," *Mademoiselle,* September 1956, pp. 158–59, 174–88. It was published in *Forty Best Stories From Mademoiselle, 1935–1960,* edited by Cyrilly Abels and Margarita G. Smith, New York: Harper & Row, 1961.

[11] Albert Marre to VSC, see above.

[12] Ibid.

[13] Ibid.

[14] John Leggett to VSC, Iowa City, Ia., April 3, 1972.

[15] Albert Marre to VSC, see above.

[16] Anne Baxter to VSC, see above.

[17] Jose Quintero to VSC, interview, Columbus, Ga., February 11, 1972.

[18] Jordan Massee to VSC, interview, New York City, July 24, 1971.

[19] Anne Baxter to VSC, see above.

[20] Glenway Wescott to VSC, Rosemont, N.J., February 7, 1972.

[21] Arthur Gelb, "Script Revision Held Increasing: Lantz Sees Need for Extensive Rewriting," New York *Times,* October 21, 1959.

[22] Anne Baxter to VSC, see above.

[23] John Leggett to VSC, see above.

[24] Carson McCullers, "A Personal Preface," *The Square Root of Wonderful,* Boston: Houghton Mifflin, 1958, ix; see also "Why Novelists Turn to Plays," New York *Times,* June 20, 1958.

[25] *The Square Root of Wonderful,* op. cit., p. 83.

[26] Cecil Beaton, *The Face of the World: An International Scrapbook of People and Places,* New York: John Day Company, n.d., p. 34.

[27] Jordan Massee to VSC, see above.

[28] Dr. Ernst Hammerschlag to VSC, New York City, January 4, 1973.

[29] Carson's "old friend" who contributed his diary entry for August 10, 1958, requested to remain anonymous.

[30] Edward Newhouse to VSC, interview, Upper Nyack, N.Y., May 22, 1971.

[31] Jordan Massee to VSC, see above.

[32] Leo Lerman to VSC, interview, New York City, March 3, 1972.

[33] Thomas Ryan to VSC, New York City, October 8, 1970.

[34] Ibid.

[35] Hilda Marks to VSC, interview, New York City, May 24, 1971.

[36] Dr. Ernst Hammerschlag to VSC, see above.

[37] CMcC to Dame Edith Sitwell, Nyack, N.Y., September 8, 1959; from the Edith Sitwell Collection, New York Public Library.

[38] Thomas Ryan to VSC, see above.

[39] CMcC to Dame Edith Sitwell, Nyack, N.Y., April 23, 1959 and September 8, 1959, see above.

[40] "An Interview with Carson McCullers," *The Marquis,* Lafayette College, Pa., 1963.

[41] Jordan Massee to VSC, interview, New York City, May 21, 1971.

[42] Dr. Ray E. Trussell to VSC, New York City, July 9, 1973.

[43] Jordan Massee to VSC, July 24, 1971, see above.

[44] Cyrilly Abels to VSC, interview, New York City, March 3, 1972; also, letter to VSC, May 8, 1972.

45 Dorothy Salisbury Davis to VSC, interview, Palisades, N.Y., May 23, 1971.
46 Paul Bowles to VSC, Tangier, Morocco, September 16, 1970.
47 Thomas Ryan to VSC, see above.
48 Carson McCullers, "The Flowering Dream: Notes on Writing," *Esquire*, December 1959, pp. 162–64. See also Margarita G. Smith, ed., *The Mortgaged Heart*, Boston: Houghton Mifflin, 1971, pp. 274–82.
49 Jean Stein vanden Heuvel to VSC, telephone interview, New York City, May 23, 1971; also letter, September 8, 1973; passage quoted from *The Member of the Wedding* (play), New York: New Directions, 1949, p. 52.
50 Thomas Lask, "Readings from Swift to Faulkner: Records," New York *Times*, May 4, 1958.
51 "Carson McCullers on Television: 'Lamp Unto My Feet,'" Columbus *Ledger*, August 19, 1958.
52 J. C. Trewin, "The World of the Theatre: One of the Party," *Illustrated London Times*, February 16, 1957, p. 276; see also reviews by T. C. Worsley, "Growing Up," *New Statesman and Nation*, February 16, 1957, p. 201; and an unsigned review, "Plays," *English*, Summer 1957, p. 185.
53 André Bay to VSC, Paris, February 19, 1973.
54 Marielle Bancou to VSC, interview, New York City, July 30, 1971.
55 Edward Newhouse to VSC, see above.
56 Eric Preminger to VSC, telephone interview, New York City, July 27, 1971; also, Marjorie Kellogg to VSC, New York City, February 26, 1972.
57 Jordan Massee to VSC, see above.
58 Marielle Bancou to VSC, see above.
59 Janet Flanner to VSC, interview, New York City, March 3, 1972.
60 Dr. Mercer did not discuss Carson McCullers with this biographer, for she felt that to do so would be a breach of the patient-psychiatrist relationship. In a letter she said that Carson McCullers was not only her friend, but her patient; and since she never discussed a patient she would have to decline the request for an interview. Mary Mercer to VSC, Nyack, N.Y., September 30, 1970. There was, however, one brief meeting in Nyack on December 13, 1970, during which Dr. Mercer answered several questions of a factual nature.
61 Isak Dinesen, "On Mottoes of My Life," *Proceedings*, Second Series, ✕10, AAAL, NEAL, pp. 345–58.
62 CMcC, "Isak Dinesen: In Praise of Radiance," *Saturday Review*, March 16, 1963, pp. 29, 83; see also *The Mortgaged Heart*, op. cit., p. 271.
63 Ibid.
64 Jordan Massee to VSC, interview, New York City, July 16, 1973.
65 Arthur Miller to VSC, Washington, D.C., May 26, 1973.
66 Ibid.
67 Arthur Miller to Aimee Alexander, New York City, November 28, 1970; Arthur Miller to VSC, see above.
68 David McDowell to VSC, interview, New York City, July 31, 1971.
69 Elizabeth Linscott to VSC, Northampton, Mass., April 2, 1973.
70 Albert Erskine to VSC, New York City, January 17, 1973.
71 Kenneth Lohf, curator, Columbia University Library, New York City, to VSC, June 7, 1972.
72 William Goyen to VSC, New York City, March 24, 1973.
73 John Leggett to VSC, see above.

[74] Jordan Massee to VSC, July 16, 1973, see above.

[75] According to Ford Foundation records, there is no evidence that Carson ever sought assistance for herself; nor did she recommend anyone during the three years she was asked to serve as a nominator (she was invited again in 1963). William H. Nims, assistant secretary of the Ford Foundation, to Aimee Alexander, New York City, November 4, 1970.

[76] CMcC to Carl Van Vechten, Nyack, N.Y., April 2, 1960; from the Carl Van Vechten Papers, Collection of American Literature, Beinecke Rare Book and Manuscript Library, Yale University, and Donald Gallup, curator and literary trustee of Van Vechten.

[77] CMcC to Newton Arvin, Nyack, N.Y., April 2, 1960; from Daniel Aaron, literary executor, Newton Arvin Papers, Smith College, Northampton, Mass.

[78] Mary E. Mercer to Carl Van Vechten, Nyack, N.Y., December 22, 1959; from the Carl Van Vechten Papers, Collection of American Literature, Beinecke Rare Book and Manuscript Library, Yale University, and Donald Gallup, curator and literary trustee of Van Vechten.

[79] "The Editor's Guest Book," *Harper's Bazaar*, July 1960, p. 31.

[80] Leon Edel to Aimee Alexander, Honolulu, Hawaii, May 28, 1971.

[81] CMcC to Mr. and Mrs. Tom Melgaard, Nyack, N.Y., January 25, 1960; from the Mary (Sames) Tucker Papers, Perkins Library, Duke University, Durham, N.C.

[82] Louise Dahl-Wolfe to VSC, Frenchtown, N.J., May 25, 1972.

[83] Jordan Massee to VSC, New York City, July 26, 1971.

[84] Tennessee Williams, "A Note on the Author," *Saturday Review*, September 23, 1961, pp. 14–15.

[85] CMcC to Oliver Evans, Nyack, N.Y., August 8, 1963; from the Oliver Evans Collection, Humanities Research Center Library, University of Texas, Austin, Tex.

[86] CMcC to John Banister, Nyack, N.Y., August 21, 1958; John R. Banister to CMcC, Columbus, Ga., September 3, 1958.

[87] Babette Deutsch to VSC, New York City, April 26, 1973.

[88] John Leggett to VSC, see above.

[89] Rex Reed to VSC, New York City, July 27, 1971.

[90] Rex Reed, *Do You Sleep in the Nude?* New York: New American Library, 1968, p. 48.

[91] Rex Reed, "'Frankie Addams' at 50," New York *Times*, April 16, 1967, sec. 2, p. D15; reprinted in *Do You Sleep in the Nude?* op. cit.

[92] Bentz Plagemann to VSC, Palisades, N.Y., April 28 and May 11, 1971; also telephone interview, July 27, 1971.

[93] Ibid.

[94] Robert Lantz to Whit Burnett, New York City, November 22, 1961; from the archives of Columbia University Library; see also Whit Burnett, ed., *Firsts of the Famous*, New York: Ballantine, 1962.

[95] Frances G. Hackett to Aimee Alexander, New York City, March 14, 1971; see also Lewis Funke, "News of the Theatre," New York *Times*, May 21, 1961.

[96] Edward Albee to VSC, New York City, October 18, 1971.

[97] Marjory Rutherford, "New Broadway Hit for Carson McCullers?" Atlanta *Journal and Constitution Magazine*, September 29, 1963, p. 10.

[98] Paul Gardner, "Rialto News," New York *Times*, August 11, 1963.

99 Thomas Lask, New York Sunday *Times,* October 27, 1963.

100 Edward Albee to VSC, see above.

101 Paul Gardner, see above.

102 Marjory Rutherford, see above.

103 *"The Marquis* Interviews Carson McCullers," *The Marquis,* Lafayette College, Pa., 1963, p. 22.

104 Describing Carson's novel from which it was made as "a strange, tender, and muted prose poem," Howard Taubman congratulated Albee for faithfully converting it into "a play flecked with weird, halting poetry." The alternation between narration and the balladier and the dramatic scenes had a two-fold effect, said Taubman: "On one hand, it keeps reminding one that this is a stage version of a tale designed to be read. On the other, it moves the play away from the routines of reality and confers on it the very poetic atmosphere embedded in the printed pages." Such demands require "a kind of bifocal vision," concluded Taubman, which is difficult and too demanding for many theatregoers. Howard Taubman, "Theater: 'The Ballad of the Sad Café,'" New York *Times,* October 31, 1963.

105 *Who's Afraid of Virginia Woolf?* opened on October 13, 1962, and closed May 16, 1964, for a total of 665 performances, exceeding by over one hundred performances Carson's *The Member of the Wedding.*

106 Edward Albee to VSC, see above.

107 Rex Reed, " 'Frankie Addams' at 50," see above.

108 Thomas G. Ryan to VSC, see above.

109 Rex Reed, *Do You Sleep in the Nude?,* see above.

110 Jordan Massee to VSC, May 21, 1971, see above.

111 Jordan Massee to VSC, interview, New York City, February 27, 1972.

112 Mary Mercer to Mary Tucker, Nyack, N.Y., October 1963.

113 Jordan Massee to VSC, July 16, 1973, see above.

114 Ibid.

115 Jordan Massee to VSC, February 27, 1972, see above.

116 Eli Avstreih to VSC, interview, Nyack, N.Y., December 14, 1970.

117 Virginia Johnston and Margaret English to VSC, interview, Nyack, N.Y., May 23, 1971.

118 David Diamond to VSC, interview, Rochester, N.Y., December 10, 1970.

119 Jordan Massee to VSC, July 24, 1971, see above.

120 Ibid.

121 Ibid.

122 Rex Reed to VSC, July 27, 1971, see above.

123 Ruth Wells to VSC, telephone interview, Nyack, N.Y., July 30, 1971.

124 Kenneth French to VSC, interview, New York City, December 15, 1970.

125 Anthony McCombe to VSC, interview, Nyack, N.Y., December 13, 1970.

126 Kenneth French, see above.

127 Charles Cordova to VSC, interview, Nyack, N.Y., May 21, 1971.

128 Mary Mercer to Mary Tucker, Nyack, N.Y., June 1, 1962; also undated letter, Nyack, N.Y., Wednesday (1962); from the Mary (Sames) Tucker Papers, Perkins Library, Duke University, Durham, N.C.

129 Andrew Sinclair, "A Choice of Festivals," *The Listener,* October 11, 1962; see also "On Cheltenham's Festival," Walter Allen, London *Sunday Telegraph,* October 7, 1962.

[130] Prizes which Carson presented at the 1962 Cheltenham Literary Festival went to actor-novelist Robert Shaw for his novel *The Sun Doctor* (Shaw received the most famous award, the Hawthornden); to Irish poet Richard Murphy, the Guinness Poetry Prize (American poet Marion Lineaweaver was one of two runners-up); and to Miss A. L. Barker, the Cheltenham Festival Award, a 500-pound award given not so much for work already accomplished, but to make it possible that further work could be done. (Miss Barker had written a collection of short stories, *Innocents*, in 1948, which won for her the Somerset Maugham Award for the year, but since that time she had been working as a secretary.)

[131] Frank Tuohy, "Writers and Patrons: Cheltenham Festival," *Spectator*, October 12, 1962.

[132] Joseph Heller to Aimee Alexander, New York City, May 10, 1971.

[133] Marielle Bancou to VSC, see above.

[134] Elizabeth Salter, *The Last Years of a Rebel: A Memoir of Edith Sitwell*, London: Bodley Head, Ltd., 1967, p. 163.

[135] Dawn Pepita Simmons, formerly known as Gordon Langley Hall, to VSC, October 28, 1971; also telephone interview, Charleston, S.C., November 13, 1971.

[136] Mrs. Simmons' story is rendered in detail in her "transsexual autobiography," *Man Into Woman*, New York: Macfadden-Bartell, 1971.

[137] *Library Journal*, vol. 89, December 15, 1964, p. 5006.

[138] Walter Gibson, New York *Times Book Review*, November 1, 1964, Part II, p. 57.

[139] *London Times Literary Supplement*, December 9, 1964, p. 114.

[140] Jordan Massee to VSC, July 26, 1971, see above.

[141] Jean Amery, *National Newspaper*, Hamburg, Germany, October 9, 1965; see also *News Bulletin* No. 2, Diogenes Publishing House, October 1965; New York *Times*, December 18, 1965.

[142] Michel Mohrt, "Les États-Unis," in *Les Littératures Contemporaines à Travers le Monde*, Jean-Claude Ibert, ed., Paris: Hachette, 1961.

[143] Angus Wilson, "Were We Afraid of Formentor?" (magazine unidentified), May 5, 1962. Uwe Johnson's ten-thousand-dollar International Publishers Prize, awarded in 1962, was based on his novel, *The Third Book About Achim*: there was still another ten-thousand-dollar Prix des Editeurs (also called the Formentor Prize) which went to Dacie Maraini, a young Italian woman novelist. This award was a ten-thousand-dollar advance on royalties for her unpublished manuscript, which would mean simultaneous publication in eleven languages. According to Alastair Reid, "Having eleven different novels with an immediate international circulation was unprecedented in the history of literature."

[144] The musical version of *The Member of the Wedding*, bearing the title *F. Jasmine Addams*, was presented off Broadway in 1972, written and directed by Theodore Mann; however, it was not a success and closed in a week. The script was entirely different from the one Carson and Mary Rodgers had worked on.

[145] Mary Rodgers Guettel to VSC, interview, New York City, February 29, 1972.

[146] Thomas Ryan to VSC, see above.

[147] Gladys Hill to VSC, Burbank, Calif., July 15, 1974.

[148] Mary Mercer to VSC, interview, Nyack, N.Y., see above.

[149] CMcC to John Huston, Nyack, N.Y.. November 18, 1966.

[150] Ken McCormick to VSC, New York City, July 18, 1973.

[151] Gladys Hill to VSC, Cuernavaca, Mexico, September 7, 1973.

[152] This manuscript, obviously written for publication, remains unpublished at present. It is housed in the personal literary archives of John Huston.

[153] Carson McCullers, "The Flowering Dream: Notes on Writing," *Esquire*, December 1959, p. 163; see also *The Mortgaged Heart*, op. cit., p. 277.

[154] Tennessee Williams to VSC, interview, New Orleans, January 30, 1972.

[155] Tennessee Williams, "Which Is My Little Boy?" *In the Winter of Cities: Collected Poems of Tennessee Williams*, New York: New Directions, 1964, p. 99.

Genealogies

CARSON-WATERS
GENEALOGY

Thomas Carson, his wife, Margaret, their seven children emigrated to Abbeville District, South Carolina, 1773, from Newry, Ireland. En route, they met the McGough family.

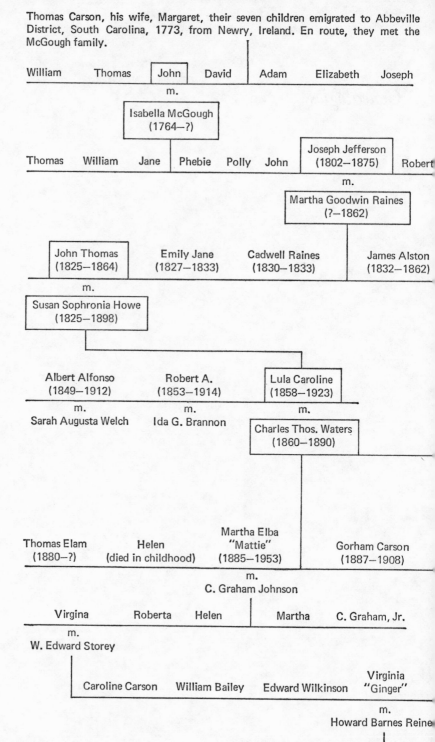

William   Thomas   John   David   Adam   Elizabeth   Joseph

m.

Isabella McGough
(1764–?)

Thomas   William   Jane   Phebie   Polly   John   Joseph Jefferson (1802–1875)   Robert

m.

Martha Goodwin Raines
(?–1862)

John Thomas (1825–1864)   Emily Jane (1827–1833)   Cadwell Raines (1830–1833)   James Alston (1832–1862)

m.

Susan Sophronia Howe
(1825–1898)

Albert Alfonso (1849–1912)   Robert A. (1853–1914)   Lula Caroline (1858–1923)

m.   m.   m.

Sarah Augusta Welch   Ida G. Brannon   Charles Thos. Waters (1860–1890)

Thomas Elam (1880–?)   Helen (died in childhood)   Martha Elba "Mattie" (1885–1953)   Gorham Carson (1887–1908)

m.

C. Graham Johnson

Virgina   Roberta   Helen   Martha   C. Graham, Jr.

m.

W. Edward Storey

Caroline Carson   William Bailey   Edward Wilkinson   Virginia "Ginger"

m.

Howard Barnes Reine

Howard Barnes, Jr.

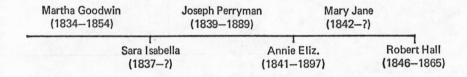

Martha Goodwin
(1834—1854)

Joseph Perryman
(1839—1889)

Mary Jane
(1842—?)

Sara Isabella
(1837—?)

Annie Eliz.
(1841—1897)

Robert Hall
(1846—1865)

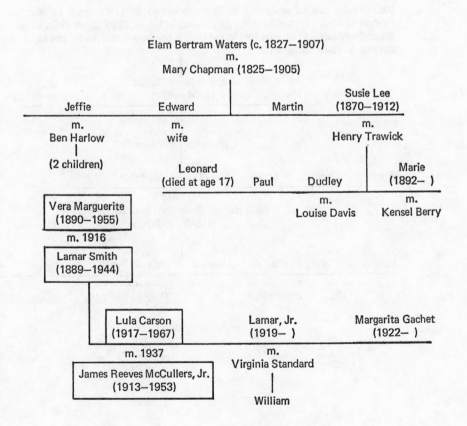

Elam Bertram Waters (c. 1827—1907)
m.
Mary Chapman (1825—1905)

Jeffie

Edward

Martin

Susie Lee
(1870—1912)

m.
Ben Harlow

m.
wife

m.
Henry Trawick

(2 children)

Leonard
(died at age 17)

Paul

Dudley

Marie
(1892—)

m.
Louise Davis

m.
Kensel Berry

Vera Marguerite
(1890—1955)

m. 1916

Lamar Smith
(1889—1944)

Lula Carson
(1917—1967)

Lamar, Jr.
(1919—)

Margarita Gachet
(1922—)

m. 1937

m.
Virginia Standard

James Reeves McCullers, Jr.
(1913—1953)

William

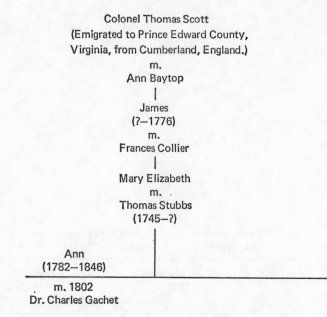

Colonel Thomas Scott
(Emigrated to Prince Edward County,
Virginia, from Cumberland, England.)
m.
Ann Baytop
|
James
(?—1776)
m.
Frances Collier
|
Mary Elizabeth
m.
Thomas Stubbs
(1745—?)

Ann
(1782—1846)
m. 1802
Dr. Charles Gachet

(Dr. Charles Gachet emigrated to Santa Domingo in 1780s from La Rochelle, France; Charles's first wife (Miss Scott) was killed in 1890 in an insurrection in Santa Domingo, and Charles fled to the United States. He met the Stubbs family on the ship en route to Savannah.)

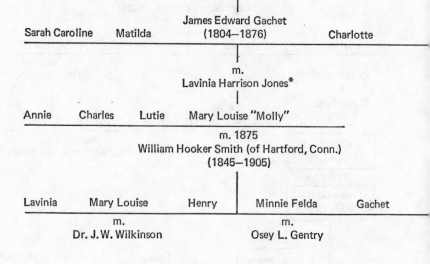

| Sarah Caroline | Matilda | James Edward Gachet (1804—1876) | Charlotte |

m.
Lavinia Harrison Jones*

| Annie | Charles | Lutie | Mary Louise "Molly" |

m. 1875
William Hooker Smith (of Hartford, Conn.)
(1845—1905)

| Lavinia | Mary Louise | Henry | Minnie Felda | Gachet |

| m. | | m. | |
| Dr. J. W. Wilkinson | | Osey L. Gentry | |

SCOTT-GACHET-SMITH
GENEALOGY

Caroline Mildred
_____

m. 1815
Charles Benjamin Gachet
(the son of her sister Ann's husband)

Adolph

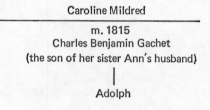

Nicholas
_____

m.
*Janie Jones (sister of Lavinia)

| Rochelle | Janie | James |

m.
?   Martiniere

Nicolas

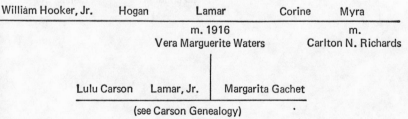

| William Hooker, Jr. | Hogan | Lamar | Corine | Myra |

m. 1916   m.
Vera Marguerite Waters   Carlton N. Richards

| Lulu Carson | Lamar, Jr. | Margarita Gachet |

(see Carson Genealogy)

McCULLERS
GENEALOGY

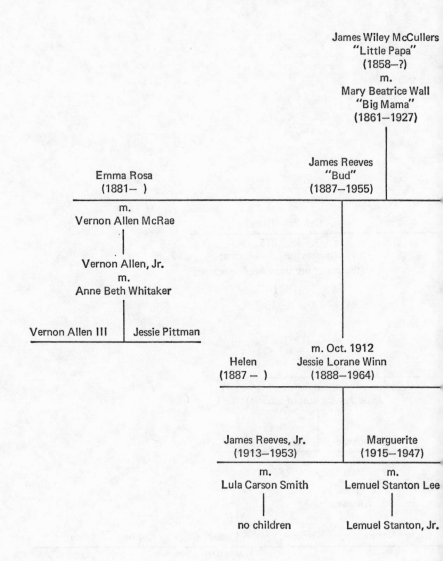

James Wiley McCullers
"Little Papa"
(1858–?)
m.
Mary Beatrice Wall
"Big Mama"
(1861–1927)

Emma Rosa
(1881–)

James Reeves
"Bud"
(1887–1955)

m.
Vernon Allen McRae

Vernon Allen, Jr.
m.
Anne Beth Whitaker

Vernon Allen III | Jessie Pittman

m. Oct. 1912

Helen
(1887–)

Jessie Lorane Winn
(1888–1964)

James Reeves, Jr.
(1913–1953)

Marguerite
(1915–1947)

m.
Lula Carson Smith

m.
Lemuel Stanton Lee

no children

Lemuel Stanton, Jr.

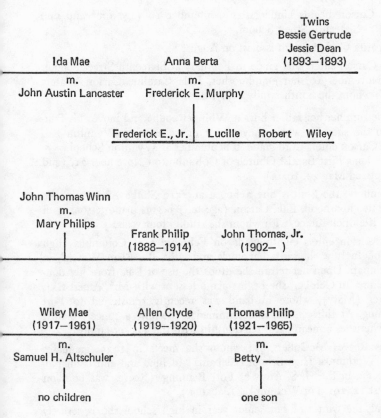

Twins
Bessie Gertrude
Jessie Dean
Ida Mae   Anna Berta   (1893—1893)
m.   m.
John Austin Lancaster   Frederick E. Murphy

        Frederick E., Jr. Lucille   Robert   Wiley

John Thomas Winn
     m.
Mary Philips
                    Frank Philip   John Thomas, Jr.
                    (1888—1914)   (1902—)

Wiley Mae   Allen Clyde   Thomas Philip
(1917—1961)   (1919—1920)   (1921—1965)
    m.   m.
Samuel H. Altschuler   Betty _____

no children   one son

A Chronology of Carson Smith McCullers

1917   Lula Carson Smith is born on February 19 at 423 Thirteenth Street, in the heart of downtown Columbus, Georgia; first child of Marguerite Waters Smith and her husband, Lamar.

1919   Lamar Smith, Jr., is born on May 13.

1921   Lula Carson begins kindergarten September 16 (age four and one half) at Sixteenth Street School.

1922   Margarita Gachet Smith is born on August 2.

1923   Lula Carson enters first grade in February at Sixteenth Street School. On November 19, her grandmother, Lula Caroline Carson Waters (with whom the Smith family lives), dies.

1925   In the summer her father buys a Whippet coupé and moves his family to the suburbs, where they rent a house at 2417 Wynnton Rd. Lula Carson enters third grade in September at Wynnton School.
        She joins First Baptist Church of Columbus on November 21, (and is baptized May 30, 1926.)

1926   In January, the Smiths buy a house at 1519 Starke Avenue in the same neighborhood. Lula Carson (age ten) begins piano lessons with Mrs. Kendrick Kierce, with whom she studies four years.

1930   Lula Carson enters eighth grade on February 3 at Columbus High School. In July, she visits her uncle and aunt, the Elam Waters', in Cincinnati. Upon her return she drops the use of Lula from her double name. In October, she begins piano lessons with Mrs. Albert S. J. Tucker (Mary), whose husband was recently transferred to Fort Benning. At thirteen she is determined to become a concert pianist and cherishes a meaningful relationship with the Tucker family.

1931   James Reeves McCullers, Jr., whom she meets in 1935, graduates from Wetumpka High School (Alabama) in June and enlists on November 3 in the U. S. Army at Fort Benning. (Reeves was born on August 11, 1913, in Wetumpka, Alabama.)

1932   During the winter of her senior year in high school she is severely stricken with rheumatic fever (incorrectly diagnosed at the time; later, the illness was thought to have contributed to her crippling strokes and other debilitating maladies). In December, during her recuperation, she announces to her friend Helen Jackson that she has decided to abandon her plans to be a concert pianist and to become a writer. She continues studying with Mary Tucker and does not tell her of her decision.

1933   Carson graduates from Columbus High School in June and begins to read voraciously the fiction of Dostoevski, Chekhov, Tolstoy, Gogol, Tergenev, and many major British and American writers, including the dramas of O'Neill. By this time she has begun to write plays (in which she casts her brother and sister) and directs them in her living room for an intimate family audience. Her first play, *The Faucet*, is an imitation of O'Neill. She writes her first short story, "Sucker," which she tries unsuccessfully several years later to sell.

1934   Through Mary Tucker Carson meets Edwin Peacock and for the first time experiences meaningful male companionship. Peacock shares her love of books and music and encourages her to become a writer. In the spring Mary Tucker tells her that her husband is to be transferred to Fort Howard, Maryland. Devastated that she is losing her "other family," Carson admits to Mrs. Tucker that she has decided to give up her piano and become a writer.

        In September, at age seventeen, Carson leaves Savannah, Georgia, by steamship for New York City—a trip financed by the sale of an heirloom diamond and emerald ring. Soon after her arrival she loses her money on the subway and is forced to work at odd jobs to save money to study creative writing at Columbia and New York University. She lives first at the Parnassus Club, then at the Three Arts Club.

        On November 2, Reeves McCullers completes his three-year enlistment as a soldier and immediately signs up for a three-year re-enlistment. Reeves, a close friend of Peacock's, is introduced by Peacock to the Smith family. Mrs. Smith welcomes him, as she did Peacock, as "one of her boys."

1935   In February, Carson enrolls in creative writing courses with Dorothy Scarborough and Helen Rose Hull at Columbia University. In June, at the end of the term she returns to Columbus, where she works a short time on the Columbus *Ledger*. A fire in the family's Starke Avenue home forces the Smiths to move elsewhere for two months while the house is renovated. During the summer she meets Reeves McCullers through Peacock, and they become a "threesome." Carson writes prolifically all summer, but most of this early work remains unpublished during her lifetime.

        In September, she sails again for New York City, enrolls at Washington Square College of New York University, and studies writing for two semesters with Sylvia Chatfield Bates.

        In November, John Vincent Adams, a friend of Reeves and Peacock's, moves to New York and urges Reeves to leave the Army, join him there, and dedicate himself to writing.

1936   In January, Reeves's aunt, Mrs. John Austin Lancaster, dies and bequeaths him three Alabama Harbor bonds, which he sells to purchase his discharge from the Army. Reeves moves to New York City and lives with Adams at 439 West Forty-third Street. In September, he enrolls at Columbia University and takes courses in journalism and anthropology. In the meantime, Carson enters the summer term at Columbia University to study with Whit Burnett, editor of *Story*. In November, she becomes seriously ill, and Reeves withdraws from Columbia to take Carson home to Columbus. Put to bed for the winter, she begins to work out the story of a deaf mute in her mind. The work eventually becomes her novel *The Heart Is a Lonely Hunter*. In December, her first published story, "Wunderkind," appears in *Story*. "Like That" is also purchased by *Story*, but remains unpublished during her lifetime.

1937   Reeves returns to New York City and moves with Adams into an apartment in Sunnyside, then to Golden Bridge at Lake Katona, where Carson joins them in the spring. In April, Adams marries and aborts a planned trip to Mexico, where he and Reeves had intended to spend the summer and write. After less than a month in New York, Carson becomes ill again and returns to Columbus by ocean steamer accompanied by Reeves. In the summer she teaches a lecture-study course in music appreciation in her home to earn money. She and Reeves plan to marry. After weeks of futile job hunting and traveling in the South, Reeves moves to Charlotte, North Carolina, where he finds work with Retail Credit Corporation. On September 20, Carson, twenty, and Reeves, twenty-four, are married in the Smith home. They return to Charlotte and move into Reeves's apartment at 311 East Boulevard, where she begins writing her novel. In a few weeks they rent the upstairs apartment at 806 Central Avenue. Although Reeves has frequently expressed a desire to write professionally, he has little time or energy to devote to it. He tells Adams that he has written a collection of essays.

1938   After eight months in Charlotte Carson and Reeves move in the spring to Rowan Street in Fayetteville, North Carolina, where Reeves has been transferred and promoted by Retail Credit Corporation. In the fall, they rent the upstairs apartment at 119 North Cool Spring Street. Carson submits six chapters and an outline of her novel to Houghton Mifflin, for which she receives a contract and the promise of a five-hundred-dollar advance.

1939   In April, Carson finishes her novel, which she entitles *The Mute*. Exhausted, she goes to Columbus to recuperate. Restless, she returns shortly to Fayetteville and writes in two months a second novel, *Army Post*, later entitled *Reflections in a Golden Eye*. In the fall, she returns to Columbus and begins to conceive the nebulous plot she thinks of as *The Bride and Her Brother*. She recognizes that her marriage has begun to disintegrate.

1940   *The Heart Is a Lonely Hunter* (formerly entitled *The Mute*) dedicated to Reeves and her mother and father, is published on June 4; a few days later she and Reeves move to New York City, determined never again to live in the South. They rent a fifth-floor Greenwich

Village apartment at 321 West Eleventh Street. In July, Carson meets Klaus and Erika Mann, Wystan Auden, and Annemarie Clarac-Schwarzenbach, a Swiss girl to whom she dedicates *Reflections in a Golden Eye*, which she sells in August to *Harper's Bazaar* for five hundred dollars (published in two parts in October and November). On August 14, she attends the two-week Bread Loaf Writers' Conference in Middlebury, Vermont, where she meets Louis Untermeyer and Eudora Welty. On August 29, she visits her editor Robert Linscott and the Houghton Mifflin offices in Boston. When she returns to Reeves and their apartment in New York she fidgets and is unhappy over the progress of her new novel. In September, she separates from Reeves and moves to 7 Middagh Street in Brooklyn Heights to live with George Davis, Wystan Auden, and Gypsy Rose Lee. Here she continues to struggle with *The Bride and Her Bother*, until Thanksgiving Day, when in a rare moment of illumination she sees the master design of her novel. Carson is ill during much of the winter of 1940–41. Her mother comes to stay with her in Brooklyn Heights, and after several weeks takes her home to Columbus to recuperate. In November, Annemarie Clarac-Schwarzenbach is hospitalized from mental illness. Later, she flees from the hospital and Carson returns to New York to be with her a few days. It is the last time they see each other.

In December, "Look Homeward, Americans" is published in *Vogue*. It is Carson's first published short piece since "Wunderkind" in 1936.

1941   On January 1, "Night Watch Over Freedom," a second prose piece, is published in *Vogue*. On February 14, *Reflections in a Golden Eye* is published by Houghton Mifflin. In February, Carson is stricken again, this time with radically impaired vision and stabbing head pains. Gradually her sight returns, but she is not ambulatory for over a month. Reeves, seeking a reconciliation, goes to Columbus and returns with her to New York City in April. In March, "Brooklyn Is My Neighborhood" is published in *Vogue*, and on March 15, her book review of *Commend the Devil* by Howard Coxe, "The Devil's Idlers," is published in *Saturday Review*. In April, *Harper's Bazaar* publishes "Books I Remember." Upon her return to New York City, Carson meets Elizabeth Ames, executive director of Yaddo Artists' Colony in Saratoga Springs, and is invited to Yaddo. On May 2, she meets through Muriel Rukeyser composer David Diamond. At Yaddo, from June 14–August 2, she meets Katherine Anne Porter and Newton Arvin. Here she writes a new tale, *The Ballad of the Sad Café*, and continues work on *The Bride and Her Brother*. In July, "The Russian Realists and Southern Literature" is published in *Decision*, a new magazine edited by her friend Klaus Mann. On July 15, "We Carried Our Banners—We Were Pacifists Too" is published in *Vogue*. On August 23, "The Jockey" is published in *The New Yorker*. She also writes "Madame Zilensky and the King of Finland" and "Correspond-

ence," which are both accepted by *The New Yorker* for publication
that winter. "Correspondence" is provoked by her not having heard
from Reeves for many months.

In July, Reeves begins to forge checks on Carson's account, and she
plans to divorce him. August 22–30 she accompanies Newton Arvin,
Granville Hicks, and his family to Quebec. She is back at Yaddo from
September 4–30, then goes to New York City to initiate divorce pro-
ceedings. From July through November 14, Reeves lives with David
Diamond and works at Samson United in Rochester, New York. In
October, Diamond dedicates his ballet *The Dream of Audubon* to
Carson and Reeves.

In the November–December issue of *Decision* her first published
poem appears: "The Twisted Trinity," which Diamond sets to music.
In mid-October, Carson returns to Columbus; in December she is
critically ill with pleurisy, strep throat, and double pneumonia—her
second major illness within the year.

1942   By February, Carson recuperates enough to resume work on her
Bride manuscript (on February 2, she finishes Part I, which she re-
fers to as "The Listener" and begins the middle section, "The Nigger
with the Glass Blue Eye"). She interrupts her novel now to write a
short story, "A Tree. A Rock. A Cloud." which is accepted immediately by *Harper's Bazaar*. On February 7, her short story "Correspondence" is published in *The New Yorker*. On March 19, Reeves,
now divorced, re-enlists in the U. S. Army (he takes his commission
on November 29 at Camp Upton, New York). Carson is notified on
March 24 that she has been awarded a Guggenheim Fellowship. She
wants to take her Guggenheim money to Mexico to write and live
with Newton Arvin and David Diamond, but her doctor and Guggenheim officials dissuade her because of her poor health. In March,
she tells David Diamond that her *Bride* manuscript is finished, but
quickly realizes that it must undergo much revision before it is finally ready for publication. Carson is invited by George Davis to return to 7 Middagh Street to live, but goes, instead, to Yaddo, where
she stays from July 2–January 17, 1943. "A Tree. A Rock. A Cloud."
is published in *Harper's Bazaar* in November. On November 29,
Reeves begins OCS at Fort Benning, where he remains until November 23, 1943. On December 1, she learns that Annemarie Clarac-
Schwarzenbach died in Sils, Switzerland, on November 15.

1943   Carson leaves Yaddo January 17 and moves again into 7 Middagh
Street with Auden and Davis. In January, she sells *The Ballad of the
Sad Café* to *Harper's Bazaar*, to be published in August. In February,
she is ill and her mother comes to Middagh Street to nurse her and
accompany her back to Columbus. In April, "Love's Not Time's Fool"
(signed by "A War Wife") is published in *Mademoiselle*. On April
9, she learns that she will receive a one-thousand-dollar Arts and Letters Grant from the American Academy of Arts and Letters and the
National Institute of Arts and Letters. On April 22, she returns to

Columbus, and on May 5, meets Reeves in Atlanta; a week later he joins her in Columbus on a five-day leave. Reeves is a company commander in the Second Ranger Battalion, Camp Forrest, Tennessee. The first of June she returns briefly to 7 Middagh Street, then proceeds to Yaddo (June 8–August 12).

In mid-August she spends a few days in New York City, then returns to Columbus. On November 15, she stays a week with Reeves at Fort Dix, his point of embarkation for Europe on November 28. They consider a remarriage, but decide against it.

1944   In January and February, Carson is ill again with influenza and pleurisy; she also suffers a severe nervous attack and fears for Reeves's safety in combat. In February, she learns that Reeves has fractured his wrist in a motorcycle accident in England.

In March, Carson's sister, Rita Smith, moves to New York City to write and find a job in publishing. On June 6, Reeves is wounded in the Normandy invasion, but recovers and participates in the September Bay of Brest seige. On June 15, Carson goes to Yaddo. On August 1, her father dies in Columbus of a heart attack. Carson leaves Yaddo and returns to Columbus for the funeral. On September 4, Carson, her sister, and mother move to Nyack, New York, and rent an apartment at 127 South Broadway. In December, *The Ballad of the Sad Café* is included in Martha Foley's *The Best American Short Stories of 1944*. On December 9, Reeves in wounded in Rötgen, Germany. Carson suffers acute eye strain and is unable to work.

1945   Carson is ill with influenza during much of January and laments her slow progress on *The Member of the Wedding*. On February 10, Reeves leaves England by ship for the United States after serving fifteen months overseas and participating in three major campaigns. He has been decorated for bravery and is a first lieutenant. On March 19, Carson and Reeves remarry in a civil ceremony in New City, New York. After being treated in various Veterans Administration hospitals in New York for a severely injured wrist and other minor combat injuries, he is sent to Camp Wheeler, near Macon, Georgia. Carson remains in Nyack. On May 15, her mother buys a house at 131 South Broadway, Nyack. Reeves returns to Nyack, having arranged for a physical disability discharge, which is granted March 16, 1946. In the meantime, he is on terminal leave and has been promoted to captain. On June 26, Carson again goes to Yaddo, determined to finish *The Member of the Wedding*. She returns to Nyack August 31, the manuscript complete. At the invitation of her former editor at Houghton Mifflin, Robert Linscott, now at Random House, she considers offering him the book for publication, but decides against it. In November, "Our Heads Are Bowed" is published in *Mademoiselle*. Reeves looks for work but cannot find a suitable job. He considers medical school, but is discouraged because of his age.

1946   In January, Part I of *The Member of the Wedding* is published in

Harper's Bazaar. On March 19, *The Member of the Wedding* is published by Houghton Mifflin, dedicated to Elizabeth Ames. Carson returns to Yaddo on March 23 (through May 31). On April 15, she is
awarded her second Guggenheim Fellowship and she and Reeves plan
to live in Paris. In June, Carson spends several weeks in Nantucket
with Tennessee Williams, whom she has not met until he greets her
at the ferry. On November 22, she and Reeves sail on the *Île de
France* for Paris, where she is enthusiastically received.

1947   In April, Carson goes on a skiing expedition in the Italian Tyrol and
visits Natalia Danesi Murray in Rome, where she meets the major
Italian writers, and again, is well received as one of America's brightest young talents. In August, Carson suffers a severe and frightening
stroke and is hospitalized in the American Hospital near Paris. In
November, another stroke occurs, which paralyzes her left side. On
December 1, she and Reeves both are flown home ill, on stretchers;
Reeves suffers from delirium tremens. On December 17, *Quick* magazine names her one of the best postwar writers in America.

1948   In the January issue of *Mademoiselle* she is named one of the ten
most deserving women in America for 1947 and is the recipient of a
Mademoiselle Merit Award. Carson remains in bed at home after being hospitalized in Nyack for several weeks upon her return from
Paris and is ill through the early spring. She and Reeves separate and
he moves to New York City. In March, Carson attempts suicide
and is hospitalized briefly at Payne Whitney Psychiatric Clinic in
Manhattan. In August, she and Reeves reconcile. In September,
"How I Began to Write" is published in *Mademoiselle,* and two poems, "The Mortgaged Heart" and "When We Are Lost," are published
in *New Directions* (Vol. 10). In the summer and fall, she revises the
play *The Member of the Wedding,* which she adapted from her novel
while in Nantucket with Tennessee Williams. In October, she joins
twenty-six other writers in public support of Harry S Truman as President.

1949   In January, Carson spends a month with Reeves in his apartment at
105 Thompson Street in Manhattan. On March 13, she returns with
her mother to Georgia for two weeks, first to Columbus, then to
Macon to visit her cousin Jordan Massee. On May 13, she and Reeves
go to Charleston, South Carolina, to visit their friends Edwin Peacock
and John Zeigler. *The Member of the Wedding* opens at the Walnut
Theatre in Philadelphia for its pre-Broadway run on December 22.
"Home for Christmas" is published in the December issue of *Mademoiselle.* On December 19, "Loneliness, an American Malady" is
published in *This Week Magazine* of the New York *Herald Tribune;*
it also appears in *Playbill.* The play is published in December by New
Directions.

1950   On January 5, *The Member of the Wedding* opens at the Empire
Theatre on Broadway; in April, it wins the New York Drama Critics'

Circle Award for the best play of the season (April 1, 1949–March 31, 1950), and the Donaldson Award as the best play of last season and the best first play by an author to be produced on Broadway. Carson is awarded a Gold Medal by the Theatre Club, Inc., as the best playwright of the year. In the spring, she is reconciled to her former piano teacher, Mary Tucker, from whom there has been a fifteen-year estrangement. In April, "The Vision Shared" is published in *Theatre Arts*. In May, "The Sojourner" is published in *Mademoiselle*. On May 20, Carson sails for Ireland to visit Elizabeth Bowen; later, joined by Reeves, she goes to Paris, then returns to Bowen's Court. Once again Carson decides to separate from Reeves. The Tuckers invite her to Virginia, where she spends several weeks. In New York she meets Dame Edith Sitwell, the beginning of a lifelong friendship.

1951   Stanley Kramer buys the screen rights to *The Member of the Wedding* for $75,000. With the money she purchases her mother's home at 131 South Broadway. *The Member of the Wedding* closes on March 17 after 501 performances. On May 24, *The Ballad of the Sad Café and Other Works* (Omnibus Edition) is published by Houghton Mifflin. On July 28, she sails to England aboard the *Queen Elizabeth*. Reeves is a stowaway until the ship has been at sea several days. He soon returns to America, but Carson remains in England three months. She stays with David Gascoyne, visits Dame Edith Sitwell, and works on a long poem begun on the ship: "The Dual Angel: A Meditation on Origin and Choice." A British doctor attempts psychiatric and hypnotic therapy to help her paralyzed left arm; the treatment fails, and Carson leaves England (October). Once home, she returns to Nyack and to Reeves; they go to New Orleans for a vacation, but she returns home ill with bronchial pneumonia and pleurisy. In the fall, Carson begins work on a manuscript she refers to as "The Pestle" (it later becomes a part of the novel *Clock Without Hands*).

1952   On January 30, Carson and Reeves sail on the *Constitution* for Naples, Italy, intending to spend another year or more in Europe. After a month in Rome (where they see David Diamond), they drive to Paris and buy a home in Bachvillers, a nearby village. On May 28, Carson is inducted in absentia into the National Institute of Arts and Letters. In midsummer, *The Ballad of the Sad Café and Collected Short Stories* is published by Houghton Mifflin. It contains "The Haunted Boy," a short story published for the first time. In July, "The Dual Angel: A Meditation on Origin and Choice" is published in *Mademoiselle*, and later in the Italian publication *Botteghe Oscure* (September–December issue, 1952). In September, Carson and Reeves return to Rome, where she works on the film script *Terminal Station* with De Sica and Selznick; it is an unsuccessful venture—except monetarily—and Carson and Reeves return to Bachvillers in October.

1953   "The Pestle" (Part I of *Clock Without Hands*) is published in the July issues of *Mademoiselle* and *Botteghe Oscure*. Carson and Reeves become increasingly unhappy and disillusioned in their marriage; both drink heavily and Reeves threatens (and attempts) suicide. He tries to talk her into a double suicide, and in the late summer she flees France, fearful of her life. On November 19, Reeves kills himself in a Paris hotel; Carson hears the news while she is visiting Lillian Smith in Clayton, Georgia. She visits Dr. Hervey M. Cleckley in Augusta before returning North to complete funeral arrangements. On December 10, she goes to Columbus upon the death of her mother's sister, Martha Waters Johnson. In the December issue of *Mademoiselle*, "The Discovery of Christmas" is published.

       On December 27, "The Invisible Wall" is presented live on television by the Ford Foundation program "Omnibus." The play is an adaptation of her short story "The Sojourner."

1954   On February 17, Carson lectures on fiction writing and drama at Goucher College. Later in the year she lectures at Columbia University and the Philadelphia Fine Arts Association. On May 8, she lectures at the Poetry Center of the Young Men and Young Women's Hebrew Association in New York City. She calls her talk "Twenty Years of Writing" and is accompanied on the platform by Tennessee Williams, who reads from her works. From April 20 through July 3, she is in residence at Yaddo, where she completes the first draft of her play *The Square Root of Wonderful* and works on *Clock Without Hands*. In midsummer she returns South and spends a month in Charleston and Charlotte before returning to Yaddo. In Charlotte, Robert Walden encourages her to adapt *The Ballad of the Sad Café* as a musical ballet. In the fall and winter, Carson is at home in Nyack or in Manhattan with friends. She meets Arnold Saint Subber, who becomes interested in producing *The Square Root of Wonderful*.

1955   In April, Carson flies to Key West to vacation with Tennessee Williams and to work on her three manuscripts then in progress: the dramatization of *The Ballad of the Sad Café*, *The Square Root of Wonderful*, and *Clock Without Hands*. She and Williams also spend a weekend in Cuba. On May 25, Carson finishes her manuscript "Who Has Seen the Wind?," a short-story version of *The Square Root of Wonderful*. On June 10, her mother dies unexpectedly in Nyack and Carson is devastated. To cope, she works almost frantically on *The Square Root of Wonderful* and establishes a meaningful personal relationship with Arnold Saint Subber, who announces that *The Square Root of Wonderful* will be his next play. In November, her short story "The Haunted Boy" is published simultaneously in *Mademoiselle* and *Botteghe Oscure*.

1956   Carson is ill during much of the year; her paralyzed left arm becomes increasingly painful and drawn. Saint Subber works with her daily in the revision of her play, which is delayed going into production for almost a year. In September, "Who Has Seen the Wind?" is published by *Mademoiselle*.

1957　"Mick" is published in the February issue of *Literary Calvacade*. On February 16, *The Member of the Wedding* opens at the Royal Court Theatre, London, by the English Stage Company, starring Geraldine McEwan. Her poem "Stone Is Not Stone" is published in *Mademoiselle* in July. On September 2, *The Square Root of Wonderful* goes into rehearsal with Anne Baxter in the leading role of Mollie Lovejoy. It has a ten-day pre-Broadway run at the McCarter Theatre in Princeton, New Jersey, opening October 10. "Playwright Tells of Pangs" is published on October 13 in the Philadelphia *Inquirer*. On October 23, George Keathley is called in to replace director Jose Quintero, who has resigned. The play opens on Broadway at the National Theatre on October 30 and closes December 7 after forty-five performances.

1958　Carson suffers acute depression after the early closing of her play and feels that she is losing her writing powers. Concerned friends seek relief for her and arrange for her to meet Dr. Mary Mercer, a specialist in child psychiatry in Nyack. They meet in February, have a brief doctor-patient relationship, and become lifelong friends. Through Dr. Mercer she regains self-confidence and is able to write again. In May, Carson makes a record with Jean Stein vanden Heuvel, entitled "Carson McCullers Reads from *The Member of the Wedding* and Other Works." In July, she lectures at Columbia University and writes "A Personal Preface" to *The Square Root of Wonderful*. The preface and play are published by Houghton Mifflin. In August, she is at work on a new "Flowering Dream" manuscript. On August 19, she participates in a panel discussion on drama in the television production of "Lamp Unto My Feet." In December, *The Member of the Wedding* is produced in French at the Alliance Française in Paris, translated and adapted by Andrè Bay and William Hope.

1959　In January, Carson attends a dinner meeting of the American Academy of Arts and Letters and the National Institute of Arts and Letters, at which Isak Dinesen is the guest speaker; later she gives a luncheon for Miss Dinesen, attended by Arthur Miller and Marilyn Monroe. Carson resumes work on the script and lyrics of *The Ballad of the Sad Café* as a musical, and by August she has finished half of *Clock Without Hands*. She has two operations on her damaged left arm and wrist, and schedules two more for the next year. When she is unable because of her health to work on her manuscripts, she begins writing children's verse. "The Flowering Dream: Notes on Writing" is published by *Esquire* in December.

1960　In April Carson's third application for a Guggenheim is denied because she has already received two earlier grants. In July, Edward Albee approaches her with the idea that he would like to adapt *The*

Ballad of the Sad Café as a dramatic play. On December 1, Carson finishes *Clock Without Hands.*

1961   In January, Thomas Ryan purchases the screen rights of *The Heart Is a Lonely Hunter.* In February, Carson finishes galley proofs of *Clock Without Hands.* In May, Kermit Bloomgarden acquires the theatre rights of *Clock Without Hands,* but abandons his plans after a few weeks of work on the script. Edward Albee invites Carson and Mary Mercer to Shelter Island to visit him and to talk about his adaptation of *The Ballad of the Sad Café.* On June 11, Carson writes an "Author's Note" regarding *Clock Without Hands* for the New York *Times Book Review.* In June, she again undergoes surgery at Harkness Pavilion. By 1962, she has begun to spend most of her sitting-up hours in a wheelchair. "To Bear the Truth Alone" (Part II of *Clock Without Hands*) is published in the July issue of *Harper's Bazaar.* On September 18, *Clock Without Hands* is published by Houghton Mifflin, dedicated to Dr. Mary Mercer. "A Child's View of Christmas" is published in the December issue of *Redbook.*

1962   Carson does little writing in 1962; what she does is in longhand. In February, she and Dr. Mercer visit Mary Tucker in Virginia. Here Carson meets with Albee, a lecturer in residence at the University of Virginia, to discuss his adaptation of *The Ballad of the Sad Café.* In May, Mary Tucker visits Carson in Nyack. On June 6, Carson's cancerous right breast is removed, and surgery is performed on every major joint of her left hand in an eight-hour operation. By August, she has recuperated enough to spend a week on Fire Island with Edward Albee, accompanied by Mary Mercer. She also visits West Point in August, where she meets William Faulkner. In October, she flies alone to England to participate in a "Symposium on Love" at the Cheltenham Festival of Literature and to attend Dame Edith Sitwell's seventy-fifth birthday celebration.

1963   In January, "The Dark Brilliance of Edward Albee" is published in *Harper's Bazaar.* On March 16, "Isak Dinesen: In Praise of Radiance" is published in the *Saturday Review.* On March 7, the Glasgow Theatre, Scotland, presents *The Square Root of Wonderful* at the Palace of Art; the play is well received by the critics. On April 12, Carson and Mary Mercer fly to Charleston to visit Edwin Peacock and John Zeigler. In the spring, Ray Stark takes an option to produce *Reflections in a Golden Eye* as a movie, to be directed by John Huston. (Shooting does not begin until 1966; the film is released October 11, 1967.) In the summer, Carson and Dr. Mercer join Edward Albee on Fire Island. "Sucker" is published in *The Saturday Evening Post* on September 28. *The Ballad of the Sad Café* opens on October 30 at the Martin Beck Theatre on Broadway, without a pre-Broadway run.

1964   *The Ballad of the Sad Café* closes on February 15 after 123 performances. In the spring, Carson breaks her right hip and shatters her left elbow. On May 25, "The Sojourner" is presented by NBC television. On November 1, her collection of children's verses, *Sweet as a Pickle, Clean as a Pig*, is published by Houghton Mifflin. On November 8, Carson signs her last will and testament. On December 1, "Selections from *Sweet as a Pickle, Clean as a Pig*" is published in *Redbook*. Throughout 1964 and 1965, Carson and Mary Tucker write each other frequently and exchange visits in Nyack and Lexington, Virginia.

1965   On July 14, Carson undergoes exploratory surgery and has her broken hip reset. Her condition is critical and she remains in the hospital three months. On December 18, she is awarded the Prize of the Younger Generation by *Die Welt*, a Hamburg, Germany, newspaper.

1966   Thomas Ryan completes his screen script of *The Heart Is a Lonely Hunter* and reads it to Carson and Mary Mercer. In October, the shooting of *Reflections in a Golden Eye* begins at Mitchell Field on Long Island, then moves to Rome. Throughout 1966, Carson's major creative endeavor is working with Mary Rodgers on an adaptation of a musical version of *The Member of the Wedding*. She also works on a manuscript referred to as *Illuminations and Night Glare*.

1967   A short story, "The March," appears in *Redbook* in March. On April 1, Carson flies to Ireland to visit John Huston. On April 30, she is named winner of the 1966 Henry Bellamann Award, a one-thousand-dollar grant in recognition of her "outstanding contribution to literature." On August 15, she suffers her final stroke, a massive brain hemorrhage, and is comatose forty-seven days. She dies on September 29 in the Nyack Hospital and is buried on October 3 in Oak Hill Cemetery, on the bank of the Hudson River in Nyack. On October 2, shooting begins on the film *The Heart Is a Lonely Hunter*. "A Hospital Christmas Eve" is published in *Redbook* in December.

1971   Margarita G. Smith, her sister, edits *The Mortgaged Heart*, the first posthumous collection of her works. It is published by Houghton Mifflin early in the year. *F. Jasmine Addams*, a musical version of *The Member of the Wedding*, opens off Broadway in May, but closes after twenty performances. The script is not Carson's (written in collaboration with Mary Rodgers), but Theodore Mann's, who produced the show.

Bibliography

PUBLISHED WORKS BY CARSON MCCULLERS

BOOKS:

The Ballad of the Sad Café and Collected Short Stories. Boston: Houghton Mifflin, 1952, 1955.
> Contains:
> *The Ballad of the Sad Café*
> "Wunderkind"
> "The Jockey"
> "Madame Zilensky and the King of Finland"
> "The Sojourner"
> "A Domestic Dilemma"
> "A Tree. A Rock. A Cloud."
> "The Haunted Boy" (first included in the 1955 edition)

The Ballad of the Sad Café and Other Works. Boston: Houghton Mifflin, 1951.
> Contains:
> *The Ballad of the Sad Café*
> "Wunderkind"
> "The Jockey"
> "Madame Zilensky and the King of Finland"
> "The Sojourner"
> "A Domestic Dilemma"
> "A Tree. A Rock. A Cloud."
> *The Heart Is a Lonely Hunter*
> *Reflections in a Golden Eye*
> *The Member of the Wedding*

Clock Without Hands. Boston: Houghton Mifflin, 1961.

The Heart Is a Lonely Hunter. Boston: Houghton Mifflin, 1940.

The Member of the Wedding. Boston: Houghton Mifflin, 1946.

The Member of the Wedding. Play. New York: New Directions, 1951.

The Mortgaged Heart, edited by Margarita G. Smith. Boston: Houghton Mifflin, 1971.

Reflections in a Golden Eye. Boston: Houghton Mifflin, 1941.

The Square Root of Wonderful. Play. New York: Houghton Mifflin, 1958.

Sweet as a Pickle and Clean as a Pig. Poems. Boston: Houghton Mifflin, 1964.

ARTICLES AND STORIES:

"Art and Mr. Mahoney." *Mademoiselle*, XXVIII (February 1949), 120, 184–86.

"Author's Note." New York *Times Book Review*, LXVI, no. 24 (June 11, 1961), 4.

"The Ballad of the Sad Café." *Harper's Bazaar*, LXXVII (August 1943), 72–75, 140–61.

"Books I Remember." *Harper's Bazaar*, LXXV (April 1941), 82, 122, 125.

"Brooklyn Is My Neighborhood." *Vogue*, XCVII (March 1941), 62–63, 138.

"A Child's View of Christmas." *Redbook*, CXVIII (December 1961), 31–34, 99–100.

"Correspondence." *The New Yorker*, XVII (February 7, 1942), 36–39.

"The Dark Brilliance of Edward Albee." *Harper's Bazaar*, XCVII (January 1963), 98–99.

"The Devil's Idlers," a review of *Commend the Devil* by Howard Coxe. *Saturday Review*, XXIII (March 15, 1941), 15.

"The Discovery of Christmas." *Mademoiselle*, XXXVIII (December 1953), 54–55, 118–20.

"A Domestic Dilemma." *New York Post Magazine Section*, September 16, 1951, pp. 10ff.

"The Flowering Dream: Notes on Writing." *Esquire*, LII (December 1959), 162–64.

"The Haunted Boy." *Botteghe Oscure*, XVI (1955), 264–78; *Mademoiselle*, XLII (November 1955), 134–35, 152–59.

"Home for Christmas." *Mademoiselle*, XXX (December 1949), 53, 129–32.

"A Hospital Christmas Eve." *McCalls*, XCV (December 1967), 96–97.

"How I Began to Write." *Mademoiselle*, XXVII (September 1948), 256–57.

"Isak Dinesen: In Praise of Radiance." *Saturday Review*, XLVI (March 16, 1963), 29, 83.

"The Jockey." *The New Yorker*, XVII (August 23, 1941), 15–16.

"Loneliness, an American Malady." *This Week Magazine*, New York *Herald Tribune*, December 19, 1949, 18–19.

"Look Homeward, Americans." *Vogue*, XCVI (December 1, 1940), 74–75.

"Love's Not Time's Fool" (signed by "A War Wife"). *Mademoiselle*, XVI (April 1943), 95, 166–68.

"Madame Zilensky and the King of Finland." *The New Yorker*, XVII (December 20, 1941), 15–18.

"The March." *Redbook*, CXXVIII (March 1967), 69, 114–23.

"The Member of the Wedding." (Part I), *Harper's Bazaar*, LXXX (January 1946), 94–96, 101, 128–38, 144–48.

"Mick." *Literary Cavalcade*, X (February 1957), 16–22, 32.

"Night Watch Over Freedom." *Vogue*, XCVII (January 1, 1941), 29.

"A Note from the Author." *The Saturday Evening Post*, CCXXXVI (September 28, 1963), 69.

"Our Heads Are Bowed." *Mademoiselle*, XXII (November 1945), 131, 229.

"A Personal Preface" to *The Square Root of Wonderful*. Boston: Houghton Mifflin, 1958, pp. 7–10.

"The Pestle." *Botteghe Oscure*, XI (1953), 226–46; *Mademoiselle*, XXXVII (July 1953), 44–45, 114–18.

"Playwright Tells of Pangs." Philadelphia *Inquirer*, October 13, 1957, 1, 5.

"Reflections in a Golden Eye." *Harper's Bazaar*, LXXIV (October–November 1940), 60–61, 131–43; 56, 120–39.

"The Russian Realists and Southern Literature." *Decision*, II (July 1941), 15–19.

"The Sojourner." *Mademoiselle*, XXXI (May 1950), 90, 160–66.

"Sucker." *The Saturday Evening Post*, CCXXXVI (September 28, 1963), 69–71.

"To Bear the Truth Alone." *Harper's Bazaar*, XCIV (July 1961), 42–43, 93–99.

"A Tree. A Rock. A Cloud." *Harper's Bazaar*, LXXVI (November 1942), 50, 96–99.

"The Vision Shared." *Theatre Arts*, XXXIV (April 1950), 28–30.

"We Carried Our Banners—We Were Pacifists Too." *Vogue*, XCVII (July 15, 1941), 42–43.

"Who Has Seen the Wind?" *Mademoiselle*, XLIII (September 1956), 156–57, 174–88.

"Wunderkind." *Story*, IX (December 1936), 61–73.

POETRY:

"The Dual Angel: A Meditation on Origin and Choice."
Poems, including "Incantation to Lucifer," "Hymen, O Hymen," "Love and the Rind of Time," "The Dual Angel," and "Father, Upon Thy Image We Are Spanned." *Botteghe Oscure*, IX (1952), 213–18; *Mademoiselle*, XXXV (July 1952), 54–55, 108.

"The Mortgaged Heart." *New Directions*, X (1948), 509; *Voices*, CXLIX (September–December 1952), 11–12.

"Stone Is Not Stone." *Mademoiselle*, XLV (July 1957), 43.

"Sweet as a Pickle and Clean as a Pig." *Redbook*, CXXIV (December 1964), 49–56.

"The Twisted Trinity." *Decision*, II (November–December 1941), 30.

"When We Are Lost." *New Directions*, X (1948), 509; *Voices*, CXLIX (September–December 1952), 12.

Index

Picture Credits

1. Photograph by Lawrence Smith, *Ledger-Enquirer*, Columbus, Georgia
2. Photograph courtesy of Marielle Bancou
3. Photograph by Jungermann's Studio, Columbus, Georgia
4. Photograph courtesy of Felda Gentry James
5. Photograph by Virginia Spencer Carr
6. Photograph courtesy of Ida Thompson
7. Photograph courtesy of Ella Kirven
8. Photograph courtesy of Helen H. Jackson
9. Photograph courtesy of Helen H. Jackson
10. Photograph courtesy of Vernon McRae
11. Photograph reproduced by Lawrence Smith, *Ledger-Enquirer*, Columbus, Georgia
12. Photograph courtesy of Lamar Smith
13. Photograph reproduced by Lawrence Smith, *Ledger-Enquirer*, Columbus, Georgia; courtesy of Edwin Peacock
14. Photograph courtesy of Vernon McRae
15. Photograph courtesy of Vernon McRae
16. Photograph courtesy of Vernon McRae
17. Photograph courtesy of Vernon McRae
18. Photograph by Virginia Spencer Carr
19. Photograph by Virginia Spencer Carr
20. Photograph by John Vincent Adams
21. Photograph courtesy of Jonathan Aldrich, Middlebury College, Vermont
22. Photograph courtesy of Edwin Peacock
23. Photograph by Henri Cartier-Bresson
24. Photograph courtesy of Lotte Lenya Weill-Detwiler
25. Photograph courtesy of Suzanne Schwarzenbach Ohman
26. Photograph by Virginia Spencer Carr
27. Photograph by Virginia Spencer Carr
28. Photograph courtesy of Elizabeth Ames
29. Photograph by Granville Hicks
30. Photograph by Helen Eustis
31. Photograph courtesy of Lamar Smith
32. Photograph courtesy of Lamar Smith
33. Photograph by Henri Cartier-Bresson
34. Photograph by Paul Stewart, *Ledger-Enquirer*, Columbus, Georgia
35. Photograph courtesy of Pancho Rodriguez
36. Photograph by Louise Dahl-Wolfe
37. Photograph by Louise Dahl-Wolfe
38. Photograph by Louise Dahl-Wolfe
39. Photograph by Henri Cartier-Bresson
40. Photograph courtesy of Jordan Massee
41. Photograph by Eileen Darby, Graphic House, Inc.
42. Photograph by Edwin Peacock
43. Photograph by Eileen Darby, Graphic House, Inc.
44. Photograph by Alfredo Valente
45. Photograph by Peter R. Kaldor
46. Photograph by Alfredo Valente
47. Photograph courtesy of Rowland E. Fullilove

48. Photograph courtesy of Rowland E. Fullilove
49. Photograph courtesy of Edwin Peacock
50. Photograph courtesy of Edwin Peacock
51. Photograph by Larry Gordon; courtesy of Lotte Lenya Weill-Detwiler
52. Charleston *Evening Post* staff photograph; courtesy of Edwin Peacock
53. Photograph courtesy of Jordan Massee
54. Photograph by Ivan Obolensky; courtesy of Jordan Massee
55. Photograph by Carl Van Vechten
56. Photograph courtesy of Jordan Massee
57. Photograph courtesy of Jordan Massee
58. Photograph by Ernst Hammerschlag
59. Photograph by Louise Dahl-Wolfe
60. Photograph by Virginia Spencer Carr
61. Photograph by Jean Paul Mannesson
62. Photograph by Hilda Marks
63. Photograph by Sir Cecil Beaton
64. Photograph by Virginia Spencer Carr
65. Photo by Werner J. Kuhn
66. Photograph by H. B. Settle, Saratoga Springs, New York
67. Photograph by David Diamond
68. Photograph by Marion Morehouse
69. Photograph by Robert Walden
70. Photograph by Ruth Orkin
71. Photograph by George S. Bolster, Saratoga Springs, New York
72. Photograph by George S. Bolster, Saratoga Springs, New York
73. Photograph by Roy Stevens; courtesy of Jordan Massee
74. Photograph by the *Irish Times*
75. Photograph by Richard Avedon